WEBSTER'S RED SEAL CROSSWORD DICTIONARY

Compiled and Edited by Norman Hill

FAWCETT POPULAR LIBRARY • NEW YORK

WEBSTER'S RED SEAL CROSSWORD DICTIONARY

Published by Fawcett Popular Library, a unit of CBS Publications, the Consumer Division of CBS Inc.

ISBN: 0-445-08299-2

EDITORIAL STAFF

Norman Hill, Editor
Laura M. Engle, Associate Editor
Lili Fenyves Hill, Consulting Editor
Naomi Bloom, Assistant Editor

PRINTED IN THE UNITED STATES OF AMERICA

28   27   26   25   24   23   22   21

FOREWORD

During the past decade the editors of this publication have done extensive research in lexicography, have edited tens of thousands of crossword puzzles, checked and evaluated hundreds of thousands of definitions and words. Now it is with great pride and pleasure that we present this new and unique reference book—a crossword puzzle dictionary conceived, designed and painstakingly compiled to best accomplish the single purpose for which a crossword puzzle dictionary is intended: to provide efficient, simplified help for the puzzle solver.

Webster's Red Seal Crossword Dictionary contains thousands of entries which are used by leading professional crossword constructors, and which appear most frequently in crossword puzzles published in magazines, books and newspapers. The definitions have been carefully edited by a staff of some of America's most experienced, most expert editors.

We have included those definitions which will be of maximum usefulness to the puzzle solver. As a result we believe you will find *Webster's Red Seal Crossword Dictionary* to be a complete, handy, reliable guide and solving aid.

Definitions are listed alphabetically, and worded just as they appear in puzzles. Where more than one answer word might fit the definition, additional possibilities are offered.

There is no confusing clutter of so-called "special categories" —no detours and confusing road signs; no meandering listings of Indian tribes, mythological beings or foreign weights and measures. What you hold in your hand is the easiest-to-use, most efficient alphabetical dictionary of crossword puzzle definitions available anywhere. We commend it to you with our best wishes for many hours of pleasurable puzzle solving.

Norman Hill
Editor

A

aardvark **ANTEATER**
aardvark's diet **ANTS**
aardwolf **HYENA**
Aare **SWISS RIVER**
Aaron **BIBLICAL PRIEST**
Ab **HEBREW MONTH**
abaca **MANILA HEMP**
abalone **MOLLUSK, ORMER**
abandon **DESERT, STRAND, MAROON**
abandoned (law) **DERELICT**
abase **DEGRADE, DEMEAN, LOWER. HUMBLE**
abasement **SHAME, DISHONOR**
abash **DISCONCERT**
abate **DIMINISH, EBB, SLACKEN, LET UP, DEDUCT, SUBSIDE**
abatement **REDUCTION, DECREASE**
abbey head **ABBOT, ABBESS**
abbreviate **SHORTEN, ABRIDGE, REDUCE**
abdicate **RESIGN, RENOUNCE**
abdomen **BELLY, STOMACH PAUNCH**
Abe Lincoln symbol
(2 wds.) **STOVEPIPE HAT**
Abel's brother **CAIN, SETH**
abet **ENCOURAGE, HELP, INCITE, SANCTION**
abhor **HATE, LOATHE, DETEST, DESPISE**
abject **BASE, WRETCHED**
able **CAPABLE, COMPETENT, QUALIFIED, SKILLED**
able to be examined **TESTABLE**
able to fly **VOLANT**
abluent **CLEANER, CLEANSER**
ablution **BATH, WASHING, CLEANSING**
ably **EFFICIENTLY, CAPABLY COMPETENTLY**
Abner's friend **LUM**
abode **DWELLING, RESIDENCE, HOME, HEARTH**
abolish **ANNUL**
abomasum **RUMINANT**
abominable **ODIOUS, HORRIBLE**

abominable snowman **YETI**
abomination **DETESTATION, ABHORRENCE**
aborigine **PRIMITIVE, NATIVE**
about **ANENT**
above **ATOP, ON, UPON, OVER, OVERHEAD, SUPERIOR**
aboveboard **OPEN, FRANK, CANDID**
abrade **SAND, SCRAPE, RUB OFF**
Abraham's father **TERAH**
abrasion **EROSION**
abroad **OVERSEAS**
abrogate **ANNUL, CANCEL**
abrupt **SUDDEN, BRUSQUE**
abscond **RUN OFF, DECAMP**
absconding soldier **DESERTER**
absence **LACK**
absence of sound **SILENCE**
absent **AWAY, LACKING**
absolute **ENTIRE, COMPLETE**
absolutely **PURELY, WHOLLY, REALLY**
absolute ruler **DESPOT, DICTATOR, TYRANT**
absolve **PARDON, FORGIVE**
absorb **CONSUME, SWALLOW**
absorb information **DIGEST, LEARN**
absorb moisture **IMBIBE**
abstain from **ESCHEW**
abstain from food **FAST**
abstain from meat
(those who) **VEGETARIAN**
abstract **STEAL, DIVERT**
abstract being **ESSE**
abstruse **PROFOUND, SUBTLE. RECONDITE**
abundantly supplied **REPLETE**
abuse **DAMAGE, INJURE**
abusive speech **TIRADE**
abyss **CHASM, PIT, GULF**
Abyssinian ruler **AMEER, AMIR, EMIR**
accelerate **SPEED**
accelerate a motor **REV**
accent **STRESS**
accented part of a verse **ARSIS**
accept as true **BELIEVE**
accepted rule **CANON**
access **DOOR**
access to a mine **ADIT**
acclaim **ECLAT, APPLAUD, HAIL, WELCOME**

accredited	APPROVED	across (prefix)	TRANS
accrue	INCREASE	acrostic	PUZZLE
accumulate	AMASS, STORE	act	FEAT, DEED,
accumulated matter	HEAP		PERFORMANCE, BEHAVIOR,
	ACCRETION		DO, PERFORM, BEHAVE,
accurate	EXACT		EMOTE, PRETEND, PRETENSE
accuse	BLAME	Actaeon	HUNTER, STAG
accustom	INURE, ENURE	act against	OPPOSE
accustomed	WONT	act as a bearer	CARRY
ace	CARD	act as a butler	BUTTLE
acerbity	RANCOR	act as a model	POSE
ache	PAIN, HURT,	act as chairman	PRESIDE
	YEARN, LONGING	act as mediator	INTERCEDE
accommodate	SERVE, OBLIGE	actin	PROTEIN
accompany	ESCORT, ATTEND	acting a role (2 wds.)	ON STAGE
accomplice	ALLY	actinia	RAY, SEA ANEMONE
accomplish	DO, COMPLETE,	actinolite	ASBESTOS,
	PERFECT		AMPHIBOLE
accomplishment	DEED, FEAT	action	DEED
accord	UNISON, HARMONIZE,	active	VIGOROUS, AGILE,
	AGREE, GRANT, BESTOW		LIVELY, BUSY, SPRY
according to fact	TRUE	active person	DOER
according to law	LEGAL	activity	MOTION
accost	GREET	act of daring	FEAT
account	TAB	act of learning	LOAN
accountable	LIABLE	act of stealing	THEFT
account book	LEDGER	act of taking for	
accounting	BILL	one's own	ADOPTION
accounting term	DEBIT, CREDIT,	actor	THESPIAN
	NET, PROFIT,	actor Ameche	DON
	LOSS, ASSET	actor Andrews	DANA
account juggler	EMBEZZLER	actor Arness	JAMES
achieve	DO, PERFORM	actor Astaire	FRED
achievement	DEED, FEAT	actor Autry	GENE
achromatic	COLORLESS	actor Backus	JIM
acid	SOUR, TART	actor Barry	GENE
aciform	SHARP	actor Blore	ERIC
acknowledge	AVOW, OWN	actor Brand	NEVIL
acknowledge a greeting	NOD	actor Brynner	YUL
acorn	NUT	actor Burr	RAYMOND
acorn tree	OAK	actor Cameron	ROD
acquaint	INFORM, TELL	actor Carney	ART
acquiesce	COMPLY, AGREE,	actor Crabbe	BUSTER
	GAIN, GET	actor Dailey	DAN
acquire by labor	EARN	actor Drury	JAMES
acquired skill	ART	actor Duryea	DAN
acquire knowledge	LEARN	actor Ferrer	JOSE, MEL
acquisitive	GREEDY	actor Flynn	ERROLL
acquit	PARDON, ABSOLVE	actor Fonda	HENRY, PETER
acrid	BITTER, TART	actor Ford	GLENN
acrimony	BITTERNESS	actor Grant	CARY
acrobatic performer	TUMBLER	actor Graves	PETER
	ROPEDANCER	actor Guinness	ALEC
acrobat's bar	TRAPEZE	actor Heflin	VAN
acrobat's feat	STUNT, SPLIT	actor Holbrook	HAL
acrobat's garment	LEOTARD	actor Hudson	ROCK
acrogen	FERN, MOSS, PLANT	actor Hunter	TAB
acrolith	STATUE	actor Jannings	EMIL
acromion	SHOULDER, SCAPULA	actor Janssen	DAVID

actor Jourdan	**LOUIS**	actress Chase	**ILKA**
actor Keith	**BRIAN**	actress Christian	**LINDA**
actor Karloff	**BORIS**	actress Claire	**INA**
actor Knotts	**DON**	actress Collins	**JOAN**
actor Kruger	**OTTO, HARDY**	actress Dahl	**ARLENE**
actor Ladd	**ALAN**	actress Davis	**BETTE**
actor Lancaster	**BURT**	actress Day	**DORIS**
actor Lugosi	**BELA**	actress Dee	**SANDRA**
actor MacAuthur	**JAMES**	actress Dennis	**SANDY**
actor MacDowell	**RODDY**	actress Dickinson	**ANGIE**
actor MacMurray	**FRED**	actress Drew	**ELLEN**
actor March	**HAL, FREDRIC**	actress Duke	**PATTY**
actor Massey	**RAYMOND**	actress Dunne	**IRENE**
actor McQueen	**STEVE**	actress Farrow	**MIA**
actor Milland	**RAY**	actress Feldon	**BARBARA**
actor Mineo	**SAL**	actress Fisher	**GAIL**
actor Mitchum	**ROBERT**	actress Fleming	**RHONDA**
actor Montand	**YVES**	actress Foch	**NINA**
actor Murray	**DON, JAN, KEN**	actress Fontaine	**JOAN**
actor Newman	**PAUL**	actress Gabor	**EVA, ZSA ZSA**
actor Nielsen	**LESLIE**	actress Gam	**RITA**
actor Nimoy	**LEONARD**	actress Gardner	**AVA**
actor O'Brien	**PAT**	actress Hagen	**UTA**
actor O'Toole	**PETER**	actress Harding	**ANNE**
actor Parker	**FESS**	actress Haver	**JUNE**
actor Perkins	**TONY**	actress Havoc	**JUNE**
actor Powell	**WILLIAM**	actress Hayworth	**RITA**
actor Price	**VINCENT**	actress Hepburn	**AUDREY,**
actor Randall	**TONY**		**KATHARINE**
actor Sharif	**OMAR**	actress Hopkins	**MIRIAM**
actor Shatner	**WILLIAM**	actress Jeanmaire	**RENEE**
actor Sinatra	**FRANK**	actress Jones	**JENNIFER,**
actor Sparks	**NED**		**SHIRLEY**
actor Steiger	**ROD**	actress Lanchester	**ELSA**
actor Stewart	**JAMES**	actress Lange	**HOPE**
actor Taylor	**ROD, ROBERT**	actress Leigh	**JANET, VIVIEN**
actor Torn	**RIP**	actress Louise	**TINA, ANITA**
actor Van Dyke	**DICK**	actress Lupino	**IDA**
actor Wallach	**ELI**	actress Magnani	**ANNA**
actor Wayne	**JOHN**	actress Mayo	**VIRGINIA**
actor Weaver	**DENNIS**	actress Medford	**KAY**
actor West	**ADAM**	actress Merkel	**UNA**
actor's audition	**TRYOUT**	actress Merrill	**DINA**
actor's hint	**CUE**	actress Mills	**JULIET, HAYLEY**
actor's part	**ROLE**	actress Moore	**TERRY, MELBA**
actors in a play	**CAST**	actress Moorehead	**AGNES**
act pretentiously		actress Neal	**PATRICIA**
(2 wds.)	**SHOW OFF**	actress Novak	**KIM**
actress Albright	**LOLA**	actress Oberon	**MERLE**
actress Angeli	**PIER**	actress O'Hara	**MAUREEN**
actress Arden	**EVE**	actress Parker	**ELEANOR**
actress Balin	**INA**	actress Pitts	**ZASU**
actress Bancroft	**ANNE**	actress-playwright	
actress Baxter	**ANNE**	Gordon	**RUTH**
actress Benaderet	**BEA**	actress Rainer	**LUISE**
actress Bernhardt	**SARAH**	actress Raines	**ELLA**
actress Blake	**AMANDA**	actress Redgrave	**VANESSA,**
actress Cannon	**DYAN**		**LYNN**
actress Charisse	**CYD**	actress Ritter	**THELMA**

actress Rush	BARBARA	adjust	ALINE, ALIGN, ADAPT
actress Shearer	NORMA	adjutant bird	ARGALA,
actress Sheridan	ANNE		MARABOU, STORK
actress Sommars	JULIE	administer	MANAGE
actress Southern	ANN	administer corporal	
actress Stanwyck	BARBARA	punishment	SPANK, LASH
actress Storm	GALE		WHIP, PADDLE
actress Taylor	LIZ, ELIZABETH	admirer	BEAU, SWAIN
actress Thomas	MARLO	admiring group	
actress Tierney	GENE	(2 wds.)	FAN CLUB
actress Toren	MARTA	admissible	WORTHY, PROPER,
actress Turner	LANA		ACCEPTABLE
actress Welch	RAQUEL	admission	ENTRY
actress Weld	TUESDAY	admit	ALLOW, OWN
actress West	MAE	admit being	
actual	REAL	true	ACKNOWLEDGE
actuality	FACT	admonish	WARN
aculeus	STING, PRICKLE	admonition	REBUKE
acumen	INSIGHT	adnate	JOINED
acuminate	SHARPEN, TAPER	ado	FUSS, HUBBUB, TO-DO
acute	SHARP	adobe	BRICK, MUD
adage	PROVERB, SAYING	adolescent	TEEN
Adam and Eve's home	EDEN	adopt	ASSUME, ACCEPT
Adam's ale	WATER	adorable	CUTE
Adam's grandson	ENOS	adorably pretty (5 wds.)	AS
Adam's mate	EVE		CUTE AS A BUTTON
adapt	ADJUST	adore	IDOLIZE, LOVE,
add	TOTAL, SUM UP		WORSHIP, DOTE
addax	ANTELOPE	adorn	DECORATE, TRIM,
adder	VIPER, SNAKE, ASP		EMBELLISH
addict	USER	Adriatic port of Italy	BARI
addicted	DEVOTED,	adroit	DEXTEROUS
ATTACHED, HABITUATED		adulterate	MIX, DEBASE
addition	INCREASE	adult female	WOMAN
additional	EXTRA, MORE,	adult insect	IMAGO
SUPPLEMENTARY		adult male	MAN
addition to a house	ELL	advance	GAIN, PROCEED, GO
addle	MUDDLE, CONFUSE,	advanced in years	AGED, OLD
SPOIL		advancement	PROGRESS
add on	ANNEX, APPEND	advantage	EDGE, HEAD START
address	SPEAK, SPEECH	advantageous	USEFUL
address with friendliness	GREET	advantageous	
add salt	SEASON	purchase	BARGAIN
add sugar	SWEETEN	adventure	INCIDENT, EVENT,
ade	FRUIT DRINK		EXPERIENCE
adduce	CITE	adventurous deed	GEST, GESTE
adequate	SUITABLE	adversary	FOE, ENEMY
adhere	STICK, CLEAVE	adverse	HOSTILE,
adherent of a king	ROYALIST,		UNFAVORABLE
TORY		adversity	DISASTER,
adhesive	STICKY		CALAMITY
adhesive strip	TAPE	advertisement	NOTICE
adhesive substance	PASTE,	advertising sign	POSTER,
GLUE			BILLBOARD, BILL
adieu	FAREWELL	advice	COUNSEL
adjacent	NEAR, NEXT	advise	COUNSEL, SUGGEST
adjoin	ABUT, CONTIGUOUS	advise (arch.)	REDE
adjuration	APPEAL, COMMAND	advise of danger	WARN, ALERT
		advocate	SUPPORT

Aegean Island,
  former name **NIOS**
aerial toy **KITE**
aerie **NEST**
aery **ETHEREAL**
Aesop's island home **SAMOS**
affable **EASY, POLITE**
affair **INCIDENT**
affectation **POSE**
affected manner **AIRS**
affection **LOVE, FONDNESS**
affectionate **LOVING,
DEMONSTRATIVE**
affirm **ASSERT, ATTEST,
AVOW, ACKNOWLEDGE,
AVER**
affirmative reply **YES, YEA,
AY, AYE**
affix a signature **SIGN,
ENDORSE**
afflatus **IMPULSE**
affliction **TROUBLE, SORROW**
affluent **WEALTHY**
afford **SPARE**
affray **MELEE, BRAWL**
affright **TERROR**
affront **INSULT**
Afghan prince **AMIR, AMEER,
EMIR**
aflame **BURNING**
afoot **BREWING**
afoul **TANGLED**
afraid **SCARED**
African antelope **ELAND, GNU**
African-Arabian
  waters (2 wds.) **RED SEA**
African dialect **BANTU,
SWAHILI, BEMBA, LINGALA,
CONGO, HAUSA, MANDINGO**
African hemp **IFE**
African hunting
  expedition **SAFARI**
African land **ALGERIA,
BOTSWANA, BURUNDI,
CAMEROON, CHAD, CONGO,
DAHOMEY, EGYPT, ETHIOPIA,
GABON, GAMBIA, GHANA,
GUINEA, KENYA, LESOTHO,
LIBERIA, LIBYA, MALAWI,
MALI, MAURITANIA,
MOROCCO, NIGER, NIGERIA,
RHODESIA, RWANDA,
SENEGAL, SOMALIA, SUDAN,
TANZANIA, TOGO, TUNISIA,
UGANDA, ZAMBIA**
African land (2 wds.) **IVORY
COAST, SOUTH AFRICA,
UPPER VOLTA**
African lily **ALOE**

African nut tree **KOLA, COLA**
African river **CONGO, JUBA,
NIGER, NILE, SHIRE,
VAAL, VOLTA, VELE**
African tree **SHEA**
Afrikaans **LANGUAGE**
Afrikander **BOER**
aft **ASTERN**
after **FOLLOWING, BEHIND,
LATER**
after-dinner candy **MINT**
aftermath **RESULT**
aftermost **LAST**
afternoon beverage **TEA**
afternoon party **TEA**
afternoon
  performance **MATINEE**
afternoon show **MATINEE**
afternoon sleep **SIESTA, NAP**
afternoon snack **TEA**
aftersong **EPODE**
afterthought (abbr.) **PS**
aftertime **FUTURE**
afterward **LATER**
again **ANEW, OVER, ENCORE**
against **ANTI, CON**
agama **LIZARD**
agapanthus **LILY**
agape **LOVE**
agar **GEL, MEDIUM**
age **ERA, EPOCH,
LIFETIME, EON**
aged **OLD, ANCIENT,
RIPENED, MATURED**
aged, as meat **CURED**
aged beer **LAGER**
ageless **ETERNAL**
agenda **PROGRAM**
agenesis **ABSENCE**
agent **DEPUTY,
REPRESENTATIVE**
age-old **ANCIENT**
age on the vine **RIPEN**
agglomeration **HEAP, MASS**
agglutinant **GLUE**
aggrandize **EXALT**
aggregate **SUM, TOTAL**
aggressive **PUSHY**
agile **NIMBLE, LIVELY,
SPRY, ACTIVE**
agitate **STIR**
Agnes Moorehead role **ENDORA**
ago **PAST**
agony **TORTURE**
agree **ACCORD, ASSENT,
CONCUR, CONSENT**
agreeable **PLEASANT**
agreement **PACT**

agreement between nations **TREATY**

agrestic **RURAL, RUSTIC**

agricultural home **FARM**

agricultural implement **HOE, HARROW, PLOW, REAPER, SICKLE**

agriculture **FARMING, HUSBANDRY**

agrimony **FLOWER**

aguardiente **BRANDY**

ague **FEVER**

ahead **FORWARD**

ah me! **ALAS**

aid **ABET, ASSIST, HELP**

Aida role **RADAMES, AMNERIS, AMONASRO**

aide **ASSISTANT**

aid in diagnosing **X-RAY**

aiguille **DRILL**

ail **SICKEN, TROUBLE**

ailanthus **TREE**

ailment **DISEASE**

aim **OBJECTIVE, DIRECT, GOAL, POINT, END**

air **AURA, ATMOSPHERE, VENTILATE, TUNE, MELODY**

airborne **ALOFT, FLYING**

air circulator **FAN**

aircraft **AIRPLANE, GLIDER, HELICOPTER, JET**

airedale **DOG, BREED**

air hero **ACE**

airman **AVIATOR, FLIER, PILOT**

airplane (Fr.) **AVION**

airplane enclosure **COCKPIT**

airplane space **SEAT**

airplane varnish **DOPE**

air pollution **SMOG**

airport, for short **DROME**

air rifle **BB**

airscrew **PROPELLER**

airstrip **RUNWAY**

Air Traffic Control (abbr.) **ATC**

air travel term **NONSTOP**

airy **LIGHT, LOFTY**

airy farewell **TATA**

ait **ISLET, EYOT**

aitch **"H"**

ajar **OPEN**

akin **RELATED**

Akkadian sun god **SHAMASH**

alacrity **SPEED**

alae **WINGS**

alar **WINGED, WINGLIKE**

alarm **FEAR, WARN, ALERT**

Alaskan native **ALEUT, ESKIMO**

Alaskan transportation **SLED, SKIDOO**

alate **WINGED**

alb **ROBE, CLOAK**

albacore **TUNA**

Albanian currency **LEK**

albeit **ALTHOUGH**

albite **FELDSPAR**

alcoholic beverage **GIN, SCOTCH, BOURBON, VODKA, RUM, MEAD, SPIRITS, WHISKEY**

alcohol lamp **ETNA**

alcove **NICHE, NOOK**

alder (var.) **OWLER**

alegar **VINEGAR**

alehouse **PUB, TAVERN, INN, BAR**

ale mug **TOBY**

alert **ATTENTIVE, WATCHFUL, WARN, ALARM**

Aleutian island **ATTU**

Aleut's home **IGLOO**

alewife **HERRING**

alexipharmic **ANTIDOTAL**

alfalfa **GRASS, FODDER**

alga **SEAWEED**

Algerian governor **DEY**

Algerian port **ORAN**

alien **FOREIGN, STRANGE, FOREIGNER**

alienate **ESTRANGE**

alight **DISMOUNT**

alike **SIMILAR, SAME**

aline **STRAIGHTEN**

alive **VITAL**

all **EVERYBODY, EVERYTHING**

allargando **SLOWER**

allay **SLAKE**

allege **AVER, STATE**

allegiance **LOYALTY**

allegorical work **FABLE**

allegro **FASTER**

alleviate **EASE, RELIEVE**

all excited **AGOG**

alley **LANE**

alliance **UNION**

allied **UNITED**

alligator **CROCODILE**

alligator pear **AVOCADO**

all male party **STAG**

allot **APPORTION, ASSIGN, DISTRIBUTE, METE, DOLE**

allow **LET, PERMIT, OWN, ADMIT**

allowable **PERMISSIBLE**

allowable under law **LEGAL, LICIT**

allowance **SHARE, RATION**

allowance for cash payment **DISCOUNT**
allowance for waste **TRET**
allow as a discount **REBATE**
allow liquid to fall **SPILL**
allow to fall **DROP**
allow to go free **RELEASE**
alloy **COMBINE, MIX, DEBASE**
all right **OK, OKAY, ROGER**
allspice **MYRTLE, PIMIENTO**
all the time (3 wds.) **DAY AND NIGHT**
all tied up (2 wds.) **EVEN STEVEN**
allude **REFER**
allure **ATTRACT, ENTICE, VAMP**
allurement **FASCINATION**
alluring sea creature **MERMAID, SIREN**
alluring woman **SIREN**
alluvion **FLOOD**
ally **CONFEDERATE**
almandine **GARNET**
almond **NUT**
almost **NEARLY, NIGH**
almost alike **SIMILAR**
alms box **ARCA**
almshouse **POORHOUSE**
aloe **LILY**
aloft **ABOVE, UP**
aloha state **HAWAII**
aloha symbol **LEI**
alone **SOLITARY, SOLO, UNACCOMPANIED**
along in years **AGED, OLD**
aloof **REMOVED**
alphabet **LETTERS**
alphabetic character **LETTER**
Alpine cottage **CHALET**
Alpine country **FRANCE, SWITZERLAND, AUSTRIA, ITALY**
Alpine peak **MATTERHORN, JUNGFRAU**
Alpine primrose **AURICULA**
Alpine region **TIROL, TYROL**
alsike **CLOVER**
also **AND, TOO, PLUS**
also-ran **LOSER**
alter **ADAPT, CHANGE, VARY, AMEND**
alterant **DYE**
alter, as a dress (2 wds.) **MAKE OVER**
altercation **QUARREL, SCRAP**
alternate **STANDBY**
alternately (2 wds.) **BY TURNS**
alternating current (abbr.) **AC**

alternative **OPTION, CHOICE**
alternative word **OR**
althea **FLOWER, HOLLYHOCK**
alto **VIOLA**
alum **ASTRINGENT, STYPTIC**
always **EVER, FOREVER**
always (poet.) **EER**
alyssum **MUSTARD**
amadavat **SONGBIRD**
amadou **PUNK, TINDER**
amalgam **ALLOY, MIXTURE, BLEND**
amalgamation **UNION, BLEND**
amass **ACCUMULATE, GATHER**
amass and conceal **HOARD**
amateur **DILETTANTE**
amateur radio operator **HAM**
amaze **ASTONISH, STUN, AWE**
amazement **SURPRISE**
Amazon tributary **APA, ICA**
ambassador **ENVOY**
ambiguous **UNCLEAR, VAGUE**
ambition **DESIRE**
amble **STROLL, MEANDER**
ambo **PULPIT**
ambush **TRAP**
amend **CORRECT, REVISE, ALTER, CHANGE**
American Beauty **ROSE**
American bird **EAGLE**
American black snake **RACER**
American blackbird **GRACKLE**
American buffalo **BISON**
American cheese **CHEDDAR**
American dish **HOTDOG, HAMBURGER**
American eagle **BALD**
American folk singer **IVES, SEEGER, GUTHRIE**
American humorist **ADE, TWAIN**
American in Britain **YANK**
American Indian **CREE, HOPI, UTE, ERIE, NAVAJO, OTO, APACHE, POHO, SIOUX, OMAHA, CROW**
American Indian tent **TEPEE, TIPI, TIPEE**
American ivy **CREEPER**
American patriot **OTIS, HALE, HENRY**
American soldiers **GI'S**
American spotted cat **MARGAY**
American symbol **EAGLE**
American vegetable **CORN, MAIZE, SQUASH**
America's uncle **SAM**
amiable **CORDIAL, AGREEABLE**
amianthus **ASBESTOS**

amicable	**FRIENDLY**
amid	**AMONG**
amidone	**METHADONE**
amiss	**ASTRAY, WRONG**
amity	**PEACE, FRIENDSHIP**
ammonia compounds	**AMINES**
ammonite	**FOSSIL**
ammunition	**SHOT, SHELLS**
among	**AMID, MID**
amoretto	**CUPID**
amorous look	**OGLE**
amorphous	**SHAPELESS**
amort	**SPIRITLESS**
amortize	**PRORATE**
amount	**SUM, TOTAL**
amount carried	**LOAD**
ampere (abbr.)	**AMP**
ampersand	**AND**
amphibian	**TOAD, FROG, SALAMANDER**
amphitheater	**ARENA**
ample	**PLENTIFUL, ENOUGH**
amplify	**ENLARGE, MAGNIFY**
amplitude	**BREADTH, SCOPE**
amulet	**CHARM**
amuse	**DIVERT, ENTERTAIN**
amusement	**GAME**
amusement enterprise	**CARNIVAL**
amusing	**COMICAL, FUNNY**
amusing play	**COMEDY**
amylaceous	**STARCHY**
amylum	**STARCH**
analyze grammatically	**PARSE**
analyze ore	**ASSAY**
Ananias	**LIAR**
anaphora	**REPETITION**
anarchy	**DISORDER**
anasarca	**DROPSY**
anatomical networks	**RETIA**
anatomical pouch	**SAC**
ancestor of the pharaohs	**RA, RE**
ancestry	**FAMILY, LINEAGE**
anchor	**MOOR, FIX, TIE**
anchor chain	**CABLE**
ancient	**OLD, OLDEN, AGED**
ancient British chariot	**ESSED, ESSEDA**
ancient Chinese capital	**SIAN**
ancient Greek coin	**OBOL**
ancient Hebrew ascetic	**ESSENE**
ancient Irish capital	**TARA**
ancient Italian	**LATIN, ROMAN OSCAN, ETRUSCAN**
ancient Italian family	**ESTE**
ancient king	**ARTHUR, DAVID, SAUL**
ancient kingdom on Persian Gulf	**ELAM**
ancient Mexican	**MAYA, AZTEC, TOLTEC**
ancient musical instrument	**LYRA, LYRE, LUTE**
ancient name of Vich	**AUSA**
Ancient of Days	**GOD**
ancient Peruvian	**INCA**
ancient Phoenician port	**SIDON, TYRE**
ancient poet	**BARD, PSALMIST**
ancient port of Rome	**OSTIA**
ancient psalmist	**DAVID**
ancient Roman garments	**TOGAS**
ancient Roman magistrate	**AEDILE, EDILE**
ancient sacred writings of Persia	**AVESTA**
ancient serf	**HELOT, ESNE**
ancient stringed instrument	**LUTE, LYRA, LYRE, KITHARA**
ancient Sudanese	**NUBIANS, NUBA**
ancient Syria	**ARAM**
ancient theatres	**ODEON, ODEUM**
ancient two-wheeled chariot	**ESSED, ESSEDA**
ancient writing	**RUNE**
ancon	**CONSOLE**
and	**ALSO, NEXT, PLUS**
and (Fr.)	**ET**
Andaman Islands' neighbor	**NICOBAR**
andante	**MODERATE**
Andes animal	**LLAMA**
Andes country	**PERU, BOLIVIA, CHILE, VENEZUELA, ECUADOR, ARGENTINA**
andesite	**FELDSPAR, GRANITE**
Andes mountain	**SORATA**
Andes vulture	**CONDOR**
and not	**NOR**
and others (2 wds., Lat. abbr.)	**ET AL**
Andrew Jackson's nickname (2 wds.)	**OLD HICKORY**
android	**ROBOT**
andromeda	**STAR**
and sign	**AMPERSAND**
and so on (2 wds., Lat. abbr.)	**ETC.**
Andy's partner	**AMOS**
anecdote	**TALE, YARN**
anechoic	**SOUNDPROOF**
anele	**ANOINT**
anemone	**BUTTERCUP**
anent	**CONCERNING, ABOUT**

anesthetic **ETHER, CHLOROFORM, GAS**
anew **AFRESH, OVER**
angel **CHERUB, SPIRIT**
angelic **HEAVENLY, GOOD**
angelic child **CHERUB**
angelica **PARSLEY**
angel's headdress **HALO**
angel's instrument **HARP**
anger **ENRAGE, IRE, WRATH, RAGE, MADDEN**
angina **SPASM**
angioma **TUMOR**
angle **BEVEL, FISH, CORNER**
angle of a leaf **AXIL**
anglepod **MILKWEED**
angler's bait **LURE**
angleworm **BAIT**
Anglo-Saxon Letter **EDH**
Anglo-Saxon slave **ESNE**
angry **CROSS, IRATE, MAD, ENRAGED, WRATHFUL**
anguish **DISTRESS, PAIN**
angular **GAUNT**
angwantibo **LEMUR**
anhydrous **WATERLESS**
ani **CUCKOO, BLACKBIRD**
anil **INDIGO**
anile **INFIRM, WEAK**
aniline product **DYE**
animal **BRUTE, BEAST, BIPED**
animal claw **TALON**
animal doctor **VET**
animal enclosure **CAGE, PEN**
animal fat **TALLOW**
animal flesh **MEAT, BEEF, PORK, HAM, VEAL, BACON, LAMB**
animal food **FODDER**
animal foot **PAW, PAD, HOOF**
animal garden **ZOO**
animal hair **FUR, MANE**
animal hide **PELT**
animal home **LAIR, DEN, BURROW, NEST**
animal nail **CLAW**
animal of South America **TAPIR, LLAMA, APARA, COATI, PACO, ALPACA**
animal of the cat family **LION, CHEETAH, TIGER, PANTHER, COUGAR, JAGUAR, OCELOT, CARACAL, LEOPARD**
animal park **ZOO**
animal's coat **FUR, PELT, HIDE, PELAGE**
animal's den **LAIR**

animal skin **PELT, FUR**
animal's limb **LEG**
animal trainer **TAMER**
animate **INSPIRE, CHEER, PROMPT**
animated **ALIVE, LIVELY**
animato (mus.) **ANIMATED**
anime **RESIN**
animosities **ENMITIES**
animus **SOUL**
anisette **LIQUEUR**
anjou **PEAR**
anklebone **TALUS**
ankle coverings **SPATS**
ankle mishap **SPRAIN**
anklet **SOCK**
annals **ARCHIVES**
Anne Bancroft role (2 wds.) **MIRACLE WORKER**
annex **ADD**
annihilate **ANNUL, EXTINGUISH, DESTROY**
announce **REVEAL, REPORT, TELL**
annoy **IRK, PESTER, TEASE, RILE**
annoying **TIRESOME**
annoying bird **PIGEON**
annoying child **BRAT**
annoying feeling **ITCH**
annoying insect **GNAT, MITE**
annoying one **PEST, NUISANCE**
annual **YEARLY**
annual contest (2 wds.) **MISS AMERICA**
annually **YEARLY**
annuity **PAYMENT**
annul **ABOLISH**
annulus **CIRCLE**
anomalous **ABNORMAL, DEVIANT**
anon **PRESENTLY, SOON, SUBSEQUENTLY**
anonymous **NAMELESS, ANON**
anopheles **MOSQUITO**
another name **ALIAS**
another name for Candia **HERAKLION**
another way around **DETOUR**
answer **RESPOND, REPLY**
answer the purpose **SERVE**
ant **EMMET, PISMIRE, TERMITE**
antagonism **ENMITY**
antagonist **RIVAL**
antarctic bird **PENGUIN**
Antarctic explorer **BYRD**
Antarctic sea **ROSS**

ant cow	APHID
antecedent	ANCESTOR
Anthony's nickname	TONY
anthracite	COAL
antiaircraft fire	FLAK
antiar	UPAS, POISON
antibiotic	SULFA
antic	CAPER, DIDO, PRANK
anticipate	AWAIT, WAIT
anticipation	HOPE
antidote	REMEDY
antimacassar	DOILY
antipasto	APPETIZER, SALAD
antipathy	HATE, HATRED
antiprohibitionists	WETS
antiquated	OLD, PASSE, AGED, ANCIENT
antique	ANCIENT, QUAINT, OLD
antiquity	YORE
antiseptic liquid	IODINE
antithesis	CONTRAST, OPPOSITE
antler	HORN
antlered animal	DEER, ELK, MOOSE
antre	CAVE, CAVERN
antrum	CAVITY
anvil (ant.)	INCUS
anxiety	CARE, WORRY, FEAR
anxious	EAGER
any	SOME
apace	SWIFTLY, QUICKLY
apart from	ASIDE, SEPARATE
apartment	FLAT
apartment (abbr.)	APT
apartment building	TENEMENT
apartment occupant	TENANT
apart (prefix)	DIS
apathy	INDIFFERENCE, PASSIVITY
ape	GORILLA, CHIMPANZEE, SIMIAN, ORANGUTAN, MIMIC, IMITATE, MONKEY, MOCK, COPY
apeak	VERTICAL
aper	COPYCAT, MIMIC
apercu	INSIGHT
aperitif	LIQUEUR, WINE
aperture	GAP, OPENING, ORIFICE
apex	SUMMIT, TOP, ACME
aphid	INSECT, LOUSE
aphorism	MAXIM, ADAGE
apiary dweller	BEE
apiece	EACH
apish	SILLY
aplomb	POISE
apocryphal	SPURIOUS
apology	PLEA
apoplexy	PARALYSIS, STROKE
Apostle Paul	SAUL
apothecary's weight	DRAM
appall	DISMAY
apalling	TERRIBLE
apparel	DRESS, RAIMENT, GARB, SUIT, COAT
apparel of skins	PELT
apparent	SEEMING
apparition	GHOST, SHADE, SPECTRE
appeal	PLEAD
appear	SEEM, SPRING UP, TURN UP
appear again	RECUR
appearance	ASPECT, FACET, LOOK
appease	PACIFY
appel	DARE, CHALLENGE
appellation	TITLE, NAME
append	ADD, ATTACH, ANNEX
appendage	TAIL, LIMB
appetite	DESIRE, RELISH
applaud	CLAP, CHEER
apple (Fr.)	POMME
apple center	CORE
apple drink	CIDER
applejack	CIDER, BRANDY
apple of one's eye	PET, FAVORITE
apple-pie order	NEAT
apple seed	PIP
Appleseed	JOHNNY
appliance	DEVICE, MACHINE, TOOL
applique	DECORATE
apply	SPREAD, PLACE, REQUEST
apply lightly	DAB
apply powder	DUST
appoint	NAME, FURNISH
appointment	DATE, TRYST
apportion	DOLE, ALLOT, METE
apposite	APT
appraise	RATE
appreciate	ESTEEM, ESTIMATE, NOTICE
appreciative	GRATEFUL
apprehend	DISCERN
apprehension	FEAR, TREPIDATION
apprentice	TRAINEE, NOVICE
apprise	TEACH, INFORM
approach	NEAR, COME
approachable	RECEPTIVE
approbate	APPROVE

appropriate	ADOPT, SEEMLY, FIT, FITTING	arachnid	SPIDER, MITE, TICK, SCORPION
approve	OK, OKAY	araneid	SPIDER
approved model	STANDARD	arbalest	CROSSBOW
approximal	ADJOINING	arbiter	UMPIRE
approximately	ABOUT, AROUND	arbitrary	ABSOLUTE, DESPOTIC
approximation	LIKENESS, NEARNESS	arbitrary assertion (colloq.)	SAY-SO
April shower	RAIN	arbor	BOWER
apron-like garment	SMOCK	arcane	HIDDEN, SECRET
apropos	TIMELY, APT	arch (Scot.)	PEND
apt	LIKELY, APRÓPOS	Archbishop of	
apteryx	KIWI	Canterbury	ANSELM, BECKET
aquarium	TANK	arched way	ARCADE, LOGGIA, PORTICO
aquarium fish	MOLLY, GUPPY, GOURAMI, PLATY	archer	BOWMAN
aquatic animal	OTTER, SEAL, WHALE, SEACOW, SEALION, SEA ELEPHANT, WALRUS, HIPPOPOTAMUS	archer's missile	ARROW
		archimage	MAGICIAN, WIZARD
		archives	ANNALS
		arch of a circle	SECTOR
aquatic bird	SWAN, TERN, DUCK, TEAL, DRAKE, GULL, PENGUIN, FALK	Arctic abode	IGLOO, IGLU
		Arctic bird	SKUA
		Arctic charr	TROUT
aquatic rodent	MUSKRAT, BEAVER	Arctic expanse	ICE
		Arctic inhabitant	ESKIMO, ALEUT
aquatic sport	SWIM, DIVE, BOAT, SAIL, FISH, SURF, WATER SKI	arctics	BOOTS, OVERSHOES
		Arctic vehicle	SLED, SLEIGH, DOGSLED
aquatint	ETCHING	ardent affection	LOVE
aquavit	LIQUOR, APERITIF	ardor	ELAN, ZEAL
aqua vitae	LIQUOR, ALCOHOL	arduous journey	TREK
aqueous	WATERY	are	EXIST
Ara	CONSTELLATION, MACAW	area	REGION, SURFACE
Arab	BEDOUIN, SEMITE, YEMENITE	area in a house	ROOM
		areca	PALM
Arab chieftain	EMIR, AMIR, AMEER	arena	AMPHITHEATER
		arenaceous	SANDY
Arab chieftain's domain	EMIRATE	argala	STORK, MARIBOU
		Argentine dance	TANGO
Arab country	YEMEN, OMAN, ADEN, SYRIA, LEBANON, EGYPT, JORDAN, MOROCCO, ALGERIA, TUNISIA, LIBYA, SUDAN, IRAQ, KUWAIT, MUSCAT	Argentine plains	PAMPAS
		argol	TARTAR
		argot	CANT, SLANG
		argue	DEBATE, REBUT, FIGHT, QUARREL
		argument	SPAT, QUARREL, DEBATE, FIGHT
Arab garment	ABA, BURNOOSE	arid	DRY, SERE
Arabian coffee	MOCHA	arid expanse	DESERT
Arabian coin	DINAR	Aries	RAM
Arabian gazelle	ARIEL	Arikara	REE
Arabian gulf	ADEN, AQABA	ariose	MELODIC
Arabian name	SAUD	arise	GET UP, COME UP, ASCEND
Arabian port	ADEN		
Arabian prince	EMIR, AMIR, AMEER, EMEER	arithmetic, for short	MATH
		arithmetic sign	PLUS, MINUS, EQUAL
Arabian ship	DHOW		
Arabian territory	OMAN		
arable grassland	LEA, LEY	Arizona college town	TEMPE

Arizona Indian **APACHE, PIMA, PAPAGO, HOPI, NAVAJO**
Arizona lizard
(2 wds.) **GILA MONSTER**
Arizona river **GILA, SALT, COLORADO**
ark **BOAT**
ark builder **NOAH**
arkose **SANDSTONE**
ark's landing place **ARARAT**
arm **LIMB, BRANCH, TENTACLE**
armada **FLEET**
arm and hand joint **WRIST**
armature **DEFENSE, COVERING**
arm bone **ULNA**
arm covering **SLEEVE**
armed band **POSSE**
armed conflict **WAR, BATTLE**
Armenian cap **CALPAC, CALPACK, KALPAK**
Armenian mountain **ARARAT, ARA, ARAGATIS, TAURUS**
Armenian people **GOMER**
arm extremity **HAND**
armistice **TRUCE**
armorbearer **SQUIRE, ARMIGER**
armored mammal **ARMADILLO**
arms **WEAPONS**
arms and legs **LIMBS**
army **FORCES, TROOPS**
army acronym **AWOL**
army base **CAMP**
army bed **COT**
army chaplain **PADRE**
army group **UNIT, CADRE**
army meal **MESS**
army officer **CAPTAIN, COLONEL, MAJOR, GENERAL, LIEUTENANT**
army shoe **BOOT**
army trader **SUTLER**
Army Transport Service
(abbr.) **A.T.S.**
army unit **CORPS, REGIMENT**
aroid **TARO**
aroma **BOUQUET, ODOR, FRAGRANCE, SCENT, SMELL**
aromatic **REDOLENT, FRAGRANT**
aromatic beverage **TEA**
aromatic gum resin **MYRRH**
aromatic herb **MINT, DILL, SPEARMINT, SAGE, CARUM**
aromatic medicinal ingredient
(2 wds.) **BAY RUM**
aromatic ointment **NARD**
aromatic product **SPICE**

aromatic seed **ANISE, CUMIN**
around **ABOUT**
around (prefix) **PERI**
arouse a response
(3 wds.) **RING A BELL**
arraign **CHARGE, ACCUSE**
arrange **ASSORT**
arrange and edit **COMPILE**
arrange in folds **DRAPE**
arrange in layers **TIER, LAMINATE**
arrange in order **SORT**
arrange in rows **ALINE, ALIGN**
arrangement **SETUP, DISPOSITION**
Arras **TAPESTRY**
array **DRESS, DECK, ADORN**
arrears **BEHIND**
arrest **NAB, STOP, CHECK**
arrive **COME**
arrive at **REACH**
arrive by plane **LAND**
arrogance **PRIDE**
arrogant **PROUD, HAUGHTY**
arrogant manner **HAUTEUR**
arrogate **USURP, TAKE**
arrow **DART, SPEAR, SHAFT**
arrow case **QUIVER**
arrow point **BARB**
arrow poison **CURARE, INEE, URARI, UPAS, ANTIAR**
arrow-shaped **HASTATE**
arroyo **BROOK, CREEK, GULCH**
art **CUNNING, KNACK**
art (Lat.) **ARS**
artery **AORTA**
art gallery **SALON, MUSEUM**
article **AN, THE, ITEM**
article of apparel **SHIRT, BLOUSE, DRESS, ROBE, JACKET, VEST, SKIRT, WAIST**
article of bedding **SHEET, SPREAD, BLANKET, PILLOWCASE**
article of cosmetics **ROUGE, LIPSTICK, MASCARA, LINER, POWDER**
article of faith **TENET, DOCTRINE, DOGMA**
article of food **CORN, RICE, BREAD, STEAK, CHOP, VEGETABLE, FRUIT**
article of furniture **TABLE, CHAIR, SOFA, SETTEE, DAVENPORT, BOOKCASE, BED, DRESSER**

article of jewelry **RING, NECKLACE, BRACELET, EARRING**
articles of merchandise **WARES**
artifice **RUSE, SUBTERFUGE**
artificer **ARTISAN, SMITH**
artificial **FALSE**
artificial butter **OLEO**
artificial coloring **DYE**
artificial front **FACADE**
artificial hairpiece **WIG, TOUPEE, FALL**
artificial ice floor **RINK**
artificial language **IDO, ESPERANTO**
artificially high voice **FALSETTO**
artificially sprouted grain **MALT**
artificial silk **RAYON**
artificial water channel **FLUME**
artificial waterway **CANAL**
artillery **CANNON**
artillery emplacement **BATTERY**
artillery fire **SALVO**
artisan **CRAFTSMAN**
artist **PAINTER, SCULPTOR**
artiste **ACTOR, PERFORMER**
artistic person **AESTHETE**
artist's cap **BERET**
artist's equipment **EASEL, PALETTE**
artist's medium **INK, OIL, TEMPERA**
artist's paint holder **PALETTE**
artist's specialty **PAINTING, LANDSCAPE, PORTRAIT, STILL LIFE, SCULPTURE, ETCHING**
artist's stand **EASEL**
artist's work **COLLAGE, PAINTING, MASTERPIECE, PORTRAIT, MINIATURE**
artist's workshop **ATELIER, STUDIO**
artless **OPEN, CANDID**
artlessness **NAIVETE**
art of discourse **RHETORIC**
art of government **POLITICS**
art of self-protection **DEFENSE**
arui **AOUDAD**
arum **CUCKOOPINT, CALLAS**
as **WHILE**
asa **PHYSICIAN, HEALER**
as a certainty **FOR SURE, SURELY**

as a close race (3 wds.) **NIP AND TUCK**
as a rule **NORMALLY**
ascend **ARISE, CLIMB, RISE**
ascenseur **ELEVATOR, LIFT**
ascertain **LEARN, PROVE**
ascertain bearing **ORIENT**
ascertain the dimensions **MEASURE**
ascertain the number **COUNT**
ascetic **HERMIT, AUSTERE**
ascot **TIE, CRAVAT, SCARF**
ascribable **DUE, ATTRIBUTABLE**
ascribe **ASSIGN**
asea **BEFUDDLED, BEWILDERED**
as far as **TO**
ash **TREE**
ash can (Brit.) **DUSTBIN**
ash-colored **GRAY**
ashen **PALE, LIVID**
Asia Minor mountain **IDA**
Asia Minor sea **AEGEAN, BLACK**
Asian country **IRAN, LAOS, VIETNAM, CHINA, THAILAND, INDIA, PAKISTAN, IRAQ, ADEN, AFGHANISTAN, CAMBODIA, JAPAN, QATAR, NEPAL, CEYLON, KOREA, KUWAIT, MACAO, MALAYSIA, PHILIPPINES**
Asian sea **ARAL, CASPIAN, DEAD**
Asian treeless tract **STEPPE**
Asian Turk **TATAR**
Asiatic fiber plant **HEMP**
Asiatic mountains **PAMIRS, ALTAI, ELBURZ, HIMALAYA, KARAKORUM, KUNLUN, TAURUS, URALS**
ask **INQUIRE, INVITE, REQUEST**
ask alms **BEG**
askew **ALOP, AWRY, OBLIQUE**
ask for **SOLICIT**
ask for a job **APPLY**
ask for charity **BEG**
ask forcibly **DEMAND**
ask for payment **DUN**
as of now (2 wds.) **TO-DATE**
aspect **APPEARANCE, PHASE, FACET, SIDE**
aspen **POPLAR**
asperity **ACRIMONY, ROUGHNESS**

asperse	DEFAME, SLANDER
aspersion	CALUMNY
asphalt	BITUMEN
aspiration	HOPE
aspiring actress	STARLET
asp	SNAKE, ADDER, VIPER
ass	DOLT, FOOL
assail	BESET
Assam worm	ERIA
assault	ATTACK
assemblage	CREW
assemble	COLLECT, GATHER, MEET, MUSTER
assembly	COMPANY, MEETING
assent	CONSENT, AGREEMENT, COMPLY
assert	AFFIRM, AVER, AVOW, ALLEGE, CLAIM
assert as fact	POSIT
assertion	DECLARATION, STATEMENT
assertion of right	CLAIM
assess	CHARGE, LEVY, ESTIMATE
assess taxes	LEVY
asset	PROPERTY, RESOURCE
assign	ASCRIBE, DELEGATE
assign a portion	ALLOT
assignation	TRYST
assigned chore	TASK, STINT, JOB
assignment	TASK
assimilate	ABSORB
assist	AID, HELP, ABET
assistance	AID, HELP, WELFARE
assistant	AIDE, HELPER
associate	COMRADE, COMPANION, PARTNER, COLLEAGUE
Associated Press (abbr.)	AP
associates	KITH
association	CLUB, LEAGUE, ORGANIZATION
assort	CLASSIFY
assortment	VARIETY
assuage	ALLAY
assume an attitude	POSE
assume an upright position	STAND
assume control (2 wds.)	TAKE OVER
assumed manner	AIRS
assumed name	ALIAS
assurance	APLOMB, TRUST
asterisk	STAR
astern	AFT

asthmatic	WHEEZY
astir	ACTIVE, UP
astonish	AMAZE, ASTOUND, STUN
astound	AMAZE
astral	STARRY, STELLAR
astride	ASTRADDLE
astringent	ALUM, STYPTIC
astronaut Cooper	LEROY
astronaut's "all right"	AOK
astronaut's feat (2 wds.)	SPACE WALK
astronaut's ferry	LEM
astronaut's garment (2 wds.)	SPACE SUIT
astronaut's report (2 wds.)	NO GO
astronomer's tool	TELESCOPE
astute	SHREWD
asunder	APART
Aswan sight	DAM
Aswan's river	NILE
as well	ALSO, TOO, AND
asylum	HAVEN
at	NEARBY
at a disadvantage (4 wds.)	OUT ON A LIMB
at a distance	AFAR, OFF
at all	EVER
at all events (3 wds.)	IN ANY CASE
at all times	EVER
at bat	UP
ate	DINED, CONSUMED, GOBBLED
at ease	POISED, RELAXED, COMFORTABLE
atelier	STUDIO
ates	SWEETSOP
at flood level	AWASH
at full speed	ALL-OUT
at hand	NEAR
Athena	PALLAS
Athenian historian	XENOPHON
Athenian lawgiver	SOLON
Athenian statesman	PERICLES
Athens' rival	SPARTA
at highest point	ZENITH, APEX, APOGEE
athletic center	GYMNASIUM, GYM
athletic contest	TOURNAMENT, GAME, BOUT, MATCH, MEET
athletic star	ACE, PRO
at home	IN
atimon	MUSKMELON
Atlantic fish	SALEMA

Atlantic island	**CANARY**	at that place	**THERE**
atlas chart	**MAP**	at that time	**THEN**
at last	**FINALLY**	at the back	**AFT, ASTERN**
at liberty	**FREE**	at the front	
at long last	**FINALLY**	(3 wds.)	**TO THE FORE**
atmosphere	**AIR, AURA,**	at the middle	**CENTRAL**
	AMBIANCE	at the middle point	**MID**
atmospheric disturbance		at the peak	**ATOP**
	STATIC, STORM	at the same time	**TOGETHER**
atmospheric weight		at the summit	**ATOP**
(2 wds.)	**AIR PRESSURE**	at the tip	**APICAL**
at no cost	**FREE, GRATIS**	at this place	**HERE**
at no time	**NEVER**	at this time	**NOW**
at odds	**OUT**	attic	**GARRET**
atoll	**ISLET, REEF**	Attila's followers	**HUNS**
atom	**WHIT, PARTICLE**	attire	**DRESS, GARB,**
atomic	**MINUTE, SMALL**		**CLOTHING, ARRAY**
atomic device	**REACTOR, BOMB**	attired	
atomic number (abbr.)	**AT. NO.**		**CLAD, DRESSED,**
atomic particle	**PROTON,**		**GARBED, BEDECKED**
	NEUTRON, ELECTRON,	attitude	**AIR, SLANT**
	ION	attorney	**LAWYER, COUNSELOR**
atomize	**SPRAY**	attorney's charge	**FEE**
atone	**EXPIATE**	attract	**ALLURE, LURE,**
atonement	**AMENDS**		**ENTICE, INVITE**
atop	**ON, UPON, OVER,**	attraction	**CHARM, LURE**
	SURMOUNTING	attractive	**CUTE, MAGNETIC,**
at present	**NOW**		**INVITING**
at rest	**EASE**	attrap	**ADORN, ARRAY**
atrocious	**CRUEL, WICKED**	attribute	**PROPERTY, REFER,**
attach	**APPEND, ANNEX**		**ASSIGN, CREDIT**
attachment	**AFFINITY**	attrition	**FRICTION**
attach to	**ANNEX**	at what place	**WHERE**
attack	**SET ON, BESET,**	at what time	**WHEN**
	ASSAULT, ASSAIL	auberge	**INN**
attack by waiting	**SIEGE**	auction	**SALE**
attacker	**ASSAILANT**	auctioneer	**SELLER**
attack on all sides	**BESET**	auctioneer's word	**SOLD,**
attack repeatedly	**PELT,**		**GOING, GONE**
	ASSAIL	auction participant	**BIDDER**
attain	**REACH**	audacious	**BOLD, INSOLENT**
attainment	**ARRIVAL**	audacity	**GALL, NERVE,**
attain recognition	**ARRIVE**		**CHEEK**
attain success	**WIN**	audible respiration	**SIGH**
attempt	**TRY, ESSAY**	audibility	**ALOUD**
attend	**ESCORT, LISTEN**	audience	**EAR, ATTENTION**
attendance	**PRESENCE**	auditorium	**HALL**
attendant	**ESCORT, SERVANT**	auditory	**OTIC, AURAL**
attendant on board		auger	**TOOL, BORE**
ship	**STEWARD**	augment	**EKE, ADD, SWELL**
attending	**AT, WITH**	augury	**OMEN, FORETOKEN,**
attend to	**SEE**		**PORTENT, SIGN**
attention	**EAR, AUDIENCE**	aura	**ATMOSPHERE, AIR,**
attention-getting sound	**AHEM,**		**EMANATION**
	PST	auricle	**EAR, PINNA**
attentive	**ALERT**	auricular	**OTIC**
attestation	**TESTIMONY**	Aurora	**EOS**
atter	**POISON, VENOM, STING**	auspices	**EGIS, AEGIS**

austere	SEVERE, HARSH
Australian animal	KOALA,
	KANGAROO, PLATYPUS,
	ECHIDNA
Australian badger	WOMBAT
Australian beverage	KAVA
Australian bird	EMU
Australian capital	CANBERRA,
	PERTH
Australian cedar	TOON
Australian city	ADELAIDE,
	SYDNEY, GEELONG,
	BRISBANE
Australian dog	DINGO
Austrian capital	VIENNA
authentic	REAL
avarice	GREED
author Bellow	SAUL
authoress Ferber	EDNA
author Fleming	IAN
author Gardner	ERLE
author Harte	BRET
author Hunter	EVAN
authoritative	
example	PRECEDENT
authoritative rule	LAW
authoritative standard	NORM
authority	POWER, SAY
authority on governmental	
law	PARLIAMENTARIAN
authorize	LICENSE
author Levin	IRA
author of "The Inferno"	DANTE
author of "Picnic"	INGE
author of "Pygmalion"	SHAW
author of "Robinson	
Crusoe"	DEFOE
author of "The Raven"	POE
author of "The Song of	
Hiawatha"	LONGFELLOW
author Tolstoy	LEO
author Turgenev	IVAN
author unknown (abbr.)	ANON
author's alias	
(2 wds.)	PEN NAME
authoritative command	FIAT,
	DECREE
auto	CAR
autocracy	MONARCHY
autocrat	DESPOT
auto frame	CHASSIS
auto fuel	GAS, PETROL,
	GASOLINE
autograph	SIGNATURE
automation	ROBOT
auto part	STARTER, CHOKE,
	TRANSMISSION, SPARK
	PLUG, CARBURETOR,
	RADIATOR, HORN

auto power source	BATTERY
autumn	FALL
autumn pear	BOSC
autumnal beverage	CIDER
auxiliary	HELPER, AID, ALLY
auxiliary verb	HAD, WAS,
	ARE, MAY, CAN, WILL,
	HAS, MUST, IS, SHALL,
	SHOULD, COULD
available	READY, HANDY
available, as fresh	
fruit	IN SEASON
available money	CAPITAL
available space	ROOM
avalanche	SLIDE, FALL
avarice	GREED
avaricious	MISERLY, STINGY
avatar	ARCHETYPE
avaunt	ADVANCE
ave	HAIL!
avenge	VINDICATE
avenge a wrong (3 wds.)	
	SETTLE A SCORE
avenue	STREET, BOULEVARD,
	ROADWAY
aver	AFFIRM, ASSERT,
	DECLARE
average	MEAN, NORM,
	MEDIAN, SO-SO,
	PAR, ORDINARY
averse	RELUCTANT
aversion	DISLIKE
avert (2 wds.)	WARD OFF
aviary	BIRDHOUSE,
	SANCTUARY
aviation	FLYING
aviator	AIRMAN, PILOT
avid	EAGER, ENTHUSIASTIC,
	GREEDY
avoid	AVERT, EVADE, SHUN,
	STEER CLEAR OF
avoid as hurtful	ESCHEW
avoirdupois weight	TON
avow	DECLARE, AVER,
	CONFESS
awabi	ABALONE
awaft	AFLOAT, ADRIFT
awaiting	PENDING
awaken	ROUSE, STIR
award	GRANT, PRIZE,
	MEDAL, RECOGNIZE
aware of	ONTO, COGNIZANT,
	CONSCIOUS
away	ABSENT, OUT
away (prefix)	APO, AP, DE
away from	ABSENT, OUT
away from the coast	INLAND
away from the wind	ALEE

awe DREAD, FEAR
awful TERRIBLE, HORRIBLE, BAD, GRISLY
awkward MALADROIT, CLUMSY, UNGAINLY, INEPT, GAUCHE
awkward person LOUT, CLOD
awning TILT, SHELTER
awry AGEE, AMISS, WRONG
ax ADZ(E), HATCHET
axiom MAXIM, SAW, LAW
axis LINE
axle PIN, SPINDLE
aye YES, YEA
azure BLUE

B

baa BLEAT
ba-ba CAKE
babacoote LEMUR
babble PRATE, PRATTLE
baboon APE
baby bear CUB
baby carriage PRAM, BUGGY
baby frog TADPOLE
babyish CHILDISH, PUERILE
Babylonian deity ANU, ISHTAR, BEL, NEBO, MAROUK, BAAL
Babylonian people ELAMITE
baby powder TALC, TALCUM
baby rabbit BUNNY
baby's apron BIB
baby's bed CRADLE, CRIB, BASSINET
baby's game PEEKABOO
baby's good-bye TATA
baby's hat BONNET
baby sheep LAMB
baby shoe BOOTEE, BOOTIE
baby's napkin BIB
baby's plaything RATTLE, TOY
baby's supervisor NURSEMAID, NANNY
baby's toy RATTLE
baby's underclothing DIAPER
Bacchanals' cry EVOE
bachelor CELIBATE
bachelor's last words (2 wds.) I DO
bacillus GERM, MICROBE, BACTERIA
back SUPPORT, UPHOLD, AFT, AID, ENDORSE
backbone SPINE

back country HINTERLAND, STICKS, BUSH
back end REAR
background REAR, EXPERIENCE
background of a play SETTING
backless chair STOOL
backless top HALTER
back of the foot HEEL
back of the neck NAPE
back out WITHDRAW
back pain NOTALGIA
back street ALLEY
back talk SASS
back up ACCUMULATE, REVERSE
backward REVERSE, SHY
backwater BAYOU
backyard barrier FENCE
bacon portion RASHER
bacteria GERMS
bacterial culture AGAR
bad EVIL, NAUGHTY
bad dream NIGHTMARE
bade ORDERED, COMMANDED, SUMMONED
badge EMBLEM, TOKEN, INSIGNIA
badger TEASE
badgerlike animal RATEL
Badger State WISCONSIN
badinage BANTER, REPARTEE
badly ILL
badness EVIL
baffle OUTWIT
baffling question POSER
bag POKE, SAC(K), POUCH, PURSE
bagatelle TRIFLE
bag closure DRAWSTRING
baggage LUGGAGE, SUITCASES, CASES, GRIPS, TRUNKS, VALISES
baggage handler PORTER, BELL HOP
baggy LOOSE
baggy knickers (2 wds.) PLUS FOURS
bagpipe horn DRONE
bail SCOOP
bait LURE
bake COOK, ROAST
bake eggs SHIRR
baker's dozen THIRTEEN
baker's shovel PEEL
bakery item PIE, CAKE, CREAM PUFF, BREAD, ROLL, BUN, TART, DANISH, PASTRY, COOKIE

baking dish **RAMEKIN, SHEET, CASSEROLE**
baking ingredient **SODA, YEAST, FLOUR, SALT**
baking chamber **OVEN, OAST, KILN**
baking item **PIN, ROLLER,**
baking pit **IMU, UMU**
baking soda **SALERATUS**
baking tin (2 wds.) **PIE PAN, CAKE PAN, COOKIE SHEET**
baksheesh **TIP, ALMS**
Balaam's mount **ASS**
balance **POISE**
balance-sheet loss **DEFICIT**
balance unsteadily **TEETER**
bald **HAIRLESS**
balderdash **NONSENSE**
bald head **PATE**
bale **BUNDLE**
Balearic island **MAJORCA**
baleful **EVIL, SINISTER, DIRE, HARMFUL, MALIGNANT**
balk **FOIL**
ball **DANCE**
ballad **SONG**
ballast **WEIGHT**
ballerina **DANCER**
ballerina's strong points **TOES**
ballet **DANCE**
ball of medicine **PILL**
ball of paper **WAD**
ball of yarn **CLEW**
ballot **VOTE, TICKET**
ballot caster **VOTER**
ball park events (2 wds.) **HOME RUN, DOUBLE PLAY, TRIPLE PLAY, BASE HIT, DOUBLE HEADER, LADY'S DAY, SHUTOUT**
ballroom dance **FOX TROT, RUMBA, SAMBA, WALTZ, TANGO, TWO STEP, CARIOCA, POLKA**
balls of fringe **TASSELS**
ball team **NINE**
ballyhoo **PUBLICITY**
balmy **MILD, INSANE**
balsam tree **FIR**
Baltic city **DANZIG**
Baltic port **RIGA**
Baltic river **ODER, NEVA, NARVA, NEMAN, DAL, VISTULA, UME, TORNE**
Baltimore **PORT**
Baltimore bird **ORIOLE**
balustrade **RAILING**
Bambi **DEER**

bambino **BABY**
Bambi's mother **DOE**
bamboolike grass **REEDS**
bamboo medicine **TABASHEER, TABASHIR**
bamboo stem **CANE**
bamboozle **HOAX**
ban **INTERDICTION, INTERDICT, PROHIBIT, PROHIBITION, FORBID, EXCOMMUNICATE**
banal **HACKNEYED, TRITE**
banana **PLANTAIN**
banana republic **HONDURAS**
band **ORCHESTRA, GROUP**
bandage **BIND, TOURNIQUET**
bandicott **RAT**
band instrument **DRUM, SNARE DRUM, SAX, TUBA, FIFE, BUGLE, FLUTE, HORN**
bandit **OUTLAW, ROBBER**
bandleader **CONDUCTOR**
bandleader Arnaz **DESI**
bandleader Weems **TED**
bandleader's stick **BATON**
bandleader's wand **BATON**
bandy **CART**
bane **RUIN, HARM, WOE**
baneful **HARMFUL**
bang **BEAT, SLAM**
bang a door **SLAM**
banishment **EXILE**
banister **RAIL, RAILING**
bank **RIVERSIDE, MOUNT, RIDGE**
bank employee **TELLER, GUARD**
bank payment (abbr.) **INT**
bankrupt **RUIN**
bank safe **VAULT**
bank transaction **LOAN**
banner **FLAG**
banquet **FEAST, REPAST**
bantam car **JEEP**
banter **BADINAGE**
Bantu language **ILA**
baptismal vessel **FONT**
baptismal water **LAVER**
bar **COUNTER, STRIPE, TAVERN, INN**
barb **THORN**
barbarian **GOTH**
barbarous **CRUEL**
barbecue **COOKOUT**
barber's concern **HAIR, BEARD**
barber's tool **RAZOR, CLIPPER**
barb of feather **PINNULA, PINNULE**

bard	**MINSTREL, POET**
Bard's river	**AVON**
bare	**EMPTY, NUDE,**
	UNDECORATED, UNVEIL
barefaced	**IMPUDENT,**
	SHAMELESS
barely	**HARDLY**
barely audible	**FAINT**
bargain	**DICKER**
bargain basement event	**SALE**
barge	**SCOW, BOAT**
barge-load of coal	**KEEL**
bar item	**ALE, BEER**
bark	**SKIN, YELP**
bark at	**BAY**
bark-like	**CORTEX**
barnyard bird	**ROOSTER,**
	GOOSE, HEN, DUCK,
	GANDER, CHICKEN
barnyard sound	**MOO, OINK,**
	CLUCK, BAA, MAA,
	QUACK, WHINNY, CROW
bar of metal	**INGOT**
bar of soap	**CAKE**
barometer line	**ISOBAR**
baronet's title	**SIR**
barracks	**CASERN**
barrage	**CANNONADE**
barranca	**RAVINE**
barrel	**KEG, CASK**
barrel band	**HOOP**
barrel organ	**HURDY-GURDY**
barrel section	**STAVE**
barrel stopper	**BUNG**
barren	**ARID, FRUITLESS,**
	CHILDLESS, DEVOID
barrier	**BAR, BLOCKADE**
barrier around a yard	**FENCE**
barrister's concern	**TRIAL,**
	BRIEF, CASE
barroom	**TAP**
barter	**SWAP, TRADE**
bartizan	**TURRET**
Bartlett	**PEAR**
Bartok	**BELA**
base	**FOUNDATION, FOUND**
baseball	**NATIONAL PASTIME**
baseball catcher	**BACKSTOP**
baseball club	**BAT, TEAM,**
	NINE
baseball coup	**NO-HITTER,**
	SHUTOUT, HOME RUN,
	TRIPLE PLAY, HOMER
baseballer Aaron	**HANK**
baseballer Agee	**TOMMY**
baseballer Berra	**YOGI**
baseballer DiMaggio	**JOE, DOM**
baseballer Gehrig	**LOU**

baseballer Hodges	**GIL**
baseballer Kaline	**AL**
baseballer Koufax	**SANDY**
baseballer Mantle	**MICKEY**
baseballer Maris	**ROGER**
baseballer Musial	**STAN**
baseballer Ott	**MEL**
baseballer Robinson	**JACK,**
	FRANK, BROOKS
baseballer Ruth	**BABE**
baseballer Seaver	**TOM**
baseballer Slaughter	**ENOS**
baseballer Williams	**TED**
baseball fan	**ROOTER**
baseball field	**DIAMOND**
baseball game	
divisions	**INNINGS**
baseball glove	**MITT**
baseball goal	**HOME**
baseball hit	**HOMER, DOUBLE,**
	TRIPLE, SINGLE
baseball nickname	**BABE,**
	LEFTY
baseball nine	**TEAM**
baseball official	**UMPIRE, UMP**
baseball player	**FIELDER,**
	PITCHER, SHORTSTOP,
	INFIELDER, OUTFIELDER,
	CATCHER, BATTER,
	CENTER FIELDER, RIGHT
	FIELDER
baseball position	**PLATE,**
	BASE, OUTFIELD,
	INFIELD, SECOND
	BASE, SHORTSTOP
baseball stick	**BAT, FUNGO**
baseball stopover point	**BASE**
baseball team number	**NINE**
based on	
experience	**EMPIRICAL**
base in Greenland	**ETAH**
baseman	**INFIELDER**
basement	**CELLAR**
base of leaf	**AXIL**
bashful	**COY, SHY, TIMID,**
	MODEST
basic	**FUNDAMENTAL**
basic food	**BREAD, RICE,**
	GRAIN, WHEAT
basin	**TANK, SINK, VESSEL**
basis	**GROUNDWORK, ROOT,**
	FOUNDATION
basis of argument	**PREMISE**
bask	**LUXURIATE**
basketball group (abbr.)	**N.B.A.**
basketball misplay	**FOUL**
basketball team	**FIVE**
basket twig	**WATTLE**

basket willow	OSIER
Basque game	PELOTA
Basque headwear	BERET
basslike marine fish	SNAPPER
basswood tree	LINDEN
bast	FIBER
baste	HEM, SEW, MOISTEN
bat	HIT, CLUB
bastion	EPAULE
bath	SAUNA, TUB
bathe	LAVE, WASH
bath house	CABANA
bathing place	TUB
bathrobe fabric	TERRY
bathroom fixture	SHOWER,
	TUB, SINK
Batman or	
Robin	CRIMEFIGHTER
baton	STICK
batter	RAM, HITTER
battery plate	GRID
battle	DUEL, WAR, FRAY,
	FIGHT, MELEE
Battle-Born State	NEVADA
battle memento	SCAR
battle with lances	JOUST
bauble	PLAYTHING
bauxite	ORE, ALUMINUM
bay	COVE, INLET, TREE
bay bird	SNIPE, PLOVER
bayou	CREEK, ESTUARY
Bay State	MASSACHUSETTS
bay tree	LAUREL
bay window	ORIEL
bazaar	FAIR
bazaar stall	BOOTH
be	EXIST
beach	SHORE, STRAND,
	SEASIDE, PLAYA
beach feature	DUNE, SAND
beacon	LIGHT
be adjacent to	ABUT
beadle	USHER
be afraid	FEAR
be agitated	SEETHE
be agreeable to	PLEASE
beak	NIB, BILL
beaker	CUP
beam	EMIT, GIRDER
be a match for	COPE
be ambitious	ASPIRE
be a member	BELONG
beam of light	RAY
bean	LIMA, SOY
bear	CARRY, GRIZZLY,
	SUPPORT, KOALA, POLAR
	TOLERATE, STAND,
	SUFFER, ABIDE, YIELD
bear (Lat.)	URSUS, URSA
bear cat	PANDA
beard of grain	AWN
bearded titmouse	REEDLING
bearing	MIEN, PRESENCE
bearlike	URSINE
bearlike animal	PANDA
bear's home	DEN
bear up under	TOLERATE
bear witness to	ATTEST
beast	ANIMAL, BRUTE
beastly	BRUTAL, CRUEL
beast of burden	ASS, CAMEL,
	HORSE, OX, MULE,
	BURRO. LLAMA,
	ELEPHANT
beast's stomach	MAW
beat	POUND, TEMPO,
	RHYTHM, WHIP, THROB,
	PULSE, PULSATE
beat back	REPULSE
beaten way	PATH
beatitude	JOY, HAPPINESS
Beatles' drummer	RINGO
Beatles' movie	HELP, HARD
	DAY'S NIGHT, YELLOW
	SUBMARINE, LET IT BE
beatnik's abode	PAD
beau	ESCORT, LOVER,
	ADMIRER
beautiful	FAIR, LOVELY,
	PRETTY
beautify	ADORN
beauty	GRACE
beauty aid	CURLER, WIG,
	COSMETIC
beauty of movement	GRACE
beauty preparation	COSMETIC
beauty shop	SALON, PARLOR
beauty spot	MOLE
beaver skin	PELT, PLEW
Beaver State	OREGON
be beholden to	OWE
be careful of	BEWARE
because	FOR, SINCE, AS
be chief feature of	DOMINATE,
	STAR
beck	BIDDING
beckon	MOTION, WAVE
be clothed in	WEAR
becloud	DARKEN, CONFUSE
become a Benedict	WED
become accustomed	INURE,
	ENURE
become adept in	MASTER
become a nun	TAKE THE VEIL
become apparent	EMERGE
become a tenant	RENT

become aware of	**SENSE**	be correct size	**FIT**
become bankrupt	**FAIL**	bed	**COT, FOUR POSTER,**
become better	**IMPROVE**		**COUCH, BUNK,**
become buoyant	**FLOAT,**		**BERTH, CHAISE**
	LEVITATE	bed and board	**HOME**
become covered with		bedaub	**SMEAR, SOIL**
fungus	**MILDEW**	bedaze	**STUN**
become crooked	**BEND**	bed board	**SLAT**
become curved	**BEND**	bed cover	**BLANKET,**
become depressed	**DESPOND**	**SPREAD,QUILT, COMFORTER,**	
become different	**ALTER**		**SHEET, COVERLET**
become dirty	**SOIL**	bedding	**LINEN**
become drowsy	**NOD**	bedeck	**ADORN**
become entangled	**MAT**	be deeply affected	
become faded	**PALE**	by	**TAKE TO HEART**
become firm	**GEL, SET**	be defeated	**LOSE**
become fond of	**TAKE TO**	be deficient	**FALL SHORT, LACK**
become formed	**TAKE SHAPE**	bedevil	**HARASS, CONFUSE**
become frayed	**WEAR**	bedim	**CLOUD**
become furious	**RAGE**	bedlam	**MADHOUSE**
become ill	**AIL**	Bedlington	**TERRIER**
become indistinct	**BLUR**	bed of flowers	**GARDEN**
become insipid	**PALL**	bed of straw	**PALLET**
become		Bedouin	**ARAB**
insufficient	**RUN SHORT**	bedroom	**CHAMBER**
become less	**ABATE**	bedroom furniture	**DRESSER,**
become less stern	**RELENT**	**VANITY, BUREAU,**	
become lively	**PERK**		**NIGHTSTAND**
become manifest	**EMERGE**	bedroom shoe	**SLIPPER, MULE**
become mature	**RIPEN, AGE**	bedside light	**LAMP**
become mellow	**AGE, RIPEN**	bedspread material	**CHENILLE**
become more genial	**THAW**	be dull	**BORE**
become more profound	**DEEPEN**	bee	**APIS**
become morose	**SOUR**	beech	**TREE**
become old	**AGE**	beef	**MEAT**
become one	**MERGE**	beef animal	**STEER**
become overcast	**DIM**	beef cattle	**LONGHORN**
become oxidized	**RUST**	beef fat	**SUET**
become reconciled	**MAKE UP**	Beehive State	**UTAH**
become ripe	**MATURE**	beekeeper	**APIARIST**
become smaller	**DWINDLE**	beelzebub	**DEVIL, SATAN**
become sound	**HEAL**	beep	**HONK**
become sour	**TART**	bee product	**HONEY**
become stale	**STAGNATE**	be enough	**DO, SUFFICE**
become submerged	**SINK**	be equal	**TIE**
become thin with use	**WEAR**	beer	**LAGER, PILSNER,**
become twisted	**GNARL**		**BREW, SUDS**
become unwoven	**RAVEL**	beer barrel	**CASK, KEG**
become very cold	**FREEZE**	beer cask	**BUTT**
become visible	**APPEAR**	beer glass	**STEIN, MUG**
become void	**LAPSE**	beer ingredient	**HOPS, MALT,**
become weary	**TIRE**		**YEAST**
become worn	**FRAY**	beerlike drink	**ALE, STOUT,**
become zealous	**ENTHUSE**		**PORTER**
becoming	**FIT, PROPER**	beer maker	**BREWER**
be compelled	**MUST**	beer mug	**STEIN**
be concerned	**CARE**	bee's home	**HIVE**
be contiguous	**ABUT**	beet	**CHARD, SUGAR**

beet genus **BETA**
beetle **DOR**
beetleheaded **STUPID**
beetlenut palm **ARECA**
befall **BETIDE, HAPPEN**
be festive **REVEL**
be finical **FUSS**
before (Lat.) **ANTE**
before (poet.) **ERE**
before (prefix) **PRE**
before all others **FIRST**
before birth **PRENATAL**
before deductions **NET**
beforehand **IN ADVANCE, AHEAD**
before long **ANON, SOON**
before noon (abbr.) **AM**
before this **ERE, SINCE**
beforetime **FORMERLY**
befoul **SOIL**
befriend **ASSIST, ABET**
befuddle **CONFUSE**
befuddled **ASEA, IN A FOG, AT SEA, CONFUSED, MUDDLED**
beg **PLEAD, ENTREAT, IMPLORE, CADGE, SPONGE, MOOCH, BESEECH**
beget **PRODUCE, PROCREATE**
begetter **PARENT**
beggar **MENDICANT, BUM, PANHANDLER, PAUPER**
beggarly **MEAN, INDIGENT**
begin **OPEN, START, SET OUT, FALL TO**
begin a battle **ATTACK**
begin a day **RISE, AWAKEN**
begin again **RENEW, REOPEN**
begin an ocean voyage **SAIL, EMBARK**
begin eating **DIG IN**
beginner **STARTER, TIRO, TYRO, NOVICE, GREENHORN, TENDERFOOT, NEOPHYTE, FRESHMAN**
beginning **ONSET, NASCENT, EMERGING, ROOT, START**
beginning of day **DAWN, SUNRISE**
beginning of flight **TAKEOFF**
beginning of marriage **HONEYMOON**
beginning of social career **DEBUT**
beginning socialite **DEB**

beginning worker **APPRENTICE, TRAINEE**
begin to develop **BUD**
begin war **ATTACK**
begird **SURROUND**
begone **SHOO, SCAT, GO, LEAVE, BEAT IT, VAMOOSE**
begonia **FLOWER**
begrime **SOIL**
begrudge **ENVY**
beguile **DECEIVE, CHEAT, DELUDE**
beguiled **AMUSED**
beguine **DANCE**
behalf **PART, SUPPORT**
behalf of **FOR**
behave **ACT**
behave badly **MISBEHAVE**
behave childishly **CRY**
behave foolishly **CARRY ON**
behave menacingly **THREATEN, FRIGHTEN**
behave theatrically **EMOTE**
behave with dignity **ACT ONE'S AGE**
behavior **COMPORTMENT, DEPORTMENT, MANNER**
behest **COMMAND**
behind **AFTER, LATE, SLOW**
behind a ship **ASTERN**
behind in payments **IN ARREARS**
behind the curtain **BACKSTAGE**
behold **LO**
behold (Lat.) **ECCE**
beige **TAN, ECRU**
be ill **AIL**
be imminent **IMPEND**
be in a fury **RAGE**
be in command **LEAD**
be in contact **TOUCH**
be in debt **OWE**
be indignant **RESENT**
being **ESSENCE, EXISTENCE**
being (Fr.) **ETRE**
being (Lat.) **ESSE**
being broadcast **ON THE AIR**
being in a fairy tale **OGRE**
being from Aladdin's lamp **GENIE**
be in harmony **AGREE**
be in store for **AWAIT**
be interested **CARE**
be irritated **FRET**
be kept waiting **COOL ONE'S HEELS**
belabor **ASSAIL**
beldam **HAG**

belfry	**TOWER**
Belgian capital	**BRUSSELS**
Belgian port	**OSTEND, ANTWERP**
belie	**DENY**
belief	**CREDO, CREDENCE, CREED, RELIGION, FAITH**
believe	**OPINE, THINK, JUDGE**
believer (suffix)	**IST**
believer in facts	**REALIST**
believer in God	**THEIST**
belittle	**DISPARAGE**
bell	**CHIME, GONG**
bellicose	**WARLIKE**
belligerent	**HOSTILE**
bellow	**ROAR**
bell-shaped flower	**TULIP**
bell-shaped hat	**CLOCHE**
bell sound	**BONG, TINKLE, DING, GONG, PEAL, TOLL, CHIME**
bell tower	**BELFRY, CAMPANILE**
be lofty	**TOWER**
belonging to him	**HIS**
belonging to me	**MINE**
belonging to the thing	**ITS**
belonging to us	**OUR, OURS**
belongings	**PROPERTY**
beloved	**DEAR**
beloved Disciple	**JOHN**
below	**BENEATH, UNDER, UNDERNEATH**
below key	**FLAT**
belt	**STRAP, BAND**
belt fastener	**BUCKLE**
belt of calm	**DOLDRUMS**
beluga	**CAVIAR**
be made up of	**CONSIST**
be master of	**POSSESS**
be merciful	**SPARE**
be mistaken	**ERR**
bemoan	**LAMENT**
be moodily silent	**SULK**
bemuse	**DAZE**
Ben Cartwright's boy	**HOSS, JOE**
bench	**SEAT, PEW, CHAIR**
bend	**CURVE**
bend down	**STOOP**
bend downward	**SAG**
bender	**SPREE**
bend low	**CROUCH**
bend over	**STOOP**
bend the head	**BOW**
be near	**STAND BY**
beneath	**BELOW, UNDER, UNDERNEATH**
beneath the earth	**UNDERGROUND**
benediction	**BLESSING, PRAYER**
benefactor	**HELPER, PATRON**
beneficial	**USEFUL**
beneficiary of a will	**HEIR**
benefit	**STEAD**
benevolence	**KINDNESS**
Bengal capitol	**CALCUTTA**
Bengal cat	**TIGER**
bent pipe	**SIPHON**
bent to one side	**WRY**
be obedient	**BEHAVE**
be of consequence	**MATTER**
be of importance	**MATTER**
be of one mind	**AGREE**
be of the opinion	**BELIEVE**
be of use	**AVAIL**
be on fire	**BURN**
be on one's feet	**STAND**
be overly fond	**DOTE**
be present	**ATTEND**
be quiet	**SH**
berate	**NAG, SCOLD**
Berber	**ARAB**
be ready for	**AWAIT**
be reluctant	**BALK**
beret	**CAP**
be revived	**COME TO**
Berliner	**GERMAN**
Berlin's divider	**WALL**
Bernstein, for short	**LEN**
berry	**CURRANT**
beseech	**BEG, ENTREAT, PLEAD, IMPLORE**
be sensitive to	**FEEL**
beset	**ATTACK, BESIEGE**
be sick	**AIL**
beside (prefix)	**PARA, PAR**
besides	**ALSO, ELSE, TO BOOT, TOO**
besiege	**BESET, ATTACK**
be situated	**LIE, SIT, SETTLED**
besmear	**SOIL**
besom	**BROOM**
be sorry for	**PITY**
be sparing	**STINT**
bespatter	**DAUB, SPLASH**
best	**OUTSTRIP, BEAT, OUT-DO, GREATEST, LARGEST**
bestial	**BRUTAL, CRUEL**
bestow	**GRANT, AWARD, GIVE**
be successful	**GO FAR**
be sufficient	**AMPLE, DO**
be suitable	**FIT**
bet	**WAGER**

betel palm	ARECA	Biblical king	ASA, HEROD,
betray	SELL		HIRAM, DAVID, SOLOMON,
betrayal	TREASON		SAUL, JOSIAH, AHAB, OMRI,
be sparing	STINT		HEZEKIAH, JEHORAM,
be undecided	WAVER		AHAZ, ELAH
be unsuccessful	FAIL	Biblical land	OPHIR, ELAM,
be victorious	WIN		MOAB, CANAAN, EGYPT
be without	LACK	Biblical liar	ANANIAS
be worthy of	DESERVE	Biblical measure	OMER
be wrong	ERR	Biblical mountain	ARARAT,
beach	SHORE, STRAND,		SINAI, CARMEL, JARMAK,
	SEASIDE, PLAYA		EBAL, THABOR, NEBO,
beach feature	DUNE, SAND		GARIZIM, LEBANON
betrothed	ENGAGED	Biblical name of Syria	ARAM
better balanced	SANER	Biblical passage	TEXT
betting factor	ODDS	Biblical Patriarch	MOSES,
betting method	PARLAY		NOAH
betting odds	PRICE	Biblical preposition	UNTO
between (Fr.)	ENTRE	Biblical pronoun	THY, THOU,
between (prefix)	INTER		THINE
bevel	SLANT	Biblical plotter	HAMAN
bevel corners	SPLAY	Biblical priest	AARON, LEVI,
beverage	TEA, ALE, BEER,		SADOC
	COFFEE, MILK, SODA, WINE	Biblical prophet	HOSEA, AMOS,
beverage container	TEAPOT,		MICAH, ISAIA, DANIEL,
	GLASS, TUMBLER, BOTTLE,		OSEE, JOEL, ABDIA, JONAH,
	CARTON, CAN, FLASK,		NAHUM, HABACUC, ELIA
	PITCHER, CUP	Biblical story	PARABLE
beverage glasses	STEMWARE,	Biblical strong man	SAMSON
	TUMBLERS	Biblical tower	BABEL
bevy	FLOCK	Biblical town	CANA, LOD,
bewail	LAMENT, MOAN		HEBRON
bewildered	AT SEA, ASEA,	Biblical tribe	ANAK, LEVI, DAN
	BEFUDDLED, LOST,	Biblical vessel	ARK
	CONFUSED	Biblical weed	TARE
bewitch	CHARM	Biblical witch's home	ENDOR
beyond	YONDER, ABOVE	Biblical word	SELAH
beyond control	OUT OF HAND	bicker	ARGUE
beyond the limit	OUT	bicuspid	TOOTH
bias	SLANT, PREJUDICE	bicycle for two	TANDEM
bias binding	TAPE	bicycle part	PEDAL
bib	TUCKER	bid	OFFER, COMMAND
Biblical angel	RAPHAEL,	biddy	HEN
	GABRIEL, MICHAEL	bide	TARRY, WAIT
Biblical boat	ARK	big	LARGE, HUGE, IMMENSE,
Biblical brother	ABEL, CAIN,		VAST, MAMMOTH, GIANT,
	JOSEPH, ESAU, JACOB,		GIGANTIC, COLOSSAL
	REUBEN, SIMEON,	big and strong	BURLY
	BENJAMIN, JUDAH	Big Bend State	TENNESSEE
Biblical character	LOT, ARA,	big book	TOME
	IRA, ABEL, JOAB, JOB,	big boy	MAN
	AMOS, MICAH, MOSES,	big bundle	BALE
	AARON, ZADOK, ELI, BOAZ	big coffee pot	URN
Biblical dancer	SALOME	big deer	ELK
Biblical garden	EDEN,	bigeye	FISH
	GETHSEMANE	big girl	WOMAN
Biblical hero	NOAH	big house	PRISON, PEN
		big leaguer	PRO

big man **TITAN, GIANT**
big monkey **APE, GORILLA, ORANGUTAN**
big name in golf **PALMER, SNEAD, HOGAN, CASPER, BEARD, NICKLAUS, WOOD**
bigoted **NARROW**
bigotry **PREJUDICE**
big top **TENT**
bijou **JEWEL, GEM**
bile **CHOLER, ANGER**
bilk **CHEAT, SWINDLE**
bill **NIB, BEAK, INVOICE, TARIFF, CHECK, NEB**
billabong **LAGOON**
billboard **SIGN, POSTER**
billiard shot **CAROM, MASSE, BANK, BREAK, DRAW, KISS**
billiard stick **CUE**
billiards **POOL**
bill of fare **MENU**
bill of lading (abbr.) **BL**
billow **SURGE, WAVE**
billowy expanse **OCEAN, SEA**
billy **CLUB**
billy or nanny **GOAT**
bin **CRIB, BOX**
binary **DOUBLE, DUAL, TWOFOLD**
bind **TIE, LASH, BANDAGE**
bind closely **ALLY, TIE**
binding custom **LAW**
bind up **GIRD, TRUSS**
binge **SPREE, TOOT**
bingo **GAME**
biographer Ludwig **EMIL**
biography **LIFE**
biological classification **GENUS**
biological determinant **GENE**
birchbark boat **CANOE**
bird **AUK, FINCH, ORIOLE, SERIN, TERN, CANARY, OWL, SPARROW, SWALLOW, SWAN, RAVEN, PARROT, PARAKEET, WREN, HAWK, CROW, EAGLE, DOVE, CHICKADEE, BLUEJAY, CARDINAL, GROSBEAK, REDPOL, BUZZARD, OSPREY, VULTURE, ERNE, ALBATROSS, PIGEON, LOON, QUAIL, GROUSE, PENGUIN, PETREL, BOOBIE, FALCON, STORK, SWIFT, GULL, DODO, THRUSH**
bird (Lat.) **AVIS**
bird (prefix) **AVI**

bird call **NOTE, TWEET, SONG, TRILL, CHIRP, TWEE**
bird clapper **SCARECROW**
bird class **AVES**
bird claw **TALON**
bird enclosure **CAGE**
bird feed **SUET, SEED**
bird home **NEST, AVIARY**
bird keeper **AVIARIST**
bird of Jove **EAGLE**
bird of peace **DOVE**
bird of prey **EAGLE, HAWK, KITE, OWL, FALCON, BUZZARD, VULTURE**
bird's arm **WING**
bird's beak **BILL, NEB**
bird's crop **CRAW**
bird's flapper **WING**
bird's food **SEED**
bird's home **NEST, AERIE**
bird's perch **ROOST**
bireme **GALLEY, SHIP**
birth **ORIGIN**
birthday figure **AGE**
birthmark **NEVUS, MOLE**
birthright **HERITAGE**
birthstone for April **DIAMOND**
birthstone for August **PERIDOT**
birthstone for December **TURQUOISE**
birthstone for February **AMETHYST**
birthstone for January **GARNET**
birthstone for July **RUBY**
birthstone for June **PEARL**
birthstone for March **AQUAMARINE**
birthstone for May **EMERALD**
birthstone for November **TOPAZ**
birthstone for October **OPAL**
birthstone for September **SAPPHIRE**
bis **TWICE**
biscuit **BUN**
bisect **HALVE**
bishop **PRELATE**
bishopric **SEE**
bishop's hat **MITRE**
bishop's throne **SEE**
bison **BUFFALO**
bisque **SOUP**
bistro **BAR**
bit **MORSEL, SCRAP**
bite **MOUTHFUL, NIBBLE, GNAW, NIP, SNAP, STING, TANG, CHEW**
bite impatiently **CHAMP**
bite off **GHAW**
biting **ACRID, CAUSTIC**

bit of floating dust	**MOTE**	blast	**EXPLOSION**
bit of news	**ITEM**	blast of wind	**GUST**
bits of fluff	**LINT**	blaze	**FLAME, FLARE, FIRE,**
bitter	**ACRID**		**CUT, FLASH**
bitter nut	**KOLA**	blaze brightly	**FLARE**
bitter vetch	**ERS**	blazing	**AFIRE**
bivalve	**CLAM, MUSSEL**	bleak	**DESOLATE**
bivouac	**CAMP, ENCAMP**	bleat	**BAA, MAA**
bizarre	**OUTRE, ODD**	blemish	**SCAR, SPOT, FLAW,**
Bizet opera	**CARMEN**		**DEFECT**
blab	**TELL, TATTLE**	blend	**MERGE, MIX**
black	**EBON, EBONY**	bless	**HALLOW**
black and blue	**LIVID**	blessed	**BLEST, HALLOWED,**
black art	**MAGIC**		**SAINT**
black-backed gull	**COB(B)**	blessing	**BOON, GRACE,**
Black Beauty	**HORSE**		**BENEDICTION**
black bird	**ANI, CROW, DAW,**	blessing (arch.)	**BENISON**
	RAVEN, GRACKLE, MERLE	blimp	**BALLOON, DIRIGIBLE**
blackboard	**SLATE**	blind fear	**PANIC**
black bread	**RYE**	blink	**WINK**
black buck	**SASIN**	blithe	**MERRY, GAY**
black dairy cow	**KERRY**	blockade	**SIEGE**
black death	**PLAGUE**	blockhead	**ASS, DOLT, DOPE,**
black diamond	**COAL**		**OAF, FOOL, DUNCE**
blacken	**CHAR**	bloke	**CHAP**
black eye	**SHINER**	blond	**GOLDEN, FAIR,**
black face	**MINSTREL**		**FLAXEN**
blackface music		blood-building meat	**LIVER**
show	**MINSTREL**	blood deficiency	**ANEMIA**
blackfin	**FISH, SNAPPER**	blood fluid	**PLASMA**
black flag	**JOLLY ROGER**	blood giver	**DONER**
black fuel	**COAL**	blood (prefix)	**HEMO, HEMA,**
black gold	**OIL**		**HEM**
blackguard	**SCOUNDREL**	blooper	**ERROR, BLUNDER**
black hole	**CELL, BRIG**	blossom	**BLOOM, FLOWER**
black lacquer	**JAPAN**	blot	**SPOT, STAIN**
black leg (Brit.)	**SCAB**	blot out	**ERASE**
black magic	**WITCHCRAFT**	blouse	**WAIST**
blackmail	**EXTORT**	blouse ruffle	**JABOT**
black mark	**DEMERIT**	blow	**HIT, STROKE**
Blackmore heroine	**LORNA**	blow a horn	**TOOT, HONK**
blacksmith shop	**FORGE**	blow hard	**BRAGGART**
black snake	**RACER**	blue	**AZURE, INDIGO, SAD,**
black tea	**BOHEA**		**MOPEY**
blackthorn fruit	**SLOE**	blue dye	**ANIL**
black-tongued dog	**CHOW**	blue fin	**TUNA**
blacktop	**PAVE**	blue flag	**IRIS**
black widow	**SPIDER**	Bluegrass State	**KENTUCKY**
black wood	**EBONY**	blue jeans material	**DENIM**
blade	**SWORD, KNIFE, DIRK**	Blue Law State	**CONNECTICUT**
blade bone	**SCAPULA**	blue or white	
blame	**ACCUSE, CENSURE**	bird	**GREAT HERON**
blameless	**INNOCENT**	blue-pencil	**EDIT**
blanch	**ETIOLATE, WHITEN**	blue pigment	**BICE, SMALT**
blanched	**PALE, WHITE**	Blue Point	**OYSTER**
blank	**VOID, EMPTY**	blue pottery	**DELFT**
blank book	**TABLET**	blueprint	**PLAN**
blase	**BORED, JADED**	blue-white star in Lyra	**VEGA**

bluff **GRUFF, RUDE, HOODWINK**
bluish gray **SLATE**
bluish-white metal **ZINC**
blunder **ERR, MISTAKE, ERROR, SNAFU**
blunt **DULL**
blur **DIM, OBSCURE**
blurt out **BLAT, BLAB**
blush **REDDEN**
blushing **ROSY**
boa **SERPENT, SNAKE, PYTHON, SCARF**
boar **PIG**
board **PLANK**
boarder **ROOMER**
boardinghouse fare **HASH**
boarhound **GREAT DANE**
boast **BLOW, BRAG**
boat **CANOE, SHIP, VESSEL**
boat basin **MARINA**
boat paddle **OAR**
boat ride **SAIL**
boat rope **HAWSER, LINE**
boat's company **CREW**
boat side **GUNWALE**
boat's radio **SHIP-TO-SHORE**
boat's power source **OUTBOARD MOTOR**
boat trip **SAIL, CRUISE**
bobble **ERR, BUNGLE, MISS, FUMBLE**
bobwhite **QUAIL**
bodice **WAIST**
body **TORSO, TRUNK**
body builders **LIFTS, WEIGHTS**
body height **STATURE**
body injuries **LESIONS**
body limb **LEG, ARM**
body of advisers **CABINET, BOARD**
body of police **POSSE**
body of ship **HULL**
body of soldiers **REGIMENT**
body of students **CLASS**
body of water **BAY, LAKE, SEA, OCEAN, POND, RIVER, STREAM, CREEK**
Boer **AFRIKANER**
boff **JOKE**
bog **MORASS, FEN, MARSH, SWAMP, MIRE**
bog down **MIRE, SLOW, IMPEDE, HINDER**
bogus **SHAM, ERSATZ**
Bohemian **ARTY**
Bohemian city **PRAGUE**
Bohemian reformer **HUSS**

boil **STEW, SIMMER, SEETHE**
boil down **CONDENSE, REDUCE**
bold **PERT, DARING, SASSY, NERVY, CHEEKY, BRAVE, VENTURESOME**
boldness **COURAGE, DARING**
bolero **DANCE, JACKET**
Bolivian mountains **ANDES**
Bolshevik **LENIN, TROTSKY**
bolster **PILLOW**
bombastic speech **HARANGUE**
bond **TIE, BAIL**
bondage **SLAVERY**
bondsman **SLAVE**
bone **OS**
boneblack **CHARCOAL**
bone-dry **ARID**
boner **BLUNDER**
bone structure **SKELETON**
bongo **DRUM**
bonito **ALBACORE**
bonnet **HAT, TOQUE**
boo **HISS**
boob **SAP, DOPE, FOOL, DOLT**
book **FOLIO, TOME**
bookbinding leather **ROAN**
book cover **BINDING**
bookish **STODGY**
bookkeeper's entry **DEBIT, CREDIT**
bookkeeping term **ENTRY, POST**
book (Lat.) **LIBER**
book leaf **PAGE**
book of a poem **CANTO**
book of fiction **NOVEL**
book of maps **ATLAS**
book of Norse myths **EDDA**
book of photographs **ALBUM**
book page **FOLIO, LEAF**
book part **PAGE, CHAPTER, LEAF, SPINE**
boom **SPAR**
boon **BLESSING, FAVOR**
Boone **DANIEL, DANL**
boorish **RUDE**
boost **LIFT**
booster **FAN**
boot **KICK**
bootblack's specialty **SHINE**
booth **LOGE, SEAT, ETALL**
booty **LOOT, SPOILS**
bop **HIT, PUNCH**
Bordeaux wine **CLARET, MEDOC, GRAVES, SAUTERNE**
border **EDGE, RIM, HEM, MARGIN, SELVAGE**

bordering tool	**EDGER**
border on	**ABUT**
border saloon	**CANTINA**
bore	**DRILL, TIRE, EAGRE**
bore into	**TAP**
bore witness	**ATTESTED**
boreal	**NORTHERN**
boredom	**ENNUI, TEDIUM**
boring	**TEDIOUS**
boring tool	**BRACE AND BIT, AUGER, DRILL**
born	**NEE**
Borneo ape	**ORANG**
borough	**BURG**
borrow dishonestly	**CADGE, PLAGERIZE**
borrow money on	**PAWN**
Bosc	**PEAR**
bosom	**BREAST**
bossy	**COW**
botch	**BUNGLE, MESS**
both	**TWO**
bother	**AIL, ANNOY, PESTER**
bottle	**FLASK**
bottle cap	**LID**
bottle cap remover	**OPENER**
bottle dweller	**GENIE**
bottle part	**NECK**
bottle sealer	**CAP, CORK**
bottle-shaped container	**FLASK**
bottle stopper	**CORK**
bottle top	**CAP**
bottom	**BASE**
bottomless	**DEEP, ENDLESS**
bottomless pit	**HELL**
bottom out	**LEVEL**
bottom surface	**BED, FLOOR**
bottom support of a column	**PEDESTAL**
bough	**BRANCH**
boulevard	**STREET, AVENUE, ROAD**
bouillon	**BROTH, STOCK**
boulder	**ROCK**
bounce	**DAP, REBOUND**
bound	**TIED, DESTINED**
boundary	**LIMIT, LINE, BORDER**
boundary line	**FENCE**
bounder	**CAD, ROUE, LOUT**
boundless	**ENDLESS, LIMITLESS**
bounteous	**AMPLE, PLENTIFUL**
bountiful	**PLENTIFUL, ABUNDANT**
bounty	**REWARD**
bouquet	**AROMA, CORSAGE, ODOR, POSY, NOSEGAY**

bourbon	**WHISKEY, CORN MASH**
bout	**PRIZEFIGHT, MATCH, SPELL**
boutonniere	**FLOWER, CARNATION**
boutonniere location	**LAPEL**
boutique	**SHOP**
bouzouki	**MANDOLIN**
bovine animal	**STEER, OX, COW, BULL**
bovine sound	**LOW, MOO**
bow	**KNOT, CURTSY, STOOP**
bowed	**BENT**
bower	**ARBOR**
bowfin	**AMIA**
bowie	**KNIFE**
bowl	**BASIN**
bowler	**HAT, DERBY**
bowlike curved line	**ARC**
bowline	**KNOT**
bowling alley	**LANE, GREEN**
bowling norm	**AVERAGE**
bowling piece	**PIN**
bowling place	**ALLEY, GREEN**
bowling term	**SPARE, STRIKE**
bowling target	**PIN, TENPIN**
bowman	**ARCHER**
bow of a ship	**PROW**
bowsprit	**BOOM, SPAR**
box	**CASE, CRATE, CARTON, FIGHT, SPAR, LOGE**
boxberry	**WINTERGREEN**
boxcars	**TWELVE**
box cautiously	**SPAR**
boxer Baer	**MAX**
boxer Clay	**CASSIUS**
boxer Palooka	**JOE**
boxer Patterson	**FLOYD**
boxer's nickname	**CHAMP**
box for alms	**ARCA**
box for coal	**BIN**
boxing blow	**JAB, HOOK, KO, KNOCKOUT, KAYO, CROSS**
boxing contest	**BOUT**
boxing coup	**KO, KAYO, KNOCKOUT**
boxing ring	**ARENA**
boxing strategy	**ONE-TWO**
box-of-evils opener	**PANDORA**
box supper	**SOCIAL**
box top	**LID**
box up	**CONFINE**
boy	**LAD, SON, MALE, TAD**
boycott	**BLOCK**
boyfriend	**BEAU**

boyhood **YOUTH**
boys and girls **CHILDREN**
boy's book author **ALGER**
Boy Scout **CUB, EAGLE**
Boy Scout activity **HIKE**
Boy Scout group **TROOP**
boy's plaything **TOY SOLDIER, CAP GUN, FOOTBALL, BASEBALL**
bozo **GUY, FELLOW**
BPOE member **ELK**
brace **PAIR, TWOSOME, SUPPORT, COUPLE**
bracer **TONIC**
bracing **CRISP**
bracket candlestick **SCONCE**
brackish **SALTY, BRINY**
brad **NAIL**
brag **BOAST**
Brahman **PUNDIT, AYA**
braid **PLAIT**
brain **MIND**
brainless **STUPID**
brainstorm **IDEA**
brainwash **CONDITION, CONVINCE**
brainy **SMART**
braise **COOK**
brake **STOP**
bran **CEREAL**
branch **ARM, BOUGH**
branch (biol.) **RAMUS**
branches of learning **ARTS**
branch of the armed forces **MARINES, NAVY, ARMY, AIR FORCE, COAST GUARD, NATIONAL GUARD**
branch off **FORK**
brand **MARK, TRADEMARK**
brandish **SHAKE, WAVE**
brass hat **GENERAL**
brass instrument **BUGLE, CORNET, TUBA, TRUMPET, TROMBONE**
brassy **BOLD**
brave **DARING, COURAGEOUS, INDIAN**
brave man **HERO**
bravery **COURAGE**
brawl **FIGHT, MELEE**
Brazilian dance **SAMBA**
Brazilian export **RUBBER**
Brazilian parrot **ARA**
Brazilian port **BELEM, RIO, NATAL, CEARA**
Brazilian river **AMAZON**
Brazilian rubber tree **SERINGA**
breach **CHASM, GAP**

breadbasket **STOMACH**
bread cakes **ROLLS, MUFFINS**
bread crust **RIND**
bread made of corn meal **PONE**
breadmaking ingredient **YEAST**
bread spread **OLEO, BUTTER, MARGARINE, JELLY, JAM, CURD, MUSTARD, MAYONNAISE**
breadwinner **DAD, PAPA, FATHER, POP**
breadwinning ability **EARNING POWER**
break **SMASH, SPLIT, SHATTER**
breakable **FRAGILE**
break asunder **DISRUPT**
breakdown in law and order **ANARCHY**
breakers **SURF, WAVES**
breakfast **MEAL**
breakfast bread **ROLLS, BUN, SCONE, COFFEE CAKE**
breakfast food **CEREAL, BACON, EGGS, PANCAKE, HOTCAKE, WAFFLE, HAM, OMELET, GRITS, OATMEAL**
breakfast fruit juice **ORANGE, GRAPEFRUIT**
breakfast sweet (2 wds.) **COFFEE CAKE**
break in two **SNAP**
break into many pieces **SHATTER**
break of day **DAWN, SUNRISE**
break out **ERUPT**
break ranks **DISBAND**
break rules **DISOBEY**
break short **SNAP**
break suddenly **BURST, SNAP**
break the seal **OPEN**
break up **SEPARATE, DISPERSE**
breakwater **PIER, JETTY**
breast **BOSOM**
breastbone **STERNUM**
breathe **RESPIRE, INHALE**
breathe hard **PANT, GASP, WHEEZE**
breathe one's last **DIE, EXPIRE**
breathe spasmodically **SIGH**
breathing **ALIVE**
breathing organ **LUNG**
bred **ENGENDERED, RAISED, REARED**
breeches **TROUSERS**
breed **CLASS**
breed of cat **SIAMESE, PERSIAN**

breed of dog **SETTER, POODLE, SPANIEL, PUG, SCHNAUZER, TERRIER, SCOTTIE, WHIPPET, CHOW, SAMOYED, COLLIE, SHEPHERD**

breed of horse **ARAB, BARB, THOROUGHBRED, CLYDESDALE, MORGAN, SHIRE**

breeze **WIND, ZEPHYR**

breezy **AIRY**

breezy farewell **TATA**

Breton **CELT**

brew **STEEP**

brick carrier **HOD**

bricklayer **MASON**

brick red **SARAVAN**

bridal

    attendant **MAID OF HONOR**

bridegroom's attendant **BEST MAN, USHER**

bride's mate **GROOM**

bride's portion **DOWERY**

bridge **SPAN**

bridge (Fr.) **PONT**

bridge expert **GOREN**

bridge play **SLAM**

bridge score **GAME**

bridge strategy **FINESSE**

bridge structure **ARCH**

bridle **HALTER, HARNESS**

bridle part **BIT, REIN, HEADSTALL**

brief **SHORT**

brief and compact **CONCISE**

brief excerpt **SCRAP**

brief in speech **CURT, TERSE**

brief look **GLIMPSE, GLANCE**

briefly brilliant star **NOVA**

brief news statement **BULLETIN**

brief outline **SKETCH**

brief preface **PROEM**

brief swim **DIP**

brier **THORN**

brig **BOAT**

brigand **PIRATE, THIEF**

bright **SHINY, BRILLIANT**

bright but cheap **TINNY**

bright color **RED, CRIMSON, SCARLET, YELLOW, GOLD, CORAL**

brighten **CLEAR UP, LIGHT UP**

brightly colored bird **ORIOLE, PEACOCK**

bright person **BRAIN, GENIUS**

bright planet **EVENING STAR, VENUS**

brilliance **ELAN, LUSTER, SHINE, GLOW**

brilliance of success **ECLAT**

brilliant **BRIGHT, VIVID**

brilliant Asian

    pheasant **TRAGOPAN**

brilliant fish **OPAH**

brilliant planet **VENUS**

brim **EDGE, RIM**

brimless hat **CAP**

bring **CARRY, FETCH**

bring about **CAUSE**

bring back **RESTORE, RETURN**

bring forth **EDUCE**

bring into existence **CREATE, GENERATE, CONCEIVE**

bring into line **ALINE, ALIGN**

bring into play **USE**

bring legal action **SUE**

bring out **ELICIT, EDUCE, EVOKE**

bring out into the open **AIR, REVEAL**

bring to a finish **GO THROUGH WITH, END, CLOSE, FINALIZE, CONCLUDE**

bring to an end **CLOSE**

bring to bay **TREE, CORNER, TRAP**

bring to earth **LAND**

bring to life **RENEW**

bring to light **DETECT, PUBLICIZE**

bring to completion **FINISH, END**

bring together **UNITE**

bring to memory **REMIND**

bring to mind **RECALL**

bring to ruin **UNDO**

bring to the attention **REMIND, RECALL**

bring up **REAR, RAISE**

bring upon oneself **INCUR**

brink **EDGE, RIM, VERGE**

briny **SALINE, SALTY**

briny expanse **SEA, OCEAN**

brioche **ROLL**

brisk **LIVELY**

bristle **AWN, SETA**

bristle (prefix) **SETI**

British airplane **SPITFIRE**

British beverage **TEA**

British car **ROLLS ROYCE**

British carbine **STEN**

British cavalryman **DRAGOON**

British coin **SHILLING, PENNY**

British colony **BAHAMA, BERMUDA, GIBRALTAR, HONG KONG**

British county **SHIRE**
British daisy **GOWAN**
British essayist **STEELE, ADDISON, CHESTERTON**
British flag **UNION JACK**
British flyers (abbr.) **R.A.F.**
British foreign minister **EDEN**
British gun **STEN**
British imperial color **RED**
British island **MALTA**
British isle **MAN, WIGHT**
British king **GEORGE, HENRY, EDWARD, RICHARD, CHARLES**
British man-of-war **GALATEA**
British manufacturing city **LEEDS**
British meal **TEA**
British nobleman **EARL, LORD, BARON, BARONET, PEER, DUKE**
British peeress **DAME, LADY, DUCHESS, BARONESS**
British pennies **PENCE**
British prep school **ETON, HARROW**
British prime minister **CHURCHILL, WILSON**
British princess **ANNE, MARGARET, ALEXANDRA**
British school **ETON, HARROW, OXFORD, CAMBRIDGE**
British sea hero **NELSON**
British streetcar **TRAM**
British taproom **PUB**
British weight **STONE**
Briton **CELT**
brittle **CRISP**
broad **WIDE, VAST**
broadcast **AIR**
broaden **WIDEN**
broad flat bottle **FLASK**
broad humor **FARCE**
broad minded **LIBERAL**
broad necktie **ASCOT**
broad scarf **SHAWL**
broad smile **GRIN**
broad street **BOULEVARD, AVENUE**
broadtail **KARAKUL**
broad thin piece **SHEET**
Broadway backer **ANGEL**
Broadway light **NEON**
Broadway musical **HAIR, CAMELOT, HELLO DOLLY, MAME, COMPANY, APPLAUSE, FANNY, FUNNY GIRL, TENDERLOIN, FIORELLO, ZORBA**

Broadway offering **DRAMA, COMEDY, MUSICAL, REVUE, PLAY**
Broadway patron **GOER**
brochette **SKEWER**
brochure **PAMPHLET**
brogan **SHOE**
broil **GRILL**
broiler **CHICKEN**
broil in covered kettle **BRAIZE**
broiling meat **STEAK**
broil on gridiron **GRILL**
broke **PENNILESS**
broke bread **ATE**
broken open **SPRUNG**
broken pottery **SHARD**
broker **AGENT, REPRESENTATIVE**
broker's advice **SELL, BUY**
bromide **CLICHE**
bronze **TAN**
brooch **PIN**
brood **COVEY, HATCH**
brook **RILL, STREAM, RIVULET**
broom **BESOM**
brose **OATMEAL**
broth **SOUP, BOUILLON**
brother **FRA**
brother (abbr.) **BR., BRO.**
brother (Fr.) **FRERE**
brotherly **LOYAL**
brother of Abel **CAIN**
brother of Cain **ABLE**
brother of Esau **JACOB**
brother of Moses **AARON**
brother's daughter **NIECE**
brother's son **NEPHEW**
brought about **DID**
brought into life **BORN**
brought up **BRED, REARED**
brow **FOREHEAD**
brown **TAN, COCOA, BEIGE, CHOCOLATE, SEPIA**
brown bread **GRAHAM, WHOLE WHEAT**
browned **RISSOLE**
brown ermine **STOAT**
brownie **CAKE, ELF**
brownish **RUSSET, UMBER**
brownish purple **PUCE**
brownish yellow **AMBER**
brown kiwi **MOA**
brown pigment **UMBER**
browse for bargains **SHOP**
bruin **BEAR**
bruise **BUMP, WELT**
brusque **CURT, TERSE, BLUNT**

brute	ANIMAL, BEAST	building wing	ELL, ANNEX, EXTENSION
brutish	COARSE, RUDE		
bryophyte	MOSS, LIVERWORT	bulb	ROOT, GLOBE
bubble	GLOBULE	bulbous vegetable	ONION
bubble up	BOIL	Bulgarian city	SOFIA
bubbling	BOILING	Bulgarian river	DANUBE
buccaneers	PIRATES, PRIVATEER, SEA ROVER	bulge	SWELL
		bulkhead	WALL, FIREWALL
buckboard	WAGON	bulky	MASSIVE, HEAVY
bucket	PAIL, TUB	bull (Sp.)	TORO
bucket handle	BAIL	bulldozer	GRADER
Buckeye State	OHIO	bullet	PELLET, SLUG
bucolic	PASTORAL, RUSTIC	bullet diameter	CALIBER
Buddha's mother	MAYA	bullfight cheer	OLE
Buddhist monk	LAMA	bullfighter	TORERO, MATADOR, PICADOR
Buddhist shrine	TOPE, STUPA		
buddy	PAL, CHUM, PARTNER, MATE, FRIEND	bully	MENACE, TOUGH, HOODLUM
budge	STIR, MOVE	bulwark	RAMPART
budget	SCHEDULE	bum	HOBO, TRAMP, BEGGAR, PANHANDLER
buff	POLISH, TAN		
buffalo	BISON	bumpkin	YOKEL, RUBE, HICK, HILLBILLY
buffalo of India	ARNA		
buffet	CUPBOARD, MEAL	bun	ROLL, BREAD, CHIGNON
buffet about	TOSS	bunch	CLUSTER
buffoon	MERRY ANDREW, JESTER, CLOWN	bunch of grass	TUFT
		bundle	BALE, PACK, WRAP, PACKAGE
bug	INSECT		
bugaboo	GOBLIN, SPECTER	bundle maker	BALER
bugbear	GHOST, BOGIE, HOBGOBLIN	bundle of cotton	BALE
		bundle of grain	SHEAF
buggy	CARRIAGE, PRAM	bundle of sticks	FAGOT
bugle	HORN	bungle	BOTCH
bugle call	TAPS, REVEILLE, RETREAT	bungling	CLUMSY
		bunk	BED
bugle note	MOT	bunny	RABBIT
build	CONSTRUCT, ERECT, MAKE, ESTABLISH	bunting	ETAMINE
		buoy	FLOAT
build castles in the air	DREAM	burden	LOAD, ONUS
building	HOUSE, SKYSCRAPER, OFFICE, CHURCH, FACTORY, SETBACK, HI RISE	burdened	LADEN
		burdensome	HEAVY
		bureau	CHEST, DRESSER, DESK, OFFICE, BUSINESS, DEPARTMENT
building addition	ELL, WING, ANNEX		
building beam	GIRDER	burglar	THIEF
building block	STONE	burglarize	ROB
building diagram	PLAN	burglary	LARCENY, THEFT
building entrance	DOOR	burgle	ROB
building front	FACADE	burgundy	WINE
building ground	LOT, PLOT, SITE	burial place	CEMETERY
		burlap fiber	JUTE
building location	SITE	burlesque	PARODY
building material	LUMBER, STEEL, STONE, WOOD, BRICK, CONCRETE	burly	BULKY, STOUT
		Burmese	LAI
		Burmese capital	RANGOON
buildings along the Rhine	CASTLES	Burmese tribe	TAI
		burn	CHAR, SINGE, SEAR, SCALD
building support	ANTA		

burning	**AFIRE, AFLAME, FLAMING, TORRID, HOT, PASSIONATE**	butter portion	**PAT**
		butter substitute	**OLEO, MARGARINE**
Burning Bush	**WAHOO**	butterfly	**IO, SATYR, MONARCH**
burning glass	**LENS**	butterfly snare	**NET**
burning mountain	**VOLCANO**	butting animal	**GOAT**
burning oil	**KEROSENE**	buttock	**RUMP**
burn in hot water	**SCALD**	butt of joke	**IT**
burnish	**GLAZE**	button	**STUD**
burro	**ASS**	button-down	**COLLAR**
burrowing animal	**MOLE, VOLE, GROUNDHOG**	button fastener	**LOOP, HOOK**
		buttress	**PILE**
burry	**PRICKLY**	buy	**PURCHASE**
bursa	**CAVITY**	buyer	**SHOPPER**
bursar	**TREASURER**	buy off	**BRIBE**
bursary	**TREASURY**	buzz	**HUM, DRONE**
burst	**ERUPT, EXPLODE**	buzzing insect	**DOR, BEE, WASP, HORNET, FLY**
burst of activity	**SPASM**		
burst of thunder	**CLAP**	by	**AT, NEAR**
burst open	**POP, EXPLODE, ERUPT**	by and by	**ANON, SOON, PRESENTLY**
bury	**INTER**	by and large	**MAINLY**
bus	**TRANSPORT**	by birth	**NEE**
busby	**HAT**	bygone days	**PAST, AGO**
bush	**SHRUB**	by itself	**ALONE, SOLO, SOLITARY, LONELY, LONE**
bushy clump (Brit.)	**TOD**		
business	**TRADE, WORK**	Byelorussian town	**PINSK, MINSK**
business agreement	**DEAL**		
business deal	**SALE**	by means of	**PER, THROUGH**
business deficit	**LOSS**	by mouth	**ORAL**
business house	**FIRM**	by-pass	**DETOUR**
business man	**TYCOON**	by reason	**RATIONAL**
business note	**MEMO, MEMORANDUM**	by slow stages	**GRADUAL**
		bystander	**ONLOOKER, WITNESS**
business program	**AGENDA**		
business organization	**CARTEL, COMPANY, CORPORATION, CONGLOMERATE**	by the side of	**BESIDE**
		byway	**PATH, LANE**
businessman	**MERCHANT, WHOLESALER**	by way of	**VIA**
		byword	**PROVERB**
bus station	**DEPOT, TERMINAL**	by word of mouth	**PAROL**
bustle	**TO-DO, HUBBUB, ADO**		
bus token	**FARE**		
busybody	**MEDDLER**		
busy insect	**ANT, BEE**		
busy place	**HIVE**		
but	**SAVE, EXCEPT**	**C**	
but (Gr.)	**ABER**		
but (Lat.)	**SED**	ca	**CALCIUM, CIRCA**
butcher	**SLAY, SLAUGHTER**	cab	**TAXI**
butcher's tool	**SLICER, KNIFE, CLEAVER, BLOCK, SCALE**	cabal	**INTRIGUE, PLOT, SCHEME**
butch's pal	**SPIKE**	cabalistic	**OCCULT**
butler	**SERVANT**	caballero	**SENOR, CAVALIER**
butlery	**PANTRY**	cabana	**BEACHHOUSE, LANAI**
butt	**RAM, TARGET**	cabbage broth	**KALE**
butte	**MESA**	cabbage dish	**SLAW, SAUERKRAUT**
butter maker	**CHURN**		

cabin **STATEROOM, SHED**
cabin bed **BERTH**
cabinet **CASE, CUPBOARD**
cable **WIRE, ROPE**
cad **BOUNDER, ROUE, LOUT**
cadence **LILT, BEAT, MEASURE**
Caesar's enemy **SULLA,**
POMPEY, CASSIUS
Caesar's language **LATIN**
cafe employee **WAITER,**
WAITRESS, COOK,
DISHWASHER, HOST,
HOSTESS, CASHIER
cafe patron **EATER, DINER**
DRINKER
cage for poultry **COOP**
cage of an elevator **CAR, CAB**
Cain's brother **ABEL**
Cairo's river **NILE**
caisson **WAGON**
cajole **COAX, WHEEDLE**
cake **PASTRY, HARDEN**
cake mix **BATTER**
cake of soap **BAR**
cake topping **ICING, FROSTING,**
SAUCE, FRUIT, WHIPPED
CREAM, ICE CREAM
calabash **GOURD**
calaboose **JAIL, PRISON**
calamity **DISASTER**
calculate **COMPUTE**
calculate
approximately **ESTIMATE**
calculation
instrument **ABACUS,**
ADDING MACHINE, COMPUTER
Calcutta hemp **JUTE**
caldron **VAT, KETTLE, POT**
Caledonian **SCOT**
calendar **ALMANAC**
calf meat **VEAL**
caliber **BORE**
California city **NAPA, SALINAS,**
SAN FRANCISCO, LOS
ANGELES, FRESNO,
SACRAMENTO
California fruit **KUMQUAT**
California mountain **SHASTA**
California rockfish **RENA**
California tree **REDWOOD**
California wine district **NAPA**
Caliph's name **ALI**
call **SHOUT, TELL, PAGE,**
PHONE, TELEPHONE,
SUMMON, VISIT, RING UP,
YELL, SHRIEK, HOLLER,
SCREAM
call for quiet **SH, HUSH**

call forth **EVOKE, SUMMON**
calling **TRADE, VOCATION**
call it quits **STOP, CEASE**
callous **UNFEELING**
callow **GREEN**
call the roll **MUSTER**
call to the phone **PAGE**
calm **SERENITY, TRANQUILITY,**
LULL, QUIET, PEACE,
PEACEFUL
calmative **SEDATIVE**
calm endurance **PATIENCE**
calumet **PIPE, PEACE PIPE**
calumny **SLANDER, LIBEL**
calyx leaf **SEPAL**
camel-like mammal **LLAMA**
camelopard **GIRAFFE**
Camelot's king **ARTHUR**
Camelot's magician **MERLIN**
camera adjustment **FOCUS**
camera glass **LENS**
Cameroon tribe **IBO, BETI,**
BULU
camp bed **COT**
camp shelter **TENT**
campus building **DORM, QUAD,**
HALL, LIBRARY, CHAPEL
can **TIN**
Canadian capital **OTTAWA,**
VICTORIA, EDMONTON,
REGINA, WINNIPEG,
QUEBEC, ST. JOHNS,
HALIFAX, FREDERICTON
Canadian mountain **LOGAN**
Canadian peninsula **GASPE**
Canadian province **ONTARIO,**
QUEBEC, NEW BRUNSWICK,
NOVA SCOTIA, BRITISH
COLUMBIA,
NEWFOUNDLAND,
MANITOBA,
SASKATCHEWAN,
ALBERTA
canal **WATERWAY**
canal near Egypt **SUEZ**
canal system in northern
Michigan **SOO**
Canal Zone lake **GATUN**
canape **APPETIZER**
canard **RUMOR**
canary **BIRD, WARBLER**
canary's home **CAGE**
cancel **ANNUL, VOID**
Cancer **CRAB**
candid **HONEST, FRANK, OPEN,**
ABOVEBOARD
candidate **NOMINEE**
candied fruit **SWEETMEAT**

candle **TAPER**
candle drippings **WAX**
candle holder **SCONCE**
candy flavor **LEMON, ORANGE, CHERRY, PEPPERMINT, CARAMEL, CHOCOLATE, MINT, LICORICE, RUM**
cane **WHIP, BEAT, THRASH, STICK, PADDLE, STEM**
cane-cutting knife **BOLO**
cane sugar **SUCROSE**
canine **TOOTH, DOG, FOX, WOLF, EYETOOTH**
canine cry **YELP, YAP, YIP, BARK, WOOF, ARF, BOWWOW, GROWL, GRR, ROWF**
canine home **KENNEL**
canine pet **DOG**
canine tooth **FANG, EYETOOTH**
canine with rabies (2 wds.) **MAD DOG**
canker **ULCER, SORE**
can metal **TIN**
cannon **GUN**
cannon fire **BARRAGE, BATTERY**
cannon handle **ANSE**
cannon shot **GRAPE**
canoe **BOAT, BIRCHBARK, PROA**
canoe of Malaysia **PROA**
canon **LAW, CODE, RULE, CRITERION**
canonized man **SAINT, ST.**
canonized woman (Fr.) **SAINTE, STE.**
canonized woman (It.) **SANTA**
canopy **ROOF**
cant **ARGOT, JARGON, SLANG, SLANT, INCLINE, TOP**
cantabile **FLOWING**
cantaloupe **MELON, MUSKMELON**
cantata **MOTET**
canteen **FLASK**
canter **GAIT, LOPE**
canticle **ODE, SONG, CHANT**
cantina **SALOON, BAR**
cantle **NOOK, SLICE**
canto **SONG, VERSE**
cantor **SOLOIST, PRECENTOR**
canvas **DUCK**
canvas bed **COT**
canvas frame **EASEL**
canvas home **TENT**
canvass **POLL**
canyon **GORGE, CHASM**

caoutchouc **RUBBER**
cap **BERET, HAT**
capa **CLOAK**
capability **CAPACITY**
capable **ABLE, COMPETENT**
capable of (2 wds.) **UP TO**
capable of cultivation **ARABLE**
capable of flying **VOLANT**
capable of learning **TEACHABLE**
capacious **LARGE, ROOMY**
capacity **VOLUME**
cape **CLOAK, HEADLAND, NESS, PROMONTORY**
Cape Kennedy launching (comp. wd.) **LIFT-OFF, BLAST-OFF**
Cape Kennedy platform **GANTRY**
Cape Kennedy rocket **AGENA, APOLLO, MERCURY, GEMINI**
Cape Kennedy routine **COUNTDOWN**
caper **ANTIC, TRICK, FROLIC**
caper about **CAVORT**
capillus **HAIR**
Capistrano resident **SWALLOW**
capital **MAIN, MAJOR**
capital of Alabama **MONTGOMERY**
capital of Alaska **JUNEAU**
capital of Albania **TIRANA**
capital of Arizona **PHOENIX**
capital of Arkansas **LITTLE ROCK**
capital of Austria **VIENNA**
capital of Bolivia (2 wds.) **LA PAZ**
capital of California **SACRAMENTO**
capital of Canada **OTTAWA**
capital of Colorado **DENVER**
capital of Connecticut **HARTFORD**
capital of Cuba **HAVANA**
capital of Delaware **DOVER**
capital of Egypt **CAIRO**
capital of Florida **TALLAHASSEE**
capital of France **PARIS**
capital of Georgia **ATLANTA**
capital of Germany **BERLIN, BONN**
capital of Greece **ATHENS**
capital of Guam **AGANA**
capital of Haiti **PORT-AU-PRINCE**
capital of Hawaii **HONOLULU**
capital of Hungary **BUDAPEST**

capital of Idaho **BOISE**
capital of Illinois **SPRINGFIELD**
capital of Indiana **INDIANAPOLIS**
capital of Indonesia **DJAKARTA**
capital of Iowa **DES MOINES**
capital of Iraq **BAGHDAD**
capital of Italia **ROMA**
capital of Italy **ROME**
capital of Kansas **TOPEKA**
capital of Kentucky **FRANKFORT**
capital of Louisiana **BATON ROUGE**
capital of Lydian Empire **SARDIS**
capital of Maine **AUGUSTA**
capital of Maryland **ANNAPOLIS**
capital of Massachusetts **BOSTON**
capital of Michigan **LANSING**
capital of Minnesota **ST. PAUL**
capital of Mississippi **JACKSON**
capital of Missouri **JEFFERSON CITY**
capital of Montana **HELENA**
capital of Morocco **RABAT**
capital of Nebraska **LINCOLN**
capital of Nevada **CARSON CITY**
capital of New Hampshire **CONCORD**
capital of New Jersey **TRENTON**
capital of New Mexico **SANTA FE**
capital of New York **ALBANY**
capital of Nicaragua **MANAGUA**
capital of Nigeria **LAGOS**
capital of North Carolina **RALEIGH**
capital of North Dakota **BISMARCK**
capital of North Vietnam **HANOI**
capital of Norway **OSLO**
capital of Ohio **COLUMBUS**
capital of Oklahoma **OKLAHOMA CITY**
capital of Oregon **SALEM**
capital of Paraguay **ASUNCION**
capital of Pennsylvania **HARRISBURG**
capital of Peru **LIMA**
capital of Philippines **QUEZON CITY**
capital of Phoenicia **TYRE**
capital of Poland **WARSAW**
capital of Rhode Island **PROVIDENCE**

capital of Senegal **DAKAR**
capital of South Carolina **COLUMBIA**
capital of South Dakota **PIERRE**
capital of Soviet Union **MOSCOW**
capital of Spain **MADRID**
capital of Tennessee **NASHVILLE**
capital of Texas **AUSTIN**
capital of Tibet **LHASA**
capital of Utah **SALT LAKE CITY**
capital of Venezuela **CARACAS**
capital of Vermont **MONTPELIER**
capital of Virginia **RICHMOND**
capital of Washington **OLYMPIA**
capital of West Germany **BONN**
capital of West Pakistan **LAHORE**
capital of West Virginia **CHARLESTON**
capital of Western Samoa **APIA**
capital of Wisconsin **MADISON**
capital of Wyoming **CHEYENNE**
capital of Yemen **SANA(A)**
capital of Yugoslavia **BELGRADE**
capsule **PILL, PELLET, TABLET**
Captain Kidd **PIRATE, BUCCANEER**
captain of a ship **SKIPPER**
captivate **ENTRANCE**
captor **TAKER**
capture **NAB, SEIZE, CATCH, GRAB, TAKE**
capture again **RETAKE, REGAIN**
capuchin monkey **SAI**
car **AUTO, AUTOMOBILE**
carabao **BUFFALO**
carafe **BOTTLE, DECANTER**
caramel **CANDY, FLAVOR**
carat **GEM WEIGHT**
caravansary **INN**
caravan station **SERAI**
caraway **SEED**
carbohydrate **STARCH**
carbon **COPY, SOOT**
carbonated beverage **POP, SODA**
carcass **BODY, CORPSE**
card **ACE, DEUCE, TREY**
card (Fr.) **CARTE**
cardboard box **CARTON**
card combination **TENACE, FLUSH, PAIR**

card game **CANASTA, GIN, LOON, PINOCHLE, POKER, HEARTS, RUMMY, BEZIQUE, CRIBBAGE, CASINO, CANFIELD, KLONDIKE, RUSSIAN BANK, MONTE CARLO, BRIDGE, WHIST**
cardigan **SWEATER, JACKET**
cardinal **BIRD**
cardinal point **NORTH, SOUTH, EAST, WEST**
cardinal's office **HAT**
cardinal's symbol (2 wds.) **RED HAT**
card of admission **PASS**
cards and letters **MAIL**
card suit **SPADES, HEARTS, DIAMONDS, CLUBS**
card wool **COMB**
care **ANXIETY, MIND, WORRY, TROUBLE, HEEDFUL, CAUTION, WISH**
careen **LURCH**
career **PROFESSION, VOCATION**
career beginning **DEBUT**
carefree **HAPPY, GAY**
careful **CAUTIOUS**
careful management **PRUDENCE**
careless **LAX, LAZY**
car entrance **DRIVEWAY**
caress **FONDLE, PET, PAT, STROKE**
caretaker **CUSTODIAN**
car fuel **GAS, PETROL, GASOLINE**
car gear **REVERSE, LOW, DRIVE, PASSING**
cargo **LOAD**
cargo compartment **HOLD**
cargo ship **TRAMP, TANKER, FREIGHTER**
cargo stower **STEVEDORE**
Caribbean island **NEVIS, GRENADA, PUERTO RICO, ANTIGUA, CUBA, JAMAICA, HAITI, BARBADOS, DOMINICA, MARTINIQUE, MONSERRAT**
caribou **MOOSE, DEER**
caricature **PARODY, BURLESQUE**
car ignition device **STARTER**
carillon **CHIME**
Carl Sandburg creation **POEM**
carmine **SCARLET**
car model **SEDAN, COUPE, CONVERTIBLE, HARDTOP**
carnal **EARTHY**

carnation **PINK**
carnival **FESTIVAL**
carnival attraction (2 wds.) **SIDE SHOW**
carousel (comp. wd.) **MERRY-GO-ROUND**
carp **CAVIL**
car part (2 wds.) **TIE ROD**
carpentry tool **AWL, HAMMER, SAW, AUGER, RASP, MITER BOX, LEVEL, PLUMB LINE, PLANE**
carpet **RUG, MAT**
carpet nap **PILE**
carport **GARAGE**
carp's home **POND**
carriage **STATURE**
carriage dog **DALMATIAN**
carried away **RAPT**
carried on the back **TOTE**
carrier **PORTER**
carrion **ROTTEN, VILE**
carry **BEAR, TOTE, LUG**
carry across water **FERRY**
carry away **REMOVE**
carrying guns **ARMED**
carry into effect **EXECUTE**
carry on **WAGE, CONTINUE, ENSUE**
carry out **PERFORM, EXECUTE**
carry tales **TATTLE**
carry the day **WIN**
cart **WAGON**
cartel **POOL, TRUST**
carter **TEAMSTER**
Carthaginian **PUNIC**
Carthaginian queen **DIDO**
cartilage **GRISTLE**
cartridge **SHELL**
carve **CUT, SLICE**
carved gem **CAMEO**
carve letters upon **ENGRAVE**
Casals' instrument **CELLO**
cascade **WATERFALL**
case **ETUI, BOX, CRATE, CARTON**
case for small articles **ETUI**
cash **MONEY**
cash drawer **TILL**
cashew **NUT**
cashmere **WOOL**
cask **BARREL, TUN**
casket **BOX, COFFIN**
cask part **STAVE**
cask's circular strip **HOOP**
cask stave **LAG**
Caspian **SEA**
cassava starch food **TAPIOCA**

cassowary	**EMU**
cast	**PLAYERS, THROW,**
	PITCH, TOSS
cast a ballot	**VOTE**
cast aside	**DISCARD, REJECT**
caste	**CLASS**
castle	**PALACE**
castle ditch	**MOAT**
castles in the air	**DREAMS**
cast off	**SHED, SLOUGH**
Castor or Pollux	**STAR**
Castro's country	**CUBA**
casual utterance	**REMARK**
casualty	**ACCIDENT**
cat	**FELINE, TABBY, PUSSY**
cataclysm	**DISASTER**
catalogue	**LIST**
catamaran	**FLOAT, RAFT**
catastrophe	**CALAMITY,**
	DISASTER
catch	**NAB, GRAB, SEIZE,**
	SNATCH, TAKE
catch on to	**GLOM**
catch sight of	**ESPY**
catch up with	**OVERTAKE**
catching implement	**HOOK**
catchword	**SLOGAN**
cat command	**SCAT, SHOO**
category	**BRACKET, CLASS**
cater	**SERVE**
catharsis	**PURGE**
Catholic cleric's cap	**BIRETTA**
Catholic prayer (Lat., 2 wds.)	
AVE MARIA, PATER NOSTER	
Catholic service	**MASS**
catkin	**AMENT**
cats and dogs	**PETS**
cat's foot	**PAW**
cat sound	**PURR, MEOW,**
MIAOW, MEW, MIAOU	
cat's prey	**MOUSE, CANARY**
cattle (arch.)	**KINE**
cattle bedding	**STRAW**
cattle enclosure	**CORRAL**
cattle genus	**BOS**
cattleman	**DROVER**
cattle thief	**RUSTLER**
Caucasian	**ARYAN**
Caucasian goat	**TUR**
caudal appendage	**TAIL**
caught in a net	**ENMESHED**
cauldron	**POT**
cause	**GIVE RISE TO, REASON**
cause dough to rise	**LEAVEN**
cause of Cleopatra's death	**ASP**
cause of tension	**STRESS**
cause to jump the track	**DERAIL**

cause to remember	**REMIND,**
	RECALL
cause to slant	**TILT**
cause to stand out	**EMBOSS**
cause to stick	**MIRE**
cause to take root	**RADICATE**
causeway	**DIKE**
causing amusement	**FUNNY**
causing feeling	**EMOTIVE**
caustic	**ACRID, BITTER**
caustic substance	**ACID, LYE**
caustic wit	**IRONIC, CUTTING,**
	SARCASTIC
cauterize	**SEAR**
caution	**WARN**
cautious	**WARY**
cautiously	**CAREFULLY,**
	GINGERLY
cavalcade	**MARCH, PARADE**
Cavalier State	**VIRGINIA**
cavalry	**TROOP**
cavalry horse	**LANCER, MOUNT**
cavalry man	**TROOPER,**
	DRAGOON
cavalry soldiers	**LANCERS**
cavalry sword	**SABER, SABRE**
cavalry unit	**TROOP**
cave	**CAVERN**
caveat	**WARNING**
cave in	**COLLAPSE**
cavern	**CAVE**
cavernous	**DEEP, HOLLOW**
caviar	**ROE**
cavil	**CARP**
caviler	**CRITIC**
cavity	**HOLE**
cavort	**PRANCE**
cay	**INLET**
cayenne	**PEPPER**
cease	**STOP, DESIST, HALT**
cease-fire	**TRUCE, ARMISTICE**
cease friendship with	
(2 wds.)	**PART COMPANY**
ceaseless	**CONTINUAL**
cebine monkey	**SAI**
Cebu hemp	**MANILA**
cedar	**TREE, SAVINE**
cede	**YIELD**
Celebes ox	**ANOA**
celebrate	**OBSERVE, REVEL**
celebrated	**FAMOUS**
celebration	**RITE, FETE,**
	FESTIVAL
celebrity	**LION, STAR**
celerity	**SPEED**
celery portion	**STALK**
celestial	**HEAVENLY**
celestial being	**ANGEL**

celestial body	**COMET, SUN, STAR, MOON, PLANET, ASTEROID**	certainty	**FACT**
celestial instrument	**HARP**	certificate	**DOCUMENT**
celestial visitor	**COMET**	certify	**ATTEST, VERIFY**
celibate	**SINGLE**	certitude	**SURENESS**
cell	**ROOM**	cerulean	**BLUE**
cellar	**BASEMENT, PANTRY**	cessation	**LULL**
Celt	**GAUL, BRITON**	cessation of war agreement (2 wds.)	**PEACE TREATY**
Celtic language	**ERSE, GAELIC, MANX, WELSH, BRETON**	cetacea	**WHALES**
Celtic peasant	**KERN**	Ceylonese canoe	**BALSA**
Celtic priest	**DRUID**	Ceylon moss	**AGAR**
Celtic sea deity	**LER**	chagrin	**SHAME**
cement	**PUTTY**	chain	**CATENA, BIND, FETTER, SHACKLE**
cemetery	**GRAVEYARD**	chain cable	**BOOM**
censurable quality	**DEMERIT**	chain of mountains	**RANGE, RIDGE**
censure	**BLAME, CONDEMN**	chain of rocks	**REEF**
cent	**PENNY**	chain part	**LINK**
Centennial State	**COLORADO**	chain reaction	**SEQUENCE**
center	**CORE, MID, MIDDLE, NUCLEUS, HUB**	chain sound	**CLANK, CLINK**
center of activity	**FOCUS**	chair	**SEAT**
center of interest	**FOCUS**	chair covers	**TIDIES**
center of sail	**BUNT**	chair of state	**THRONE**
center of target	**EYE**	chair part	**LEG, SPLAT, SEAT, BACK, ARM**
Central American country	**NICARAGUA, HONDURAS, GUATEMALA, EL SALVADOR, COSTA RICA, PANAMA**	chaise	**CHAIR, CARRIAGE**
Central American Indian	**CARIB, MAYA**	chalcedony	**AGATE, SARD**
		Chaldean city	**UR**
Central American oil tree	**EBOE**	chalet	**CABIN, HUT**
Central American rodent	**PACA**	chalice	**GOBLET, CUP**
central point	**PIVOT**	chalice cover	**PALL**
century plant	**AGAVE, MAGUEY, ALOE**	chalk	**CRAYON**
		chalk remover	**ERASER**
ceramic earth	**CLAY**	chalk up	**SCORE**
ceramic piece	**VASE, PITCHER, POT, PLATE**	chalky	**PALE, WHITE**
		challenge	**DARE, DEFY**
ceramic square	**TILE**	chalumeau	**CLARINET, REED**
ceramics	**POTTERY**	chamber	**ROOM**
ceramics maker	**POTTER**	chamber beneath the Vatican	**CATACOMB**
cerated	**WAXED**	chamberlain	**ATTENDANT, STEWARD**
cere	**ANOINT, WAX**	chameleon	**LIZARD**
cereal	**GRAIN, BRAN**	chamfer	**BEVEL**
cereal dish	**BOWL**	champ	**BITE**
cereal grain	**OAT, RICE, RYE, BARLEY, WHEAT, CORN**	champagne	**WINE**
		champagne bucket	**ICER, COOLER**
cereal grass	**OAT, RICE, RYE, WHEAT, BARLEY**	champion	**DEFENDER, WINNER**
		chance	**FATE, LUCK**
cereal spike	**EAR**	chancel seats	**SEDILIA**
ceremonial	**FORMAL, RITUAL**	chancel table	**ALTAR**
ceremonial post	**TOTEM**	change	**ALTER, AMEND, VARY**
ceremony	**RITE**	changeable	**ERRATIC, FICKLE**
cerise	**RED**	change a constitution	**AMEND**
certain	**SURE**	change a manuscript	**REVISE**
certainly	**OF COURSE, YES**	change an alarm	**RESET**
certainly not	**NO**	change color	**DYE, FADE**

change course **VEER, TACK**
change direction **TURN, VEER**
changed state **MUTATION**
change for the better **REFORM**
change from evil **REPENT**
change into bone **OSSIFY**
changeling (arch.) **IDIOT**
change off **TAKE TURNS**
change one's address **MOVE**
change order of **TRANSPOSE**
change position **TURN OVER, MOVE, SHIFT, REVERSE**
change the decor **REDO**
change the mind **RECONSIDER**
channel **VEIN, RIVER, STRAIT**
Channel Island **JERSEY, SARK, GUERNSEY, ALDERNEY**
channel marker **BUOY**
chant **INTONE, SINGSONG**
Chantilly product **LACE**
chaos **MESS**
chap **FELLOW**
chaparral **THICKET**
chaparral cock **ROAD RUNNER**
chapeau **HAT**
chapel **SANCTUARY**
chaperon **DUENNA**
chaplain **MINISTER, PADRE, PRIEST**
chaplet **ANADEM, BEADS, WREATH**
chapter of Koran **SURA**
char **BURN, SEAR, SCORCH, TASK**
character **PERSONALITY, NATURE**
characteristic **TRAIT, EARMARK**
characterization **ROLE**
characterize **REPRESENT**
characterized by (suffix) **MORPH**
character of a people **ETHOS**
character part **ROLE**
characters in a play **CAST**
charcoal **FUEL**
charcoal grill **BRAZIER**
charge **FEE, RATE**
charged atom **ION**
charge for use of road **TOLL**
charge with crime **ACCUSE**
charge with gas **AERATE**
chariot **CART**
charisma **GRACE, CHARM**
charitable **GENEROUS**
charity **ALMS, GIVING**
charity gift **DOLE, ALMS, DONATION**
charlatan **QUACK, FRAUD**
Charles Goren's domain
(2 wds.) **CONTRACT BRIDGE**

Charles Lamb **ELIA**
charley horse **CRAMP**
Charlotte Corday's
victim **MARAT**
charm **ENAMOR, ENTHRALL, FASCINATE, TALISMAN, TOKEN**
charming **WINSOME**
chart **GRAPH, MAP**
charter **HIRE, GRANT**
chary **FRUGAL, WARY, SHY**
chase **PURSUE**
chase away **ROUT**
chaste **PURE, VESTAL**
chasten **DISCIPLINE, PUNISH**
chastise **BERATE, CHASTEN, SCOLD**
chastity **PURITY, VIRTUE**
chat **GAB, CHATTER, PRATE, CHIN, CHEW THE RAG, CHEW THE FAT, GABBLE**
chatter **PRATE, PRATTLE**
cheap **INEXPENSIVE, TINNY**
cheap metal **TIN**
cheat **SWINDLE, DUPE**
check **REIN, TAB, BILL, STOP, ARREST**
check by danger **DAUNT**
checkers **DRAFTS, DRAUGHTS**
cheer **RAH, BRAVO, BRAVA, OLE, HURRAH, HURRAY, LIVEN, ELATE, GLADDEN**
cheerful **ROSY, PLEASANT**
cheerful expression **SMILE, GRIN**
cheerless **BLEAK, DRAB, DULL, DEPRESSING**
cheese dish **RAREBIT, FONDUE**
cheese variety **EDAM, GOUDA, BRIE, GRUYERE**
chef **COOK**
chef's garment **APRON**
chef's specialty **SALAD**
chelonian **TURTLE, TORTOISE**
chemical analysis **ASSAY**
chemical compound **ESTER**
chemical element **ANTIMONY, BARIUM**
chemical particle **ION**
chemical product of the
body **HORMONE**
chemical salts **SALS**
chemical suffix **ANE, ASE, IDE, ITE, INE**
chemist's
burner **BUNSEN, ETNA**
chemist's shop **PHARMACY**
chemist's workplace **LAB**

cherish	**LOVE, TREASURE, HOLD DEAR**
cherished	**DEAR**
cherished animal	**PET**
cherry	**OXHEART, MORELLO, BING**
cherry-colored	**CERISE**
cherry orange	**KUMQUAT**
cherry seed	**PIT**
chess move	**GAMBIT**
chess piece	**MAN, PAWN, KING, QUEEN, KNIGHT, BISHOP, CASTLE, ROOK**
chess victory	**CHECKMATE, MATE**
chest	**BOX, CASE, STRONGBOX**
chest bone	**RIB**
chestnut horse	**ROAN**
chest of drawers	**DRESSER, BUREAU, COMMODE**
chest sound	**RALE**
chew	**MASTICATE, GNAW, MUNCH, BITE**
chewing gum	**CHICLE**
chewing gum flavor	**SPEARMINT**
chew the cud	**RUMINATE**
chewy candy	**CARAMEL, TAFFY, TOFFEE, NOUGAT**
chic	**MODISH, STYLISH**
chick's mother	**HEN**
chicken	**HEN, CAPON, FOWL, FRYER**
chicken feed	**MASH**
chicken pen	**COOP**
chicory	**HERB, ENDIVE**
chide	**SCOLD, BERATE**
chief	**MAIN, HEAD**
chief character	**HERO**
chief executive	**PRESIDENT**
chief of fairies	**PUCK**
chief ore of lead	**GALENA**
chief part	**MAIN**
chief ruler	**GOVERNOR**
chiffonier	**CABINET**
chignon	**BUN, KNOT**
child	**KID, TOT, YOUNGSTER, TODDLER**
childish	**PUERILE, INFANTILE**
child of necessity	**INVENTION**
child's cry	**SNIVEL**
child's game	**JACKS, TAG, MARBLES, KICK THE CAN, RED ROVER, HIDE AND SEEK, JUMP ROPE, HOPSCOTCH**
child's hat	**BONNET, TAM, BERET, CAP**
child's marble	**AGATE, TAW**
child's play	**EASY, SIMPLE**
child's salary	**ALLOWANCE**
child's sock	**ANKLET**
child's stroller (comp. wd.)	**GO-CART**
child's toy	**YOYO**
child's vehicle	**SCOOTER, BIKE, WAGON, CARRIAGE**
Chilean coin	**CONDOR**
Chilean export	**NITER, NITRATES**
Chilean Indian	**ONA**
Chilean mountains	**ANDES**
chill	**FREEZE, ICE, COOL**
chilling tale (2 wds.)	**GHOST STORY**
chilly attitude	**STANDOFF**
chime	**PEAL, RING**
chimney dirt	**SOOT**
chimney passage	**FLUE**
chimpanzee	**APE**
chinaware	**DISHES**
Chinese	**SINIC**
Chinese drink	**TEA**
Chinese dynasty	**MING, CHING, SUNG, TANG, WEI**
Chinese fish sauce	**SOY, SOYA**
Chinese fruit	**LITCHI, LICHEE**
Chinese idol	**JOSS, GHOS**
Chinese island	**AMOY, FORMOSA**
Chinese laborer	**COOLIE**
Chinese measure	**LI, TU**
Chinese nurse	**AMAH**
Chinese pagoda	**TAA**
Chinese philosophy	**TAO**
Chinese poet (2 wds.)	**LI PO**
Chinese porcelain	**MING**
Chinese port	**AMOY**
Chinese ship	**JUNK**
Chinese society	**TONG**
Chinese staple grain	**RICE**
Chinese temple	**TAA**
Chinook State	**WASHINGTON**
chip of stone	**SPALL**
chirp	**PEEP, PIP, TWEET, TWEE, CHEEP, CHIRRUP**
chisel	**CUT, GOUGE, SHAPE**
chiseler	**MOOCHER, SPONGER**
chitchat (2 wds.)	**SMALL TALK**
chivalrous	**VALIANT, GALLANT**
chocolate tree	**CACAO**
choice	**OPTION, SELECTION**
choice cut of beef	**SIRLOIN**
choice morsel	**TIDBIT**
choice part	**ELITE**
choice seashore location	**OCEANFRONT**
choir leader	**CANTOR**

choir voice **ALTO, SOPRANO, BASS, BARITONE, TENOR**
choke **OBSTRUCT, STRANGLE**
choke back **REPRESS, STIFLE**
choke coil **REACTOR**
choke up **CLOG, SPEECHLESS**
choler **IRE, SPLEEN**
choleric **ANGRY**
Chomolungma's other name **EVEREST**
choose **ELECT, SELECT, OPT, PICK**
choose over **PREFER**
choosy **PARTICULAR, FINICKY**
chop **HEW, CUT, DICE, MINCE**
chop-chop **QUICKLY, HURRY**
chop finely **DICE, MINCE**
chop off **LOP**
chopped cabbage dish **SLAW**
chopped meat dish **HASH, MINCE, HAMBURGER**
chopping tool **AX, AXE, HATCHET, KNIFE**
choppy **ROUGH, JERKY**
chord **HARMONY**
chord composition **CANTATA**
chore **ERRAND, TASK**
chortle **CHUCKLE**
chorus **REFRAIN**
Chosen **KOREA**
chosen few **ELITE**
chosen field **CAREER**
chosen people **ISRAELITES, HEBREWS**
christen **DUB, NAME**
Christian **GENTILE**
Christian era (abbr.) **A.D.**
Christiania **OSLO**
Christmas **HOLIDAY, NOEL, YULE, YULETIDE**
Christmas carol **NOEL**
Christmas Carol character **TIM, SCROOGE**
Christmas decoration **HOLLY, IVY, TREE**
Christmas plant **HOLLY, MISTLETOE**
Christmas song **CAROL, NOEL**
Christmas trimming **TINSEL**
chromosome **GENE**
chronic **CONSTANT**
chronicle **ACCOUNT, HISTORY**
chubby **PLUMP**
chum **FRIEND, PAL, BUDDY, PARTNER**
chunk **SLAB**
chunky **LUMPY, PLUMP**
church **BASILICA, CATHEDRAL**

church bench **KNEELER, PEW**
church body **CANON, SYNOD, CONGREGATION**
church calendar **ORDO**
church canticle **VENITE**
church council **SYNOD**
church court **ROTA**
church dignitary **PRELATE**
church district **PARISH**
church fast **LENT**
church gallery **LOFT**
church hymn **ANTHEM**
church law **CANON**
church minister **PASTOR, PRIEST**
church morning service **MATINS**
Church of Latter-day Saints **MORMON**
church officer **SEXTON, WARDEN**
church official **ELDER, DEACON, CARDINAL**
Church of Rome **LATERAN, CATHOLIC**
church part **ALTAR, APSE, NAVE, CHANCEL, CHOIR LOFT, VESTRY, BAPTISTRY**
church pulpit **AMBO**
church seat **PEW**
church service **MASS**
church singing group **CHOIR**
church tower **STEEPLE, SPIRE**
church vault **CRYPT**
church vestry room **SACRISTY**
churl **BOOR**
churlish **SURLY**
chute **FLUME, SLIDE**
chutney **RELISH**
CIA employee **SPY, AGENT**
cicada **LOCUST**
cicatrix **SCAR**
cider source **APPLE**
cigar **STOGIE, PANATELA, PANATELLA**
cigar residue **ASH**
cigarette **FAG, CIG, BUTT**
cigarette end **STUB, BUTT**
cilium **EYELASH**
cinch **GIRTH, SNAP**
cinchona **QUININE**
Cincinnati ball club **REDS**
cincture **BELT**
cinder **ASH**
cinema house **THEATER, THEATRE, MOVIE**
cinnabar **ORE**
cinnamon **CASSIA**
cipher **CODE, ZERO**

circle	**SET, CLIQUE**
circle a planet	**ORBIT**
circle of light	**HALO**
circle of persons	**CORDON**
circle part	**ARC**
circlet	**HOOP, RING**
circlet of light	**AUREOLE(A)**
circuit	**CYCLE, LOOP**
circuit-breaker	**FUSE**
circuit rider	**ITINERANT,**
	BIRMINGHAM, MANCHESTER
	MINISTER
circuitous	**ROUNDABOUT**
circular	**OVAL, ROUND**
circular cloak	**CAPE**
circular figure	**LOOP**
circulate	**DIFFUSE, MIX**
circumference	**PERIMETER**
circumscribe	**ENCLOSE, LIMIT**
circumspect	**DISCREET**
circumstance	**EVENT**
circumvent	**EVADE, AVOID**
circus	**ARENA**
circus (2 wds.)	**BIG TOP**
circus animal	**LION, TIGER,**
	ELEPHANT, APE, HORSE,
	CHIMPANZEE, GORILLA,
	SEAL
circus attraction	**SIDE SHOW,**
	FREAK, CLOWN
circus caller	**BARKER**
circus ring	**ARENA**
circus shelter	**TENT**
circus tent (2 wds.)	**BIG TOP**
Cisalpine land	**ITALY, GAUL**
Cistercian monk	**TRAPPIST**
cistern	**TANK**
citadel	**FORT, REFUGE**
citadel in Texas	**ALAMO**
citation	**SUMMONS**
cite	**QUOTE**
cite as proof	**ADDUCE**
citizen	**SUBJECT, NATIVE**
citrus drink	**ADE**
citrus fruit	**LEMON, LIME,**
	ORANGE, GRAPEFRUIT
city	**TOWN, METROPOLIS**
city dirt	**SOOT**
city district	**WARD**
city division	**DISTRICT,**
	PRECINCT
city executive	**MAYOR**
city in Alabama	**MOBILE,**
	SELMA, MONTGOMERY,
	BIRMINGHAM
city in Alaska	**JUNEAU,**
	FAIRBANKS
city in Arizona	**TUCSON,**
	PHOENIX
city in Brazil	**RIO**

city in Brittany	**NANTES**
city in California	**SAN MATEO,**
	SANTA BARBARA, LOS
	ANGELES, FRESNO, SAN
	FRANCISCO, PALO ALTO,
	SACRAMENTO, SAN DIEGO
city in Delaware	**WILMINGTON**
city in England	**OLDHAM,**
	LONDON, LIVERPOOL,
	BIRMINGHAM, MANCHESTER
city in Florida	**OCALA, TAMPA,**
	MIAMI, MIAMI BEACH,
	TALLAHASSEE, ORLANDO
city in Georgia	**ATLANTA**
city in Germany	**EMDEN, ESSEN,**
	ULM, BERLIN, BONN
city in Hawaii	**HONOLULU, HILO**
city in Illinois	**PEKIN, CHICAGO,**
	SPRINGFIELD, PEORIA
city in India	**AGRA, NEW DELHI,**
	VARANASI, MADRAS,
	CALCUTTA, KAPUR
city in Indiana	**SOUTH BEND,**
	GARY, INDIANAPOLIS,
	TERRE HAUTE, HAMMOND
city in Iowa	**AMES**
city in Italia	**ROMA, MILANO,**
	FIRENZE, PISA, NAPOLI, SIENA
city in Italy	**ASTI, MILAN, ROME,**
	NAPLES, GENOA, FLORENCE,
	PARMA, VENICE
city in Kansas	**HUTCHINSON,**
	TOPEKA, WICHITA
city in Kentucky	**LOUISVILLE**
city in Kwangtung province	**MACAO, CANTON**
city in Louisiana	**NEW ORLEANS**
city in Michigan	**NILES,**
	LANSING, DETROIT, SAGINAW,
	ANN ARBOR
city in Minnesota	**ROCHESTER,**
	MINNEAPOLIS
city in Mississippi	**NATCHEZ,**
	JACKSON, BILOXI,
	GULFPORT, VICKSBURG,
	GREENVILLE
city in Montana	**BUTTE**
city in Nebraska	**OMAHA,**
	LINCOLN
city in Nevada	**ELKO, RENO**
city in New Hampshire	**KEENE**
city in New Jersey	**ORANGE,**
	NEWARK, PATERSON,
	TRENTON
city in New Mexico	**ALBUQUERQUE**
city in New York	**OLEAN,**
	SYRACUSE, UTICA, TROY,
	SCHENECTADY, WHITE PLAINS

city in Nicaragua **LEON**
city in Normandy **CAEN**
city in North Carolina **RALEIGH, DURHAM**
city in North Dakota **MINOT**
city in northern France **LILLE**
city in North Vietnam **HANOI**
city in Norway **OSLO, HAMMAR, BERGEN**
city in Ohio **DAYTON, TOLEDO**
city in Oklahoma **ADA, TULSA, ENID**
city in Oregon **SALEM, EUGENE, PORTLAND**
city in Pakistan **LAHORE**
city in Pennsylvania **ALTOONA, YORKTOWN, SCRANTON, PHILADELPHIA, PITTSBURGH, ERIE**
city in Peru **LIMA**
city in Poland **LODZ, POSEN**
city in Quebec **MONTREAL**
city in Russia **OREL, MOSCOW, LENINGRAD, MINSK, PINSK**
city in Sicily **ENNA**
city in Spain **JAEN, AVILA, CADIZ, MADRID, TOLEDO, BARCELONA**
city in Tennessee **MEMPHIS, NASHVILLE, KNOXVILLE, JACKSON**
city in Texas **DALLAS, WACO, EL PASO, HOUSTON, LUBBOCK**
city in The Netherlands **ROTTERDAM, AMSTERDAM, THE HAGUE**
city in Turkey **ISTANBUL**
city in Utah **OGDEN**
city in Washington **TACOMA, SEATTLE**
city in Wyoming **LARAMIE**
city man **DUDE, SLICKER**
city manager **MAYOR**
city official **ALDERMAN, MAYOR**
City of Light **PARIS**
city of Manasseh **ANER**
city of Paris **TROY**
city of Pied Piper legend **HAMELIN**
City of Rams **CANTON**
City of Saints **MONTREAL**
City of Wheels **DETROIT**
city on Lake Ontario **OSWEGO**
city on the Allegheny **OLEAN**
city on the Arno **PISA**
city on the Danube **ULM**
city on the Loire **NANTES**

city on the Mississippi gulf coast **BILOXI, GULFPORT, PASCAGOULA**
city on the Mohawk **UTICA**
city on the Nile **CAIRO**
city on the Oka **OREL**
city on the Po **TURIN**
city on the Rhone **ARLES**
city on the Seine **PARIS**
city on the Thames **LONDON**
city on the Truckee **RENO**
city on the Vltava **PRAGUE**
city problem **SMOG, CRIME, HOUSING, SANITATION, TRAFFIC**
city prosecutor (abbr.) **D.A.**
city slicker **DUDE, SOPHISTICATE**
city square **BLOCK, PLACE**
city thoroughfare **STREET, AVENUE, BOULEVARD, ROAD**
city train **EL, SUBWAY**
civet **CAT**
civic **URBAN**
civic corruption **GRAFT**
civil **POLITE**
civil defense item (2 wds.) **GAS MASK**
civil disorder **RIOT**
civilian clothes **MUFTI**
civilian, to gobs **LANDLUBBER**
civilities **AMENITIES**
civilized **REFINED**
Civil War general **LEE, GRANT, MEADE, SHERMAN**
civil wrong **TORT**
clad **ATTIRED**
claim **ASSERT, AVER**
claimant **PRETENDER**
claim as due **DEMAND**
clairvoyant **SEER**
clam dish **CHOWDER**
clam genus **MYA, VENUS**
clammy **DAMP, DANK**
clamor **NOISE**
clamor of pursuit (3 wds.) **HUE AND CRY**
clamorous **LOUD**
clamp **VISE**
clan **TRIBE, FAMILY**
clandestine **SECRET**
clan quarrel **FEUD**
clap **APPLAUD**
claret **WINE**
clash **CONFLICT**
clasp **EMBRACE, HUG, FASTEN**
class **SORT, KIND, RANK, GENRE, TYPE, VARIETY**

classical Chinese poet
(2 wds.) **LI PO**
classification of plants **GENUS**
classified item **AD**
classify **SORT, RATE, ASSORT**
classroom favorite
(2 wds.) **TEACHER'S PET**
classroom period **HOUR**
classroom talk **LECTURE**
clatter **RATTLE, DIN**
clause **ARTICLE, STIPULATION**
claw **TALON**
clay and sand mixture **LOAM**
clay building block **BRICK**
clayey earth **MARL**
clay worker **POTTER**
clean **WASH**
clean a floor **SCRUB, MOP,
SWEEP, SWAB**
clean and neat (comp.
wd.) **WELL-GROOMED**
clean a painting **RESTORE**
cleaning implement **DUSTER,
MOP, DUSTPAN, VACUUM,
CLOTH**
cleanse **PURIFY**
cleanse of impurities **PURGE**
cleanse of soap **RINSE**
cleanse the feathers **PREEN**
cleansing agent **SOAP,
DETERGENT, WATER**
clean up **POLICE**
clear **BRIGHT, LUCID**
clear a space
(2 wds.) **MAKE ROOM**
clear-cut **DECIDED**
clear of accusations **ABSOLVE,
ACQUIT**
clear profit **NET**
clear up **SOLVE**
cleave **REND, RIVE, SEVER,
SPLIT, CUT**
clef **BASS, TREBLE**
cleft **RIFT, CRACK, SPLIT**
clemency **LENIENCY, MERCY**
clement **MILD**
clench **CLUTCH, GRASP**
clenched hand **FIST**
Cleopatra's handmaiden **IRAS,
CHARMIAN**
Cleopatra's river **NILE**
Cleopatra's snake **ASP**
clergyman **CLERIC, PRIEST,
VICAR, MINISTER, PASTOR,
RECTOR, PARSON, RABBI,
MONK**
clergyman's residence **MANSE,
RECTORY**

clergyman's speech **SERMON**
clergyman's title **REVEREND**
cleric **CLERGYMAN**
clerical collar **RABAT**
clerical mantle **COPE**
clerical vestment **ALB**
cleric of early Irish
Church **ERENACH**
Cleveland's first name **GROVER**
Cleveland's waterfront **ERIE**
clever **CUTE, WITTY**
cleverness **WIT**
clever phrase **MOT**
cliche **PLATITUDE, BROMIDE**
click **SNAP**
cliff **BLUFF**
climate (poet.) **CLIME**
climax **PEAK, APEX**
climax of a joke
(2 wds.) **PUNCH LINE**
climb **ASCEND, SCALE**
climb down **DESCEND**
climbing device **LADDER**
climbing plant **IVY, LIANA,
VINE**
climb on all fours **CLAMBER**
climb on top of **MOUNT**
clime **CLIMATE**
clinch **SEAL, SECURE**
cling **ADHERE, STICK**
clinging crustacean **BARNACLE**
clinic **INFIRMARY, HOSPITAL**
clinical **IMPERSONAL**
Clio **MUSE**
clip **SNIP, TRIM, SHEAR**
clipped **SHORN**
clipper **LINER, SHIP**
clique **CLAN, SET, GROUP**
cloak **MANTLE, ROBE**
clock **TIMEPIECE**
clock dial **FACE**
clock face **DIAL**
clock sound **TICKTOCK, TICK,
TOCK**
clod **LUMP**
clodhopper **LOUT, DOLT**
clog **BLOCK, JAM**
cloister **ABBEY, CONVENT**
cloistered **SECLUDED**
cloistered woman **NUN**
close **NEAR, SHUT, END,
COVER**
close acquaintance **FRIEND**
close at hand **NEARBY**
close by **AT, HANDY, NEAR**
closed car **SEDAN**
close falcon eyes **SEEL**
close firmly **BAR, SEAL**

closefisted	**STINGY, MISERLY**
close friend	**CHUM, PAL, BUDDY**
closemouthed	**TACITURN**
closeness	**INTIMACY**
close noisily	**SLAM**
close relative	**NIECE, NEPHEW, AUNT, UNCLE, BROTHER, SISTER, MOTHER, FATHER, SON, DAUGHTER, PARENT, SIBLING**
close securely	**SEAL**
close tightly	**CLENCH, SEAL**
close to	**AT, BESIDE, NEAR**
close to tears	**SAD**
closet	**WARDROBE, LOCKER**
clot	**MASS, THICKEN**
cloth	**FABRIC**
cloth belt	**SASH**
cloth dealer	**DRAPER**
clothe	**DRESS, GARB**
clothe with authority	**VEST**
clothes	**APPAREL**
clothes (colloq.)	**TOGS**
cloth gaiters	**SPATS**
clothing	**GARB, ATTIRE, TOGS, DRESS**
clothing fabric	**HOPSACKING, TRICOT, COTTON, SERGE, WORSTED, TWEED, WOOL, CORDUROY, DENIM, LINEN, VELVET, FUR, VELOUR, PONGEE, CHIFFON, SATIN, NYLON, ACETATE, SUEDE, LEATHER, SILK, RAYON**
cloth made of flax	**LINEN**
cloth measurements	**YARD**
cloth of gold	**LAME**
cloth piece	**BOLT**
cloth ridge	**WALE**
cloth scrap	**RAG, REMNANT**
cloth used as wall hanging	**TAPESTRY**
cloth worn over the head	**SCARF, KERCHIEF, MANTILLA, VEIL**
clothes moth	**TINEA**
clothespress	**WARDROBE**
clothes tinter	**DYER**
clothes tree	**COATRACK**
cloud	**CUMULUS, NIMBUS, CIRRUS, STRATUS**
clouded	**OBSCURE, OVERCAST**
cloud of smoke	**FUME**
cloud region	**SKY**
cloudy	**DIM, GLOOMY**
clout	**SWAT**

clown	**BUFFOON, COMEDIAN, COMIC**
clownish	**AWKWARD**
cloy	**GLUT, SATE**
club	**BAT, CUDGEL**
club fees	**DUES**
clublike weapon	**MACE**
clue	**HINT, INKLING**
clump	**WAD**
clumsy	**ALL THUMBS, AWKWARD**
clumsy boat	**ARK, TUB**
clumsy fellow	**LOUT, OAF**
cluster	**TUFT**
cluster of flowers	**BUNCH**
cluster of shrubs	**BUSH**
clutch	**GRASP, BUNCH, NUMBER, CLUSTER**
clutch at wildly	**CLAW, GRIP**
coach	**CAR, STAGE**
coach and four	**TALLY-HO**
coach dog	**DALMATIAN**
coagulate	**CLOT, GEL, SET**
coagulum	**CLOT, CURD**
coal	**ANTHRACITE, FUEL**
coal bed	**SEAM**
coal digger	**MINER**
coalesce	**MERGE, UNITE**
coal excavation	**MINE**
coal fuel product	**COKE**
coal hod	**SCUTTLE**
coalition	**ALLIANCE**
coal mine	**PIT, COLLIERY**
coal oil	**KEROSENE**
coal pit	**MINE, STRIP-MINE**
coal product	**TAR, COKE**
coal scuttle	**HOD**
coal tar	**EOSIN**
coal tunnel entrance	**ADIT**
coal unit	**TON**
coarse	**ROUGH, CRUDE**
coarse and sticky	**TACKY**
coarse cord	**TWINE, ROPE**
coarse corn meal	**SAMP**
coarse file	**RASP**
coarse grain	**MEAL**
coarse grass	**REED**
coarse hair	**SETA**
coarse hairnet	**SNOOD**
coarse hominy	**GRITS, SAMP**
coarse part	**DREGS**
coarse tobacco	**SHAG**
coarse wool cloth	**TWEED**
coast	**SEASHORE, SHORE**
coastal projection	**CAPE, NESS**
coaster	**SLED, DISK**
Coast Guard lady	**SPAR**
coast of India	**MALABAR**

coat	**COVER**
coat arm	**SLEEVE**
coat collar	**LAPEL**
coat lapel	**FLAP**
coat of arms	**CREST**
coat of mail	**ARMOR**
coat sleeve	**ARM**
coat with color	**PAINT**
coat with gold	**GILD**
coat with icing	**GLAZE**
coat with metal	**PLATE**
coating on grain	**BRAN**
coating on iron	**RUST**
coating on teeth	**ENAMEL**
coax	**URGE, WHEEDLE, CAJOLE**
cob vegetable	**CORN**
cobbler's form	**LAST**
cobbler's tool	**AWL**
cock	**ROOSTER**
cocktail seafood	**SHRIMP,**
	OYSTER, CLAM, HERRING
cocktail snack	**CANAPE**
coconut tree	**PALM**
codfish dish	**SCROD**
coelenterate	**HYDRA, POLYP,**
	CORAL
coerce	**FORCE**
coercion	**DURESS**
coffee (sl.)	**JAVA**
coffee bean	**NIB**
coffee container	**CUP, MUG**
coffee dispenser	**URN, POT,**
	PERCOLATOR, CARAFE
coffee grinder	**MILL**
coffee house	**CAFE**
cogent	**POTENT, STRONG**
cogitate	**THINK**
cognizant	**AWARE, CONSCIOUS**
cognomen	**NAME**
cogwheel	**GEAR**
coil	**WIND, SPRING**
coin	**MONEY, DIME, NICKEL,**
	QUARTER, MINT
coincide	**AGREE**
coincide in part	**OVERLAP**
coin factory	**MINT**
coin manufacture	**MINTAGE**
coin of ancient Greece	**OBOL,**
	DRACHMA
coin of Bulgaria	**LEV**
coin of France	**ECU, SOU,**
	CENTIME, FRANC
coin of India	**RUPEE**
coin of Iran	**RIAL**
coin of Italy	**LIRA**
coin of Japan	**SEN, YEN**
coin of Mexico	**PESO**
coin of the Bible	**TALENT**

coin of the realm	**SPECIE**
coin opening	**SLOT**
coin's date space	**EXERGUE**
cola purchase	**SIXPACK**
colander	**SIEVE**
colate	**FINISH, STRAIN**
cold	**ALGID, FRIGID, CHILLY,**
	COOL
cold Adriatic wind	**BORA**
cold and bleak	**RAW**
cold and damp	**RAW**
cold cubes	**ICE**
cold dish	**SALAD, ASPIC, ICE**
	CREAM, SHERBET
cold feet	**COWARDICE**
cold season	**WINTER**
cold storage	**DEEP FREEZE,**
	FREEZER
cold wind (Fr.)	**BISE**
coliseum	**STADIUM**
collaborate	**AID**
collapse	**DEFLATE**
collarbone	**CLAVICLE**
collar fastener	**STUD, BUTTON**
collar of a coat	**LAPEL**
collar shape	**VEE**
collate	**COMPARE, ASSEMBLE**
collect	**ASSEMBLE, AMASS,**
	GATHER
collect gradually	**GLEAN**
collection set	**GROUP**
collection of animals	**ZOO,**
	MENAGERIE
collection of facts	**ANA, DATA**
collection of papers	**DOSSIER**
collection of sayings	**ANA**
collection of tents	**CAMP**
collection of type	**FONT**
collective	**CO-OP**
collectivism	**SOCIALISM**
colleen	**LASS**
college	**SCHOOL**
college administrator	**DEAN**
college building, for short	
	DORM
college campus	**QUAD**
college cheer	**RAH**
college course	**SEMINAR, LOGIC**
college court	**QUAD**
college dance	**HOP, PROM**
college degree (abbr.)	**BA, BS,**
	MA, MS, PHD, AB, BFA,
	LLD, MD, DDS
college discussion	
group	**SEMINAR**
college examination	**ORAL**
college girl	**COED**
college graduate	**ALUMNUS**

college group **DEBATING TEAM, FOOTBALL TEAM, FRATERNITY, FRAT, SORORITY**
college half-year **SEMESTER**
college head **DEAN**
college official **DEAN**
college president (sl.) **PREXY**
college song **GLEE**
college student **JUNIOR, SENIOR**
college subject **ECONOMICS, ANATOMY, BIOLOGY, CHEMISTRY, TRIGONOMETRY, CALCULUS, LITERATURE**
college term **SEMESTER, TRIMESTER**
collegian's jacket **BLAZER**
collide **CLASH**
collie (2 wds.) **SHEEP DOG**
colliery **MINE**
collision **CRASH**
colloidal substance **GAL**
colloquy **DISCOURSE, SPEECH**
Cologne (Ger.) **KOLN**
Colombia city **BOGOTA**
colonist **SETTLER**
colonize **PLANT, SETTLE**
colonnade **STOA**
colony **SETTLEMENT**
color **DYE, HUE, TINT, PAINT, SHADE, BLUSH, REDDEN, RED, YELLOW, BLUE, CERISE, SCARLET, BEIGE, BROWN, TAN, ECRU, CORAL, OLIVE, GREEN, PURPLE, VIOLET, PINK, AZURE**
color (suffix) **CHROME**
Colorado city **ASPEN, DENVER**
Colorado Indian **UTE**
Colorado mountain (2 wds.) **PIKES PEAK**
Colorado park **ESTES**
Colorado ski resort **ASPEN**
Colorado tributary **GILA**
color a picture **TINT**
color-changing lizard **AGAMA**
color graduation **SHADE, TONE, TINE, HUE**
color of moleskin **TAUPE**
color slightly **TINGE, TINT**
colorful **PICTURESQUE, VIVID**
colorful bird **BLUE JAY, BALTIMORE ORIOLE, PEACOCK**
colorful fabric **CHINTZ PRINT**
colorful lizard **AGAMA**
colorful parrot **MACAW**

colorful warm-water denizen (2 wds.) **PARROT FISH**
colorless **ASHEN, DRAB, PALE, PALLID, TRANSPARENT**
colorless alcohol **NEROLI**
colorless crystalline compound **TAURINE**
colossal **HUGE, IMMENSE**
colt **YEARLING**
coltish **FRISKY**
colt's father **SIRE**
colt's mother **DAM, MARE**
Columbus' birthplace **GENOA**
Columbus' departure port **PALOS**
Columbus' ship **NINA, PINTA, SANTA MARIA**
Columbus' sponsor **ISABELLA, SPAIN**
column **PILLAR**
column shaft **SCAPE**
columnist's entry **ITEM**
columnist Wilson **EARL**
comatose **TORPID**
comb rat **GUNDI**
combat **FIGHT, BATTLE, WAR, DUEL**
combatant **FIGHTER**
combat vehicle **TANK**
combination **UNION, MERGER**
combine **MERGE, UNITE, WED, MARRY, MELD, MIX**
combustion **FIRE, BURNING**
combustion remnant **ASH**
come **APPROACH, ARRIVE, NEAR**
come across **FIND**
come back **RETURN**
come between **MEDDLE**
come by **GET, GAIN**
come close to **NEAR, APPROACH**
comedian Abbott **BUD**
comedian Benny **JACK**
comedian Caesar **SID**
comedian Carney **ART**
comedian Conway **TIM**
comedian DeLuise **DOM**
comedian Durante **JIMMY**
comedian Hill **NORMAN**
comedian Hope **BOB**
comedian Kamen **MILT**
comedian Kaye **DANNY**
comedian King **ALAN**
comedian Knotts **DON**
comedian Lahr **BERT**
comedian Mostel **ZERO**

comedian Shriner **HERB**
comedian Skelton **RED**
comedian Sparks **NED**
comedienne Arden **EVE**
comedienne Ball **LUCILLE**
comedienne Prentiss **PAULA**
come forth **EMERGE, EMANATE**
come in **ENTER**
come in first **WIN**
come in second **LOSE**
come into port **LAND**
come into sight **APPEAR**
come into view **LOOM**
comely **PRETTY**
come-on **TEASER**
come out **EMERGE**
come to **REACH**
come to an end **HALT, STOP,
CEASE, TERMINATE**
come to earth **ALIGHT, LIGHT,
LAND**
come to nothing **FIZZLE**
come to rest **STOP**
come to terms **AGREE**
come together **MEET, MERGE,
UNITE, AGREE**
comet's train **TAIL**
comet tail **STREAMER**
come up **ARISE, VISIT**
come upon **FIND**
come upon (2 wds.) **MEET WITH**
come upon unawares
(3 wds.) **TAKE BY SURPRISE**
comfort **EASE, SOLACE,
SOOTHE**
comfortable **PLEASANT**
comfortable chair **RECLINER**
comforter **QUILT, BLANKET**
comic **FUNNY, DROLL**
comical **AMUSING**
comic section **FUNNIES**
comic strip
detective **DICK TRACY**
comic strip sailor **POPEYE**
coming into being **GENESIS**
coming-out party **DEBUT**
comma **CAESURA, PAUSE**
command **ORDER, BID, EDICT**
commander **LEADER**
commander-in-chief
PRESIDENT
commandment **LAW, PRECEPT**
command to a horse **GEE,
WHOA, HAW, GIDDYAP**
commemorate **CELEBRATE**
commemoration **MEMORY**
commemorative pillar **STELE**
commence **BEGIN, INITIATE**

commend **PRAISE, APPROVE**
comment **REMARK**
commentator Sevareid **ERIC**
comment on **NOTE**
commerce **TRADE**
commercial building **MART**
commercial flight
(2 wds.) **AIR TRAVEL**
commercial ship **STEAMER**
commercial spiel
(2 wds.) **SALES PITCH**
commiserate **CONDOLE**
commission **PERCENTAGE**
commit a faux pas **ERR**
commit theft **ROB**
commode **CHEST**
commodious **SUITABLE,
COMFORTABLE**
common **ORDINARY**
common (prefix) **CENO**
common adder **ASP**
common ailment **COLD, FLU**
common ancestor **ADAM, EVE**
common ant **PISMIRE**
common conjunction **AND**
common level **PAR**
common metal **IRON, TIN,
NICKEL, STEEL, COPPER,
BRASS**
common newt **EFT**
common people **DEMOS**
commonplace **TRITE, BANAL,
HACKNEYED**
commonplace
remark **PLATITUDE**
common practice **USAGE**
common sailor
(2 wds.) **DECK HAND**
common tree **ELM, OAK,
MAPLE, PINE**
common verb **ARE, IS, BE**
common viper **ADDER**
commonwealth **STATE**
commotion **ADO, TO-DO,
NOISE, STIR, RACKET,
DISTURBANCE**
communalism **SOCIALISM**
commune in Belgium **NIEL**
communicant **MEMBER**
communicate **CONVEY**
communicating instrument **TV,
PHONE, TELEGRAPH,
SATELLITE, TELSTAR**
communication **MESSAGE,
LETTER, WIRE, CALL**
communion **FELLOWSHIP,
SHARE**
communion cloth **CORPORAL**

communion plate	**PATEN**
communion table	**ALTAR**
communion vessel	**PYX**
communique	**MESSAGE**
communist	**RED**
commute	**EXCHANGE, SUBSTITUTE**
compact	**DENSE, SOLID, SNUG, SERRIED**
compact body of troops	**PHALANX**
companion	**MATE, PAL, BUDDY, FRIEND, SPOUSE, ASSOCIATE, PARTNER**
companionable	**SOCIAL**
companion for ham	**EGGS**
companion of odds	**ENDS**
company	**GUESTS**
company (Fr. abbr.)	**CIE**
company of people	**CREW, GANG**
company of troupers	**CAST**
comparable to (3 wds.)	**AS GOOD AS**
comparative	**RELATIVE**
comparative conjunction	**THAN**
compare	**CONTRAST, LIKEN**
compare critically	**EXAMINE**
comparison	**SIMILE**
compartment aboard a ship	**CABIN, GALLEY, STATEROOM, BERTH**
compass point	**ENE, NNE, SSE, SSW, ESE, WSW, WNW, NNW, NE, NW, SE, SW, NORTH, SOUTH, EAST, WEST**
compassion	**TENDERNESS, PITY**
compassionate	**TENDER**
compatible	**AGREEABLE**
compatriot	**COLLEAGUE**
compel	**FORCE**
compendium	**SUMMARY**
compensate	**PAY**
compensate for	**RECOUP**
compensation	**PAY, REWARD**
compete	**VIE**
compete in a race	**RUN**
competence	**ABILITY**
competent	**ABLE, CAPABLE**
competition	**CONTEST, RACE**
competition between retailers (2 wds.)	**PRICE WAR**
competitive game	**SPORT, TENNIS, BASEBALL, HOCKEY**
competitor	**RIVAL**
compilation	**REPORT, DIGEST**
compile	**AMASS, EDIT**
compiler of game rules	**HOYLE**
complacent	**SMUG**
complacently self-satisfied	**SMUG**
complain	**MOAN, GRIPE, BEEF**
complainant	**PLAINTIFF**
complaining	**QUERULOUS**
complain loudly (3 wds.)	**RAISE THE ROOF**
complaint	**ILLNESS, AILMENT**
complaisance	**COURTESY, AMENITY**
complaisant	**CIVIL**
complement	**ADJUNCT**
complete	**ENTIRE, WHOLE, TOTAL, UTTER, FINISH, ACCOMPLISH**
complete agreement	**UNISON**
complete collection	**SET**
completed	**DONE**
complete failure	**WASHOUT**
completely mistaken (2 wds.)	**OFF BASE**
completely waterless (comp. wd.)	**BONE-DRY**
complex	**INTRICATE, CONFUSED**
compliment	**FLATTER**
complimentary ticket	**PASS**
comply	**SUBMIT, OBEY**
comply with	**OBSERVE**
comply with commands	**OBEY**
component	**UNIT, PART**
component of atom	**PROTON, ION**
comport	**BEHAVE**
comportment	**BEHAVIOR**
compose	**WRITE**
composed	**CALM**
composer	**AUTHOR**
composer Bernstein	**LEONARD**
composer Dvorak	**ANTON(IN)**
composer Stravinsky	**IGOR**
composite picture	**MONTAGE**
composition	**ESSAY**
composition for two	**DUET**
composure	**POISE, SERENITY**
compound	**COMBINE, ESTER**
compound tincture	**ELIXIR**
comprehend	**UNDERSTAND, GRASP**
comprehensive	**EXTENSIVE, WIDE**
comprise	**INCLUDE**
compulsion	**DURESS**
compunction	**REMORSE, REGRET**
compute	**CALCULATE, COUNT**

computerized production **AUTOMATION**
comrade **MATE, COMPANION, FRIEND, PAL, CHUM, COLLEAGUE**
conceal **COVER, HIDE, MASK**
conceal by false appearance **DISGUISE**
concealed **HID, HIDDEN, COVERT**
concede **ADMIT**
conceit **EGO, VANITY**
conceited **VAIN**
conceited person **EGOTIST**
conceive **IMAGINE, SUPPOSE**
concentrate **FOCUS**
concentration **ATTENTION**
concept **IDEA**
conception **NOTION, DESIGN**
concern **CARE, INTEREST**
concerned **ANXIOUS**
concerning **AS TO, IN RE, ANENT, ABOUT, RE**
concerning a title **TITULAR**
concerning origin **GENETIC**
concerning the ear **OTIC**
concernment **WORRY, ANXIETY**
concert by single performer **RECITAL**
concert grand **PIANO**
concert halls **ODEA, ODEONS**
concert instrument **OBOE, PIANO, VIOLIN, HARP, CELLO, FLUTE, TUBA**
concession **FAVOR**
conch **SHELL**
concierge **CUSTODIAN, SUPER**
conciliate **PACIFY, MOLLIFY**
conciliatory bribe **SOP**
concise **LACONIC, TERSE, BRIEF**
concise summary **PRECIS**
conclave **MEETING**
conclude **CLOSE, END, FINISH**
concluding passage **CODA**
conclusion **END, FINALE, FINIS, CLIMAX**
conclusive **DECISIVE, FINAL**
concoct **BREW**
concoction **INVENTION**
concord **AGREEMENT, UNISON**
concordat **COVENANT**
concrete **SOLID, FIRM**
concrete surface **PAVEMENT**
concretion **PEARL**
concur **AGREE**
condemn **CONVICT, DOOM**
condensation **DEW**

condense **ABRIDGE**
condensed representation **EPITOME**
condign **DESERVED, SUITABLE**
condiment **RELISH, SEASONING**
condition **CIRCUMSTANCE, STATE**
conditional release from prison **PAROLE**
conditional stipulation **PROVISO**
condition made **PREMISE**
conditions **TERMS**
condone **FORGIVE, PARDON**
conducive to peace **IRENIC**
conduct **BEHAVIOR, LEAD**
conduct oneself **BEHAVE**
conductor **DIRECTOR, LEADER**
conductor's stick **BATON**
conduit **CHANNEL, TUBE**
cone-bearing tree **FIR, PINE**
cone-shaped cap **FEZ**
confederate **ALLY**
Confederate soldier **REB**
Confederate States Army (abbr.) **CSA**
confederation **UNION, LEAGUE**
confer **BESTOW**
conference site, 1945 **YALTA**
confess (3 wds.) **OWN UP TO**
confession of faith **CREDO, CREED**
confide **TRUST, RELY**
confidence **TRUST**
confident **CERTAIN, SURE**
confine **COOP UP, PEN**
confine by bars **JAIL, CAGE**
confined to a locality **ENDEMIC**
confinement **DETENTION**
confirm **RATIFY**
confiscate **SEIZE**
conflagration **FIRE, BLAZE**
conflict **STRIFE CLASH, WAR, BATTLE, MELEE**
conform **ADAPT**
conform to shape **FIT**
confound **AMAZE, ASTONISH**
confront **FACE, MEET**
confuse **ADDLE, MIX UP**
confused **ASEA, AT SEA**
confused fight **MELEE, FREE-FOR-ALL**
confused mess **MISHMASH**
confused state **MESS**
confusion **DISORDER, CHAOS**
confute **DENY**
congeal **FREEZE, ICE**
congenial **FRIENDLY**

conger **EEL**
congressional office **SPEAKER, SENATORSHIP, WHIP**
congressman (abbr.) **REP**
congressman's trip **JUNKET**
coniferous tree **FIR, PINE, LARCH**
conjecture **GUESS**
conjugal **BRIDAL, MARITAL**
conjunction **AND, OR, BUT, NOR**
conjunction (Fr.) **ET**
conjunction (Ger.) **UND**
conjunction (Lat.) **ET**
conjunction (Sp.) **Y**
conjure **INVOKE**
conjuror's handiwork **SPELL**
connect **JOIN, WED, MARRY, WELD**
connected group **NEXUS**
Connecticut university **YALE**
connection **LINKAGE, RELATION**
connective **AND**
conquer **BEST, BEAT, WIN**
conscious **AWARE, AWAKE**
consecrate **BLESS**
consecrated **HOLY, BLESSED, BLEST**
consent **AGREE, ASSENT**
consequence **RESULT**
conservationist **FORESTER, ECOLOGIST**
conservative group (2 wds.) **OLD GUARD**
consider **PONDER**
considerable **NOTABLE**
considerable amount **WAD**
considerate **KIND**
consideration **ESTEEM, ATTENTION**
considering **SINCE**
consign **SEND, DELIVER**
consistent **REGULAR**
consolation **COMFORT**
console **SOLACE, COMFORT, SOOTHE**
consolidate **UNITE, COMBINE**
consomme **SOUP**
consort **SPOUSE, PARTNER**
consort of Amon-Ra **MUT**
conspicuous **NOTICEABLE, SALIENT**
conspiracy **CABAL, INTRIGUE**
constant **TRUE, STEADY, REGULAR**
constantly **AT EVERY TURN, ALWAYS**

constellation **ARA, ORION, LEO, CENTAURUS, LYRA, BOOTES, VIRGO, AQUILA, GEMINI, SCORPIUS, CYGNUS, CRUX, CETUS, COMA, ARIES, GRUS, PAVO, VELA, DORADO, CARINA, AURIGA, TAURUS, LYNX**
consternation **DISMAY, ALARM**
constituent **COMPONENT, FACTOR**
constituent part **ELEMENT**
Constitution State **CONNECTICUT**
constrain **CHECK, CURB**
constraint **DURESS**
constrict **CONTRACT**
construct **MAKE, ERECT, BUILD**
construct anew **REMAKE**
construction beam (2 wds.) **I BAR, T BAR**
constructive **CREATIVE**
constructor **BUILDER**
construe **INTERPRET**
consul of old Rome **CATO**
consult **CONFER**
consultation **CONFERENCE, DISCUSSION**
consume **EAT, USE**
consummate **COMPLETE, IDEAL**
consumption **TUBERCULOSIS**
contact **TOUCH**
contact by phone **CALL**
contagious **INFECTIOUS**
contain **HOLD**
container **CAN, TIN, VAT, CRATE, CARTON**
container for face powder **COMPACT**
container for oranges **CRATE**
containing air **PNEUMATIC**
containing fine soil **SILTY**
containing fire **IGNEOUS**
containing gold **AURIC**
containing iron **FERRIC**
containing orifices **POROUS**
contaminate **TAINT**
contemn **SCORN, RIDICULE**
contemplate **CONSIDER**
contemplative **THOUGHTFUL, SEDATE**
contemporary **MODERN**

contemporary painter **DALI, WYETH, WARHOL, TAMAYO, PICASSO, RAY O'KEEFFE, RIVERS, MIRO, MOTHERWELL, OLDENBURG, GUSTON, INDIANA, POLLOCK, KUPKA, LEVINE, DINE, EVERGOOD, CHIRICO, CHAGALL, ALBERS, ARP, BACON, BENTON, BRAQUE, DIX**
contempt **DISDAIN, SCORN**
contemptible **MEAN**
contemptibly cheap person **PIKER**
contend **COPE, VIE**
content **HAPPY, PLEASED**
contention **STRIFE**
contentment **PLEASURE**
contest **COMPETITION, RACE, GAME**
contestant **ENTRANT**
contestant for office **CANDIDATE**
contest at law **LITIGATE**
contest necessity **BOX TOP**
contiguous **TOUCHING**
continent **AFRICA, ASIA, NORTH AMERICA, EUROPE, AUSTRALIA, SOUTH AMERICA**
contingent **CAUSAL**
continual **CONSTANT**
continue **ENDURE, PERSIST**
continue a journey (2 wds.) **PUSH ON**
continuing story **SERIAL**
contract **CHARTER**
contraction **SPASM**
contract of ownership **DEED**
contradict **DENY, REBUT**
contradiction **PARADOX, DENIAL, REBUTTAL**
contrary **UNLIKE, OPPOSITE**
contrary current **EDDY**
contrast **COMPARE**
contribute **SHELL OUT, DONATE, GIVE**
contribution **DONATION, GIFT, BEQUEST**
contrivance **DEVICE, TRICK**
contrive **CONCOCT**
control **CHECK, DIAL, MASTERY, REGULATE, MANAGE**
control of emotions **RESTRAINT**
controversial **POLEMIC**

controversy **DEBATE, DISPUTE**
conundrum **RIDDLE**
convene **MEET, SIT, CALL**
convenient **HANDY**
convent **CLOISTER**
convent inmate **NUN**
convent room **CELL**
convention **MEETING**
conventional **ACCEPTED, CORRECT**
convention representative **DELEGATE**
conventions **MORES**
converge **FOCUS**
conversant **FAMILIAR, SKILLED**
conversation **CHAT, TALK**
conversational pause **ER, UH, AHEM**
converse **TALK, CHAT, GAB**
convert **CHANGE**
convert into money **CASH**
convert into ordinary language **DECODE**
convertible **CAR, COUCH, SOFA**
convex molding **OVOLO**
convey **BRING**
conviction **FAITH, BELIEF**
convince **ASSURE**
convivial **FESTIVE, GAY**
convoke **SUMMON**
cook **CHEF**
cook bacon **FRY**
cook by simmering **STEW**
cooked fruit dish **COMPOTE, APPLESAUCE**
cooked sufficiently **DONE**
cooker **STOVE, RANGE, POT**
cookery **CUISINE**
cookie **SNAP**
cook in an oven **BAKE, ROAST**
cook in fat **FRY, SAUTE**
cooking device **GRIDDLE, STOVE**
cooking fat **LARD, OIL, GREASE, BUTTER, SUET**
cooking mixture **BATTER**
cooking pot **OLLA**
cooking vessel **PAN, POT, SAUCEPAN, SKILLET**
cook in water **BOIL**
cook lightly in liquid **POACH**
cookout **BARBECUE**
cook over live coals **BROIL, GRILL**
cook quickly **FRY, SEAR**
cook's formula **RECIPE**
cook's measure **TABLESPOON, TEASPOON, CUP, PINCH, DASH**

cook slowly	**STEW**	corn spike	**EAR, COB**
cookstove	**RANGE**	corny	**TRITE, BANAL**
cook up	**CONCOCT, DEVISE**	corny actor	**HAM**
cook with dry heat	**BAKE,**	coronet	**TIARA, CROWN**
	ROAST	corporal	**BODILY**
cool	**CHILLY, FROSTY**	corporation	**BODY**
cool and reserved	**ALOOF**	corpse	**BODY, CADAVER**
cooled	**ICED**	corpulence	**FAT, OBESITY**
cooled lava	**AA**	corpulent	**FAT, OBESE**
cooler	**JAIL, ICER**	corral	**PEN, RING**
coolheaded	**CALM**	correct	**AMEND, EMEND,**
coolie	**LABORER**		**TRUE, REVISE, EDIT,**
cooling beverage	**ADE**		**RIGHT**
cooling device	**FAN**	correct a manuscript	**EDIT**
cool off	**CHILL**	corrida cheer	**OLE**
cool season	**FALL**	corridor	**HALL**
cool to low point	**FREEZE**	corrode	**RUST, EAT**
coonskin	**CAP**	corrupt	**LOW, BASE**
coop	**CAGE, PEN**	corruption	**VICE**
cooperate	**ASSIST, CONSPIRE**	corsage	**BOUQUET**
cooperate secretly	**CONNIVE**	corset string	**LACE**
cootie	**LOUSE, BUG**	cortege	**PARADE, RETINUE,**
cope	**CONTEND**		**PROCESSION**
copious	**PLENTIFUL**	cortex	**BARK, RIND**
copper and tin alloy	**BRONZE,**	cos	**LETTUCE**
	PEWTER	cosmetic	**ROUGE, CREAM,**
copper coin	**CENT, PENNY**		**LIPSTICK, SHADOW,**
Copperfield's wife	**DORA,**		**MASCARA, LINER, BASE,**
	AGNES		**POWDER**
copter	**GIRO**	cost	**PRICE, RATE**
copy	**APE, MIMIC, CARBON,**	costly	**DEAR, EXPENSIVE**
	XEROX	costly fur	**SABLE, MINK,**
copycat	**APER**		**ERMINE**
coral island	**ATOLL**	cost of membership	**DUES**
coral reef	**KEY**	cost of passage	**FARE**
coral ridge	**REEF**	costume	**ATTIRE, CLOTHING**
corbel	**BRACKET**	cot	**BED**
Corcyra	**CORFU**	cote	**COOP**
cord	**STRING, TWINE**	coterie	**CLIQUE, SET**
cord-and-stone weapon	**BOLA**	cote sound	**COO**
corded fabric	**REP(P)**	cottage cheese lumps	**CURDS**
cordial	**GENIAL**	cotton bundle	**BALE**
cordon	**CIRCLE**	cotton fabric	**LISLE, PIMA,**
cord on an Arab			**MUSLIN, PERCALE, VOILE,**
headdress	**AGAL**		**FLANNEL**
cord ornament	**TASSEL**	cotton pod	**BOLL**
cordwood measure	**STERE**	cottontail	**HARE, RABBIT,**
core	**HEART, CENTER**		**PETER**
cornbread	**PONE**	cottonwood	**TREE**
corncob	**PIPE**	couch	**SOFA, SETTEE, DIVAN,**
corner	**NOOK, TREE**		**DAVENPORT**
cornered	**ANGULAR, CAUGHT**	cougar	**PUMA, CAT**
cornet	**TRUMPET, HORN**	counsel	**ADVICE**
cornfield weed	**DARNEL**	count	**NUMBER**
corn-heating utensil	**POPPER**	count calories	**DIET, REDUCE**
Cornhusker State	**NEBRASKA**	countenance	**FACE, VISAGE**
cornice	**EAVE**	counter	**OPPOSE, BAR**
corn porridge	**SAMP, MUSH**		

counterfeit	**BOGUS, FAKE, PHONY, SHAM, IMITATION, ERSATZ**
counterfeit coin	**SLUG**
countermand	**ABOLISH, CANCEL**
counterpane	**COVER**
counterpart	**DUPLICATE, TWIN**
countersign	**PASSWORD**
counter tenor	**ALTO**
counting of votes cast	**POLL**
countless	**INFINITE**
Count of music	**BASIE**
country	**STATE, LAND, NATION, WOODS**
country bumpkin (sl.)	**RUBE, HICK**
country by-way	**LANE**
country estate	**VILLA**
country festival	**FAIR**
country hotel	**INN**
country place	**VILLA, CABIN, FARM**
country road	**LANE**
countrywide	**NATIONAL**
county	**PARISH**
county in England	**SHIRE**
coup	**BLOW, UPSET**
coupe	**AUTO, CAR**
couple	**PAIR, TWO, TWOSOME, DUO, LINK**
couple together	**BRACKET**
courage	**HEART, METTLE, BRAVERY, NERVE**
courageous	**BRAVE**
courageous man	**HERO**
courant	**GAZETTE**
courier	**MESSENGER**
course	**PATH, WAY, ROUTE, PATHWAY**
course of instruction	**CLASS**
court	**WOO**
court case	**TRIAL, SUIT**
court cry	**OYES, OYEZ, HEAR YE**
courteous	**CIVIL, POLITE**
court game	**TENNIS, SQUASH**
court hearing	**OYER**
court order	**FIAT, WRIT**
court proceedings	**TRIAL**
court reporter's machine	**STENOTYPE**
courtroom panel	**JURY**
courtroom procedure	**TRIAL, SUIT**
court session	**ASSIZE**
courtyard	**PATIO**
cousin of Absalom	**AMASA**
couth	**REFINED, POLISHED**
couturiere	**MODISTE**
cove	**BAY, INLET**
covenant	**BOND, CONTRACT**
cover	**CONCEAL, LID, TOP**
cover a package	**WRAP**
covered avenue	**ARCADE**
covered porch	**VERANDA**
covered with frost	**HOARY**
covered with moisture	**DEWY**
covered with velvety growth	**MOSSY**
cover girl	**MODEL**
covering of trees	**BARK**
coverlet	**BEDSPREAD**
covert	**HIDDEN, PRIVATE**
cover the face	**MASK**
cover the inside	**LINE**
cover up	**CONCEAL**
cover with a sheath	**GLOVE**
cover with asphalt	**PAVE**
cover with cloth	**DRAPE**
cover with concrete	**PAVE**
cover with gold paint	**GILD**
cover with turf	**SOD**
covet	**DESIRE**
covey	**BEVY, FLOCK**
cow	**DAUNT, TERRIFY**
coward	**CRAVEN**
cowardice	**FEAR**
cowbell	**CAMPION**
cowboy	**RIDER, ROPER**
cowboy country	**WEST**
cowboy event	**RODEO**
cowboy gear	**STIRRUP, SADDLE, RIATA, LASSO LARIAT, CHAPS**
cowboy movie	**WESTERN, OATER**
cowboy Rogers	**ROY**
cowboy's breeches	**CHAPS**
cowboy's concern	**HERD**
cowboy's nickname	**TEX**
cowboy's rope	**LARIAT, RIATA, LASSO**
cowboy's shoes	**BOOTS**
cower	**CRINGE**
cowfish	**GRAMPUS**
cow genus	**BOS**
cowgirl Evans	**DALE**
cowl	**HOOD**
cows	**CATTLE, KINE**
cow's chewed food	**RUMEN, CUD**
cow's home	**BARN**
cow's low	**MOO**
cow's offspring	**CALF**
cowskin	**HIDE**

cow sound	MOO
coy	DEMUR, SHY
Coyote State	SOUTH DAKOTA
cozen	CHEAT
cozy	SNUG
cozy home	NEST
cozy room	DEN
cozy talk	CHAT
crab	CANCER
crab's pincer	CLAW
crack	BREAK, SPLIT
Cracker State	GEORGIA
crackle	SNAP, CRUNCH, POP
crackpot	NUT, LUNATIC
crack through which water escapes	LEAK
cradle	BASSINET, CRIB
cradle song	LULLABY
craft	BOAT, ART, SKILL
craft of the far north	KAYAK, ICEBREAKER
crafty	SLY, WILY, CLEVER
crag	TOR, PRECIPICE
cram	STUFF, RAM, STUDY
cramp	SPASM, ACHE
crane	DERRICK
crane arm	GIB
cranium	SKULL
crank	GROUCH, HANDLE
cranky	TESTY, CROSS
crash against	RAM
crate	CASE, CARTON
cravat	TIE
crave	DESIRE
craven	AFRAID, COWARDLY
craving	LUST, HUNGER, DESIRE
crawl	CREEP
crawling animal	REPTILE
crayon drawing	PASTEL
craze	FAD, MANIA
crazy	DAFT, NUTS, NUTTY, CRACKED, MAD
cream	ELITE
crease	FOLD
create	ORIGINATE, MAKE, BUILD
create pictures	PAINT, DRAW
creative person	ARTIST
creator of Fantasyland	DISNEY
creator of the Thesaurus	ROGET
creature	ANIMAL, BEING
credence	TRUST
credential	VOUCHER, PASS
creed	RELIGION, BELIEF
creek	INLET, STREAM, BAYOU
creep	CRAWL

creep furtively	SNEAK
creeping creature	WORM, SNAKE, REPTILE
Creole State	LOUISIANA
crescent point	CUSP
crestfallen	ASHAMED
crest of hair	TOPKNOT
crew	TEAM, GANG
crew member	MAN
cricket team	ELEVEN
crime	SIN, OFFENSE
criminal	FELON, CROOK, HOODLUM, MISCREANT
crimson	RED
cringe	COWER
crinkled fabric	CRAPE, CREPE
crinoline	PETTICOAT, SLIP
cripple	DISABLE, MAIM
crippled	LAME
crisis	EMERGENCY
crisp and fragile	BRITTLE
crisp cookie	SNAP
criterion	RULE, TEST, BASIS
critical	ACUTE
criticize	CARP, CAVIL
criticize severely (colloq.)	PAN
critic's account	REVIEW
critic's place (2 wds.)	AISLE SEAT
croak	CAW
Croatian	SERBIAN
crochet	HOOK, KNIT
crockery	CHINA
crocodile	ALLIGATOR
crone	HAG
crony	CHUM, PAL
crook	BEND, THIEF, ROBBER
crooked	ASKEW, AWRY
croon	SING
crooner Crosby	BING
crooner Vallee	RUDY
crop	HARVEST
cross	TRAVERSE
cross a river	FORD
crossbar	AXLE
crossbeam	TRAVE
crossed wood framework	LATTICE
cross in a church	ROOD
cross out	DELE
crouch	BEND, STOOP
crouch in fear	COWER
crow	ROOK
crowbar	LEVER
crowd	HORDE, PACK, MOB
crowded	DENSE
crown	DIADEM, TIARA, CORONET

crow's call	CAW
crucible	POT
crucifix	CROSS
crude	RAW
crude metal	ORE
crude rubber	PARA
crude watercraft	RAFT
cruel	MEAN, BRUTAL, SADISTIC
cruel joke	HOAX
cruel person	BRUTE, MEANIE, SADIST BULLY
cruet	VIAL
cruise	SAIL
crumb	BIT, PIECE
crumble	MOLDER
Crusader's enemy	SARACEN
crush	MASH
crustacean	CRAB, SHRIMP
cry	SOB, WEEP, BAWL
cry of a lamb	BLEAT, BAA, MAA, BLAT
cry of an owl	HOOT
cry of despair	ALAS
cry of pain	OUCH, YIPE, OW
cry of sorrow	ALAS
cry of surprise	OH, HO, OHO, AHA
cry of triumph	AHA, EUREKA
cry out	SCREAM, SHOUT
crypt	VAULT
cryptic	SECRET, OCCULT
crystal	GLASS
crystalline gem	IOLITE
Cuban capital	HAVANA
Cuban dance	CONGA
cubicle	CELL
cubic meter	STERE
cuboid	BONE
cub's home	DEN
cuckoo	ANI
cuckoopoint	ARUM
cucumber	PICKLE
cud	RUMEN
cud chewer	COW
cuddle	NESTLE, SNUGGLE
cuddy	CABIN, GALLEY
cudgel	CLUB, STAVE
cue	HINT, SIGNAL
cuff	SLAP, STRIKE
cuff ornament	STUD, LINK, BUTTON
culinary expert	CHEF
cull	CHOOSE, SORT
culmination	CLIMAX, ACME
culpability	GUILT
cult	SECT

cultivate	FARM, PLOW, GROW, RAISE, REFINE
cultivate the soil	TILL, FARM
cultivator	HOER
culture	ART, POLISH
culture medium	AGAR
culvert	CONDUIT, UNDERPASS
cummerbund	SASH, BELT
cunning	SLY, CLEVER, ART, SLYNESS
cup	MUG
cupbearer of gods	HEBE
cupboard	CABINET, CLOSET, PANTRY
Cupid	AMOR. EROS
Cupid's mother	VENUS
Cupid's title	DAN
cupidity	AVARICE, GREED
cupola	DOME
cup rim	LIP
cuprum	COPPER
cup-shaped flower	TULIP
cur	MONGREL, MUTT
curate	PRIEST
curative	REMEDY
curb	ARREST, CHECK
cure	HEAL, REMEDY
curious	ODD
curl	TRESS, RINGLET
curl the lip	SNEER
curly cabbage	KALE, ENDIVE
curly-haired dog	POODLE
curly letter	ESS
curmudgeon	MISER
currant	BERRY
currency	MONEY
currency exchange premium	AGIO
current	TIDE, PRESENT
current events	NEWS
current fad	CRAZE
current fashion	MODE
current of air	DRAFT, BREEZE
current style	FAD, TREND
curry a horse	GROOM
curse	SWEAR, HEX, OATH
cursory	HASTY, CARELESS
curt	ABRUPT
curtail	SHORTEN
curtain	DRAPE
curtain fabric	NINON, SCRIM
curtain pole	ROD
curtsy	BOW
curve	ARC, BEND, HOOK, TWIST, BOW
curved bone	RIB
curved doorway	ARCH
curved garland	FESTOON

curved glass	**LENS**	cut of meat	**CHOP, STEAK, LOIN**
curved inward	**ADUNCOUS,**	cut one's teeth	**TEETHE**
	CONCAVE	cut on slant	**BEVEL**
curved molding	**OGEE**	cut out	**OMIT, ELIMINATE**
curved roof	**DOME**	cut out for	**FIT, SUITED**
curvy letter	**ESS**	cut-price deal	**SALE, BARGAIN**
cushion	**PAD, MAT, PILLOW,**	cut short	**CROP, LOP**
	SOFTEN	cut timber	**LUMBER**
Cush's father	**HAM**	cut to deep slope	**SCARP**
Cush's son	**NIMROD, SEBA**	cut up	**KIBITZ, CARVE**
cushy	**EASY**	cut with scissors	**SNIP**
custard	**FLAN**	cute	**ADORABLE, LOVABLE,**
custodian	**CARETAKER,**		**DARLING**
	JANITOR	cuticle	**PELLICLE, SKIN**
custody	**CHARGE, TRUST**	cutter	**SLOOP**
custom	**HABIT, USAGE, MODE**	cutting	**SHARP**
customary	**USUAL**	cutting diamond	**BORT**
customary method	**HABIT**	cutting edge	**BLADE**
customer	**BUYER, CLIENT,**	cutting implement	**KNIFE,**
	USER, PATRON		**SHEARS, SCISSORS, SAW,**
customs	**MORES**		**BLADE, RAZOR, AX, AXE**
cut	**HEW, SEVER, SAW, SLICE**	cuttlefish ink	**SEPIA**
cut across	**TRANSECT**	Cyclades island	**DELOS**
cut apart	**SEVER**	cylindrical	**TERETE**
cut at random	**SLASH**	cymbal	**TAL**
cut back	**PINCH, REDUCE,**	Cymric	**WELSH, BRETON,**
	DECREASE		**CORNISH**
cut dead	**SNUB**	cyprinoid fish	**IDE**
cut down	**HEW**	Cyprus city	**NICOSIA**
cut down a tree	**FELL**	cyst	**POUCH, SAC**
cut down wood on land	**CLEAR**	czar	**PETER, IVAN**
cut fine	**DICE, MINCE**	czardas	**DANCE**
cut for insertion in			
mortise	**TENON**		
cut grass	**MOW**		
cut hair	**CLIP, BOB, STYLE,**		
	TRIM	**D**	
cut in	**INTERRUPT**		
cut in small pieces	**HASH**	dabber	**PAD**
cut in squares	**DICE, CUBE**	dad	**FATHER, PAPA, DADDY,**
cut into cubes	**DICE, MINCE**		**SIRE**
cut into pieces	**CHOP**	daffy	**WACKY, BATTY, NUTS**
cut into slices	**CARVE**	dagger	**DIRK**
cut in two	**HALVE, SEVER,**	dagger thrust	**STAB**
	SPLIT, BISECT	daily record	**DIARY, JOURNAL**
cut it out	**STOP**	dainty	**CHIC, CUTE,**
cut jaggedly	**SNAG**		**FASTIDIOUS**
cut lengthwise	**SLIT**	dairy animal	**COW**
cut lumber	**SAW**	dairy product	**CHEESE, MILK,**
cut of beef	**EYE ROAST,**		**CREAM, BUTTER, EGG**
FLANK, SIRLOIN, RUMP		dais	**STAND, PLATFORM**
ROAST, T-BONE, STEAK,		daisy phrase	
RIB ROAST, CHUCK		(3 wds.)	**HE LOVES ME**
cut off	**LOP, SNIP**	Dakota	**SIOUX**
cut off the beard	**SHAVE**	dale	**VALLEY, VALE, DELL**
cut off tops	**CROP**	dally	**LINGER**
cut of lamb	**LEG, SHOULDER,**	Dalmatian (2 wds.)	**COACH DOG**
CHOP, ROAST, CROWN		dam	**BLOCK, RESTRAIN**

damage	HARM, SPOIL, MAR, RUIN
damask	LINEN, PINK
dame	WOMAN, GIRL
damp	HUMID, MOIST, WET
damp and cold	DANK
damsel	MAID
damson	PLUM, BULLACE
dance	WALTZ, POLKA, SAMBA, RHUMBA, CONGA, BALL, PROM, HOP, JIG, TANGO, FRUG, TWIST, BALLET, TAP
dance orchestra	BAND, COMBO, GROUP
dancer	HOOFER, TAPPER, BALLERINA
dancer Astaire	FRED
dancer Bolger	RAY
dancer Charisse	CYD
dancer Chase	BARRIE
dancer for Herod	SALOME
dancer Kelly	GENE
dance routine (2 wds.)	TIME STEP
dancer Rogers	GINGER
dancer Tallchief	MARIA
dancer Verdon	GWEN
dance step	CHASSE, PAS, GLISSADE
dancing mate	PARTNER
dancing shoe	PUMP, SLIPPER
dandelion	WEED
dandy	FOP
danger	PERIL
dangerous	RISKY
dangerous fish	SHARK
dangerous woman	SIREN
danger signal	ALARM, ALERT, SIREN
dangle	HANG
Danish coin	KRONE
dank	DAMP, SOGGY
danseuse	BALLERINA
Danube tributary	ENNS, ISAR
dapper	NATTY
dapple	FLECK
dappled	PIED
dare	CHALLENGE, VENTURE
daring	BOLD, HEROIC, NERVE
daring deed	FEAT
dark	DIM, DUSKY, INKY, BLACK, UNLIGHTED
dark blue	NAVY
dark brown fur	SABLE, MINK, BEAVER
darken	DIM, SHADOW
dark gray	TAUPE

dark-haired girl	BRUNETTE
dark mood	ANGER
darkness (prefix)	SCOTO
dark-skinned	DUSKY, SWARTHY
darling	MINION, PET
darn	MEND
dart	ARROW, FLIT
dash	SHATTER, TEAR, RACE
data	INFORMATION, FACTS, STATISTICS
date	APPOINTMENT
date book	CALENDAR
dated	PASSE
date tree	PALM
datum	FACT
daub	SMEAR
daughter of Cadmus	INO
daughter of Eioneus	DIA
daunt	SCARE, COW
davenport	SOFA, COUCH, DIVAN, SETTEE
David Copperfield's first wife	DORA
David Copperfield villain	HEEP
David's daughter	TAMAR, THAMAR
David's father	JESSE
David's son	AMNON, SOLOMON, ABSALOM
David's wife	MICHAL, ABITAL, ABIGAIL, BATHSHEBA
dawdle	MOPE, LINGER
dawn	SUNUP, DAYBREAK, SUNRISE
dawn (Sp.)	ALBA
dawn moisture	DEW
day (Fr.)	JOUR
day (Heb.)	YOM
day before a feast	EVE
daybreak	DAWN, SUNUP, SUNRISE
daydream	CHIMERA
day of rest	SABBATH
days long gone (2 wds.)	OLDEN TIMES, ANCIENT HISTORY
daytime performance	MATINEE
day work	LABOR
daze	STUN
dazzle	BLIND
dazzling	BRILLIANT
dead city (2 wds.)	GHOST TOWN
deaden the sound of	MUFFLE
deadfall	SNARE, TRAP
dead heat	TIE
dead language	LATIN
deadly	FATAL, LETHAL
deadly snake	ASP, VIPER
deadlock	STALEMATE

Dead Sea city **SODOM**
dead tired **WEARY**
deal **PACT**
dealer **DISTRIBUTOR,**
SALESMAN, RETAILER
dealer in salvaged
trash **JUNKMAN**
deal sparingly **DOLE**
deal with
beforehand **ANTICIPATE**
dear **BELOVED**
dear one (Fr.) **CHERI**
death **DECEASE, DEMISE**
deathly pale **ASHEN, ASHY**
debar **EXCLUDE**
debase **DEGRADE**
debatable **MOOT, ARGUABLE**
debate **ARGUE, DISCUSS**
debilitated **FEEBLE, INFIRM**
debit **CHARGE**
debonair **URBANE, SUAVE**
debonair fellow
(2 wds.) **CITY SLICKER**
debris **RUBBLE**
debt **OBLIGATION**
debtor's note **IOU**
Debussy opus (2 wds.) **LA MER**
decade **TEN**
decadence **DECAY**
decamp **FLEE**
decant **POUR**
decanter **BOTTLE**
decay **ROT, SPOIL**
decay of timber
(2 wds.) **WET ROT**
deceit **GUILE, CHICANERY**
deceitful **TRICKY, FALSE**
deceive **FOOL, TRICK,**
BEGUILE, DELUDE, DUPE,
MISLEAD
deceived easily **GULLIBLE**
December song **CAROL, NOEL**
December 24th
(2 wds.) **CHRISTMAS EVE**
December visitor **SANTA**
decent **PROPER**
deception **FRAUD**
deceptive **ILLUSORY**
decide **SETTLE**
decimal unit **TEN**
decimeter **LITER**
decipher **READ, DECODE**
decision **RESOLUTION**
decisive **CONCLUSIVE**
deck hand **TAR, SALT, GOB,**
SAILOR
deck out **ARRAY**
declaim **ORATE**

declaim violently **RANT**
declamation **ORATORY**
declaration **AVOWAL,**
STATEMENT
declaration of allegiance **OATH,**
PLEDGE
declare **AVER, AVOW, ASSERT,**
ALLEGE, SAY, STATE
declare invalid **ANNUL**
declare untrue **DENY**
declination **REFUSAL**
decline **DESCENT, EBB,**
REFUSE
declining **DECADENT**
declivity **SCARP**
decode **TRANSLATE**
decompose **ROT, DECAY**
decompression sickness **BENDS**
decorate **ADORN, TRIM,**
PAINT, GILD, BEDECK, DECK,
ORNAMENT
decorated **ORNATE**
decorate with
woodworking **PANEL, INLAY**
decorating metal **NIELLO**
decoration **DECOR, MEDAL,**
BADGE, ORNAMENT
decorative **ORNAMENTAL**
decorative fold **PLEAT**
decorative hanging **FESTOON**
decorative pellet **BEAD**
decorative stamp **SEAL**
decorous **STAID**
decorum **DIGNITY, PROPRIETY**
decoy **LURE**
decrease **ABATE, WANE, EBB**
decree **EDICT, BULL**
decree beforehand **DESTINE**
decreed **FATED**
decrement **LOSS, WASTE**
decrepit **INFIRM, SENILE**
decry **BELITTLE, BOO**
decrypt **DECODE**
dedicate **DEVOTE**
deduce **DERIVE, INFER**
deduct **SUBTRACT**
deduct from bill **REBATE**
deduction **REBATE**
deed **ACT, ACTION, FEAT,**
CONTRACT, BOND
deem **JUDGE**
deep **PROFOUND**
deep affection **LOVE**
deep apprehension **FEAR,**
FOREBODING
deep blue pigment **SMALT**
deep blue stone
(2 wds.) **LAPIS LAZULI**

deep bow	**SALAAM**	deform	**MAIM**
deep canyon	**CHASM**	defraud	**CHEAT, MULCT**
deep crimson	**CARMINE**	defray	**MEET, SETTLE, PAY**
deep dish	**BOWL**	deft	**ADEPT**
deep ditch	**TRENCH**	defy	**OPPOSE**
deepen a channel	**DREDGE**	degenerate	**DECAY, DEPRAVE**
deep gorge	**RAVINE**	degradation	**DISHONOR,**
deep hole	**PIT**		**DISGRACE**
deep in tone	**LOW**	degrade	**ABASE, DEBASE,**
deeply engrossed	**RAPT**		**DEMEAN**
deeply tinge	**IMBUE**	degree	**STEP, STAGE**
deep mud	**MIRE**	degree of a slope	**GRADE**
deep sleep	**TRANCE**	deign	**CONDESCEND**
deep space	**OUTER SPACE**	deity	**GOD**
deep valley	**RAVINE**	deity (name of) *See under*	
deer	**HIND, DOE, STAG, ROE,**	*Greek deity, Norse deity, etc.*	
	HART	dejected	**SAD, MOROSE, GLUM**
deer meat	**VENISON**	Delaware Indian	**LENAPE**
deer pathway	**RUN**	Delaware town	**CHESTER**
deer's horn	**ANTLER**	delay	**RETARD, DETAIN, HOLD**
deface	**MAR**		**UP, PUT OFF**
defamation	**SLANDER, LIBEL**	dele	**ERASE**
defamatory statement	**LIBEL**	delete's opposite	**STET**
defame	**SMEAR, LIBEL**	delegate (abbr.)	**REP**
default	**FAILURE, NEGLECT**	delete	**ERASE, REMOVE**
defeat	**BEAT, THWART, ROUT,**	deliberate	**CAREFUL, CAUTIOUS**
	SUBDUE	delicacy	**TACT**
defeat at bridge	**SET**	delicate	**FRAIL, FRAGILE,**
defeated one	**LOSER**		**TENDER**
defeat soundly	**ROUT**	delicate plant	**MOSS**
defect	**FLAW, IMPERFECTION**	delicate skill	**FINESSE**
defection	**DESERTION**	delicious	**TASTEFUL, TASTY**
defective	**BAD, POOR**	delicious beverage	**NECTAR**
defective bomb	**DUD**	delight	**JOY, PLEASE**
defective vision	**ANOPIA,**	delightful	**NICE**
	MYOPIA	delightful abode	**EDEN**
defend	**PROTECT, SHIELD**	delight in	**LOVE, SAVOR**
defendant's answer	**PLEA**	delineate	**DRAW**
defense	**BULWARK,**	delirious	**RAVING**
	PROTECTION	deliver	**BRING, RENDER**
defenseless	**NAKED**	deliver an address	**SPEAK**
defense missile	**NIKE, ICBM**	deliver formally	**PRESENT**
defense organization		dell	**VALLEY, VALE, DALE**
(abbr.)	**NATO**	delude	**DUPE, FOOL**
defensible	**TENABLE**	deluge	**FLOOD, SWAMP**
defensive slope	**GLACIS**	demand obedience	
defensive wall	**PARAPET**	(3 wds.)	**SNAP THE WHIP**
defensive work	**FORT,**	demand payment	**DUN**
	RAMPART	demean	**DEBASE, ABASE,**
defer	**DELAY, RETARD**		**DEGRADE**
defer temporarily	**TABLE**	demeanor	**MANNER**
deficient	**DEFECTIVE, SCARCE**	demented	**INSANE**
defile	**CORRUPT, SOIL**	Democrat's symbol	**DONKEY**
define	**DESCRIBE**	demolish	**DESTROY**
definite	**FIXED, EXACT**	demon	**DEVIL, FIEND**
definite article	**THE**	demon of Arabian lore	**JINN(I),**
definition	**MEANING**		**DJINN, GENIE**
deflect	**DIVERT**	demonstrate	**PROVE, SHOW**

demonstrative pronoun **THAT**
demoralize **DISCOURAGE**
demos **POPULACE, PEOPLE**
demur **OBJECT, BALK, HESITATE**
demure **SHY, COY**
den **LAIR**
denomination **SECT, CULT, CLASSIFICATION**
denote **SIGNIFY, MEAN**
denounce **ACCUSE, BLAME**
dense **COMPACT**
dense growth of trees **FOREST**
dense row of shrubs **HEDGE**
dent **BATTER**
dental filling **INLAY**
dentine **IVORY**
dentist's degree (abbr.) **DDS**
denude **BARE, STRIP, EXPOSE**
deny **REPUDIATE, WITHHOLD**
depart **GO, LEAVE**
departed **GONE, LEFT, WENT, DECEASED**
department **FIELD, SECTION**
department of France **EURE**
depart secretly **ABSCOND**
depart suddenly **BOLT**
depart this life **DIE**
departure **EXIT**
departure port of
Columbus **PALOS**
depend **RELY**
dependable **RELIABLE**
dependent **SUBJECT**
depend upon **HINGE**
depict **PORTRAY**
deplete **DRAIN, EXHAUST**
deplorable **WRETCHED**
deplore **BEMOAN**
deploy **SPREAD, SCATTER**
deport **BANISH, EXILE**
deportment **AIR, BEHAVIOR**
deposit **LAY, PUT, PLACE**
deposit, as a ballot **CAST**
deposit of resources **FUND**
depositor's concern **INTEREST**
depot **WAREHOUSE, STATION, TERMINAL**
depraved **EVIL, BAD**
depravity **CORRUPTION, EVIL**
deprecate **DECRY, BELITTLE**
depress **SADDEN**
depressed **LOW, BLUE**
depression **GLOOM**
depression initials **NRA**
depress with fear **COW**
deprivation **LOSS**
deprive **DEBAR, DISPOSSESS**

deprived of (Fr.) **SANS**
deprived of social
rights **UNDERPRIVILEGED**
deprive of sensation **NUMB**
deprived of strength **ENERVATED, DEBILITATED**
deputy **AGENT, REP, ASSISTANT**
deranged **INSANE, DEMENTED**
derby **HAT, BOWLER**
deride **RIDICULE**
derision **SCORN, CONTEMPT**
derivation **ORIGIN, CAUSE**
derive **DEDUCE, INFER, ORIGINATE**
derogatory **SNIDE**
descend (2 wds.) **GO DOWN**
descendant **SCION, HEIR**
descent **FALL**
describe grammatically **PARSE**
descriptive name **TITLE**
desert **ABANDON, STRAND, LEAVE, WASTELAND**
desert animal **CAMEL**
desert dweller **ARAB, BEDOUIN**
deserted in love **LORN, FORLORN, BEREFT**
deserter **RAT**
Desert Fox **ROMMEL**
desert green spot **OASIS**
desert hallucination **MIRAGE**
desert illusion **MIRAGE**
desert in Asia **GOBI**
desertlike **ARID**
desert nomad **ARAB**
desert plant **AGAVE, CACTUS, YUCCA**
desert region of Africa **SUDAN**
desert region of shifting
sand **ERG**
desert ship **CAMEL**
desert shrub **TETEM**
desert train **CARAVAN**
desert wind **SIROCCO, SIMOON, SAMIEL**
deserve **EARN, MERIT**
deserving of
reproach **BLAMABLE**
desiccated **DRY, ARID**
design **PATTERN, PLAN**
designate **NAME, APPOINT**
design of initials **MONOGRAM**
design on fabric **BATIK**
desirable **VALUABLE**
desire **COVET, WANT, ASPIRE, WISH, HOPE, YEN, YEARN**
desire a lofty object **ASPIRE**
desist **CEASE, STOP**

desk	ESCRITOIRE, SECRETARY, BUREAU
desolate	BLEAK, FORSAKEN, STARK
desolation	RUIN
despair	HOPELESSNESS
desperate	FRANTIC
despise	HATE, LOATHE, SCORN
despondent	FORLORN
despot	TSAR, TYRANT, DICTATOR
dessert pastry	PIE, CAKE, ECLAIR, TART
destination	GOAL
destine	DOOM
destined	FATED, IN THE CARDS
destiny	FATE, LOT
destitute	DEVOID, NEEDY, POOR
destitute of light	DARK
destitution	POVERTY, WANT
destroy	RUIN
destroyed	KAPUT
destroyed by fire	BURNT
destroyer	SHIP
destroy most of	DECIMATE
destroy power of	ANNUL
destruction	ERADICATION, LOSS, RUIN
destructive	HARMFUL
destructive insect	PEST
destructive prowler	VANDAL
destructive rodent	RAT
destructive storm	TORNADO, HURRICANE, GALE, SQUALL, BLIZZARD
desultory	CURSORY, RAMBLING
detach	SEPARATE, SEVER
detached	UNCONCERNED
detail	ITEM
detain	HOLD, KEEP
detect	DISCOVER
detecting device	RADAR, SONAR
detective Queen	ELLERY
detective's case (sl.)	CAPER
detective Spade	SAM
detention	DELAY
deter	WARN, DISSUADE
detergent	SOAP
deteriorate	DEGRADE, DEBASE
deterioration	DECAY, DECLINE
determination	GRIT, RESOLVE
determine	WILL
determined	FIRM, RESOLUTE
detest	ABHOR, LOATHE. HATE
detraction	DEROGATION
detriment	HARM, LOSS
Detroit baseball team	TIGERS
deuce	CARD, TWO
DeValera's land	ERIN, EIRE
devastate	RAVAGE
devastation	HAVOC
develop	UNFOLD
develop into	BECOME
deviate	DEFLECT
device	MACHINE, GADGET
device for runners (2 wds.)	STARTING BLOCK
devil	DEMON, SATAN, FIEND
devilfish	MANTA, RAY
devise	INVENT, CONTRIVE
devise unfairly (2 wds.)	TRUMP UP
devoid	LACKING
devoid of light	DARK
devotion of nine days	NOVENA
devour	EAT, CONSUME
devout	HOLY, PIOUS
dew	MOISTURE
dexterity	AGILITY
dexterous	ADROIT, DEFT
diabetic's need	INSULIN
diabolical	FIENDISH
diacritical mark	TILDE
diagonal	CATERCORNER, SLANT
diagram	GRAPH, MAP
dialect	IDIOM, LINGO, SLANG, ARGOT
dial pointer	HAND
diamond	GEM, JEWEL, STONE
diamond call (2 wds.)	BATTER UP, PLAY BALL
diamond man	PITCHER, CATCHER, BATTER
diamond ring	SOLITAIRE
diamonds (sl.)	ICE, ROCKS
Diamond State	DELAWARE
diamond surface	FACET
diaphanous	SHEER
diary	JOURNAL, LOG
dictate	COMMAND, DIRECT
diction	STYLE
dictionary	LEXICON, GLOSSARY
dido	ANTIC, TRICK, CAPER
die	EXPIRE, DECEASE
diesel engine	MOTOR
diet	REGIMEN
dieter's concern	FLAB, FAT, POUNDS, CALORIES, BULGE, PAUNCH
diet fruit	GRAPEFRUIT

differ	**VARY**	dinner	**MEAL, BANQUET**
different	**ELSE, OTHER**	dinner bell	**GONG**
differentiate	**CONTRAST,**	dinner course	**DESSERT,**
	DISTINGUISH		**ENTREE, SALAD, FISH,**
differently	**OTHERWISE**		**MEAT, SOUP, APPETIZER**
difficult	**HARD**	dinner jacket	**TUXEDO**
difficult journey	**TREK**	dinosaur	**LIZARD**
difficult problem	**POSER**	Dinsmore	**ELSIE**
difficult sailing		dint	**FORCE**
(3 wds.) **AGAINST THE WIND**		diocese	**SEE, BISHOPRIC**
difficult		dip	**IMMERSE, DUNK, SOP**
situation	**PREDICAMENT**	dip Easter eggs	**TINT, DYE**
difficulty	**SNAG**	dip into liquid	**RINSE**
diffident	**TIMID, SHY**	diploma	**CERTIFICATE,**
diffuse	**SPREAD, EXPAND**		**DEGREE**
diffused with color	**IRIDESCENT**	diplomacy	**TACT**
dig	**EXCAVATE**	diplomat	**CONSUL**
dig cherrystones	**CLAM**	diplomatic	**TACTFUL**
digging implement	**SPADE,**	diplomat's aide	**ATTACHE**
	SHOVEL	dip out	**BAIL**
digit	**FINGER, TOE, NUMBER,**	dipper	**LADLE**
	NUMERAL	dire	**DISASTROUS, DREADFUL,**
dignified	**SEDATE**		**FATAL, CRITICAL**
dignify	**ENNOBLE**	direct	**LEAD, MANAGE, AIM**
dignity	**DECORUM, MAJESTY**	direct attention	**REFER**
dig ore	**MINE**	direction	**GUIDANCE, EAST,**
digress	**DEVIATE**		**NORTH, SOUTH, WEST,**
dig up	**UNEARTH**		**EASTWARD, WESTWARD,**
dike	**LEVEE**		**NORTHWARD, SOUTHWARD,**
dilate	**EXPAND, WIDEN**		**RIGHT, LEFT**
dilemma	**PLIGHT, PROBLEM**	direction mark	**ARROW**
dilettante	**AMATEUR,**	directive	**ORDER**
	DABBLER	director	**LEADER, MANAGER**
diligence	**CARE, INDUSTRY**	director Kazan	**ELIA**
dill	**ANET, SPICE**	director Penn	**ARTHUR**
dim	**PALE**	director Preminger	**OTTO**
dimension	**LENGTH, HEIGHT,**	dirge	**LAMENT**
	WIDTH	dirigible	**BLIMP**
diminish	**ABATE, LESSEN,**	dirk	**DAGGER, SNEE**
	PETER OUT, TAPER	dirndl	**SKIRT**
diminish gradually	**TAPER**	dirt	**FILTH, GRIME, SOIL,**
diminutive	**SMALL, PETITE**		**SOOT**
diminutive being	**GNOME, ELF,**	dirty	**IMPURE, SOOTY,**
DWARF, BROWNIE, GREMLIN			**FILTHY, GRIMY, SOILED**
diminutive suffix	**ETTE, ULE**	disability	**WEAKNESS**
dimwit	**DUNCE, FOOL, DOLT**	disable	**CRIPPLE**
din	**CLATTER, NOISE,**	disadvantage	**HANDICAP**
	UPROAR, RACKET	disagree	**DIFFER, ARGUE**
dine	**EAT, SUP**	disagreeable	**NASTY,**
dine at home (2 wds.)	**EAT IN**		**UNPLEASANT**
diner	**EATERY, EATER**	disagreeable child	**BRAT**
ding	**RING**	disagreeable person	**CRAB,**
dinghy	**ROWBOAT**		**GROUCH**
dingy	**DUSKY, DRAB, WORN,**	disagreeable sight	**EYESORE**
	SHABBY	disagreeable woman	**SHREW**
dining room furniture	**TABLE,**	disagreement	**CLASH, DISPUTE**
CHAIR, SERVER, CART,		disappear	**VANISH**
	BUFFET	disappoint	**FAIL**

disapproval **CENSURE**
disarray **CONFUSION, DISORDER**
disassemble (2 wds.) **TAKE APART**
disaster **CALAMITY, CATASTROPHE**
disastrous **DIRE, TRAGIC**
disavow **RETRACT**
disburse **SPEND**
disc **RECORD**
discard **SET ASIDE, THROW AWAY, TOSS OUT, SCRAP**
discern **DETECT, PERCEIVE**
discharge **DISMISS, UNLOAD, EMIT, FIRE**
discharge a debt **PAY, PAY UP**
discharge a gun **SHOOT, FIRE**
disciple **STUDENT, FOLLOWER**
discipline **CHASTEN**
disclaim **DISAVOW**
disclaimer **DENIAL**
disclaim formally **ABJURE**
disclose **BARE, REVEAL**
discomfit **THWART, FOIL, ROUT**
discompose **UNSETTLE**
disconcert **ABASH**
disconnect **SEPARATE**
disconsolate **SAD**
discontent **RESTLESS**
discontinue **STOP, HALT**
discord **CONTENTION, STRIFE**
Discordia **ERIS**
discount **REBATE, KICKBACK**
discourage **DAUNT**
discourage through fear **DETER**
discourse **LECTURE, DEBATE**
discourteous **RUDE, IMPOLITE**
discover **ESPY, FIND, DETECT**
discover by chance
(2 wds.) **RUN ACROSS**
discoverer of
America **COLUMBUS**
discover suddenly
(2 wds.) **HIT ON**
discovery-minded
traveler **EXPLORER**
discreet **CAUTIOUS, PRUDENT**
discrepancy **VARIANCE**
discretion **TACT**
discrimination **PRUDENCE**
discuss **DEBATE**
discussion basis **TOPIC**
disdain **SCORN**
disease **AILMENT, MALADY**
disembark **LAND**
disencumber **RID, RELIEVE**
disfigure **DEFACE, MAR, SCAR**

disgrace **SHAME**
disguise **MASK, CAMOUFLAGE**
disgust **DISTASTE, DISLIKE**
disgusting **NASTY**
dish **PLATE, BOWL, SAUCER, CUP**
dishes **CHINA**
dish of appetizers
(2 wds.) **RELISH TRAY**
dish of cabbage **SLAW**
dish of greens **SALAD**
dish of stewed fruit **COMPOTE**
dishonest **FALSE, UNTRUE**
disinclined **AVERSE**
disinclined to work **LAZY**
dislike **HATE, LOATHE, DESPISE**
disloyal **FALSE, UNTRUE**
dismal **GLOOMY, DREARY**
dismal failure **FLOP**
dismantle **STRIP**
dismantled ship **HULK**
dismay **APPALL, COW, DAUNT**
dismiss **DISCHARGE, DROP**
dismissal (Fr.) **CONGE**
dismiss forcibly **EXILE**
dismiss from office **AMOVE, REMOVE, IMPEACH**
dismount **ALIGHT, UNSEAT**
disobedient **NAUGHTY**
disobey **DEFY, REBEL**
disorder **MESS**
disorderly **UNRULY**
disorderly crowd **MOB**
disorderly flight **ROUT**
disorganize **CONFUSE**
disown **RENOUNCE**
disparage **BELITTLE**
disparaging remark **SLUR**
disparity **ODDS, INCONGRUITY**
dispatch **SEND**
dispatch boat **AVISO**
dispel **DISPERSE, BANISH**
disperse **SCATTER**
disperse in defeat **ROUT**
display **SHOW, FLAUNT**
display cards for a score **MELD, DECLARE**
display stand **RACK**
displease **ANNOY, VEX**
displeased **OUT OF HUMOR, CROSS**
dispose **ARRANGE**
disposed **PRONE**
dispossess **DIVEST**
dispute **HAGGLE, WRANGLE, QUARREL, CONTEST, FIGHT, DEBATE**

disregard **PASS OVER, IGNORE, NEGLECT**
disreputable **LOW, BASE**
disrespectful **RUDE**
disrupt **REND, TEAR**
dissent **DISAGREE, DIFFER**
dissenting vote **NAY**
dissertation **TRACT, THESIS, TREATISE**
dissipate **DIFFUSE**
dissolve **MELT, THAW**
dissuade **DETER**
distance measure **MILE, FOOT, ROD, YARD, INCH**
distant **FAR, AFAR**
distant (prefix) **TELE**
distaste **AVERSION, DISGUST**
distasteful **BITTER**
distemper **AILMENT, VIRUS**
distend **DILATE, SWELL**
distinct **CLEAR, PLAIN**
distinct (comp. wd.) **CLEAR-CUT**
distinct part **UNIT**
distinction **HONOR, RENOWN, DIFFERENCE**
distinctive **PECULIAR**
distinctive air **AURA**
distinctive character **CACHET**
distinctive manner of writing **STYLE**
distinctive mark **STAMP**
distinctive quality **TALENT**
distinctive taste **SAVOR**
distinguish **DISCERN**
distinguished **EMINENT**
distinguishing feature **TRAIT**
distort **WARP**
distorted **AWRY**
distract **DIVERT**
distress **TROUBLE, ANGUISH**
distress call **SOS, HELP**
distribute **ALLOT, DOLE, APPORTION**
distribute cards **DEAL**
district **AREA, REGION, TERRITORY**
district attorney (abbr.) **DA**
district in Saudi Arabia **ASIR**
distrust **DOUBT**
disturb **TROUBLE, WORRY**
disturbance **UPROAR**
disturb suddenly **STARTLE, ALARM**
disturb the peace **RIOT**
disunite **SEVER, DIVORCE**
disuse **DISCARD**
ditch **TRENCH, RHINE, RINE**

ditch around a castle **MOAT**
ditty **SONG, AIR**
divan **SOFA, COUCH, SETTEE**
diva's forte **ARIA**
dive **PLUNGE, RUSH**
divers **SUNDRY**
diver's disease **BENDS**
diversion **GAME, SPORT, AMUSEMENT**
divest **DEPRIVE**
divest of office **DEPOSE**
divide **CLEFT, PART, SPLIT, SEPARATE, SUNDER**
divided into two lobes **BIFID**
divide into regular steps **GRADUATE**
divide into strata **LAYER**
divide in two parts **BISECT**
dividing wall **SEPTUM, PARTITION**
divine **HOLY, SACRED**
divine being **DEITY, GOD**
divine gift **BLESSING**
diving bird **AUK, LOON, GREBE**
diving duck **SMEE, SCOTER**
divinity **FUDGE**
division **SEGMENT, SECTION, RIFT, PART, PORTION**
division of ancient Greece **ELIS**
division of a poem **PASSUS, CANTO, VERSE, COUPLET**
division of Great Britain **WALES, SCOTLAND, ENGLAND, IRELAND**
division of the year **SEASON, MONTH**
division preposition **INTO**
divorce **SEPARATE, DISUNITE**
divorce capital **RENO**
divorced person **EX**
divot **CLOD, TURF**
divulge **TELL, INFORM**
Dixie **SOUTH**
Dixieland **JAZZ**
dizziness **VERTIGO**
dizzy **GIDDY**
do **PERFORM, ACT**
do a jackknife **DIVE**
do a risky deed (3 wds.) **BELL THE CAT**
do away with **ABOLISH**
dobbin **HORSE**
docile **GENTLE, TAME**
dock **PIER, WHARF**
docket **TICKET**
doctor **PHYSICIAN**
doctor's assistant **NURSE**

doctors' group **AMA**
doctor's helper (abbr.) **RN**
doctrine **ISM, TENET, CREDO**
doctrine adherent (suffix) **IST**
doctrine of
  inevitable **FATALISM**
doctrine of selfishness **EGOISM**
doc's penmanship **SCRAWL**
document **PAPER**
document addition **RIDER**
document file **DOSSIER**
documentary **FILM**
dodder **TREMBLE, TOTTER**
dodderer **CODGER**
doddering old age **SENILITY**
do detective work
  (2 wds.) **TRACK DOWN**
dodge **DUCK, ELUDE**
dodge an issue **SIDESTEP**
dodo **FOGY**
doe **HIND, DEER**
doer **ACTOR**
doer of odd jobs
  (2 wds.) **HANDY MAN**
do farm work **HOE, SOW, MILK,**
REAP, PLOW, HARVEST
doff **REMOVE**
dog **PET, CANINE**
dog doctor, for short **VET**
dog-drawn vehicle **SLED**
dogged **STUBBORN**
doggerel **NONSENSE VERSE**
doggie-in-window locale
  (2 wds.) **PET SHOP**
dog house **KENNEL**
dogie **CALF**
doglike animal **WOLF. FOX**
dogma **TENET, BELIEF,**
TEACHING
dogmatic sayings **DICTA**
dog salmon **KETA**
dog-tired (2 wds.) **ALL IN**
dog's delight **BONE**
dog's foot **PAW**
dog's growl **GNAR, ROWF,**
GRRR
dog's lead **LEASH**
dog's name **FIDO, ROVER,**
KING, REX, LADY, LASSIE
dog's tail movement **WAG**
dog's tooth **FANG**
dog's treats **BONES**
dog's wagger **TAIL**
dogwood **TREE**
do housework **CLEAN, DUST,**
SWEEP, POLISH, WAX,
WASH, MOP

doily **MAT**
do in **KILL**
do intensive research **DELVE**
do laundry **WASH**
dolce **SWEET, SMOOTH**
doldrums **CALM**
dole **ALLOTMENT, ALLOCATE,**
DISTRIBUTE, ALLOT,
APPORTION, METE, PORTION
doleful **SAD**
doll **TOY, PUPPET**
dollar bill **ONE, SINGLE**
dollop **LUMP, HELPING**
dolman **SLEEVE**
dolor **GRIEF, SORROW**
dolphin **PORPOISE**
dolt **BLOCKHEAD**
domain **FIELD, REALM**
dome **CUPOLA**
domestic **TAME, NATIVE**
domestic animal **CAT, DOG,**
PET, CANARY, PARAKEET,
COW, SHEEP, HORSE, HEN,
ROOSTER. DUCK, BULL,
STEER, RAM. EWE, GOAT
domestic animals **CATTLE**
domesticate **TAME**
domestic employee **SERVANT,**
MAID, HOUSEBOY, BUTLER,
COOK
domestic
  establishment **MENAGE**
domicile **ABODE, RESIDENCE**
dominant **CHIEF, SUPREME**
dominate **REIGN, RULE**
dominating **BOSSY**
domination **RULE**
domineer **BULLY, TYRANNIZE**
domineering **OVERBEARING**
Dominican friar **JACOBIN**
dominion **TERRITORY**
domino **MASK, TILE, ROBE**
don **TUTOR**
Don Adams program
  (2 wds.) **GET SMART**
donate **GIVE. CONTRIBUTE**
donating **GIVING**
donation **GRANT, GIFT**
done **FINISHED, OVER**
done for **DEAD**
done in **TIRED**
donjon **KEEP. TOWER**
Don Juan's mother **INEZ**
do newspaper work **EDIT,**
REPORT. REWRITE
donkey **ASS, BURRO**
donkey's cry **BRAY**
donna **LADY, MADAM**

donor	**GIVER**	draft animals	**OXEN**
Don Quixote's steed	**ROSINANTE**	draftsman	**DRAWER**
doodad	**TRINKET, BAUBLE**	draftsman's need	
doodle	**SCRIBBLE**	(2 wds.)	**GRAPH PAPER**
doom	**FATE**	drag	**HAUL, TOW, PULL**
door	**PORTAL**	drag loosely	**TRAIL**
door (Ital.)	**PORTA**	drama	**THEATER, PLAY**
doorbell	**CHIME**	drama division	**ACT, SCENE**
door clasp	**HASP, KNOB**	dramatic part	**ROLE**
door column	**ANTA**	dramatis personae	**CAST**
door fastening	**LATCH**	draped garment	**TOGA**
door frame	**JAMB**	drastic social change	**REFORM**
door joint	**HINGE**	draught	**DOSE, PORTION**
door molding	**ASTRAGAL**	draw	**PULL, SKETCH,**
door-to-door			**DELINEATE**
salesman	**PEDDLER**	draw a mark below	**UNDERLINE**
doorway sign	**EXIT**	draw back	**RECEDE**
doorway structure	**ARCH**	draw close	**NEAR**
dope	**NARCOTIC, OPIUM**	drawer knob	**PULL**
dor	**BEETLE**	drawforth	**EDUCE, EVOKE**
dormant	**LATENT**	draw game	**STALEMATE**
dormer window	**LUCARNE**	drawing	**SKETCH**
do sums	**ADD**	drawing room	**SALON, PARLOR**
dot	**PERIOD, SPOT, SPECK**	draw letters	**PRINT**
dote on	**ADORE**	draw off	**SIPHON**
do the crawl	**SWIM**	draw out	**ELICIT**
doting	**FOND**	draw through thin paper	**TRACE**
double	**TWIN, TWOFOLD**	draw tight	**CINCH**
double chair		dread	**FEAR**
(2 wds.)	**LOVE SEAT**	dreadful	**DIRE**
double curve	**ESS**	dream	**FANTASY, REVERIE**
doubt	**DEMUR, DISTRUST**	dreamer	**VISIONARY**
dough	**PASTE, MONEY, BREAD**	dreamland	**SLEEP**
doughnut-shaped roll	**BAGEL**	dreary	**BLEAK**
do up	**PREPARE**	dreary (poet.)	**DREAR**
dour	**GLOOMY**	dredge	**SCOOP**
dove	**PIGEON**	dregs	**LEES, SEDIMENT**
doves' home	**COTE**	drench	**SOAK, SOP, SOUSE**
dove sound	**COO**	Dresden	**PORCELAIN, CHINA,**
dowdy	**SHABBY**		**MEISSENWARE**
dowdy woman	**FRUMP**	dress	**CLOTHE, FROCK,**
down	**FUZZ**	**GOWN, CLOTHING, GARB,**	
down (arch.)	**ADOWN**	**APPAREL, ATTIRE**	
down (prefix)	**DE**	dressage	**HORSEMANSHIP**
downcast	**BLUE, SAD**	dress border	**HEM**
downpour	**RAIN, TORRENT**	dress carefully	**PREEN, PRIMP**
downright	**CANDID**	dress down	**SCOLD**
downtown Chicago	**LOOP**	dressed	**CLAD**
downwind	**LEEWARD**	dressed pelt	**FUR**
down with (Fr., 2 wds.)	**A BAS**	dresser	**BUREAU, VALET**
downy	**SOFT**	dress feathers	**PREEN**
downy duck	**EIDER**	dress flax	**TED**
downy surface	**NAP**	dressing	**TOPPING, STUFFING,**
do wrong	**ERR**		**SAUCE**
doxology	**HYMN, FORMULA**	dressing gown	**NEGLIGEE,**
doze	**DROWSE, NAP, SLEEP**		**ROBE, WRAPPER**
drab	**COLORLESS, DULL**	dressmaker	**MODISTE**
draft	**DOSE, PORTION**		

dress material **SILK, CREPE, COTTON, SATIN, RAYON, NYLON, ARNEL**
dress style **EMPIRE, SACK, A-LINE, MOD**
dress the hair **COMB**
dress trimming **RUCHE, RUFFLE**
dress up **PRIMP**
dress warmly (2 wds.) **BUNDLE UP**
dressy **STYLISH, ELEGANT**
dribble **TRICKLE**
dried cut grass **HAY**
dried plum **PRUNE**
dried up **SERE**
drift **TENDENCY, TREND, FLOAT, PILE**
drill **BORE**
drill into again **RETAP**
drink **IMBIBE, QUAFF**
drink heavily **TOPE**
drinking cup **MUG, TOBY**
drinking salutation **PROSIT**
drinking tube **STRAW**
drinking vessel **CUP, MUG, GLASS, STEIN**
drink like a dog **LAP**
drink slowly **SIP**
drink to excess **TIPPLE**
drink to health of **TOAST**
drip **TRICKLE**
drip-dry **NO IRON**
dripping wet **SODDEN**
drive **IMPEL, PROPEL**
drive a golf ball (2 wds.) **TEE OFF**
drive at **AIM**
drive away **SHOO**
drive back **REPULSE, REPEL**
drive backward **REVERSE**
drive forward **IMPEL, PROPEL**
drive frantic **BEDEVIL**
drive-in **RESTAURANT, MOVIE**
drive insane **MADDEN**
drive obliquely **SLICE**
drive out **EXPEL**
driver **CHAUFFEUR**
driver's compartment **CAB**
driveway covering **GRAVEL**
drizzle **RAIN**
droll **FUNNY**
dromedary **CAMEL**
drone **HUM, BUZZ, BEE**
drool **SLAVER**
droop **SAG, WILT**
drooping on one side **ALOP**
drooping tree **WILLOW**

droopy **TIRED**
drop **FALL, GLOBULE**
drop down suddenly **DIP, PLUNGE**
drop from sight **VANISH**
drop heavily **PLOP**
drop in **VISIT, CALL**
droplet **BEAD**
drop off **DECLINE, DECREASE**
drop slowly **SINK**
dropsy **EDEMA**
dross **WASTE**
dross of metal **SLAG**
drove **FLOCK**
drown **INUNDATE, SUBMERGE**
drowse **DOZE, NOD**
drowsy **SLEEPY**
drudge **SLAVE**
drudgery **LABOR, GRIND**
drug **MEDICINE, OPIATE, DOPE**
drug container **CAPSULE**
druggist **APOTHECARY, PHARMACIST**
drug plant **ALOE, POPPY**
drugstore **PHARMACY**
drug-yielding crocus **SAFFRON**
drum **TAMBOR, KETTLE**
drunkard **SOT, SOUSE, TIPPLER**
dry **ARID, SEAR, SERE**
dryad **NYMPH**
dry, as wine **SEC**
dry dishes **WIPE**
dryer **BLOWER**
dry goods dealer (Brit.) **DRAPER**
drying cloth **TOWEL**
drying kiln **OAST**
dry outer part **HUSK**
dry river bed **WADI**
dry rot **FUNGUS**
dry run **REHEARSAL**
duad **PAIR, COUPLE**
dual **TWOFOLD**
dub **TAP, NAME**
dubious **DOUBTFUL**
duck **MALLARD, TEAL, SMEE, PINTAIL**
ducklike bird **COOT**
duck's call **QUACK**
duct **CANAL, TUBE**
ductile **DOCILE, FACILE**
dud **FLOP, FIZZLE**
dude **TENDERFOOT**
due **OWING**
duel **CONTEST**

duelist's aide **SECOND**
duet **TWO, TWOSOME, DUO**
due to motion **KINETIC**
duffer's bugaboo **TRAP**
duke (Fr.) **DUC**
duke's wife **DUCHESS**
dukedom **DUCHY**
dull **DREARY, BLUNT,**
BORING, TEDIOUS, DRAB
dull blow **THUD**
dull color **GRAY, GREY**
dull fellow **CLOD**
dull pain **ACHE**
dull routine **RUT**
dull thump **THUD**
duly **PROPERLY**
Dumas character **ARAMIS**
dumb **MUTE**
dumbbell **DUNCE**
dumb girl **DORA**
dump dweller **RAT**
dun **TAN**
dunce **FOOL**
dunderhead **ASS**
duo **PAIR, TWOSOME, DUET,**
TWO
dupe **TRICK, FOOL**
duplicate **REPLICA, COPY,**
CARBON
duplicate part **SPARE**
duplication **COPY, REPLICA**
durable **LASTING, CONSTANT**
duramen **HEARTWOOD**
duration **TERM, TIME, SPAN,**
TENURE
duress **IMPRISONMENT,**
FORCE
during the time that **WHILE**
dusk **GLOAM, TWILIGHT**
dusky **DARK**
dust cloth **RAG**
dust matter **LINT**
dust speck **MOTE**
dustbowl victim **OKIE**
Dutch cheese **EDAM, GOUDA**
Dutch coin **STIVER, GUILDER**
Dutch commune **EDE**
Dutch embankment **DIKE**
Dutch flower **TULIP**
Dutch Guiana **SURINAM**
Dutch landholder **PATROON**
Dutch measure **AHM, AUM**
Dutch pottery **DELFT**
Dutch South African **BOER**
Dutch uncle **EME**
duty **TASK, TARIFF**
dwarf **ELF, RUNT**
dwell **ABIDE, RESIDE, LIVE**

dweller **TENANT**
dwelling place **ABODE, HOME,**
DOMICILE, RESIDENCE,
HOUSE, APARTMENT, VILLA,
FARM, RANCH, ESTATE,
DUPLEX, PENTHOUSE, COOP
dwell on unduly **HARP**
dwindle **TAPER, WANE**
dyad **PAIR, COUPLE**
dybbuk **SPIRIT**
dye **COLOR, STAIN, TINT,**
ANIL, TINGE
dye compound **ANILINE,**
EOSIN
dye for butter **ACHIOTE,**
ANNATTO, ARNATO
dyed rabbit fur **LAPIN**
dyeing tub **TANK, VAT**
dyer **STAINER**
dynamic **POTENT**
dynamite explosion **BLAST**
dynamo **GENERATOR**
dyspeptic **GLOOMY,**
GROUCHY, MOROSE

E

each **APIECE, EVERY,**
EVERYONE, ALL
each and every **ALL**
eager **AGOG, ANXIOUS,**
ARDENT, AVID,
ENTHUSIASTIC, KEEN,
IMPATIENT
eagerness **ALACRITY, FERVOR**
eagerness for action **ELAN**
eagle **ERN, ERNE**
eagle's claw **TALON**
eagle's nest **AERIE, EYRIE,**
EYRY, AERY
ear **AURICLE**
ear (prefix) **OT, OTO**
earache **OTALGIA**
eared seal **OTARY**
earlier **PRIOR**
earliest **FIRST, SOONEST**
earliest born **ELDEST, FIRST**
early **PREMATURE**
early Briton **PICT, CELT,**
ANGLE, JUTE
early dwelling place **CAVE**
early mattress
stuffing **STRAW**
early part of day **MORN,**
MORNING
early part of night **EVENING**

early stringed
instrument **LUTE, LYRE**
early violin **REBEC**
earn **MERIT, DESERVE**
earnest **SINCERE, ZEALOUS**
earnest effort **UTMOST, BEST**
earnings **SALARY, WAGES,
PROFIT**
ear of corn **SPIKE**
ear ornament **EARRING**
ear part **LOBE**
ear shell **ABALONE**
earshot **HEARING**
earsplitting **LOUD**
earth **WORLD, LAND, SOIL,
PLANET**
earth deity **TARI, GEB, KEB**
earth deposit **SILT**
earthenware **CROCKERY**
earthenware jar **OLLA**
earthenware vessel **JAR, OLLA**
earthly **MUNDANE, PROFANE**
earth mover **BULLDOZER**
earthnut **TRUFFLE**
earthquake **TREMOR, SEISM**
earth's axis end **POLE**
earth's satellite **MOON**
earth's sister planet **VENUS**
earth's star **SUN, SOL**
earthworm **ANNELID**
earthy **SENSUAL**
earthy deposit **MARL**
earwax **CERUMEN**
ease **ALLEVIATE, RELIEVE,
LUXURY, SOOTHE**
easel **STAND**
ease off **ABATE**
ease up **RELENT**
easily broken **FRAGILE**
easily cut, as a steak **TENDER**
easily deceived **GULLIBLE**
easily fooled person **DUPE**
easily frightened **SKITTISH**
easily hurt **SENSITIVE**
easily managed **DOCILE**
east **ORIENT**
Easter flower **LILY**
eastern **ORIENTAL**
eastern caravansary **SERAI**
eastern Catholic **UNIATET**
eastern potentate **RAJAH**
eastern priest **ABBA**
eastern title **AGA**
Easter preparatory
season **LENT**
East Indian bird **SHAMA**
East Indian cedar **DEODAR**
East Indian cereal grass **RAGI**

East Indian island **BALI**
East Indian pepper plant **BETEL**
East Indian sailor **LASCAR**
East Indian timber tree **TEAK**
East Indian tree **POON**
East Indian weight **BAHAR, SER**
East Indian wood **ENG, ALOES**
east wind god **EURUS**
easy **FACILE**
easy does it **CAREFUL**
easy gait **LOPE**
easy gallop **CANTER**
easy-going horse **PADNAG**
easy-going walker **AMBLER**
easy job **SINECURE**
easy mark (2 wds.) **SOFT TOUCH**
easy task **CINCH, SNAP**
easy winner
(comp. wd.) **SHOO-IN**
eat **CONSUME, DEVOUR, DINE,
SUP, ERODE**
eat at eight **DINE**
eat away **ERODE**
eat by regimen **DIET**
eatery **DINER**
eat grass **GRAZE**
eat greedily **GOBBLE**
eating alcove **DINETTE**
eating utensil **FORK, SPOON,
KNIFE**
eat noisily **SLURP**
eat peanuts **MUNCH**
eat sparingly **DIET**
eau de vie **BRANDY**
eavesdrop **LISTEN**
ebb **ABATE, RECEDE,
SUBSIDE**
ebb and flow **TIDE**
ebony **BLACK**
ebullient **BUBBLING**
eccentric **ODD, QUEER**
eccentric piece **CAM**
ecclesiastic **PRIEST**
echinoderm **STARFISH**
echo **REVERBERATE,
RESOUND, REPEAT, APE,
MIMIC**
eclat **ACCLAIM**
eclipse **DARKEN**
economical **FRUGAL, THRIFTY**
economize **SAVE, SCRIMP**
ecstasy **RAPTURE**
ectoskeleton **SHELL**
Ecuador capital **QUITO**
Ecuador islands **GALAPAGOS**

ecumenical **UNIVERSAL, GENERAL, WORLDWIDE, ALL**
eddy **SWIRL, WHIRLPOOL**
Eden **PARADISE**
edge **ADVANTAGE, BRINK, VERGE, BORDER, BRIM, RIM, MARGIN, LIP**
edge of a molding **ARRIS**
edge of a street **CURB, KERB**
edge of woven fabric **SELVAGE**
edging **HEM**
edgy **NERVOUS, TENSE**
edible bean **LENTIL**
edible bivalve **MUSSEL, CLAM, OYSTER**
edible bulb **ONION**
edible crustacean **LOBSTER, CRAB**
edible fish **CARP, TUNA**
edible fruit **PLUM, PEAR, APPLE, ORANGE**
edible fungus **MUSHROOM**
edible green pod **OKRA**
edible Japanese shoot **UDO**
edible marine fish **GRUNT**
edible nut **ALMOND, CASHEW, FILBERT, PECAN, WALNUT, PEANUT, HAZELNUT**
edible part of fruit **PULP**
edible root **CARROT, RADISH, POTATO, BEET, PARSNIP, TURNIP, TARO**
edibles **FOODS**
edible seaweed **DULSE**
edible seed **BEAN, PEA**
edible tuber **POTATO, OCA, YAM**
edict **DECREE**
edification **INSTRUCTION**
edifice **BUILDING**
edify **INSTRUCT, ENLIGHTEN**
edit **REVISE**
Ed Sullivan, e.g. **EMCEE**
educate **TEACH, TRAIN, SCHOOL**
education **TRAINING**
educe **ELICIT, EVOKE**
eel **LAMPREY, CONGER**
eerie **SPOOKY, WEIRD**
efface **ERASE, EXPUNGE**
effect **FINISH, FULFILL, RESULT**
effective **USEFUL, EFFICIENT**
effeminate **WOMANLY**
effervescent **VOLATILE**
efficiency **ABILITY, EFFICACY**
efficient **ABLE, CAPABLE, COMPETENT, VALID**

eft **NEWT**
egg **GOAD, INCITE**
egg (prefix) **OVI**
egg cell **OVUM**
egg center **YOLK, NUCLEUS**
egg covering **SHELL**
egg dish **OMELET, SOUFFLE**
egg drink **NOG**
egg layer **HEN**
egg on **URGE**
egg part **YOLK, WHITE**
egg-shaped **OVAL, OVATE, OVOID**
egg white **ALBUMEN**
egis **AUSPICES, PATRONAGE**
ego **SELF, CONCEIT**
egotism **CONCEIT, VANITY**
egotistic **VAIN**
egress **EXIT**
egret **HERON**
Egyptian **COPTIC, COPT**
Egyptian astral body **KA**
Egyptian beetle **SCARAB**
Egyptian boat **BARIS**
Egyptian dam site **ASWAN**
Egyptian dancing girl **ALME**
Egyptian deity **SEB, SET(H), APET, OPET, ISIS, AMON, ANUBIS, OSIRIS, BUBASTIS, MA, THOTH, RA, BES, AANI, HAPI, PTAH, SATI, HORUS, ATON, HERSHEF**
Egyptian governor **PASHA**
Egyptian king **PTOLEMY, FAROUK**
Egyptian king's crown **ATEF**
Egyptian lily **LOTUS, CALLA**
Egyptian measure **ABDAT, CUBUT**
Egyptian paper **PAPYRUS**
Egyptian peninsula **SINAI**
Egyptian queen of gods **SATI**
Egyptian reed **PAPYRUS**
Egyptian river **NILE**
Egyptian sacred bull **APIS**
Egyptian seaport **SUEZ**
Egyptian stone **ROSETTA**
Egyptian sun disk **ATEN**
Egyptian sun god **RA**
Egyptian symbol **SCARAB**
Egyptian tomb **PYRAMID**
eider **DOWN, DUCK**
eight (comb. form) **OCTO**
Eire **IRELAND, ERIN**
Eisenhower memorial museum site **ABILENE**

Eisenhower's nickname	**IKE**	elevator	**LIFT**
either	**OR**	elevator direction	**UP, DOWN**
ejaculate	**EXCLAIM**	elf	**SPRITE, PIXIE, GNOME,**
eject	**OUST**		**BROWNIE**
eke	**SUPPLEMENT**	elicit	**EVOKE, EDUCE**
elaborate	**FANCY**	elide	**OMIT, SLUR**
elaborate meal	**FEAST**	eligible	**FIT, WORTHY**
elan	**ARDOR, ENTHUSIASM,**	eliminate (2 wds.)	**RULE OUT**
	VERVE, DASH	elite	**CREAM**
elapse	**EXPIRE, PASS**	elk	**MOOSE**
elastic	**PLIABLE**	elk's horn	**ANTLER**
elate	**GLADDEN**	elliptical	**OVAL, OVATE**
elation	**GLADNESS, JOY,**	elm	**TREE**
	HAPPINESS	Elmo Roper item (2 wds.)	
elder	**OLDER, SENIOR**		**STRAW VOTE**
elderly	**AGED, OLD, ANCIENT**	elongate	**LENGTHEN,**
elderly person			**STRETCH**
(2 wds.)	**SENIOR CITIZEN**	elope	**ABSCOND**
elder statesman of Japan		eloquence	**RHETORIC,**
	GENRO		**ORATORY**
eldest of the Pleiades	**MAIA**	eloquent	**EXPRESSIVE**
elect	**CHOOSE, SELECT**	else	**OTHERWISE**
elector	**VOTER**	elucidate	**EXPLAIN,**
electrical device	**RESISTOR**		**ILLUSTRATE**
electrical engineer (abbr.)	**EE**	elude	**EVADE, AVOID**
electrically charged particle		emaciated	**LEAN, SKINNY**
	ION, PROTON	emanate	**ISSUE, FLOW**
electrical unit	**AMP, FARAD,**	emanation	**AURA**
	OHM, VOLT, WATT, MHO	emancipate	**LIBERATE, FREE**
electric current (abbr.)	**AC, DC**	embankment	**LEVEE**
electric current path	**CIRCUIT**	embark	**SAIL**
electrician	**WIRER**	embarrass	**ABASH**
electrified particle	**ION**	embarrassment	**SHAME**
electromotive unit	**VOLT**	embellish	**ADORN, DECORATE**
electronic beam	**LASER**	ember	**COAL**
electronic speed-check	**RADAR**	embezzle	**STEAL**
elegance	**GRACE, POLISH**	emblem	**BADGE, TOKEN**
elegance of manners		emblem of grief	**RUE**
	REFINEMENT	emblem of United States	**EAGLE**
elegant	**REFINED, POLISHED**	embody	**EMBRACE, COMPRISE**
elegant appetizer	**CAVIAR,**	embolden	**STIMULATE**
	PÂTÉ	embrace	**CLASP, HUG**
elegant attire	**ARRAY**	embroidery	**NEEDLEWORK**
element	**INGREDIENT, FACTOR**	embroidery silk	**FLOSS**
elementary	**PRIMARY**	embroil	**PERPLEX, TROUBLE**
elementary schoolbook	**PRIMER**	emcee Linkletter	**ART**
elephant call	**TRUMPET**	emcee Mack	**TED**
elephant cry	**BARR**	emcee Sullivan	**ED**
elephant dentin	**IVORY**	emend	**CORRECT**
elephant driver	**MAHOUT**	Emerald Isle	**EIRE, ERIN,**
elephant saddle	**HOWDAH**		**IRELAND**
elephant's ear	**TARO**	emerge from an egg	**HATCH**
elephant's tooth	**TUSK**	emergency	**CRISIS, NECESSITY**
elephant's tusk	**IVORY**	emergency sum (2 wds.)	
elevate	**EXALT, RAISE,**		**MAD MONEY**
	UPLIFT, REAR	emery	**CORUNDUM**
elevated railroad	**EL**	emigrant	**SETTLER**
elevation	**HILL**	emigrate	**MIGRATE, MOVE**

Emily Post behavior (2 wds.) **GOOD MANNERS**
eminent **ILLUSTRIOUS, PROMINENT**
emissary **AGENT**
emit **DISCHARGE, VENT**
emit rays of light **RADIATE**
emit vapor **REEK, STEAM**
emmet **ANT**
emote **OVERACT, ACT, HAM**
emotion **SENTIMENT, FEELING**
emotionally detached **CLINICAL**
emotional shock **TRAUMA**
empathy **COMPASSION**
emperor **RULER**
emphasis **STRESS, ACCENT**
emphasize **ACCENT, STRESS, UNDERSCORE, PLAY UP**
emphatic **STRONG, FORCEFUL**
emphatic request **DEMAND**
Empire State (2 wds.) **NEW YORK**
Empire State city **OLEAN, YONKERS, UTICA, ALBANY, TROY**
Empire State of the south **GEORGIA**
employ **HIRE, TAKE ON, USE, UTILIZE**
employee **HAND, HELP**
employee's hourly record **TIME CARD**
employer **BOSS**
employment **WORK**
emporium **STORE, MART**
empower **ENABLE, ENTITLE**
empty **BARE, VOID, BLANK, INANE, UNOCCUPIED**
empty bullet **SHELL**
empty place **SPACE, BLANK, SHELL, VACANT, VOID**
emulate **IMITATE**
emulation **RIVALRY, IMITATION**
emulsion **PAP**
enable **EMPOWER, PERMIT**
enact **DECREE**
enamel **GLAZE, PAINT**
enamor **CHARM**
enchant **CHARM, BEWITCH**
enchantment **SPELL**
enchantress **SIREN**
encina **OAK**
encircle **ENCLOSE, RING**
encircled **GIRT**
encircling strap **BELT, CINCTURE**
enclose **ENVELOP, FENCE**
enclosed automobile **SEDAN**

enclosed in this **HEREWITH**
enclose in paper **WRAP**
enclosure **CAGE, PEN**
enclosure for horses **CORRAL**
encomiast **EULOGIST**
encomium **PRAISE**
encompass **INCLUDE**
encore **AGAIN, BIS**
encounter **MEET, MEET WITH**
encourage **ABET, PROD, EGG ON**
encroach **TRESPASS**
encroach on **INVADE**
encrust **CAKE**
encumber **HINDER**
encumbrance **BURDEN**
encyclopedic **COMPREHENSIVE**
end **CONCLUDE, CONCLUSION, FINISH, TERMINATE, TERMINUS, OUTCOME, RESULT, AIM, GOAL, OMEGA, PURPOSE**
end (Lat.) **FINIS**
endanger **IMPERIL**
endearment **CARESS**
endeavor **ATTEMPT, STRIVE**
endemic **NATIVE**
endless **ETERNAL**
endocrine **GLAND, GLANDULAR**
end of a pencil **STUB, ERASER**
end of a spar **YARDARM**
endowment **GIFT, BEQUEST**
endurable **BEARABLE**
endurance **PATIENCE, TOLERANCE**
endure **LAST, BEAR, TOLERATE**
enemy **FOE**
energetic **VIGOROUS**
energize **ACTIVATE**
energy **VIM, VIGOR, PEP**
energy unit **ERG**
enervate **WEAKEN, SAP**
enfeeble **WEAKEN**
enfold **WRAP, ENVELOP**
enforce **EXECUTE**
enfranchise **FREE**
engage **HIRE, WIN**
engage, as gears **MESH**
engage in a contest **COMPETE**
engage in reverie **DREAM**
engage in small talk **CHAT, GAB, JAW**
engage in sport **PLAY**
engage in winter sport **SKI, SKATE**
engagement **TROTH, DATE, BETROTHAL**

engagement ring	SPARKLER	engrave	ETCH
engender	BREED	engraver's tool	BURIN
engine	MOTOR	engross	ABSORB
engineer	DESIGNER	engrossed	ENRAPT, RAPT
engineer's helper	OILER	engulf	DROWN, SWAMP
English actor	TREE, MILLS,	enigma	RIDDLE
	REDGRAVE	enjoin	ORDER, DIRECT
English admiral	NELSON	enjoy	LIKE
English air force	R.A.F.	enjoy a book	READ
English architect	WREN	enjoy a cigar	SMOKE
English architecture	TUDOR	enjoy a meal	DINE, EAT, SUP
English bard	SCOP	enjoyment	FUN, AMUSEMENT
English cathedral city	ELY,	enlarge	WIDEN, PROJECT
COVENTRY, ST. ALBANS		enlarge a hole	REAM
English city	BRISTOL,	enlighten	INFORM, TEACH
	LIVERPOOL	enlist	ENROLL
English coin	SHILLING, PENNY	enlisted man	GI
English coins	PENCE	enliven	ANIMATE
English college	OXFORD, ETON	enmity	MALICE
English composer	ARNOLD,	ennui	TEDIUM, BOREDOM
BLIS, BRITTEN, ELGAR,		enormity	VASTNESS
PURCELL		enormous	HUGE, VAST,
English conservative	TORY		LARGE, BIG
English count	EARL	enough	ADEQUATE, PLENTY
English county	SHIRE	enrage	ANGER, MADDEN
English derby town	EPSOM	enrapture	ENCHANT, CHARM
English dynasty	TUDOR,	enroll	ENTER, REGISTER
	STUART	en route (3 wds.)	ON THE WAY
English game	CRICKET	ensconce	CONCEAL, HIDE
English heather	LING	ensign (abbr.)	ENS.
English island	WIGHT	ensnare	ENTRAP, NET
English manufacturing city		ensue	FOLLOW
LEEDS, LIVERPOOL		entangle	SNARL
English nursemaid	NANNY	enter	BEGIN
English poet	MILTON, BYRON,	enter in writing	SET DOWN
SHELLEY, KEATS		enterprise	VENTURE
English policeman	BOBBY	entertain	AMUSE, TREAT,
English porcelain	SPODE		REGALE
English potter	SPODE	entertain at one's	
English prep school	ETON,	own expense	TREAT
	HARROW	entertainer	ACTOR, STAR
English princess	ANNE,	entertaining	AMUSING
	MARGARET	entertain lavishly	FETE,
English professor	DON		REGALE
English pudding	PUD	entertainment	FUN, PLEASURE
English racetrack	ASCOT		SHOW
English region (2 wds.)		entertainment group (abbr.)	
LAKE DISTRICT,			USO
HOME COUNTIES		enthrall	FASCINATE
English resort	BATH,	enthralled	RAPT
	BRIGHTON	enthusiasm	ELAN
English river	AVON, DEE,	enthusiast	FAN
HUMBER, THAMES		enthusiastic	AVID, EAGER
English rowboat	PUNT	enthusiastic applause	OVATION
English school	ETON, HARROW	enthusiastic review	RAVE
English statesman	PITT	entice	ALLURE, LURE, TEMPT
English streetcar	TRAM	enticement	TEMPTATION
English tavern	PUB, TAPROOM	enticing woman	SIREN

entire **ALL, TOTAL, WHOLE**
entirety (2 wds., sl.)
    WHOLE HOG
entire range **GAMUT**
entirely **ALL**
entity **BEING, UNITY**
entourage **TRAIN**
entrance **DOOR, ACCESS**
entrance fee **ADMISSION**
entrance hall **FOYER**
entrance to a garden **GATE**
entrance way **ENTRY**
entrancing **RAVISHING**
entrant **CONTESTANT, PARTICIPANT**
entrap **CATCH, ENSNARE**
entreat **BEG, BESEECH, PRAY, PLEAD**
entreaty **PLEA**
entrechat **LEAP**
entry **ENTRANCE, ACCESS**
entwine **ENLACE, LACE, TWIST**
enumerate **COUNT, LIST**
enunciate **UTTER, ARTICULATE**
enure **HARDEN**
envelop **ENCLOSE**
envelop in paper **WRAP**
envious **JEALOUS, COVETOUS**
environment **LOCALE, SURROUNDINGS**
envision **SEE**
envoy **MESSENGER**
envy **JEALOUSY**
enzyme (suffix) **ASE**
eoan **AURORAL**
eon **ETERNITY, ERA, AGE**
ephemeral **TRANSIENT, FLEETING**
epi **FINIAL**
epic **HEROIC**
epic poem **EPOS, EPODE, EPOPEE**
epic story **SAGA**
epicurean **SENSUAL**
epidemic **PLAGUE**
episode **SCENE**
epistle **LETTER, MISSIVE**
epithet **NAME, APPELATION**
epitome **SYNOPSIS, PRECIS**
epoch **ERA, AGE**
epoxy **ENAMEL, RESIN**
equable **EVEN, STEADY**
equal **EVEN, PEER**
equal (Fr.) **EGAL**
equality **PAR**
equality (Fr.) **EGALITE**
Equality State **WYOMING**

equalize (2 wds.) **LEVEL OFF**
equanimity **POISE**
equation **FORMULA**
equidistant lines **PARALLEL**
equilibrium **BALANCE**
equine **HORSE, ZEBRA, ASS**
equine father **SIRE**
equine gait **CANTER, TROT, GALLOP, LOPE**
equine mother **DAM**
equine sound **SNORT, WHINNY, NEIGH**
equine trappings **CAPARISON**
equinox **VERNAL, AUTUMNAL**
equip **RIG, FIT OUT, OUTFIT**
equipage (arch.) **CREW, RETINUE**
equipment **GEAR**
equitable **FAIR, IMPARTIAL**
equitably **FAIRLY**
equitation **DRESSAGE**
equity **FAIRNESS**
equivalent to **TANTAMOUNT**
equivocal **UNCERTAIN**
equivocate **LIE**
equivocation **EVASION**
equivoque **PUN**
era **AGE, EPOCH, EON**
eradicate (2 wds.) **ROOT OUT**
erase **DELE, EXPUNGE, RUB OUT**
Erato **MUSE**
ere **BEFORE, RATHER**
erect **BUILD, UPRIGHT**
ere long **ANON, SOON**
eremite **HERMIT, RECLUSE**
eremite's hut **CELL**
erenow **HERETOFORE**
ergo **THUS, HENCE**
ergot **FUNGUS**
Erin **IRELAND, EIRE**
Erinyes **FURIES**
Erle Stanley Gardner stories **MYSTERIES**
ermine **STOAT**
ern **OSPREY**
Ernest Borgnine role **MARTY**
erode **EAT, WEAR**
Eros **AMOR, CUPID**
erose **WORN, JAGGED**
erotic **SENSUAL**
err **MISDO, SIN**
errand **SHORE, MISSION, TASK**
errand boy **PAGE, MESSENGER**
errant **ITINERANT**
errantry **CHIVALRY**
erratic **ECCENTRIC**
erroneous **MISTAKEN**

error	BLUNDER, LAPSE, MISTAKE, SLIP, FALLACY	eternally	ALWAYS, EVER, E'ER, FOREVER
ersatz	SYNTHETIC, ARTIFICIAL, BUTTER, OLEO	eternity	EON
		ethanol	ALCOHOL
Erse	GAELIC	ether	ANAESTHETIC
erst	ONCE, FORMERLY	ether compound	ESTER
erudite	LEARNED, WISE	ethereal	AIRY
erupt	BURST, EJECT	ethereal being	SYLPH
Esau's brother	JACOB	ethereal salt	ESTER
Esau's country	EDOM	ethical	MORAL
Esau's wife	ADA, JUDITH, BASEMATH, MAHELETH	ethics	MORALS
		Ethopian lake	TANA
escape	ELUDE, EVADE, FLEE, LAM	Ethiopian native	GALLA
		Ethiopia's neighbor	ERITREA
escargot	SNAIL	Etruscan deity	LAR, LARES (PL.)
eschew	AVOID, SHUN	Eucharistic plate	PATEN
escort	CHAPERONE, USHER	eulogize	LAUD, GLORIFY
eskers	OSAR	eulogy	ELOGE
Eskimo	AMERIND, ALEUT	Euphrates tributary	TIGRIS
Eskimo boat	UMIAK, KAYAK, OOMIAK	European apple	SORB
		European beetle	DOR
Eskimo house	IGLOO, IGLU	European blackbird	MERL
Eskimo knife	ULU	European capital	BERN, BONN, OSLO, PARIS, ROME, MADRID
Eskimo vehicle	SLED		
espouse	EMBRACE, ADOPT	European dormouse	LEROT
esprit de corps	MORALE, SPIRIT, UNITY	European farmer	PEASANT
		European flatfish	TURBOT
espy	SEE	European gull	MEW
essay	TRY, ATTEMPT, THEME	European mountain district	TYROL
essay	THEME, TOPIC		
essence	PERFUME	European mountains	ALPS
essential	IMPERATIVE, NECESSARY	European river	ELBE, RUHR
		European sandpiper	TEREK
essential part	PITH, CORE, CRUX, GIST	European shad	ALOSE
		European shark	TOPE
establishment	SHOP	evade	CIRCUMVENT, ELUDE, AVOID, ESCAPE
establish the truth	PROVE		
estate	MANOR, PROPERTY	evade, as a question	PARRY
estate employee	GARDENER, GATEMAN	evade, as duty	SHIRK
		evaluate	RATE
esteem	RESPECT, REVERE	evanesce	DISAPPEAR, VANISH
esthetic judgment (2 wds.)	GOOD TASTE	evanescent	FLEETING
		evangelical	GOSPEL
estimable	WORTHY	Evangeline's home	ACADIA
estimate	ASSESS, GUESS, RATE	evaporate (2 wds.)	DRY UP
estimated worth	VALUE	even	LEVEL, FLAT
estimation	ESTEEM, REGARD	even (Lat.)	ENIM
estop	BAR, PROHIBIT	even (poet.)	E'EN
estrange	ALIENATE	even a little bit (2 wds.)	AT ALL
estuary	BAY, FIRTH	evening	TWILIGHT, DUSK
etape	STOREHOUSE	evening (Ger.)	ABEND
etch	ENGRAVE	evening (poet.)	EVE
etching fluid	ACID	evening cloak	WRAP
eternal	AGELESS, ENDLESS, PERPETUAL	evening dress	GOWN
		evening in Italy	SERA
Eternal City native	ROMAN	evening party	SOIREE

evening song	**SERENADE, VESPER**	examination	**TEST, FINAL, MIDTERM**
evening star	**VENUS, VESPER**	examine	**TEST**
even one	**ANY**	examine eggs under a light	
even score	**TIE**		**CANDLE**
event	**OCCURRENCE**	examine judicially	**TRY**
eventual	**ULTIMATE, FINAL**	examine minutely	**SIFT**
ever	**ALWAYS**	example	**MODEL, SAMPLE**
ever (poet.)	**E'ER**	exanimate	**DEAD, INERT**
Everglade	**SWAMP**	exasperate	**RILE**
evergreen shrub	**JUNIPER, MYRTLE**	exasperation	**ANNOYANCE**
		exclamation of pity	**ALAS**
Evergreen State	**WASHINGTON**	excavate	**DIG**
evergreen tree	**CEDAR, FIR, SPRUCE, YEW. PINE**	excavation	**PIT, HOLE, CAVITY**
		excavator	**SHOVEL**
everlasting	**ETERNAL**	exceed	**OUTDO, EXCEL**
evermore	**FOREVER, ALWAYS**	exceedingly	**VERY**
every	**ALL, ANY, EACH**	excel	**EXCEED OUTDO**
everyday	**COMMON, ORDINARY**	excellence	**VIRTUE**
everything	**ALL**	excellent	**FINE, SPLENDID**
everything counted		excelling others	**BEST**
(2 wds.)	**ALL TOLD**	except	**SAVE, BUT**
every 24 hours	**DAILY**	except for	**SAVE**
Eve's mate	**ADAM**	except that	**ONLY**
Eve's origin	**RIB**	exception	**DISSENT**
evict	**EJECT, OUST**	exceptional	**UNCOMMON, RARE**
evidence	**PROOF**	excerpt	**EXTRACT**
evident	**OBVIOUS**	excess	**OVERAGE**
evil	**BAD, BADNESS, SIN, MALEVOLENT, WICKED**	excessive	**EXORBITANT, UNDUE**
		excessive interest	**USURY**
evil deed	**SIN**	excessively	**UNDULY, TOO**
evil giant	**OGRE**	exchange	**SWAP, TRADE, BARTER**
evil grin	**LEER, SNEER**		
evil omen	**KNELL**	exchange discount	**AGIO**
evil one	**DEVIL, SATAN**	exchange for money	**SELL**
evil spirit	**DEMON**	exchange letters	**CORRESPOND**
evince	**SHOW, MANIFEST**	exchange place	**FAIR, MARKET, MART**
evocation	**INDUCTION**		
evoke	**SUMMON**	exchange premium	**AGIO**
evolution	**DEVELOPMENT**	exchequer	**TREASURY**
evolutionary	**GENETIC**	excise	**TAX, DUTY**
ewer	**PITCHER**	excite	**PROVOKE, WORK UP, ENTHUSE**
ewe's mate	**RAM**		
exacerbate	**IRRITATE**	excite the attention of	
exact	**PRECISE**		**INTEREST**
exacting	**STRENUOUS**	excite to action	**ROUSE**
exactitude	**PRECISION, ACCURACY**	excited	**AGOG**
		excitement	**ADO, STIR**
exact likeness	**COPY**	exciting	**HECTIC**
exactly (3 wds.)	**TO A T, TO A TEE**	exclaim	**CRY OUT**
		exclamation	**AHA, OHO**
exactness	**PRECISION**	exclamation of	
exact opposite	**ANTIPODE**	annoyance	**DRAT**
exact satisfaction	**AVENGE**	exclamation of	
exaggerate	**OVERDO, OVERSTATE**	approval	**BRAVO**
		exclamation of	
exalt	**ELATE, ELEVATE, HONOR**	disappointment	**AW**
exaltation of spirit	**ELATION**	exclamation of disbelief	**BAH**

exclamation of disgust	UGH, POOH
exclamation of doubt	HUMPH
exclamation of horror (2 wds.)	OH NO
exclamation of pity	ALAS
exclamation of sorrow	ALAS
exclamation of surprise	WOW, OH, HO
exclamation of triumph	AHA, AH
exclude	BAR, RULE OUT, DEBAR
exclusive	SELECT
exclusive news story	SCOOP
exclusive right	PATENT
excoriate	CHAFE, IRRITATE
excruciate	TORTURE
excruciating	PAINFUL
exculpate	ACQUIT
excursion	JUNKET, TRIP, TREK, TOUR
excuse	ALIBI, PLEA
execrate	ABHOR, CURSE, CONDEMN
execute	EFFECT, PERFORM
executive ability	LEADERSHIP
executive's bag	BRIEFCASE
executor's responsibility	ESTATE
exemplar	MODEL
exemplify	ILLUSTRATE
exempt	FREE, CLEAR
exercise	ACTIVITY
exercising device (2 wds.)	LONG HORSE
exertion	DINT
exhale	RESPIRE, EMIT
exhaust	DEPLETE, FAG, SPEND, BUSH, WEAR OUT
exhausted	TIRED, SPENT
exhaustion	FATIGUE
exhibit	DISPLAY
exhibition at its best	SHOWCASE
exhilarate	ELATE
exhort	URGE
exhortation	PLEA, SERMON
exhume	DISCLOSE, REVEAL
exigency	EMERGENCY, NEED
exigent	URGENT
exile	DEPORT
exist	AM, ARE, IS, BE, LIVE
existed	BEEN, WAS, WERE
existence	BEING, LIFE
existence (Lat.)	ESSE
existent	ALIVE
exit	EGRESS
exodus	HEGIRA
exonerate	CLEAR
exorbitant	EXCESSIVE
exorbitant interest rate	USURY
exotic	ALIEN, STRANGE
expand	DEVELOP, DILATE, ENLARGE
expanse	REACH, SPREAD
expansion	INCREASE, GROWTH
expansive	BROAD, WIDE
expatriate	EXILE, BANISH
expect	AWAIT
expectation	HOPE
expedient	POLITIC, WISE
expedite	HASTEN
expedition	EXCURSION, JOURNEY
expel	OUST, EVICT, EJECT
expend	DISBURSE, CONSUME
expenditure	OUTLAY
expense	COST
expensive	DEAR, COSTLY
expensive fur	MINK, SABLE, ERMINE
experience anew	REENACT
experiment	TEST
expert	PRO, ADEPT, SKILLED, ACE
expert bridge player	MASTER
expert flyer	ACE
expert golfer	ACE, PRO
expertise	SKILL
expiate	ATONE
expire	DIE, RUN OUT, LAPSE
explain	INTERPRET, DEFINE
explain a word	DEFINE
explanation	DESCRIPTION
expletive	GOSH, GEE
explicit	CLEAR
explode	BURST, POP, DETONATE, ERUPT
explode in muffler	BACKFIRE
exploit	FEAT, USE, DEED
explore	EXAMINE, SEARCH
explorer	PIONEER
explosion	BLAST
explosive	TNT, NITRO
explosive device	BOMB, GRENADE, MINE
explosive noise	POP
expose	BARE
exposed	BARED, BARE, OPEN, FRANK
expose to view	OPEN
expound	ORATE
express	DECLARE, TELL
express a choice for	PREFER

express an idea **OPINE**
express disapproval **ADMONISH**
express discontent **COMPLAIN**
express disdain **SNIFF**
express gratitude **THANK**
express impatience **TUT**
expressing love **ROMANTIC**
express in words **PHRASE, SAY, STATE**
expression of contempt **BOO**
expression of good will **VIVA**
express merriment **LAUGH**
express road **FREEWAY**
express scorn **SNEER**
express sorrow **LAMENT**
express sympathy **CONDOLE, CONSOLE**
expunge **ERASE, DELE, DELETE**
exquisite **PERFECT**
extant **BEING, EXISTENT**
extemporaneous **IMPROMPTU**
extempore (comp. wd.) **AD-LIB**
extend **OFFER, REACH**
extend across **SPAN**
extend a loan **LEND**
extend a subscription **RENEW**
extend over **COVER**
extend to **REACH**
extend upward **RISE**
extensive **LONG, VAST**
extensive plain **PRAIRIE**
extent **RANGE, SCOPE, LENGTH**
extent of influence **SCOPE**
exterior **OUTER**
exterminate **ANNIHILATE, DESTROY**
external **OUTER**
extinct **DEAD**
extinct bird **DODO, MOA**
extinct wild ox **URUS, AUROCHS**
extinguish **DOUSE, QUELL**
extol **PRAISE**
extract **EDUCE**
extraction **ORIGIN, STOCK**
extraneous **EXTERNAL, FOREIGN**
extraordinary **RARE, SINGULAR**
extra pay **BONUS**
extrasensory perception (abbr.) **ESP**
extra small pup **RUNT**
extra supplies **RESERVES**
extra tire **SPARE**
extravagance **WASTE**
extravagant **FANCY**
extreme **DIRE, RADICAL, DRASTIC**
extreme alarm **PANIC**

extreme anger **RAGE**
extreme conservative **DIEHARD**
extreme fear **HORROR, TERROR, PANIC**
extreme fondness **LOVE**
extremely **AWFULLY, VERY**
extremely poor **DESTITUTE**
extremely violent argument (comp. wd.) **KNOCK-DOWN-AND-DRAG-OUT**
extremist **RADICAL**
extremity **END, TOE, FINGER**
extricate **DISENTANGLE**
exuberant **PROLIFIC**
exudation **SECRETION**
exude **EMIT, SPEW, SEEP, OOZE**
exult **ELATE**
exultant **JUBILANT**
exultation **GLEE, JOY**
exult maliciously **GLOAT**
exuviate **MOLT**
eye **ESPY, OBSERVE, SCRUTINIZE, WATCH**
eye amorously **OGLE, LEER**
eye boldly **STARE**
eye disease **GLAUCOMA, TRACHOMA**
eye drop **TEAR**
eyeglass **LENS, MONOCLE**
eyelashes **CILIA**
eye make-up **MASCARA**
eye membrane **RETINA**
eyes (slang) **GLIMS**
eyesight **VISION**
eyetooth **CANINE**
eyre **COURT, TOUR, CIRCUIT**

F

fable **PARABLE, MYTH**
fabled bird **ROC**
fabled marine creature **MERMAID**
fabled one-horned animal **UNICORN**
fabliau **TALE, STORY**
fabric **TEXTILE, MATERIAL, CLOTH**
fabricate **MAKE**
fabrication **LIE, FIB**
fabric glaze **CIRE**
fabric junction **SEAM**
fabric woven from flax **LINEN**
fabulist **AESOP**
fabulous **WONDERFUL**
fabulous beast **DRAGON**

fabulous bird	ROC
fabulous one-horned animal	UNICORN
facade	FACE, FRONT
face	VISAGE
face covering	VEIL, MASK
face part	CHIN, NOSE, LIP, MOUTH, CHEEK, EYE
face with stone	REVET
facet	SIDE, ASPECT, PHASE
facetious	SARCASTIC, WITTY
facile	EASY
facilitate	AID, ASSIST
facility	EASE, FLUENCY
facing	TOWARD
facsimile	LIKENESS
fact	DATUM
faction	SIDE
factitious	ARTIFICIAL, SHAM
factor	AGENT, ELEMENT
factory	MILL, PLANT
factory fuel	COAL
factory superintendent	FOREMAN
factotum	HANDYMAN
facts and figures	DATA
factual	TRUE
faculty	ABILITY
fad	RAGE, CRAZE, MANIA
fade	PALE, DIM
fade away	EVANESCE
faded star (comp. wd.)	HAS-BEEN
Faerie Queene	UNA
fail	MISS, FLUNK
fail in duty	LAPSE
failing	FAULT
fail to follow suit	RENEGE
fail to hit	MISS
fail to mention	OMIT
fail to win	LOSE
failure	FLOP, DUD
failure at Cape Kennedy (2 wds.)	NO GO
faint	FEEBLE
fair	JUST
fair grade	CEE
fairly	SOMEWHAT
fair to middling	PASSABLE
fairy	ELF, SPRITE
fairy stick	WAND
fairy tale creature	ELF, GNOME, OGRE, TROLL
faith	CONVICTION, TRUST
faithful	TRUE, LOYAL
faithful counselor	MENTOR
faith healer Roberts	ORAL
faithless	FALSE

fake	COUNTERFEIT, PHONY, FRAUD, SHAM, PRETEND, ERSATZ, FORGERY
fake coin	SLUG
fake jewelry	PASTE
fakir	YOGI, DERVISH
Falasha	HAMITE
falchion	SWORD
falcon	KESTREL
falderal	NONSENSE
fall	AUTUMN
fallacious	CRAFTY, DECEITFUL
fallacy	ERROR
fall back	RECEDE, RETREAT
fall back into former state	RELAPSE
fall back on	RELY, DEPEND
fall behind	LAG
fall flower	ASTER, MUM
fall guy	PATSY, CHUMP, MARK
fallible	HUMAN
fall in	MEET, COLLAPSE
fall in drops	DRIP
fall in flakes	SNOW
falling sickness	EPILEPSY
fall month	SEPTEMBER, OCTOBER
fall noisily	CRASH
fall off	DECLINE
fall of rain	SHOWER
fall out	DISAGREE, QUARREL
fall over	TOPPLE
fallow	IDLE, INACTIVE
fall short	FAIL
fall suddenly	DROP, SLUMP, COLLAPSE
fall to	BEGIN, START
fall upon	ASSAIL, ATTACK
false	RECREANT, UNFAITHFUL, UNTRUE
false appearance	GUISE
false belief	DELUSION
false claim	PRETENSE
false coin	SLUG
false face	MASK
false front	POSE
false god	IDOL
false hairpiece	WIG, PERUKE, FALL, TOUPEE
falsehood	LIE, FIB
false jewelry	PASTE
false name	ALIAS
false report	CANARD, RUMOR
false show	TINSEL
false signature	FORGERY
false step	SLIP
false teeth	DENTURE
falsify	FORGE, LIE

falter	**HESITATE, STUMBLE**
faltering speech	**STUTTER**
fame	**HONOR, RENOWN, NAME,**
	REPUTE
familiar	**INTIMATE**
familiar emblem	**EAGLE**
familiarity	**FRIENDSHIP**
familiar with	**CONVERSANT**
family	**HOUSE, CLAN**
family car	**AUTO, SEDAN,**
	COUPE, STATION WAGON
family group	**CLAN**
family imp	**BRAT**
family man	**FATHER**
family member	**MAMA, PAPA,**
	MOM, DAD, SISTER,
	BROTHER, JUNIOR, SIS
family name	**SURNAME**
family of kings	**DYNASTY**
family of medieval	
Ferrara	**ESTE**
famine	**HUNGER, SHORTAGE**
famish	**STARVE**
famous	**EMINENT, KNOWN**
famous uncle	**SAM**
fan	**ENTHUSIAST, SUPPORTER**
fanatic	**CRANK, ZEALOT**
fanatical	**RABID**
fanatic devotion	**CULT**
fanciful	**WHIMSICAL**
fanciful reverie	**DAYDREAM**
fancy	**ELABORATE**
fancy dive	**GAINER**
fancy fabric	**LACE**
fancy trappings	**REGALIA,**
	FINERY
fancy vase	**URN**
fane	**BANNER, PENNANT**
Fanny Farmer specialty	**RECIPE**
fantastic	**BIZARRE**
fantastic trick	**ANTIC**
fantasy	**DREAM**
far	**DISTANT, REMOTE**
far (prefix)	**TEL(E)**
farce	**COMEDY**
farcical	**ABSURD**
far down	**DEEP**
fare	**DIET, PASSAGE, GO**
Far East	**ORIENT**
farer	**TRAVELER**
farewell	**ADIEU**
farewell (Sp.)	**ADIOS**
farewell party (comp. wd.)	
	SEND-OFF
farewell to the Islands	**ALOHA**

farm animal	**CALF, SOW, COW,**
	BULL, STEER, HORSE,
	SHEEP, MARE, EWE,
	RAM, GOAT
farm animals	**LIVESTOCK,**
	CATTLE
farm building	**BARN, SILO**
farm implement	**REAPER,**
	GIN, TRACTOR, PLOW
farming	**AGRICULTURE**
farm laborer	**HAND**
farm measure	**ACRE**
farm out	**HIRE, LET**
farm product	**CROP**
farm tenant	**COTTER, COTTIER**
farmyard sound	**MOO, BAA,**
	BLEAT, OINK, CLUCK,
	WHINNY
far-off	**DISTANT**
far-reaching	**VAST**
farrow	**PIG**
far-sighted	**SHREWD**
fascinate	**CHARM**
fashion	**CRAZE, FAD, MODE,**
	STYLE, MODEL, FORM,
	MANNER, ASPECT, SORT,
	VOGUE
fashionable	**CHIC**
fashionable resort	**SPA**
fashionable section	
of Boston	**BACK BAY**
fashionably elegant	**SWANK**
fashion name	**DIOR, CHANEL,**
	PARNIS, BROOKS,
	CARDIN, PUCCI,
	VALENTINO, GRES
fast	**FLEET, RAPID, QUICK**
	SPEEDY
fast car	**RACER**
fast driver	
(2 wds.)	**SPEED DEMON**
fasten	**GLUE, NAIL, RIVET, TIE,**
	LACE, CLASP, CLIP, PIN,
	SNAP, LATCH
fastener	**CLASP, PIN**
fasten firmly	**ANCHOR, BIND,**
	NAIL
fastens	**CLASPS**
fasten shut	**BAR**
fasten with stitches	**SEW**
fasten with string	**TIE**
fastidious	**NEAT, DAINTY**
fastidious man	**DUDE, FOP**
fasting period	**LENT**
fast plane	**JET**
fat	**CORPULENT, OBESE,**
	PLUMP, LARD, GREASE,
	STOUT, ROTUND, CHUBBY

fatal	**LETHAL**	fear	**DREAD, TERROR, FRIGHT,**
fatality	**DEATH**		**ALARM**
fata morgana	**MIRAGE**	fearful	**ANXIOUS, AWFUL,**
fate	**DESTINY, DOOM, KARMA,**		**DREADFUL**
	KISMET	fearless	**BOLD, BRAVE**
fateful time for Caesar	**IDES**	fearsome	**AWFUL, AWESOME,**
Fates	**PARCAE, ATROPOS,**		**TIMID**
	CLOTHO, LACHESIS	feasible	**POSSIBLE**
father	**DAD, SIRE, POP, DADDY,**	Feast of Booths	**SUCCOTH,**
	POPPA, PAPA, PA, PAW		**SUKKOTH**
father (Fr.)	**PERE**	Feast of Lights	**CHANUKAH**
father (Lat.)	**PATER**	Feast of Lots	**PURIM**
father (poetic)	**SIRE**	Feast of Nativity	**CHRISTMAS**
father (Sp.)	**PADRE**	Feast of Weeks	**SHAVUOT,**
fatherhood	**PATERNITY**		**SHABUOTH**
father of Enos	**SETH**	feat	**ACHIEVEMENT, DEED**
father of Horus	**OSIRIS**	feather	**PLUME**
father of Zeus	**KRONOS,**	feather barb	**PINNULA**
	CRONUS, CRONOS	feathered friend	**BIRD**
father or mother	**PARENT**	feathers	**PLUMAGE, DOWN**
father's wife	**MOTHER**	feather scarf	**BOA**
fathom	**DELVE**	feature	**QUALITY, MOTIF**
fatigue	**TIRE, WEARY,**	febrile	**FEVERISH**
	WEARINESS	fecund	**FERTILE**
Fatima's husband	**ALI,**	federal	**NATIONAL**
	BLUEBEARD	federate	**UNITE**
fat lot	**LITTLE, NOTHING**	federation	**ALLIANCE**
fat of swine	**LARD**	fedora	**HAT**
fat of the land	**LUXURY**	fee	**CHARGE**
fattened, as cattle (comp. wd.)		feeble	**WEAK, PUNY**
	CORN-FED	feeble-minded person	**MORON,**
fatty	**ADIPOSE**		**DOLT, IDIOT,**
fatuity	**STUPIDITY**		**IMBECILE**
fatuous	**FOOLISH**	feed	**NOURISH**
faubourg	**SUBURB, QUARTER,**	feed the kitty	**ANTE**
	SECTION	feed to fill	**SATE**
faucet	**SPIGOT, TAP**	feel	**TOUCH, SENSE**
fault	**FLAW, FAILING**	feel affection for	**LIKE**
faultfinder	**CARPER**	feel contrite	**REPENT**
faultfinding	**CENSORIAL**	feeler	**TENTACLE, ANTENNA,**
faultless	**PERFECT, PURE**		**BARBEL**
faulty	**AMISS**	feel indignation	**RESENT**
faun	**SATYR**	feel indisposed	**AIL, SICK**
faux pas	**ERROR**	feeling	**SENSATION, EMOTION**
favor	**RESPECT, INDULGENCE,**	feeling deeply	**INTENSE**
	PARTIALITY	feeling of resentment	**PEEVE**
favorable	**HELPFUL**	feeling of weariness	**ENNUI**
favorable to progress	**LIBERAL**	feel in the dark	**GROPE**
favoring	**FOR, PRO**	feel intuitively	**SENSE**
favoring neither	**NEUTRAL**	feel melancholy	**GRIEVE**
favorite	**PET**	feel one's way	**GROPE**
favoritism	**BIAS, PREJUDICE**	feel regret	**REPENT, RUE**
fawn	**DEER**	feel sorrow	**MOURN**
fawning	**SERVILE, OBSEQUIOUS**	feign	**SHAM, PRETEND,**
fay	**FAIRY**		**PUT ON, ACT**
faze	**DISTURB, DISCONCERT**	feign illness	**MALINGER**
feal	**LOYAL, FAITHFUL**	feint	**SHAM**
fealty	**LOYALTY, HOMAGE**	feisty	**AGGRESSIVE**

felicitate	**CONGRATULATE, GREET**
felicity	**BLISS, RAPTURE**
feline	**CAT**
feline sound	**MEW, MIAO, MEOW**
feline treat	**CATNIP**
fell	**CUT, BEAT**
fellow	**CHAP**
fellowship	**COMPANY, BROTHERHOOD**
felon	**CRIMINAL**
felonious	**MALICIOUS**
felony	**CRIME**
female	**WOMAN, GIRL**
female antelope	**DOE**
female bird	**HEN**
female child	**GIRL**
female colt	**FILLY**
female deer	**DOE**
female deity	**GODDESS**
female domestic	**MAID**
female elephant	**COW**
female goat	**NANNY**
female hog	**SOW**
female horse	**MARE**
female host	**HOSTESS**
female knight	**DAME**
female monster	**GORGON, MEDUSA, STHENO, EURYALE**
female ovine	**EWE**
female parent	**MOTHER**
female pig	**SOW**
female relative	**AUNT, MOTHER, DAUGHTER, SISTER, GRANDMA**
female religious (abbr.)	**SR.**
female ruff	**REEVE, REE**
female sailor	**WAVE**
female saint (abbr.)	**STE.**
female sandpiper	**REEVE, REE**
female servant	**MAID**
female sheep	**EWE**
female sibling	**SISTER**
female's mate	**MALE, HUSBAND**
female soldier	**WAC**
female sovereign	**PRINCESS, QUEEN**
female spirit	**BANSHEE, BANSHIE**
female student	**COED**
female swimmer	**MERMAID**
female voice	**ALTO, SOPRANO**
female warrior	**AMAZON**
feminine	**FEMALE, WOMANLY**
feminine (suffix)	**ETTE**
feminine garment	**SKIP, SKIRT, DRESS, BRA**
feminine title	**MADAM, MISS, MAM**
femininity	**WOMEN**
femme fatale	**SIREN**
femur	**THIGH**
fen	**MARSH, SWAMP, BOG**
fence	**WALL, HEDGE, RAIL**
fence opening	**GATE, TURNSTILE**
fence post	**STAKE**
fencer	**DUELIST**
fence stake	**POST**
fence step	**STILE**
fence straddler's domain (4 wds.)	**MIDDLE OF THE ROAD**
fence timber	**RAIL**
fencing hit	**PUNTO, TOUCHE**
fencing position	**CARTE**
fencing sword	**EPEE, FOIL, SABER**
fend	**PARRY, RESIST**
fender	**BUMPER**
fender mishap	**DENT**
fennel genus	**NIGELLA**
fenstra	**OPENING**
fen water	**MIRE**
feral	**WILD, SAVAGE**
fermented drink	**ALE, CIDER, WINE, BEER**
fermenting vat	**GYLE**
fern genus	**ANEMIA**
fern leaf	**FROND**
ferocious	**FIERCE, VIOLENT**
ferret	**WEASEL**
ferrous metal	**IRON**
ferry	**CARRY. TRANSPORT**
fertile	**FRUITFUL, FECUND**
fertile spot in a desert	**OASIS**
fertilizer	**MARL**
fervent	**ARDENT**
fervent appeal	**PLEA**
fervor	**ARDOR, ZEAL**
festival	**FETE, GALA, FAIR, FIESTA**
festival of Passover	**SEDER**
festive	**GALA**
festivity	**MIRTH, REVEL**
feta	**CHEESE**
fetch	**BRING**
fete	**GALA**
fetid	**RANK**
fetish	**TOTEM, IDOL**
fetter	**MANACLE, CHAIN**
fettel	**CONDITION**
feud	**DISPUTE, VENDETTA**
feudal castle	**MANOR**

feudal chief	**LORD, OVERLORD, BARON**
feudal estate	**FIEF**
feudal slave	**SERF, ESNE**
feudal tenant	**VASSAL**
fever	**HEAT, FIRE**
feverish	**FEBRILE, EXCITED**
fewer	**LESS**
fewest	**LEAST**
fey	**ODD**
fez ornament	**TASSEL**
fiance	**BETROTHED, INTENDED**
fiasco	**FAILURE**
fiat	**DECREE, EDICT**
fib	**LIE**
fiber	**STAPLE, SISAL, KAPOK**
fiber cluster	**NEP**
fiber plant	**FLAX, HEMP, SISAL**
fibril	**HAIR**
fibula	**BUCKLE, CLASP**
fickle	**UNSTABLE, FAITHLESS**
fiction	**NOVEL**
fictional story	**TALE, YARN, NOVEL, FABLE, ROMANCE**
fictitious	**FALSE**
fictitious name	**ALIAS**
fiddling emperor	**NERO**
fidelity	**DEVOTION, LOYALTY**
Fidel's capital	**HAVANA**
fidget	**FUSS, FRET**
fidgety	**NERVOUS, RESTIVE**
Fido	**DOG**
Fido's offspring	**PUPPY, PUP**
Fido's treasure	**BONE**
fiduciary	**TRUSTEE**
fief	**FEE**
field	**LOT, CLEARING, AREA**
field edge	**RAND**
field flower	**DAISY**
field mouse	**VOLE**
field of action	**ARENA**
field of granular snow	**NEVE, FIRN**
fiend	**DEMON, DEVIL**
fiendish	**MALICIOUS**
fierce	**VIOLENT, FIERY**
fiery	**ARDENT, FIERCE, HOT**
fiery jewel	**OPAL**
fiesta	**FESTIVAL, HOLIDAY**
fifteenth century royal family	**PLANTAGENET, YORK, TUDOR, LANCASTER**
fifth tire	**SPARE**
fifth zodiac sign	**LEO**
fiftieth state	**HAWAII**
fifty percent	**HALF**

fight	**STRUGGLE, BATTLE, WAR, QUARREL**
fight against	**RESIST**
fighter pilot	**ACE**
fighter's exercise	**LEG WORK**
fighting equipment	**ARMS**
figure	**NUMBER, SHAPE**
figure applied to fabric	**APPLIQUE**
figure in a Millet painting	**GLEANER**
figure on a card	**SPADE, HEART, CLUB, DIAMOND**
filament	**THREAD**
filament for cloth	**FIBER**
filch	**PILFER, STEAL**
file	**RASP**
fill	**GLUT, SATE**
fill again	**REPLENISH**
fill a gun	**LOAD**
fill a suitcase	**PACK**
filled with interstices	**AREOLAR**
fill with ambition	**INSPIRE**
fill with determination	**STEEL**
fill with ennui	**BORE**
fill with joy	**ELATE**
fill with love	**ENAMOR**
fill with pride	**ELATE**
filly	**MARE**
film	**MOVIE, CINEMA**
film spool	**REEL**
filmy	**SHEER**
filter	**STRAIN**
filth	**DIRT**
filthy	**CRUDDY, DIRTY, SOILED**
filthy hut	**STY**
finagle	**SCHEME, CONTRIVE**
final	**LAST, ULTIMATE**
finale	**FINISH, CODA**
finalize	**COMPLETE**
finally (2 wds.)	**AT LAST**
finally and decisively (4 wds.)	**ONCE AND FOR ALL**
final opportunity (2 wds.)	**LAST CHANCE**
final performer (2 wds.)	**ANCHOR MAN**
financial	**FISCAL, PECUNIARY**
financial center in N.Y. (2 wds.)	**WALL STREET**
financially solvent (3 wds.)	**IN THE BLACK**
financial sponsor	**PATRON**
find	**DISCOVER, LOCATE**
find a sum	**ADD**
find direction	**ORIENT**
find fault	**NAG, CARP, CAVIL**

find guilty	**CONVICT**
finding	**CONCLUSION, SOLUTION**
find of treasure	**TROVE**
find out	**DISCOVER, DETECT**
find position of	**LOCATE**
find the answer	**SOLVE**
fine	**EXCELLENT, PENALTY, TARIFF**
fine bits of thread	**LINT**
fine cord	**THREAD**
fine cotton fabric	**BATISTE**
fine English china	**SPODE**
fine jet of water	**SPRAY**
fine line, in printing	**SERIF**
fine linen	**CAMBRIC**
finely	**NICELY**
fine porcelain	**SPODE, LIMOGES**
fine rock debris	**SAND**
finery	**GAUD, LUXURY**
fine sensitiveness	**DELICACY**
fine soil	**SILT**
finesse	**CUNNING, SUBTLETY**
finest	**BEST**
fine suiting	**TWEED, SERGE**
fine whetstone	**HONE**
finger	**DIGIT**
finger jewelry	**RING**
fingernail moon	**LUNULE**
fingerprint mark	**LOOP, WHORL**
finial	**EPI**
finis	**END**
finish	**END, CONCLUDE, TERMINATE, COMPLETE**
finished	**OVER, DONE**
finished garment edge	**HEM**
finish line	**TAPE**
finite	**LIMITED**
Finland	**SUOMI**
Finnish city	**HELSINKI, ABO**
Finnish lake	**ENARE**
Finnish steam bath	**SAUNA**
fiord	**INLET**
fire	**FLAME, BLAZE**
fire a gun	**SHOOT**
firearm	**GUN, RIFLE**
firebug's crime	**ARSON**
firecracker	**PETARD**
firedog	**ANDIRON**
fire god	**VULCAN, YAMA**
fireman	**STOKER**
fire opal	**GIRASOL**
fireplace	**GRATE, HEARTH**
fireplace facing	**MANTEL**
fireplace fuel	**LOGS, COAL, PEAT**
fireplace shelf	**HOB, MANTLE**
fireplug	**HYDRANT**

fire residue	**ASH, ASHES**
fire-stirring rod	**POKER**
firewater	**WHISKEY, LIQUOR**
fire whistle	**SIREN**
firewood	**FUEL**
fireworks	**ROCKETS, SPARKLERS**
firm	**HARD, SOLID, STRICT, STERN**
firmament	**SKY, HEAVEN**
firm grasp	**GRIP**
firmly established	**DEEP-SET**
firn	**NEVE**
first	**PRIMAL, LEADING**
first appearance	**DEBUT**
first beginning	**ORIGIN**
first class	**PRIME**
first day	**SUNDAY**
first drawing	**DRAFT**
first garden	**EDEN**
first Hebrew letter	**ALEPH, ALEF**
first king of Israel	**SAUL**
first king of Rome	**ROMULUS**
first man	**ADAM**
first performance	**DEBUT, PREMIERE**
first person	**I, ME**
first principle	**ELEMENT**
first-rate	**SUPER, A ONE, TOP NOTCH**
first reader	**PRIMER**
first-row position (2 wds.)	**IN FRONT, UP FRONT**
first state	**DELAWARE**
first water	**BEST, PUREST**
first woman	**EVE**
first word of Caesar's boast	**VENI**
first word on the wall	**MENE**
first zodiac sign	**ARIES**
firth	**ESTUARY**
fisc	**TREASURY, EXCHEQUER**
fiscal	**FINANCIAL**
fiscal department	**TREASURY**
fiscal officer	**TREASURER, CONTROLLER**
fish	**ANGLE, DACE, IDE, TUNA, GAR, CARP, SHAD, SOLE, PIKE, PORGY, RAY, SHARK, SKATE**
fish appendage	**FIN**
fish bait	**WORM**
fish basket	**CREEL**
fish bowl	**AQUARIUM**
fish-catching fence	**WEIR**
fish-eating diving bird	**LOON**

fish-eating mammal	**OTTER, WHALE, DOLPHIN, SEAL, PORPOISE**
fish eggs	**ROE**
fisherman's boot	**WADER**
fisherman's snare	**NET**
fish fin (Sp.)	**ALETA**
fish from moving boat	**TROLL**
fish gig	**SPEAR**
fish hawk	**OSPREY**
fishhook leader	**SNELL**
fishhook part	**BARB**
fishing appurtenance	**CORK, FLOAT**
fishing cork	**FLOAT**
fishing duck	**MERGANSER, SHELDRAKE**
fishing eagle	**OSPREY**
fishing float	**BOBBER**
fishing fly	**LURE**
fishing gear	**TACKLE**
fishing lure	**BAIT**
fishing net	**SEINE, TRAWL**
fishing pole	**ROD**
fishing rod	**POLE**
fishing snare	**NET**
fishing vessel	**SMACK, BOAT, TRAWLER**
fish limb	**FIN**
fish lung	**GILL**
fish lure	**BAIT**
fish nostril	**GILL**
fish of the carp family	**DACE**
fishpound	**WEIR**
fish roe	**CAVIAR, EGGS**
fish sauce	**ALEC**
fish spear	**GIG**
fish through ice	**CHUG**
fish trap	**EELPOT, WEIR**
fish with a moving line	**TROLL**
fishy	**SUSPECT**
fissile rock	**SHALE**
fission	**DIVISION**
fissure	**CLEFT**
fisticuffs	**BOXING**
fistula	**CAVITY**
fit	**SUITABLE, PROPER**
fit for farming	**ARABLE**
fitful	**RESTLESS**
fitness	**DECORUM**
fit of anger	**HUFF, RAGE**
fit of petulance	**RAGE, TANTRUM**
fit of resentment	**PIQUE**
fit of temper	**TANTRUM**
fit out	**EQUIP**
fit together closely	**DOVETAIL**
fit to one's use	**ADAPT**

fix	**REPAIR**
fix definitely	**SETTLE**
fixed	**SET**
fixed charge	**FEE, RATE**
fixed in position	**STABILE**
fixed pay	**STIPEND, SALARY**
fixed period of time	**TERM**
fixed prices	**RATES**
fixed residence	**HOME**
fixed routine	**ROTE**
fixed star	**VEGA**
fixed time period	**TERM**
fix up	**MEND**
fizz	**HISS, BUBBLE**
flabby	**WEAK, LIMP**
flaccid	**LIMP**
flag	**BANNER, IRIS, CATTAIL**
flag flower	**IRIS**
flagon	**FLASK, BOTTLE**
flagrant	**GLARING**
flagstone	**SLAB**
flail	**BEAT, FLOG**
flair	**KNACK, TALENT**
flair for gardening (2 wds.)	**GREEN THUMB**
flaky storm	**SNOW**
flam	**CHEAT, TRICK**
flamboyant	**ORNATE, GARISH**
flame	**BLAZE, FIRE**
flaming	**ARDENT**
flaming light	**TORCH**
flame-loving insect	**MOTH**
Flanders treaty city	**GHENT**
flank	**SIDE**
flare	**FLAME, FLICKER**
flash	**FLARE, BLAZE**
flash lamp	**STROBE**
flashlight (Brit.)	**TORCH**
flash of lightning	**BOLT**
flash out	**GLINT**
flashy	**GAUDY, GARISH**
flask	**AMPULE, CANTEEN**
flat	**LEVEL, EVEN, SMOOTH, TENEMENT, APARTMENT**
flat and even	**LEVEL**
flatbed	**TRUCK**
flat-bottomed boat	**BARGE, DORY, PUNT, SCOW**
flat cap	**BERET**
flat circular plate	**DISK**
flat disc-like sea urchin (2 wds.)	**SAND DOLLAR**
flatfish	**SOLE**
flat fold in cloth	**PLEAT**
flatfoot	**COP, DETECTIVE**
flat hat	**CAP**
flatland form	**MESA**
flat shallow container	**TRAY**

flat surface **PLANE**
flat tableland **MESA**
flatten **DEPRESS, EVEN**
flatter **COMPLIMENT, PRAISE**
flattery (2 wds.) **SWEET TALK**
flaunt **BRANDISH**
flavor **SAPOR, TASTE, SEASON**
flavoring plant **ANISE**
flavorsome **TASTY**
flaw **DEFECT**
flawless **PERFECT**
flaxen **WHITE, TOW**
flax fabric **LINEN**
flaxseed **LINSEED**
flay **REPROVE**
fled **RAN**
flee **LAM, RUN, SPLIT, ESCAPE**
fleecy white clouds **CIRRI**
flee in panic, as cattle
STAMPEDE
fleet **FAST**
fleet of ships **NAVY, ARMADA**
Flemish **DUTCH**
flesh **MEAT**
flesh and blood **MORTAL**
fleshy **BEEFY, PLUMP**
fleshy berry **PEPO**
fleshy fruit **PEAR, APPLE, PEACH**
fleur de lis **LILY, IRIS**
flex **BEND, CONTRACT**
flexible **LIMP, PLIABLE**
flexible tube **HOSE**
flexor **MUSCLE**
flick **MOVIE**
flicker **WAVER**
Flickertail State
NORTH DAKOTA
flier **AVIATOR, PILOT**
flight **FLYING, HOP**
flightless bird **EMU, MOA, RATITE**
flight of steps **STAIRS**
flighty person **RATTLEBRAIN**
flimflam **NONSENSE, SWINDLE**
flimsy **THIN, TRANSPARENT**
flinch **WINCE**
fling **TOSS, CAST, THROW**
flint **FIRESTONE, CHERT**
flip **TOSS**
flippant **GLIB**
flipper **FIN**
flippered animal **SEAL**
flirt **OGLE**
flit **DART**
float **RAFT, WAFT**
floating home **HOUSEBOAT**

floating ice mass **BERG, FLOE, ICEBERG**
float in the air **SOAR, LEVITATE**
float of logs **RAFT**
float on water **BOB**
float upward **RISE, SURFACE**
flock **BEVY, HERD**
flock member **EWE, RAM, LAMB**
flock of herons **SEDGE**
flock tender **SHEPHERD**
floe **BERG**
flog **LASH**
flood **DELUGE**
flooded stream **FRESHET**
flood gate **SLUICE**
floor **STORY**
floor covering **CARPET, RUG, MAT, TILE, LINELOEUM, SKIN**
flooring square **TILE**
flora **PLANTS**
flora and fauna **BIOTA**
floral emblem of Wales **LEEK**
floral ornament **ROSETTE**
Florentine family **MEDICI**
Florentine iris **ORRIS**
florid **ORNATE**
Florida city **MIAMI, TAMPA, SARASOTA, OCALA**
Florida county **DADE**
Florida food fish **POMPANO**
Florida game fish **SNAPPER**
Florida Indian **SEMINOLE**
Florida islets **KEYS**
Florida key **LARGO, WEST**
Florida race track **HIALEAH**
Florida region **EVERGLADES**
flotilla **NAVY, FLEET**
flounder **FISH**
flourish **GROW, PROSPER**
flour manufacturer **MILLER**
flout **JEER, SCORN, SPURN**
flow **RUN**
flow back **EBB, RECEDE**
flower **ASTER, CANNA, LILY, DANDELION, ROSE, DAHLIA, ZINNIA, PEONY, TULIP, MUM, DAISY, POSY, PRIMROSE, LILAC, ARUM, PANSY, GERANIUM, VIOLET, PHLOX, PETUNIA, BEGONIA, PINK, CARNATION, STOCK, SEDUM, MARIGOLD, ANEMONE, POPPY, CLOVER, IRIS, FOXGLOVE, GEUM, CROCUS**
flower band **WREATH**
flower circle **WREATH**
flower holder **VASE, URN**

flowering climbing plant **SMILAX**
flower leaf **PETAL, SEPAL**
flowerless plant **MOSS, VINE, FERN, IVY**
flower of Holland **TULIP**
flower part **PETAL, SEPAL, STEM, STALK**
flower plot **BED**
flower stalk **STEM**
flower-to-be **BUD**
flowing **FLUENT, COPIOUS**
flowing forth **EMANATE**
flowing garment **ROBE, CAPE**
flowing oil well **GUSHER**
flub **BLUNDER**
fluctuate **WAVER**
flue **CHIMNEY**
fluent **LIQUID, SMOOTH**
fluent in speech **GLIB**
fluff **DOWN, FLOSS**
fluff from cloth **LINT**
fluffy **SOFT**
fluid **LIQUID, WATER**
fluid measure **DRAM, PINT, QUART, CUP**
fluid rock **LAVA**
flunk **FAIL**
flurry **ADO, BUSTLE**
flush **BLUSH, REDDEN**
flush with success **ELATE**
flute **WOODWIND**
flutelike instrument **OBOE**
flutter **FLAP, WAVE, WAVER**
flutter over **HOVER**
fly **SOAR, WING, AVIATE**
fly before the wind **SCUD**
flyer **PILOT, ACE**
fly high **SOAR**
flying (3 wds.) **ON THE WING**
flying boat **SEAPLANE**
flying body **METEOR**
flying creature **BIRD**
flying equipment **WING**
flying fish **SAURY**
flying honker **GOOSE**
flying machine **PLANE**
flying mammal **BAT**
flying saucer (abbr.) **UFO**
flying toy **KITE**
fly quickly **FLIT**
fly's enemy **SPIDER**
flyspeck **ERROR, FLAW, SPOT**
foal **HORSE, COLT**
foam **SPUME, FROTH, LATHER**
foaming **SPUMOUS, SUDSY**
fob **POCKET, CHAIN**
focus **CENTER, CONVERGE**
fodder **FEED, SILAGE**

fodder storage structure **SILO**
fodder tower **SILO**
foe **ADVERSARY, ENEMY**
fog **MIST, HAZE**
fog and smoke **SMOG**
foggy **CLOUDY, DIM**
foghorn **SIREN**
foible **WEAKNESS**
foil **FRUSTRATE, SWORD**
fold **NAP, CREASE**
folder **LEAFLET**
folding bed **COT**
folding money **DOLLAR**
fold of cloth **PLEAT**
fold of skin **DEWLAP**
fold over **LAP**
foliage **LEAVES**
folio **BOOK**
folk **PEOPLE**
folk knowledge **LORE**
folklore **LEGENDS**
folklore creatures **GNOME, TROLL, ELF, SPRITE**
folklore genie **SANDMAN**
folksinger Ives **BURL**
folksinger Guthrie **WOODY, ARLO**
folksinger Seeger **PETE**
folk song **BLUES**
folkways **MORES**
follow **ENSUE, TAIL, CHASE**
follower **ITE, ADHERENT**
follow exactly **TRACE**
following **AFTER**
following story **SEQUEL**
follow orders **OBEY**
follow secretly **SHADOW**
follow the chase **HUNT**
folly **MADNESS**
fond **LOVING**
fondle **CARESS, PET**
fondly **TENDERLY**
fondness **AFFECTION, LOVE**
font **POOL, POND, BASIN**
food **CHOW, EATS, VICTUALS, GRUB, EATABLES, EDIBLES, NOURISHMENT**
food constituent **VITAMIN**
food container **CAN, TIN, JAR, BOX**
food counter **BAR**
food dressing **SAUCE**
food fish **COD, BASS, SOLE, SHAD, TROUT, EEL, HALIBUT, TUNA, SALMON**
food for animals **FORAGE**
food for cattle **FODDER**
food for infants **PAP**

food from heaven	**MANNA**
food of the gods	**AMBROSIA**
food quickly prepared (2 wds.)	
	SHORT ORDER
food regimen	**DIET**
food sauce	**CONDIMENT**
food scrap	**ORT**
food served	**MENU**
food shortage	**FAMINE**
foodstuff	**CEREAL**
food topping	**SAUCE, GARNISH**
fool	**ASS, IDIOT**
fool away	**FRITTER**
foolhardy	**BRASH, RASH**
fool hen	**GROUSE**
foolish	**INANE, SILLY**
foolish act	**FOLLY, BONER**
foolishness	**NONSENSE**
foolish person	**GOOSE, DOLT**
foolish show	**FARCE**
foolproof	**SIMPLE**
foolscap	**PAPER**
fool's gold	**PYRITE**
fool's paradise	**LIMBO**
foot	**PES, HOOF**
foot affliction	**CORN**
footage	**LENGTH**
football cheer	**RAH**
football in England	**RUGBY**
football kick	**PUNT**
football pass	**LATERAL**
football play	**DROP KICK,**
TOUCHDOWN, PUNT, RUN,	
	PASS
football player	**BACK, END,**
CENTER, TACKLE,	
FULLBACK, HALFBACK	
football score	**TOUCHDOWN**
football team	**ELEVEN**
foot bone	**TARSUS**
footboy	**PAGE**
foot covering	**SHOE, BOOT,**
	SOCK
foot digit	**TOE**
footed vase	**URN**
footing	**POSITION**
foot it	**SCUD**
footless	**APOD**
foot lever	**PEDAL**
footlike part	**PES**
footlocker	**TRUNK**
footloose	**FREE**
footnote	**ADDITION, P.S.**
foot part	**TOE, HEEL, INSTEP,**
ARCH, SOLE, BALL	
footpath	**TRAIL**
footprint	**STEP, TRACK**
footrace	**DASH**

footrest	**OTTOMAN, HASSOCK**
foot trail	**PATH**
footwear	**SHOES**
foozle	**BUNGLE**
fop	**DANDY**
for	**PRO**
for (Sp.)	**POR**
forage	**BROWSE**
forage acre	**PASTURE**
forage grass	**REDTOP**
forage plant	**CLOVER**
foray	**RAID**
forbear	**ABSTAIN**
forbearance	**MERCY**
forbid	**BAN**
forbidden	**TABOO**
Forbidden City	**LHASA, LASA**
forbidding	**GRIM**
force	**COMPEL, OBLIGE, DINT,**
	POWER, STRENGTH
force (Lat.)	**VIS**
forced	**COMPELLED,**
	COMPULSORY
forced laborer	**SLAVE**
forceful blow	**BASH**
force into less space	**COMPRESS**
force onward	**URGE**
force to go	**DRIVE OUT**
force unit	**DYNE**
for credit	**ON THE CUFF**
ford a stream	**WADE**
for each	**PER**
for each person	**APIECE**
forearm bone	**ULNA**
forebear	**ANCESTOR**
forebode	**AUGUR**
foreboding	**OMEN,**
	PREMONITION
forebrain	**PROSENCEPHALON**
forecast	**PRESAGE**
forecaster	**SEER**
foreclose	**DEBAR, PREVENT**
forefather	**ANCESTOR**
forefinger	**INDEX**
forego	**PRECEDE**
foregoing	**FORMER**
forehead	**BROW**
foreign	**STRANGE, ALIEN**
foreign agent	**SPY**
foreigner	**ALIEN**
foreign service residence	
	CONSULATE
foreknow	**PRECONCEIVE**
foreknowledge	**PRESCIENCE**
forlock	**BANGS**
foreman	**BOSS, MANAGER**
foremost	**LEADING, FIRST**

forenoon (abbr.)	**A.M.**
forensic	**RHETORICAL**
foreordain	**DESTINE**
forepiece of a cap	**VISOR**
forest	**WOODS**
forestall	**AVERT**
forest animal	**DEER, BEAR**
forest clearing	**GLADE**
forest god	**PAN**
forest home	**CABIN**
forest open space	**GLADE**
forest ox	**ANOA**
forest warden	**RANGER**
foretell	**BODE**
foretoken	**OMEN**
forever	**ALWAYS, AYE**
foreword	**PREFACE**
for example (abbr.)	**E.G.**
for fear that	**LEST**
forfeit	**LOSE, PENALTY**
forge	**SMITHY**
forget	**OMIT**
forgive	**CONDONE, PARDON**
forgo	**QUIT, WAIVE**
for instance	**AS**
fork over	**PAY**
fork prong	**TINE**
forlorn	**FORSAKEN, DESOLATE**
form	**MOLD, SHAPE**
form a jelly	**GEL**
formal	**STIFF**
formal argument	**DEBATE**
formal attitude	**POSE**
formal dance	**BALL**
formal dress	**GOWN**
formal letter	**EPISTLE**
formalities	**ETIQUETTE**
formality	**CEREMONY**
formal meeting	**CONFERENCE**
formal objection	**PROTEST**
formal procession	**PARADE**
formal speech	**ORATION, ADDRESS**
formal structure	**FORMATION**
form a spider web	**SPIN**
format	**PLAN**
formed at the base of mountains	**PIEDMONT**
formed by the sea	**MARINE**
formed like a needle	**ACERATE**
formed like lips	**LABIAL**
for men only	**STAG**
former	**ONE TIME, ONCE**
former boy	**MAN**
former candidate Stevenson	**ADLAI**
former college man	**ALUMNUS**
former European coin	**DUCAT**
former French premier	**DE GAULLE**
former German coin	**TALER, KRONA**
former Japanese statesman	**ITO**
former labor group (abbr.)	**IWW**
formerly	**ERST, ONCE**
formerly Persia	**IRAN**
former Moslem edict	**IRADE**
former New York governor	**DEWEY**
former Russian ruler	**TZAR, CZAR**
former screen star (2 wds.)	**GRETA GARBO, PEARL WHITE, THEDA BARA**
former Soviet leader	**LENIN, STALIN, KHRUSHCHEV**
former state in Germany	**PRUSSIA**
former time	**PAST**
former Turkish president	**INONU**
former President's nickname	**IKE**
formicary	**ANTHILL**
formidable	**ALARMING, APPALLING**
forming container	**MOLD**
form of architecture	**DORIC, IONIC**
form of hoisting crane	**DAVIT**
form of polite address	**MADAM**
Formosa	**TAIWAN**
Formosa city	**TAIPEI**
formula	**RECIPE**
for nothing	**GRATIS**
forsake	**LEAVE, DEPART, GO, DESERT, ABANDON, STRAND**
forsaken	**DESOLATE**
forswear	**REJECT, RENOUNCE**
fort	**STRONGHOLD**
forth	**FORWARD**
forthcoming	**DUE**
for the most part	**IN GENERAL, MAINLY**
forthwith	**AT ONCE**
fortification	**REDAN**
fortify	**ARM**
fortitude	**STRENGTH**
fortress	**TOWER**
fortuitous	**ACCIDENTAL**
fortuity	**CHANCE**
fortunate	**LUCKY**
fortune	**LOT, LUCK, FATE**

forty winks	**NAP**
forward	**ON**
forward part	**FRONT**
forward part of a ship	**PROW, BOW**
for what reason	**WHY**
foss	**DITCH, MOAT**
fossil	**BONE**
foster	**PROMOTE**
foul	**FILTHY, NASTY**
foulard	**SCARF, TIE**
found	**BASE, ESTABLISH**
foundation	**BASE, BASIS**
founded on experience	**EMPIRICAL**
founder	**STUMBLE, FAIL**
founder of Carthage	**DIDO**
foundling	**WAIF, ORPHAN**
fountain	**WELLHEAD**
fountain drink	**COLA, SODA, SHAKE, MALTED, FLOAT, COOLER**
fountain man (2 wds.)	**SODA JERK**
fountain nymph	**NAIAD**
four	**TETRAD**
four (Ger.)	**VIER**
four (prefix)	**TETRA, TETR**
four-door car	**SEDAN**
four-flush	**BLUFF**
four-in-hand	**TIE, CRAVAT**
fourpenny	**NAIL**
four-poster	**BED**
fourth estate	**PRESS**
fourth month	**APRIL**
fowl	**BIRD**
fowl product	**EGG**
fox's foot	**PAD**
foxy	**SLY, CRAFTY**
foyer	**LOBBY**
fracas	**SET-TO**
fraction	**PART, DIVISION**
fractious	**CROSS, FRETFUL**
fracture	**BREAK**
fragile	**DELICATE, BREAKABLE, FRAIL**
fragment	**CHIP, PIECE, SCRAP, SHRED, WISP, SHARD**
fragment left at meal	**ORT**
fragment of earthern vessel	**SHARD**
fragrance	**AROMA, ODOR, SCENT, BOUQUET, PERFUME**
fragrant	**OLENT, REDOLENT**
fragrant ointment	**BALM, NARD**
fragrant plant	**MINT**
fragrant root in perfume	**ORRIS**
fragrant wood	**CEDAR**
frail	**WEAK, DELICATE, FRAGILE**
frailty	**WEAKNESS**
frambesia	**YAWS**
frame	**FORM, CONSTRUCT, OUTLINE**
frame for stretching	**TENTER**
frame of mind	**MOOD**
framework	**LATTICE**
France	**GAUL**
franchise	**RIGHT, LICENSE**
franchised	**PATENTED**
Franciscan	**FRIAR, MONK**
Franco's land	**SPAIN**
frangible	**FRAGILE**
frank	**OPEN, CANDID**
Frankish	**GALIC**
Franklin	**BEN**
frankness	**CANDOR**
frantic	**FRENZIED**
frantic cry	**HELP**
frappe	**ICED**
fraternal	**BROTHERLY**
fraternal member	**ELK**
fraternize	**ASSOCIATE**
fraud	**FAKER, FAKERY, PHONY**
fraud (2 wds.)	**MARE'S NEST**
fraudulent	**FAKE, CUNNING**
fraught	**LADEN**
fray	**RAVEL, BATTLE**
frazzle	**WEAR, FRAY**
freak	**MONSTER, QUIRK**
freakish	**ODD, QUEER**
freckle	**SPOT**
Fred Astaire's sister	**ADELE**
free	**LOOSE, UNFETTERED, RELEASE, RID, LIBERATE, GRATIS**
free access (2 wds.)	**OPEN DOOR**
free and easy	**INFORMAL**
free commercial	**PLUG**
freedom	**LIBERTY, LICENSE**
freedom from activity	**REST, RESPITE**
freedom from narrow restrictions	**LATITUDE**
freedom from strife	**PEACE**
freedom from worry (3 wds.)	**PEACE OF MIND**
freedom of access	**ENTREE**
freedom of action	**LEEWAY**
free entertainment	**TREAT**
free food or money	**HANDOUT**
free-for-all	**FRACAS**

free from bacteria	ASEPTIC
free from coarseness	REFINED
free from danger	RESCUE, SAFE, SECURE
free from guilt (3 wds.)	IN THE CLEAR
free from liability	EXEMPT
free from suspicion	ABSOLVE, CLEAR
freely	WILLINGLY
free ticket	PASS
free time	LEISURE
freeway	PIKE
freeze	CHILL, ICE
freezing rain	SLEET
freight	CARGO
freighted	LADEN
freighter	SHIP
French annual income	RENTE
French article	LE, LA, LES, UN, UNE
French author	DUMAS, HUGO
French capital	PARIS
French cheese	BRIE
French chemist	PASTEUR
French city	BREST, PARIS, NICE, NIMES, METZ, LILLE
French cleric	ABBE, PERE
French coin	SOU, ECU, FRANC
French composer	BIZET, RAVEL
French conjunction	ET
French dance	CANCAN
French dog	POODLE
French dramatist	RACINE, ANOUILH
French duke	DUC
French edict	ARRET
French father	PERE
French friend	AMI
French impressionist	MANET, MONET
French island	ILE
French cream	CREME
Frenchman	GAUL
French negative	NON
French noble	DUC
French painter	DEGAS, MANET, MONET, RENOIR, DAVID
French pirate in America	LAFITTE
French police	SURETE
French resort	NICE, NIMES, CANNES
French revolutionary leader	MARAT

French river	ISERE, LOIRE, OISE, SEINE
French school	ECOLE, LYCEE
French sculptor	RODIN
French service cap	KEPI
French shooting contest	TIR
French short story	CONTE
French singer	CHANTEUSE
French stock exchange	BOURSE
French street	RUE
French subway	METRO
frenzied	FRANTIC, MAD
frenzy	FUROR, RAGE
frequent	FAMILIAR, USUAL
frequent a place	HAUNT
frequently	OFTEN
frequently (poet.)	OFT
fresh	NEW, STRONG
freshen	PERK
freshet	STREAM
freshwater duck	TEAL
freshwater fish	CARP, IDE, DACE, PIKE
freshwater porpoise	INIA
fret	WORRY, STEW
fretful	CROSS
friar	MONK
friar's title	FRA
friend	CHUM, PAL, BUDDY, MATE
friend (Fr.)	AMI
friend (Sp.)	AMIGO
friendly correspondent (2 wds.)	PEN PAL
Friendly Islands	TONGA
friendly talk	CHAT
friend of Peter Pan	WENDY
friendship	AMITY
frieze	BORDER
frigate	SHIP
fright	PANIC, FEAR
frighten	SCARE, TERRIFY
frighten away	SHOO
frightful	AWFUL, HORRIBLE
frigid	COLD, ICY, FROZEN
frill	RUCHE, LACE
frilly trimming	LACE, RUFFLE
fringe	EDGE
fringed ornament	TASSEL
frisk	FROLIC, CAVORT
frisky	PLAYFUL
frisson	CHILL, SHIVER
frivolous	PETTY, TRIVIAL
frock	DRESS
froglike amphibian	TOAD
frog's sound	CROAK
frolic	CAPER, REVEL, ROMP, SPREE

from	**OF**	fruit seed	**PIP, PIT**
from a distance	**AFAR**	fruit skin	**PEEL, RIND**
from head to foot (comp. wd.)	**CAP-A-PIE**	fruit spread	**JELLY, JAM, PRESERVE, MARMALADE**
from now on	**HENCEFORTH**	fruit stone	**PIT**
from one side to the other	**ACROSS**	fruit sugar	**FRUCTOSE**
from the heart	**SINCERE**	frump	**DOWDY**
from the time of	**SINCE**	frustrate	**FOIL**
from this place	**NATIVE**	frustrator of plan	**MARPLOT**
frond	**LEAF**	fry	**YOUNG, BROOD**
front	**FORE, VAN**	fryer	**CHICKEN**
frontage	**FACADE, EXPOSURE**	frying pan	**SPIDER, GRIDDLE, SKILLET**
frontier merchant	**TRADER**	fry quickly	**SAUTE**
frontiersman	**BOONE, CROCKETT**	fuchsia	**PURPLE**
		fucus	**PAINT, DYE**
frontier transportation	**STAGE**	fudge	**CANDY**
front lawn	**YARD**	fuel	**COAL, WOOD, GAS, PEAT, OIL**
front part of a coat	**LAPEL**		
frontrunner	**LEADER**	fuel-carrying ship	**COALER, OILER, TANKER**
frost a cake	**ICE**		
frosting	**ICE, ICING**	fuel-conveying tube. (2 wds.)	**GAS PIPE**
frosty	**ICY, HAUGHTY**		
frothy	**FOAMY, SPUMOUS**	fugitive	**REFUGEE, RUNAWAY**
frothy brew	**ALE**	Fujiyama, e.g.	**VOLCANO**
frothy dessert	**MOUSSE**	fulcrum	**SUPPORT, PROP**
froufrou	**SWISH, RUSTLE**	fulfill	**FINISH, COMPLETE**
frown	**SCOWL**	fulfill a command	**OBEY**
frowsy	**UNKEMPT, MESSY**	fulfill the demands of	**SATISFY**
frozen dessert	**FRAPPE, ICE, ICE CREAM, GLACE**	full	**REPLETE, SATED**
		full-length	**UNABRIDGED, UNCUT**
frozen pendant	**ICICLE**		
frozen rain	**SLEET, HAIL**	fulness	**PLENUM**
frozen water	**ICE**	full of (suffix)	**OSE**
fructuous	**FRUITFUL**	full of ecstatic joy	**RAPTUROUS**
frugal	**SAVING, THRIFTY**	full of happenings	**EVENTFUL**
frugality	**ECONOMY**	full of holes, as a roof	**LEAKY**
fruit	**LEMON, LIME, ORANGE, APPLE, PEAR, MELON, PEACH**	full of life	**ANIMATE**
		full of meaning	**PITHY**
		full of ringlets	**CURLY**
fruit center	**CORE**	full of small openings	**POROUS**
fruit covering	**PERICARP**	full of vigor	**PEPPY**
fruit decay	**BLET**	full of zest	**RACY**
fruit drink	**ADE, CIDER, NECTAR, JUICE**	fully	**WHOLLY, UTTERLY**
		fully grown	**ADULT, MATURE**
fruitful	**FERTILE**	fully sufficient	**ADEQUATE**
fruit in bunches	**BANANA, GRAPE**	fulsome	**INSINCERE**
		Fulton's folly	**CLERMONT**
fruition	**FULFILLMENT**	fume	**REEK, SMOKE**
fruit jar rubber ring	**LUTE**	fun	**AMUSEMENT, SPORT**
fruitless	**VAIN, IDLE**	function	**ROLE**
fruit of a palm	**DATE, FIG**	fund	**STOCK, STORE**
fruit of Jove	**PERSIMMON**	fundamental	**BASAL, BASIC**
fruit of paradise	**POMELO**	funeral bell	**TOLL, KNELL**
fruit of pine	**CONE**	funeral hymn	**DIRGE**
fruit or vegetable dish	**SALAD**	fungus	**MILDEW, MOLD**
fruit pastry	**PIE, TART**	funny	**COMIC, AMUSING**
fruit preserve	**COMPOTE**		

fur-bearing animal	**MARTEN, OTTER, SEAL, MINK, RABBIT, SABLE**	gain courage (2 wds.)	**TAKE HEART**
fur-cloak	**PELISSE**	gainer	**DIVE**
furious	**IRATE, MAD, ANGRY**	gainful	**PROFITABLE**
furlough	**LEAVE**	gain knowledge	**LEARN**
furnace	**OVEN, OAST, KILN**	gain on	**NEAR**
furnish	**PROVIDE, DECORATE**	gain over expense	**NET, PROFIT**
furnished with shoes	**SHOD**	gainsay	**DENY**
furnish food	**CATER**	gain victory	**OVERCOME, WIN, TRIUMPH**
furnish with weapons	**ARM**	gait	**CANTER, PACE, TROT**
furnishings	**FURNITURE**	gaited horse	**PACER**
furniture item	**BED, COUCH, CHAIR, TABLE, SOFA, DAVENPORT**	gaiters	**SPATS**
		gala	**FESTIVAL, FETE, BALL, FESTIVE, FIESTA**
furniture polish	**WAX**	Galatea's lover	**ACIS**
furniture set	**DINETTE, SUITE**	gale	**STORM**
furniture wheel	**CASTER**	gall	**NERVE**
furor	**HOOPLA**	gallant	**NOBLE, HEROIC**
furrow	**SEAM**	gallery hanging	**OIL**
furs	**PELTRY**	galley sweep	**OAR**
further	**ADVANCE**	Gallic affirmative	**OUI**
further direction	**REFERRAL**	gallop	**GAIT**
furthermore	**MOREOVER**	gamble	**BET, WAGER**
furtive	**SNEAKY, STEALTHY**	gambler	**BETTOR**
furtive glimpse	**PEEP, PEEK**	gambler's capital	**STAKE**
fur wrap	**STOLE**	gambling cubes	**DICE**
fury	**RAGE**	gambling game	**FARO, POKER, BLACKJACK**
furze genus	**ULEX**	gambol	**CAPER, FRISK**
fuse	**CIRCUIT**	gambrel	**ROOF**
fused by heat	**MOLTEN**	game	**SPORT**
fuse together	**WELD**	game animal	**DEER, ELK, MOOSE**
fuss	**ADO, TO-DO, POTHER, BOTHER, STIR, STEW**	game at cards	**FARO, LOO**
		game at marbles	**TAW, MIB**
fusty	**MUSTY, MOLDY**	gamecock spur	**GAFF**
futile	**USELESS, VAIN**	game collection	**BAG**
fuzz	**LINT, FLUFF**	game fish	**BASS, CERO, TARPON, TROUT, PIKE**
fylfot	**SWASTIKA**	game like bowling	**TENPINS**
		game of checkers	**DRAUGHTS**

G

		game of strategy	**CHESS, GO**
gab	**CHAT, CHATTER, GABBLE**	game played on horseback	**POLO**
gabble	**BABBLE, CHATTER, JABBER**	game played with clubs	**GOLF**
gaberdine	**COAT**	game result	**SCORE**
Gabriel, for one	**ANGEL**	game stealer	**POACHER**
gad	**ROVE, ROAM**	gamester	**GAMBLER**
Gaelic	**ERSE**	gamin	**URCHIN, WAIF**
gag	**JOKE**	gaming cubes	**DICE**
gage	**SECURITY**	gammon	**BACON**
gaiety	**MIRTH**	gamut	**RANGE, SCOPE**
gain	**ACQUIRE, PROFIT**	gamy	**SPOILED**
gain a victory	**WIN, TRIUMPH**	gander	**GOOSE**
gain as clear profit	**NET**	gang	**CREW**
gain by labor	**EARN**	gangling	**LANKY**
gain command of	**MASTER**	gangster	**HOODLUM, THUG**
gain control (2 wds.)	**SEW UP**		

gangster Capone	**AL**
gangster's girl friend	**MOLL**
gang up on	**ATTACK, OPPOSE**
gaol	**PRISON**
gap	**OPENING, HOLE, LACUNA, HIATUS**
gape	**YAWN, STARE**
gar	**NEEDLEFISH**
garb	**ATTIRE, CLOTHE, CLOTHING**
garbage	**TRASH**
garbage barge	**SCOW**
garbanzo	**BEAN, CHICKPEA**
garble	**DISTORT**
garcon	**WAITER**
garden amphibian	**TOAD, FROG**
garden flower	**PETUNIA, ROSE, PEONY, ASTER, ZINNIA, DAHLIA, PANSY**
garden for animals	**ZOO**
garden implement	**HOE, RAKE, TROWEL**
garden moisture	**DEW**
garden party	**FETE**
garden pest	**APHID, WEED, BEETLE**
garden plant	**RADISH, TOMATO, BEAN, CARROT, POTATO, ASPARAGUS, BEET, TURNIP, PEA**
garden plot	**BED**
garden portulaca (2 wds.)	**ROSE MOSS**
Garden State	**NEW JERSEY**
garden tool	**HOE, RAKE, TROWEL**
garden walk	**PATH**
gargantuan	**HUGE, GIGANTIC**
gargle	**RINSE**
gargling liquid	**MOUTHWASH**
gargoyle	**SPOUT**
garish	**GAUDY, LOUD**
garland	**WREATH, LEI, ANADEM**
garlic-like herb	**SHALLOT**
garlic part	**CLOVE**
garment	**WRAP**
garment edge	**HEM**
garment maker	**TAILOR**
garment of old Rome	**TOGA**
garment piece	**SLEEVE, YOKE, COLLAR, LAPEL**
garment protector	**APRON, BIB, SMOCK**
garner	**GATHER, COLLECT**
garnish	**ADORN, EMBELLISH**
garret	**ATTIC**
garrison	**POST, FORT**
garrote	**STRANGLE**
garrulous	**TALKY, TALKATIVE**
garter	**SUPPORT**
gas	**FUEL, PETROL, VAPOR, FUME**
gas burner	**JET**
gaseous compound	**ETHANE**
gaseous element	**ARGON, NEON**
gaseous hydrocarbon	**ETHANE**
gash	**CUT, SLASH**
gasoline container	**TANK**
gasoline in Britain	**PETROL**
gasoline rating	**OCTANE**
gasp	**PANT**
gastronome	**EPICURE, GOURMET**
gastropod	**ABALONE, SNAIL**
gastropod genus	**OLIVA**
gat	**CHANNEL**
gate	**DOOR, PORTAL**
gatefold	**FOLD-OUT, INSERT**
gatekeeper	**WARDEN**
gateway	**ENTRY, PORTICO**
gather	**AMASS, ASSEMBLE, REAP, ACCUMULATE, COLLECT, GLEAN**
gathering of people	**MEETING, ASSEMBLY**
gather in sails	**FURL**
gather into folds	**PLEAT, SHIRR**
gauche	**AWKWARD, CLUMSY**
gaucho	**COWBOY**
gaucho's weapon	**BOLA(S)**
gaudy	**GARISH, LOUD**
gaudy trifle	**GEWGAW**
gauge	**METER, MEASURE**
Gaul	**FRENCHMAN**
gaunt	**BONY, SKINNY**
gauntlet	**GLOVE**
gay	**CHEERY, JOYOUS, MERRY**
gay city	**PAREE, PARIS**
gay time	**LARK, SPREE**
gaze	**PEER, STARE**
gazelle	**ARIEL, GOA**
gaze with greed	**GLOAT**
gear	**EQUIPMENT**
gear tooth	**COG**
gee	**GOLLY**
gekko	**LIZARD**
gelatinous substance	**AGAR, AGAR-AGAR**
gem	**JEWEL, STONE**
gem carved in relief	**CAMEO**
gem face	**FACET**
gem of the mountains	**IDAHO**
Gem State	**IDAHO**
gem surface	**FACET**
gem weight	**CARAT**

gender	**SEX**
Gene Tierney role	**LAURA**
genealogical record	**TREE**
genealogy	**LINEAGE, PEDIGREE**
general	**COMMON, UNIVERSAL**
general course	**TREND**
general Eisenhower	**IKE**
generally	**USUALLY**
general's aides	**STAFF**
general's assistant	
	AIDE-DE-CAMP, AIDE
generate	**PRODUCE**
generation	**AGE, ERA**
generic	**TYPICAL**
generous	**OPEN-HANDED,**
	CHARITABLE
genesis	**BIRTH, ORIGIN**
genial	**CORDIAL, WARM**
genius	**TALENT**
genteel	**POLITE, POLISHED**
gentle	**MILD, TAME, KIND,**
	SOFT
gentle blow	**TAP**
gentle creature	**LAMB**
gentlefolk	**NOBILITY**
gentleman	**SIR**
gentleman (Sp.)	**SENOR**
gentleman's gentleman	**VALET**
gentlemen's agreement	
	HANDSHAKE
gentle reproof	**ADMONITION**
gentle tap	**PAT**
genuflect	**KNEEL**
genuine	**REAL, BONA FIDE,**
	PURE, TRUE
genus	**CLASS**
genus of African tree	**COLA**
genus of ants	**ECITON**
genus of apes	**SIMIA**
genus of apple trees	**MALUS**
genus of bees	**APIS**
genus of beetles	**SITOPHILUS**
genus of cattle	**BOS**
genus of chickpeas	**CICER**
genus of currants	**RIBES**
genus of frogs	**RANA**
genus of maples	**ACER**
genus of olive trees	**OLEA**
genus of palms	**ARECA**
genus of rodents	**MUS**
genus of sheep	**OVIS**
genus of snakes	**OPHIDIA**
geographical dictionary	
	GAZETTEER
geographical division	**ZONE**
geological period	**ERA**

geometrical figure	**CONE,**
	CUBE, POLYGON,
	SQUARE, OCTAGON
geometrical line	**RADIUS,**
	DIAMETER
George Gershwin's brother	**IRA**
George Sand classic	**LELIA**
Georgia city	**AUGUSTA,**
	MACON, ATLANTA
germ	**SEED**
German	**TEUTON**
German article	**DAS, DER, DIE**
German city	**BADEN, ESSEN,**
	EMDEN, BONN, BERLIN,
	FRANKFURT, HAMBURG
German coin	**TALER**
German composer	**LEHAR,**
	STRAUS, BRAHMS, WAGNER
German dive bomber	**STUKA**
German fascist	**NAZI**
German folk dance	**ALLEMANDE**
German goblin	**KOBOLD**
German-made pistol	**LUGER**
German measles	**RUBELLA**
German negative	**NEIN**
German philosopher	**KANT,**
	HEGEL
German river	**ELBE, ISAR,**
	ODER, RHINE
German submarine	
(comp. wd.)	**U-BOAT**
German title	**HERR, FRAU**
germ culture	**AGAR**
gesture	**ACT, MOTION**
get	**RECEIVE, OBTAIN,**
	PROCURE, GAIN
get along	**MANAGE**
get a scolding	
(2 wds., colloq.)	**CATCH IT**
get as deserved	**EARN, MERIT**
get away	**ESCAPE, FLEE**
get back	**REDEEM**
get better of	**BEST**
get bigger	**GROW, INCREASE**
get by force	**EXTORT, PRY**
get by reasoning	**DERIVE**
get lost	**STRAY**
get on	**BOARD**
get on a horse	**MOUNT**
get out (sl.)	**SCRAM**
get ready	**PREPARE**
get rid of (2 wds.)	**CLEAR OFF**
get the advantage of	**BEST**
get the best of	**MASTER**
get the point	**UNDERSTAND,**
	SEE
get up	**ARISE, STAND**
get-up	**OUTFIT**

get well **RECOVER, HEAL, MEND**
gewgaw **TRINKET**
Ghandi's country **INDIA**
ghastly **HIDEOUS**
ghat **PASS, STAIRS**
gherkin **CUCUMBER, PICKLE**
ghost **SPIRIT, SPOOK, SHADE**
ghostly **EERIE, EERY**
giant **TITAN**
giant beggar of Ithaca **IRUS**
giant of fairy tales **OGRE**
gibberish **CHATTER, JARGON**
gibbon **APE**
gift **PRESENT**
gibe **SNEER, SCOFF**
giddy **DIZZY**
gift bearer **GREEK, DONOR**
gift recipient **DONEE**
gifted speaker **ORATOR**
gift to the needy **ALMS**
gigantic **HUGE, IMMENSE**
giggle **LAUGH, TITTER, SNICKER**
giggling sound **TEHEE**
gilding **GILT**
gill **SMALL LIQUID MEASURE**
gimcrack **GEWGAW, TRINKET**
gimpy **LAME**
gin-and-tonic garnish **LIME**
ginger **PEP**
ginger cookie **SNAP**
gingerly **CAREFULLY**
gingili **SESAME**
gin mixer **TONIC**
giraffe-like animal **OKAPI**
gird **BIND, BELT**
girl **GAL, LASS, MAID, MAIDEN**
girl of song **MARIE, LOLA, DAISY, MARY, JEANNIE, LAURA, MARTA, WENDY**
girl of the Twenties **FLAPPER**
girl servant **MAID**
girth **HOOP, BAND**
GI's ID (2 wds., colloq.) **DOG TAG**
gist **POINT, MEAT**
give **DONATE**
give an account of **RELATE, REPORT, TELL**
give and take **BANDY**
give a new title to **RENAME**
give another title to **RENAME**
give assent **AGREE**
give away **BESTOW, GRANT**
give back **REPAY, RETURN, RESTORE**
give claim to **ENTITLE**

give consent **ACCEDE**
give due credit **PRAISE**
give ear **HEED, LISTEN**
give evidence **TESTIFY**
give forth **EMIT**
give in **RELENT**
give information **REPORT**
give legal force to **VALIDATE**
give light **SHINE, GLOW**
give meaning to **DEFINE**
give name to **DUB, TITLE**
give notice **WARN**
given to loose chatter **GOSSIPY**
give off fumes **REEK**
give one's word **PROMISE**
give outlet to **VENT**
give out sparingly **DOLE, METE**
give silent assent **NOD**
give temporarily **LEND**
give the alarm **WARN, ALERT**
give the meaning of **DEFINE**
give up **CEDE, YIELD**
giving **GENEROUS**
glacial epoch (2 wds.) **ICE AGE**
glacial ice **SERAC**
glacial ridge **ESKER**
glacial sand **NEVE**
glacial term **STOSS**
glad **HAPPY, JOYFUL**
gladden **ELATE**
glade **VALE**
glamour **CHARM, ALLURE**
glance **LOOK, PEEK**
glare **SHINE, GLEAM**
glaring **OBVIOUS**
Glasgow resident **SCOT**
glass bottle **CARAFE**
glass container **JAR, BOTTLE**
glass-enclosed room **SOLARIUM, SUNROOM**
glasses part **LENS, FRAME**
glass to reflect image **MIRROR**
glassy **SMOOTH**
gleam **GLINT, SHINE**
glee **EXULTATION, JOY, BLISS, ELATION**
glib **FLIP, SMOOTH**
glide aloft **SOAR**
glide on snow **SKI**
glide over ice **SKATE**
glider **SWING**
glimpse **ESPY, NOTICE**
glisten **GLITTER, SHINE**
glisten brightly **SPARKLE**
glitter **GLARE, SHINE**
globe **SPHERE, ORB, WORLD, PLANET, BULB**
globule **DROP**

gloom	**DARKNESS**
gloomy	**GLUM, BLUE, SAD**
glorify	**PRAISE**
glorious	**SPLENDID, NOBLE**
glory	**GRANDEUR, HONOR**
gloss	**LUSTER, POLISH, SHEEN, SHINE**
glossa	**TONGUE**
glossy	**SHINY**
glossy black bird	**RAVEN**
glossy fabric	**SATEEN, SATIN**
glossy paint	**ENAMEL**
glossy shoe material (2 wds.)	**PATENT LEATHER**
glove	**GAUNTLET, MITTEN**
glove leather	**CALF, KID**
glow	**SHINE**
glowing coal	**EMBER**
glucose	**SUGAR**
glue	**PASTE**
glue shut	**SEAL**
glum	**SULLEN, SAD**
glut	**SATE, SATIATE**
glutton (colloq.)	**HOG, PIG**
gluttony	**GREED**
glyph	**CARVING**
gnarl	**KNOT, SNARL**
gnash	**GRIND**
gnat	**MIDGE**
gnaw	**CHEW**
gnome	**ELF, GREMLIN, TROLL, BROWNIE**
gnu	**WILDEBEEST**
go	**DEPART, LEAVE**
go (poet.)	**WEND**
go aboard, at depot	**ENTRAIN**
goad	**INCITE, PROD, SPUR, URGE, EGG ON**
go ahead	**CONTINUE, PROCEED**
goal	**AIM, OBJECTIVE, END, TARGET**
go along with	**AGREE**
go around	**DETOUR**
go astray	**ERR, SIN**
goat	**KID**
go at	**ATTACK**
goatee	**BEARD**
go away	**SCRAM, SHOO, DEPART, LEAVE, SCAT**
gob	**TAR, SAILOR**
go back	**RETURN**
go back on a promise	**RENEGE**
go back to	**REVERT, RETURN**
go bad	**SPOIL, ROT**
gobble	**EAT**
gobbler	**TURKEY**
go before the wind	**SCUD**
go-between	**AGENT**
go beyond	**OVERREACH**
goblet	**GLASS**
goblet part	**STEM**
goblin	**SPRITE, GHOST, HAUNT**
go by	**ELAPSE, PASS**
go by car	**RIDE**
go by ship	**SAIL**
god	**IDOL, DIETY**
god-fearing	**DEVOUT, PIOUS**
godforsaken	**DESOLATE, FORLORN**
god, goddess (name of)—(See under Greek deity, Norse deity, etc.)	
godliness	**PIETY**
godly	**DIVINE**
god of the east	**ALLAH**
go easily	**AMBLE**
go forward	**ADVANCE, PROGRESS**
go from store to store	**SHOP**
go furtively	**SNEAK, STEAL**
goggle	**STARE, GAPE**
goggles	**GLASSES**
go in	**ENTER, PENETRATE**
gold	**WEALTH, MONEY**
gold (Sp.)	**ORO**
gold cloth	**LAME**
Gold Coast	**GHANA**
gold coin	**EAGLE**
gold color	**YELLOW**
gold in heraldry	**OR**
gold in mass	**BULLION**
gold leaf	**GILT**
gold plated statuette	**OSCAR**
golden	**GILT**
golden bird	**ORIOLE**
golden bronze	**ORMOLU**
golden calf	**IDOL**
golden fish	**CARP**
golden fleece seeker	**JASON**
golden horde	**MONGOLS**
Golden State	**CALIFORNIA**
golf club	**WOOD, PUTTER, IRON, DRIVER**
golf club face	**LOFT**
golf course	**LINKS**
golf course item	**HOLE**
golfer Hogan	**BEN**
golfer Lema	**TONY**
golfer Palmer	**ARNOLD**
golfer Sarazen	**GENE**
golfer Snead	**SAM**
golf expert	**PRO**
golf gadget	**TEE**
golf hazard	**BUNKER, TRAP**
golf hole	**CUP, BYE**
golf mound	**TEE**

golf norm	**PAR**	go swiftly	**FLIT, RACE, RUN,**
golf score	**BIRDIE, PAR,**		**HIE, HASTEN, SCUD**
	EAGLE, BOGEY	go swimming	**BATHE**
golf shout	**FORE**	Gothic arch	**OGIVE**
golf term	**BIRDIE, FORE**	Gothic window	**ORIEL**
Golgotha	**CALVARY**	go through	**EXPERIENCE**
goliard	**MINSTREL, JESTER**	go through with	**COMPLETE**
Goliath	**GIANT**	go to bed	**RETIRE, TURN IN**
Goliath's slayer	**DAVID**	go together	**MATCH**
golly	**GEE, GOSH**	go too far	**OVERSTEP**
gondola	**BOAT**	go to the bottom	**SINK**
gone	**LEFT, AGO**	goulash	**STEW**
gone by	**PAST, AGO**	go under	**FAIL**
gone from home	**AWAY, OUT**	Gounod's opera	**FAUST**
goober	**PEANUT**	go up	**RISE, ASCEND, CLIMB**
good	**HONEST**	gourd	**PEPO, MELON**
good (Fr.)	**BON**	gourmand	**EPICURE, GOURMET**
good (Scot.)	**GUDE**	govern	**RULE**
good-by	**FAREWELL, TA-TA**	governess	**NANNY**
good-by, in Madrid	**ADIOS**	governing board member	
good-by, in Tokyo	**SAYONARA**		**REGENT**
good-for-nothing	**IDLER**	government agent	
good fortune on first venture		(comp. wd.)	**T-MAN, G-MAN**
	BEGINNER'S LUCK	government assistance	
good judgment	**PRUDENCE**	(2 wds.)	**FEDERAL AID**
good luck symbol	**MASCOT,**	government by a few	
	TALISMAN		**OLIGARCHY**
good name	**CREDIT, HONOR**	government levy	**TAX**
goodness	**VIRTUE**	governor	**REGENT**
good news	**EVANGEL**	Gower Champion's wife	**MARGE**
goods	**MATERIAL, WARES**	gown	**DRESS**
goods for sale	**WARES**	go wrong	**ERR, SIN**
good turn	**FAVOR**	grace	**CHARM**
gooey	**STICKY**	graceful	**ELEGANT**
gooey mud	**SLIME**	graceful animal	**DEER**
goof	**BLUNDER**	graceful bird	**SWAN**
go off	**EXPLODE**	graceful horse	**ARAB**
go on	**CONTINUE**	graceful loser (2 wds.)	**GOOD**
go on a cruise (2 wds.)	**SET SAIL**		**SPORT**
go one better	**OUT DO**	gracious	**BENIGN, KIND**
go on foot	**WALK, MARCH**	gradation	**STEP**
goose egg	**O, ZERO**	grade	**RANK**
goose genus	**ANSER**	gradual	**SLOW**
go over	**EXAMINE**	graduate	**ALUMNUS**
go over a bridge	**CROSS**	graduate of Annapolis (abbr.)	
go over and change	**REVISE**		**ENS**
gore	**PIERCE**	graduate's memento	
gorge	**CANYON**	(2 wds.)	**CLASS RING**
gorgeous	**MAGNIFICENT,**	grafted (Her.)	**ENTE**
	SPLENDID	grafting twig	**SCION, CION**
gorgon	**MEDUSA**	grain	**OAT, RICE, WHEAT,**
gorilla	**APE**		**BARLEY, SEED**
gorse	**FURZE**	grain for beer	**BARLEY**
gosh	**GEE, GOLLY**	grain for bread	**WHEAT**
go softly	**TIPTOE**	grain for grinding	**GRIST**
gospel	**TRUTH**	grain for weddings	**RICE**
gossamer	**FILMY, THIN**	grain for whiskey	**RYE**
gossip	**TALK, TATTLER, DIRT**	grain grinding place	**MILL**

grain mildew	**RUST**
grain of corn	**KERNEL**
grain warehouse	**ELEVATOR**
grainy	**GRANULAR**
grammarian's concern	**SYNTAX**
grammatical mark	**TILDE**
grampus	**ORC**
grand	**GREAT, EPIC**
Grand Canyon State	**ARIZONA**
grandee	**NOBLEMAN**
grandeur	**MAJESTY**
grange	**FARM**
Granite State	**NEW HAMPSHIRE**
grant	**CEDE**
granting that	**IF**
grant temporarily	**LEND**
granular	**GRAINY**
granular snow	**NEVE**
grape plant	**VINE**
graph	**CHART**
graphic	**VIVID, LUCID, CLEAR**
graphic layout	**MAP**
grapple	**WRESTLE**
grasp	**CLUTCH, HOLD, TAKE**
grasp firmly	**CLENCH**
grasp grimly	**GRIP**
grasping	**AVID, GREEDY**
grasping device	**TONGS**
grasp roughly	**GRAB**
grass	**LAWN, CEREAL**
grass cloth	**JUTE, HEMP**
grass cutter	**MOWER**
grass dried for fodder	**HAY**
grassland	**LEA, PASTURE**
grass leaf	**BLADE**
grasshopper's cousin	**CICADA, LOCUST, MANTIS**
grass roots	**BASICS**
grassy area	**LAWN, PASTURE, LEA, SAVANNA**
grassy field (poet.)	**MEAD**
grate	**RASP, SCRAPE**
grateful	**APPRECIATIVE, GLAD**
gratify	**PLEASE**
gratify one's vanity	**FLATTER**
grating	**GRID**
gratis	**FREE**
gratitude	**THANKS**
gratuitous	**BASELESS**
gratuity	**TIP**
grave	**SERIOUS, SOBER**
grave robber	**GHOUL**
gravy	**SAUCE**
gravy server	**BOAT**
gray	**DISMAL, NEUTRAL**
grayish blue	**SLATE**
grayish red (2 wds.)	**ASH ROSE**
gray with age	**HOARY**

grazing land	**PASTURE, LEA**
grease	**OIL, FAT, LARD**
great	**LARGE, VAST, BIG, HUGE**
Great Britain principality	**WALES, SCOTLAND**
greater in number	**MORE**
greatest	**EXTREME, UTMOST**
great folly	**MADNESS**
great-hearted	**BRAVE, GENEROUS**
great in size	**VAST, GIGANTIC**
great knowledge	**LORE**
Great Lake	**ERIE, HURON, MICHIGAN, ONTARIO, SUPERIOR**
great lie (colloq)	**WHOPPER**
greatly	**MUCH**
greatly excited	**ENTHUSED, AGOG**
greatly happy	**BLISSFUL, JOYFUL, ELATED**
great misfortune	**DISASTER**
great Mogul emperor	**AKBAR**
great number	**MULTITUDE**
great operatic tenor	**CARUSO**
great part	**BULK**
great personage	**MOGUL**
great pleasure	**DELIGHT**
great plenty	**ABUNDANCE**
great realm	**EMPIRE**
great respect	**AWE**
great success	**HIT**
Great White Way	**BROADWAY**
great world	**SOCIETY**
greedy	**AVID**
greedy person	**MISER**
Greek assembly	**AGORA**
Greek biographer	**PLUTARCH**
Greek capital	**ATHENS**
Greek city	**SPARTA**
Greek coin	**OBOL**
Greek colonnade	**STOA**
Greek colony	**IONIA**
Greek column	**CARYATID**
Greek commune	**DEME**
Greek cupid	**EROS**
Greek cynic	**TIMON**
Greek dialect	**DORIC, AEOLIC, EOLIC**
Greek deity	**AMPHITRITE, APHRODITE, APOLLO, ARES, POSEIDON, ZEUS, HERMES, HERA, HECATE, ARTEMIS, HEBE, ERIS, ATHENA, EROS, EOS, DEMETER, DIONYSUS, NIKE, PAN, PLUTO, TRITON, MOIRA, CYBELE, NEMESIS, BACCHUS**

Greek district	**DEME**
Greek dog	**GREYHOUND**
Greek epic poem	**ILIAD,**
	ODYSSEY
Greek epic poet	**HOMER**
Greek games city	**NEMEA**
Greek god—(See Greek deity)	
Greek goddess of agriculture	
	DEMETER
Greek goddess of discord	**ERIS**
Greek goddess of peace	**IRENE**
Greek goddess of the dawn	**EOS**
Greek goddess of the moon	
	ARTEMIS
Greek goddess of victory	**NIKE**
Greek goddess of youth	**HEBE**
Greek god of love	**EROS**
Greek goddess—(See Greek deity)	
Greek hero	**THESEUS, AJAX**
Greek island	**CRETE, SAMOS,**
	CORFU
Greek Juno	**HERA**
Greek lawgiver	**SOLON**
Greek letter	**BETA, ALPHA,**
THETA, KAPPA, PI, PSI, RHO,	
OMEGA, CHI, ETA, DELTA,	
PHI, TAU, MU, EPSILON,	
GAMMA, ZETA, ETA, IOTA,	
LAMBDA, NU, XI, OMICRON,	
SIGMA, UPSILON	
Greek malignant spirit	**KER**
Greek marker	**STELE**
Greek mathematician and	
inventor	**ARCHIMEDES**
Greek measure	**DAKTYLOS,**
	BEMA
Greek money	**DRACHMA**
Greek monster	**GORGON**
Greek mountain	**OSSA, PELION**
Greek muse	**ERATO, CLIO,**
CALLIOPE, EUTERPE,	
MELPOMENE, POLYMNIA,	
TERPSICHORE, THALIA,	
URANIA	
Greek mythological youth	
	ADONIS
Greek nymph	**OREAD**
Greek paradise	**ELYSIUM**
Greek people	**DEMOS**
Greek philosophers	**PLATO,**
	SOCRATES
Greek philosophy school	**STOIC**
Greek physician	**GALEN**
Greek platform	**BEMA**
Greek poet	**HOMER, ARION**
Greek poetess	**SAPPHO**
Greek port	**CORFU, PIRAEUS**

Greek portico	**STOA**
Greek ruler	**EPARCH**
Greek sea	**AEGEAN, IONIAN**
Greek slave	**HELOT**
Greek sorceress	**MEDEA**
Greek sun god	**APOLLO**
Greek sylvan deity	**SATYR**
Greek temple	**NAOS**
Greek theater	**ODEUM, ODEA**
green	**UNRIPE, ENVIOUS**
greenback	**DOLLAR, BILL**
Green Bay football team	
	PACKERS
green citrus fruit	**LIME**
green-eyed	**JEALOUS**
green (Fr.)	**VERT**
green gem	**JADE, EMERALD**
green herbage	**GRASS**
Greenland's colonizer	**ERIC**
Greenland settlement	**ETAH**
green light	**GO-AHEAD, GO**
Green Mountain State	**VERMONT**
green onion	**SCALLION**
green plum	**GAGE**
green quartz	**PRASE**
green rock-growth	**MOSS**
green rust	**PATINA**
green spot	**OASIS**
green stone	**EMERALD, JADE**
greensward	**LAWN, SOD**
greet	**ACCOST, HAIL, SALUTE**
greeting	**HULLO, HELLO, HI**
greeting message	**CARD**
gregarious	**SOCIAL**
gremlin	**GNOME, BROWNIE,**
	ELF, SPRITE
Gretna Green figure	**ELOPER**
grief	**SORROW**
grieve	**LAMENT**
grieve bitterly (4 wds.)	**EAT**
	ONE'S HEART OUT
grievous	**LAMENTABLE**
grill	**BROIL**
grim	**AUSTERE**
grimace	**MOUE, SNEER**
grime	**DIRT, SOOT, DUST**
grin	**SMILE**
grind	**CRUSH**
grinding machine	**MILL**
grinding stone	**EMERY**
grinding tooth	**MOLAR**
grind with the teeth	**CHEW,**
	MASH, GNASH
grip	**GRASP, VALISE**
grisly	**GHASTLY, GRIM**
gristle	**CARTILAGE**
grit	**SAND**

grizzly **BEAR**
groan **MOAN**
grooming aid **COMB, BRUSH,**
TALC, TONIC, RAZOR
groom's attendant
(2 wds.) **BEST MAN**
groove **RUT**
grotesque **BIZARRE**
grotto **CAVE, CAVERN**
grotto (poet.) **GROT**
grouchy person **CRAB, CRANK**
ground **LAND, SOIL**
ground-breaking tool **SPADE**
ground grain **MEAL**
groundless **UNFOUNDED**
ground plot **LOT**
grounds **BASIS**
ground squirrel **GOPHER**
group **LOT**
grouper **MERO**
group of actors **CAST, TROUPE**
group of animals **HERD**
group of criminals **GANG**
group of customers **CLIENTELE**
group of eight **OCTET**
group of facts **DATA**
group of families **TRIBE, CLAN**
group of five **QUINTET, PENTAD**
group of Indians **TRIBE**
group of lions **PRIDE**
group of musicians **BAND,**
ORCHESTRA, COMBO,
DANCE BAND
group of nine **ENNEAD**
group of persons **TEAM, CROWD**
group of pictures **SET**
group of points **LOCI**
group of related species **GENUS**
group of rooms **SUITE**
group of seamen **CREW**
group of seven **HEPTAD**
group of ships **FLEET, ARMADA**
group of singers **CHOIR**
group of six **SEXTET**
group of states **EMPIRE**
group of students **CLASS**
group of ten **DECADE, DECAD**
group of three **TRIAD, TRIO**
group of two **DYAD, DUET, DUO,**
PAIR, BRACE
group of Western allies **NATO**
group spirit **MORALE**
group transportation
(2 wds.) **CHARTERED BUS**
grove of trees **COPSE, FOREST**
grovel **FAWN, CRINGE**
grow **EXPAND, RAISE**
grow dim **FADE, WANE**

grow drowsy **NOD**
growing in pairs **BINATE**
grow in length **ELONGATE**
growl **SNARL**
grow molars **TEETHE**
grow more intense **DEEPEN**
grown boy **MAN**
grown up ugly duckling **SWAN**
grow old **AGE**
grow out of **DEVELOP**
grow quickly **SPROUT**
growth **RISE, INCREASE**
grow thin **EMACIATE**
grow tiresome **BORE**
grow weary **TIRE**
grow worse **DETERIORATE**
grub **FOOD, VICTUALS**
grubby **MESSY, UNTIDY**
grudge **SPITE, ENVY**
gruesome **LURID, MACABRE**
gruff **ABRUPT, BRUSQUE**
grumble **COMPLAIN**
Guam capital **AGANA**
Guam seaport **APRA**
guanaco **LLAMA**
guarantee **ASSURE**
guaranty **PLEDGE, WARRANTY**
guard **SENTINEL**
guardhouse **BRIG**
guardian **PATRON,**
CUSTODIAN
guard spirit of old Rome **LAR**
Guatemalan **MAYAN**
Gudrun's husband **ATLI**
guess **SUPPOSE, ESTIMATE**
guessing game **CHARADE**
guest **LODGER, VISITOR**
guide **LEAD**
guide a car **STEER,**
DRIVE
guide a plane **PILOT**
guide to solution of
a mystery **CLUE**
guidon **PENNANT, BANNER**
Guido's high note **ELA**
guile **CRAFT, CUNNING**
guileless **NAIVE**
guillotine **BEHEAD**
guilty **CULPABLE,**
BLAMABLE
guilty person **CULPRIT**
guilty regret **REMORSE**
guinea pig **CAVY**
guise **ASPECT, SEMBLANCE**
gulch **RAVINE**
gulf **ABYSS**
gulf between Africa
and Arabia **ADEN**

gulf of Australia	**CARPENTARIA**
gullet	**MAW, THROAT**
gullible fellow	**DUPE**
gull-like bird	**TERN**
gully	**GUTTER**
gum	**RESIN**
gumbo	**OKRA, SOUP**
gumption	**NERVE**
gums	**ULA**
gum tree	**SAPODILLA**
gun	**FIREARM, MUSKET,**
	RIFLE, PISTOL
gun an engine	**REV**
gun barrel cleaner	**RAMROD**
gun cavity	**BORE**
gun dog	**SETTER**
gunny bag	**SACK**
gunpowder ingredient	**NITRE**
gun tube	**BARREL**
guru	**TEACHER**
gush	**POUR, SPURT**
gush forth	**SPEW**
gusto	**ZEST, ELAN**
guy	**CHAP, FELLOW**
gymnasium pad	**MAT**
gyp	**CHEAT, SWINDLE**
gypsy man	**ROM**
gyrate	**WHIRL, ROTATE**

H

habiliment	**CLOTHING,**
	DRESS, ATTIRE
habit	**CUSTOM, WONT,**
	OUTFIT, ATTIRE
habitat	**LOCALITY**
habitation	**ABODE**
habitual	**USUAL, CUSTOMARY**
habitual drunkard	**SOT**
habituate	**INURE**
hack	**TAXI**
hackamore	**HALTER, BRIDLE**
hackle	**BRISTLE**
hackneyed	**BANAL, TRITE,**
	STALE
hack up	**CHOP**
hades	**HELL, INFERNO**
hag	**CRONE**
haggard	**GAUNT, WEARY**
Haggard novel	**SHE**
haggle	**BARGAIN, DICKER**
hail	**AVE, GREET, SLEET**
hair	**TRESSES, MANE**
hair curler	**ROLLER**
hair-do	**AFRO, SET, STYLE**
hair-do holder	**NET**
hair dye	**HENNA**

hair grooming aid	**COMB,**
	BRUSH
hairless	**BALD**
hair ointment	**POMADE**
hair on horse's foot	**FETLOCK**
hair on lion's neck	**MANE**
hair pad	**RAT**
hair piece	**SWITCH, FALL,**
	WIG, TOUPEE
hair ribbon	**SNOOD**
hair ringlet	**TRESS, CURL**
hair roll	**CHIGNON**
hair style	**UPDO, SHINGLE**
hair tint	**RINSE**
hairy man	**ESAU**
Haitian city	**PORT-AU-**
	PRINCE
Haitian magic	**OBEAH, OBI**
halcyon	**TRANQUIL, CALM**
hale	**HEALTHY, ROBUST**
half	**PART, PARTIAL**
half (prefix)	**SEMI, DEMI, HEMI**
half a quart	**PINT**
half a score	**TEN**
half-diameter	**RADIUS**
half gainer	**DIVE**
half hitch	**KNOT**
half man and half bull	**CENTAUR**
half mask	**DOMINO**
half moon	**CRESCENT**
half-suppressed laugh	**SNICKER**
halfway	**MID**
halfwit	**FOOL, DOLT**
hall	**PASSAGE, CORRIDOR**
Halley's constellation	**APUS**
hallow	**DEDICATE, BLESS**
hallowed place	**SHRINE**
Halloween alternative	**TRICK,**
	TREAT
Halloween beverage	**CIDER**
hall rug	**RUNNER**
hallucination	**DELUSION**
hallux	**BIG TOE**
halo	**AURA, NIMBUS**
halt	**CEASE, STOP,**
	DESIST, ESTOP
halter	**LEAD**
halve	**BISECT**
hambletonian	**TROTTER, RACE**
hamburger garnish	**ONION,**
	PICKLE,
	MUSTARD, CATSUP, RELISH
hame	**HARNESS**
Hamilton bill	**TEN**
Hamite	**SOMALI**
hamlet	**TOWN, VILLAGE, DORP**
Hamlet's home	**ELSINORE,**
	DENMARK

Hamlet's sweetheart	**OPHELIA**
hammer	**SLEDGE**
hammer part	**PEEN, CLAW,**
	HEAD
hammerhead	**SHARK**
hammerlike tool	**MALLET**
hammock cord (comp. wd.)	
	TIE-TIE
hamper	**BASKET, IMPEDE**
Ham's son	**CUSH**
hamstring	**DISABLE**
hand	**WORKER**
handbag	**PURSE**
handball point	**ACE**
hand blow	**SLAP**
handcuff	**MANACLE**
Handel masterwork	**MESSIAH**
hand down	**BEQUEATH**
handicap	**BURDEN, PENALTY**
hand implement	**SHOVEL,**
	PICK, HOE
handkerchief	**BANDANA,**
	HANKY
handle	**LEVER, TREAT**
handle of a knife	**HAFT**
handle of a sword	**HILT**
handle of a whip	**CROP**
handle roughly	**MAUL**
handle rudely	**PAW**
handle well	**COPE**
handling	**TREATMENT,**
	CONTROL
handsome man	**ADONIS**
hand-to-hand fight	**MELEE**
handy carryall (2 wds.)	
	SHOPPING BAG
hang	**PEND, SUSPEND**
hang above	**HOVER**
hang around	**LOITER**
hanger on	**PARASITE**
hang in folds	**DRAPE**
hanging tuft of threads	**TASSEL**
hang loosely	**LOLL, SAG, DROOP**
hangman's knot	**NOOSE**
hang on	**PERSEVERE**
hang on to	**HOLD, KEEP,**
	RETAIN
hang overhead	**HOVER**
hank	**SKEIN**
hanker	**ITCH, YEN, DESIRE**
hank of twine	**RAN**
haphazard (3 wds.)	**HIT OR MISS**
haphazardly (2 wds.)	
	AT RANDOM
happen	**BETIDE, OCCUR,**
	TAKE PLACE
happen again	**RECUR**
hapless	**UNLUCKY**
happening	**EVENT**
happen to	**BEFALL**
happily	**LUCKILY**
happiness	**GLADNESS, JOY,**
	ELATION, BLISS
happy	**GLAD, JOYFUL,**
	BLISSFUL
happy bird	**LARK**
happy cat sound	**PURR**
happy expressions	**SMILE, GRIN**
harangue	**ORATE**
harass	**ANNOY, PLAGUE**
harbinger	**HERALD**
harbor	**HAVEN, PORT**
harbor boat	**TUG**
harbor city	**PORT**
harbor craft	**FERRYBOAT,**
	TUGBOAT
harbor guide	**PILOT**
harbor sight	**SHIP**
hard	**DIFFICULT, SOLID**
hard and fast	**STRICT**
hard ball	**BASEBALL**
hard-bitten	**STUBBORN, TOUGH**
hard-boiled	**TOUGH, CALLOUS**
hard candy	**LEMON DROP**
hard cash	**MONEY**
hard coal	**ANTHRACITE**
hard core	**ABSOLUTE**
hard cover	**BOUND**
hard drawn	**TENSE**
hard drinker	**TOPER, SOT,**
	SOUSE
harden	**SET, STEEL, GEL, INURE**
hardened	**CALLOUS, FROZEN**
hard finish	**ENAMEL**
hard-fisted	**STINGY, MISERLY**
hard handed defense	**KARATE**
hard hearted	**CRUEL, MEAN**
hard lump of earth	**CLOD**
hardly	**BARELY**
hardly ever	**RARELY**
hard metal	**IRON, STEEL**
hardness	**RIGOR**
hard-nosed	**SHREWD**
hard of hearing	**DEAF**
hard question	**POSER**
hard resin	**COPAL**
hard rock	**SLATE**
hard-shelled fruit	**NUT**
hardship	**PRIVATION, RIGOR**
hard to describe	**NONDESCRIPT**
hard up	**NEEDY, LACKING**
hardware	**TOOLS**
hardwood	**TEAK**
hardwood tree	**MAPLE, OAK**
hard work	**LABOR, TOIL**
hard worker	**DEMON**

hardy **BOLD, DARING**
hardy cabbage **KALE**
hardy person **SPARTAN**
Hardy's heroine **TESS**
harebrained **RECKLESS, RASH**
harem apartment **ODA**
hark **LISTEN**
harm **DAMAGE, MAR, HURT**
harmless **GENTLE, DOCILE**
harmonious **AGREEABLE**
harmonize **AGREE, BLEND**
harmony **UNISON, ACCORD**
harmony in pitch **TUNE**
harness attachment **REIN**
harry **HARASS, ANNOY**
harsh **SEVERE**
harshest **SEVEREST**
harsh speech **TIRADE**
hart **DEER, STAG**
Harvard's rival **YALE**
harvest **CROP, REAP**
harvest fly **CICADA**
hash **MINCE**
hash over **DISCUSS**
hassle **CONTENTION**
hassock **FOOTSTOOL**
haste **SPEED, SWIFTNESS**
hasten **HIE, RUN, SPEED**
hasty **HURRIED, FLEET**
hasty meal **SNACK**
hat **BONNET, CAP, BERET,
CHAPEAU**
hat accessory **VEIL, RIBBON**
hatch **PLOT, PLAN**
hatchet **AX, AXE**
hat crown **POLL**
hate **ABHOR, DETEST, LOATHE**
hateful **ODIOUS**
hat material **FELT, STRAW**
hatred **ODIUM, DISLIKE**
haughtiness **ARROGANCE,
PRIDE**
haughty **PROUD, ALOOF**
haughty one **SNOB**
haul **DRAG, TOW, TUG**
haul down flag **STRIKE**
hauling charge **CARTAGE**
hauling wagon **DRAY**
haulm **STRAW**
haul up **REST, STOP**
haunch **HIP**
haunt **DEN, HABIT**
hausen **BELUGA**
hautboy **OBOE**
have **OWN, POSSESS, HOLD**
have affection for **LIKE, LOVE**
have ambitions **ASPIRE**
have a meal **EAT, DINE, SUP**

have another opinion **DIFFER**
have a quarrel (2 wds.) **FALL OUT**
have at **ATTACK, STRIKE**
have being **ARE**
have benefit **ENJOY**
have courage (2 wds.) **BEAR UP**
have debts **OWE**
have done **FINISH**
have effect **ENURE, INURE**
have faith **TRUST**
have high regard for **ADMIRE**
have interest in **CARE**
have life **LIVE, EXIST**
have need of **LACK**
have reference to **PERTAIN**
have the ability **CAN**
have the courage **DARE TO**
have to **MUST**
have to do with **DEAL**
haven **HARBOR, PORT,
ASYLUM**
having a backbone **VERTEBRATE**
having a beak **ROSTRATE**
having a good memory
RETENTIVE
having antlers **HORNED**
having a tail **CAUDATE**
having auricles **EARED**
having boots **SHOD**
having equality of measure
ISOMETRICAL
having feet **PEDATE**
having fine scenery **SCENIC**
having knowledge **AWARE**
having leaves **FOLIAR**
having left a will **TESTATE**
having less hair **BALDER**
having liberty **FREE**
having limits **FINITE**
having little warmth **COLD**
having made a will **TESTATE**
having offensive odor **OLID**
having one foot **UNIPED**
having onionlike forms **BULBED**
having pile **NAPPY**
having ringlets **CURLY**
having wealth position, etc.
SUCCESSFUL
having wings **ALAR, ALATE**
Hawaiian city **HILO, HONOLULU**
Hawaiian Dance **HULA**
Hawaiian export **COPRA,
PINEAPPLE**
Hawaiian food fish **LANIA, ULUA**
Hawaiian food staple **TARO**
Hawaiian garland **LEI**
Hawaiian goddess **PELE**
Hawaiian greeting **ALOHA**

Hawaiian guitar **UKULELE, UKE**
Hawaiian hawk **IO**
Hawaiian island **OAHU**
Hawaiian lava **AA**
Hawaiian mahogany **KOA**
Hawaiian pepper **AVA**
Hawaiian porch **LANAI**
Hawaiian root **TARO**
Hawaiian salutation **ALOHA**
Hawaiian town **HILO**
hawker **PEDDLER**
Hawkeye State **IOWA**
hawk-like bird **KITE**
hawk's claws **TALON**
hawkshaw's **SLEUTH**
hawk's victims **PREY**
Hawthorne heroine **HESTER**
hay fever **POLLEN**
hay field **MEADOW**
hayseed **RUBE, HICK**
haystack **STADDLE**
haywire **CRAZY, WACKY**
hazard **RISK**
hazardous **UNSAFE, RISKY**
haze **MIST, FOG**
hazelnut **FILBERT**
hazy **CLOUDY, MURKY**
he (Fr.) **IL**
head **PATE, CHIEF, NOODLE,**
NOGGIN, BEAN
headache **MIGRAINE**
headache remedy **ASPIRIN**
headcloth **SCARF**
head cook **CHEF**
head covering **CAP, HAT, HOOD,**
SCARF, BERET, VEIL
headdress **FEATHER**
headed pin **RIVET**
heading **TITLE, BEARING,**
DIRECTION
headland **CAPE, NESS, RAS**
headless (Fr.) **ETETE**
headline **CAPTION**
headliner **STAR**
headlong **RECKLESS, HASTY**
headman **CHIEF**
head money **BOUNTY**
head of a monastery **ABBOT**
head of a nunnery **ABBESS**
head skin **SCALP**
headstrong **RASH**
heal **CURE, MEND**
heal, as bone **KNIT**
healer **BALM**
healing **CURATIVE**
healing profession **MEDICINE**
health resort **SPA**
healthy **HALE, ROBUST**

healthy (Lat.) **SANA**
heap **MOUND, PILE, STACK**
heap of stone **CAIRN**
hear **HEED, LISTEN**
hear about **LEARN**
hearing organ **EAR**
hearken **HEED, LISTEN**
hearsay **RUMOR, GOSSIP**
heart **CORE**
heartbeat **PULSE**
heartbreak **GRIEF, SORROW**
hear tell **LEARN**
hearten **CHEER**
hearth **FIRESIDE**
heartless **COLD, HARD, CRUEL**
heart of the matter **GIST**
hearty **WARM**
hearty enjoyment **ZEST**
hearty laugh (comp. wd.) **HA-HA**
hearty meat dish **STEW**
hearty relish **GUSTO**
heat **WARMTH, PRESSURE**
heat content **ENTHALPY**
heater **STOVE, OVEN**
heath (Brit.) **MOOR**
heathen (arch.) **PAYNIM**
heathen deity **IDOL**
heather **LING, ERICA**
heath plant **ERICA**
heath tree **BRIER, BRIAR**
heating apparatus **ETNA,**
OVEN, OAST, KILN,
BOILER, BRAZIER,
STOVE
heating chambers **OVEN**
OAST, KILN
heating material **FUEL, OIL,**
GAS, WOOD
heave **HOIST, LIFT**
heave to **STOP**
heaven **PARADISE**
heavenly **DIVINE, SUBLIME,**
CELESTIAL
heavenly altar **ARA**
heavenly being **ANGEL**
heavenly body **COMET, STAR,**
PLANET, SUN,
MOON, METEOR
heavenly city **ZION, VALHALLA**
heavenly instrument **HARP**
heavens **SKY**
heavenward **UP**
heavily built **STOCKY**
heavily loaded **LADEN**
heavy **WEIGHTY, LEADEN**
heavy affliction **WOE**
heavy board **PLANK**
heavy blow **CLOUT**

heavy book	**TOME**	height	**STATURE**
heavy burden	**LOAD**	heighten	**ENHANCE**
heavy cord	**ROPE**	heinous	**HIDEOUS,**
heavy curtain	**DRAPE**		**OUTRAGEOUS**
heavy element	**LEAD**	heir	**SON, SCION**
heavy-footed	**SLOW, DULL**	held in readiness (2 wds.)	**ON ICE**
heavy grouping of reeds	**CLUMP**	hell	**HADES, INFERNO**
heavy-handed	**CLUMSY, HARSH**	hello	**HI, GREETING**
heavy-hearted	**SAD**	helmsman	**PILOT**
heavy hydrogen	**DEUTERIUM**	help	**ABET, AID, ASSIST**
heavy impact	**SLAM**	helper	**ALLY, AIDE, ASSISTANT**
heavy metal	**LEAD**	helpful	**USEFUL**
heavy nail	**SPIKE**	help in crime	**ABET**
heavy rainfall	**STORM**	helping	**PORTION**
heavy-set	**STOUT, STOCKY**	help in solving a mystery	**CLUE**
heavy shoe	**BOOT, BROGAN,**	helpless	**POWERLESS**
	CLOG	helpmate	**WIFE**
heavy sleepers	**SNORERS,**	Helsinki native	**FINLANDER**
	BUNTING	helter-skelter	**RUSHED,**
heavy spar	**BARITE**		**DISORDERLY**
heavy string	**CORD, TWINE,**	hem	**BORDER, EDGE**
	ROPE	hemi	**HALF**
heavy twilled cotton	**DENIM**	hem in	**ENCLOSE**
heavy volume	**TOME**	hemorrhage	**BLEEDING**
heavy weight	**TON**	hemp	**FENNEL, SISAL**
heavy with moisture	**SODDEN**	hemp cord	**ROPE**
Hebrew	**SEMITE, SEMITIC**	hen	**CHICKEN, PULLET**
Hebrew abode of dead	**SHEOL**	henchman	**MINION**
Hebrew ascetic	**ESSENE**	hen fruit	**EGG**
Hebrew lawgiver	**MOSES**	hens	**POULTRY**
Hebrew letter	**ALEF, BETH,**	herald	**MESSENGER**
	GIMEL, DALETH, MEM,	heraldic bearing	**ORLE**
	TETH, PE, YOD, HE,	heraldic cross	**PETTEE,**
	VAU, ZAYIN, CHETH,		**POMMEE, MOLINE, TAU,**
	VODH, CAPH, LAMEDH,		**MALTESE, FOURCHEE,**
	NUN, SAMEKH, AYIN,		**BOTONEE, CROSSLET**
	SADHE, KOPH, RESH,	Hera's husband	**ZEUS**
	SIN, SHIN. TAV	Hera's son	**ARES, HEPHAETOS**
Hebrew lyre	**ASTOR**	herb	**SAGE, ANISE, BASIL**
Hebrew marriage custom		herb of the teasel family	
	LEVIRATE		**SCABIOSA**
Hebrew measure	**OMER**	Hercules' captive	**IOLE**
Hebrew month	**TISHRI, ADAR,**	herd	**DROVE, FLOCK**
	ELUL, AB, KISLEV	here (Fr.)	**ICI**
Hebrew patriarch	**ABRAHAM,**	hereditary	**INHERENT, INNATE**
	ISAAC, JACOB	hereditary factor	**GENE**
Hebrew prophet	**MOSES,**	heretic	**DISSENTER, TRAITOR**
	DANIEL, AMOS,	heritage	**LEGACY, BIRTHRIGHT**
	HOSEA, MICAH	hermit	**EREMITE, RECLUSE**
Hebrew prophetess	**DEBORAH**	hermit's hut	**CELL**
Hebrew Sabbath	**SATURDAY,**	hernia support	**TRUSS**
	SHABBAT	hero of comics	**SUPERMAN,**
Hebrew school	**CHEDER**		**BATMAN, DICK TRACY**
Hebrew teacher	**RABBI**	heroic	**EPIC**
heckle	**BADGER, PESTER**	heroic tale	**SAGA**
hectic	**FEVERISH**	heroine of A Doll's House	**NORA**
hedge shrub	**PRIVET**	heroine of The Rose Tattoo	
heed	**HEAR**		**ROSA**

heroism	**VALOR, BRAVERY**
heron	**EGRET**
hero's award	**MEDAL**
herring	**CISCO, SPRAT**
herring alec	**PICKLE**
herring family fish	**ALEWIFE**
he-she dispute (2 wds.)	
	LOVERS' QUARREL
hesitate	**DEMUR, FALTER,**
PAUSE, STUMBLE, WAVER	
hesitation of speech	**STUTTER**
heterogeneous	**VARIANT, MIXED,**
	DISSIMILAR
hew	**CUT, CHOP**
hew out	**CARVE**
hex	**JINX**
Heyerdahl's raft (2 wds.)	
	KON TIKI
Hialeah event (2 wds.)	
	HORSE RACE
hiatus	**GAP, PAUSE**
Hiawatha's nurse	**NOKOMIS**
Hibernian	**ERSE**
hickory nut	**PECAN**
hidden	**INNER, LATENT,**
	COVERT
hidden obstacle	**SNAG**
hidden supply	**CACHE**
hide	**CONCEAL, COVER,**
MASK, PELT, SKIN	
hideous	**GHASTLY, HORRIBLE**
hideous giant	**OGRE**
hiding place	**CACHE, LAIR**
hie	**HASTEN, HURRY,**
	SPEED, RUN
hiemal	**WINTRY**
hieratic	**SACERDOTAL**
hieroglyphic	**SYMBOL**
hierology	**LORE, FABLE**
hi-fi	**STEREO**
high	**TALL, LOFTY**
highbinder	**SWINDLER**
highborn	**NOBLE**
highboy	**BUREAU, CHEST**
highbrow	**INTELLECTUAL**
high card	**ACE**
high-class	**SUPERIOR**
high craggy hill	**TOR**
high day	**FESTIVAL, HOLIDAY**
higher than	**ABOVE**
highest note	**ELA**
highest point	**ACME, APEX,**
	SUMMIT
high-flying bird	**LARK, EAGLE**
high-hatter	**SNOB**
high honkers (2 wds.)	
	WILD GEESE
high in pitch	**ALT**

high intensity light beam	**LASER**
high in value	**DEAR**
high keyed	**TENSE**
highlander	**SCOT**
highlander's cap	**TAM**
highly	**EXTREMELY**
highly seasoned dish	**OLLA,**
	PODRIDA
highly sensible	**PRUDENT**
high male singing voice	**TENOR**
high-minded	**NOBLE**
high mountain	**ALP**
high note	**ELA, ALT**
high-pitched	**SHRILL**
high plateau	**MESA**
high pointed hill	**TOR**
high priced	**COSTLY**
high priest of Israel	**ELI**
high rank	**EMINENCE**
high regard	**ESTEEM, RESPECT,**
	HONOR
high rubber boot	**WADER**
high school dance	**HOP, PROM**
high school student	
(comp. wd.)	**TEENAGER**
high sea	**MAIN**
high shoe	**BOOT**
high spirits	**ELATION, GLEE**
high structure	**TOWER**
high strung	**TENSE, NERVOUS**
high temperature	**HEAT**
high time	**SPREE**
high up	**ALOFT**
highway	**ROAD, ROUTE, PIKE**
highway charge	**TOLL**
highway curve	**ESS**
highway division	**LANE**
highway exit	**RAMP**
highway Inn	**MOTEL**
highwayman (2 wds.)	
	ROAD AGENT
highway sight	**BILLBOARD**
highway to the far north	**ALCAN**
high winds	**GALE, SQUALL,**
	STORM, HURRICANE,
	TORNADO, CYCLONE
high wire	**TIGHTROPE**
hijack	**STEAL, CAPTURE**
hike	**MARCH, TRAMP**
hilarious	**FUNNY, MERRY**
hilarious comedy	**FARCE**
hilarity	**GLEE, MIRTH**
hill	**HEAP, MOUND**
hill (Sp.)	**MORRO**
hill dweller	**ANT**
hillock	**KNOLL**
hill of beans	**TRIFLE**
hillside (Scot.)	**BRAE**

hilly **RUGGED, STEEP**
Hilo garland **LEIS**
hilt **HANDLE**
Himalayan animal **PANDA**
Himalayan monkshood **ATIS**
Himalayan mountain **EVEREST**
Himalayan ox **YAK**
hind **DOE, DEER**
hinder **DETER, STOP, SET BACK**
hinder (law) **ESTOP, ESTOPPEL**
Hindi dialect **URDU**
hindrance **OBSTACLE, BURDEN, IMPEDIMENT**
Hindu ascetic **SADHU, SADDHU, YOGI**
Hindu ascetic practice **YOGA**
Hindu chief **SIRDAR**
Hindu coin **ANAA**
Hindu cymbals **TAL**
Hindu deity **DEVI, VAC, UMA, KALI, MATRIS, AGNI, SIVA, DEVA, KAMA, RAMA, YAMA, VISHNU, KRISHNA, INDRA, USAS, SURYA, VARUNA, SHAKTI, GANESA**
Hindu doctrine **KARMA**
Hindu garment **SARI**
Hindu guitar **SITAR**
Hindu incarnation **AVATAR**
Hindu king **RAJAH**
Hindu literature **VEDA**
Hindu noble **RAJAH**
Hindu queen **RANEE, RANI**
Hindu religious teacher **SWAMI**
Hindu sacred city **BENARES, BANARAS**
Hindu social class **CASTE**
hinged tabletop folding to wall **DROP TABLE**
hint **CLUE, CUE, SUGGESTION**
hint (Brit.) **CLEW**
hinterland **BACKWOODS**
hip (sl.) **AWARE, COOL**
hipbone **ILIUM, ILIA (pl.)**
hippie's home **PAD**
hippocampus (2 wds.) **SEA HORSE**
Hippocrates **PHYSICIAN**
hippodrome **ARENA**
hippopotamus (2 wds.) **RIVER HORSE**
hire **EMPLOY, ENGAGE, RENT, LEASE, LET, CHARTER**
hired help **HAND**
hireling **SERF, MERCENARY**
hirsute **HAIRY**
hirundine **SWALLOW**

hiss **SIBILANCE**
hissing sound **SISS**
historian **CHRONICLER**
historical records **ANNALS**
historic island of the Philippines **LEYTE**
historic period **ERA, EPOCH**
history **ACCOUNT, RECORD**
histrionics **THEATRICS**
hit **STRIKE, BAT**
hitch **CATCH, TWIST**
hitchhike **THUMB**
hit hard **SWAT, SMOTE, SMITE, SLAP**
hither **HERE**
hithermost **NEAREST**
Hitler follower **NAZI**
hit lightly **TAP**
hit or miss **CARELESS**
hit out at **ATTACK, CRITICIZE**
hit-show sign (abbr.) **S.R.O.**
hit the road **SCRAM**
hit with the open hand **SLAP**
hive dweller **BEE, WASP, HORNET**
hive product **HONEY**
hoard **SAVE**
hoarder **MISER**
hoarfrost **RIME**
hoarse **HARSH, GRATING**
hoax **FOOLER**
hobble along **LIMP**
hobbling **LAME**
hobby **AVOCATION, PURSUIT**
hobgoblin **IMP, SPRITE**
hobo **BUM, TRAMP, VAGRANT**
hock **PAWN**
hockey game **BANDY**
hockey player **SKATER**
hodgepodge **MESS, MIXTURE, HOTCHPOTCH**
hoe **WEED, DIG**
hog **PIG, SWINE**
hog food **SLOP**
hog meat **HAM, PORK, BACON**
hogshead **CASK**
hoi polloi **RABBLE**
hoist **HEAVE, LIFT**
hoisting device **CRANE**
hold **GRASP, KEEP, CLASP**
hold an opinion **DEEM**
hold back **DELAY, DETAIN, PREVENT, RESTRAIN, RETARD**
hold dear **CHERISH**
hold fast **CLING, ADHERE**
hold firmly **CLASP, GRASP, GRIP**

hold in check	**CURB, REIN**
holding device	**CLAMP, VISE**
holding of property	**TENURE**
hold in greater favor	**PREFER**
hold out	**ENDURE, LAST**
hold session	**SIT, MEET**
hold spellbound	**ENTHRALL,**
	MESMERIZE, HYPNOTIZE
hold sway	**RULE**
hold up	**ROB, ROBBERY**
hold up well	**WEAR**
hold within fixed limits	**CONTAIN**
hole	**CAVITY, PIT,**
	EXCAVATION, CAVE, CAVERN
hole enlarger	**REAMER**
hole in a mold	**SPRUE**
hole in a pan	**LEAK**
hole-in-one	**ACE**
hole-making tool	**AWL**
holey cheese	**SWISS**
holiday	**FESTIVAL**
holiness	**SANCTITY, PIETY**
holler	**ROAR, YELL**
hollow	**EMPTY**
hollow grass	**REED, BAMBOO**
holly tree	**ILEX**
Hollywood event	**ACADEMY**
	AWARDS, PREMIERE,
	SCREENING, SHOWING
Hollywood hopeful	**STARLET**
Hollywood luminary	**STAR**
Hollywood's elephant boy	**SABU**
holm	**AIT**
holm oak	**ILEX**
holocaust	**DESTRUCTION**
holy (Fr.)	**SACRE**
holy city of Islam	**MECCA**
holy image	**ICON**
Holy Land	**PALESTINE**
holy person	**SAINT**
Holy Roman Empire (abbr.)	**H.R.E.**
holy souvenir	**RELIC**
holy water receptacle	**FONT**
homage	**HONOR**
homard	**LOBSTER**
homburg	**HAT**
home	**ABODE, DWELLING,**
	HOUSE, APARTMENT,
	FIRESIDE, HEARTH,
	RESIDENCE
home base	**PLATE**
home-grown	**DOMESTIC**
home in Madrid	**CASA**
homeless child	**WAIF**
homelike	**HOMEY**
homely	**UGLY, PLAIN**

homemade	**DOMESTIC**
home of Abraham	**UR**
home of Adam and Eve	**EDEN**
home of Irish kings	**TARA**
home of Scarlett O'Hara	**TARA**
home party (2 wds.)	**OPEN**
	HOUSE
Homeric epic	**ILIAD, ODYSSEY**
Homeric poem	**EPIC, ILIAD,**
	ODYSSEY
Homeric wise man	**NESTOR**
homesickness	**NOSTALGIA**
homesite	**LOT**
homesteader	**SETTLER**
homicide	**MURDER**
homily	**ADAGE, SERMON**
hominy	**SAMP, GRITS**
homogeneous	**UNIFORM, ALIKE**
homo sapiens	**MAN**
Honduras Indian	**LENCA**
hone	**SHARPEN, WHET**
honest	**TRUTHFUL, JUST,**
	FRANK, OPEN, CANDID, FAIR
honesty	**SINCERITY,**
	FRANKNESS, CANDOR
honey (pharm.)	**MEL**
honey badger	**RATEL**
honey bee genus	**APIS**
honeycomb cell	**ALVEOLUS**
honeycomb product	**BEESWAX**
honey maker	**BEE**
honk	**TOOT, BEEP**
honor	**EXALT**
honorable	**HONEST, EXALTED,**
	ESTEEMED
honorary disc	**MEDAL**
honorary title for retired VIP's	**EMERITUS**
Honshu bay	**ISE**
hood	**COWL**
hooded cape	**AMICE, DOMINO**
hooded vestment	**COPE**
hoodwink	**DUPE**
hoofbeat sound	**CLOP, CLIP**
hoofer	**DANCER**
hook	**GAFF**
Hoosier State	**INDIANA**
hoot	**JEER, HISS**
hop	**LEAP, JUMP**
hope	**ASPIRATION, WISH**
hopeful time	**TOMORROW**
hopeless	**DESPERATE**
hop kiln	**OAST**
hopping insect	**FLEA**
hop stem	**BINE**
horde	**CROWD, MULTITUDE,**
	HOST, MOB
horizon	**SKYLINE**

horizontal **PLANE, LEVEL**
horn **CORNET, BUGLE,**
ANTLER, CORNUCOPIA
horn blare **FANFARE, TANTARA**
horned animal **STAG, ELK,**
MOOSE
horned cud-chewer **GOAT, COW**
horned viper **ASP**
horn of plenty **CORNUCOPIA**
horns **BRASS**
horn sound **TOOT, HONK**
horrible **HATEFUL, REPULSIVE**
horror **DISGUST, AVERSION**
hors d'oeuvre mixture **DIP**
horse **FOAL, ROAN, MARE,**
NAG, PLUG
STALLION, STEED,
horse and buggy **RIG**
horseback game **POLO**
horse bet **PARLAY, WAGER**
horse color **ROAN**
horse command **GEE, HAW,**
WHOA
horsedoctor, for short **VET**
horsefeathers **NONSENSE,**
BUNK
horse food **HAY, OATS, FODDER**
horsehair **CRINOLINE**
horselaugh **GUFFAW**
horselike mammal **MULE,**
DONKEY, BURRO, ZEBRA
horseman **EQUESTRIAN, RIDER,**
JOCKEY
horseman's goad **SPUR**
horse measure **HAND**
horse opera **WESTERN**
horse race **DERBY**
horse racing (4 wds.)
THE SPORT OF KINGS
horse rope **HALTER,**
HACKAMORE
horse's ankle **HOCK**
horse's foot **HOOF**
horse's gait **LOPE, TROT,**
CANTER, GALLOP
horse's gear **HARNESS, REIN,**
SADDLE, BRIDLE, BLINDER
horse's long neck-hair **MANE**
horse soldiers **CAVALRY**
horse's shoe spur **CALK**
horse-training rope **LONGE**
horticulturist **FLORIST,**
GARDENER
hose **STOCKINGS**
hospitable **FRIENDLY, CORDIAL**
hospital **INFIRMARY, CLINIC**
hospital assistant (2 wds.)
NURSE'S AIDE

hospital doctor **INTERN,**
RESIDENT
hospitalization **INSURANCE**
hospital section **WARD**
host **ARMY, MULTITUDE**
hostelry **INN, TAVERN, HOTEL,**
MOTEL
hostile **CONTRARY, OPPOSED**
hostile criticism **CENSURE**
hostile feeling **ANGER**
hostile force **ENEMY, FOE**
hostile incursion **RAID**
hostility **WAR, BATTLE, FIGHT**
hostler **GROOM**
hot **TORRID**
hot and humid **STICKY, TROPIC,**
TORRID
hot chocolate **COCOA**
hotel **INN, HOSTEL**
hotel guest **PATRON**
hotheaded **RASH, HASTY**
hothouse **GREENHOUSE**
hot Mexican specialty **TAMALE**
hot spring **GEYSER, SPA**
hot vapor **STEAM**
hot water tank **BOILER**
hound **DOG**
hound's quarry **HARE, FOX**
hour and minute **TIME**
hourglass **TIMER**
hourglass contents **SAND**
hourly **HORAL, HORARY**
house **RESIDENCE, DWELLING**
house (Sp.) **CASA**
house addition **ELL, WING**
house and grounds **PREMISES**
House and Senate **CONGRESS**
houseboat **BARGE**
house-breaker **BURGLAR**
housebroken **TRAINED**
house broker **REALTOR**
housecoat **ROBE**
house fuel **GAS, OIL, COAL,**
WOOD
household **MENAGE**
household animal **PET, DOG,**
CAT
household appliance **WASHER,**
DRIER, STOVE, IRON,
TOASTER, BLENDER, MIXER,
REFRIGERATOR
household gods **LARES,**
PENATES, LARS
household linen **NAPERY**
housekeeper **MATRON**
house member **LEGISLATOR,**
REP
housemother **CHAPERONE**

house of healing **HOSPITAL**
house of logs **CABIN**
house pet **DOG, CAT, FISH, CANARY, PARAKEET**
house plant **FERN, IVY**
house projection **DORMER**
housetop **ROOF**
housetop feature **GABLE, EAVE**
housewifely **DOMESTIC**
housewife's title (abbr.) **MRS.**
house wing **ELL, ADDITION**
housing **LODGING, SHELTER**
Houston ballplayer **ASTRO**
hovel **HUT**
hover **LINGER, SUSPEND**
however **YET**
howl **BAY, WAIL**
hoyden **TOMBOY**
hub **CENTER**
hubbub - **ADO, TO-DO, STIR**
hub of a wheel **NAVE**
Huckleberry Finn character **JIM**
Huckleberry Finn's craft **RAFT**
huckster **HAWKER, PEDDLER**
huddle **CONFER**
hue **COLOR, TINT, SHADE**
huffy **TESTY, TOUCHY**
hug **CLASP, CARESS, FONDLE, HOLD**
huge **BIG, ENORMOUS, LARGE, VAST**
huge animal **ELEPHANT, HIPPO, RHINO**
huge continent **ASIA**
huge stone **BOULDER**
Huguenot **PROTESTANT**
huitre **OYSTER**
hulky **HEAVY**
hull **HUSK**
hullabaloo **HUBBUB**
hulled corn **SAMP**
hum **DRONE, BUZZ**
human being **ADAMITE, MAN, MORTAL, PERSON, WOMAN**
human bondage **SLAVERY**
humane **KIND, MERCIFUL**
humanity **MANKIND**
human trunk **TORSO**
humble **ABASE, MEEK, MODEST**
humbug **ROT, BAH**
humdrum **MONOTONOUS, TRITE, BANAL**
humid **DANK, MOIST, DAMP**
humiliate **SHAME, DISGRACE**
humility **MODESTY**
hummock **KNOLL**
humor **WIT**

humorist **COMIC, WIT, WAG, COMEDIAN, SATIRIST**
humorous **COMIC, FUNNY**
humorous play **FARCE, COMEDY**
humor to excess **PAMPER**
hump **BULGE, LUMP**
hump-backed animal **CAMEL, DROMEDARY**
Hun **VANDAL**
hunch **INTUITION**
hunchback **QUASIMODO**
hundredth anniversary **CENTENNIAL**
Hungarian **MAGYAR**
Hungarian wine **TOKAY**
hunger pain **PANG**
hungery **STARVING, UNFED**
hungry rodent **SHREW**
Hung Wu dynasty **MING**
hunt **CHASE, SEARCH, SEEK**
hunt for bargains **SHOP**
hunter **NIMROD, CHASER, SEEKER**
hunter's shelter **LODGE, CAMP, TENT**
hunter's shoe **BOOT**
hunting dog **BASSET, SETTER, POINTER, BEAGLE, HOUND**
hunting expedition **SAFARI**
hurdle **JUMP, BARRIER**
hurl **THROW, FLING, SLING, TOSS**
hurly-burly **TUMULT**
hurrah, for short **RAH**
hurricane **GALE, TEMPEST, STORM**
hurricane center **EYE**
hurry **RACE, DASH, HASTEN, SPEED, RUN, HIE, SHAKE A LEG, GET A MOVE ON**
hurt **ACHE, PAIN, WOUND**
husband **MAN, SPOUSE**
husbandman **FARMER**
husband of Bathsheba **URIAH**
husband of Isis **OSIRIS**
husband of Minnehaha **HIAWATHA**
husbandry **FARMING**
hush **QUIET, CALM**
hush-hush business process (2 wds.) **TRADE SECRET**
husk **HULL**
husk of wheat grain **BRAN**
hustle **RUSH, DRIVE**
hustler **PROMOTER**
hut **HOVEL, SHANTY**

hutch **CHEST**
hygiene **SANITATION**
hymn of joy **PEAN, PAEAN**
hymn of thanksgiving **TE DEUM**
hymn's finale **AMEN**
hypersensitivity **ALLERGY**
hyphen **DASH**
hypnotic spell **TRANCE**
hypocrisy **SHAM**
hypocrite **DECEIVER**
hypocritical **FALSE, INSINCERE**
hypocritical sorrow (2 wds.)
CROCODILE TEARS
hypothesis **THEORY**
hyssop **MINT, FIGWORT**

I (Ger.) **ICH**
Iago's wife **EMILIA**
iatric **MEDICAL**
Iberian lady **DONA**
ibex **GOAT**
Ibsen character **ASE, NORA,**
PEER GYNT, HEDDA GABLER,
LONA, HELMER
ice **COOL, FROST, FRIGID**
ice carrier **TONGS**
ice cream drink **SODA, SHAKE,**
MALTED, FROSTED, FLOAT
ice cream holder **CONE**
iced **GLACE**
ice fishing gear **GIG**
Icelandic epic **EDDA**
Icelandic giant **ATLI**
Icelandic legend **SAGA**
Icelandic literary work **EDDA**
ice mass **BERG, FLOE**
ice runner **SKATE**
ice tower **SERAC**
ichneumon **MONGOOSE**
icicle **STALACTITE**
icing **GLAZE**
icon **IMAGE**
icy **FRIGID, FROSTY, COLD**
icy precipitation **SLEET, HAIL**
Idaho city **BOISE**
ide **FISH**
idea **BRAINSTORM, THOUGHT,**
CONCEPTION, INSPIRATION,
OPINION, CONCEPT, NOTION
idea (prefix) **IDEO**
ideal **PERFECT**
identical **TWIN, SAME, ALIKE,**
SIMILAR
identical sibling **TWIN**
identify **RECOGNIZE, NAME**

idiocy **FOLLY**
idiom **PHRASE**
idiomatic **COLLOQUIAL**
idiot **FOOL, IMBECILE**
idiotic **INANE, FOOLISH**
idle **INACTIVE, LAZY**
LOITER
idle away time **LOAF**
idle rumor **GOSSIP**
idle talk **PATTER, PRATE**
idler **LOAFER**
idol **HERO, GOD, IMAGE,**
DEITY, WORSHIP
idolize **ADORE, DEIFY,**
WORSHIP
idyll **POEM**
if **PROVIDED, PROVISO**
if not **ELSE**
igloo builder **ESKIMO, ALEUT**
igneous rock **BASALT**
ignite **LIGHT, FIRE**
ignoble **MEAN, BASE**
ignominious **VILE**
ignominy **SHAME, INFAMY**
ignorant **UNTAUGHT, DENSE**
ignore **ELIDE, NEGLECT**
I have found it **EUREKA**
ilk **KIND, TYPE**
ill **SICK, AILING, TROUBLE,**
WOE, BAD
ill-boding **DIRE**
ill-bred person **CAD**
illegal business **RACKET**
illegal eavesdropping device
WIRETAP
Illinois city **PEORIA, CHICAGO**
illiterate signature **EX**
ill-tempered person **CRAB**
ill-tempered woman **SHREW**
illusion **CHIMERA**
illustration **EXAMPLE, DRAWING**
illustration placed within
another **INSET**
illustrator **ARTIST**
illustrious **EMINENT, GRAND**
ill will **RANCOR**
illuminate **LIGHT**
I love you (Lat.) **AMO**
image **ICON, IDOL, LIKENESS,**
PICTURE
imaginary **FANCIFUL,**
ILLUSORY
imaginary marine creature
MERMAID
imagination **FANCY**
imagine **DREAM, CONCEIVE**
imbecile **DOLT, MORON**
imbed firmly (2 wds.) **SET IN**

imbibe	**DRINK**	imposing	**IMPRESSIVE, STRIKING**
imbue	**COLOR, SUFFUSE**	imposing series	**ARRAY**
imbue thoroughly	**STEEP, SATURATE**	imposture	**RUSE, PRETENSE**
imitate	**MIMIC, APE, COPY**	impotent	**BARREN, STERILE**
imitate Sam Spade	**TAIL**	impoverished	**NEEDY, POOR**
imitation	**COPY, ERSATZ, MIMICRY**	impregnable	**INVINCIBLE, SECURE**
immaculate	**PURE**	impression	**DENT, IDEA, STAMP**
immature	**INFANTILE, YOUNG**		
immediately	**ANON, SOON, AT ONCE**	impressive	**AWESOME**
		imprison	**IMMURE**
immediately following	**NEXT**	imprisonment	**DURESS**
immense	**VAST, HUGE, LARGE, ENORMOUS**	impromptu (2 wds.)	**AD LIB**
		improve	**BETTER**
immerse	**DIP, DUNK**	improvident	**PRODIGAL**
imminent	**IMPENDING, THREATENING**	improvise (2 wds.)	**AD LIB**
		imprudent	**RASH, HASTY**
immoral	**CORRUPT, EVIL**	impudence	**BRASS, SASS**
immortal	**ETERNAL**	impudent	**BRASSY, FRESH, SASSY, PERT**
immortal spirit	**ANGEL**		
immunity	**EXEMPTION**	impugn	**ATTACK, CHALLENGE, REFUTE**
imp	**PIXIE**		
impair	**MAR, WEAR, INJURE**	impulse	**URGE, WHIM**
impalpable	**VAGUE, INTANGIBLE**	impulsive	**RASH, HASTY**
impart	**CONVEY, BESTOW**	impure	**UNCLEAN, CORRUPT**
impartial	**FAIR, EQUITABLE**	impute	**ASCRIBE, ATTRIBUTE**
impart knowledge to	**EDUCATE, TEACH**	inability	**IMPOTENCE**
		in abundance	**GALORE**
impassive	**STOICAL, STOLID, APATHETIC**	inaccuracy	**ERROR, MISTAKE**
		inaccurate	**FAULTY**
impatient	**EAGER**	inactive	**IDLE, INERT**
impeach	**CENSURE, DENOUNCE**	inactivity	**INERTIA**
impeccable	**SPOTLESS, PERFECT**	in addition	**ALSO, TOO, AND, YET**
impede	**HINDER**	inadequate	**WANTING**
impediment	**OBSTACLE, SNAG**	in a difficult position	**TREED**
impel	**URGE, PROD, EGG ON, SPUR, PROPEL**	in a direct line (4 wds.)	**AS THE CROW FLIES**
impend	**LOOM**	in agreement (2 wds., Fr.)	**EN RAPPORT**
impersonate	**MAKE LIKE, MIMIC**	in a line	**ALONG, AROW**
impervious to rain	**LEAKPROOF**	in all places	**EVERYWHERE**
impetuous	**RASH, BRASH, HASTY**	in ancient times	**EARLY**
		inane	**POINTLESS, TRITE, FOOLISH**
impetuous person	**HOTHEAD**		
implement	**TOOL**	inanimate	**INERT, LIFELESS**
implement of warfare	**WEAPON**	in another direction	**AWAY**
impolite	**RUDE**	in another place	**ELSEWHERE**
importance	**MOMENT, VALUE**	in any case	**ANYWAY**
important	**VITAL**	in any manner	**SOMEWAY**
important bridge card	**TRUMP**	in any way (2 wds.)	**AT ALL**
important occurrence	**EVENT**	in a pile	**AHEAP**
important part	**PITH, LEAD**	inappropriate	**INEPT, UNFIT**
importune	**URGE, COAX, BEG, PLEAD**	in a row	**ALINED, AROW**
		in a sheltered place	**ALEE**
impose a tax	**ASSESS, LEVY**	in a short time	**SOON, ANON**
impose restrictions (2 wds.)	**CLAMP DOWN**	inaugurate	**START**

in bad temper	**CROSS**
in behalf of	**FOR**
in between	**MID**
inborn	**INNATE, NATURAL**
inbred	**INNATE**
Inca country	**PERU**
incandescence	**GLOW**
incapable of being obliterated	
	INDELIBLE
incapacity of	**QUA**
incarnate	**EMBODIED,**
	PERSONIFIED
incarnation of Vishnu	**RAMA**
in case that	**IF, LEST**
incense	**ENRAGE, INFURIATE**
incense burner	**CENSER,**
	THURIBLE
incentive	**MOTIVE**
inception	**START, INITIATION**
incessant	**UNENDING**
inch along	**EDGE, CREEP**
incident	**EVENT**
incidental information	
	SIDELIGHT, TRIVIA
incite	**GOAD, SPUR, URGE**
incivility	**DISRESPECT**
inclement	**SEVERE, STORMY**
inclination	**SLOPE, TREND,**
	TENDENCY
incline	**SLANT, SLOPE, TILT**
inclined walkway	**RAMP**
incline the head	**BOW, NOD**
include	**CONTAIN, INVOLVE**
incoherent	**GARBLED**
income	**REVENUE, SALARY,**
	WAGES
income from housing	**RENTAL**
in common	**ALIKE**
in company of	**WITH**
incomparable	**UNRIVALED,**
	PEERLESS, SUPREME
incompatible	**CONTRARY**
incompetence	**INABILITY**
incompetent	**INEPT**
incomplete	**UNFINISHED**
in conflict (2 wds.)	**AT WAR**
incongruous expression	
(2 wds.)	**IRISH BULL**
inconsistent	**VARYING**
inconstant	**CHANGING,**
	UNSTABLE
in controversy (2 wds.)	**AT ISSUE**
incorrect (prefix)	**MIS-**
increase	**INCREMENT, GROWTH**
increased by	**PLUS**
increase in size	**GROW, SWELL**
increase in wages (2 wds.)	
	PAY RAISE
increment	**INCREASE**
incrustation	**SCAB**
inculcate	**INSTILL, IMBUE**
incumbent	**BINDING, REQUIRED**
in current style	**MODISH**
incursion	**RAID, INROAD**
incus	**ANVIL**
in debt	**OWING**
indeed	**AYE, YES, REALLY,**
	OF COURSE
indefatigable	**TIRELESS,**
	UNTIRING
indefinite	**UNCERTAIN, VAGUE**
indefinite amount	**SOME, ANY**
indefinite article	**AN, A**
indefinite number	**MANY,**
	SEVERAL, SOME, ANY
indelible	**FIXED**
indemnify	**GUARANTEE**
independent	**FREE,**
	UNENCUMBERED,
	AUTONOMOUS
independent thing	**ENTITY**
index	**FILE, LIST**
India, class of	**CASTE**
India rubber	**CAOUT CHOUC**
Indian	**CREE, ERIE, OSAGE,**
	PAWNEE, UTE, SIOUX,
	APACHE, PIMA, NAVAHO
Indiana city	**GARY, SOUTH**
	BEND, TERRE HAUTE,
	FORT WAYNE,
	INDIANAPOLIS
Indianapolis competitor	**RACER,**
	DRIVER
Indianapolis 500	**RACE**
Indian boat	**CANOE**
Indian buffalo	**ARNA, ARNEE**
Indian coin	**ANNA**
Indian drum	**TOMTOM**
Indian garment	**SARI**
Indian group	**TRIBE**
Indian maize	**CORN**
Indian mercenary	**SEPOY**
Indian of Peru	**INCA**
Indian of Yucatan	**MAYA**
Indian pony	**CAYUSE**
Indian rainy season	**MONSOON**
Indian ruler	**RAJAH**
Indian state	**NEPAL**
Indian tent	**TEPEE, WIGWAM,**
	TIPEE, TIPI
Indian territory	**OKLAHOMA**
Indian tribe	**ERIE, SIOUX**
Indian trophy	**SCALP, COUP**
Indian unit of weight	**SER**
Indian warrior	**BRAVE**
Indian woman	**SQUAW**

indicate assent	**NOD**
indicate beforehand	**PORTEND, PRESAGE**
indication	**CLUE, SIGN, HINT**
indifference	**APATHY**
indifferent	**ALOOF, BLASE, DISINTERESTED, SO-SO**
indigence	**WANT, POVERTY, NEED**
indigenous	**NATIVE, INNATE**
indignation	**ANGER, IRE**
indignity	**INSULT, AFFRONT**
indigo dye	**ANIL**
indirect	**DEVIOUS**
indirect allusion	**HINT, CLUE**
indiscreet	**RASH**
in disorder	**ASKEW, MESSY, UNTIDY**
indispensable	**ESSENTIAL, NECESSARY**
indistinct	**DIM, VAGUE, FAINT**
individual	**ONE, PERSON, UNIT**
Indo-European	**ARYAN**
indolent	**OTIOSE, LAZY**
Indonesian capital	**DJAKARTA**
Indonesian island	**BALI, JAVA, SUMATRA**
indorse	**RATIFY, CONFIRM**
induce	**EVOKE, LEAD**
indulge	**PAMPER, FAVOR**
indulger in fantasy	**DREAMER**
industrial fuel	**COKE**
industrious	**BUSY, DILIGENT**
industrious creature	**ANT, BEE**
industry	**ACTIVITY**
inebriated	**DRUNK**
in effect	**OPERATIVE**
ineffective	**USELESS**
inept serviceman (2 wds.)	**SAD SACK**
in equal degree	**AS**
in error	**WRONG, MISTAKEN**
inert	**IDLE, INACTIVE, PASSIVE**
inert gas	**ARGON, NEON**
inevitable outcome	**DOOM, FATE, DESTINY**
in excess	**OVER, TOO**
in existence	**ALIVE**
inexpensive	**CHEAP**
inexpensive cigar	**STOGIE**
inexperienced	**RAW, YOUNG, GREEN, NEOPHYTE, NOVICE, TYRO**
infallible	**UNERRING**
infamous	**CONTEMPTIBLE, BASE**
infamous Roman emperor	**NERO**
infamy	**DISHONOR, DISGRACE**

infant	**BABY**
infant cupid	**AMOR**
infant enclosure	**CRIB, PLAYPEN**
infant food	**PAP, PABLUM, FORMULA, MILK**
infant garment	**DIAPER, SACQUE, BUNTING**
infant's bed	**CRIB, CRADLE, BASSINET**
in favor of	**PRO, FOR**
infect	**POISON, POLLUTE**
infer	**DEDUCE**
inference	**CONCLUSION**
inferior	**BENEATH, POOR**
inferior in size	**PUNY, RUNTY**
inferior race horse	**PLATER**
inferior ship accommodations	**STEERAGE**
infernal	**SATANIC, DEMONIC, HELLISH, DAMNABLE**
infielder	**BASEMAN**
infiltrate	**PENETRATE**
infinite	**UNLIMITED, BOUNDLESS**
infinity of time	**EON**
infirm	**WEAK, FEEBLE**
inflame	**IRRITATE, CHAFE**
inflame with love	**ENAMOR**
inflate	**EXPAND**
inflexible	**STIFF, FIRM**
inflict	**IMPOSE**
in flight (3 wds.)	**ON THE WING**
influence	**IMPRESS, PRESTIGE**
influence with flattery	**WHEEDLE, PANDER**
infold	**WRAP**
informal chat at meal (2 wds.)	**TABLE TALK**
informal letter	**NOTE**
informal talk	**CHAT, GAB**
information	**DATA, DOPE, INFO, FACTS**
informed	**AWARE, HEP, HIP**
infrequent	**RARE**
infrequently	**SELDOM, RARELY**
infringe	**TRESPASS, VIOLATE**
in front	**AHEAD**
infuriate	**ENRAGE**
infuse	**INSTILL, IMBUE**
in general favor	**POPULAR**
ingenious	**CLEVER**
ingenuous	**NAIVE**
in good condition	**SOUND, FIT, HEALTHY**
in good order	**NEAT**
ingratiate	**CHARM, FLATTER**
ingredient	**ELEMENT**
inhabitant	**DENIZEN, RESIDENT**
inhabitant of (suffix)	**ITE**

inhabited by a ghost	**HAUNTED**
inherent character	**NATURE**
inheritor	**HEIR**
in high spirits	**MERRY**
iniquity	**EVIL**
initiate	**START, BEGIN**
in itself (2 wds.)	**PER SE**
injure	**DAMAGE, HARM,**
	WOUND, MAR, HURT
injure seriously	**MAIM, CRIPPLE**
injure with a knife	**STAB**
injure with horns	**GORE**
injurious	**DELETERIOUS**
injury	**WOUND, HURT, DAMAGE**
injury mark	**CICATRIX, SCAR,**
	SCAB
injustice	**WRONG, INEQUITY**
ink	**DRAW, WRITE**
inkling	**CLUE, HINT, IDEA**
ink stain	**BLOT**
ink writing instrument	**PEN,**
	QUILL, PRESS
inky	**BLACK**
inland sea	**LAKE**
inlay	**FILLING**
inlay work	**MOSAIC**
inlet	**BAY, RIA**
in line	**AROW**
in lower position	**DOWN, BELOW**
in manner of (Fr.)	**A LA**
in motion	**ASTIR**
inn	**HOTEL, TAVERN, MOTEL,**
	HOSTEL
innate	**INHERENT**
innate skill	**TALENT, ABILITY,**
	FLAIR
in neat layers	**STACKED**
inner	**INSIDE, INTERIOR**
Inner Hebrides island	**IONA**
inner self	**EGO**
inner surface of the hand	**PALM**
innocent	**NAIVE, PURE**
innocuous	**HARMLESS**
in no manner	**NOT**
in no way	**NOWISE**
inordinate	**EXCESSIVE, UNDUE**
inordinate self-esteem	**EGO,**
	CONCEIT
inorganic substance	**METAL,**
	PLASTIC
in other words (4 wds.)	
	THAT IS TO SAY
in place of	**INSTEAD**
in present conditions (2 wds.)	
	AS IS
in progress	**AFOOT**
in proper manner	**DULY**
in pursuit of	**AFTER**
inquire	**ASK, REQUEST**
inquire curiously	**PRY**
inquiry	**QUESTION, RESEARCH**
inquiry for lost goods	**TRACER**
inquisition	**PURGE, INQUEST**
inquisitive	**PRYING, CURIOUS**
inquisitive (sl.)	**NOSY**
in rags	**TATTERED**
in recent times	**LATELY**
in regard to (Scot.)	**ANENT**
inroad	**RAID, INCURSION**
insane	**CRAZY, MAD**
insane person	**LUNATIC,**
	MADMAN
insanity	**MANIA, LUNACY**
insatiable	**GREEDY**
inscribe	**ENGRAVE, WRITE**
inscribed tablet	**STELE**
inscription	**EPIGRAPH, LEGEND**
inscrutable	**MYSTERIOUS**
insect	**ANT, BEE, BEETLE,**
	ROACH, BUG, KATYDID,
	MANTIS, APHID, LOCUST,
	FLY, WASP, TICK, FLEA,
	MOTH, TERMITE
insect antenna	**FEELER**
insect at a picnic	**ANT**
insect bite	**STING**
insect egg	**NIT**
insect feeler	**PALP**
insect pupa	**CHRYSALIS**
insect stage	**PUPA, LARVA,**
	EGG, ADULT
insect trap	**WEB**
insecticide	**PARIS GREEN, DDT**
insidious	**DECEITFUL**
insight	**INTUITION**
insignificant	**PETTY, SLIGHT**
insignificant matter	**TRIVIALITY**
insinuate	**INTIMATE, HINT**
insipid	**TASTELESS, WATERY**
in so far as (Lat.)	**QUA**
insolence (2 wds.)	**BACK TALK**
insolent	**OFFENSIVE, RUDE**
insolvent	**BANKRUPT**
in some other place	**ELSEWHERE**
in sour spirits	**CROSS**
inspiration	**IDEA**
inspire	**AWE**
in spite of	**DESPITE**
instant	**MOMENT, SECOND,**
	WINK, MINUTE, TRICE
instead	**LIEU**
instigate (2 wds.)	**STIR UP,**
	SPUR ON, ROUSE UP,
	URGE ON
instruct	**EDUCATE, TEACH,**
	COACH, TUTOR
instructor, for short	**PROF**
instrument board	**PANEL**

insubordination **DEFIANCE, REVOLT**
in such a manner **SO, THIS**
insult **AFFRONT, INDIGNITY**
in support of **FOR, BEHIND**
insurance payment **PREMIUM**
insurgent **REBEL**
intact **WHOLE, COMPLETE**
integer **NUMERAL, UNIT, ENTITY**
integrity **HONESTY**
intellect **MIND**
intellectual **EGGHEAD**
intelligence **SENSE, WIT**
intelligent **SMART, BRAINY, BRIGHT**
intelligible **CLEAR, LUCID**
intemperance **EXCESS**
intend **AIM, MEAN, PLAN**
intensify **ENHANCE**
intensity **ENERGY, FORCE**
intent **RAPT**
intent look **STARE**
intention **AIM, GOAL, END**
intentional **DELIBERATE**
intentionally (2 wds.) **ON PURPOSE**
inter **BURY**
interdict **CUT, DEBAR, BAN**
interdiction **BAN**
interest **PROFIT, CONCERN**
interest-bearing certificate **BOND**
interfere **MEDDLE, INTRUDE, TAMPER**
interfering **MEDDLESOME**
interim **MEANTIME**
interim ruler **REGENT**
interior **INNER, INSIDE**
interjection **ALAS, OH**
interlace **ENTWINE, WEAVE**
interlaced design **FRET, LACE**
interlock **KNIT, UNITE**
interloper **INTRUDER**
intermediate (law) **MESNE**
intermediate (prefix) **MES**
interminable **ENDLESS, INFINITE**
intermittent **BROKEN, PERIODIC**
intermittently (3 wds.) **OFF AND ON**
internal **INNER**
internal revenue supporter **TAXPAYER**
international monopoly **CARTEL**
international tennis cup **DAVIS**
international treaty **PACT**

international understanding **ENTENTE**
interpose **INTERCEDE**
interpret **EXPLAIN, TRANSLATE**
interpretation **EXPLANATION**
interrupt (2 wds.) **CUT IN, BUTT IN**
intersect **CROSS, CUT**
intersection of lines **ANGLE**
intersection sign **STOP, YIELD**
interstice **PORE, CHINK, CREVICE, INTERVAL**
intertwine **LACE**
interurban railroad **EL**
interval of relief **RESPITE**
intervene (2 wds.) **STEP IN, MEDDLE IN**
intervening (law) **MESNE**
interweave **MAT**
in that case **THEN**
in that place **THERE**
in the center **AMID**
in the direction of **TOWARD, TO**
in the future **LATER**
in the interim **MEANWHILE**
in the know **AWARE, HEP, HIP**
in the last month **ULTIMO**
in the middle of **AMID**
in the offing **NEAR, SOON**
in the past **AGO**
in the place **AT**
in the same place (abbr.) **IBID.**
in the time of **DURING**
in this manner **SO, THUS**
in this place **HERE**
intimate **CLOSE, FAMILIAR**
intimation **HINT, CLUE**
intimidate **DAUNT, DISMAY**
intolerable **UNBEARABLE**
intone **CHANT**
intoxicating liquor **SPIRITS**
intrepid **BRAVE, BOLD**
intricate **COMPLEX**
intrigue **CABAL, PLOT**
intrinsic **GENUINE**
introduction **PREFACE, PRELUDE**
introductory discourse **PROEM, PREFACE**
introductory performance **PRELUDE, OVERTURE**
in truth **INDEED, VERILY**
intuitive feeling **HUNCH**
inundation **FLOOD**
invading throng **HORDE, MOB**
invent **DEVISE, CREATE**
invention protection **PATENT**
inventor Whitney **ELI**

invigorating medicine	TONIC
invisible	UNSEEN
invisible emanation	AURA
invitation	BID
invite	ASK, ATTRACT, LURE
invocation	PRAYER, SERMON
invoice	BILL
invoke	ELICIT
involve	ENTAIL, INCLUDE
inward	INNER, INTERN
in what place	WHERE
in what way	HOW
in what way (Lat.)	QUO MODO
iota	JOT
IOU endorser	OWER
Iowa college town	AMES
Iran	PERSIA
Iran's neighbor	IRAQ, IRAK
Irani ruler	SHAH
irate	ANGRY, MAD, WRATHFUL, FURIOUS
ire	ANGER, CHOLER
Ireland	ERIN, EIRE, EMERALD ISLE
irenic	SERENE, PEACEFUL
iridescent	OPALINE
iridescent gem	OPAL
iris	IXIA, FLAG, RAINBOW
iris with fragrant roots	ORRIS
Irish	CELTIC, ERSE
Irish cattle	KERRY
Irish chemist	BOYLE
Irish city	BELFAST, CORK
Irish clan	SEPT
Irish county	MAYO, CORK
Irish dagger	SKEAN
Irish dance	REEL
Irish dish	STEW
Irish emblem	SHAMROCK
Irish expletive	ARRAH, GO-ON
Irish fairy	BANSHEE
Irish Free State	EIRE
Irish fuel	PEAT
Irish-Gaelic	ERSE
Irish island group	ARAN
Irish king's home	TARA
Irish lass	COLLEEN
Irish moss	CARRAGEEN
Irish poet	WILDE, YEATS
Irish republic	EIRE
Irish sea god	LER
Irish seaport	COBH
irk	ANNOY
iron bar	ROD
iron clothes	PRESS
iron coating	RUST
iron compound	FERRITE, STEEL
iron rod	BAR

irrational	FOOLISH, ABSURD
irregularly notched	EROSE
irrelevant	EXTRANEOUS
irreligious	IMPIOUS
irresolute	UNDECIDED
irresponsible	UNRELIABLE
irrigate	WATER
irrigation dike	LEVEE
irritable	FRETFUL, TESTY
irritate	IRK, RILE, NETTLE, TEASE
irritated	SORE
irritation	PIQUE
is	EXISTS
is (Sp.)	ES, ESTA
Isaac's mother	SARAH
Isaac's son	DSAU, JACOB
is able to	CAN
is angered at	RESENTS
is appropriate	SUITS
is aware of	KNOWS
is compelled	MUST
is concerned	CARES
is curious	WONDERS
is disposed kindly toward (2 wds.)	TAKES TO
is excessively fond of	DOTES
Ishmael's mother	HAGAR
is human	ERRS
is inclined	LEANS
is indebted to	OWES
isinglass	MICA
is in store for	AWAITS
Isis' husband	OSIRIS
Islamic holy city	MECCA, MEDINA
Islamic name	ALI
island (Fr.)	ILE
island (Ital.)	ISOLA
island in the Mediterranean	ELBA, MALTA, CYPRUS, CORSICA, SICILY
island in the West Indies	CUBA, JAMAICA
island nation	HAITI, IRELAND, JAPAN, FORMOSA
island near Athens	SALAMIS
island near Corsica	ELBA, SARDINIA
island near Greece	CRETE
island near Italy	MALTA
island of exile	ELBA, ST. HELENA
island off China	NATSU HAINAN
island off Mozambique	IBO
island off Scotland	IONA
island of saints	ERIN

island of the Aegean **LEROS, IOS, DELOS, MELOS, NAXOS**
island of the Bahamas **BIMINI**
island of the Cyclades **DELOS, ANDROS, TENOS, NAXOS, MELOS**
island of the Philippines **SAMAR**
island republic **EIRE, IRELAND, PHILIPPINES**
islands between North and South America (2 wds.) **WEST INDIES**
islands near Florida **BAHAMAS, KEYS**
island south of Australia **TASMANIA**
island south of Sicily **MALTA**
isle in a river **AIT**
isle in the Bay of Naples **CAPRI**
isle off coast of Ireland **ARAN**
islet **AIT**
ism **DOCTRINE**
is no more **GONE**
is not (arch.) **NIS**
is not well **AILS**
is obliged to **MUST**
isolate **SEPARATE, SECLUDE**
isolation **SOLITUDE**
isometrics **EXERCISES**
is on fire **BURNS**
is overfond **DOTES, SPOILS**
is possible **MAY**
is present at **ATTENDS**
Israel, formerly **PALESTINE**
Israeli coins **MILS**
Israeli folk dance **HORA**
Israeli port **HAIFA, ELATH**
Israeli round dance **HORA**
is situated **LIES**
is successful **WINS, TRIUMPHS**
issue **EMIT, FLOW**
issue forth **EMANATE**
is suitable to **BECOMES**
isthmus **NECK**
is unable to (contr.) **CAN'T**
is unsuccessful **FAILS**
is worthy of **DESERVES**
Italian actress **LOREN, MAGNANI**
Italian affirmative **SI**
Italian art center **SIENA, ROME, VENICE, FLORENCE**
Italian capital **ROME**
Italian city **GENOA, TURIN**
Italian coin **LIRA**
Italian commune **ASOLA**

Italian delicacy **RAVIOLI, SPAGHETTI, PASTA, ANTIPASTO**
Italian epic poet **TASSO**
Italian family **ESTE, BORGIA**
Italian family of violin makers **AMATI**
Italian house **CASA, VILLA**
Italian housewife's title **SIGNORA**
Italian innkeeper **PADRONE**
Italian island **LIDO, SICILY**
Italian lady **DONNA**
Italian lake **ALBANO, COMO**
Italian monetary unit **LIRA**
Italian monk **FRA**
Italian poet **DANTE**
Italian port **GENOA, NAPLES, BARI**
Italian resort **LIDO, CAPRI**
Italian river **ARNO, PO, TIBER**
Itch **HANKER, URGE**
item **DETAIL, PARAGRAPH**
itemize **DETAIL**
item of clothing **TOG**
item of gossip **RUMOR**
item often tossed **SALAD, COIN, BALL**
item of value **ASSET**
itinerant **ARRANT, ERRANT, NOMAD**
itinerary **ROUTE**
it is (contr.) **'TIS, IT'S**
itty-bitty **TINY**
Ivan the Terrible **TSAR**
ivory **DENTINE**
ivy **VINE**
Ivy League member **YALE, HARVARD, PRINCETON, DARTMOUTH, COLUMBIA**
ixia **IRIS**

J

jab **POKE, THRUST, BLOW, PUNCH**
jabber **CHATTER, PRATE, PRATTLE**
jabberwocky **NONSENSE, GIBBERISH**
jabot material **LACE**
jack at cards **KNAVE**
jacket **COAT**
jack-in-the-pulpit **ARUM**
jackrabbit **HARE**
jacks or better **OPENERS**

Jack Sprat's meat **LEAN**
Jack Tar's drink **GROG**
Jacob's brother **ESAU**
Jacob's father **ISAAC**
Jacob's father-in-law **LABAN**
Jacob's first wife **LEAH, LEI**
Jacob's son **JOSEPH, LEVI, DAN, RUBEN, AS(H)ER, BENJAMIN, SIMEON, JUDA, ISSACHAR, ZABULON, GAD, NEPHTHALI**
Jacob's wife **LEAH, RACHEL**
jacquard **LOOM**
jade **TIRE**
jagged **ROUGH**
jai alai **PELOTA**
jail (Brit.) **GAOL**
jail breaker **ESCAPEE**
jail room **CELL**
jalousie **BLIND, SHUTTER**
Jamaican witchcraft **OBEAH**
Jane Austen title **EMMA**
Jane Eyre author **BRONTE**
Japan **NIPPON**
Japanese aborigine **AINO, AINU**
Japanese-American **NISEI, SANSEI, ISSEI, KIBEI**
Japanese beverage **SAKE, TEA**
Japanese coin **SEN, YEN**
Japanese drama **NO, NOH**
Japanese metropolis **KYOTO, TOKYO**
Japanese musical instrument **KOTO**
Japanese outlaw **RONIN**
Japanese pagoda **TAA**
Japanese plant **UDO**
Japanese port **KOBE, OSAKA**
Japanese robe **KIMONO**
Japanese sash **OBI**
Japanese statesman **ITO**
Japanese zither **KOTO**
jar **JOLT, SHAKE**
jar cover **LID, TOP**
jardiniere **URN, VASE, POT**
jargon **CANT, ARGOT**
Jason's ship **ARGO**
jaunt **TRIP**
jaunty **PERKY**
java **COFFEE**
Javanese tree **UPAS**
Jayhawk State **KANSAS**
jazz music **BEBOP**
jealous **ENVIOUS**
jealousy **ENVY**
jeer **MOCK, JIBE**
jeer at **TAUNT**
jelly **ASPIC, GELATIN**
jerk (colloq.) **YANK**

jerky **CHOPPY, MEAT**
jest **JOKE, JAPE, QUIP**
jesting talk **JAPERY**
jet **FLY, BLACK, PLANE**
jet black **RAVEN**
jet pilot **FLYER**
jetty **WHARF, PIER**
Jew **SEMITE, HEBREW**
jewel **GEM**
jeweled coronet **TIARA**
jeweler's weight **CARAT**
Jewish ascetic **ESSENE**
Jewish bible **TORAH**
Jewish Day of Atonement **YOM KIPPUR**
Jewish feast **PASSOVER, SEDER, PESACH**
Jewish leader **RABBI**
Jewish month **HESHVAN, KISLEV, TEBET, SHEBAT, ADAR, VEADAR, NISAN, IYAR, SILVAN, TAMMUZ, TISHRI, AB, ELUL**
Jewish nation **ISRAEL**
Jewish prayer book **SIDDUR**
Jewish quarter **GHETTO**
Jewish school **(C)HEDER**
Jewish scripture **TORAH**
Jewish spiritual leader **RABBI**
Jewish teacher **RABBI**
jib **BOOM, CRANE**
jibe **TAUNT**
jiffy **INSTANT**
jiggle **VIBRATE**
jingle **TINKLE, VERSE**
jinx **HEX**
job **CHORE, TASK**
job for Perry Mason **CASE**
Job's home **UZ**
jocose **JOKING, PLAYFUL**
jocular **COMICAL**
jocund **CHEERFUL**
jog **TROT**
joggle **DOWEL**
johnnycake **PONE**
Johnson's vice president **HUMPHREY**
join **ADD, CONNECT, UNITE, WED, MARRY, TIE, WELD, MELD, SOLDER, YOKE**
join forces **UNITE**
join securely **TENON**
join strands **SPLICE**
joint **ELBOW, KNEE, ANKLE**
join the army **ENLIST**
join the colors **ENLIST**
join the race **RUN**

joint on which a door swings **HINGE**
joke **GAG, JEST**
joke anthology **ANA**
jokester **WAG, WIT**
jollity **MIRTH**
jolly **JOCULAR, MERRY**
jolly boat **SKIFF, YAWL**
jolt **JAR**
Jonah **JINX**
josh **TEASE**
Joshua's partner to Canaan **CALEB**
Joshua tree **YUCCA**
jostle **SHOVE, PUSH**
jot **IOTA**
jounce **JOLT, BOUNCE**
journal **NEWSPAPER, PAPER, DIARY, RECORD, LOG**
journalist **REPORTER**
journalist Sevareid **ERIC**
journey **TOUR, TRAVEL, TRIP, TREK**
journey for another **ERRAND**
journey's interruption **STOPOVER**
joust **TILT**
jovial **JOLLY**
jowl **CHOP, JAWBONE**
joy **GLEE, ELATION, HAPPINESS, BLISS**
Joyce Kilmer poem **TREES**
joyful **ELATED, GLAD, GAY MIRTHFUL, JUBILANT**
joyous **HAPPY, GLAD**
Jubal **MUSICIAN**
jubilant **ELATED, JOYFUL**
jubilation **REJOICING**
Judas tree **CERCIS, REDBUD**
Judean king **ASA, HEROD**
judge **DEEM, OPINE**
judge in a dispute **ARBITER**
judge's aide (2 wds.) **COURT CLERK**
judge's bench **BANC**
judge's chambers **CAMERAS**
judge's command (4 wds.) **ORDER IN THE COURT**
judge's concern **CASE**
judge's gown **TOGA, ROBE**
judge's hammer **GAVEL**
judgeship **CHAIR**
judgment **DECISION**
judicial order **WRIT**
judiciary **BENCH**
judicious **WISE, PRUDENT**

Judy Garland movie **WIZARD OF OZ, A STAR IS BORN, THE PIRATE, EASTER PARADE**
jug **EWER, PITCHER**
juice drink **ADE**
juicer **REAMER**
juicy **SUCCULENT**
juicy fruit **ORANGE, LEMON, GRAPEFRUIT, PEAR, PLUM, PEACH, LIME**
Juliet's lover **ROMEO**
Julliard specialty **MUSIC**
jumbled medley **OLIO**
jumbled type **PI**
jump **LEAP, HOP**
jumping insect **FLEA**
jumping stick **POGO**
jump on **SCOLD**
jump suit **OVERALLS**
junction **MEETING, UNION**
juncture **SEAM, JOINT**
june bug **DOR**
jungle cat **TIGER, PANTHER, LION**
jungle drum **TOM-TOM**
jungle snake **BOA**
junior **NAMESAKE**
Junior League event (2 wds.) **DEBUTANTE BALL**
junior or senior (2 wds.) **COLLEGE STUDENT**
junior's father **SENIOR**
juniper bush **SAVIN**
juniper tree **CEDAR**
junket **TOUR, TRIP**
jupe **SKIRT**
Jupiter **JOVE**
jurisdiction **AUTHORITY**
jury **PANEL**
just **ONLY, FAIR**
just gone by **PAST**
justice **FAIRNESS**
justify **WARRANT**
just perfect **IDEAL**
just right (3 wds., sl.) **ON THE BEAM**
Jute leader **HORSA, HENGIST**
Jutland native **DANE**
juvenile **YOUNG, YOUTHFUL, CHILDISH, CHILD**

K

Kaddish **PRAYER**

karate blow	**CHOP**	killer whale	**ORC**
karma	**FATE**	killick	**ANCHOR**
kasha	**MUSH, GROATS**	Kilmer poem	**TREES**
katydid	**INSECT, GRASSHOPPER**	kiln	**OAST, OVEN**
kayak	**CANOE**	kiloliter	**STERE**
keen	**SHARP**	kilt	**PLEAT, SKIRT**
keen enjoyment	**ZEST**	kimono	**ROBE**
keen insight	**ACUMEN**	kimono sash	**OBI**
keen intuitive power (2 wds.)		kin	**FAMILY, RELATIVES**
	SIXTH SENSE	kind	**ILK, SORT, TYPE, CLASS,**
keenly desirous	**EAGER, AVID**		**GENTLE, NICE, GENRE**
keenly eager	**AVID**	kindle	**LIGHT, FIRE**
keenly honed	**SHARP**	kindly	**NICE**
keenness	**ACUMEN**	kindness	**COMPASSION**
keen relish	**GUSTO**	kind of	**SOMEWHAT, RATHER**
keep	**RETAIN, HOLD, RESERVE,**	kind of art	**POP, OP, MODERN**
	MAINTAIN	kind of automobile	**STATION**
keep afloat	**BUOY**		**WAGON, SEDAN, COUPE,**
keep clear of	**EVADE, SHUN**		**ROADSTER, HOT ROD**
keeper	**GUARD, WARDEN**	kind of bark	**CANELLA**
keeper of an elephant	**MAHOUT**	kind of beaver	**EAGER**
keep going	**SUSTAIN**	kind of beer	**LAGER, BITTER,**
keep in check	**RESTRAIN**		**PILSNER**
keeping	**CUSTODY, CHARGE**	kind of bread	**RYE, WHITE,**
keepsake	**TOKEN, MOMENTO**		**WHEAT, CORN**
keepsake box	**CHEST**	kind of cheese	**EDAM, BRIE,**
keep within one's			**GOUDA, SWISS, CHEDDAR,**
means (4 wds.)			**STILTON**
	MAKE BOTH ENDS MEET	kind of clock	**ALARM**
keg	**BARREL, CASK**	kind of cloth	**COTTON, SILK,**
kelp	**ALGA**		**SATIN, RAYON, NYLON, LINEN**
ken	**UNDERSTANDING**	kind of corn bread	**PONE**
kennel dwellers	**CANINE, DOG**	kind of couch	**DIVAN, SETTEE,**
kennel sound	**YAP, YELP, YIP,**		**LOVE SEAT**
	WOOF, BOWWOW,	kind of dog	**PUG, POM, PEKE,**
	ROWF, GRRR		**MUTT, CUR, SPANIEL, HOUND**
Kentucky blue grass	**POA**	kind of fabric	**CORD, SCRIM**
Kentucky college	**BEREA**	kind of feed	**BRAN**
Kentucky Derby entry	**HORSE**	kind of firecracker	**DEVIL**
kernel	**CORN, SEED, GERM**	kind of fuel	**GAS, OIL, PEAT,**
kerosene	**OIL**		**COAL, WOOD**
kerosene lantern	**LAMP**	kind of grain	**WHEAT, OATS**
ketch	**SAIC**	kind of hammer	**PEEN, GAVEL**
ketone	**ACETONE**	kind of income	**RENT**
kettle	**POT**	kind of lettuce	**COS, BIB,**
kettle drum	**TYMPANUM**		**BOSTON, ICEBERG,**
key	**OPENER, SOLUTION**		**ROMAINE**
keyboard instrument	**ORGAN,**	kind of marble	**AGATE, TAW**
	PIANO,	kind of meat	**PORK, HAM, BEEF,**
	SPINET		**VEAL, STEAK, LAMB**
keyhole	**SLOT**	kind of moth	**LUNA, MILLER**
Keystone State	**PENNSYLVANIA**	kind of music	**OPERA, POP,**
kick	**BOOT**		**ROCK, BLUES,**
kick a football	**PUNT**		**COUNTRY, JAZZ**
kid	**CHILD, GOAT**	kind of nut	**PECAN, ALMOND,**
kill	**SLAY, MURDER**		**WALNUT**
kill a fly	**SWAT**	kind of onion	**LEEK**
killed	**SLEW, SLAIN**	kind of overshoe	**GAITER**

kind of paper	**RICE**
kind of pastry	**PIE, CAKE, TART, COOKIE**
kind of pie	**MINCE, APPLE, PUMPKIN**
kind of power	**ATOMIC, ELECTRIC**
kind of race	**RELAY**
kind of rocket	**RETRO**
kind of salesmen (comp. wd.)	**DOOR-TO-DOOR, HOUSE-TO-HOUSE, TRAVELING**
kind of sea food	**SHRIMP, CLAM, CRAB, LOBSTER**
kind of signal	**DANGER, ALARM, STOP, GO**
kind of singing club	**GLEE**
kind of slipper	**MULE**
kind of soil	**LOAM**
kind of stew	**POTTAGE**
kind of test	**ORAL**
kind of trowel	**PLANE**
kind of velvet	**PANNE**
kind of violin (sl.)	**STRAD**
kind of weapon	**BAZOOKA, GUN, RIFLE, ARROW, CANNON**
kind or class	**SORT**
king	**RULER, MONARCH**
king (Fr.)	**ROI**
king (Lat.)	**REX**
King Arthur's capital	**CAMELOT**
King David's grandfather	**OBED**
kingdom	**REALM**
kingfish	**OPAH**
King James' translation	**BIBLE**
kingly	**REGAL, ROYAL**
King Minos' daughter	**ARIADNE**
King Mongkut's land	**SIAM**
King Mongkut's tutor	**ANNA**
king of beasts	**LION**
king of birds	**EAGLE**
king of fairies	**OBERON**
king of gods	**JUPITER**
king of Israel	**AHAB, DAVID, SAUL**
king of Judah	**ASA**
king of Judea	**HEROD**
king of Norway	**OLAF**
king of Persia	**DARIUS**
king of the golden touch	**MIDAS**
king of the Huns	**ATLI, ATTILA**
king of the Lapithae	**IXION**
king of the Visigoths	**ALARIC**
king of Troy	**PRIAM**
king's baton	**SCEPTER**
king's blue	**COBALT**
king's chair	**THRONE**
king's hat	**CROWN**
king's representative	**VICEROY**
king (Sp.)	**REY**
king's son	**PRINCE**
king's yellow	**ORPIMENT**
kinship	**AFFINITY**
kinsman	**RELATIVE**
Kirghiz mountain range	**ALAI**
kiss	**SMOOCH, BUSS**
kit	**OUTFIT, GEAR**
kitchen appliance	**TOASTER, OPENER, STOVE, REFRIGERATOR, GRILL**
kitchen gadget	**CORER, DICER, RICER, PRESS, CUTTER, HILL**
kitchen garment	**APRON**
kitchen implement	**SPATULA, KNIFE, SPOON, SCRAPER, SIEVE**
kitchen rug	**MAT**
kitchen stove	**RANGE**
kitchen vessel	**KETTLE, POT, PAN, SAUCEPAN**
kite	**ELANET**
kite part	**TAIL**
kith	**FRIENDS**
kitsch	**SHALLOW, POP**
kitten's cry	**MEW, MEOW**
Kiwanis member	**MAN**
kiwi	**BIRD**
klatch (klatsch)	**GATHERING, HEN PARTY, BREAK**
knack	**ART, TALENT, FLAIR**
knapsack	**BAG**
knave	**RASCAL, JACK**
knead	**MASSAGE**
knee	**PATELLA, JOINT**
kneehole and rolltop	**DESKS**
knickknack	**NOTION, WHATNOT**
knife edge	**BLADE**
knife for dissecting	**SCALPEL**
knife maker	**CUTLER**
knife swinger	**SLASHER**
knight	**CAVALIER, SIR**
knight errant	**PALADIN**
knightly champion	**PALADIN**
knightly quest	**GRAIL**
knight's assistant	**PAGE**
knight's clothing	**ARMOR**
knight's lance banner	**GONFALON**
knight's title	**SIR**
knit	**WEAVE**
knitting stitch	**LOOP, PURL, CABLE, KNIT**
knitting wool	**YARN**
knives	**CUTLERY**

knob	**NODE**
knock	**RAP, TAP**
knock about	**WANDER**
knock against	**BUMP**
knock down	**FLOOR, KO, KAYO**
knock it off	**STOP**
knock off	**QUIT, KILL**
knockout	**KO, KAYO**
knoll	**HILL**
knot	**NODE, BOW, NOOSE**
knot in cotton fiber	**NEPS**
knot in wood	**GNARL, KNAR**
knot in wool	**NOIL**
knot of hair	**BUN**
knotty	**INTRICATE**
knout	**FLOG**
know	**WIST, REALIZE**
knowhow	**SKILL**
knowing	**ALERT, SCIENT, AWARE**
knowledge	**KEN, LORE**
knuckle under	**YIELD**
knurl	**NODULE, KNOT**
kobold	**GNOME, GOBLIN**
kohlrabi	**CABBAGE**
Konrad Adenauer's nickname	**DER ALTE**
kooky	**SILLY, CRAZY**
Korea	**CHOSEN**
Korean Border river	**YALU**
Korean city	**SEOUL**
Korean seaport	**PUSAN**
kosher	**CLEAN, RIGHT, PROPER**
Krupp works site	**ESSEN**

L

laager	**CAMP**
Laban's daughter	**RACHEL, LEAH**
lab burner	**ETNA, BUNSEN**
lab substance	**AGAR**
label	**STICKER, TAB, TAG, TRADEMARK**
labial	**LIP**
labor	**TOIL, WORK**
laboratory tube	**PIPETTE**
laborer	**COOLIE, TOILER, WORKER, HAND**
labor group	**UNION, ILO, CIO, AFL, GUILD**
laborious	**ARDUOUS, DIFFICULT**
labor stoppage	**STRIKE**
Labrador dog	**RETRIEVER NEWFOUNDLAND**

labyrinth	**MAZE**
lac	**RESIN**
lace	**DASH, FRILL, SHOESTRING**
lace collar	**RUFF**
lacelike fabric	**NET**
lacerate	**RIP, TEAR, SCRATCH, CUT**
lachrymal drop	**TEAR**
lack	**ABSENCE, NEED, WANT**
lackadaisical	**LISTLESS**
lackey	**TOADY, FOOTMAN**
lacking	**SHY, SHORT**
lacking boldness	**TIMID**
lacking good taste	**INDECOROUS, UNSEEMLY**
lacking hair	**BALD**
lacking heat	**COLD**
lacking money	**POOR, NEEDY, INDIGENT**
lacking strength	**WEAK**
lackluster	**DULL**
lack of energy	**ATONY**
lack of interest	**APATHY**
laconic	**TERSE, CONCISE**
lacquer	**ENAMEL**
lacquered metalware	**TOLE**
lacuna	**GAP, HIATUS**
lacy	**DELICATE, FILMY**
lacy frill	**RUCHE, ROUCHE**
lacy plant	**FERN**
lad	**BOY, STRIPLING**
ladder round	**RUNG, STEP, RUNDLE**
lade	**LOAD**
laden	**FREIGHTED**
ladies' man	**ROMEO, CASANOVA, DON JUAN**
lading	**CARGO, LOAD**
ladle	**DIPPER, SCOOP**
ladrone	**BANDIT, THIEF**
lady	**DAME, WOMAN, MADAM, DONNA**
lady (Sp.)	**SENORA**
ladylike	**FEMININE**
lady's gown	**DRESS, FROCK**
lag	**DELAY, LINGER**
lag behind	**LOITER, TARRY**
lager	**BEER**
laggard	**SLUGGISH, STRAGGLER**
lagniappe	**GRATUITY**
lagoon	**POND**
laic	**SECULAR, LAITY**
lair	**DEN**
laity	**LAYMEN**
lake	**POOL**
lam	**FLEE, ESCAPE**
Lama land	**TIBET**

lambaste **THRASH, SCOLD**
lambent **GLOWING, LUMINOUS**
lamblike **GENTLE, MEEK**
lamb's father **RAM**
lamb's mother **EWE**
Lamb's pen name **ELIA**
lambskin leather **SUEDE**
lame **CRIPPLED, GIMPY**
lamebrain **NUMBSKULL**
lament **BEMOAN, MOAN, RUE, SIGH, WAIL**
lamentation **GRIEF**
lamia **VAMPIRE**
lamp **LIGHT, TORCH**
lampblack **SOOT**
lampoon **SATIRE**
lamprey **EEL**
lampshade **GLOBE**
lanai **VERANDA**
lanate **WOOLLY**
lance **SPEAR**
lance contest **JOUST**
lancer **SOLDIER**
land **DISEMBARK, ALIGHT, SOIL, TERRAIN, COUNTRY CARRIAGE, WAGON**
land broker **REALTOR**
land contract **DEED**
land drawing **MAP**
land measure **ACRE, AREA, PLOT, LOT**
land parcel **LOT**
land title **DEED**
landed property **ESTATE, REAL ESTATE**
landing boat **LST**
landing pier **WHARF**
landing place **AIRPORT, RUNWAY, AIRSTRIP, STOLPORT**
Land of Alley Oop **MOO**
Land of Enchantment **NEW MEXICO**
Land of Opportunity **ARKANSAS**
Land of Rising Sun **JAPAN**
Land of Ten Thousand Lakes **MINNESOTA**
Land of the Midnight Sun **ALASKA**
Land of the Sheiks **ARABIA**
land on **CRITICIZE, SCOLD**
landscape **SCENERY, VIEW**
landscape feature **SCENERY**
landslide **AVALANCHE**
lane **ALLEY**
language **TONGUE**

language of ancient Rome **LATIN**
language of North Africa **ARABIC**
language peculiarity **IDIOM**
language spoken in Brazil **PORTUGUESE**
languid **WEAK, SLOW**
languish **AIL, PINE, YEARN, ACHE**
languor **ENNUI**
lanky **GAUNT, THIN**
lap **FOLD, LIP**
Lapp **SCANDINAVIAN**
lap robe **BLANKET, RUG**
lapse **ERROR, MISTAKE**
larceny **THEFT, ROBBERY**
lard **FAT, SHORTENING, GREASE**
larder **PANTRY**
large **BIG, HUGE, VAST, ENORMOUS**
large amount **SCADS**
large antelope **GNU, ELAND**
large ape **GORILLA, ORANGUTAN**
large armadillo **PELUDO**
large artery **AORTA**
large Australian shark **MAKO**
large bag **SACK**
large barb of a feather **HERL, HARL**
large basin **TANK**
large bell **GONG**
large bird **EMU, MOA, OSTRICH, STORK**
large board **PLANK, SLAT**
large book **TOME**
large bundle **BALE**
large burrowing mammal **AARDVARK**
large candlestick **FLAMBEAU**
large canine **MASTIFF**
large canoe **BUNGO**
large cask **TUN**
large cat **LION, TIGER, PANTHER**
large Central American snake **BUSHMASTER**
large Central American tree **SAPODILLA**
large chest **TRUNK**
large cistern **TANK**
large conduit **MAIN**
large container **VAT, TUN**
large continent **ASIA**
large country house **CHATEAU, ESTATE, MANOR**

large crude boat	ARK
large cup	MUG
large cupola	DOME
large cut	SLAB
large deer	ELK
large dog (2 wds.)	
	SAINT BERNARD
large drinking vessel	FLAGON
large East Indian tree	NEEM
large fish	OPAH, TUNA
large fruit	MELON
large gateway	PYLON
large gray wolf	LOBO
large heavy hammer	SLEDGE
large in scope	GENERAL
large kettle	CALDRON
large knife	SNEE, BOLO
large ladle	SCOOP
large-leaved beet	CHARD
large lizard	ALLIGATOR,
	CROCODILE
large mass of people	HORDE,
	MOB, CROWD, HOST,
	MULTITUDE
large mouthed pot	OLLA
large number	MYRIAD
large of body	BURLY
large parrot	MACAW
large porch	VERANDA
large pulpit	AMBO
large quantity	MUCH, RAFT
large rock	BOULDER
large rodent	PACA, RAT
larger than life	HEROIC
large scissors	SHEARS
large sea duck	EIDER
large seagoing vessel	LINER
large seal (2 wds.)	SEA LION
large snake	BOA
large sofa	DIVAN
large South African antelope	
	SASSABY
large spoon	LADLE
largess	BOUNTY, GENEROSITY
largest amount	MOST
largest continent	ASIA
large stewpot	OLLA
largest ocean	PACIFIC
largest of the Kuriles	ETOROFU
large stout cord	ROPE
largest planet	JUPITER
large stream	RIVER
large tooth	TUSK
large town	CITY
large truck	VAN
large tub	VAT
large vase	URN
large volume	TOME

large wading bird	CRANE, IBIS
large warship (2 wds.)	
	AIRCRAFT CARRIER
large wasp	HORNET
large web-footed bird	PELICAN
large white bear	POLAR
large wicker basket	HAMPER
large wooden cask	BARREL
largo	SLOW
lariat	LASSO, REATA,
	RIATA, ROPE
laridae	GULLS
lark	FROLIC, SPREE
larkspur	DELPHINIUM
larrigan	MOCCASIN
larva	GRUB
larval stage	PUPA
lascivious	LEWD
laser	BEAM
lash	WHIP, FLOG
lash out	STRIKE
lass	GIRL, MAID, MAIDEN
lassitude	TORPOR, LANGUOR
lasso	LARIAT, REATA,
	RIATA, ROPE, NOOSE
lasso expert	ROPER, COWBOY
last	ENDURE, FINAL, PERSIST,
	OMEGA
last dinner course	DESSERT
last frontier	ALASKA
last Greek letter	OMEGA
lasting	PERMANENT
lasting a brief time	EPHEMERAL
last inning	NINTH
last in the race	LOSER
last letter	ZED, ZEE, OMEGA
lastly	FINALLY
last named	LATTER
last offer	ULTIMATUM
last part	END
last queen of Spain	ENA
last-resort device (2 wds.)	
	PANIC BUTTON
last word	AUTHORITY
latch	LEVER, LOCK
late	OVERDUE, TARDY,
	RECENT
lateen	SAIL
lately	RECENTLY
latent	HIDDEN, COVERT,
	POTENTIAL, DORMANT
later	AFTERWARD
lateral	SIDE, SIDEWARD
lateral part	SIDE
latest	NEWEST
latest happenings	NEWS
latex	RUBBER
lath	SLAT

lathe operator	**TURNER**	lawn party	**FÊTE, BARBECUE**
lather	**FOAM, SUDS**	lawn wrecker	**MOLE**
Latin	**ROMAN**	law of Moses	**TORAH**
Latin conjunction	**ET**	law officers	**POLICE**
Latin god	**DEUS**	law precedent (2 wds.)	**RES JUDICATA**
Latin poet	**OVID, VIRGIL**	lawsuit	**CASE**
Latvia's capital	**RIGA**	lawyer	**ATTORNEY,**
laud	**PRAISE**	**BARRISTER, COUNSELOR,**	
laudable	**WORTHY**	**COUNSEL, SOLICITOR,**	
laudanum	**OPIATE**	**ADVOCATE**	
laugh	**GIGGLE**	lawyer's charge	**FEE, RETAINER**
laughable	**COMIC, FUNNY**	lawyer's customer	**CLIENT**
laugh boisterously	**ROAR,**	lawyer's fee	**RETAINER**
	SNORT	lawyer's patron saint	**IVES**
laugh brokenly	**CACKLE**	lax	**NEGLIGENT**
laugh contemptuously	**SNORT**	laxative	**PURGATIVE,**
laughing	**RIANT**	**CATHARTIC**	
laughing bird	**LOON**	laxity	**LOOSENESS**
laughingstock	**BUTT**	lay	**PUT, PLACE, DEPOSIT**
laugh loudly	**ROAR**	lay in plaits	**FOLD**
laugh raucously	**CACKLE**	layer	**PLY, TIER, STRATUM**
laugh syllable	**HA, HO, TEE, HEE**	layer of cloth	**PLY**
laughter	**MIRTH**	layer of floors	**TILER,**
laugh to scorn	**DERIDE**	**CARPENTER**	
launch	**DISCHARGE, START**	layer of eye	**UVEA**
launching site	**PAD**	layer of paint	**COAT**
launder	**WASH, LAVE**	layer of skin	**DERMA**
launderable	**TUB-FAST,**	lay out	**EXPEND, SPEND**
	WASHABLE, COLORFAST	layover	**STOP**
laundering finale	**RINSE**	lay up	**DISABLE**
laundry appliance	**WRINGER,**	lay waste	**RAVAGE**
	DRYER, WASHER	laze	**LOAF**
laureate	**DISTINGUISHED,**	laziness	**LETHARGY**
	HONORED	lazy	**INDOLENT, IDLE**
laurel	**BAY**	lazy animal	**SLOTH**
lava	**LATITE, SCORIA**	lazybones	**SHIRKER, IDLER**
lavaliere	**PENDANT**	lazy way to fish	**TROTLINE,**
lavatory	**BASIN**	**SETLINE, TRAWL**	
lave	**WASH**	LBJ's state	**TEXAS**
lavender	**PURPLE**	lea	**MEADOW**
lavish	**PROFUSE**	leachy	**POROUS**
lavish party	**FÊTE**	lead	**DIRECT, GUIDE**
law	**ACT, RULE, STATUTE,**	leaden	**HEAVY**
CANON, DECREE, EDICT,		leader	**CHIEF, HEAD**
ORDINANCE		lead-in	**INTRODUCTION**
law (Lat.)	**LEX, LEGES (PL.)**	leading	**AHEAD**
law charges	**COSTS**	leading actor	**STAR**
law degree (abbr.)	**LLB**	leading man	**HERO, STAR**
lawful	**LEGAL, LICIT**	lead into error	**DELUDE**
lawless	**ILLEGAL, UNRULY**	lead on	**LURE**
lawless crowd	**MOB, GANG**	leaf	**PAGE, SEPAL**
lawmaker	**SENATOR,**	leaf-cutter	**ANT**
	LEGISLATOR	leaf fat	**LARD**
lawman	**SHERIFF, MARSHAL**	leafless plant	**FERN**
lawn	**GREENSWARD**	leaflet	**PAMPHLET**
lawn covering	**GRASS, TURF**	leaf of a book	**PAGE**
lawn mower's path	**SWATH**	leaf of a calyx	**SEPAL**

leafstalk	**PETIOLE**
leafstalk used for sauce	**RHUBARB**
leafy-headed vegetable	**CABBAGE, LETTUCE**
league	**CLUB**
League of Nations city	**GENEVA**
Leah's sister	**RACHEL**
leak	**ESCAPE, FLAW, CRACK, DRIP**
leak out	**SEEP, OOZE**
lean	**RARE, SPARE, THIN, LANK, GAUNT, TILT**
lean, as a ship	**CAREEN, HEEL**
leaned over	**CANTED**
leaning	**ALOP, TREND, TENDENCY**
lean-to	**SHED**
leap	**JUMP, SKIP, HOP, SPRING**
leaping creature	**TOAD, FROG**
leaping insect	**CRICKET, FLEA**
leaps and bounds	**RAPIDLY**
learn	**ASCERTAIN, MASTER**
learned	**VERSED**
learned man in India	**PANDIT**
learned person	**SCHOLAR**
learning	**LORE, KNOWLEDGE**
lease	**LET, RENT**
lease payment	**RENT**
leash	**CURB, RESTRAIN**
least	**MEREST**
least appropriate (3 wds.)	**OF ALL THINGS**
least bit	**IOTA**
leather	**HIDE**
leatherback	**TURTLE**
leather belt	**STRAP**
leather bottle	**MATARA**
leather fastener	**STRAP, THONG**
leather gaiter	**PUTTÉE, SPAT**
leatherneck	**MARINE**
leather punch	**AWL**
leather ribbon	**STRAP**
leather source	**STEERHIDE**
leather splitting tool	**SKIVER**
leather strap	**THONG, BELT**
leather strip	**STRAP**
leather whip	**KNOUT**
leathery	**TOUGH**
leave	**DEPART, GO**
leave empty	**VACATE**
leave isolated	**MAROON, STRAND, ABANDON, DESERT**
leavening agent	**YEAST**
leave of absence	**FURLOUGH, SABBATICAL**
leave off	**CEASE**

leave out	**OMIT, SKIP, REMOVE, CUT, DELETE**
leave port	**SAIL, EMBARK**
leaves	**FOLIAGE**
leave suddenly (2 wds.)	**MAKE OFF**
leaving	**RESIDUE**
leaving a will	**TESTATE**
lectern	**DESK, STAND**
lecture	**DISCOURSE, SERMON**
lecture platform	**DAIS**
ledge	**SHELF**
ledger entry	**CREDIT, DEBIT**
lee	**SHELTER**
leech	**PARASITE**
leek	**ONION**
leer	**OGLE**
leery	**WARY**
leeward	**DOWNWIND**
leeway	**ROOM, PLAY**
left	**GONE, LIBERAL**
Left Bank location	**PARIS**
leftist	**RADICAL, RED**
leftover	**SCRAP**
leg	**CALF, GAM**
legacy	**BEQUEST**
legal	**LAWFUL, LICIT**
legal claim	**LIEN**
legal conveyance	**DEED**
legal critic	**CENSOR**
legal decree	**EDICT**
legal defense	**ALIBI**
legal document	**DEED, WRIT**
legal holiday	**LABOR DAY, MEMORIAL DAY, LINCOLN'S BIRTHDAY, WASHINGTON'S BIRTHDAY, COLUMBUS DAY, ARMISTICE DAY**
legally authorized	**LICENSED**
legal matter	**RES**
legal order	**WRIT**
legal paper	**WRIT**
legal plea	**ALIBI**
legal profession	**BAR**
legal warning	**CAVEAT**
legal writ to insure payment	**ELEGIT**
leg armor	**GREAVE**
legate	**ENVOY**
legatee	**HEIR**
legation	**MISSION**
leg bone	**SHIN, TIBIA**
legend	**MYTH, SAGA**
legendary	**MYTHICAL**
legendary bird	**ROC**
legendary British king	**LUD, ARTHUR**

legendary enchantress **CIRCE**
legendary hero **PALADIN**
legendary magician **MERLIN**
legendary sea creature **MERMAID**
legerdemain **MAGIC, TRICKERY**
leghorn **CHICKEN**
legible **READABLE**
legion **ARMY, MULTITUDE**
legislate **ENACT**
legislative body **SENATE, CONGRESS, HOUSE, PARLIAMENT**
legislative enactment **LAW**
legislator **SENATOR, CONGRESSMAN, REPRESENTATIVE, MP, ASSEMBLYMAN**
legislature **ASSEMBLY, CONGRESS**
legitimate **LAWFUL, LICIT**
leg joint **HIP, KNEE**
legume **PEA, BEAN, VEGETABLE**
lei **GARLAND, WREATH**
leisure **REST, EASE**
leisure activity **HOBBY**
leisure time **EASE**
leitmotif **THEME**
lemming **RODENT**
lemon **DEFECTIVE, CITRUS**
lemon drink **ADE**
lemonlike fruit **CITRON, LIME**
lemur **TARSIER**
lemur of Java **LORIS**
Lenape **DELAWARE**
lend **LOAN**
lend a hand **AID, HELP, ASSIST**
lend dignity to **ENNOBLE**
lene **NONASPIRATE**
length **EXTENT**
lengthen **EXTEND**
length of office **TERM**
length of railroad **TRACK**
length of service status **SENIORITY**
length of 3/4 of an inch **DIGIT**
length unit **ROD, YARD, FOOT, INCH, MILE**
lengthwise **ALONG**
lengthy **LONG**
leniency **MERCY**
lenient **TOLERANT**
Lenin's country **RUSSIA**
Lenten observers goal (comp. wd.) **SELF-DENIAL**

lentigo **FRECKLE**
lento **SLOW**
leonine hair **MANE**
leonine sound **ROAR**
leopard **PANTHER, CHEETAH**
leotard **TIGHTS**
Leo's home **LAIR**
Leo's son **LIONET**
lepidopteran **BUTTERFLY**
leporid **HARE**
leprechauns (2 wds.) **LITTLE PEOPLE**
lesion **INJURY, WOUND**
Leslie Caron role **LILI**
less **FEWER**
less adulterated **PURER**
less bad **BETTER**
less common **RARER**
less difficult **EASIER**
lessee **RENTER, TENANT**
lessen **ABATE, WANE, EASE**
lessen the strength of **ENERVATE, DEBILITATE**
lessen the tension of **RELAX**
lesser **MINOR, INFERIOR**
less expensive **CHEAPER**
less fancy **BARER**
less good **WORSE**
lesson **EXERCISE, UNIT**
lessor **LANDLORD**
less refined **COARSER**
less risky **SAFER**
less stale **FRESHER**
less than **UNDER**
less than 100 shares stock (2 wds.) **ODD LOT**
less wild **TAMER**
let **ALLOW, HIRE, RENT, PERMIT**
let down **LOWER, DISAPPOINT**
let fall **DROP**
let go **RELEASE, RELAX**
lethal **FATAL, DEADLY**
lethargic **SLEEPY, DULL**
lethargy **STUPOR, LANGUOR, TORPOR**
let in **ADMIT**
let it stand **STET**
let off **EXCUSE**
let run out **SPILL**
letter **NOTE, PRINT, MISSIVE, EPISTLE, CHARACTER**
letter carrier **POSTMAN, MAILMAN**
letter cutter **OPENER**
lettered **LITERATE**
letterhead **STATIONERY**

letter of agreement	**CARTEL**
lettuce	**ICEBERG, BOSTON, ROMAINE, BIBB, HEAD, COS**
lettuce dish	**SALAD**
let up	**RESPITE**
Levant	**EAST, ORIENT**
Levantine ketch	**SAIC**
levee	**DIKE, PIER**
level	**EVEN, FLAT, RAZE, RASE**
leveler	**PLANE**
levelheaded	**SENSIBLE**
level of command	**ECHELON**
level of equality	**PAR**
lever	**PRY, CROWBAR**
leveret	**HARE**
leviathan	**MONSTER**
levis	**JEANS**
levitate	**RISE, FLOAT**
levity	**GAIETY, FRIVOLITY**
levy a fine	**AMERCE**
lewd	**OBSCENE**
Lewis Carroll character	**ALICE**
lexicon	**DICTIONARY**
liability	**DEBT**
liable	**APT, PRONE, LIKELY, SUBJECT**
liaison	**INTIMACY**
liana	**VINE**
liar	**PERJURER, PREVARICATOR, FIBBER**
lias	**LIMESTONE**
libation	**DRINK, POTION**
Liberace's instrument	**PIANO**
liberal	**FREE**
liberate	**FREE, RELEASE**
Liberian natives	**VAI, VEI**
liberty	**FREEDOM, PRIVILEGE**
libidinous	**LEWD, WANTON**
library (2 wds.)	**READING ROOM**
library piece	**BOOKCASE**
library's study enclosure	**CARREL(L)**
library treasure	**BOOK**
Libyan city	**TRIPOLI, BENGASI**
license	**PERMIT, SANCTION**
license plate	**TAG**
license tag	**PLATE**
licentious	**WANTON, LIBERTINE**
lichen	**MOSS**
lichen dye	**LITMUS**
lick an envelope	**SEAL**
lick up	**LAP**
licorice herb	**ANISE**

lid	**COVER**
lid clasp	**HASP**
Lido	**RESORT, BEACH**
lid remover	**OPENER**
lie	**EQUIVOCATE, FIB, FALSEHOOD, STORY, RECLINE, FABRICATE**
lie in ambush	**LURK**
lie in warmth	**BASK**
Liebfraumilch	**WINE**
Liederkranz	**CHEESE**
lief	**WILLINGLY, GLADLY**
lieu	**STEAD, PLACE**
lieutenant	**SHAVETAIL, OFFICER**
life	**BIOGRAPHY, EXISTENCE**
life and death	**DIRE**
lifeboat	**RAFT**
life jacket	**MAE WEST**
lifeless	**INERT, DEAD**
lifetime	**AGE**
lift	**RAISE, BOOST, ELEVATOR**
lifting device	**LEVER, CRANE**
lifting machine	**CRANE**
lift the hat	**DOFF**
lift up	**BOOST, ELEVATE, RAISE**
lift with effort	**HEAVE, STRAIN**
light	**IGNITE, LAMP, CANDLE, BLITHE, TRIVIAL, AIRY, FAIR, ASPECT**
light anchor	**KEDGE**
light and airy	**ETHEREAL**
light anew	**REKINDLE**
light beam	**RAY**
light beer	**LAGER**
light boat	**CANOE, SUNFISH, SAILFISH, SKIFF**
light breeze	**AIR, ZEPHYR**
light brown	**ECRU, TAN, BEIGE**
light coating	**FILM**
light crimson	**PINK**
lighted	**LIT, ILLUMINATED**
lighten	**EASE**
light-footed	**NIMBLE**
light four-wheeled carriage	**PHAETON**
light globe	**BULB**
light-headed	**GIDDY, DIZZY**
lighthouse	**BEACON, PHAROS**
lighting device	**LAMP, TORCH, CANDLE, BEACON**
light meal	**LUNCHEON, SNACK, TEA**
lightning bug	**FIREFLY**
light open wagon	**CART**

light portable sunshade **PARASOL**
light red **PINK**
light refractor **PRISM**
light sarcasm **IRONY**
light shoe **SLIPPER, SANDAL**
light soup **BROTH**
lights out **TAPS**
light tan **ECRU, BEIGE, KHAKI**
light touch **DAB**
light up **ILLUMINE, BRIGHTEN**
light weight **DRAM**
light wood **BALSA**
lignite **COAL**
likable **NICE, PLEASING, ATTRACTIVE**
like **SIMILAR, ENJOY**
like a leopard **SPOTTED**
like a modern refrigerator (comp. wd.) **SELF-DEFROSTING**
like an old maid **SPINSTERISH, FINICKY, FUSSY**
like a routine police case (3 wds.) **OPEN AND SHUT**
like a warm spring day **BALMY**
like a wing **ALAR**
like better **PREFER**
like expensive beef (comp. wd.) **TOP-GRADE**
like metal **STEELY**
likely **APT, LIABLE, PRONE**
likely to turn out well **PROMISING**
liken **COMPARE**
likeness **IMAGE**
like peanut brittle **CRUNCHY**
like seawater **SALTY**
like some diets (comp. wd.) **SALT-FREE**
like sweater weather **COOL**
like unfilleted fish **BONY**
likewise **ALSO, DITTO, TOO**
liking **TASTE**
lilac color **MAUVE**
lilliputian **TINY**
lilt **CADENCE, AIR, TUNE, MELODY**
lily **ALOE, CALLA**
Lily Maid **ELAINE**
lily of the sea **CRINOID**
lily palm **TI**
lily plant **ALOE**
Lily Pons, for one **DIVA**
lily-white **PURE, BLAMELESS**
lima **BEAN**

limb **BRANCH, RAMAGE, LEG, ARM**
limber **AGILE, SPRY, NIMBLE**
limbo **HELL**
limbless reptile **SNAKE**
Limburger **CHEESE**
lime **CITRUS, CEMENT**
limestone pit **QUARRY**
lime twig **SNARE**
limit **END, BOUNDARY, EXTENT, RESTRICT, CONFINE, BOUND**
limited **FINITE, NARROW**
limiting **RESTRICTIVE**
limitless **VAST, INFINITE**
limp **FLACCID, FLABBY**
limpid **BRIGHT, LUCID**
Lincoln Center offering **OPERA, CONCERT, PLAY, BALLET**
Lindbergh book **WE**
line **ROPE, ROW, QUEUE, BOUNDARY**
lineage **PEDIGREE**
line delivered to the audience **ASIDE**
linen **NAPERY**
line of cliffs **PALISADES**
line of guards **CORDON**
line of travel **ROUTE**
line ornamenting type **SERIF**
liner **STEAMSHIP, PLANE**
liner's roster (2 wds.) **PASSENGER LIST**
lineup **ROSTER**
line with panels **WAINSCOT**
ling **HAKE, BURBOT**
linger **TARRY, WAIT**
linger close by **HOVER**
linger idly **LOITER**
linger over a triumph **GLOAT**
lingo **LANGUAGE, JARGON, CANT**
linguine **PASTA**
linguist **POLYGLOT**
link **CONNECTION**
linn **POOL, RAVINE, WATERFALL**
linoleum **FLOORING**
lint **FLUFF**
lion **CAT**
lioness in *Born Free* **ELSA**
lion's cry **ROAR**
lion's den **LAIR**
lion's lair **DEN**
lion's neck hair **MANE**
lion's share **ALL**
lip **LABIUM, RIM**

liquefy	THAW, MELT, DEFROST, CONDENSE
liqueur	CORDIAL
liqueur flavoring	ANISE, MINT, COFFEE, ORANGE, CHERRY
liquid	FLUID, WATER
liquidate	SETTLE
liquid dressing	SAUCE
liquid food	SOUP, BROTH
liquid measure	LITRE, PINT, CUP, QUART, GALLON
liquor	SPIRITS, WHISKEY
liquor vessel	DECANTER
lisle	CLOTH, THREAD
lissome	AGILE, SUPPLE
list	CATALOGUE, REGISTER
listel	FILLET, MOLDING
listen	HARK, HEED, HEAR
listen furtively	EAVESDROP
listening	ATTENTIVE
list individually	ITEMIZE
listless	BORED
list of candidates	SLATE
list of foods	MENU
list of investments	PORTFOLIO
list of names	ROLL
list of performers	CAST
list of persons	ROTA
litany	PRAYER, RECITAL
literal	TRUE, EXACT
literalism	REALISM
literally	REALLY, ACTUALLY
literary appendix	ADDENDUM
literary composition	ESSAY
literary drudge	HACK
literary irony	SATIRE
literary man	AUTHOR, WRITER
literary miscellany	ANA
literary parody	TRAVESTY
literature	LORE, WRITINGS
lithe	LIMBER, SUPPLE
litigant	SUITOR
litigate	CONTEST
little	SMALL, TINY, WEE
little (mus.)	POCO
little arrow	DART
little bone	OSSICLE
little branch	TWIG
little brook	RILL
little by little	GRADUALLY
little child	TOT, TAD
Little Corporal	NAPOLEON
little devil	IMP
little fellow	SHAVER
little piece	MORSEL
Little Rhody	RHODE ISLAND
little whirlpool	EDDY
liturgy	RITE, RITUAL

live	EXIST, RESIDE, DWELL
live coal	EMBER
liveliness	ANIMATION
lively	NIMBLE, AGILE, PEPPY, ACTIVE, PERT, SPRY
lively celebration	GALA
lively dance	GALOP, JIG, POLKA, REEL, FANDANGO
lively frolic	SPREE, CAPER
lively song	LILT
liver fluid	BILE
liverwort	HEPATICA
livestock	CATTLE
livid	PALE, ASHEN
living	ALIVE, VITAL
living being	ANIMAL, CREATURE
living room	PARLOR
living room piece	DIVAN, SOFA, COUCH, END TABLE, COFFEE TABLE, LAMP, RUG
living thing	CREATURE, ANIMAL
lizard	ANOLE
lizardlike amphibian	SALAMANDER
llama	ALPACA
llano	PLAIN
lo	BEHOLD
load	BURDEN, LADE, CARGO, PACK
loaf about	LOITER, LOLL, IDLE
loafer	SHOE, MOCASSIN
loam	SOIL
loam deposit	LOESS, SILT
loan	LEND
loan shark	USURER
loath	UNWILLING, RELUCTANT
loathe	DESPISE, HATE, DETEST, ABHOR
loathing	AVERSION
loathsome	DETESTABLE
lobby	FOYER, HALL
lobe	EARLAP
lobo	TIMBERWOLF
lobster claw	CHELA, PINCER
local	REGIONAL, AREAL
local businessman (2 wds.)	RETAIL MERCHANT
local citizen (2 wds.)	NATIVE SON
local dialect	IDIOM
locale	AREA, SITE, ENVIRONMENT
local geography	TERRAIN
localism	CUSTOM
locality	PLACE, SPOT, SITE
locate	FIND, SITUATE

location **PLACE, SITE, SPOT**
loch in Scotland **NESS, LEVEN, TAY, KATRINE**
lock **GATE, BOLT**
lock away **STORE, SAVE**
lockjaw **TETANUS**
lock of hair **TRESS**
lock opener **KEY**
locomotive **ENGINE**
locomotive and cars **TRAIN**
locomotive cowcatcher **PILOT**
locomotive track **RAIL**
locule **CAVITY**
locus **PLACE, SITE**
locust **CICADA**
locust tree **ACACIA, CAROB**
lode **VEIN**
lodestone **MAGNET**
lodge **CABIN**
lodge member **ELK**
lodger **ROOMER**
lodging **ROOM, QUARTERS**
lodging house **HOTEL, INN, HOSTEL**
loess **LOAM, SILT**
loft **ATTIC**
lofty **HIGH, TALL, ALPINE, GRAND, NOBLE**
lofty goal **IDEAL**
lofty mountain **EVEREST**
lofty place **PEAK, PINNACLE**
log **DIARY, RECORD**
log dwelling **CABIN**
loge **BOX, MEZZANINE**
log float **RAFT**
logger's boot **PAC**
loggia **GALLERY**
logical **SOUND, VALID**
logrolling **BIRLING**
logrolling contest **ROLEO**
logy **DULL, SLUGGISH**
Lohengrin's bride **ELSA**
loiter **DALLY, LAG, LINGER, TARRY, IDLE, LOLL**
loll **LOUNGE, LAZE, LINGER**
London district **CHELSEA, SOHO, MAYFAIR**
Londoner **COCKNEY**
London literature **ADELPHIAN**
London's cafe district **SOHO**
London trolley **TRAM**
lone **SOLE, SOLITARY**
loneliness **ISOLATION, SOLITUDE**
lonely **LONESOME, SOLITARY**
lone performance **SOLO**
loner **SINGLETON**
Lone Star State **TEXAS**

long **EXTENSIVE, LENGTHY, YEARN, PINE**
long ago **YORE**
long and slender **REEDY, LANK**
long and tiresome **TEDIOUS, BORING**
long cape **CLOAK**
long creeping reptile **SNAKE**
long curl of hair **RINGLET, TRESS**
long discourse **TIRADE**
long distance (2 wds.) **COUNTRY MILE**
long distance runner **MILER**
long dry period **DROUGHT**
longe **ROPE, RING**
long essay **TREATISE**
Longfellow hero **ALDEN**
long fish **EEL, GAR**
long for **COVET, PINE, YEARN, CRAVE**
long green **MONEY**
longhair **INTELLECTUAL**
longhand **WRITTEN**
long-handled brush **BROOM**
long heroic poem **EPOS**
longing **ACHE, YEN, DESIRE**
longing for friends **LONELY, HOMESICK**
long inlet **RIA**
long journey **ODYSSEY, TREK**
long-legged bird **STORK, STILT**
long life **LONGEVITY**
long live (Fr.) **VIVE**
long narrative **SAGA**
long narrow pennant **STREAMER**
long narrow piece **STRIP**
long-necked bird **SWAN, GOOSE**
long nose **SNOUT**
long-nosed fish **GAR**
long period of time **EON, AGE, CENTURY**
long piece of timber **BEAM**
long piece of wood **POLE**
long poem's division **CANTO**
long rolling wave **SWELL**
long seat **BENCH**
longshoreman **STEVEDORE**
long spear **LANCE**
long staff **POLE**
long step **STRIDE**
long-suffering **PATIENT**
long tale **SAGA**
long time **EON, AGE**
long tooth **TUSK, FANG**
long tube **PIPE**
long vocal solo **ARIA**

long weapon	**SWORD**	lorgnette	**EYEGLASSES**
look	**SEE, VIEW**	loris	**LEMUR**
look after	**TEND, MIND**	lorry	**TRUCK**
look-alike	**TWIN, DOUBLE**	lory	**PARROT**
look askance	**LEER, OGLE**	Los Angeles area	**WATTS**
look at	**ESPY, EYE, SEE,**	Los Angeles ball club	**ANGELS,**
	WATCH, REGARD		**DODGERS**
look at flirtatiously	**OGLE, LEER**	Los Angeles quarterback	**RAM**
look back	**RECALL**	Los Angeles specialty	**SMOG**
look closely	**PEER, PRY,**	Los Angeles suburb (2 wds.)	
	EXAMINE		**SANTA MONICA**
look for	**SEEK, HUNT, SEARCH**	lose	**MISLAY, MISPLACE**
look for game	**HUNT**	lose balance	**TRIP**
look for ore	**PROSPECT**	lose by neglect	**FORFEIT**
look forward to	**ANTICIPATE**	lose color	**FADE, PALE**
looking for trouble (4 wds.)		lose courage	**DESPAIR**
	UP TO NO GOOD	lose feathers	**MOLT**
looking glass	**MIRROR**	lose force	**WANE**
look in on	**VISIT, CHECK**	lose freshness	**FADE**
look on	**OBSERVE, REGARD**	lose hair	**SHED**
lookout	**SENTRY**	lose luster	**DIM, FADE**
look over	**SCAN, PORE**	lose out	**FAIL**
look slyly	**PEEP, PEEK**	lose patience	**TIRE**
look steadily	**GAZE, STARE**	lose weight	**REDUCE**
look sullen	**POUT**	loser's alibi (2 wds.)	
look to	**RELY**		**SOUR GRAPES**
look to be	**SEEM**	loss	**DEPRIVATION**
look up to	**RESPECT**	loss of memory	**AMNESIA**
loom	**IMPEND, SHAFT**	loss of reason	**AMENTIA**
loom bar	**EASER**	loss of speech	**APHASIA**
loom frame	**LATHE**	lost	**GONE, MISSING**
loom harness	**LEAF**	lot	**GROUP, PLOT, FATE, LUCK**
loon	**DIVER**	Lothario	**RAKE**
loop	**CURL**	lottery	**RAFFLE**
loop for lifting	**TAB**	loud	**NOISY**
loop in a rope	**NOOSE**	loud clamor	**RACKET, DIN**
loop on lace	**PICOT**	loud guffaw	**ROAR**
loose	**BAGGY, SLACK**	loud noise	**BANG, DIN**
loose garment	**ROBE, SIMAR,**	loud rushing noise	**WHOOSH**
	CAPE, CLOAK	loud-voiced person	**STENTOR**
loose-jointed	**LIMBER**	Louisiana bird	**PELICAN**
loosen	**UNPIN, UNTIE, UNDO**	Louisiana county	**PARISH**
loosen up	**RELAX**	Louisiana patois	**CREOLE**
looseness	**SLACK**	lounge	**LOLL, LOAF, LAZE**
loose rock particles	**SAND**	lout	**OAF, BOOR, CAD**
loose soil	**DIRT**	lovable	**AMIABLE, ENDEARING**
loot	**BOOTY, PLUNDER**	love	**FONDNESS**
lop	**CUT**	love affair	**AMOUR**
lop off	**BOB**	love apple	**TOMATO**
lope	**STRIDE**	love deity	**CUPID**
lopsided	**ALIST, ATILT, AWRY**	love in Rome	**AMORE**
loquacious	**TALKATIVE**	loveliness	**PULCHRITUDE**
lord	**NOBLEMAN**	lovelock	**TRESS**
lordly beast	**LION**	lovely	**BEAUTIFUL, HANDSOME,**
Lord's Day	**SUNDAY**		**COMELY**
lord's wife	**LADY**	love of travel	**WANDERLUST**
lore	**KNOWLEDGE**	lover	**ROMEO, SWEETHEART,**
Lorelei	**SIREN**		**PARAMOUR**

lover of Heloise **ABELARD**
lover's heartbeat (comp. wd.) **PIT-A-PAT**
lovers' meeting place **TRYST**
lovers' quarrel **SPAT**
lover's song **SERENADE**
love seat **DIVAN**
love story **ROMANCE**
love to excess **ADORE, DOTE**
love token **AMORET**
loving **FOND**
loving cup **TROPHY**
low **BASE, DEEP**
lowbred **VULGAR, COARSE**
low chirping note **TWEET**
low-cost dwelling **TENEMENT**
lower **ABASE**
lower limb **LEG**
lower world **HADES, ORCUS**
lowest **LEAST**
lowest class of animal **AMOEBA**
lowest deck **ORLOP**
lowest form of wit **PUN**
lowest point **NADIR**
lowest singing voice **BASS**
low female voice **ALTO**
low green shrub **ERICA**
lowland **BOTTOM**
low male voice **BASS**
low spirits **BLUES**
low step-in shoe **LOAFER**
low tide **NEAP, EBB**
low tufted plant **MOSS**
low waters (2 wds.) **EBB TIDE**
loyal **TRUE, CONSTANT, FAITHFUL**
loyalist **PATRIOT, TORY**
loyal supporter **FAN**
loyalty **DEVOTION, FEALTY**
Loyolite **JESUIT**
lozenge **PASTILLE**
luau food **POI**
lubricant, for short **LUBE**
lubricate **OIL, GREASE**
lucid **BRIGHT, CLEAR**
Lucifer **FALLEN ANGEL, SATAN, DEVIL**
Lucifer's state **PERDITION**
luck **CHANCE**
lucky **FORTUNATE**
lucky event **HIT**
lucky number **SEVEN**
lucky token **AMULET**
lucrative **GAINFUL**
ludicrous **COMICAL**
luggage item **TRUNK, SUITCASE, BAG, GRIP, ETUI, VALISE**

lukewarm **TEPID**
lull **HUSH, CALM**
lumber **WOOD, TIMBER**
lumberman's boot **PAC**
lumberman's tool **AXE, AX, SAW**
luminary **SUN, STAR**
luminous **RADIANT, SHINY**
luminous heavenly body **COMET, STAR, MOON, PLANET**
lump **BLOB, MASS**
lump of butter **PAT**
lump of cottage cheese **CURD**
lump of earth **CLOD**
lump of earth on the fairway **DIVOT**
lump of tobacco **WAD**
lunar flight control center **HOUSTON**
lunacy **MADNESS, INSANITY**
lunatic **MANIAC**
lunchroom **TEA SHOP, SNACK BAR, COFFEE SHOP, CAFE, CAFETERIA, RESTAURANT**
lunchtime **NOON**
lune **MOON, CRESCENT**
lunge **LEAP, SPRING**
lurch **CAREEN**
lure **BAIT, ENTICE, TEMPT**
lure by artifice **DECOY**
lurid **SENSATIONAL**
lurk **SKULK, SNEAK**
lurk about **SNEAK**
luscious **TASTY, SWEET**
lush **JUICY, PROFUSE**
lust **PASSION**
luster **GLOSS, POLISH, SHEEN, SHINE**
lusterless **DEAD, MAT**
lustrous cloth **PANNE**
lustrous resin **COPAL**
luxuriate **BASK**
luxurious **SYBARITIC**
luxurious fabric **SILK, SATIN, VELVET**
luxurious fur **SABLE, MINK, ERMINE**
luxury **EASE**
Luzon headhunter **IGOROT**
lying **DISHONEST, PRONE**
lying across **TRANSVERSE**
lying flat **PRONE**
lying on the back **SUPINE**
lynx **CAT, WILDCAT**
lyric **POETIC**
lyricist Gershwin **IRA**
lyric poem **ODE, EPODE**
lysergic acid diethylamide **LSD**

M

macabre **WEIRD, EERIE, EERY, GRIM, GHASTLY, GRUESOME**
macaco **LEMUR, MONKEY**
macadamia **NUT**
Macao coin **AVO**
macaroni **PASTA**
macaw **ARA, PARROT**
Macbeth's title **THANE**
maccaboy **SNUFF**
mace **SPICE**
macedoine **MEDLEY**
macerate **SOFTEN, TORMENT**
machination **SCHEME, PLOT**
machine **ENGINE, MOTOR, GADGET**
machine part **CAM, GEAR, TAPPET, PAWL**
machine tool **BAND-SAW, FILE, LATHE**
machismo **VIRILITY**
mackerel's relative **BONITO, CERO**
mackinaw **BLANKET, COAT**
mackintosh **RAINCOAT**
mackle **BLUR**
macrocosm **UNIVERSE**
macroscopic **VISIBLE**
macruran **LOBSTER, SHRIMP**
maculate **DEFILE**
mad **ANGRY, INSANE, RABID**
Madagascar mammal **LEMUR**
mad, as a dog **RABID**
madcap **RECKLESS**
madden **ENRAGE, CRAZE**
madder **DYE, CRIMSON**
made of (suffix) **INE**
made of a hard wood **OAKEN**
made of cereal **OATEN**
made of fired clay **EARTHEN, CERAMIC**
made of flax **LINEN**
made of grain **CEREAL**
made of iron **METALLIC**
made of silver **ARGENT**
made on a loom **WOVEN**
madhouse **BEDLAM**
Madison Avenue technique (2 wds.) **HARD SELL, SOFT SELL**
madman **LUNATIC, MANIAC**
madness **LUNACY, INSANITY**
Madras hemp **SUNN**
Madrid boulevard **PRADO**
madrigal **LYRIC, POEM**

maelstrom **WHIRLPOOL**
Mae West role **LOU, LIL**
magazine official **EDITOR**
magic **LEGERDEMAIN, SORCERY, VOODOO, ALCHEMY, NECROMANCY**
magic charm **AMULET**
magician's rod **WAND**
magic lamp owner **ALADDIN**
magic stick **WAND**
magistrate **JUDGE**
magistrate's staff **MACE**
magnanimous **GENEROUS**
magnetic metal **IRON**
magnetic recording strip **TAPE**
magnificent **GRAND**
magnify **ENLARGE**
magnitude **SIZE**
magnolia **TREE**
Magnolia State **MISSISSIPPI**
mahatma (2 wds.) **HOLY MAN**
mah-jongg piece **TILE**
maid **GIRL, LASS, SERVANT**
mail **POST, SEND**
mail container **SACK**
mail room employee (2 wds.) **OFFICE BOY**
mailbag **POUCH**
maim **CRIPPLE, DISFIGURE**
main **CHIEF, PRIME**
main artery **AORTA, BOULEVARD**
main course **ENTREE**
Maine capital **AUGUSTA**
Maine city **BANGOR**
Maine lake **SEBAGO**
main idea **GIST**
main impact **BRUNT**
mainland **CONTINENT**
main meal **DINNER**
main movie **FEATURE**
main part **BULK**
maintain **KEEP**
maintain one's dignity (2 wds.) **SAVE FACE**
maize **CORN**
majestic **REGAL, ROYAL, STATELY, GRAND**
major appliance **RANGE, STOVE, REFRIGERATOR, WASHER, DRYER, OVEN**
majority **PLURALITY**
make **CONSTRUCT, CREATE, ERECT, MANUFACTURE**
make a beginning **START, BEGIN, COMMENCE**
make a brief visit **CALL**
make a cake **BAKE**

make a choice	**OPT, ELECT, SELECT**
make a contented sound	**PURR**
make active	**ENERGIZE**
make a decision	**DECIDE**
make a difference	**MATTER**
make a garment	**SEW**
make airtight	**SEAL**
make allusion to	**MENTION**
make a loan	**LEND**
make amends	**REDRESS, ATONE**
make a mess of	**PI(E)**
make a mistake	**ERR**
make an address	**SPEAK, ORATE**
make an edging	**TAT, BIND**
make angry	**RILE, MADDEN, IRE**
make an offer	**BID**
make a picture	**DRAW, PAINT, ILLUSTRATE, SKETCH**
make a promise	**PLEDGE, VOW**
make a proposal	**OFFER**
make a rasping sound	**GRATE**
make a recording	**TAPE**
make a speech	**ORATE**
make a vow	**SWEAR**
make bare	**DENUDE**
make beer	**BREW**
make believe	**PRETEND**
make beloved	**ENDEAR**
make better	**AMEND, REFORM, RENOVATE, REPAIR, RENEW, RESTORE, REHABILITATE**
make bigger	**ENLARGE, MAGNIFY**
make brief note	**JOT**
make broader	**WIDEN**
make brown	**TAN**
make butter	**CHURN**
make calm	**ALLAY, COMPOSE**
make certain	**ENSURE**
make cheerful	**ENLIVEN**
make choice	**OPT, SELECT**
make cloth	**WEAVE**
make cloudy	**BLUR**
make content	**SATISFY**
make corrections	**AMEND**
make designs on metal	**ETCH**
make different	**CHANGE**
make even	**LEVEL**
make eyes at	**OGLE**
make float in air	**LEVITATE, FLY**
make free	**RID, LIBERATE**
make fresh again	**RENEW**
make full	**FILL**
make fun of	**RIDICULE**

make gay	**LIVEN, ELATE**
make gentle	**TAME**
make happen	**CAUSE**
make happy	**ELATE**
make hard	**FREEZE, STEEL**
make headway	**ADVANCE, PROGRESS**
make holy	**HALLOW, SANCTIFY, BLESS, CANONIZE**
make impossible	**PRECLUDE**
make improvements	**REVISE**
make inquiry	**ASK**
make into coin	**MINT**
make into law	**ENACT, LEGISLATE**
make into leather	**TAN**
make keen, as the appetite	**WHET**
make known	**DISCLOSE, AIR, PUBLISH, ADVERTISE, REVEAL**
make lace	**TAT**
make less dense	**RAREFY**
make level	**TRUE**
make lively	**ANIMATE**
make love	**WOO**
make lusterless	**FLATTEN**
make merry	**REVEL**
make money	**EARN, COIN, MINT**
make muddy	**ROIL**
make multiform	**DIVERSIFY**
make neat	**GROOM, TIDY**
make objection	**DEMUR, REMONSTRATE, PROTEST**
make out clearly	**DISCERN**
make over	**REDO**
make pale	**CHALK**
make payment	**PAY, REMIT**
make perplexed	**BAFFLE**
make possible	**ENABLE**
make precious	**ENDEAR**
make preparations (2 wds.)	**GET READY**
make progress	**ADVANCE, GAIN**
make proud	**ELATE**
make purchases	**SHOP, BUY**
make quiet	**HUSH, SILENCE**
maker	**CREATOR, MANUFACTURER**
make ready	**PREPARE**
make report	**TELL**
maker of earthenware	**POTTER, CERAMIST**
maker of laws	**LEGISLATOR**
maker of pottery	**CERAMIST**
make slow	**RETARD**
make smaller	**DECREASE, SHRINK**

make small talk	CHAT	male pig	BOAR
make soundproof	DEAFEN,	male sheep	RAM
	INSULATE	male sibling	BROTHER
make sport of	DERIDE	male singer	TENOR, BASS,
make tardy	DELAY, RETARD		BARITONE, CROONER
make thread	SPIN	male swan	COB
make unfriendly	ALIENATE	male swine	BOAR
make untidy	MUSS, MESS-UP	male title	MR., SIR
makeup	COSMETICS	male turkey	TOM
make up for	ATONE	male witch	WARLOCK, WIZARD
make use of	AVAIL, EMPLOY	malevolent	EVIL
make void	ANNUL	malice	SPITE
make watertight	SEAL, CALK	malicious	SPITEFUL
make weary	BORE, TIRE	malicious burning	ARSON
make well	CURE	malicious look	LEER
make white	BLANCH	malign	SLANDER, DEFAME
make wine	VINTAGE	malignant	POISONOUS
make worse	AGGRAVATE,	mall	PROMENADE
	IRRITATE	mallard	DUCK
making a profit (3 wds.)		mallet	GAVEL, HAMMER,
	IN THE BLACK		SLEDGE
maladroit	INEPT	malodorous	RANK, FOUL
malady	ILLNESS, AILMENT	malt beverage	ALE, BEER
malagma	POULTICE	malt froth	BARM
Malamud novel (2 wds.)		malt infusion	WORT
	THE FIXER	malt liquor	BREW
malarial fever	AGUE	maltreat	INJURE, ABUSE
Malay ape	LAR	maltworm	TOPER
Malay archipelago garment		mama	MOTHER, MOM,
	SARONG		MOMMY, MA
Malay buffalo	CARIBOU	mama hog	SOW
Malay island	JAVA	mama's husband	PAPA
Malaysian state	PERAK	mamba	COBRA, SNAKE
male	MASCULINE	Mamie's man	IKE
male adult	MAN	mammoth	COLOSSAL,
male ancestor	SIRE		IMMENSE
male bee	DRONE	man	MALE, MASCULINE
male bird	ROOSTER	man about town	SOPHISTICATE
male bovine	BULL, STEER, OX	manacle	HANDCUFF
male cat	TOM	manage	RUN, ADMINISTER,
male chicken	ROOSTER		DIRECT, OPERATE
male child	SON, BOY	manageable	DOCILE
male deer	HART, STAG	management	DIRECTION,
male deity	GOD		CONTROL
male descendant	SON	manage well (2 wds.)	GET ALONG
malediction	CURSE	manager	BOSS, LEADER
male elephant	BULL	manatee (2 wds.)	SEA COW
malefactor	VILLAIN	man child	BOY, SON
male falcon	TERCEL, TIERCEL	Manchurian border river	AMUR
male garment	SHIRT, TIE,	Mandan	SIOUAN, SIOUX
TRUNKS, ASCOT, TUXEDO,		mandrill	BABOON
OVERCOAT, JACKET		mane	HAIR
male horse	STALLION, STUD	man-eater	CANNIBAL, SHARK
Malemute	HUSKY	maneuver	TACTIC
male or female	SEX	man from Amsterdam	
male parent	DAD, SIRE,	NETHERLANDER, DUTCHMAN	
FATHER, POP, DADDY,		man from Bangkok	THAI
POPPA, PAPA, PA, PAW		man from Edinburgh	SCOT

man from Glasgow **SCOT**
man from Stockholm **SWEDE**
man from Tel Aviv **ISRAELI**
mangle **IRON**
mangy **SORDID, SQUALID, SHABBY, SEEDY**
maniac **LUNATIC, MADMAN**
manicuring tool **SCISSORS, BRUSH, CLIPPER, FILE, BUFFER**
manifest **CLEAR, REVEAL**
manifold **DIVERSE, SUNDRY**
manioc **CASSAVA**
man in charge **BOSS, FOREMAN**
man in the street **PEDESTRIAN**
manipulate **JUGGLE, WIELD, RIG, HANDLE**
manlike device **ROBOT**
manlike robot **ANDROID**
manly **BOLD, BRAVE, MASCULINE**
man-made **SYNTHETIC, ARTIFICIAL**
manner **AIR, MIEN**
manner of walking **GAIT**
man next door **NEIGHBOR**
man of action **DOER**
man of God **SAINT, PRIEST, RABBI, MINISTER**
man of great valor **HERO**
man of great wealth **MIDAS**
man of influence **VIP**
man of law **ATTORNEY**
man of learning **SCHOLAR**
man of letters **AUTHOR**
Man of Sorrows **MESSIAH, CHRIST**
man of the hour **HERO**
man-of-war **FRIGATE, WARSHIP, JELLYFISH**
man on the bench **JUDGE**
manor house **MANSION**
Mansard's extension **EAVES**
man's best friend **DOG**
manservant **VALET, BUTLER, CHAUFFEUR, HOUSEBOY, GARDENER, CHEF**
man's garment **SUIT, SHIRT, PANTS, POLO SHIRT, SPORTS JACKET, TUXEDO, OVERCOAT, TIE**
man's mate **WOMAN**
man's opera headgear **TOP HAT**
man's purchase (2 wds.) **RAZOR BLADE, SHAVE CREAM**
man's title **SIR, MR.**
manta **DEVILFISH, RAY**

mantle **CLOAK, CAPE, CONCEAL**
manual **HANDBOOK**
manual art **CRAFT**
manual digit **THUMB**
manufacture **MAKE, PRODUCE**
manufactured products **WARE**
manuscript (abbr.) **MS, MSS (pl.)**
manuscript part **PAGE, FOLIO**
many **NUMEROUS**
many times **OFTEN, FREQUENTLY**
Maori tribe **ATI**
map **PLAN, CHART, ARRANGE**
map abbreviation **ALT, LAT, LONG**
map book **ATLAS**
maple **TREE**
maple genus **ACER**
map within a map **INSET**
maquillage **MAKEUP, COSMETICS**
mar **DAMAGE, IMPAIR, INJURE, SPOIL**
marabou **STORK**
marauder **BRIGAND**
marble **AGATE, TAW, MIB**
Marc Antony's wife **OCTAVIA**
Marcel Marceau's routine **MIME, PANTOMIME**
march **DRILL, HIKE, WALK, PARADE**
marching order (2 wds.) **ABOUT FACE, RIGHT FACE, LEFT FACE, DOUBLE TIME**
march into **ENTER**
March King **SOUSA**
Margaret Mitchell hero (2 wds.) **RHETT BUTLER**
Margaret Mitchell heroine (2 wds.) **SCARLETT O'HARA**
margarine **OLEO**
margin **EDGE, BORDER, RIM**
marijuana (sl.) **POT, REEFER, MARY JANE, JOINT, GRASS, TEA**
marina **BASIN, DOCK**
marina sight **YACHT, BOAT, SAILS**
marine **NAVAL**
marine crustacean **CRAB, CRAYFISH, CRAWDAD**
marine fish **HAKE, OPAH, BLUE, TUNA**
marine growth **SEAWEED**
mariner **SAILOR, SEAMAN**

marionette	**DOLL, PUPPET**	martini garnish	**OLIVE, TWIST**
marital	**CONJUGAL**	martini ingredient	**OLIVE, GIN,**
maritime	**NAVAL, NAUTICAL**		**VERMOUTH, TWIST,**
mark	**TRAIT, SCAR, STAIN**		**ICE, VODKA**
markdown	**DISCOUNT, SALE**	Martinique volcano	**PELEE**
marked aversion	**DISGUST**	marvel	**MIRACLE, WONDER**
marked by denial	**NEGATIVE**	marvelous	**WONDERFUL**
market	**MART, STORE, SHOP,**	mascara wearer	**EYELASH**
	SELL, VEND	masculine	**MALE**
market again	**RESELL**	mash	**PULVERIZE, CRUSH**
market place	**AGORA**	masher	**WOLF**
mark of a wound	**SCAR**	mask	**HIDE, CONCEAL,**
mark of disgrace	**STIGMA**		**SCREEN, DOMINO**
mark of omission	**CARET**	masked animal, for	
mark of respect	**HONOR**	short	**COON**
mark with spots	**MOTTLE**	ma's mate	**PA**
marksman	**SHOT**	masonry fence	**WALL**
marksman's goal	**TARGET**	mass	**BULK, WAD**
marl	**FERTILIZER**	Massachusetts cape	**ANN, COD**
marmalade	**JELLY**	Massachusetts city	**SALEM,**
maroon	**STRAND, ABANDON,**		**BOSTON, CAMBRIDGE**
	DESERT	Massachusetts island	
marriage	**WEDDING, WEDLOCK**		**NANTUCKET**
marriage announcement		massacre	**SLAUGHTER**
	BANNS	massage	**RUB**
marriage ceremony	**WEDDING,**	massive	**HUGE, HEAVY**
	NUPTIALS	mass of bread	**LOAF**
marriage notice	**BANNS**	mass of trees	**FOREST**
marriage termination	**DIVORCE**	mass vestment	**AMICE**
marriage vow (2 wds.)	**I DO**	mast	**POLE, SPAR**
married	**WED, WEDDED**	master	**CHIEF, LORD**
married woman	**WIFE**	master in India	**SAHIB**
married woman's title (Fr.)		master in music	**MAESTRO**
	MADAME	master of ceremonies	**EMCEE**
marron	**CHESTNUT**	master plan	**STRATEGY**
marrow	**MEDULLA, PITH**	Master Sawyer	**TOM**
marrowbone	**KNEE**	master stroke	**COUP**
marry	**WED**	mastery (2 wds.)	**UPPER HAND**
marry again	**REWED**	masticate	**CHEW**
marry a woman	**WIVE**	mat	**RUG**
marry in haste	**ELOPE**	matador's opponent	**TORO,**
Mars (2 wds.)	**RED PLANET**		**BULL**
marsh	**BOG, FEN, SWAMP,**	match	**MATE**
	MIRE, MORASS	matched group	**SET**
marshal's badge	**STAR**	matched group of china	
Marshal Dillon's nickname		(2 wds.)	**TEA SET**
	MATT	matched pair	**MATES**
marsh bird	**RAIL, SNIPE, STILT**	matchless	**PEERLESS**
marsh crocodile	**GOA**	mate	**COMRADE, SPOUSE,**
marsh elder	**IVA**		**HUSBAND, WIFE,**
marsh gas	**METHANE**		**COMPANION**
marshy	**BOGGY, WET**	material for making molds	
marshy hollow part	**SWALE**	(3 wds.)	**PLASTER OF PARIS**
marsupial	**KOALA, KANGAROO**	maternity bird	**STORK**
mart	**MARKET, EMPORIUM**	mate's kin	**IN-LAW**
marten	**WEASEL**	mathematics	**ARITHMETIC**
martenlike mammal	**SABLE**	math exercise	**PROBLEM**
martial	**MILITARY**	math term	**SINE, COSINE**

matriculate	**ENROLL**	means of entry	**ACCESS, DOOR,**
matrimonial	**CONJUGAL,**		**GATE, ENTRY**
	MARITAL	means of escape	**LOOPHOLE**
matter	**SUBSTANCE**	meantime	**INTERIM**
mature	**AGE, RIPE, RIPEN**	measles	**RUBELLA**
mature person	**ADULT**	measly	**SKIMPY**
maturing agent	**AGER**	measure	**METE**
maudlin	**EMOTIONAL, MUSHY**	measured	**UNIFORM**
mausoleum	**TOMB, CRYPT**	measured duration	**TIME**
mauve	**LILAC, PURPLE**	measure of distance	**MILE**
maw	**CRAW, CROP**	measure of heat	**CALORIE,**
maw's husband	**PAW**		**THERM**
maxilla and mandible	**JAWS**	measure of land	**ACRE, ARE,**
maxim	**ADAGE, MOTTO,**		**LOT, PLOT**
	SAYING, SAW	measure of length	**FOOT, ROD,**
maximum	**MOST, LIMIT**		**METER, YARD,**
maybe	**PERHAPS, POSSIBLY,**		**INCH, MILE**
	PERCHANCE	measure of paper	**REAM**
Mayday signal	**SOS**	measure of time	**HOUR,**
mayhem	**DESTRUCTION,**		**MINUTE, SECOND, DAY,**
	VIOLENCE		**WEEK, MONTH, YEAR**
May 30th	**MEMORIAL DAY,**	measure of type	**EN, EM, POINT**
(2 wds.)	**DECORATION DAY**	measure of weight	**POUND,**
maze	**TANGLE, CONFUSION**		**OUNCE**
maze of the Minotaur		measure of wood	**CORD**
	LABYRINTH	measure out	**ALLOT**
mazzard	**CHERRY**	measure swords	**DUEL**
McGuffey opus	**READER**	measurer	**RULER, GAUGE,**
McIntosh	**APPLE**		**SURVEYOR**
McLuhan's field	**TV, MEDIA**	measuring strip	**TAPE**
McNally's partner	**RAND**	meat	**FLESH, PORK, BEEF,**
m.c. Mack	**TED**		**HAM, LAMB**
m.c. Sullivan	**ED**	meat cut	**RASHER, LOIN**
mead	**DRINK, BREW**	meat dish	**HASH, STEW**
meadow	**LEA**	meat jelly	**ASPIC**
meadow mouse	**VOLE**	meat pastry	**RISSOLE**
meadow saffron	**COLCHIUM**	meat sauce	**GRAVY**
meager	**POOR, SCANT, SCANTY**	meaty	**SUBSTANTIAL**
meal	**DINNER, LUNCH,**	mechanical	**AUTOMATIC,**
	SNACK, SUPPER, TEA,		**REFLEX**
	REPAST, BREAKFAST	mechanical man	**ROBOT**
meal fragment	**ORT**	mechanics of	
mealtime prayer	**GRACE**	motion	**DYNAMICS**
mealy	**FRIABLE**	mechanism	**APPARATUS, TOOL**
mean	**INTEND, CRUEL, NASTY,**	medal	**BADGE, PLAQUE**
	AVERAGE	meddler	**BUSYBODY**
meander	**ROAM, WANDER**	meddle (with)	**TAMPER**
mean dog	**BITER**	Mede	**ARYAN**
meaning	**IMPORT, SENSE,**	mediate	**INTERCEDE**
	INTENT	medical fluid	**SERUM**
meaningful	**SIGNIFICANT**	medical patient	**CASE**
meaningless	**EMPTY**	medical picture	**X RAY**
meaningless ritual		medical suffix	**IATRIC, OMA**
(2 wds.)	**MUMBO JUMBO**	medicated lozenge	**PASTILLE**
meanness	**SPITE**	medicinal plant	**ALOE, HERB,**
mean proportion	**AVERAGE**		**SENNA**
means	**RESOURCE, WEALTH**	medicinal remedy	**ANTIDOTE**
		medicinal root	**IPECAC**

medicinal unit	**DOSE**	meloid	**BEETLE**
medicine	**DRUG**	melon	**CANTALOUPE, PEPO,**
medicine bottle	**VIAL**		**HONEYDEW**
medicine man	**SHAMAN**	melon-like fruit	**GOURD**
medicine pellet	**PILL**	melon pear	**PEPINO**
medicine portion	**DOSE**	melt	**DISSOLVE, THAW,**
medico	**PHYSICIAN, SURGEON**		**DEFROST**
medieval dance refrain	**RONDO**	melt away	**DWINDLE**
medieval instrument	**LUTE**	melt down, as lard	**RENDER**
medieval Jewish automaton		melted rock	**LAVA**
	GOLEM	melting pot	**CRUCIBLE**
medieval poem	**LAI, LAY,**	melt ore	**SMELT**
	BALLAD, ROMANCE	melt together	**FUSE**
medieval slave	**SERF, ESNE**	member	**LIMB, ELEMENT**
medieval story	**SAGA, ROMANCE**	member of an Indian sect	
medieval viol	**REBEC**		**PARSI, PARSEE**
mediocre	**SO-SO**	member of boys' group	**SCOUT**
meditate	**PONDER, BROOD,**	member of crew	**HAND**
	THINK	member of Parliament	
Mediterranean	**SEA**		**LORD, MP**
Mediterranean area	**RIVIERA**	member of state	**CITIZEN**
Mediterranean island	**CRETE,**	member of the clergy	**CLERIC,**
	CYPRUS, MALTA		**MINISTER, PRIEST, RABBI**
Mediterranean sailing vessel		member of the firm	**PARTNER**
	SETTEE	member of a work crew	**MAN**
Mediterranean tree	**CAROB**	members of the fourth	
Mediterranean wind	**SOLANO,**	estate	**PRESS, REPORTER**
	MISTRAL	membership charge	**DUES**
medium	**MIDDLE, HALF**	membrane	**TELA**
medium (pl.)	**MEDIA**	membranous pouch	**CYST**
medium of exchange		memento	**RELIC, REMINDER,**
	CURRENCY		**SOUVENIR**
medley	**OLIO**	memento case	**LOCKET,**
medulla	**MARROW**		**RELIQUARY**
meek	**HUMBLE**	memo	**NOTE**
meerschaum	**PIPE**	memoir	**RECORD, REPORT**
meet	**ENCOUNTER, SIT,**	memorable	**NOTABLE**
	CONVENE, ASSEMBLE,	memorial mound	**CAIRN**
	CONFRONT	memory	**RECOLLECTION**
meet by chance (2 wds.)	**COME**	memory aid	**MNEMONIC**
	ACROSS, RUN INTO	menace	**THREATEN**
meeting	**SESSION**	menage	**HOUSEHOLD**
meeting program	**AGENDA**	menagerie	**ZOO**
mel	**HONEY**	mend	**REPAIR, DARN, FIX,**
melancholy	**LOW, SAD, BLUE,**		**KNIT, HEAL**
	SOMBER	mendacity	**LYING, DECEIT**
Melanesian native	**FIJI**	mender of pots	**TINKER**
melange	**MEDLEY, MIXTURE**	mendicant	**BEGGAR**
melee	**RIOT**	menial	**SERVILE**
mellow	**RIPE, AGE, RIPEN**	men in blue	**POLICE**
melodic	**ARIOSE**	Mennonite sect	**AMISH**
melodic sounds	**MUSIC,**	men's party	**STAG, SMOKER**
	HARMONY	mental	**RATIONAL**
melodious	**MUSICAL,**	mental acumen	**WIT**
	AGREEABLE	mental anguish	**DOLOR**
melodist	**COMPOSER**	mental disposition	**TEMPER,**
melody	**ARIA, SONG, TUNE,**		**MOOD**
	AIR, REFRAIN	mentality	**ACUMEN**

mentally sound	**SANE**
mental position (3 wds.)	**POINT OF VIEW**
mental slip	**LAPSE**
mental strain	**TENSION**
mention	**CITE, NAME**
mentor	**TEACHER**
menu (3 wds.)	**BILL OF FARE**
menu item	**PRIME RIBS,** **STEAK, CHOPS, SALAD,** **VEGETABLE, DESSERT,** **ROAST BEEF, ENTREE**
Mephistopheles	**SATAN, DEVIL**
mephitic	**POISONOUS, FOUL**
mercantile	**COMMERCIAL**
mercenary	**HIRELING**
merchandise	**GOODS, WARES**
merchant	**DEALER, TRADER,** **SELLER, VENDOR**
merciful	**CLEMENT**
merciless	**STONY**
Mercury's winged cap	**PETASOS**
mercy	**LENIENCY, PITY**
mere	**ONLY, SIMPLE**
mere handful	**WISP**
merely	**JUST, ONLY**
merest bit	**IOTA**
mere taste	**SIP, BIT**
meretricious	**VULGAR, GAUDY,** **TAWDRY**
merganser	**SMEW, SHELDRAKE**
merge	**BLEND, MELD,** **COALESCE, COMBINE**
meridian	**MIDDAY, NOON**
merino	**SHEEP, WOOL**
merit	**DESERVE, EARN, WORTH,** **VALUE**
meritorious	**WORTHY**
mermaid	**SIREN**
mero	**GROUPER, GUASA**
merriment	**GAIETY, GLEE**
merry	**GAY, HILARIOUS**
merry adventure	**LARK, SPREE**
merry andrew	**CLOWN, ZANY,** **BUFFOON**
merry-go-round	**CAROUSEL**
merrymaking	**REVEL**
merry prank	**CAPER**
merry tune	**LILT**
mesa	**TABLELAND, PLATEAU**
mescal cactus of Mexico	**PEYOTE**
mesh	**NET, NETWORK**
mess	**HODGEPODGE**
message	**COMMUNICATION,** **TELEGRAM, NOTE**
message boy	**PAGE**
messenger	**ENVOY, HERALD**
messenger of the gods	**HERMES**
messiah	**SAVIOR**
messy	**UNTIDY**
Met solo	**ARIA**
metal	**LEAD, TIN, ZINC, STEEL,** **IRON**
metal bar	**INGOT**
metal-bearing lode	**VEIN**
metal bolt	**RIVET**
metal cement	**SOLDER**
metal container	**CAN, TIN**
metal cord	**WIRE**
metal deposit	**LODE**
metal disc	**PATEN, MEDAL**
metal dross	**SLAG**
metal fastener	**NAIL, PIN,** **RIVET, SNAP, BOLT, SCREW**
metal globe	**POME**
metallic paper	**FOIL**
metallic fabric	**LAME**
metallic sound	**CLING, CLANK,** **PING, BANG**
metallic vein	**LODE**
metal tag on shoelace	**AGLET**
metal thread	**WIRE**
metal tube	**PIPE**
metal worker	**TINNER, TINKER**
metal workshop	**SMITHY,** **FORGE**
metamorphosis	**CHANGE**
metaphor	**TROPE**
metaphysical entity	**ENTIUM,** **(pl.) ENTIA**
metatarsus	**FOOT**
mete	**ALLOT, APPORTION,** **DOLE, DISTRIBUTE**
meteorological device	**SONDE**
meter	**RHYTHM**
methane hydrocarbon	**PARAFFIN**
method	**MODE, SYSTEM, WAY**
method of payment (2 wds.)	**INSTALLMENT PLAN**
methyl alcohol (2 wds.)	**WOOD SPIRIT**
meticulous	**FASTIDIOUS,** **PRECISE**
metier	**LINE, JOB**
metrical	**RHYTHMIC**
metrical stress	**ICTUS**
metric foot	**IAMB**
metric land measure	**ARE**
metric measure	**STERE**
metric quart	**LITER**
metric unit	**GRAM, STERE,** **LITER, DECARE, KILO,** **METER, ARE**
metric weight	**KILO, GRAM**

mettle	**SPIRIT, STAMINA**	mild	**GENTLE, TAME, TENDER,**
Mexican blanket	**SERAPE**		**KIND, PLEASANT, NICE,**
Mexican coin	**PESO**		**FAIR, CLÉMENT**
Mexican corn cake	**TORTILLA**	mild cheese	**GOUDA, BRIE**
Mexican cottonwood	**ALAMO**	mildew	**MOLD**
Mexican dance	**HAT**	mild expletive	**DANG, DRAT,**
Mexican dish	**TAMALE**		**HECK, GAD, EGAD,**
Mexican dollar	**PESO**		**PFUI, DARN,**
Mexican garment	**SERAPE,**	mild oath	**EGAD**
	PONCHO	mild oath in Britain	**GOR, GAD**
Mexican gentleman	**SENOR**	mild pinch	**TWEAK**
Mexican Indian	**AZTEC, YAQUI**	militant	**HOSTILE**
Mexican laborer	**PEON**	military	**MARTIAL**
Mexican lake	**CHAPALA**	military acronym	**AWOL**
Mexican peninsula	**YUCATAN**	military aircraft	**CHOPPER,**
Mexican rubber tree	**ULE**		**PURSUIT PLANE, BOMBER,**
Mexican sandwich	**TACO**		**FIGHTER PLANE**
Mexican's hat	**SOMBRERO**	military assistant	**AIDE**
Mexican shrub	**CHIA**	military automobile	**JEEP**
Michaelmas daisy	**ASTER**	military award	**MEDAL**
Michelangelo masterpiece		military base	**FORT, POST,**
	PIETA,		**CAMP**
	DAVID, MOSES	military cap	**KEPI**
Michigan metropolis	**DETROIT,**	military depot	**BASE**
	LANSING, ANN ARBOR	military device	**SONAR, RADAR**
Mickey Mouse inventor	**DISNEY**	military ditch	**TRENCH**
microcosm	**UNIVERSE**	military division	**PLATOON,**
microorganism	**BACTERIUM,**		**SQUAD**
	GERM, VIRUS	military dress hat	**SHAKO**
microscopic	**MINUTE, TINY**	military exercise	**DRILL,**
microscopic organism	**AMOEBA**		**PARADE, BIVOUAC**
microwave amplifier	**MASER**	military expedition to Holy	
mid	**CENTRAL**	Land	**CRUSADE**
midday	**NOON**	military force	**LEGION, TROOP**
midday nap	**SIESTA**	military fugitive	**AWOL**
midday refreshment	**LUNCH**	military greeting	**SALUTE**
middle	**CENTER, MID**	military guard	**SENTRY**
Middle Eastern nation	**ISRAEL,**	military horsemen	**CAVALRY**
	SYRIA, JORDAN,	military inspection	**REVIEW,**
	EGYPT, LEBANON		**PARADE**
middle (law)	**MESNE**	military instrument	**BUGLE**
Midianite king	**REBA**	military offense	**DESERTION**
midshipman	**CADET**	military officer	**CAPTAIN,**
midst	**AMONG**		**COLONEL, SERGEANT,**
midway attraction	**RIDE, SHOW,**		**CORPORAL, LIEUTENANT,**
	SIDESHOW		**MAJOR, GENERAL**
midwestern college	**ANTIOCH,**	military operation	**SIEGE, RAID**
	OBERLIN, KENT, WAYNE,	military orchestra	**BAND**
	NOTRE DAME	military review	**PARADE**
mien	**BEARING**	military salute	**SALVO**
miff	**OFFEND**	military storehouse	**ETAPE**
might	**POWER, MAY**	military student	**CADET**
mighty	**POTENT, STRONG**	military supplies and	
mighty cataract	**NIAGARA**	weapons	**ORDNANCE**
mighty mite	**ATOM**	military truck	**CAMION**
mignon	**DELICATE**	military unit	**REGIMENT, TROOP**
migraine	**HEADACHE**	milk	**DRAIN**
migration	**TREK**	milk and egg dish	**CUSTARD**

milk cattle farm	**DAIRY**	Minotaur's owner	**MINOS**
milk giver	**COW**	minstrel	**BARD**
milk glass	**OPALINE**	minstrel's instrument	**LUTE**
milkman's daily course	**ROUTE**	minstrel's song	**LAY, LAMENT**
milky gem	**OPAL**	mint	**COIN, CANDY, PLANT,**
milquetoast	**SISSY, CASPER**		**HERB, GARNISH**
Milwaukee brew	**BEER**	mint camphor	**MENTHOL**
mime	**CLOWN, COPY, APE**	minuet	**DANCE**
mimeo master	**STENCIL**	minus	**LESS**
mimic	**APE, COPY, IMITATE**	minuscule	**PETTY, TINY**
minaret	**TOWER**	minute	**SMALL, TINY**
mince	**CHOP, DICE**	minute difference	**SHADE**
minced dish	**HASH**	minute groove	**STRIA**
minced oath	**EGAD**	minute insect	**GNAT**
mincing	**DAINTY**	minute opening	**PORE**
mind	**CARE, TEND, INTELLECT,**	minute particle	**ATOM, IOTA**
	OBEY, BRAIN	minutes	**RECORD, PROCEEDING**
mindful	**AWARE**	minutes of court	**REGISTER,**
mind's eye	**IMAGINATION**		**RECORD, ACTA**
mine	**PIT, DIG**	minutia	**DETAIL**
mine car	**TRAM**	minyan	**QUORUM, TEN**
mined fuel	**COKE**	miracle	**MARVEL, WONDER**
mine entrance	**ADIT**	mirage	**CHIMERA**
mine explosion hole	**CRATER**	mire	**MUD**
mine level	**STOPE**	mirror	**GLASS, REFLECT**
mine passage	**DRIFT, ADIT,**	mirth	**GAIETY, GLEE**
	SHAFT	mirthful	**MERRY**
mine product	**ORE, COAL,**	misanthrope	**CYNIC**
	STONES, MINERAL	misbehave (2 wds.)	**ACT UP,**
mineral	**ORE**		**CUT UP**
mineral deposit	**LODE**	misbehaving (3 wds.)	
mineral jelly	**PETROLATUM**		**OUT OF LINE**
mineral pitch	**ASPHALT**	miscalculate	**ERR**
mineral spring	**SPA**	miscellaneous	**VARIOUS**
mineral tar	**MALTHA**	miscellaneous items	**SUNDRIES**
mine shaft	**ADIT, INCLINE,**	miscellany	**OLLA, MIXTURE,**
	TUNNEL		**OLIO**
mingle	**MIX**		
miniature	**TINY**	mischievous	**NAUGHTY**
minim	**SMALLEST**	mischievous child	**IMP**
minimal	**LEAST**	mischievous person	**RASCAL**
minimize	**BELITTLE**	mischievous sprite	**ELF**
minimum	**LEAST**	miscreant	**VILLAIN, WRETCH**
minister	**HELP, ATTEND**	misdeed	**CRIME**
minister's assistant	**DEACON**	misdemeanor	**CRIME**
minister's home	**MANSE,**	misdo	**ERR, BLUNDER**
	RECTORY, PARSONAGE	miser	**SCROOGE**
minister's speech	**SERMON,**	miserable	**UNHAPPY**
	HOMILY	miserly	**STINGY**
ministration	**SERVICE**	misery	**SORROW**
ministry	**CLERGY**	misfortune	**ILL, EVIL, WOE**
minium	**VERMILION**	mishandle	**ABUSE**
mink	**FUR**	mishap	**ACCIDENT**
minklike animal	**WEASEL,**	misinterpret	**MISREAD**
	STOAT	mislay	**LOSE, MISPLACE**
minor	**LESSER, INFERIOR**	mislead	**DECEIVE, DELUDE**
minority	**FACTION**	misplace	**LOSE, MISLAY**
minor river	**BAYOU**	misrepresent	**DISTORT, BELIE**

miss	**GIRL, LASS, MAID, MAIDEN**	mock sun	**PARHELION**
misshapen	**DEFORMED**	mock-up	**MODEL, LAYOUT**
missile	**DART, ARROW, ICBM, NIKE**	mode	**CUSTOM, MANNER, FASHION, STYLE**
missing	**LOST**	model	**PATTERN, SAMPLE, EXAMPLE**
missing link	**APEMAN, PITHECANTHROPUS, JAVA-MAN**	model of perfection	**PARAGON**
		model of solar system	**ORRERY**
mission	**ERRAND, DELEGATION, CHURCH**	mode of speech	**PARLANCE**
		mode of standing	**POSTURE**
Mississippi resort	**BILOXI**	moderate	**LIMITED, FAIR**
Mississippi River sight	**LEVEE**	moderately cold	**COOL**
missive	**LETTER, EPISTLE**	moderation	**RESTRAINT**
Miss Kett of the comics	**ETTA**	moderator	**ARBITER**
Miss O'Hara	**SCARLETT**	modern	**NEW**
Miss Oyl	**OLIVE**	modern appliance	**WASHER, DRYER**
misstep	**ERROR, TRIP**		
mist	**FOG, HAZE**	modern epiclike narrative	**SAGA**
mistake	**ERR, ERROR, BLUNDER, BONER, GOOF**	modern fabric	**NYLON, RAYON, ARNEL, ORLON, DACRON**
mistaken	**WRONG**	modernize	**RENOVATE**
mistake in printing	**ERRATUM**	modern painter	**DALI, STELLA, WARHOL, PICASSO, MIRO**
mister (Sp.)	**SENOR**		
mistreat	**ABUSE**	modern philosophy	**EXISTENTIALISM**
mistress	**DAME**		
mistrust	**DOUBT**	modern phonograph	**STEREO**
misty	**FOGGY, DIM**	modest	**SHY**
misuse	**ABUSE**	modesty	**HUMILITY**
Mitch Miller's instrument	**OBOE**	mod fashion	**MINISKIRT, MIDISKIRT, MAXICOAT**
Mitchell novel (4 wds.)	**GONE WITH THE WIND**	modify	**AMEND, ALTER, CHANGE, DEFINE**
mite	**TICK**		
mitigate	**LESSEN**	modish	**CHIC, STYLISH**
mix	**BLEND, STIR, MINGLE**	modiste	**DRESSMAKER, COUTURIERE**
mixed breed	**MONGREL**		
mixed greens	**SALAD**	mod paintings (2 wds.)	**POP ART**
mixed type	**PI**	modulation	**TONE**
mixed with	**AMONG**	Mohammedan prince	**AMIR, EMIR, AMEER**
mix playing cards	**SHUFFLE**		
mixture	**MEDLEY, OLIO, HODGEPODGE, POTPOURRI, BLEND**	Mohammedan religion	**ISLAM**
		Mohammed's birthplace	**MECCA**
mixture of snow and rain	**SLEET**	Mohammed's daughter	**FATIMA**
mizzen	**MAST**	Mohammed's flight	**HEGIRA**
moa	**BIRD, OSTRICH**	Mohammed's son	**ALI**
moa genus	**APTERYX**	moist	**DAMP, WET**
moan	**GROAN**	molar	**TOOTH**
moat	**TRENCH, DITCH**	molasses	**SIRUP, SYRUP**
mob	**CROWD, RABBLE, HORDE, GANG**	molasses (Brit.)	**TREACLE**
		mold	**FORM, SHAPE**
mobile	**MOVABLE**	moldy	**MUSTY**
mobile home	**TRAILER, CAMPER**	moleskin color	**TAUPE**
mocassin	**PAC, SHOE**	molest	**INJURE, DISTURB**
mock	**DERIDE, RIDICULE, APE, MIMIC**	mollify	**ASSUAGE**
		mollusk	**CLAM, OYSTER**
mocker nut	**HICKORY**	molt	**SHED**
mockery	**FARCE**	molten rock	**LAVA**

moment	**IMPORT, MINUTE,**
	TRICE, SECOND
mom or dad	**PARENT**
mom's mate	**DAD**
monastery	**PRIORY, CONVENT,**
	ABBEY
monastery head	**ABBOT**
monastery occupant	**MONK,**
	FRA
monastery room	**CELL**
monastic	**ASCETIC**
monastic officer	**PRIOR, ABBOT**
monastic title	**DOM**
monetary	**FINANCIAL**
monetary penalty	**FINE**
monetary unit	**DOLLAR**
monetary unit of Japan	**YEN,**
	SEN
money	**CURRENCY**
money factory	**MINT**
money handler	**CASHIER**
money holder	**WALLET, BANK,**
	PURSE
money in India	**RUPEE**
money in Rome	**LIRA**
money on hand	**CASH**
money opening	**SLOT**
money saving campaign	
(2 wds.)	**ECONOMY DRIVE**
money (sl.)	**GREEN, MOOLAH,**
	GELT, BREAD
money vault	**SAFE**
Mongol conqueror	**TAMERLANE**
Mongolian monk	**LAMA**
mongrel dog	**CUR, MUTT**
monk	**FRIAR**
monkey	**APE**
monkey's treat	**BANANA**
monk's hood	**ATIS, COWL**
monk's title	**FRA**
monocle	**EYEGLASS, LENS**
monogram	**INITIAL, CIPHER**
monolith	**MENHIR, PILLAR**
monomania	**LUNACY, DELIRIUM**
monopoly	**GAME**
monotonous	**HUMDRUM,**
	TEDIOUS
monotonous song	**CHANT**
monotony	**TEDIUM**
monster	**GIANT, OGRE, TROLL**
monstrous	**ATROCIOUS, VAST**
Montana city	**BUTTE, MISSOULA**
Montana river	**TETON**
month	**JANUARY, FEBRUARY,**
	MARCH, APRIL, MAY, JUNE,
	JULY, AUGUST, SEPTEMBER
	OCTOBER, NOVEMBER,
	DECEMBER

month (Fr.)	**JANVIER, FEVRIER,**
	MARS, AVRIL, MAI, JUIN,
	JUILLET, AOUT, SEPTEMBRE,
	OCTOBRE, NOVEMBRE,
	DECEMBRE
month (Sp.)	**ENERO, FEBRERO,**
	MARZO, ABRIL, MAYO, JUNIO,
	JULIO, AGOSTO, SEPTIEMBRE,
	OCTUBRE, NOVIEMBRE,
	DICIEMBRE
monument	**TOMBSTONE**
moo	**LOW**
mood	**TEMPER**
moody	**CAPRICIOUS**
moody person	**MOPER**
moon goddess	**LUNA, DIANA,**
	ARTEMIS
moor	**ANCHOR, HEATH**
mooring post	**BITT**
mop	**SWAB**
mope	**SULK, BROOD**
moppet	**BABY, DOLL**
moral	**ETHICAL**
morale	**SPIRIT**
morale-raising speech	
(2 wds.)	**PEP TALK**
moralist	**PRIG**
morals	**ETHICS**
moral transgression	**SIN**
morass	**SWAMP, BOG, FEN,**
	MIRE
moray	**EEL**
morbid	**UNHEALTHY**
morbid sound	**RALE**
mordant	**CAUSTIC**
more	**ADDITIONAL, GREATER**
more agreeable	**NICER**
more ancient	**OLDER**
more arid	**DRIER**
more austere	**STERNER**
more banal	**TRITER**
more cautious	**WARIER**
more cerulean	**BLUER**
more clever	**SMARTER**
more competent	**ABLER**
more crafty	**FOXIER, SLYER**
more cunning	**SLYER**
more delicate	**FINER**
more difficult	**HARDER**
more disabled	**LAMER**
more distant	**FARTHER,**
	REMOTER
more distended	**FULLER**
more docile	**TAMER**
more domesticated	**TAMER**
more elegant	**FINER, SMARTER**
more expensive	**DEARER**
more famous	**GREATER**

more fastidious	**NEATER, TIDIER, DAINTIER, NICER,**	more up-to-date	**NEWER**
		more wary	**CAGIER**
more foxy	**SLYER, SLIER**	more willingly	**RATHER**
more frigid	**ICIER, COOLER, COLDER**	moribund	**DYING**
		morion	**HELMET**
more gentle	**TAMER**	Mormon of secret sect	**DANITE**
more inclement	**RAWER, ROUGHER**	Mormon State	**UTAH**
		morning	**DAWN**
more infrequent	**RARER**	morning (poetic)	**MORN**
more insolent	**BRASHER, SASSIER**	morning after	**HANGOVER**
		morning coat	**CUTAWAY**
more intelligent	**SMARTER, BRIGHTER**	morning glory genus	**IPOMOEA**
		morning moisture	**DEW**
more learned	**WISER**	morning performance	**MATINEE**
more likely	**APTER**	morning prayer	**MATINS**
morello	**CHERRY**	morning reception	**LEVEE**
more mature	**OLDER, RIPER**	morning's light	**DAWN**
more meager	**SCANTIER**	morning song	**ALBA**
more mellow	**RIPER**	morning star	**MARS, VENUS**
more miserly	**MEANER**	Moroccan capital	**RABAT**
more modern	**NEWER**	Moroccan native	**BERBER**
more optimistic	**ROSIER, BRIGHTER**	Moroccan ruler	**SULTAN**
		Moroccan soldier	**ASKAR**
more or less	**SOME**	moro chief	**DATO**
more orderly	**NEATER, TIDIER**	moron	**IMBECILE**
moreover	**AND, BESIDES**	morose	**GLUM**
more painful	**SORER**	morphine derivative	**HEROIN**
more pallid	**PALER**	morro	**HILL**
more precious	**DEARER**	morsel	**BIT, BITE, ORT**
more precipitous	**STEEPER**	morsel left at meal	**ORT**
more profound	**DEEPER**	mortal	**HUMAN, PERSON, FATAL**
more rapid	**FASTER**		
more rational	**SANER**	mortar	**BOWL, PUTTY**
more recent	**LATTER**	mortar mixer	**RAB**
more refined	**NICER**	mortar tray	**HOD**
mores	**CUSTOMS**	mortgage	**LIEN, LOAN**
more sagacious	**WISER**	mortification	**CHAGRIN**
more scarce	**RARER**	mosaic piece	**INSET, TILE**
more secure	**SAFER**	moselle (2 wds.)	**WHITE WINE**
more seedy	**SHABBIER**	Moses' brother	**AARON**
more severe	**STERNER**	Moslem bible	**KORAN**
more slippery	**ICIER, SLICKER**	Moslem commander	**AGA**
more so	**YEA**	Moslem countries	**ISLAM**
more sour	**TARTER**	Moslem deity	**ALLAH**
more spacious	**ROOMIER, LARGER**	Moslem headgear	**FEZ, TURBAN**
		Moslem judge	**CADI**
more strange	**ODDER**	Moslem lawyer	**MUFTI**
more suitable	**BETTER**	Moslem nymph	**HOURI**
more tardy	**LATER**	Moslem officer	**AGA**
more tender	**SORER**	Moslem priest	**IMAM**
more than	**ABOVE, OVER**	Moslem prince	**AMIR, EMIR, AMEER**
more than enough	**AMPLE**	Moslem title	**AGA**
more than one	**MANY, PLURAL**	mosquito-eating bird	**MARTIN**
more tidy	**NEATER**	mosquito genus	**AEDES**
more uncanny	**EERIER**	mosquito larva	**WIGGLER**
more uncivil	**RUDER**	most attractive	**PRETTIEST, CUTEST**
more uncommon	**RARER**		

most beloved	**DEAREST**	mother of Romulus	
most brazen (sl.)	**NERVIEST**	and Remus	**ILIA**
most courageous	**GAMEST,**	mother or father	**PARENT**
	BRAVEST	mother sheep	**EWE**
most desirable	**BEST**	mother's sister	**AUNT**
most difficult	**HARDEST**	mother turned to stone	**NIOBE**
most distant planet	**PLUTO**	motherly	**MATERNAL**
most distant point in		moth larva	**CATERPILLAR**
an orbit.	**APOGEE**	motif	**THEME**
most excellent	**BEST**	motion	**GESTURE**
most ill-boding	**DIREST**	motionless	**INERT, STILL**
most independent	**FREEST**	motion picture	**FILM**
most intelligent	**SMARTEST**	motion picture light	**KLIEG**
mostly	**CHIEFLY, USUALLY**	motion picture machine	
most modern	**NEWEST**		**PROJECTOR**
most outstanding	**BEST**	motivate	**INSPIRE**
most pallid	**PALEST**	motive	**REASON**
most peculiar	**ODDEST**	motive force	**POWER**
most pleasant	**NICEST**	motley	**DIVERSE, MIXED**
most precious	**DEAREST**	motor	**ENGINE, TURBINE**
most precipitous	**STEEPEST**	motorcar	**AUTOMOBILE**
most profound	**DEEPEST**	motor coach	**BUS**
most rapid	**FASTEST**	motor control	**STARTER**
most recent	**LATEST**	motor court	**MOTEL**
most ridiculous	**SILLIEST**	motorist	**DRIVER**
most sagacious	**WISEST**	motorist's nightmare (2 wds.)	
most savory	**TASTIEST**		**TRAFFIC JAM**
most sensible	**SANEST**	motorist's problem (2 wds.)	
most sensitive	**SOREST**		**PARKING SPACE**
most spirited	**LIVELIEST**	motorist's tool	**JACK, WRENCH**
most tardy	**LATEST**	motorless airplane	**GLIDER**
most terrible	**DIREST**	motorman	**CONDUCTOR**
most unique	**ODDEST**	mottled horse	**PINTO**
most untouched	**PUREST**	mottled marking	**DAPPLE**
most unusual	**ODDEST, RAREST**	mottled soap	**CASTILE**
most wonderful	**BEST**	motto	**ADAGE, MAXIM, SAW**
mot	**RETORT, SAYING**	mould	**MATRIX**
mote	**PARTICLE**	mound	**HEAP, TEE**
motel feature	**POOL**	mount	**ASCEND, CLIMB**
motet	**ANTHEM**	mountain at earth's center	
moth-eaten	**OLD, WORN**		**MERU**
mother **MA, MOM, MAW, MAMA,**		mountain cat	**BOBCAT,**
MOMMY, MOMMA, DAM,			**COUGAR, PUMA**
MADONNA		mountain crest	**ARETE, RIDGE**
mother (Lat.)	**MATER**	mountain home	**CHALET**
mother (Sp.)	**MADRE**	mountain in Thessaly	**OSSA**
mother and father	**PARENTS**	mountain lake	**TARN**
Mother Carey's chicken	**PETREL**	mountain lion	**PUMA**
Mother Carey's goose	**FULMAR**	mountain near ancient	
Mother Goose author	**PERRAULT**	Troy	**IDA**
Mother Hubbard	**GOWN**	mountain nymph	**OREAD**
mother of Castor and Pollux		mountain pass	**COL, GAP**
	LEDA	mountain pass in India	**GHAT,**
mother of Hiawatha	**NOKOMIS**		**GHAUT**
mother of mankind	**EVE**	mountain peak	**TOR**
mother-of-pearl	**NACRE**	mountain pheasant	**GROUSE**
mother of Peer Gynt	**ASE**	mountain pool	**TARN**
mother of Perseus	**DANAE**	mountain ridge	**ARETE, CREST**

Mountain State **WEST VIRGINIA**
mountain system in Europe **ALPS**
mountain system in South America **ANDES**
mountaintop **PEAK**
mourn **LAMENT, GRIEVE**
mournful **DOLEFUL**
mournful cry **ALAS, ALACK, WOE IS ME**
mournful poem **ELEGY, LAMENT**
mournful song **DIRGE**
mournful sound **KNELL, MOAN, KEEN**
mourning **SORROW, GRIEF**
mouse family **RODENT**
mouser **CAT**
mouth **SPEAK, SAY**
mouthful **BITE, MORSEL, SIP**
mouth organ **HARMONICA**
mouth part **LIP, PALATE, TONGUE, GUM, TOOTH**
movable **MOBILE**
movable cover **LID, AWNING**
movable door part **HINGE**
move **STIR, BUDGE**
move along **MOSEY**
move apart **SEPARATE**
move, as Fido's tail **WAG**
move aside (2 wds.) **MAKE WAY**
move aside suddenly **DODGE**
move, as the wind **BLOW**
move back **RECEDE, RETREAT**
move back and forth **SHUTTLE**
move before the wind **SCUD, SAIL**
move forward **ADVANCE**
move furtively **LURK, SLINK, SNEAK, TIPTOE, CREEP, STEAL, SIDLE**
move in water **SWIM, FLOAT**
move like a crab **SIDLE**
move lazily **LOLL**
movement **MOTION**
movement of the hands **GESTURE**
move out **VACATE**
move over water **SAIL, FLOAT**
move quickly **RUN, SCUD, HIE, SPEED, HASTEN, BUSTLE, HUSTLE, RACE**
mover's truck **VAN**
move rhythmically **DANCE**
move sideways **SIDLE**
move slightly **BUDGE, STIR**
move slowly **EDGE, INCH**
move smoothly **SLIDE, GLIDE**
move spasmodically **TWITCH**

move stealthily **SLINK**
move suddenly **DART**
move swiftly **SCUD, DART**
move with an easy gait **LOPE, AMBLE, STROLL**
move with difficulty **WADE**
movie house **THEATRE, CINEMA**
movie queen **STAR**
movie version of a novel **ADAPTATION**
movie V.I.P. **DIRECTOR, STAR, ACTOR, PRODUCER, WRITER**
moving **ASTIR, ACTIVE**
moving air **WIND**
moving force **AGENT**
moving mechanical part **ROTOR**
moving stairway **ESCALATOR**
Mr. Bumpstead **DAGWOOD**
Mr. Claus **SANTA**
Mr. Heep **URIAH**
Mr. Kettle **PA**
Mr. Spade **SAM**
Mr. Van Winkle **RIP**
Mrs. Charles Chaplin **OONA**
Mrs. Dick Tracy **TESS**
Mrs. Eddie Cantor **IDA**
Mrs. Eisenhower **MAMIE**
mrs. in Madrid **SRA.**
Mrs. Kettle **MA**
Mrs. Nixon **PAT**
Mrs. Roosevelt **ELEANOR**
Mrs. Roy Rogers (2 wds.) **DALE EVANS**
Mrs. Truman **BESS**
Mrs. Washington **MARTHA**
much **LOTS**
much larger **HUGER**
much loved **DEAR**
much the same **ALIKE**
mucilage **GLUE, ADHESIVE**
muck **MIRE, MUD**
mud **MIRE**
muddle **MESS**
muddy **MURKY, OBSCURE**
mudguard **FENDER**
mud pie **PATTY**
mud puppy **SALAMANDER**
mud volcano **SALSE**
muffin **CRUMPET, POPOVER, SCONE**
muffle **DAMPEN, MUTE, DEADEN**
muffler **SCARF**
mug **CUP**
mugger **HAM**
muggy **HUMID, DAMP**
muir **MOOR**

mukluk	**BOOT**
mulberry cloth	**TAPA**
mulch	**SAWDUST**
mulct	**FINE, AMERCE**
mule	**SLIPPER**
muley	**COW, HORNLESS**
mulish	**STUBBORN**
mull	**PONDER**
muller	**PESTLE**
mullet hawk	**OSPREY**
mulligan	**STEW**
mulligatawny	**SOUP**
multicolored	**ROAN, PIED**
multifold	**MANY**
multiform	**DIVERSE**
multiplication word	**TIMES**
multitude	**HORDE, HOST, MOB**
munch, comic strip style	**CHOMP**
mundane	**WORLDLY**
municipal corporation	**CITY, BOROUGH**
municipality	**CITY**
municipal official	**MAYOR**
munificent	**GENEROUS**
mural painting	**FRESCO**
murder	**KILL, SLAY**
murder mystery character	**SUSPECT**
murky	**OBSCURE, DARK**
murmur	**WHISPER**
murmuring, as a brook	**BABBLING**
murmuring sound	**HUM**
muscle	**TENDON**
muscle cramp	**CRICK**
muscular	**HUSKY**
muscular tone	**TONUS**
muse	**MEDITATE, PONDER**
muse	**CALLIOPE, CLIO, ERATO, EUTERPE, MELPOMENE, POLYHYMNIA, TERPSICHORE, THALIA, URANIA**
musette	**BAGPIPE**
museum keeper	**CURATOR**
museum pieces	**ART, COLLECTION**
mush	**ATOLE**
music	**HARMONY, TUNE**
musical	**TUNEFUL, MELODIC, SHOW**
musical adaptation	**ARRANGEMENT**
musical author	**COMPOSER**
musical bells	**CHIME**
musical character	**CLEF, NOTE**
musical chord	**TRIAD**
musical composition	**ETUDE, CONCERTO, SONATA, SYMPHONY, RONDO**
musical direction	**PIANO, LARGO**
musical disk	**RECORD**
musical drama	**OPERA**
musical ending	**CODA**
musical exercise	**ETUDE, SCALE**
musical feature	**MOTIF**
musical group	**OCTET, TRIO, QUARTET, QUINTET, BAND, ORCHESTRA, COMBO**
musical group of nine	**NONET**
musical half-tone	**MINIM**
musical instrument	**FLUTE, PIPE ORGAN, BASS DRUM, FIFE, TUBA, PIANO, ORGAN, DRUM, KETTLE DRUM, TRIANGLE, LUTE, OBOE, VIOLA, VIOLIN, WOODWIND, CORNET, TRUMPET, HORN, TROMBONE, HARP, LYRE, PICCOLO, BASSOON, CELLO, GUITAR, BANJO, CLARINET, SAXOPHONE, TIMPANI, BASS**
musical interval	**SEMITONE, REST**
musical measured beat	**PULSE**
musical medley	**OLIO**
musical movement	**RONDO**
musical nocturne	**SERENADE**
musical note	**BREVE**
musical organization	**BAND, ORCHESTRA**
musical pair	**DUO, DUET**
musical pause	**REST**
musical performance	**CONCERT**
musical phrase	**LEITMOTIF**
musical pipe	**REED**
musical pitch	**TONE**
musical play	**OPERA**
musical show	**OPERETTA, REVUE**
musical sign	**REST, CLEF, NOTE, STAFF, SHARP, FLAT**
musical sound	**NOTE, TONE**
musical staff	**BAR**
musical study	**ETUDE**
musical syllable	**DO, RE, MI, FA, SO, SOL, LA, TI, TRA**
musical term	**TACET**
musical time marker	**METRONOME**

musical tone	CHORD
musical work	OPUS, OPERA, OPERETTA, SYMPHONY, CONCERTO, SONG
music buff's purchase	STEREO, ALBUM, LP, HIFI, RECORD, SPEAKER
music by two	DUET
music hall	ODEUM
musician	PLAYER
music played under lady's window	SERENADE
music syllable	DO, RE, MI, FA, SO, LA, TI
musk cat	CIVET
musket	GUN
muskmelon	CASABA
Muslim judge	CADI
Muslim mendicant	FAKIR
musty	MOLDY, FUSTY
mute	SILENT, SPEECHLESS, MUFFLE, SILENCE, QUIET
mutilate	MAIM, CRIPPLE, DISABLE
mutineer	REBEL
mutinous	RESTIVE, REBELLIOUS
mutiny	REVOLT
mutter	MUMBLE, GRUMBLE
muttonchop	SIDEBURN, WHISKERS
muzzle	GAG, RESTRAIN
my (Lat.)	MEA
myopic	NEARSIGHTED
myself	ME
mysterious	EERY, SECRET, STRANGE, WEIRD, PUZZLING
mystery	SECRET, ENIGMA
mystery tale	STORY
mystery writers' award	EDGAR
mystic	OBSCURE, OCCULT
mystic art	CABALA, CABBALA, CABBALAH
mystify	BAFFLE
myth	FABLE, LEGEND, TALE, BELIEF
mythical	FABULOUS, LEGENDARY
mythical aviator	ICARUS
mythical bird	ROC
mythical Greek bowman	EROS
mythical hunter	ORION
mythical king of Pylos	NESTOR
mythical one-horned animal	UNICORN

N

nab	GRAB, SEIZE, SNATCH
nabob	VIP, CELEBRITY, BIG WHEEL, BIG SHOT
nag	HORSE, SCOLD, FIND FAULT, CAVIL, CARP, WHINE
nagging pain	ACHE
nail container	KEG
naive	UNSOPHISTICATED, ARTLESS
naked	BARE, NUDE
name	TITLE
name for a cat	TABBY, PUSS, PUFF, KITTY
name for a dog	SPOT, FIDO, ROVER, LASSIE, REX, LADY, KING
nameless	INDEFINABLE, ANONYMOUS, OBSCURE
namely (2 wds.)	TO WIT
name of a thing	NOUN
name the letters of a word	SPELL
name to office	APPOINT
nanny	NURSE
nap	DOZE, SLEEP, SNOOZE, FORTY WINKS
nape	SCRUFF
napery	LINEN
Naples island	CAPRI
nappy leather	SUEDE
narcotic	OPIATE, DRUG
narrate	RELATE, TELL
narration	ACCOUNT
narrative	TALE, YARN, STORY
narrative poem	BALLAD, EPIC
narrator	RACONTEUR
narrow	SLENDER, THIN
narrow aperture	SLOT, SLIT
narrow band	STRIPE, TAPE, RIBBON
narrow board	SLAT, LATH
narrow boat	CANOE
narrow channel	STRAIT
narrow country road	LANE
narrow gauge	RAILROAD
narrow inlet	RIA
narrow-minded	BIGOTED, PREJUDICED
narrow opening	SLIT, SLOT
narrow path	LANE
narrow ravine	GORGE
narrow shelf	LEDGE
narrow squeak (2 wds.)	CLOSE SHAVE

narrow strip of cloth	**TAPE, RIBBON**	nature spirit	**GENIE**
narrow strip of leather	**THONG**	naught	**ZERO, NOTHING**
narrow strip of wood	**SLAT**	naughty	**BAD**
narrow thoroughfare	**ALLEY, LANE**	naughty look	**LEER**
		nausea	**QUALM**
narrow valley (Brit.)	**COMBE**	nauseate	**SICKEN**
narrow waterway	**STRAIT**	nauseous	**DISGUSTING**
narthex	**VESTIBULE**	nautical	**MARITIME**
nary	**NO, NOT ANY**	nautical assent	**AYE**
nary a soul (2 wds.)	**NO ONE**	nautical command	**AVAST, BELAY**
nasal intonation	**TWANG**	nautical cry	**AHOY, AVAST**
NASA's capsule booster	**ROCKET**	nautical line	**MARLINE, RATLINE**
NASA's realm	**SPACE**	nautical measure	**KNOT, FATHOM**
nascent	**BEGINNING**		
nasty	**DIRTY, SOILED, UNPLEASANT**	nautical mop	**SWAB**
		nautical pole	**SPAR, MAST**
natal	**NATIVE**	nautical rope	**TYE, LINE, SHEET**
natator	**SWIMMER**	nautical speed unit	**KNOT**
nation	**COUNTRY, LAND**	nautical term	**ALEE**
national	**COUNTRYWIDE**	Nautilus	**SUBMARINE**
national bird	**EAGLE**	Navaho hut	**HOGAN**
national monogram	**USA**	naval	**MARINE, NAUTICAL**
native	**SON**	naval commander in	
native-born	**INDIGENOUS**	ancient Sparta	**LYSANDER**
Native Dancer	**HORSE**	naval force	**FLEET**
native lump of gold	**NUGGET**	naval meal	**MESS**
native metal	**ORE**	naval officer	**REAR ADMIRAL,**
native name for Norway	**NORGE**		**ENSIGN, CAPTAIN**
native of (suffix)	**ITE**	naval strength (2 wds.)	
native of Attu	**ALEUT**		**SEA POWER**
native of Copenhagen	**DANE**	nave	**HUB**
native of Dundee	**SCOT**	navel	**ORANGE**
native of Edinburgh	**SCOT**	navigate	**GUIDE, SAIL**
native of Glasgow	**SCOT**	navigate in air	**AVIATE**
native of Istanbul	**TURK**	navigating instrument	
native of Madagascar	**HOVA**		**COMPASS**
native of Muscat	**OMANI**	navigation device	**LORAN,**
native of Ontario	**CANADIAN**		**SONAR**
native of Stockholm	**SWEDE**	navy	**BLUE**
native of Tel Aviv	**ISRAELI**	navy force	**FLEET**
native of the United States		navy line officer	**MUSTANG**
	AMERICAN	navy recruit (sl.)	**BOOT**
native South African village		naysay	**DENIAL**
	STAD	near	**APPROACH, AT, CLOSE**
nativity	**CHRISTMAS, CRECHE**	nearest	**NEXT**
natty	**NEAT, SPRUCE**	nearly	**ALMOST**
natural	**INNATE, INBORN, NATIVE**	nearly all	**MOST**
		nearly corresponding	**SIMILAR**
natural ability	**TALENT, GIFT**	near-sighted	**MYOPIC**
natural color	**ECRU, FLESH**	near-sighted cartoon	
natural condition	**NORM**	character	**MAGOO**
natural incline	**SLOPE**	near the beginning	**EARLY**
naturalism	**REALISM**	near the horizon	**LOW**
naturalize	**ACCUSTOM**	neat	**TIDY, TRIM**
nature	**DISPOSITION, ESSENCE**	neatly smart in dress	**NATTY**
nature's mythical maiden		neb	**BILL, BEAK**
	NYMPH	Nebraska city	**OMAHA**

Nebraska county **OTOE**
Nebraska Indian **PAWNEE**
necessary **ESSENTIAL**
necessitate **COMPEL, OBLIGE**
necessity **MUST**
neck and neck **EVEN, CLOSE**
neck artery **CAROTID**
neckerchief **SCARF**
neck frill **RUFF**
neck hair **MANE**
necklace bauble **BEAD**
neck of water **STRAIT**
neckpiece **SCARF, TIE, CRAVAT, ASCOT, COLLAR**
necktie **CRAVAT, ASCOT**
nectar of the gods **AMBROSIA**
nee **BORN**
need **LACK, REQUIRE, WANT**
neediness **POVERTY**
needing support **DEPENDENT**
needle case **ETUI**
needle (comb. form) **ACU**
needlefish **GAR**
needle hole **EYE**
needle-like body **SPICULE**
needle puncture **PRICK**
needlework **SEWING, DARNING, CREWEL, EMBROIDERY**
needy **IMPOVERISHED, POOR**
nefarious **EVIL, BAD**
negate **DENY**
negation **NOT**
negative **MINUS, NO**
negative answer **NAY, NO**
negative conjunction **NOR**
negative electrode **CATHODE**
negative ion **ANION**
negative particle **NOT**
negative prefix **NON, UN**
negative sign **MINUS**
neglect **OMIT, OVERLOOK, FORGET, SLIGHT, SHIRK**
negligence **CARELESSNESS**
negligent **LAX, REMISS, CARELESS**
negligible **NOMINAL**
negotiate **TREAT**
Negrito of Philippines **ATA, ITA**
neigh **WHINNY**
neighborhood **VICINITY**
neighborhood playing area **SANDLOT, PLAYGROUND**
neighboring **ADJACENT**
neighborly **FRIENDLY, SOCIABLE**
neither masculine nor feminine **NEUTER**
nemesis **FATE**

neophyte **NOVICE, TYRO**
Nepal capital **KATMANDU**
nephew of Daedalus **TALUS**
nepotism **PATRONAGE**
Neptune's scepter **TRIDENT**
Nero's successor **GALBA**
nerve **DARING, CHEEK, COURAGE**
nerve part **AXON**
nervous **EDGY, JITTERY, TENSE**
nervous twitch **TIC**
ness **HEADLAND**
nest **AERIE, EYRIE**
nestle **CUDDLE**
nestling pigeon **SQUAB**
nest of pheasants **NIDE**
net **MESH, SEINE, SNARE, PROFIT**
nether **LOWER, UNDER**
Netherlander **DUTCH**
Netherlands city **HAGUE, UTRECHT**
Netherlands commune **EDE, TIEL**
nethermost **LOWEST**
nether world **HELL**
netlike fabric **LACE**
netlike hat **SNOOD**
nettle **IRK, IRRITATE**
network **MESH, RETE, RESEAU, WEB**
neuter pronoun **IT**
neutral **IMPARTIAL**
Nevada city **RENO, CARSON**
Nevada lake **TAHOE**
neve **FIRN, GLACIER**
never (contr.) **NE'ER**
nevertheless **ALL THE SAME, JUST THE SAME, YET, STILL**
new **MODERN, RECENT, UNUSED**
new (prefix) **NEO**
newborn infant **BABE, BABY**
newborn threesome **TRIPLETS**
newcomer **STRANGER**
New England cape **COD, ANN**
New England native **YANKEE**
New England university **YALE, DARTMOUTH, HARVARD, BOSTON**
newel **STAIRPOST**
New Guinea export **COPRA**
New Hampshire city **DOVER, KEENE**
New Hampshire resort **SUNAPEE**
New Haven tree **ELM**
New Jersey city **NEWARK, TRENTON, ORANGE**

New Jersey river **RARITAN**
New Mexico art colony **TAOS**
New Mexico river **GILA, PECOS**
newly married woman **BRIDE**
news **TIDINGS**
news article **ITEM**
news gatherer **REPORTER**
newspaper **GAZETTE, JOURNAL**
newspaper article **ITEM**
newspaper columnist (2 wds.)
ROVING REPORTER
newspaper edition **DAILY,
WEEKLY, ISSUE, MORNING,
FIRST, LATE**
newspaper executive (abbr.) **ED.**
newspaper files **MORGUE**
newspaper notice (abbr.) **OBIT,
AD**
newspaperman **REPORTER,
EDITOR, COLUMNIST,
JOURNALIST**
news sheet **PAPER, JOURNAL**
newsstand fiction of 1930's
(2 wds.) **DIME NOVEL**
news story beginning **DATELINE**
news story title **HEADLINE**
new star **NOVA**
new suit (2 wds.) **SUNDAY BEST**
newt **EFT**
New Testament book **ACTS,
COLOSSIANS, CORINTHIANS,
EPHESIANS, GALATIANS,
HEBREWS, JAMES, JOHN,
JUDE, LUKE, MARK,
MATTHEW, PETER, PHILEMON,
PHILIPPIANS, REVELATION,
ROMANS, THESSALONIANS,
TIMOTHY, TITUS**
newton ingredient **FIG**
New Year's, Christmas, etc.
HOLIDAYS
New York ball club **METS, JETS,
YANKEES, GIANTS, KNICKS**
New York City stadium **SHEA,
YANKEE**
New York ghetto **HARLEM**
New York Indian **ONEIDA,
MOHAWK**
New York lake **SARANAC**
New York newspaper **TIMES,
NEWS, POST**
New York river **HUDSON, EAST,
HARLEM**
New York State city **ELMIRA,
OLEAN, UTICA, ALBANY,
BUFFALO, ITHACA**
New Zealand aborigine **MAORI**
New Zealand bird **MOA**

New Zealand clan **ATI**
New Zealand parrot **KEA**
New Zealand tree **AKE,
MAKOMAKO**
next **NEAREST, AFTER**
nice **PLEASANT, FINE**
niche **ALCOVE, NOOK**
nick **DENT**
nickel **COIN**
nickname for a
good dancer **TWINKLETOES**
nickname for a Scot **MAC**
nicotinic acid **NIACIN**
Nigerian city **EDE, LAGOS**
Nigerian tribesman **EBOE, IBO**
niggardly **STINGY**
nigh **NEAR, CLOSE**
night before a holiday **EVE**
night bird **OWL**
night clothes **PAJAMAS**
nightclub **CAFE**
nightclub solo (2 wds.)
TORCH SONG
nightcrawler **WORM, BAIT**
nightfall **DARK, TWILIGHT, DUSK**
night letter **TELEGRAM**
nightmare **INCUBUS**
nightshade **MOREL**
night twinkler **STAR**
nihil **NOTHING**
nil **NOTHING**
Nile bird **IBIS**
Nile queen, for short **CLEO**
Nile River dam **ASWAN**
Nile River falls **RIPON**
nilgai **ANTELOPE**
nimble **AGILE, SPRY**
nimbus **AURA, HALO**
nine days' devotion **NOVENA**
nine-headed monster **HYDRA**
ninny **FOOL, GOOSE**
nip **BITE, PINCH**
nippy **BITING, BRISK**
niter **SALTPETER**
nitrate **ESTER, SALT**
nitric acid **AQUAFORTIS**
Nixon **REPUBLICAN,
PRESIDENT, DICK**
Nixon's V.P. **AGNEW**
no (colloq.) **NIX**
Noah's boat **ARK**
Noah's son **SHEM, HAM**
nob **HEAD**
nobility **RANK, PEERAGE**
noble **GRAND, HIGH**
nobleman **BARON, EARL, LORD,
PEER, THANE, COUNT, DUKE**

noblewoman **DAME, LADY, DUCHESS, COUNTESS**
nobody **NONE, NONENTITY**
no charge **GRATIS, FREE**
nocturnal bird **OWL, BULLBAT, NIGHTINGALE**
nocturnal mammal **LEMUR**
nocturne **LULLABY, SERENADE**
Noel **CHRISTMAS, YULE**
noise **DIN, CLATTER, RACKET, SOUND**
noiseless **SILENT, STILL**
noisome **NOXIOUS, ROTTEN**
noisy dispute **FRACAS, ROW, BRAWL**
noisy impact **SLAM**
noisy swallow **SLURP**
no kidding **REALLY**
no longer active **RETIRED**
no longer are **WERE**
no longer chic **PASSE**
nomad **MIGRANT, VAGRANT**
no matter which **ANY**
nom de plume (2 wds.) **PEN NAME**
nominal **FORMAL, MERE**
nominate **NAME**
no more than **MERE, ONLY**
no one **NONE**
nonchalant **INDIFFERENT, CASUAL**
non-citizen **ALIEN**
nonconforming belief **HERESY**
none (Scot.) **NANE**
non-iron fabric (2 wds.) **DRIP DRY, PERMANENT PRESS**
nonmetallic element **BORON, IODINE**
nonpareil **PEERLESS**
nonplus **PERPLEX, STUMP**
non-productive **STERILE**
non-professional **AMATEUR, LAYMAN**
nonsense **INANITY, ROT**
nonsense poem **LIMERICK**
non-union laborer **SCAB**
nonworker **DRONE**
nook **ALCOVE**
noon **MIDDAY, TWELVE**
noonday rest **SIESTA**
noon meal **LUNCH**
noose **LOOP**
norm **STANDARD, PAR**
normal **PAR**
Norse **SCANDINAVIAN**

Norse deity **BALDUR, ODIN, FRIGGA, LOKI, HELA, BRAGI, THOR, FREY, FREYA, FRIGG, TYR, URDUR, VERDANDI, SKULD, IDUNA, HEIMDALL, FENRIS, HERMOD**
Norse god **(see Norse deity)**
Norse legend **SAGA, EDDA**
Norse letter **RUNE**
Norseman **VIKING**
Norse navigator **ERIC**
Norse night **NATT, NOTT**
Norse patron saint **OLAF**
Norse poets **SKALDS**
Norse tale **SAGA, EDDA**
Norse toast **SKOAL**
North African capital **TUNIS**
North African colony **IFNI**
North African fruit **DATE**
northeaster **STORM, GALE**
northern Britisher **SCOT**
northern constellation **LYRA**
northern European **FINN, DANE, SWEDE, LAPP**
northern horned mammal **REINDEER**
North Pole discoverer **PEARY**
North Star State **MINNESOTA**
North Vietnamese capital **HANOI**
Norwegian **NORSE**
Norwegian dramatist **IBSEN**
Norwegian sea inlet **FJORD, FIORD**
nose **PROBOSCIS, SNOUT, SNOOT**
nosegay **POSY**
nostalgic **WISTFUL, HOMESICK**
nostrils **NARES**
nosy **SNOOPY, PRYING**
notable **KNOWN, FAMOUS**
not aboveboard **EVASIVE**
not alike **UNEQUAL, DIFFERENT**
not alive **DEAD**
not all **SOME**
notandum **ENTRY, MEMO**
not any **NO, NONE**
not appropriate **INAPT**
notarize **SEAL**
not artificial **NATURAL**
not as advanced **SLOWER**
not as common **RARER**
not as early **LATER**
not as high **LOWER**
not as large **SMALLER**
not asleep **AWAKE**
not as much **LESS**
not a soul (2 wds.) **NO ONE**

not as strong	**WEAKER**
not as taut	**LOOSER**
not at all	**NEVER, NOHOW, NOWISE**
not at home	**AWAY, OUT**
notation	**MEMO, ENTRY, RECORD**
not at leisure	**BUSY, WORKING**
not a winner	**LOSER**
not bad	**GOOD**
not better	**WORSE**
not boastful	**MODEST, SHY**
not brave	**TIMID**
not brief	**LONG**
not bright	**PALE, STUPID, DUMB**
not busy	**IDLE**
notch	**NICK**
notched bar	**RATCH**
not clearly defined	**INDISTINCT**
not closed	**OPEN**
not C.O.D.	**POSTPAID, CHARGED**
not cold	**HOT, WARM**
not cooked	**RAW**
not covered	**BARE**
not dead	**ALIVE**
not definite	**TENTATIVE**
not difficult	**EASY**
not docile	**WILD**
not down	**UP**
not dry	**WET**
note	**MESSAGE, MEMO**
note contents of	**LABEL**
noted	**FAMOUS, FAMED, RENOWNED, SEEN**
note duration of	**CLOCK, TIME**
not efficient	**LAME**
not either	**NEITHER**
note (Lat.)	**NOTA**
not employed	**IDLE**
note of Guido's scale	**UT, DO, RE, MI, FA, SOL, LA**
note of the scale	**DO, RE, MI, FA, SO, LA, TI**
noteworthy	**SPECIAL**
noteworthy act	**FEAT**
not even a soul (2 wds.)	**NO ONE**
not false	**TRUE**
not fast	**SLOW**
not fastened	**LOOSE**
not fat	**LEAN, SLIM, THIN**
not feral	**TAME**
not figurative	**LITERAL**
not firm	**LOOSE**
not flexible	**RIGID**
not for publication (3 wds.)	**OFF THE RECORD**
not forward	**MODEST, SHY**
not fresh	**STALE**
not general	**LOCAL**
not genuine	**ERSATZ, FAKE, COUNTERFEIT**
not good	**BAD**
not hard	**EASY, SOFT**
not having made a will	**INTESTATE**
not heavy	**LIGHT**
not high	**LOW**
nothing	**NIL, ZERO, NAUGHT**
nothing but	**ONLY, MERE**
nothing doing	**NIX**
nothing (Fr.)	**RIEN**
nothing less than	**SAME**
nothing more than	**MERE**
not hollow	**SOLID, FILLED**
notice	**SEE, ESPY, OBSERVE**
noticeable	**SIGNIFICANT**
notify	**ANNOUNCE, INFORM**
not illuminated	**DARK**
not imaginary	**REAL**
not in	**OUT**
not in motion	**STABLE, FIXED**
not interested	**BORED**
notion	**IDEA, THOUGHT, OPINION**
not joking	**EARNEST, SERIOUS**
not living	**DEAD**
not long	**SHORT**
not long ago	**RECENTLY**
not many	**FEW**
not minor	**MAJOR**
not moist	**DRY**
not new	**OLD, USED**
not now	**LATER**
not odd	**EVEN**
not of the clergy	**LAIC, LAY**
not one	**NONE**
not open	**CLOSED, SHUT**
notoriety	**ECLAT, PUBLICITY**
notorious	**INFAMOUS**
not out	**IN, HOME, AVAILABLE**
not plump	**LEAN, SLIM, THIN**
not pretty	**UGLY, PLAIN**
not professional	**AMATEUR, LAIC**
not qualified	**UNFIT, INEXPERIENCED**
not quite	**NEARLY**
not ready	**UNPREPARED**
not regular	**UNSTEADY, SPORADIC**
not rich	**POOR**
not rigid	**LIMP, SOFT**
not ripe	**GREEN**
not separable	**INDIVISIBLE**
not shaky	**STEADY, SOLID**
not sharp	**DULL**
not short	**LONG**

not shortened, as a book	**UNABRIDGED**	novelist Glasgow	**ELLEN**
not shut	**OPEN**	novelist Hunter	**EVAN**
not skinny **FAT, PLUMP, STOUT**		novelist Jackson	**SHIRLEY**
not slow	**FAST**	novelist Kazan	**ELIA**
not smooth	**ROUGH**	novelist on the Orient (2 wds.)	
not so, in law	**SECUS**		**PEARL BUCK**
not soft	**HARD**	novelist Uris	**LEON**
not so much	**LESS**	novelist Zola	**EMILE**
not sound	**LAME**	novelty	**NEWNESS**
not speaking **MUTE, SILENT**		November event	**ELECTION**
not straight	**CROOKED**	novice	**TYRO, TIRO**
not straightforward	**EVASIVE**	novice athlete	**ROOKIE**
not suitable **INAPT, UNFIT**		novocain	**PROCAINE**
not sweet	**SOUR**	now	**PRESENT**
not talking	**SILENT**	now and then	**SOMETIMES**
not tame	**WILD**	noxious **HARMFUL, POISONOUS**	
not taut	**SLACK**	nozzle	**SPOUT, NOSE**
not these	**THOSE**	nuance	**SHADE**
not thick	**THIN**	nub	**POINT**
not those	**THESE**	nubble	**LUMP, KNOB**
not tight	**LOOSE**	nubby fabric	**TWEED**
not to be considered (4 wds.)		nucleus	**CORE, HEART**
	OUT OF THE QUESTION	nude	**BARE, NAKED**
not to be pacified **IMPLACABLE**		nudge	**POKE, PROD, JAB**
not together **APART, SPLIT**		nugget	**LUMP**
not tough	**TENDER**	nuisance **PEST, ANNOYANCE**	
not true	**FALSE**	null	**INVALID**
not up **ABED, DOWN, SLEEPING**		nullah	**GULLY, RAVINE**
not warm	**COOL, COLD**	nullify	**CANCEL, ANNUL**
not waterproof	**POROUS,**	numb	**TORPID, FROZEN**
	LEAKY	number	**DIGIT, NUMERAL**
not well	**BADLY, ILL**	number again	**RENUMERATE**
not well planned (comp. wd.)		numbered chart	**TABLE**
	HALF-BAKED	number one	**FIRST, BEST**
not wide	**NARROW**	number's third power	**CUBE**
not wild	**TAME**	numeral style **ARABIC, ROMAN**	
notwithstanding **DESPITE, YET,**		numerous	**MANY**
	HOWEVER	nun	**SISTER**
not working	**IDLE**	nuncio	**DELEGATE**
not yet settled	**MOOT**	nunnery **CLOISTER, CONVENT**	
not young	**OLD**	nun's dress	**HABIT**
nougat **CANDY, TAFFY**		nun's headdress	**WIMPLE**
nought **BAD, WORTHLESS**		nun's room	**CELL**
noun **WORD, NAME**		nuptial	**BRIDAL**
noun suffix **ENT, ESE, IER, IST,**		nuptials	**WEDDING**
	ITE	Nureyev's milieu	**BALLET**
nourish	**FEED**	Nureyev specialty	**LEAP**
nourishment **FOOD, NUTRIENT**		nurse	**TEND, FEED**
Nova Scotia	**ACADIA**	nursemaid	**NANNY**
Nova Scotia mountain ash		nursery bed	**CRIB**
	DOGBERRY	nurse's assistant	**AIDE**
Nova Scotian	**BLUENOSE**	nurture	**FEED**
Nova Scotian resort	**DIGBY**	nut **ACORN, PECAN, WALNUT,**	
novel	**STORY, BOOK,**		**HAZELNUT, FILBERT,**
	UNUSUAL, NEW		**PEANUT, ALMOND**
novelist Bagnold	**ENID**	nutant **NODDING, DROOPING**	
novelist Ferber	**EDNA**	nutation	**NOD**
		nut-bearing tree	**BEECH**

nutmeg spice **MACE**
Nutmeg State **CONNECTICUT**
nut of the oak **ACORN**
nut pine of the
Southwest **PINON**
nutramin **VITAMIN**
nutriment **FOOD, ALIMENT**
nutritious **HEALTHY**
nutty **CRAZY**
nuzzle **NESTLE, SNUGGLE**
nyala **ANTELOPE**
nylon **STOCKING, FABRIC**
nymph **SYLPH, SIREN**

O

oaf **BLOCKHEAD, LOUT, CLOD**
oak **TREE**
oak-to-be **ACORN**
oakum **HEMP**
oar **PADDLE, ROW**
oar blade **PEEL**
oarlock **THOLE**
oarsman **ROWER**
oasis **WADI, REFUGE**
oasis feature (2 wds.)
WATER HOLE
oast **KILN, OVEN**
oat **GRAIN**
oath **CURSE, VOW**
oatmeal **PORRIDGE**
obdurate **STUBBORN**
obeah **WITCHERY, VOODOO**
obedience **SUBMISSION**
obedient **DUTIFUL, LOYAL**
obeisance **HOMAGE**
obelisk **NEEDLE, PILLAR,
MONOLITH**
obelus **DAGGER**
obese **FAT, STOUT, PLUMP,
OVERWEIGHT**
obey **HEED, MIND, LISTEN**
obfuscate **BEWILDER,
CONFUSE, DIM**
obi **SASH**
object **AIM, END, INTENT,
THING**
objection **QUARREL, PROTEST**
objective **END, INTENTION,
AIM, GOAL**
object of art **CURIO**
object of dread **BOGEY**
object of worship **IDOL, GOD**
object to **DEMUR, PROTEST**
objurgate **ABUSE, CHIDE,
SCOLD, REBUKE**

objurgation **REBUKE, REPROOF**
obligate **BIND**
obligation **DEBT, DUTY**
obligatory **REQUIRED**
oblige **GRATIFY, PLEASE**
obliging **AGREEABLE**
oblique **INDIRECT, ASKEW**
obliterate **ERASE**
oblivious **UNAWARE,
FORGETFUL**
obloquy **REPROACH, DISGRACE**
obnoxious **HATEFUL**
oboe **HAUTBOY, REED,
HAUTBOIS**
obscene **LEWD, DIRTY**
obscuration **ECLIPSE**
obscure **DIM, MURKY, BLUR,
DARK, DARKEN**
obscure corner **NOOK**
obscurity **DIMNESS**
obsequious **SERVILE, FAWNING**
observance **CEREMONY, RITE**
observant **ATTENTIVE,
WATCHFUL**
observe **NOTE, NOTICE, SEE,
EYE**
observe Lent **FAST, ABSTAIN**
observer **WITNESS, SPECTATOR**
obsess **PREOCCUPY**
obsession **MANIA, PASSION**
obsolete **PASSE**
obstacle **IMPEDIMENT, SNAG**
obstinate **STUBBORN, MULISH**
obstreporous **TURBULENT,
UNRULY**
obstruct **BAR**
obstruction **BARRIER, SNAG**
obtain **GET, FIND, PROCURE**
obtain as profit **GAIN**
obtain by reasoning **DERIVE**
obtain by searching **FIND**
obtain by threat **EXTORT**
obtain information **LEARN**
obtest **BEG, PLEAD, ENTREAT**
obtrusive **MEDDLING, PUSHY**
obtuse **BLUNT, DULL**
obverse **FRONT**
obviate **AVOID, PREVENT**
obvious **EVIDENT, PATENT**
ocarina **FLUTE**
occasion **TIME, EVENT**
occasional **IRREGULAR, CASUAL**
occasionally (2 wds.) **AT TIMES**
occident **WEST**
occlusion **BITE, BLOCK**
occult **SECRET, DARK**
occultism **CABALA**
occult power **MAGIC**

occupant	**TENANT**	of a branch	**RAMOUS**
occupation	**VOCATION,**	of a chamber	**CAMERAL**
	CAREER, JOB	of a few words	**TERSE**
occupied	**BUSY, ENGAGED**	of age (Lat., abbr.)	**AETAT, AET**
occupy	**FILL**	of aircraft	**AREO**
occupy a chair	**SIT**	of a musical	
occur	**HAPPEN, TAKE PLACE,**	group	**ORCHESTRAL**
	COME TO PASS	of an artery	**AORTAL**
occurrence	**EVENT**	of an era	**EPOCHAL**
occurring after death		of an opposite color	
	POSTHUMOUS		**CONTRASTING**
occurring frequently	**COMMON**	of a part of the brain	**CORTICAL**
occurring occasionally		of a wife	**UXORIAL**
	SPORADIC	of basic alteration	**MUTANT**
occurring often	**FREQUENT**	of better quality	**FINER**
ocean	**SEA, ATLANTIC,**	of cities	**URBAN**
PACIFIC, INDIAN, ARCTIC,		of course	**YES**
ANTARCTIC, MAIN		of course not	**NO**
oceanic	**PELAGIC, VAST, HUGE**	of course (sl.)	**NATCH**
ocean liner (abbr.)	**SS**	of different kinds	**MOTLEY**
ocean mammal	**WHALE**	of equal score	**EVEN, PAR, TIED**
ocean movement	**TIDE**	off base illegally (Army sl.)	
ocean route	**LANE**		**AWOL**
ocean ship	**LINER**	offend	**DISPLEASE**
ocean shore	**SEACOAST,**	offend God	**SIN, BLASPHEME**
	STRAND, BEACH	offense	**AFFRONT**
oceans of the world (2 wds.)		offensive	**ABOMINABLE**
	SEVEN SEAS	offensively obtrusive	**BLATANT**
ocellus	**EYESPOT**	offer	**BID, TENDER**
ocelot	**CAT**	offering	**GIFT, SACRIFICE**
ocher	**PIGMENT, YELLOW**	offer marriage	**PROPOSE**
octave	**EIGHT**	offhand	**IMPROMPTU**
octopus	**POLYP**	office	**CHARGE, FUNCTION**
octopus arm	**TENTACLE**	office cabinet	**FILE**
ocular	**OPTIC**	office expense account	
odalisque	**SLAVE, CONCUBINE**	(2 wds.)	**PETTY CASH**
odd	**PECULIAR, STRANGE**	office holder	**IN**
odd-jobs doer (2 wds.)		office item (2 wds.)	**RUBBER**
	HANDY MAN		**BAND, PAPER CLIP,**
oddly amusing	**DROLL**		**CARBON PAPER**
oddment	**SCRAP, REMNANT**	office machine	**ADDER,**
odds	**ADVANTAGE**		**TYPEWRITER**
odds (Scot.)	**ORRA**	office record	**FILE**
odds and ends	**SCRAPS**	office routine (2 wds.)	
ode	**POEM, CANTICLE**		**DESK WORK, PAPER WORK**
odeon	**GALLERY, HALL**	officer's assistant	**AIDE**
odious	**HATEFUL**	officer's insignia	**STRIPE**
odium	**HATRED**	office table	**DESK**
odontalgia	**TOOTHACHE**	office worker	**STENO, CLERK,**
odor	**AROMA, BOUQUET,**		**TYPIST**
SCENT, FRAGRANCE,		official	**AUTHENTIC, REAL**
SMELL, PERFUME		official decree	**FIAT**
odorous	**REDOLENT**	official grade	**RANK**
Oedipus' father	**LAIUS**	official proclamation	**UKASE,**
Oedipus' mother	**JOCASTA**		**EDICT**
oeillade	**GLANCE, OGLE**	official records	**ACTA,**
of	**FROM**		**REGISTER**
of (Fr.)	**DE**	official seal	**STAMP**

officious **OBTRUSIVE**
offshore coral growth **REEF**
offshore radar platform
  (2 wds.) **TEXAS TOWER**
offspring **SON, DAUGHTER,
CHILD, CHILDREN,
PROGENY, DESCENDANT**
off the rack (comp. wd.)
READY-TO-WEAR
off the track **ASTRAY**
off-white **GRAY, GREY, ECRU,
CREAM, IVORY**
of government **POLITICAL**
of great depth **PROFOUND,
DEEP**
of great importance
MOMENTOUS
of great size **HUGE**
of great weight **PONDEROUS,
HEAVY**
of healing (abbr.) **MED**
of highest quality **BEST**
of little importance **TRIVIAL**
of low birth **IGNOBLE, COMMON**
of marriage **MARITAL, NUPTIAL**
of medicine **MEDICAL**
of milk **LACTIC**
of mothers and fathers
PARENTAL
of musical quality **TONAL**
of no avail **FUTILE**
of no value **USELESS**
of ocean movement **TIDAL**
of one's country **NATIONAL**
of planet's path **ORBITAL**
of punishment **PENAL**
of secondary importance
INCIDENTAL
of sound **TONAL**
of speech **PHONETIC**
of superior quality **BETTER**
often **FREQUENTLY**
often-dented item **FENDER**
often-pickled vegetable **BEET,
CUCUMBER, MELON,
CAULIFLOWER, BEAN,
ARTICHOKE, MUSHROOM**
often-read item **PALM**
of that kind **SUCH**
of the backbone **SPINAL**
of the cheek **MALAR**
of the city **URBAN**
of the country **RURAL**
of the ear **OTIC**
of the hour **HORAL, TIMELY,
CURRENT**
of the mouth **ORAL**
of the nose **NASAL**

of the Orient **EASTERN**
of the pope **PAPAL**
of the same kind **AKIN**
of the sea **MARINE, MARITIME**
of the side **LATERAL**
of the skull **CRANIAL**
of the spring **VERNAL**
of the sun **SOLAR**
of the teeth **DENTAL**
of the USN **NAVAL**
ogee **ARCH**
ogle **EYE, LEER, FLIRT,
MAKE EYES**
ogre **MONSTER, GIANT**
Ohio city **TOLEDO, AKRON**
oil **LUBRICATE, OLEO, FAT,
GREASE, LUBRICANT**
oil (suffix) **OL, OLE**
oilbird **GUACHARO**
oil of rose petals **ATTAR**
oil plant **SESAME**
oil source **OLIVE, PEANUT**
oily **UNCTUOUS, GREASY**
oily fruit **OLIVE**
oily tissue **FAT, ADIPOSE**
ointment **SALVE, NARD**
okay **ALL RIGHT, YES,
SATISFACTORY**
Oklahoma city **ADA, TULSA**
Oklahoma Indian **OSAGE,
PAWNEE**
Oklahoma mountain **OZARK**
Oklahoma river **RED**
old **ANCIENT, ELDERLY,
AGED**
old boat **TUB**
old car **CRATE, JALOPY**
old card game **LOO, WHIST**
Old Colony State
MASSACHUSETTS
old Dominion **VIRGINIA**
old English bard **SCOP**
old English coin **GROAT, RYAL,
NOBLE**
old English pronoun **YE**
older **ELDER, SENIOR**
old expletive **EGAD**
Old Faithful **GEYSER**
old-fashioned **DATED, PASSE,
QUAINT**
old-fashioned heating unit
  (2 wds.) **FRANKLIN STOVE**
old-fashioned photo **TINTYPE**
Old Franklin State **TENNESSEE**
old French coin **ECU, SOU, SOL,
LOUIS**
old French dance **GAVOTTE**

old frontier region of US
(2 wds.) **WILD WEST**
Old Glory **FLAG**
old Greek music hall **ODEON**
old Greek township **DEME**
old horse **NAG**
Old Line State **MARYLAND**
old maid **SPINSTER**
old movie **RERUN**
old musical instrument **LUTE**
old musical note **ELA, UT**
Old North State
NORTH CAROLINA
old pal **CRONY**
old picture card **TAROT**
old poet **BARD, SCOP**
old Roman official **AEDILE,**
EDILE, MAGISTRATE
old sailor **SALT**
old salt **TAR, GOB**
old saying **ADAGE, SAW**
old Scottish chief **THANE**
old slave **ESNE, SERF**
old sledge **SEVEN-UP**
old sol **SUN**
old squaw **DUCK**
old stringed instrument **LUTE,**
LYRE
Old Testament Apocrypha book
TOBIT, JUDITH, WISDOM OF
SOLOMON, ECCLESIASTICUS,
MACCABEES
Old Testament book **AMOS,**
CHRONICLES, DANIEL,
DEUTERONOMY, ESTHER,
ECCLESIASTES, EXODUS,
EZEKIEL, EZRA, GENESIS,
HABAKKUK, HAGGAI, HOSEA,
ISAIAH, JEREMIAH, JOB, JOEL,
JONAH, JOSHUA, JUDGES,
KINGS, LAMENTATIONS,
LEVITICUS, MALACHI, MICAH,
NAHUM, NEHEMIAH,
NUMBERS, OBADIAH,
PROVERBS, PSALMS, RUTH,
SAMUEL, SONG OF SOLOMON
(SONG OF SONGS), ZECHARIAH,
ZEPHANIAH
old time **YORE**
old violin **AMATI, STRADIVARI**
old wagon train route
OREGON TRAIL
old weapon **MACE, LANCE**
old witch **CRONE**
old woman **CRONE, HAG**
old-womanish **ANILE**
oleaginous **OILY, UNCTUOUS**
oleo **MARGARINE**

oleoresin **ELEMI**
olfactory organ **NOSE**
olid **FETID**
olio **HODGEPODGE, MEDLEY,**
MIXTURE
olive genus **OLEA**
oliver **HAMMER**
olla **JUG, POT**
oloroso **SHERRY**
Olympic event **SHOT-PUT,**
DASH, RELAY, GAME,
MARATHON, RACE
ombre **SHADED**
omega **END, LAST**
omen **AUGURY, FOREBODING,**
FORETOKEN, PORTENT,
PRESAGE, SIGN
ominous **FATEFUL, SINISTER**
omit **EXCLUDE, OVERLOOK**
omit a vowel in pronunciation
ELIDE
omit, in printing **DELE**
on **ATOP, UPON**
on (prefix) **EPI**
on a cruise **ASEA**
on a large scale **GIANT**
on all sides **AROUND, ABOUT**
on and on **TEDIOUSLY**
on behalf of **FOR**
once **FORMERLY**
once and again **TWICE**
once and future king **ARTHUR**
once around a track **LAP**
once famous person
(comp. wd.) **HAS-BEEN**
once, formerly **ERST**
once in a while **OCCASIONALLY**
once more **AGAIN, ANEW**
once upon a time **FORMERLY**
on condition that **IF**
one **AN, UNIT, UNITED,**
UNITY, SINGLETON
one (Fr.) **UN, UNE**
one (Ger.) **EINE, EIN**
one (Sp.) **UNO, UNA**
one against **ANTI**
one and all **EVERY**
one and only **SOLE**
one at a time (2 wds.) **SINGLE**
FILE
one-celled animal **AMOEBA**
one devoted to religious work
OBLATE
on edge **TENSE, WARY,**
NERVOUS
one having special talents
GENIUS

one horse carriage **CARIOLE, GIG**
one hundred cents **DOLLAR**
one hundred per cent **ALL, ENTIRETY WHOLE, ENTIRE**
one in authority **MANAGER, FOREMAN, CHAIRMAN BOSS**
one in favor of **FOR, PRO**
one in opposition **ANTI**
one issue of a newspaper **EDITION**
one kind of secretary **DESK, EXECUTIVE**
one lacking courage **COWARD**
one-man performance **SOLO**
one missing **ABSENTEE**
one of a deck **CARD**
one of an ancient race **MEDE**
one of Atilla's followers **HUN**
one of Columbus' ships **NINA, PINTA, SANTA MARIA**
one of Hamlet's alternatives **TO BE, NOT TO BE**
one of the Barrymores **ETHEL, JOHN, LIONEL**
one of the Bears **URSA**
one of the Evangelists **MARK, MATTHEW, LUKE, JOHN**
one of the Gershwins **IRA, GEORGE**
one of the Kettles **PA, MA**
one of the Muses **ERATO, CLIO, CALLIOPE, EUTERPE, MELPOMENE, POLYHYMNIA, TERPSICHORE, THALIA, URANIA**
one of the reindeer **DASHER, DANCER, PRANCER, VIXEN, COMET, CUPID, DONNER, DONDER, BLITZEN, RUDOLPH**
one of the senses **SIGHT, TOUCH, HEARING, TASTE, SMELL**
one of the Twelve **MATTHEW, JOHN, PETER, JUDAS, THOMAS, ANDREW, JAMES, PHILIP, BARTHOLOMEW, JUDE, SIMON, MATTHIAS**
one of two equal parts **HALF**
one or the other **EITHER**
one racing circuit **LAP**
onerous **HEAVY, DIFFICULT**
one seeking political asylum **REFUGEE**
one-sided **BIASED, SLANTED, PARTIAL**

one-spot **ACE**
one's self **EGO**
one's strong point **FORTE**
one time **QUONDAM**
one time only **ONCE**
one undergoing change **MUTANT**
one way up **STAIR**
one who abandons **DESERTER**
one who avoids the company of others **LONER**
one who consumes food **EATER**
one who dies for a cause **MARTYR**
one who digs for coal **MINER**
one who entertains **HOST**
one who excels **ACE**
one who fails to win **LOSER**
one who feels superior **SNOB**
one who fights for noble cause **CRUSADER**
one who forwards goods **CONSIGNOR**
one who fustrates a plan **MARPLOT**
one who goes by **PASSER**
one who governs **RULER**
one who lubricates **OILER**
one who makes forays **RAIDER**
one who roams about furtively **PROWLER**
one who stitches **SEAMSTRESS, TAILOR**
one who tells **RELATER, NARRATOR, SNITCH**
one without courage **COWARD**
on grand scale **EPIC**
on guard **ALERT**
onion **BULB**
onion genus **ALLIUM**
onion-like herb **CHIVE**
onion-like vegetable **LEEK, SCALLION**
on its way **GONE**
onlooker **WITNESS**
only **MERE, SOLE**
only fair (comp. wd.) **SO-SO**
onset **BEGINNING, START, OPENING**
onslaught **ATTACK**
Ontario capital **TORONTO**
on the affirmative side **PRO**
on the bottom **SUNK**
on the briny **ASEA, AT SEA**
on the contrary **BUT**
on the decline **DECADENT**
on the fritz **OUT OF WHACK, BROKEN**

on the go	**ACTIVE**
on the left side	
(nautical)	**APORT**
on the move	**ASTIR**
on the ocean	**ASEA**
on the peak	**ATOP**
on the roof of	**ATOP**
on the sheltered side	**ALEE**
on the summit	**ATOP**
on this	**HEREON**
onus	**BURDEN**
onward	**FORWARD**
oodles	**LOTS**
Oolong	**TEA**
oomph	**ENERGY**
Oopak	**TEA**
ooze	**SEEP, EXUDE**
opah	**FISH**
opal	**GIRASOL**
opaque	**DARK, OBSCURE**
open	**AJAR, FRANK, CANDID,**
UNFOLD, UNWRAP, UNLOCK	
open a package	**UNDO, UNTIE**
open declaration	**AVOWAL**
open for discussion	**MOOT**
open-handed blow	**SLAP**
opening	**GAP, HOLE, MOUTH,**
VENT	
opening for coins	**SLOT**
openings	**ORA**
open-mouthed	**AGAPE**
open out	**SPREAD**
open place in forest	**GLADE**
open shoe	**SANDAL**
open to view	**OVERT**
open wide, as the mouth	**YAWN**
openwork fabric	**LACE**
opera by Bizet	**CARMEN**
opera by Massenet	**MANON**
opera by Verdi	**AIDA**
opera division	**ACT**
opera glass	**LORGNETTE**
opera hat	**TOPPER**
opera highlight	**ARIA**
opera prince	**IGOR**
opera singer (2 wds.)	
PRIMA DONNA	
opera star	**DIVA**
operate	**MANAGE, RUN**
operate a car	**DRIVE**
operation	**WORK, PROCEDURE**
operational	**READY**
operative	**AGENT**
ophidian	**REPTILE, SERPENT**
opthalmic	**OCULAR**
opthamologist	**OCULIST**
opiate	**NARCOTIC**
opine	**THINK**

opinion	**IDEA, THOUGHT**
opinionated	**BIASED**
opinionated faction	**SECT**
opinion opposed to doctrine	
	HERESY
opinion register	**POLL**
opium	**DRUG, DOPE**
opium drug	**CODEINE,**
	MORPHINE
opponent	**ENEMY, RIVAL, FOE,**
	COMPETITOR
opportune (comp. wd.)	
	HEAVEN-SENT
opportunity	**CHANCE, OPENING**
oppose	**RESIST, COMBAT**
opposed	**ANTI**
opposite	**ANTITHESIS,**
	ANTONYM
opposite side	**REVERSE**
oppress	**AFFLICT, PERSECUTE**
oprobrious	**INFAMOUS**
opt	**CHOOSE**
optic	**EYE**
optical glass	**LENS**
optical illusion	**MIRAGE**
optical membrane	**RETINA**
optical organ	**EYE**
optimist	**HOPER**
optimistic	**ROSY**
option	**CHOICE**
optional	**VOLUNTARY**
oracular	**WISE**
oral	**SPOKEN, VOCAL, VERBAL**
oral cavity	**MOUTH**
orange and black bird	**ORIOLE**
orange genus	**CITRUS**
orange oil	**NEROLI**
orange pekoe	**TEA**
orange-red	**CORAL**
orange seed	**PIP**
orange skin	**RIND, PEEL**
orangutan	**APE**
orate	**DECLAIM, HARANGUE,**
	TALK, SPEAK
oration	**SPEECH**
orator	**SPEAKER**
oratory	**ELOCUTION**
orb	**EYE**
orbit	**CIRCUIT**
orbital point	**APSIS**
orc	**GRAMPUS**
orchestra	**BAND**
orchestra leader	**CONDUCTOR**
orchestra leader's stick	**BATON**
orchestra section	**REEDS,**
BRASS, STRINGS, TYMPANY	
orchestra's location	**PIT,**
	BANDSTAND

orchestrate	**ARRANGE**
ordain	**ENACT**
ordeal	**TEST, TRIAL**
order	**COMMAND, DIRECT,**
	DIRECTIVE, NEATNESS, BID
order for girl Friday (3 wds.)	
	TAKE A LETTER
order for writ	**PRECIPE,**
	PRAECIPE
order of frogs and toads	**ANURA**
order of whales	**CETE**
orderly	**NEAT**
ordinal	**REGULAR**
ordinance	**STATUTE, LAW**
ordinary	**MERE, COMMON**
ordinary writing	**PROSE**
ordnance	**ARMOR, ARMS**
ore deposit	**MINE, LODE, VEIN**
ore digger	**MINER**
ore vein	**LODE**
Oregon city	**SALEM, PORTLAND**
Oregon mountain	**HOOD**
Orel's river	**OKA**
organ	**MEDIUM, VEHICLE**
organic compound	**ESTER**
organic substance	**RESIN**
organization	**SETUP,**
	ASSOCIATION
organize	**ARRANGE, FORM**
organized athletics	**GAMES,**
	SPORTS
organized criminal society	
	MAFIA, COSA NOSTRA,
	SYNDICATE
organized march	**PARADE**
organized migration	**TREK,**
	EXODUS
organ of hearing	**EAR**
organ of sight	**EYE**
organ of speech	**TONGUE, LIP**
organ part	**REED, STOP**
organ pipe	**FLUE, REED**
organ stop	**OBOE, ORAGE**
organ tube	**PIPE**
Orient	**ASIA, EAST**
Oriental caravansary	**SERAI**
Oriental chief	**KHAN**
Oriental coin	**DINAR**
Oriental cymbal	**TAL**
Oriental destiny	**KISMET**
Oriental flower	**LOTUS**
Oriental grain	**RICE**
Oriental guitar	**SITAR**
Oriental headdress	**TURBAN**
Oriental marketplace	**BAZAAR**
Oriental nation	**JAPAN, CHINA,**
	KOREA, VIETNAM
Oriental nurse	**AMAH**

Oriental pagoda	**TAA**
Oriental periodic wind	
	MONSOON
Oriental potentate	**AMIR, EMIR,**
	AMEER, EMEER
Oriental river boat	**SAMPAN**
Oriental ruler	**CALIPH, SULTAN**
Oriental salute	**SALAAM**
Oriental sash	**OBI**
Oriental sauke	**SOY**
Oriental staple grain	**RICE**
Oriental title	**PASHA, AGA**
Oriental women's	
quarters	**ODA, HAREM**
origin	**GERM, ROOT, SEED**
original	**FIRST, PRIMARY**
originate	**ARISE, CREATE,**
	DERIVE
Orion	**CONSTELLATION,**
	HUNTER
orison	**PRAYER**
ormer	**ABALONE**
ornament	**BANGLE**
ornamental	**DECORATIVE**
ornamental ball	**BEAD**
ornamental bottle	**DECANTER**
ornamental button	**STUD**
ornamental fabric	**LACE**
ornamental flower holder	**URN,**
	JARDINIERE
ornamental knob	**STUD**
ornamental knot	**BOW**
ornamental setting	**DECOR**
ornamental stamp	**SEAL**
ornamental tuft	**TASSEL**
ornamental vase	**URN**
ornate	**OPULENT, FLORID**
orthodontist's concern	**BITE**
osar	**ESKER**
Oscar	**AWARD**
oscillate	**WAVER, VACILLATE**
osier	**WILLOW**
Osiris' wife	**ISIS**
osprey	**ERN**
ostentation	**DISPLAY, BRAVADO**
ostentatious	**POMPOUS,**
	PRETENTIOUS
ostentatiously fashionable (sl.)	
	SWANK
ostiole	**APERTURE, STOMA**
ostracize	**BLACKBALL, OUST**
ostrichlike bird	**EMU**
Othello villain	**IAGO**
other	**ELSE**
others (Lat.)	**ALIA**
otherwise	**ELSE, OR**
otiose	**VAIN, FUTILE**

ottoman	SOFA, STOOL, FOOTREST	outward	EXTERNAL
Ottoman Empire	TURKEY	outwit	FOIL, THWART
Ottoman governor	PASHA	ova	EGGS
oubliette	DUNGEON	oval	ELLIPTICAL
ought to	SHOULD	oven	KILN, OAST
ouija	PLANCHETTE	oven device	TIMER
our (Fr.)	NOTRE	over	ABOVE, ATOP, ACROSS, DONE, FINISHED
our country (abbr.)	USA	over (Ger.)	UBER
our planet	EARTH	over (poetic)	O'ER
oust	EJECT, EVICT	over (prefix)	SUR
out	ABSENT, AWAY	overabundance	EXCESS, SURPLUS
out-and-out	ARRANT	overact	EMOTE
outback	BUSH	over-adorned	ORNATE
outbreak	RASH	over again	ANEW, ENCORE
outbuilding	SHED, LEAN-TO, WC	overalls material	DENIM
outcast	VAGRANT, CASTAWAY	over and above	TOO
out class	EXCEL, SURPASS	over and over	REPEATEDLY
outcome	END, RESULT	overbearing	ARROGANT, HAUGHTY
outcry	HUE	overburden	OPPRESS
outdo	EXCEED, BEAT	overcast	CLOUDY
outdoor activity	SPORT	overcome	SUBDUE, CONQUER
outdoor blaze	CAMPFIRE, BONFIRE	overcome with fear	DAUNT
outer	ECTAL	overdue	LATE
outer (prefix)	ECTO	overflow	SPILL
outer garment	COAT, JACKET	over fond of	DOTE
outer layer	SKIN	over-friendly politician	HANDSHAKER
outer skin	EPIDERMIS	overhang	JUT, PROJECT
outfit	KIT, RIG	overhasty	RASH
outgrowth	EMERGENCE	overhaul	RENOVATE
outing	EXCURSION, JAUNT	overhead	ABOVE
out in the open	OVERT	overhead railroad	EL
outlandish	UNUSUAL	overjoy	ELATE
outlaw	CRIMINAL, FUGITIVE	overlapping part	FLAP
outlet	VENT	overlook	CONDONE, NEGLECT, FORGET, MISS, OMIT
outline	DRAFT, SKETCH	overpass approach	RAMP
out-migrant	EMIGRE	overpower	CRUSH, MASTER
outmoded	PASSE, DATED	overrun	RAVAGE, BESET
out of	FROM	oversee	SUPERINTEND
out of bed	ARISEN, RISEN	overseer of morals	CENSOR
out of danger	SAFE	overshadow	ECLIPSE
out of date	PASSE, DATED, OLD-FASHIONED	oversight	OMISSION, SLIP
out of place	INEPT, INAPPROPRIATE	oversized	BIG
out of style	PASSE, DATED, OLD-FASHIONED	overt	PUBLIC
out of the way	ASIDE	overtake	PASS
out of town	AWAY	over there	YONDER
outrage	INSULT, FURY	overthrow	DEFEAT, ABOLISH
outrageous	WANTON, FLAGRANT	overture	PRELUDE
outside portion	RIM	overturn	UPEND, UPSET, CAPSIZE
outspoken	CANDID, FRANK	overweight	OBESE, FAT, PLUMP
outstanding	PROMINENT	overwhelm	AWE, CRUSH
outstrip	BEST		

overwrought	**SPENT, DISTURBED**
overzealous	**FANATIC**
ovine creature	**EWE, RAM, LAMB, SHEEP**
ovine mama	**EWE**
ovine papa	**RAM**
ovolo	**ELLIPSE**
ovule	**EGG, SEED**
ovum	**EGG**
owed	**DUE**
owl-like	**STRIGINE**
owl parrot	**KAKAPO**
owl's cry	**HOOT**
own	**ACKNOWLEDGE, HAVE, POSSESS**
own (Scot.)	**AIN**
owner	**PROPRIETOR**
own up	**CONFESS, ADMIT**
oxalis plant	**OCA**
oxen harness	**YOKE**
oxeye	**DUNLIN**
oxford	**SHOE**
ox-headed antelope	**GNU**
oxidation	**RUST**
oxide of iron	**RUST**
oxygen	**ELEMENT, AIR**
oxygen compound	**OXIDE**
oyster	**BIVALVE**
oyster eggs	**SPAWN**
oyster gem	**PEARL**
Ozark State	**MISSOURI**
ozone	**GAS, AIR**

P

pac	**MOCCASIN**
paca	**RODENT**
pace	**STEP, WALK, STRIDE, GAIT, MEASURE**
pace the field	**LEAD**
pachyderm	**ELEPHANT, RHINO, HIPPO**
pacific	**CALM, SERENE**
Pacific island	**BALI, SAMOA, WAKE, GUAM, TAHITI**
Pacific shark	**MAKO**
pacify	**ASSUAGE, PLACATE**
pack	**STUFF, BIND, BUNDLE, HEAP, GROUP, SET, GANG, BAND, RIG**
package	**PARCEL, ENCASE, BUNDLE, WRAP**
package of pepper	**ROBBIN**
package of wool (Australian)	**FADGE**
pack animal	**BURRO, LLAMA**

pack animal of Tibet	**YAK**
pack away	**STOW**
pack down	**TAMP**
packet	**BUNDLE, PARCEL**
pack in	**CRAM, WEDGE**
packing box	**CASE, CRATE, CARTON**
packing plant	**CANNERY**
pack it in	**GIVE UP, ADJOURN, QUIT**
pack off	**DISCHARGE, FIRE, DISMISS**
pack of hounds	**KENNEL**
pack of playing cards	**DECK**
pack the jury	**RIG**
packthread	**TWINE**
pack together	**COMPRESS**
pact	**AGREEMENT, ENTENTE, TREATY**
pad	**CUSHION**
paddle	**OAR, ROW, SPANK, TODDLE**
paddock	**FIELD, ENCLOSURE**
pad for hair	**RAT**
pad for horse's saddle	**HOUSING, TRAPPINGS**
padre	**CHAPLAIN, PRIEST**
padrone	**MASTER, PROPRIETOR**
paean	**HYMN, PRAISE**
pagan	**HEATHEN**
pagan image	**IDOL**
page	**FOLIO, LEAF**
pageantry	**POMP, SPECTACLE**
pagoda	**TA, TAA**
pagoda finial	**TEE**
paid escort	**GIGOLO**
paid golfer	**PRO**
paid notice	**AD**
pail	**BUCKET**
paillette	**SPANGLE**
pain	**HURT, ACHE**
painful	**SORE, ACHING**
painkiller	**ANALGESIC**
painstaking	**DILIGENT**
paint	**COLOR, ENAMEL**
painter	**ARTIST**
painter's stand	**EASEL**
painting and sculpture	**ART**
painting medium	**TEMPERA, OIL, ACRYLIC, PASTEL**
paint layer	**COAT**
paint splash	**BLOB**
paint the town	**CAROUSE**
pair	**COUPLE, DUO, DUET, TWO, TWOSOME, BRACE**
pair-oar	**SHELL, BOAT**
pair of horses	**TEAM, SPAN**
paisley	**SHAWL, DESIGN**

pal	**BUDDY, CHUM, FRIEND, COMRADE, MATE**
palace	**CASTLE, RESIDENCE**
palace officer	**PALATINE**
paladin	**KNIGHT, HERO**
palatable	**SAPID, TASTY, SAVORY, FLAVORFUL**
palate	**TASTE**
palate part	**UVULA**
palatial	**ORNATE**
palaver	**CONFER, CHATTER**
pale	**ASHEN, ASHY, DIM, FADE, PALLID, WAN**
pale bluish-green	**BERYL**
pale bluish-purple	**MAUVE**
pale color	**PASTEL**
pale red	**PINK**
Palestine	**HOLY LAND, ISRAEL**
paletot	**OVERCOAT**
pale yellow	**FLAXEN, MAIZE**
paling	**FENCE**
palisade	**CLIFF**
pall	**CLOY, SICKEN**
pallet	**BED, QUILT**
palliate	**CONCEAL**
pallid	**PALE, WAN, ASHY, ASHEN**
palm	**ARECA**
Palmetto State	**SOUTH CAROLINA**
palm fiber	**TAL**
palm fruit	**DATE**
palmyra palm fiber	**TA**
palpable	**PLAIN, OBVIOUS**
palpitation	**PITAPAT**
paltry	**PETTY, VILE, TRASH**
pamper	**CODDLE, FONDLE, SPOIL**
pan	**SKILLET, BASIN**
panacea	**CURE, REMEDY**
Panama city	**COLON**
Panama passage	**CANAL**
pandemonium	**RIOT, RACKET, HUBBUB**
pander	**CATER**
pane (2 wds.)	**WINDOW GLASS**
panel	**JURY**
pang	**THROE, SPASM**
panhandler	**BEGGAR, BUM**
panic	**ALARM, TERROR**
pant	**GASP**
pantomime	**MIME**
pantry	**LARDER**
papa	**DADDY, FATHER, DAD**
Papal court	**CURIA**
Papal envoy	**LEGATE**
Papal letter	**BULL**
Papal ring	**FISHERMAN'S**
Papal scarf	**ORALE**
Papal seal	**BULLA**
Papal throne	**PETER'S**
papa's wife	**MAMA**
paper	**BOND, TISSUE, DOCUMENT, JOURNAL**
paper container	**POKE, BAG, SACK**
paper of indebtedness	**IOU**
paper quantity	**REAM**
paper size	**LEGAL, CROWN, NOTE**
par	**NORMAL, EQUAL**
parade feature	**FLOAT, BAND**
paradise	**HEAVEN, EDEN**
paradise dweller	**ADAM, EVE**
"Paradise Lost" author	**MILTON**
paradox	**ENIGMA, PUZZLE**
paragon	**MODEL, IDEAL**
paragraph	**ITEM**
Paraguay tea	**MATE**
parallel	**CONCENTRIC**
parallelogram	**RHOMBUS, RHOMBOID**
paramount	**SUPREME, EMINENT**
parapet	**RAMPART, WALL**
paraphernalia	**APPARATUS, GEAR, TRAPPINGS, EQUIPMENT**
parasite	**SYCOPHANT**
parasitic insect	**TICK, LOUSE, FLEA**
parcel	**PACKAGE**
parcel of land	**ACRE, LOT**
parcel out	**METE**
parch	**SCORCH, SEAR**
parched	**SERE, ARID**
parchment	**VELLUM, FORREL**
parchment roll	**SCROLL**
pardon	**FORGIVE**
pare	**PEEL**
parent	**MOTHER, FATHER**
pariah	**OUTCAST**
parley	**CONFER**
Paris airport	**ORLY**
Paris art exhibition	**SALON**
Paris subway	**METRO**
park for wild animals	**ZOO**
park in Copenhagen	**TIVOLI**
parking area	**LOT, GARAGE**
parking payment container	**METER**
paroxysm	**FIT, ATTACK, OUTBURST, SPASM**
parrot	**LORY, MACAW**
parsimonious	**STINGY**
parsonage	**MANSE, RECTORY**

part	**SEPARATE, SPLIT, PORTION, SHARE, ROLE, PIECE, DIVORCE**	part of a printing press	**PLATEN**
		part of Arabia	**ASIR**
		part of a ship	**KEEL, BRIDGE, DECK**
partake	**SHARE**		
parterre	**GARDEN**	part of a ship's bottom	**BILGE**
partial	**BIASED, UNFAIR**	part of a shoe	**SOLE, UPPER, LACE, TONGUE, TOE, HEEL**
partiality	**FAVOR**		
partial refund	**REBATE**		
participant	**ENTRANT**	part of a sonnet	**SESTET**
participant on a discussion show	**PANELIST**	part of a stair	**RISER, TREAD**
		part of a theater	**LOGE, STAGE, GALLERY, BALCONY, PARTERRE, LOBBY, MEZZANINE, BOX**
participate	**SHARE**		
participate in an auction	**BID**		
participle ending	**ING**		
particle	**ATOM, IOTA**	part of a typewriter	**PLATEN, ROLLER, KEY, RIBBON**
particle, as of dust	**MOTE**		
parti-colored	**PIEBALD, PIED**	part of a yard	**FOOT**
particular	**EXACT, DISTINCT, FASTIDIOUS**	part of chow mein	**NOODLES**
		part of infinitive	**TO**
particular instance	**CASE**	part of speech	**NOUN, VERB, ADVERB, ADJECTIVE, CONJUNCTION, PREPOSITION, PRONOUN**
particular place	**SPOT**		
particular taste	**SAVOR**		
particularly	**ESPECIALLY**		
particularly miserable	**WRETCHED**	part of telephone number (2 wds.)	**AREA CODE**
partisan	**FOLLOWER**	part of the day	**MORN, NOON, MORNING, EVENING, AFTERNOON, NIGHT**
partition	**SCREEN, WALL**		
partly fermented grape juice	**STUM, MUST**		
		part of the ear	**LOBE, DRUM**
partly fused	**FRIT**	part of the eye	**IRIS, LENS, UVEA, CORNEA, RETINA**
partly open	**AJAR**		
partner	**PARD, MATE, PAL**		
part of a bird's wing	**ALULA**	part of the hand	**FINGER, NAIL, KNUCKLE, PALM, THUMB**
part of a book	**LEAF, PAGE, CHAPTER**		
		part of the leg	**CALF, SHIN, KNEE, THIGH, ANKLE**
part of a bottle	**NECK**		
part of a bridle	**BIT**	part of the mouth	**LIP, PALATE, TONGUE**
part of a chain	**LINK**		
part of a church	**NAVE, APSE, CHANCEL**	part of the psyche	**EGO, ID, SUPEREGO**
		part of to be	**AM, IS, ARE, WAS, WERE**
part of a circle	**ARC**		
part of a day	**HOUR**		
part of a desk set	**PEN, PENCIL**	part of Viet Nam	**ANNAM**
part of a dogma	**TENET**	part of Yugoslavia	**CROATIA**
part of a door lock	**BOLT**	part played	**ROLE**
part of a dovetail	**TENON, MORTISE**	partridge flock	**COVEY**
part of a flower	**SEPAL, PETAL**	part worked with feet	**PEDAL, TREADLE**
part of a fortress	**REDAN**		
part of a goblet	**STEM**	party	**COMPANY, FACTION**
part of a leaf	**STIPEL**	party for a bride	**SHOWER**
part of a list	**ITEM**	party for men	**STAG**
part of an old auto	**CRANK**	party giver	**HOST, HOSTESS**
part of a plant	**SEPAL, ROOT, PETAL, LEAF, STEM, STALK**	pascal	**CELERY**
		pa's mate	**MA**
		pass	**OVERTAKE**
part of a poem	**STANZA, VERSE, CANTO**	passable	**SOSO, NOT BAD, NOT SO BAD**

passage	**CORRIDOR**	patience	**FORTITUDE,**
passageway	**AISLE**		**ENDURANCE**
passageway of shops	**ARCADE**	patient	**COOL, CALM,**
pass a law	**ENACT**		**CONSTANT, TOLERANT**
pass, as time	**ELAPSE**	patio	**COURTYARD, TERRACE**
passe	**DATED**	patio stove	**GRILL, BARBECUE**
passenger	**FARE, RIDER**	Patrick Dennis creation	**MAME**
passenger vehicle	**BUS, CAB,**	patrimony	**HERITAGE, LEGACY**
	TRAIN	patriotic monogram	**USA**
passenger vessel	**LINER**	patron	**CLIENT, CUSTOMER,**
passing fashion	**FAD, CRAZE**		**BENEFACTOR**
passion	**ARDOR, ZEAL**	patron of shepherds	**PAN**
passionate	**ARDENT, FERVENT**	patron saint of	
passive	**INERT**	England	**GEORGE**
pass lightly over	**SKIM, SLUR**	patron saint of sailors	**ELMO**
pass on	**RELAY**	patronymic	**SURNAME**
Passover feast	**SEDER**	pattern	**MODEL, MOLD**
pass over smoothly	**GLIDE**	pause	**HESITATE, RESPITE,**
passport	**CONGE**		**LETUP, BREATHER, REST**
passport endorsement	**VISA**	pave	**BLACKTOP**
pass slowly	**DRAG**	paving liquid	**TAR**
pass through a sieve	**SIFT**	paving stone	**SETT**
past	**AGO**	paw	**PATTE**
pasta	**SPAGHETTI, MACARONI,**	pawn	**HOCK, CHESSMAN**
	FETTUCINE, PASTINA, PASTE	Pawnee	**INDIAN**
paste	**GLUE**	pay	**REMIT, SETTLE**
pastel	**CRAYON, HUE, PALE**	pay a bill	**REMIT**
past events	**HISTORY**	payable	**DUE**
pastime	**SPORT, HOBBY**	pay a call	**VISIT**
pastoral	**RURAL**	pay attention	**HEED, LISTEN**
pastoral cantata	**SERENATA**	pay court to	**WOO**
pastoral deity	**FAUN**	pay dirt	**ORE**
pastoral home	**FARM**	pay heavily	**SMART**
pastoral pipe	**REED**	payment back	**REBATE**
pastoral poem	**BUCOLIC, IDYL**	payment for recovered item	
pastry	**PIE, TART**		**REWARD**
pastry chef	**BAKER**	payment owing	**DUE**
past time	**YORE**	payoff	**BRIBE**
pasturage	**GRASS**	payola	**GRAFT**
pasture grass	**GRAMA**	pay one's share	**ANTE**
pasture ground	**FIELD,**	pay out	**SPEND, EXPEND**
	PASTURAGE	pea	**LEGUME, VEGETABLE**
pasture land	**LEA**	peace	**AMITY, SERENITY,**
pasture sound	**MOO, MAA, BAA**		**TRANQUILITY**
pat	**TAP, CARESS, PET,**	peace agreement	**TREATY**
	FONDLE, STROKE	peace disturbance	**RIOT**
patch	**COVER, MEND**	peaceful	**IRENIC**
patch of ground	**PLOT**	peace pipe	**CALUMET**
patchwork	**QUILT**	peace symbol	**DOVE**
pate	**HEAD**	peach	**FREESTONE, PEEN-TO**
patella	**KNEE**	peach-like fruit	**APRICOT,**
paten	**PLATE**		**NECTARINE**
patent	**PLAIN, GRANT,**	peach seed	**PIT**
	OBVIOUS	Peach State	**GEORGIA**
pat gently	**DAB**	peacock genus	**PAVO**
path	**LANE, ROUTE, TRAIL**	peacock ore	**BORNITE**
pathetic	**SAD, PITIFUL**	peacock wing marking	**EYESPOT**
		peage	**WAMPUM**

pea holder	**POD**	pelt	**SKIN, FUR**
peak	**SUMMIT, APEX**	pelvic bones	**ILIA**
peal	**RING**	pen	**BALLPOINT, WRITE,**
peal of thunder	**CLAP**		**CONFINE, STY, PIGSTY**
peanut	**GOOBER**	penalize	**PUNISH, FINE**
pear	**BOSC, ANJOU**	penalty	**FINE, PUNISHMENT,**
pearl	**GEM, ORIENT**		**HANDICAP**
pear-like fruit	**AVOCADO**	penance	**CONTRITION**
peasant	**BOOR, RUSTIC, RUBE**	penchant	**BENT**
peasant's shoe	**SABOT**	pencil	**DRAW, SKETCH**
pea's home	**POD**	pencil point	**LEAD**
peat	**FUEL, MOSS**	pencil rubber	**ERASER**
pebble	**STONE**	pend	**AWAIT**
pecan	**NUT**	pendant	**AIGLET, AGLET**
pecan covering	**SHELL**	pending	**DUE**
peccadillo	**FAULT**	penetrate	**ENTER**
peck	**PRICK, JERK**	penetrating	**SHARP, ACUTE**
peculate	**EMBEZZLE, DEFRAUD**	penetrating ointment	**LINIMENT**
peculiar	**ODD, STRANGE,**	penetration	**ENTRANCE**
	OUTLANDISH	penetration in perception	
peculiarity	**QUIRK, ODDITY**		**ACUMEN**
pedal digit	**TOE**	pen fluid	**INK**
pedant	**PRIG, TEACHER**	penicillin	**MIRACLE DRUG**
pedant's specialty	**LESSON**	penitence	**REMORSE, REGRET**
peddle	**HAWK, SELL**	penitential period	**LENT**
peddler	**VENDOR, HAWKER,**	penitentiary inmate	**PRISONER**
	MONGER	penman	**SCRIBE**
pedestal part	**DADO**	pen name (Fr., 3 wds.)	
pedestal rest	**PLINTH**		**NOM DE PLUME**
pedestrian	**WALKER**	pen name of Charles Lamb	
pedicel	**STEM, STALK**		**ELIA**
peel	**PARE, RIND, SKIN**	pennant	**FLAG, BANNER**
peen	**HAMMER**	penniless	**BROKE, POOR**
peep	**PEEK, SPY**	pennon	**BANNER, PENNANT,**
peep out	**PEER**		**FLAG**
peer	**GAZE, LOOK, STARE,**	Pennsylvania city	**ALTOONA,**
	DUKE, EARL, BARON		**READING**
peerage	**RANK, LINEAGE**	Pennsylvania port	**ERIE**
peeress' coronet	**TIARA**	penny	**CENT**
Peer Gynt's mother	**ASE, AASE**	pennypincher	**MISER**
peerless	**MATCHLESS**	pen point	**NEB, NIB**
peer of the realm	**LORD**	pension	**SUBSIDY, INN**
peer's cognomen	**TITLE**	pensive	**THOUGHTFUL**
peeve	**ANNOY, PROVOKE**	Pentateuch	**TORAH**
peevish	**PETULANT**	penury	**PRIVATION, LACK,**
peg	**STAKE, PIN**		**DEARTH, DESTITUTION**
peignoir	**NEGLIGEE,**	peon	**SLAVE**
	DRESSING GOWN	people	**PERSONS, RACE**
pekoe	**TEA**	people in church	**LAYMEN**
pelage	**HAIR, FUR, WOOL**	people in general	**FOLK**
pelagic	**MARINE, OCEANIC**	people of action	**DOERS**
pelerine	**CAPE**	people of ancient Iran	**MEDES**
pelf	**BOOTY, SPOIL**	people of Belgrade	**SERBS**
Pelican State	**LOUISIANA**	people of County Cork	**IRISH**
pellet	**BULLET**	people on the town	
pellucid	**LIMPID, CLEAR,**	(2 wds.)	**CAFE SOCIETY**
	TRANSPARENT	people waiting for	
pelota	**JAI ALAI**	relief	**BREADLINE**

pep	ENERGY, ZEST, VIM, VIGOR	periodical	REGULAR, RECURRENT, PUBLICATION, MAGAZINE
peplum	FLOUNCE	period in history	ERA, EPOCH, AGE
pepo	FRUIT	period of dryness	DROUGHT
pepper	SPICE	period of holding	TENURE
pepper beverage	KAVA	period of time	SPELL, YEAR, MONTH, WEEK
peppermint stick (2 wds.)	CANDY CANE		
pepper pot	STEW, SOUP	period of work	SHIFT
peppery	FIERY	period without war	PEACE
peppy	ENERGETIC	periphery	PERIMETER
Pepys' signoff (4 wds.)	AND SO TO BED	perish	DIE
		perjurer	LIAR
per	THROUGH	perk up	LIVEN
perambulator	PRAM, CARRIAGE	perky	JAUNTY, LIVELY
perceive	SEE, NOTICE, ESPY	permanent	LASTING
perception	SENSE	permanent acting group	REPERTORY
perch	ROOST, FISH, SIT		
percheron	HORSE	permeate	IMBUE, PENETRATE
percolate slowly	SEEP	permission	CONSENT, LICENSE
percussion instrument	DRUM, CYMBAL	permission granted	LEAVE
		permit	ALLOW, LET, LICENSE
peremptory	ARBITRARY	perpetual	ETERNAL
peremptory request	DEMAND	perplex	PUZZLE, BEWILDER
perennial	PERPETUAL, CONSTANT	perplexing point	PROBLEM
		perplexity	DOUBT
perfect	IDEAL	perquisite	PRIVILEGE, RIGHT
perfect model	IDEAL	persecute	HARASS, OPPRESS
perfecto	CIGAR	perseverance	TENACITY
perfect serve in tennis	ACE	persevere	PLOD, CARRY ON
perfidious	DISLOYAL, FALSE	Persia	IRAN
perfidious fellow	SNEAK	Persian cat	ANGORA
perfidy	TREACHERY, TREASON	Persian coin	RIAL, RIYAL
perforate	PUNCH, BORE, PIERCE	Persian fairy	PERI
		Persian hat	FEZ, TURBAN
perforation	BORE, HOLE	Persian king	SHAH
perform	ACT, DO	Persian lynx	CARACAL
performance	ACT, EXPLOIT, PRESENTATION, DEED, FEAT	Persian money	DINAR
		Persian nymph	PERI, HOURI
performer	ACTOR	Persian or Siamese	CAT
perform in a play	ACT	Persian poet	OMAR
perform surgery	OPERATE	Persian priest	MAGUS
perfume	AROMA, SCENT, ESSENCE, ATTAR	Persian product	RUG
		Persian ruler	KHAN
perfume bottle	VIAL, ATOMIZER, FLACON	person	INDIVIDUAL, ONE
		person against	ANTI
perfume ingredient	ATTAR, AMBERGRIS	personal	PRIVATE
		personal affair (2 wds.)	PRIVATE MATTER
perfume quantity	OUNCE, DRAM	personal belongings	EFFECTS
		personal conviction	OPINION
perfumery root	ORRIS	personality	SELF, EGO
perfume with spice	INCENSE	person held prisoner	CAPTIVE
perfunctory	INDIFFERENT	person loved to excess	IDOL, HERO
perhaps	MAYBE		
peril	DANGER	personnel	STAFF
perimeter	BOUNDARY	person of power	TITAN
period	AGE, DOT, ERA, TIME		

person of prominence **BIG SHOT**, **NABOB**

person regarded as the finest (4 wds.) **SALT OF THE EARTH**
persons **PEOPLE**
person's manner **MIEN, STYLE**
persons over here **THESE**
person under age **MINOR**
person with very loud voice **STENTOR**

perspicacity **ACUMEN**
perspire **SWEAT, SWELTER**
persuade **ACTUATE, URGE, PROD, COAX**
pert **LIVELY, SASSY, SAUCY, SPRIGHTLY, PEPPY**
pertain **RELATE**
pertaining to (suffix) **AR**
pertaining to a city **URBAN**
pertaining to a kidney **RENAL**
pertaining to an age **ERAL**
pertaining to bees **APIAN, APIARIAN**
pertaining to birds **AVIAN, ORNITHIC**
pertaining to dawn **EOAN**
pertaining to dogs **CANINE**
pertaining to form **MODAL**
pertaining to Middle Ages **MEDIEVAL**
pertaining to Norway **NORSE**
pertaining to poles **POLAR**
pertaining to sheep **OVINE**
pertaining to ships **NAVAL**
pertaining to the moon **LUNAR**
pertaining to the pope **PAPAL**
pertaining to touch **TACTUAL**
pert girl **MINX**
pertinent **RELEVANT**
perturbation **WORRY**
Peru's capital **LIMA**
Peruvian beast of burden **LLAMA**
Peruvian coin **SOL**
Peruvian Indian **INCA**
Peruvian plant **OCA**
perverse **CONTRARY, STUBBORN**
pessimistic **GLOOMY, CYNICAL**
pest **NUISANCE**
pester **ANNOY, TEASE**
pet **FAVORITE, DOG, CAT, FONDLE, CARESS, STROKE**
petard **BOMB**
pet bird's home **CAGE**
petiole **STALK, STEM**
petite **SMALL, TINY, LITTLE**

petition **SUE, PLEAD**
petitioner **PLEADER**
petits fours **CAKES**
pet mammal **CAT, DOG, HORSE**
peto **WAHOO**
petrified body **FOSSIL**
petrol **GAS**
petroleum **OIL**
petroleum processor **REFINER**
petroleum product **NAPHTHA**
petroleum source (2 wds.) **OIL WELL**
petticoat **SLIP**
pettish **PEEVISH, CROSS**
petty **SMALL, TRIVIAL, SPITEFUL, MEAN**
petty malice **SPITE**
petty objection **CAVIL**
petty prince **SATRAP**
petty quarrel **SPAT, TIFF**
petulant **FRETFUL, TOUCHY**
Pfc's bed **COT**
phantom **GHOST, SHADE, SPOOK, HAUNT, JET**
Pharaoh's ancestor **RA**
pharos **BEACON, LIGHTHOUSE**
phase **ASPECT, STAGE, FACET**
pheasant duck **MERGANSER**
philatelist **COLLECTOR**
Philippine island **LEYTE, SAMAR, BOHOL**
Philippine knife **BOLO**
Philippine native **MORO**
Philippine plant **ABACA**
phlegmatic **DULL, SLUGGISH**
phone greeting **HELLO**
phonograph disc **RECORD**
phonograph machine **HI-FI, JUKE BOX, STEREO**
phonograph machine part **ARM, TURNTABLE, CHANGER, SPEAKER, TUNER**
phonograph record **DISC**
phosphate **SODA**
photograph **SHOT, SNAP**
photographer's flash tube **STROBE**
photographer's request **SMILE**
photographic bath **TONER**
photographic device **CAMERA**
phrase **SLOGAN, SENTENCE**
phrase of apology (2 wds.) **PARDON ME**
phrase of dismay (2 wds.) **OH NO**
phrase of understanding (2 wds.) **I SEE**

phrase with two meanings (2 wds.)	**DOUBLE ENTENDRE**
Phrygian god of vegetation	**ATTIS**
Phyllis Diller's husband	**FANG**
physical	**CORPORAL, TANGIBLE, CHECK-UP**
physician	**DOCTOR**
physician's association (abbr.)	**AMA**
physiognomy	**FACE, EXPRESSION**
physique	**BUILD**
pianist Brubeck	**DAVE**
pianist Cliburn	**VAN**
piano adjuster	**TUNER**
piano key	**IVORY**
piano piece	**SONATA, ETUDE**
piano student's exercise	**SCALE**
piazza	**SQUARE**
picayune	**PETTY, TRIVIAL**
pick	**CULL, PLUCK**
pick carefully	**CULL**
picket	**FENCE, FORTIFY, STRIKER, STAKE**
pickle	**MARINATE**
pickle bottle	**JAR**
pickled fruit	**OLIVE**
pickling spice	**DILL**
pick out	**CHOOSE, SELECT**
pick up the check	**TREAT**
picnic	**OUTING**
picnic dishes (2 wds.)	**PAPER PLATES**
picnic pest	**ANT**
picture	**IMAGE**
picture exhibit room	**GALLERY**
picture house	**CINEMA**
picture mounting	**FRAME**
picture puzzle	**REBUS**
picturesque	**SCENIC, CHARMING**
picture stand	**EASEL**
picture taker	**CAMERA, PHOTOGRAPHER**
pie	**CHAOS, JUMBLE, MESS**
piebald horse	**PINTO**
piece	**PART, PORTION**
piece of a tree trunk	**LOG**
piece of baked clay	**TILE**
piece of candy	**KISS**
piece of china	**PLATE, SAUCER, CUP, BOWL, TEACUP**
piece of coal	**LUMP**
piece of corn	**EAR**
piece of cutlery	**FORK, KNIFE, SPOON**
piece of evidence	**FACT**
piece of garlic	**CLOVE**

piece of ice	**FLOE, BERG, CUBE, BLOCK**
piece of information	**DATUM**
piece of jewelry	**CLIP, RING, EARRING, HATPIN, BRACELET, NECKLACE, EARDROP, BROOCH**
piece of land	**FARM, LOT, ACRE**
piece of luggage	**GRIP, TRUNK, BAG, ETUI, VALISE**
piece of lumber	**BOARD**
piece of mail	**LETTER**
piece of merchandise	**WARE**
piece of money	**COIN**
piece of open ground	**FIELD**
piece of pasteboard	**CARD**
piece of postage	**STAMP**
piece of property	**ASSET**
piece of rock	**STONE**
piece of sculpture	**BUST**
piece of stage scenery	**PROP, FLAT**
piece of sugar	**LUMP**
piece of work	**TASK, CHORE**
piece out	**EKE**
pie covering	**CRUST**
pied	**DAPPLED**
pied animal	**PINTO**
pied diver (Brit.)	**SMEW**
pie fruit	**APPLE, PEACH, LEMON, BERRY**
pieplant	**RHUBARB**
pie plate	**TIN**
pier	**WHARF**
pierce	**GORE, STAB**
piercing	**SHRILL, ACUTE**
piercing tool	**AWL, NEEDLE**
pierce with the horns	**GORE**
pier glass	**MIRROR**
pie shell	**CRUST**
piety	**DEVOTION, HOLINESS**
piffle	**NONSENSE, TWADDLE**
pig	**HOG, PORKER, SWINE**
pigeon	**DOVE**
pigeonhole	**CLASSIFY**
pigeon pea	**DAL**
pigeon shelter	**COTE**
piggery	**PEN, STY**
piggin	**PAIL, DIPPER**
piggish	**GREEDY, SELFISH**
pigheaded	**STUBBORN**
pig meat	**HAM, PORK, BACON, CHITLINS, TENDERLOIN**
pigment	**COLOR, PAINT**
pigmy	**DWARF**
pigpen	**STY, HOVEL**
pigpen sound	**GRUNT, OINK**

pigskin	FOOTBALL
pigsty	HOVEL, PEN
pigtail	QUEUE
pike	FREEWAY, HIGHWAY, ROAD
piker	SHIRKER
pilaster	COLUMN
pile	HEAP
pile driver head	TUP
pile of hay	MOW, STACK
pile up a fortune	AMASS
pilfer	FILCH, STEAL, SWIPE
pilgrim	TRAVELER
pilgrimage	JOURNEY
Pilgrim settler	PURITAN
Pilgrims' ship	MAYFLOWER
pill	PELLET, TABLET
pillage	PLUNDER, SACK, LOOT, ROB, BOOTY
pillar	COLUMN, POST
pillar of air course	PYLON
pillar of a staircase	NEWEL
pillar projecting from wall	PILASTER
pillbox	HAT, FORT
pillory	STOCKS
pillow	CUSHION, PAD
pillow covering	SHAM, TICK
pillow material	FOAM RUBBER, HAIR, DOWN
pilot	AVIATOR, FLYER, AIRMAN, GUIDE, STEER
pilot biscuit	HARDTACK
pilsener	BEER
pima	COTTON
pimento	ALLSPICE
pin	BROOCH, PEG, FASTEN
pinafore	APRON
pince-nez	LORGNETTE
pincer	CLAW
pincers	FORCEPS, PLIERS
pinch	NIP, SQUEEZE
Pindar opus	ODE
pine	FIR, TREE, EVERGREEN
pineapple	PINA
pine fruit	CONE, NUT
pine gum	SANDARAC
pine leaf	NEEDLE
pine tar hydrocarbon	RETENE
pine tree	LARCH, SPRUCE
pine tree exudation	RESIN
Pine Tree State	MAINE
pinion	FEATHER
pink	CARNATION
pinnacle	PEAK, APEX
pin one's ears back	DEFEAT, SCOLD
pintail	SMEE

pioneer	SETTLER, EARLIEST, FIRST
pious	DEVOUT
pipe	TUBE, MEERSCHAUM, CORNCOB
pipe fitting	TEE
pipe of peace	CALUMET
pipette	DROPPER
piquant	SHARP, ZESTY, SPICY
pique	IRE, ANGER
pirate	SEA ROVER, BUCCANEER, PRIVATEER
pirate flag (2 wds.)	JOLLY ROGER
pismire	ANT
pistol attachment	SILENCER
pistol (sl.)	PIECE, ROSCOE, GAT
pit	HOLE, CAVITY
pitch	TAR, THROW, TOSS
pitcher	EWER
pitcher ear	HANDLE
pitcher handle	EAR
pitcher's motions	WINDUP
piteous	PATHETIC
pitfall	TRAP
pith	GIST, ESSENCE
pith helmet	TOPEE
pithy statement	APHORISM
pitiful	WOEFUL, SAD
Pius	POPE
pivot	SLUE, TURN, SWING
pivotal	FOCAL
pixie	ELF, IMP, SPRITE, BROWNIE, FAIRY
placard	POSTER
place	PUT, LAY, LOCATION, LOCALE, LIEU, STEAD, SET
place (prefix)	TOPO
place a bet	WAGER
place a phone call	DIAL
place at intervals	SPACE
place between	INSERT
place confidence in	RELY, TRUST
place end for end	REVERSE
place for a drama critic	AISLE
place for animals	ZOO, MENAGERIE
place for art exhibit	MUSEUM, GALLERY
place for coal	BIN
place for exercise	GYM, GYMNASIUM, HEALTH CL
place for fish	AQUA
place for money	

place for sheets, towels, etc.
(2 wds.) **LINEN CLOSET**
place for skating **RINK**
place for the press **BOX**
place for unclaimed
mail (abbr.) **DLO**
place in proximity **APPOSE, NEAR**
place of business **OFFICE, STORE, SHOP, MARKET**
place of entrance **ENTRY, FOYER, LOBBY**
place of recreation **PARK, RESORT**
place of retreat **HIDEAWAY, DEN**
place of shelter **HAVEN, REFUGE**
place of worship **ALTAR, CHURCH, CHAPEL, TEMPLE**
places **LOCI**
place to live **HOUSE, FLAT, APARTMENT**
place to sit **CHAIR, BENCH, SEAT**
place to ski **SLOPE**
place to sleep **BED, COT, BEDROOM**
placid **SERENE**
plagiarize **CRIB, PURLOIN**
plague **HARASS, FEVER**
plague carrier **RAT**
plaid **TARTAN**
plain **HOMELY, EVIDENT**
Plains Indian **OTOE, SIOUX, CROW**
plain song **CHANT**
plaintiff **SUER, PETITIONER, COMPLAINANT**
plaintive **WISTFUL, PATHETIC**
plait **FOLD, BRAID**
plan **SCHEME, PLOT, BLUEPRINT, MAP**
plane **EVEN, LEVEL**
planet **MARS, PLUTO, VENUS, NEPTUNE, MERCURY, EARTH, URANUS, SATURN, SPHERE, JUPITER**
planet nearest sun **MERCURY**
　　　rest us **VENUS**
ELLIPSE
MARPLOT
BOARD
OW, FACTORY, MILL
BANANA

plant beginning **SEED**
plant by strewing **SOW**
plant disease **ERGOT, SMUT**
plant embryo **SEED**
plant exudation **SAP, RESIN**
plant firmly **IMBED**
plant fluid **SAP**
plant hemp **JUTE**
plant louse **APHID**
plant opening **STOMA**
plant part **ROOT, STEM, STALK, LEAF, PETAL, CORM, SEPAL**
plant protection **MULCH**
plant root **RADIX**
plants, collectively **FLORA, VEGETATION**
plant seed **SOW**
plant stalk **STEM**
plant superintendent **FOREMAN**
plant with prickly leaves **THISTLE**
plasterer **MASON**
Plaster of Paris **GESSO**
plastic **DUCTILE, PLIANT**
plate **DISH, PATEN, PLATTER, REPRODUCTION, METALWARE**
platform **STAGE, ELEVATION, POLICIES**
plating metal **TIN**
platitude **CLICHE**
platoon **UNIT**
platter **PLATE, RECORD, DISC**
plaudit **APPLAUSE, PRAISE**
plausible **LIKELY, PROBABLE**
play **DRAMA, SPORT**
play a banjo **STRUM**
play area **YARD, PARK**
play a role **ACT**
play at courtship **FLIRT**
play at tenpins **BOWL**
play boisterously **ROMP**
play busybody **NOSE, SNOOP, PRY**
play characters **CAST**
play division **ACT, SCENE**
player **ACTOR, GAMBLER**
player's morale (2 wds.) **TEAM SPIRIT**
player's part **ROLE**
play for time **STALL**
playful talk **BADINAGE, BANTER**
playful water mammal **OTTER**
playing card **ACE, DEUCE, TREY, TEN, KING, QUEEN, JACK, KNAVE**
playing field **DIAMOND, GRIDIRON, COURT**

playing marble **AGATE, TAW, MIB**
playing the wrong role **MISCAST**
playlet **SKIT**
play on words **PUN**
play outline **SCENARIO**
play setting **SCENE**
play the first card **LEAD**
plaything **TOY**
play unfairly **CHEAT**
play up **PLUG, ADVERTISE**
play up to **FLATTER**
play without dialogue **MIME, PANTOMIME**
playwright **DRAMATIST**
playwright Albee **EDWARD**
playwright Anouilh **JEAN**
playwright Coward **NOEL**
playwright Jones **LE ROI**
playwright Rattigan **TERENCE**
plaza **SQUARE, MALL**
plaza cheer **OLE**
plea **APOLOGY, ENTREATY, PRAYER**
pleach **PLAIT, PLASH**
plead **BEG, ENTREAT, PRAY, PETITION**
pleader **ADVOCATE, SUER**
pleasant **AGREEABLE, NICE**
pleasant expression **SMILE**
pleasant manners **AMENITIES**
please **SUIT**
pleased **GLAD, HAPPY**
please greatly **DELIGHT**
pleasing odor **AROMA, PERFUME, BOUQUET, FRAGRANCE**
pleasure **JOY, PREFERENCE**
pleasure boat **BARGE, YACHT**
pleasure ground **PARK**
pleasure seeker **EPICURE**
pleasure ship **YACHT**
pleasure trip **JAUNT, JUNKET, CRUISE, VACATION**
pleat **FOLD**
plebeian **COMMON, VULGAR**
plebiscite **DECREE, VOTE**
pledge **PROMISE, OATH, TOAST**
pledged faith **TROTH**
plenary **COMPLETE, FULL**
plentiful **AMPLE**
plenty **ENOUGH**
plethora **EXCESS**
pliant **SUPPLE**
plight **DILEMMA**
plod **TRUDGE**

plot **PLAN, SCHEME**
plot of land **LOT, PLAT**
plowed land (Sp.) **ARADA**
pluck **COURAGE, GRIT, PICK**
pluck a guitar **STRUM**
plug **PEG**
plug up **STOP**
plume **FEATHER**
plump **FAT, OBESE, PUDGY, ROLY-POLY**
plunder **LOOT, SACK, RANSACK, BOOTY, SPOILS**
plunge **DIVE**
plunge in boiling liquid **POACH**
plunge in liquid **DIP**
plunk **STRUM, TWANG**
plurality **MAJORITY**
plus **AND, ALSO**
plus fours **KNICKERS**
plush **RICH, ELEGANT**
Plutarch work **LIVES, BIOGRAPHY**
ply **FOLD, LAYER, STRAND, WIELD, SUPPLY, SAIL, WORK, STEER**
PM beverage **TEA**
poach **TRESPASS**
pocketbook **BAG, PURSE, HANDBAG, BILLFOLD**
pocosin **SWAMP**
pod **COCOON, HERD**
podagra **GOUT**
podium **DAIS**
pod vegetable **PEA**
poem **ODE, VERSE, SONG, SONNET**
poem part **REFRAIN, EPODE**
Poe's bird **RAVEN**
poesy **VERSE**
poet **BARD**
poetess Lowell **AMY**
poetic **LYRIC**
poetic contraction **E'EN, E'ER, 'TIS**
poetic fiction **MYTH**
poetic foot **IAMB, IAMBUS**
poetic possessive **THINE, THY**
poetic preposition **ERE**
poetic unit **VERSE, LINE**
poet Pound **EZRA**
poetry **POESY, VERSE**
poet Sandburg **CARL**
poet-singer McKuen **ROD**
pogonip **FOG**
pogrom **SLAUGHTER, PERSECUTION**
poignant **PIERCING, BITTER, MOVING**

point	MEANING, NUB, PROMONTORY	polish	BUFF, GLOSS, LUSTER, SHINE, SHEEN, RUB
point a gun	AIM	Polish city	CRACOW, WARSAW
point at stake	ISSUE	polished	ELEGANT, REFINED
point-blank	BLUNT, DIRECT	polishing stone	EMERY
pointed (Heb.)	URDE	polite	CIVIL, REFINED
pointed arch	OGIVE	polite society (2 wds.)	BON TON
pointed tool	AWL	politic	PRUDENT
pointed weapon	DAGGER, SPEAR, SWORD, ARROW, DART, LANCE	political group	BLOC, PARTY, CLUB, LOBBY
		political meeting	RALLY
pointer	SETTER	political party	REPUBLICAN, DEMOCRATIC, LIBERAL, COMMUNIST, CONSERVATIVE, SOCIALIST
pointing signal	ARROW		
pointless	INANE, SILLY		
point of departure	ZERO		
point of difference	CONTRAST		
point of land	SPIT	politician	STATESMAN, CANDIDATE
point of orbit, in astronomy	APSIS		
point of view	ANGLE, SLANT	pollack fish	SEY, COD
point opposite zenith	NADIR	pollen bearer	BEE
point out	INDICATE	polliwog	TADPOLE
points in a game	SCORE	pollute	CONTAMINATE, TAINT, DEFILE
point the way	DIRECT		
poise	BALANCE, CALM	polo stick	MALLET
poison	VENIN, ARSENIC, VENOM	Polynesian	HAWAIIAN, SAMOAN, TAHITIAN, MAORI, TONGAN
poison ash	SUMAC		
poison from a snake	VENOM	Polynesian dance	HULA
poisonous	NOXIOUS, TOXIC	Polynesian fabric	TAPA
poisonous shrub	SUMAC	Polynesian god	ATEO, TIKI
poisonous snake	ASP, COBRA, VIPER, ADDER, RATTLER	Polynesian occupation (2 wds.)	PEARL DIVER
poke	JAB, PROD, NUDGE, SACK, BAG	pompous	HAUGHTY, ARROGANT
poke around	ROOT	pompous show	PARADE
poke fun at	RIDICULE, DERIDE	poncho	SARAPE, SERAPE
poker game	STUD, DRAW	pond	POOL, LAGOON
poker holding	PAIR, STRAIGHT, FULL HOUSE, FLUSH	pond duck	MALLARD
		ponder	MULL, MUSE, THINK
poker kitty	ANTE	ponderous	HEAVY, INERT, DULL, MASSIVE
poker money	CHIP		
poker player	GAMBLER	pone	CORNBREAD
poker stake	ANTE	pongee	SILK, SHANTUNG, TUSSAH
Polar exploration base	ETAH		
polar explorer	BYRD, PEARY	Pons specialty	ARIA
polar lights	AURORA BOREALIS	pontiff	BISHOP
polar region	NORTH, ARCTIC, ANTARCTICA	pontoon	BOAT, BRIDGE
		pooch	DOG
pole	ROD, SHAFT	pool	LINN, RESERVOIR
polecat	SKUNK	poolside dressing room	CABANA
polemic	CONTROVERSIAL		
police (colloq.)	COPS, FUZZ	poop	STERN, DECK, DATA
police action	RAID	poor	MEAGER, NEEDY
policeman (sl.)	FLATFOOT	poor area	SLUM, GHETTO
policeman's shield	BADGE	poor person (comp. wd.)	HAVE-NOT
policy	PRINCIPLE, PLAN		

pop	**SODA, BURST, FATHER, DADDY**
pope's headdress	**MITRE**
pope's scarf	**FANON, ORALE**
pop into the oven	**BAKE**
poplar	**ASPEN, TREE**
popover	**MUFFIN**
poppycock	**NONSENSE**
pop's wife	**MOM**
pop the question	**PROPOSE**
populace	**DEMOS**
popular	**LIKED**
popular dessert	**PIE, CAKE, ICE CREAM**
popular flower	**ROSE, DAISY, MUM**
popular girl	**BELLE**
popularly supposed	**REPUTED**
popular Mother's Day gift (2 wds.)	**POTTED PLANT**
popular snack	**BURGER, CHIPS, WIENER, FRANK, DANISH**
popular success	**HIT**
popular TV program	**WESTERN, SOAP OPERA, COMEDY**
populate	**PEOPLE**
population center	**CITY, MEGALOPOLIS**
porcelain clay	**KAOLIN**
porcelain ware	**CHINA**
porch	**PORTICO, VERANDA, STOA**
porch swing	**GLIDER**
porcine animal	**PIG, HOG**
porcine home	**PIGSTY, STY, PEN**
porcine mother	**SOW**
porcupine	**HEDGEHOG**
porcupine quill	**SPINE**
pore	**STUDY, STOMA**
pork fat	**LARD**
pork pie	**HAT**
porpoise	**DOLPHIN**
porridge	**CEREAL, MEAL**
porringer	**BOWL**
port	**WINE, HARBOR, HAVEN**
portable	**MOVABLE, MOBILE**
portable home	**TRAILER**
portable light	**LANTERN, FLASHLIGHT**
portable lodge	**TENT, CAMPER**
portable steps	**LADDER**
portable sunshade	**PARASOL**
portal	**GATE, DOOR**
portcullis	**GATE, SHUT, BAR, GRATING**
portend	**BODE, FORETOKEN**
portent	**OMEN, SIGN, EVENT**
porter	**ALE, DOORMAN**
portico	**STOA, PORCH, COLONNADE**
portion	**PART, SHARE**
portion of bacon	**RASHER**
portion of land	**LOT, PARCEL, ACRE**
portion of medicine	**DOSE**
portion out	**ALLOT, DOLE, METE**
portly	**OBESE, PLUMP, FAT**
portmanteau	**BAG, CASE**
port of Rome	**OSTIA**
port of the South Seas	**APIA**
port on the Weser River	**BREMEN**
portrait	**PHOTO, PICTURE**
portrait by Da Vinci (2 wds.)	**MONA LISA**
portrait on fifty dollar bill	**GRANT**
portrait on five dollar bill	**LINCOLN**
portrait on one dollar bill	**WASHINGTON**
portrait on one hundred dollar bill	**FRANKLIN**
Portugal and Spain	**IBERIA**
Portuguese coin	**REI**
Portuguese islands	**AZORES**
Portuguese lady	**DONA**
Portuguese title	**DOM**
pose	**SIT**
posh	**ELEGANT**
position	**PLACE, POST, SITE, STANCE, ARRANGE, JOB**
position halfway between	**MIDPOINT, CENTER**
position in education	**DEAN, TEACHERAGE, CHAIR, PROFESSORSHIP, CHAIRMAN, PRESIDENT, PRINCIPAL**
positive	**CERTAIN, SURE**
positive electrode	**ANODE**
positive pole	**ION**
positive quantity	**PLUS**
possess	**HAVE, OWN, HOLD**
possessed	**MAD, BEWITCHED**
possession	**ASSET**
possessive pronoun	**HER, HERS, HIS, MY, YOUR, OUR, THEIR, MINE, THEIRS, OURS**
possible	**FEASIBLE, LIKELY**
possibly	**MAYBE**
post	**PILLAR, COLUMN, MAIL**
postage stamp paper	**PELURE**
post a letter	**MAIL, SEND**

post and wire barrier **FENCE**
post boat **PACKET**
postcard message (4 wds.)
WISH YOU WERE HERE
poster **BILL, PLACARD**
postpone **DEFER, DELAY,**
TABLE
postpone indefinitely **SHELVE**
postponement **RESPITE, RAIN**
CHECK, DELAY,
DEFERMENT
post service **MAIL**
postulate **CLAIM, STIPULATE**
posture **ATTITUDE, STANCE**
posy **NOSEGAY, FLOWER,**
BOUQUET
pot **PAN, KETTLE, SAUCEPAN**
potash **NITER, SALIN**
potassium carbonate **POTASH**
potassium compound **ALUM**
potation **DRAFT, DRINK**
potato **SPUD, TUBER**
potato bud **EYE**
potato masher **RICER**
potato squasher **MASHER**
pot cover **LID**
potent **POWERFUL, STRONG**
potentate **RULER**
potential **LATENT, POSSIBLE**
potential prune **PLUM**
potential steel **IRON**
potential trouble source
TINDERBOX
pother **ADO, FUSS, ROW**
potiche **VASE**
potion **DRAFT, DOSE**
potpourri **OLIO, COMBINATION,**
MIXTURE
potsy **HOPSCOTCH**
pottage **SOUP, STEW**
potter's clay **ARGIL**
pottery **CERAMICS**
pottery clay **KAOLIN**
pottery fragment **SHARD**
SHERD,
potto **LEMUR, KINKAJOU**
pouch **BAG, SAC**
poultry **CHICKENS, HENS**
poultry product **EGG, CHICKEN,**
DUCK
pounce **SPRING, LEAP**
pound **BEAT**
pound (abbr.) **LB.**
pound down **TAMP**
pounder **PESTLE**
pour **TEEM**
pourboire **TIP**
pour down **RAIN**

pour forth **GUSH, SPOUT**
pout **SULK, MOPE**
poverty **LACK, INDIGENCE**
poverty-stricken **NEEDY,**
POOR, DESOLATE
powder base **TALC**
powdery dirt **DUST**
power **ENERGY, STRENGTH,**
LEVERAGE
powerful **HEFTY, POTENT,**
STRONG
powerful businessman
TYCOON,
MAGNATE
powerful explosive **TNT**
powerful light beam **LASER**
powwow **CONFERENCE**
practical **PRAGMATIC,**
WORKABLE
practical joke **HOAX, CAPER,**
TRICK
practice **CUSTOM, DRILL**
practice a performance
REHEARSE
pragmatic **PRACTICAL,**
DOGMATIC
prairie **PLAIN, STEPPE**
Prairie State **ILLINOIS**
praise **COMPLIMENT, LAUD,**
EXALT
praise insincerely **FLATTER**
prance **CAPER, CAVORT,**
CURVET
prank **DIDO, TRICK, CAPER,**
ANTIC
prate **CHATTER, PRATTLE,**
TWADDLE
prattle **PRATE, CHATTER**
prawn **SHRIMP**
pray **ASK, PLEAD**
prayer **PLEA, ENTREATY,**
AVE, THANKS
prayer beads **ROSARY**
prayer book **MISSAL**
prayer ending **AMEN**
prayer shawl **TALLIS, TALLITH**
praying insect **MANTIS**
praying figure **ORANT**
preach **ORATE, SERMONIZE**
preacher **PARSON, MINISTER**
pre-adult insect **PUPA**
Preakness **RACE**
preamble **PREFACE**
precarious **INSECURE,**
DUBIOUS
precarious situation (3 wds.)
TOUCH AND GO
precedence **PRIORITY**

preceding	**PRIOR, PREVIOUS**
precept	**LAW, RULE**
precious	**DEAR**
precious jewel	**GEM, PEARL, DIAMOND, RUBY, EMERALD, GARNET, OPAL**
precious metal	**GOLD, SILVER, PLATINUM**
precious stone	**GEM, AGATE**
precipice	**CRAG**
precipitate	**HASTY, RASH, RUSH, HURRY**
precipitation	**RAIN, SNOW, SLEET, HAIL**
precipitous	**STEEP**
precis	**SUMMARY, EPITOME**
precise	**ACCURATE, CORRECT**
preclude	**BAR, AVERT**
predatory	**PREYING, DESTRUCTIVE**
predecessor of the bus	**HORSECAR, TROLLEY**
predetermine	**DESTINE, ORDAIN**
predicament	**SCRAPE**
predicate (abbr.)	**PRED**
predict	**AUGUR, BODE**
prediction	**PROPHECY, FORECAST**
predominant	**UPPERMOST**
preen	**PRIMP**
preface	**FOREWORD, PROLOGUE**
prefer	**FAVOR, SELECT**
preferably	**RATHER**
preference	**TASTE, CHOICE**
prehistoric dwelling	**CAVE**
prehistoric era (2 wds.)	**STONE AGE**
prehistoric man (2 wds.)	**CAVE DWELLER, APE MAN**
preholiday period	**EVE**
prejudice	**BIAS**
preliminary draft	**SKETCH, OUTLINE**
prelude	**PREFACE, PROEM**
premeditated	**INTENTIONAL**
premier	**CHIEF, FIRST**
preoccupied	**ENRAPT**
prep school in England	**ETON, HARROW**
prepare	**ARRANGE**
prepare a salad	**TOSS**
prepare, as beer	**BREW**
prepare copy	**EDIT**
prepared	**READY, READIED**

prepare food by canning	**PRESERVE**
prepare for war	**ARM**
prepare the way for	**PAVE**
prepare to fire	**AIM**
prepare to testify (3 wds.)	**TAKE THE STAND, TAKE AN OATH**
preposition	**INTO, OF, ON, IN, OFF, FROM, BY, FOR, ONTO**
preposterous	**ABSURD, SILLY**
prerecord a broadcast	**TAPE**
prerogative	**PRIORITY, RIGHT**
presage	**OMEN, PORTEND**
presbyter	**MINISTER, ELDER**
prescribe	**LIMIT, ORDER**
prescribed amount	**DOSE**
presence	**AIR, MIEN**
present	**HERE, GIVE, GIFT**
present as a gift	**BESTOW, DONATE**
present for acceptance	**OFFER**
presentiment	**PREMONITION**
presently	**ANON, SOON**
present time	**NOW, TODAY**
preserve	**SAVE**
preserve vegetables	**CAN, FREEZE, PICKLE**
president	**GEORGE WASHINGTON, JOHN ADAMS, THOMAS JEFFERSON, JAMES MADISON, JAMES MONROE, JOHN QUINCY ADAMS, ANDREW JACKSON, MARTIN VAN BUREN, WILLIAM HENRY HARRISON, JOHN TYLER, JAMES KNOX POLK, ZACHARY TAYLOR, MILLARD FILLMORE, FRANKLIN PIERCE, JAMES BUCHANAN, ABRAHAM (ABE, HONEST ABE) LINCOLN, ANDREW JOHNSON, ULYSSES SIMPSON (HIRAM ULYSSES) GRANT, RUTHERFORD B. HAYES, JAMES ABRAM GARFIELD, CHESTER ALAN ARTHUR, GROVER CLEVELAND, BENJAMIN HARRISON, WILLIAM McKINLEY, THEODORE ROOSEVELT, WILLIAM HOWARD TAFT, WOODROW WILSON, WARREN G. HARDING, JOHN CALVIN (CAL, SILENT CAL) COOLIDGE, HERBERT CLARK HOOVER, FRANKLIN DELANO**

ROOSEVELT, HARRY S.
TRUMAN, DWIGHT DAVID
(IKE) EISENHOWER, JOHN
FITZGERALD KENNEDY,
LYNDON BAINES JOHNSON,
RICHARD MILHOUS NIXON

president (abbr.)	**PRES.**
presidential advisers	**CABINET**
president of the Confederacy	
	DAVIS
president of Yugoslavia	**TITO**
president's no	**VETO**
presiding officer	**CHAIRMAN**
presiding officer of the House	
	SPEAKER
presiding officer's mallet	
	GAVEL
press	**FORCE, URGE**
press agent's concern	
	PUBLICITY
press clothes	**IRON, STEAM**
press down	**RAM, TAMP**
press for payment	**DUN**
pressure	**STRESS**
prestidigitator	**MAGICIAN,**
	CONJURER, JUGGLER
prestige	**INFLUENCE**
presume	**ASSUME**
presumption	**AUDACITY**
presumptuous	**INSOLENT,**
	ARROGANT
presuppose	**POSIT**
pretend	**SHAM, LET ON,**
	SUPPOSE, ACT, FAKE,
	FEIGN, POSE, SEEM
pretender	**CLAIMANT**
pretense	**ACT, POSE, SHAM**
pretentious	**AFFECTED**
pretext	**EXCUSE**
pretty	**BONNY, CUTE,**
	BEAUTIFUL
prevail	**REIGN**
prevail upon	**PERSUADE**
prevalent	**RIFE**
prevaricate	**LIE, FIB**
prevent	**AVERT, DETER, WARD**
	OFF, ESTOP, BAR, DEBAR
previous	**PRIOR, FORMER**
prey	**QUARRY**
prey upon	**HUNT, PLUNDER**
price	**RATE, COST, FARE, FEE**
price label	**TAG, TAB**
price of passage	**FARE**
price per unit	**RATE**
prick	**PIERCE**
prickle	**THORN, NETTLE**
prickly fin	**ACANTHA**
prickly heat	**MILIARA**

prickly plant	**THISTLE**
prickly seed	**BUR, BURR**
prickly sensation	**TINGLE**
prickly shrub	**BRIAR**
prick painfully	**STING**
pride	**VANITY, CONCEIT**
priest	**PASTOR, CLERIC,**
	FATHER, PADRE
priest's assistant	**ACOLYTE**
priest's mantle	**COPE**
priest's vestment	**STOLE, ALB,**
	EPHOD, AMICE
prig	**PRUDE, PEDANT**
priggish	**PRIM**
prim	**SEDATE, PRISSY**
prima donna	**DIVA**
primary	**PRINCIPAL, CHIEF**
primary color	**BLUE, RED,**
	YELLOW
primate	**APE-MAN, APE,**
	HUMANOID
prime	**FIRST, ORIGINAL**
prime minister	**PREMIER**
primeval	**ANCIENT, PRIMITIVE**
primitive	**CRUDE, SIMPLE**
primitive chisel	**CELT**
primitive wind instrument	
	PANPIPE
primitive word	**ETYMON**
primp	**PREEN**
primrose	**YELLOW**
Prince Albert	**COAT**
prince in India	**RAJA, RAJAH**
princely	**REGAL, AUGUST**
Prince of Darkness	**DEVIL,**
	SATAN
Prince of Denmark	**HAMLET**
prince of evil	**DEVIL, SATAN,**
	LUCIFER, MEPHISTOPHELES
Prince of the Church	**CARDINAL**
Princeton's mascot	**TIGER**
principal	**MAIN, CHIEF**
principal actor	**STAR**
principal commodity	**STAPLE**
principle	**TENET**
print	**PUBLISH, LETTER**
printed defamation	**LIBEL**
printed fabric	**PERCALE,**
	CHINTZ
printer's aid	**DEVIL**
printer's commodity	**INK, TYPE,**
	PLATE
printer's direction	**STET, DELE**
printer's mark	**CARET**
printer's measure	**EN, EM**
printing error	**ERRATUM**
printing for the blind	**BRAILLE**
printing machine	**PRESS**

printing necessity **INK**
printing process **OFFSET**
prior to **ERE, BEFORE**
priority **PRECEDENCE**
priory **CLOISTER**
prison **JAIL, CAGE, GAOL, PEN**
prison dweller **INMATE**
prisoner **CAPTIVE, INMATE**
prison official **WARDEN**
prison room **CELL**
pristine **PURE, UNTOUCHED**
private **PERSONAL, SOLDIER**
private entrance **POSTERN**
privateer **RAIDER, PIRATE, BUCCANEER**
private eye **SHAMUS**
private high school (colloq.) **PREP**
private pupil **TUTEE**
private road **DRIVEWAY**
private room **DEN**
private teacher **TUTOR**
privation **NEED, WANT**
privilege **RIGHT**
prize **AWARD, TROPHY, CUP**
prize bestowed **AWARD**
prizefight **BOUT**
prize money **PURSE**
prize ring **ARENA**
pro **FOR**
proa **OUTRIGGER**
probable **LIKELY**
probe **EXAMINE, SEARCH**
problematic **UNCERTAIN, UNSETTLED**
proboscis **NOSE, SNOUT, TRUNK**
procedure **ORDER, SYSTEM**
proceed **GO, GET ON**
proceeding **ACTION, PROCESS**
proceeds **PROFIT, INCOME**
process **METHOD**
process crude oil **REFINE**
procession **PARADE**
process leather **TAN**
proclaim **DECLARE**
proclamation **EDICT**
proclivity **BENT, LEANING**
procrastinate **DELAY, PUT OFF**
proctor **AGENT**
procurator of Judea **PILATE**
procure **ACQUIRE, SECURE**
prod **GOAD, NUDGE, POKE, URGE**
prodigy **MARVEL**
produce **GENERATE, YIELD, BEAR**

produce offspring **BREED, PROCREATE**
producer-director Preminger **OTTO**
productive **FERTILE, CREATIVE**
product of milk coagulation **CURD**
product of Pittsburgh **STEEL**
product of worms **SILK**
proem **PRELUDE, PREAMBLE**
profane **IMPURE, SECULAR**
profess **AVOW, STATE, SAY**
profession **CAREER, JOB, VOCATION, DECLARATION**
professional **EXPERT, PAID**
professional charge **FEE**
professional poet **BARD**
professional tramp **HOBO**
professor **TEACHER**
proffer **TENDER, OFFER**
proficient **ABLE, CAPABLE**
profile **CONTOUR, OUTLINE**
profit **GAIN, NET**
profit by **CAPITALIZE**
profligate **CORRUPT, VICIOUS**
profound **DEEP**
profound sleep **SOPOR, COMA, STUPOR**
profuse **LAVISH, COPIOUS**
profusion **ABUNDANCE**
progenitor **SIRE, FATHER**
progeny **SONS, OFFSPRING, CHILDREN, DESCENDANTS**
prognosis **FORECAST**
program **AGENDA, SCHEDULE**
programmer's direction (2 wds.) **READ OUT**
progress **GROWTH, ADVANCE**
progressive **LIBERAL**
prohibit **BAN, TABU, TABOO, DEBAR, ESTOP, FORBID**
prohibition **DRY**
prohibition on commerce **EMBARGO**
project **JUT, PLAN, SCHEME**
projectile **MISSILE**
projecting work, in fortification **REDAN**
prolix **WORDY, VERBOSE**
prolonged and wordy **PROLIX**
prominent **IMPORTANT**
promise **PLEDGE, WORD**
promise solemnly **VOW**
promontory **CAPE, NESS, HEADLAND, POINT**
promote **ADVANCE, ADVERTISE**

promulgate	**PUBLISH, DECLARE**	prosperous (2 wds.)	**WELL OFF**
prone	**LIKELY**	prostrate	**POWERLESS, OVERCOME**
prone to change	**MUTABLE**	protagonist	**HERO**
prong	**TINE**	protean	**VARIABLE**
pronged instrument	**FORK**	protect	**DEFEND, PRESERVE**
pronoun	**HER, HIM, IT, ME, YOU, US, WE, HE, SHE, THEY, THEM, THIS, THOSE**	protect an invention	**PATENT**
		protect from the sun	**SHADE**
		protection	**EGIS**
pronounce	**ARTICULATE**	protective barrier	**SCREEN, GATE**
pronounce indistinctly	**SLUR, GARBLE**	protective case for a light	**LANTERN**
pronouncement	**DICTUM, DICTA (pl.)**	protective covering	**ARMOR**
		protective ditch	**MOAT**
pronto	**QUICK**	protective garment	**APRON, COAT, SMOCK, OVERALLS**
proof	**EVIDENCE**		
proof of ownership	**DEED**	protective layer	**COAT**
proof of payment	**RECEIPT**	protective slope	**GLACIS**
proofreader's mark	**CARET**	protege	**WARD**
pro or con	**VOTE**	proteinase	**PEPSIN, TRYPSIN**
prop	**LEG, SUPPORT, BRACE**	protozoan	**AMEBA**
propel	**DRIVE**	protract	**EXTEND**
propel with oars	**ROW**	protracted	**LONG**
propensity	**INCLINATION**	protracted speech	**TIRADE**
proper	**DUE, MEET**	protrude	**JUT**
property	**ASSET, ESTATE, LAND, REAL ESTATE**	protuberance	**BULGE, NODE**
		protuberance on a camel	**HUMP**
property manager	**TRUSTEE**	proud	**ARROGANT, VAIN**
property right	**LIEN**	prove	**VERIFY, TEST**
prophecy	**ORACLE**	provender	**FODDER**
prophesy	**AUGUR, PREDICT**	provenience	**ORIGIN, SOURCE**
prophet	**SEER, AMOS, HOSEA, MICAH, ISAIAH, JOEL, OBADIAH, JONAH, NAHUM, HABAKKUK, ZEPHANIAH, HAGGAI, ZECHARIAH, MALACHI**	proverb	**ADAGE, MAXIM, SAW**
		proverbial back-breaker (2 wds.)	**LAST STRAW**
		prove satisfactory (3 wds.)	**RING THE BELL**
prophetic	**FATEFUL**	prove to be false	**BELIE, REFUTE**
prophetic sign	**OMEN**	provide	**FURNISH**
propinquity	**NEARNESS**	provide food and service	**CATER**
propitiate	**CONCILIATE, APPEASE**		
propitious	**FAVORABLE**	provide free food	**TREAT**
proportion	**RATIO**	provident	**FARSIGHTED, FRUGAL**
proposal	**OFFER, DESIGN**		
propose	**OFFER, BID**	provide schooling for	**EDUCATE**
proprietor	**OWNER**	provide weapons	**ARM**
propriety	**DECORUM**	provide (with qualities)	**ENDUE, IMBUE**
prosaic	**DRAB, INSIPID**		
proscribe	**FORBID, OUTLAW**	province in Canada	**ONTARIO, ALBERTA, BRITISH COLUMBIA, MANITOBA, NEW BRUNSWICK, NOVA SCOTIA, QUEBEC, SASKATCHEWAN, NEWFOUNDLAND**
prosecute	**SUE**		
proselyte	**CONVERT**		
prospect	**VISTA, VIEW**		
prospector's find	**ORE**		
prosper	**SUCCEED, THRIVE**		
prosperity	**WEAL, WELFARE**		
Prospero's helper	**ARIEL**	provincial	**RURAL**

provincial bishop	**PRIMATE**
provision	**FOOD**
proviso	**IF, CLAUSE**
provoke	**EXCITE, STIR**
prow	**STEM**
prowess	**ABILITY, VALOR**
prowl	**SNOOP, PRY, SNEAK**
proximal	**NEXT**
proximity	**NEARNESS**
proxy	**AGENT, PROCURATOR**
prudent	**DISCREET, WISE**
prudish one (colloq.)	
	BLUENOSE
prune	**TRIM**
pry	**WRENCH, LEVER, SNOOP**
pry bar	**LEVER**
prying	**CURIOUS**
psalm	**HYMN**
psalmist	**DAVID**
pseudonym	**ALIAS, NOM DE PLUME, PEN NAME**
psyche	**MIND**
psychotic	**INSANE**
pub	**TAVERN, BAR, SALOON**
pub beverage	**ALE, STOUT, BEER**
public	**OPEN, OVERT**
public discussion	**DEBATE**
public disturbance	**RIOT**
public garden	**PARK**
public house	**INN, TAVERN, PUB**
publicity	**BALLYHOO**
public notice	**AD**
public official	**NOTARY**
public park	**COMMONS**
public procession	**PARADE**
public road	**STREET, AVENUE, BOULEVARD, PIKE**
public service	**UTILITY**
public speaker	**LECTURER, ORATOR**
public storehouse	**ETAPE**
public vehicle	**BUS, CAB, TAXI, TRAIN**
public walk	**MALL**
publish	**ISSUE, PRINT**
puck	**SPRITE, ELF, DISC**
puddle	**POOL**
pudgy	**DUMPY**
Pueblo Indian	**HOPI, ZUNI**
puerile	**CHILDISH, JUVENILE**
Puerto Rican resort	**PONCE**
puff	**PANT, GASP**
Puff's friend	**SPOT**
pugilist	**BOXER**
pugnacious	**MILITANT**

puissance	**STRENGTH, MIGHT, FORCE, POWER**
pulchritude	**BEAUTY, COMELINESS**
pull	**HAUL, TOW, TUG, LUG, DRAG, YANK, DRAW**
pull down	**DEMOLISH**
pullet	**HEN**
pull into a fold	**TUCK**
pullman	**SLEEPER**
pull one's leg	**HOAX**
pull out	**EXTRACT**
pullover	**SWEATER**
pull to pieces	**TEAR, RIP, REND**
pulpit	**ROSTRUM**
pulpy substance	**POMACE**
pulsate	**THROB, BEAT**
pulse	**THROB**
pulverize	**GRIND, MASH**
pulverizing machine (2 wds.)	**ROD MILL**
puma	**COUGAR**
pummel	**BATTER, BEAT**
pump	**SHOE**
punch	**CUFF, SOCK**
Punch and Judy	**PUPPETS**
punching tool	**AWL**
punch server	**LADLE, BOWL**
punctilious	**FORMAL, PRECISE**
punctual	**PROMPT**
punctuation mark	**COLON, PERIOD, COMMA**
pungent	**ACRID, SPICY, TANGY, ZESTY**
pungent bulb	**ONION**
pungent flavoring	**GARLIC**
pungent refrigerant	**AMMONIA**
pungent shrub	**SAGE**
punish	**DISCIPLINE, CHASTISE, FINE**
punish a child	**SPANK**
punishing	**PENAL**
puny	**FEEBLE, LITTLE**
pupil	**STUDENT**
pupil (Fr.)	**ELEVE**
pupil's assignment	**LESSON, HOMEWORK**
pupil's record (2 wds.)	**REPORT CARD**
puppet	**DOLL**
puppeteer Lewis	**SHARI**
puppy sound	**YIP, YAP, YELP**
purchase	**BUY**
purchase back	**REDEEM**
purdah	**VEIL**
pure	**CHASTE, UNADULTERATED**

pure air	**OZONE**
purified wool fat	**LANOLIN**
purify	**REFINE**
purl	**LOOP**
purloin	**STEAL, FILCH**
purple	**AMETHYST, VIOLET**
purple flower	**VIOLET, IRIS**
purple fruit	**PLUM, GRAPE**
purple plum	**DAMSON**
purport	**OBJECT, SENSE**
purpose	**AIM, INTENT, END, DESIGN, MEANING**
purse	**BAG, HANDBAG, POCKETBOOK**
pursue	**CHASE, GO AFTER, TAIL, FOLLOW**
purvey	**CATER, PROVIDE, FURNISH**
push	**SHOVE**
push aside	**SHUNT**
pushcart	**BARROW**
push gently	**NUDGE**
push up	**BOOST**
push with the head	**BUTT**
pussy cat	**TABBY, KITTY**
put	**DEPOSIT, PLACE, SET**
put away for later (2 wds.)	**SET ASIDE**
put back	**RESTORE, REPLACE**
put down	**LAY**
put forth	**EXERT**
put in	**INSERT**
put in glass container	**BOTTLE**
put in opposition	**PIT**
put in order	**ARRANGE**
put in place	**SET**
put in scabbard	**SHEATHE**
put in shape	**TRIM**
put in tins	**CAN**
put into a secret language	**CODE, ENCODE**
put into cipher	**ENCODE**
put into office	**ELECT**
put into practice	**USE**
put into words	**STATE, EXPRESS, VERBALIZE**
put in writing	**REDACT**
put it there	**SHAKE**
put off	**DELAY, POSTPONE**
put on	**DON**
put on guard	**WARN**
put on the payroll	**HIRE, EMPLOY**
put out	**ANGER, OUST**
put out a tenant	**EVICT**
put out money	**SPEND**
put out of sight	**HIDE, HID, CONCEAL, CONCEALED**

put to proof	**TEST**
put to use	**APPLY**
put upon	**IMPOSE**
put up stake	**ANTE**
put up with	**ABIDE, TOLERATE**
puttee	**GAITER**
putty	**CEMENT, SOFT, PLIABLE**
puzzle	**ENIGMA, POSER, CROSSWORD, RIDDLE**
puzzler's friend	**DICTIONARY**
pyramid	**TOMB**
pyxis	**VASE, CASE**

Q

quadrille	**DANCE, SQUARE**
quaff	**DRINK**
quagmire	**MARSH, BOG**
quahog	**CLAM**
quail	**COWER, QUAKE, BIRD**
quaint	**CURIOUS, ODD**
quake	**TREMBLE**
qualified	**ABLE, CAPABLE, COMPETENT**
quality	**ESSENCE, CHARACTER**
quality of sound	**TONE**
qualm	**TWINGE, PANG**
quandary	**DILEMMA**
quantity of coal	**TON**
quantity of cookies	**BATCH**
quantity of medicine	**DOSE**
quantity of one baking	**BATCH**
quantity of paper	**REAM**
quantity of yarn	**HANK**
quarrel	**ROW, SPAT, FEUD, FALL OUT, TIFF**
quarry	**PREY**
quart	**FOURTH**
quarter-acre	**ROOD**
quarterly item due I.R.S. (2 wds.)	**ESTIMATED TAX**
quarter-round molding	**OVOLO**
quartet	**FOUR, FOURSOME**
quartet member	**TENOR, BARITONE, BASS**
quartz	**AGATE, SILICA**
quaver	**TREMBLE, FALTER**
quay	**LEVEE, EMBANKMENT**
queasy	**DELICATE**
queenly	**REGAL**
queen of Carthage	**DIDO**
queen of India	**RANEE, RANI**
queen of Olympian deities	**HERA**
queen of the fairies	**MAB**
queer	**ODD, STRANGE, EERIE, EERY, WEIRD**

queer (Scot.)	ORRA	race	CONTEST, RUN, SPEED
quell	SUBDUE, ALLAY	race between teams	RELAY
quench the thirst	SLAKE	racecourse	TRACK, OVAL
querulous	FRETFUL, PEEVISH	racehorse	PACER, TROTTER
query	QUESTION, ASK	racetrack character	TOUT
quest	SEARCH	racetrack shape	OVAL
question	INTERROGATE, QUERY	racetrack surface	TURF
		racetrack term	ODDS
questionable	IFFY, FISHY	Rachel's father	LABAN
queue	LINE	Rachel's sister	LEAH
quibble	EVADE	racing program	CARD
quick	FAST, SPEEDY, HASTY, RAPID	racket	NOISE, CLATTER, DIN
		racket string material	GUT, CATGUT
quick look	PEEK, GLIMPSE	radar screen image	BLIP
quick lunch place	DINER, EATERY	radiance	BRILLIANCE
		radiate	SHINE, GLOW
quick plunge	DIP	radical	EXTREME
quicksilver	MERCURY	radio detecting device	RADAR
quick sound	POP	radio interference	STATIC
quick to learn	APT, CLEVER, BRIGHT	radio or television system	NETWORK
quidnunc	GOSSIP	radio waves' medium	ETHER
quiescent	STILL, SERENE	radium discoverer	CURIE
quiet	STILL, SILENT, PEACEFUL	radium emanation	RADON
		radius	SCOPE
quill	PEN, FEATHER	radix	ROOT
quilt part	PATCH	rag	TATTER
quilting party	BEE	rage	RAVE, STORM
quintessential	PUREST	ragged edge	JAG
quintet	FIVE, FIVESOME	raging woman	MENAD, MAENAD
quip	SALLY, RETORT		
quit	STOP, GIVE UP, LEAVE	raglan	COAT, SLEEVE
quite a few	MANY	ragout	STEW
quiver	SHAKE, QUAKE, TREMBLE	rah	CHEER
		raid	FORAY
quivering motion	TREMOR	raider	PRIVATEER, PIRATE
quixotic	IDEALISTIC	rail at	SCOLD
quiz	EXAM, TEST, QUESTION	rail bird	SORA
quondam	FORMER	railroad bridge	TRESTLE
Quonset	HUT	railroad car	COACH, DINER, SLEEPER, PULLMAN
quota	PORTION, RATION		
quote as an authority	CITE	railroad car connecting rod	DRAWBAR
quote by Poe's raven	NEVERMORE	railroad locomotive	ENGINE, DIESEL
quote from memory	RECITE	railroad signal	SEMAPHORE
quotidian	DAILY, COMMON	railroad sleeper	TIE
		railroad station	DEPOT, TERMINAL
R		railroad track layer (2 wds., sl.)	GANDY DANCER
rabbet	GROOVE, JOINT		
rabbit	BUNNY, HARE	railroad vehicle	CAR
rabbit snare	NOOSE	rail-splitter	LINCOLN
rabbit tail	SCUT	railway car	TRAM
rabble	MOB, RIFFRAFF	railway mail service (abbr.)	R.M.S.
rabid	MAD, FRANTIC		
raccoon-like animal	PANDA, COATI	raiment	APPAREL

rain	**DOWNPOUR, POUR, SHOWER**	rapid	**FAST, SWIFT, QUICK, SPEEDY**
rain and snow	**SLEET**	rapidity	**HASTE**
rainbow	**IRIS**	rapidly	**APACE**
rainbow fish	**GUPPY**	rapier	**SWORD**
raincoat	**SLICKER**	rap on the knuckles	
rain hard	**POUR**		**REPRIMAND**
rain sound	**PATTER**	rapport	**ACCORD**
rain unit	**INCH**	rapture	**BLISS**
rainy	**WET**	rapturous feeling	**EXALTATION**
rainy season in India		rare	**INFREQUENT, SCARCE,**
	MONSOON		**UNCOMMON, UNUSUAL**
raise	**ELEVATE, REAR, ERECT, GROW, LIFT, BREED, UP, HOIST, BOOST**	rare art object	**CURIO**
		rarefy	**DILUTE**
		rarely	**SELDOM**
raise crops	**FARM**	rare thing	**ODDITY**
raised border	**RIM**	rascal	**ROGUE, SCAMP**
raised platform	**DAIS, STAGE**	rash	**HEEDLESS, IMPRUDENT,**
raised stripe	**RIDGE**		**OUTBREAK**
raise high	**EXALT**	rasher	**SLICE**
raise nap	**TEASE**	rasp	**FILE, GRATE**
raise to the third power	**CUBE**	rat	**RODENT**
rajah's wife	**RANEE, RANI**	ratchet	**BOBBIN, WHEEL**
rake	**ROUE, BOUNDER**	rate	**APPRAISE, PRICE, RANK,**
rakish	**DASHING, JAUNTY**		**CLASSIFY, CLASS**
rally	**SUMMON, STIR**	rate of movement	**PACE,**
ram	**TUP, SHEEP**		**SPEED**
ramadan	**FAST**	rather	**SOMEWHAT**
Rama's spouse	**SITA**	rather than	**INSTEAD**
ramble	**ROVE, WANDER, STROLL, STRAY**	rather than (poetic)	**ERE**
		ratification	**AMEN**
rambunctious	**UNRULY, WILD**	ratify	**CONFIRM**
ramification	**OFFSHOOT, BRANCH**	ration	**PORTION, SHARE**
		rational	**SANE**
ram in the zodiac	**ARIES**	rationale	**REASON**
ram into	**CRASH**	ratite	**OSTRICH**
ramp	**GRADING**	rat-like rodent	**VOLE**
rampant	**VIOLENT, RIFE**	ratline	**RIGGING**
rampart	**PARAPET, REDAN**	rattan	**CANE**
ram's horn	**SHOFAR**	rattle	**AGITATE, CLATTER**
ram's mate	**EWE**	rattler's sound	**HISS**
ranch animal	**EWE, RAM, COW, SHEEP, HORSE, MARE, BULL, STEER**	rattling sound	**CLATTER**
		raucous	**HOARSE**
		ravage	**DESTROY, DESPOIL**
rancher	**COWBOY**	rave	**RAGE, RANT**
rancid	**FOUL, ROTTEN**	ravel	**FRAY**
rancor	**SPITE, BITTERNESS**	ravelings	**LINT**
random	**CASUAL, AIMLESS**	raven	**BLACK**
range	**COOKSTOVE, STOVE**	raven-haired girl	**BRUNETTE**
range of sight	**KEN, SCOPE**	ravenous	**STARVING**
range of stables	**MEWS**	ravine	**ARROYO, GULCH**
rank	**CLASS, DEGREE, GRADE, RATE**	ravish	**ENRAPTURE**
		raw	**INEXPERIENCED, UNCOOKED, GREEN**
rankle	**FESTER**		
ransack	**PILLAGE, PLUNDER**	rawboned	**LEAN**
ransom	**REDEEM**	raw herb dish	**SALAD**
rant	**RAVE**	rawhide	**PELT**
rap	**KNOCK, TAP**	rawhide whip	**QUIRT**
rapacious	**GREEDY**	raw metal	**ORE**

raw steel	**IRON**	reata	**LARIAT, LASSO**
ray	**BEAM, SKATE**	rebate	**DISCOUNT**
raze	**TEAR DOWN, LEVEL**	rebel	**RISE, REVOLT**
razorback	**HOG**	rebellion	**REVOLT, MUTINY**
razor clam	**SOLEN**	rebellious demonstration	**RIOT**
razor sharpener	**STROP**	rebound	**BOUNCE**
razz	**HECKLE**	rebuff	**REJECT, SLAP,**
re **CONCERNING, REGARDING**			**REPULSE, SNUB**
reach	**EXTEND**	rebuild	**RENEW**
reach across	**SPAN**	rebuke	**REPROACH, CHIDE**
reach a destination	**COME,**	rebus	**PUZZLE**
	ARRIVE	rebut	**DISPROVE**
reach in time	**CATCH**	recalcitrant	**STUBBORN,**
reach maturity	**RIPEN**		**REBELLIOUS**
reach out	**STRETCH**	recall **REMEMBER, RECOLLECT**	
react	**RESPOND**	recant	**RETRACT**
reaction	**RESPONSE**	recap	**TIRE**
reactionary	**TORY**	recapitulate	**SUMMARIZE**
reactivation	**RENEWAL**	recede	**EBB**
read	**SCAN, PORE, PERUSE**	receive **GET, GAIN, ACCEPT**	
readable	**LEGIBLE**	receive advantage	**BENEFIT**
reader	**PRIMER, LECTOR**	receive a scolding (2 wds.)	
readily	**WILLINGLY**		**GET IT**
reading desk	**LECTERN**	receive information	**HEAR**
reading room	**DEN, STUDY,**	receiver of property	**ALIENEE**
	LIBRARY	receiver of stolen property	
reading table	**DESK**		**FENCE**
read rapidly	**SKIM**	receiving set	**RADIO**
read up on	**STUDY**	recent	**NEW**
ready	**PREPARED, RIPE**	recently **OF LATE, LATELY**	
ready (arch.)	**YARE**	recently acquired	**NEW**
ready answers	**REPARTEE**	recent (prefix)	**NEO**
ready cash	**MONEY**	receptacle	**CASE**
ready for action (2 wds.)		receptacle for carrying	
	IN SHAPE, ON TAP	things	**TRAY**
ready for harvest	**RIPE**	reception	**LEVEE, TEA**
ready money	**CASH**	reception room **HALL, ENTRY,**	
ready to act (3 wds.)			**PARLOR, FOYER**
	ON THE ALERT	recess	**NOOK**
ready to receive visitors		recession	**WITHDRAWAL**
(2 wds.)	**AT HOME**	recipe	**FORMULA**
reaffirm	**REASSERT**	recipient of a bequest	
Reagan's state	**CALIFORNIA**		**LEGATEE**
real **GENUINE, TRUE, ACTUAL**		recipient of a gift	**DONEE**
real estate map	**PLAT**	recipient of a gratuity	**TIPPEE**
real event	**FACT**	recite	**READ, RELATE**
realistic	**VIVID**	recite musically	**CHANT,**
reality	**FACT**		**INTONE**
realize	**KNOW**	reckless	**HASTY, RASH,**
realm	**DOMAIN**		**IMPRUDENT**
realm of fancy (2 wds.)		reckon **CONSIDER, SUPPOSE**	
	DREAM WORLD	reclaim **RECOVER, REDEEM**	
reamer	**JUICER**	recline	**LIE**
reap	**HARVEST**	recline indolently	**LOLL**
rear	**RAISE, FOSTER**	recluse **EREMITE, HERMIT**	
reason	**CAUSE, MOTIVE**	recognize	**KNOW**
reasonable	**LOGICAL,**	recoil	**SHY**
	SENSIBLE	recollect **RECALL, REMEMBER**	

recollection	**MEMORY**	reduce	**BATE, CUT, LESSEN**
recommence	**RESUME**	reduced price offers	**TWOFERS**
recompense	**REWARD, WAGE,**	reduce gradually	**TAPER**
	PAY	reduce in rank	**DEMOTE**
recondite	**ERUDITE, LEARNED**	reduce in value	**LOWER**
reconnoiter	**SCOUT, SURVEY**	reduce light	**DIM**
record	**DISC, ENTER**	reduce speed	**SLOW**
record for TV	**TAPE**	reduce to a lower grade	
record holder	**FILE**		**DEMOTE, DEGRADE**
record keeper	**REGISTRAR**	reduce to a mean	**AVERAGE**
record of a patient	**CHART,**	reduce to ashes	**CREMATE**
	MEDICAL HISTORY	reduce to fine spray	**ATOMIZE**
record of events	**ANNAL**	reduce to powder	**GRIND**
record of the past	**HISTORY**	reducing program	**DIET**
record player, for short		reduction	**DISCOUNT, REBATE**
	STEREO, PHONO	redundant	**EXCESS, WORDY**
record speed	**TIME, RPM**	red wine	**CLARET, PORT**
recount	**REPORT**	redwood	**TREE**
recover	**REGAIN, MEND**	ree	**SANDPIPER, ARIKARA**
recreation	**SPORT**	reed instrument	**OBOE**
recreation area	**CAMP, PARK**	reef material	**CORAL**
rectify	**CORRECT, REVISE**	reek	**FUME**
recurring pattern	**CYCLE**	reel	**STAGGER**
red	**CERISE, CRIMSON,**	reel's companion	**ROD**
	SCARLET, COMMUNIST	refer	**ALLUDE, MENTION**
red (prefix)	**RHOD**	referee	**UMPIRE**
redact	**EDIT**	reference book	**ATLAS,**
redan	**FORTIFICATION**		**DICTIONARY**
red-breasted bird	**ROBIN**	reference mark	**ASTERISK**
red chalcedony	**SARD**	reference table	**INDEX**
redden	**BLUSH**	refer to (Lat. abbr.)	**VID.**
reddish	**RUDDY**	refinement	**POLISH**
reddish brown	**RUST,**	refine metal	**SMELT**
	AUBURN, MAROON	reflect	**CONSIDER**
reddish horse	**ROAN**	reflection	**IMAGE**
reddish liqueur (2 wds.)		reform	**IMPROVE, BETTER**
	SLOE GIN	refrain	**CHORUS, FORBEAR,**
reddish yellow	**AMBER, CORAL**		**MELODY**
redeem	**SAVE, RESCUE**	refrain from noticing	**IGNORE**
redeem from captivity		refresh	**REVIVE, BRACE**
	RANSOM	refreshing beverage	**ICED TEA,**
red gem	**GARNET, RUBY**		**ICED COFFEE, ADE,**
red herring	**DISTRACTION**		**SODA, POP**
red-letter day	**HOLIDAY**	refrigerate	**ICE, CHILL, COOL**
red light	**DANGER**	refuge	**HAVEN, OASIS,**
red man	**INDIAN**		**SHELTER**
red meat	**STEAK, BEEF**	refugee	**EMIGRE**
redness of skin	**RUBOR,**	refund money	**REPAY**
	BLUSH	refuse	**DECLINE, PASS UP,**
redolent	**FRAGRANT**		**BALK, DENY,**
redolent wood	**CEDAR**		**DROSS, TRASH**
red planet	**MARS**	refuse from mills	**SLAG**
redress	**REPAIR**	refuse from sugar making	
red root vegetable	**BEET,**		**BAGASSE**
	RADISH	refuse to accept	**REJECT**
red round vegetable	**TOMATO**	refuse to give up	**PERSIST,**
Red Sea gulf	**AQABA**		**PERSEVERE**
Red Square name	**LENIN**	refute	**DENY, DISPROVE**

regal	**GRAND, KINGLY, ROYAL, STATELY**	relating to ebb and flow	**TIDAL**
		relating to grandparents	**AVAL**
regal attendant	**COURTIER**	relating to Hindu literature	
regal chair	**THRONE**		**VEDIC**
regale	**TREAT, FETE**	relating to measurement	
regal fur	**ERMINE**		**METRICAL**
regal residence	**PALACE, CASTLE**	relating to Paul VI	**PAPAL**
		relating to the eye	**OPTIC**
Regan's father	**LEAR**	relating to the moon	**LUNAR**
regard	**RESPECT, ESTEEM, LOOK, WATCH**	relating to time	**ERAL**
		relative	**KIN**
regard highly	**ADMIRE, ADORE, ESTEEM, RESPECT**	relative of bingo	**KENO**
		relatives	**KIN**
regarding	**RE, IN RE**	relax	**REST, SLACKEN**
regardless	**DESPITE**	relaxation	**EASE, REST**
regatta	**RACE**	relay	**RACE**
regent	**RULER**	release	**FREE, UNTIE**
regimen	**DIET**	release from an obligation	**EXEMPT**
regimental commander	**COLONEL**	release from restraint	**FREE**
regimented trip	**TOUR**	release on condition	**PAROLE**
regina	**QUEEN**	relegate	**ASSIGN, REFER**
region	**AREA, ZONE**	relent	**YIELD, DEFER**
regional	**LOCAL**	relentless	**IMPLACABLE**
region of the patella	**KNEE**	relevant	**PERTINENT**
register	**LIST, ENROLL**	reliable	**CERTAIN, SURE, DEPENDABLE**
registering of votes	**POLL**		
register opposition	**PROTEST**	reliance	**HOPE, DEPENDENCE**
regret	**REPENT, RUE**	relic	**SOUVENIR**
regretful	**PENITENT, SORRY, RUEFUL**	relief	**SUCCOR, COMFORT**
		relief-carved gem	**CAMEO**
regular	**CUSTOMARY, ORDINARY**	relief organization	**CARE**
		relieve	**ALLAY, EASE**
regular method	**SYSTEM**	religion	**BELIEF, CREED**
regulate	**ADJUST**	religious	**DEVOUT**
regulate food intake	**DIET**	religious assembly	
regulate pitch	**KEY**		**CONGREGATION**
regulation	**RULE**	religious belief	**CREED**
rehearsal	**DRILL**	religious ceremony	**RITE**
rehearse	**PRACTICE, REPEAT**	religious discourse	**RITUAL, MASS**
reign	**RULE**	religious discourse	**SERMON**
reigning beauty	**BELLE**	religious denomination	**SECT**
reimburse	**REPAY, REFUND**	religious holiday	**EASTER, CHRISTMAS, PASSOVER**
rein	**CHECK, CONTROL**		
reindeer	**CARIBOU**	religious observance	**FAST**
reinforce	**BOLSTER**	religious poem	**PSALM**
reiterate	**REPEAT**	religious recluse	**EREMITE**
reject	**REBUFF, SPURN, TURN DOWN, VETO**	religious service	**MASS, RITE, RITUAL**
rejoice	**CELEBRATE**	religious sister	**NUN**
rejoice in triumph	**EXULT**	relinquish	**WAIVE, CEDE, YIELD**
rejoinder	**RETORT**		
relapse	**BACKSLIDE**	relinquish throne	**ABDICATE**
relate	**PERTAIN, TELL, REPORT**	reliquary	**SHRINE**
		relish	**GUSTO, SAVOR**
related	**AKIN, KINDRED**	reluctant	**AVERSE**
related group	**CLAN**	rely	**DEPEND**
relating to branches	**RAMAL**	remain	**STAY**

remainder	**REST**	renounce (2 wds.)	**SWEAR OFF**
remaining	**LEFT, OVER**	renovate	**REDO, RENEW,**
remain on the feet	**STAND**		**REMODEL**
remains	**ASHES, CORPSE,**	renown	**ECLAT, FAME, NOTE,**
	STAYS		**ACCLAIM**
remain suspended above		rent	**HIRE, LET, LEASE**
	HOVER	rental contract	**LEASE**
remain undecided	**PEND**	rental sign (2 wds.)	**TO LET**
remark	**NOTICE**	renter	**TENANT**
remarkable	**NOTEWORTHY**	renunciation	**DISCLAIMER**
remarkable person (sl.)	**ONER,**	rep	**CORD, RIBBING**
	CORKER, LULU	repair	**MEND, FIX**
remedy	**CURE, ANTIDOTE**	repair shoes	**SOLE**
remember	**RECALL,**	reparation	**ATONEMENT**
	RECOLLECT	repartee	**RETORT, RIPOSTE**
remembrance	**MEMENTO,**	repast	**MEAL**
	SOUVENIR	repayment	**REBATE**
remind	**REMEMBER**	repeal	**CANCEL, RECALL**
reminder	**MEMO**	repeat	**ECHO, RECUR,**
remiss	**NEGLIGENT, LAX**		**ITERATE**
remit	**PAY**	repeatedly (3 wds.)	
remnant	**LEFTOVER**		**OVER AND OVER**
remodel (2 wds.)	**MAKE OVER**	repeat from memory	**RECITE**
remonstrate	**PROTEST**	repeating from memory	**ROTE**
remorse	**COMPUNCTION,**	repeat mechanically	**PARROT**
	REGRET	repeat performance	**ENCORE**
remorseful	**SORRY**	repeat showing	**RERUN**
remote	**FAR, DISTANT, ALOOF**	repel	**REPULSE, DISGUST**
remount a gem	**RESET**	repent	**RUE**
remove	**DISPLACE, SUBTRACT**	repentance	**REMORSE**
remove by cleaning	**SCOUR,**	repercussion	**EFFECT**
	SCRUB	repertory	**THEATER**
remove by clipping	**TRIM**	repetition	**ROTE, ECHO**
remove cover	**UNCAP**	repetition, in psychology	
removed	**DISTANT, REMOTE**		**ECHOLALIA**
remove from office	**OUST,**	repetition of a note	**TREMOLO**
	DISPLACE	repetitive	**REDUNDANT**
remove from print	**DELETE,**	repine	**COMPLAIN, FRET**
	DELE, ERASE	replace	**RESET, RESTORE**
remove moisture	**WRING, DRY**	replenish	**RENEW**
remove rind	**PARE, SKIN**	replete	**SATED, FULL**
remove the beard	**SHAVE**	replica	**COPY, DUPLICATE**
remove the clothes	**STRIP**	reply	**ANSWER, RESPOND**
remunerate	**PAY**	report	**RUMOR**
Remus' brother	**ROMULUS**	reporter	**JOURNALIST**
renaissance	**REBIRTH**	repose	**REST, SLEEP**
rend	**SPLIT, TEAR, RIP,**	repository	**VAULT**
	DELIVER	reprehension	**GUILT, BLAME**
render	**GIVE, DEPICT**	represent (2 wds.)	**STAND FOR**
rendezvous	**TRYST**	representation	**PORTRAYAL**
rendition	**VERSION, DELIVERY**	representative	**AGENT,**
renegade	**TRAITOR**		**ENVOY, DELEGATE**
renege (colloq., var.)	**RENIG**	representative part	**SAMPLE**
renege (3 wds.)	**GO BACK ON**	reprimand	**ADMONISH,**
renew	**REBUILD, RESTORE,**		**CENSURE**
	REACTIVATE, REDO,	reproach	**SLUR**
	RENOVATE	reproach insultingly	**TAUNT**
Reno's river	**TRUCKEE**	reprobate	**IMMORAL, SINNER**

reproduction	**REPLICA**
reprove	**TAKE TO TASK,**
	CHASTISE, REPRIMAND
reptile	**SNAKE, LIZARD**
reptilian	**SAURIAN**
Republican party,	
familiarly	**GOP**
Republican symbol	**ELEPHANT**
Republic of Ireland	**EIRE**
repudiate	**DENY**
repugnant	**ADVERSE, INIMICAL**
repulse	**REPEL**
repulsive	**OFFENSIVE**
reputation	**FAME, RENOWN**
repute	**CREDIT, REGARD**
request	**ASK, PRAYER**
requiem	**DIRGE**
require	**DEMAND, NEED**
requisition	**ORDER**
rescind	**REVOKE, CANCEL**
rescue	**SAVE, REDEEM**
research	**STUDY**
research room	**LAB**
reseau	**NETWORK**
resemblance	**LIKENESS,**
	SIMILARITY
resembling	**LIKE**
resembling bone	**OSSEOUS**
resembling man	**ANDROID**
resembling sheep	**OVINE**
resembling wool	**LANATE**
resentment	**ANGER, IRE**
reserve	**HOLD**
reserved	**TAKEN**
reserved in manner	**ALOOF**
reserve fund (2 wds.)	
	NEST EGG
reservoir	**STORE**
reside	**DWELL, LIVE, ABIDE**
residence	**ABODE, DWELLING,**
	DOMICILE, HOME
residency	**TENURE**
resident of (suffix)	**ITE**
resident of Ankara	**TURK**
resident of Avila	**SPANIARD**
resident of Bagdad	**IRAQI**
resident of Bahia	**BRAZILIAN**
resident of Bali	**INDONESIAN**
resident of Berlin	**GERMAN**
resident of Boise	**IDAHOAN**
resident of Buda	**HUNGARIAN**
resident of Cebu	**PHILIPPINE,**
	FILIPINO
resident of Copenhagen	**DANE**
resident of Edinburgh	**SCOT**
resident of Ghent	**BELGIAN**
resident of Glasgow	**SCOT**
resident of Havana	**CUBAN**
resident of Helsinki	**FINN**
resident of Mecca	**ARAB**
resident of Ocala	**FLORIDIAN**
resident of Perth	**AUSTRALIAN**
resident of Rangoon	**BURMESE**
resident of Rotterdam	**DUTCH**
resident of Selma	**ALABAMAN**
resident of Sitka	**ALASKAN**
resident of Sophia	**BULGARIAN**
resident of Stockholm	**SWEDE**
resident of Tirana	**ALBANIAN**
resident of Vienna	**AUSTRIAN**
resident of Warsaw	**POLE**
resident of Yuma	**ARIZONAN**
residue	**ASH, SIFTINGS,**
	DREGS, LEES
resign	**BOW OUT, QUIT,**
	ABDICATE
resilient	**ELASTIC, SUPPLE**
resin	**LAC**
resinous	**PINY**
resinous wood	**TEAK**
resist	**OPPOSE**
resist authority	**REBEL**
resist change (2 wds.)	
	STAND PAT
resister	**OPPOSER, REBEL**
resolute	**DETERMINED**
resolve	**DECIDE**
resonance	**SONORITY**
resonant	**SONOROUS,**
	VIBRATING
resort	**SPA**
resort city in Florida	**MIAMI,**
	MIAMI BEACH
resort hotel feature	**CABANA,**
	POOL
resort near Venice	**LIDO**
resort of New Mexico	**TAOS**
resound	**ECHO, PEAL,**
	REVERBERATE
resound vibrantly	**TRILL**
resource	**ASSET**
resourceful	**SHARP**
resources	**MEANS**
respect	**ESTEEM, HONOR,**
	REGARD
respectable	**DECENT**
respectful title	**SIR**
respective	**INDIVIDUAL**
respiratory organ	**LUNG**
respire	**BREATHE**
respite	**LETUP, REST, LULL,**
	POSTPONEMENT
resplendent	**RADIANT,**
	SPLENDID
respond	**REACT, ANSWER**
response	**REPLY**

responsibility	**ONUS**
responsible	**RELIABLE, LIABLE**
rest	**PAUSE, RELAX, REPOSE,**
	REMAINDER
restaurant	**CAFE, DINER**
restaurant bill	**CHECK, TAB**
restaurant employee	**WAITER,**
	WAITRESS, COOK,
	BUSBOY, HEADWAITER
restful	**SERENE, SOOTHING**
resting	**ABED, DORMANT**
restitution	**REPARATION**
restive	**FIDGETY, UNEASY,**
	IMPATIENT, EDGY
restless	**NERVOUS, ANXIOUS**
rest on the knees	**KNEEL**
restore	**RENEW, RENOVATE**
restore confidence to	
	REASSURE
restore to health	**HEAL, CURE**
restrain	**LEASH, REIN, HOLD**
	BACK, CHECK, REPRESS
restraint	**CONTROL**
restrained in actions	
	RESERVED
restrict	**LIMIT**
restyle	**REDO, REMODEL**
result of rainy weather	**MUD**
result of supply and	
demand	**PRICE**
resumé	**SUMMARY**
resurface	**RETOP**
resurface a building	**FACE**
resuscitate	**REVIVE**
ret	**SOAK**
retail shop	**STORE, BOUTIQUE**
retain	**KEEP, HOLD**
retainer	**FEE**
retaining wall	**REVETMENT**
retaliate	**AVENGE, REVENGE,**
	PAY BACK
retard	**SLACKEN, SLOW**
rete	**NETWORK**
retention	**MEMORY**
reticent	**TACITURN**
retinue	**ENTOURAGE**
retired	**ABED**
retirement allotment	**PENSION**
retiring	**SHY, MODEST, TIMID**
retort	**RIPOSTE, REPARTEE**
retract	**RECANT, TAKE BACK**
retreaded tire	**RECAP**
retreat	**DEN, LAIR**
retrieve	**RECOVER**
retriever	**DOG**
retribution	**REPRISAL,**
	REVENGE
return	**REVERT, COME BACK**

return a loan	**REPAY**
return an argument	**RETORT**
return like for like	**RETALIATE**
reveal	**DIVULGE, DISCLOSE**
reveler	**MERRYMAKER**
reveler's cry	**EVOE**
revelry	**RIOT**
revenant	**GHOST, PHANTOM**
revenge	**RETALIATE**
revengeful	**VINDICTIVE**
revenue	**INCOME**
revenue (Fr.)	**RENTE**
reverberant	**RESONANT**
reverberate	**ECHO, RESOUND**
revere	**VENERATE, WORSHIP**
reverence	**AWE, RESPECT**
reverent fear	**AWE**
reverential regard	**HOMAGE**
reverie	**FANTASY, DREAM**
reversal	**HINDRANCE, SNAG**
reverse	**CONTRARY, OPPOSITE**
revert	**RETURN, REGRESS**
review	**GO OVER, RECAP**
revise	**EDIT, EMEND, CHANGE**
revive	**WAKE, FRESHEN**
revoke a law	**REPEAL**
revoke at cards	**RENEGE**
revolt	**ARISE, REBEL, RISE UP**
revolting	**OFFENSIVE**
revolution	**ROTATION,**
	REBELLION, UPRISING
revolutionary	**RED, REBEL**
revolutions per minute	
(abbr.)	**RPM**
revolve	**ROTATE, TURN, SPIN**
revolver	**PISTOL, GUN**
revolving	**ROTARY**
revolving machine part	**CAM**
revolving storm	**TORNADO,**
	CYCLONE
revulsion	**AVERSION**
reward	**BONUS, RECOMPENSE**
rewarding	**BENEFICIAL**
rhea	**EMU**
Rhine nymph	**LORELEI**
Rhine tributary	**RUHR**
Rhine wine	**MOSELLE**
Rhone tributary	**YSER**
rhumba country	**CUBA**
rhythm	**BEAT, TEMPO,**
	METER, CADENCE
rhythmic	**POETIC**
rhythmical beating	**PULSE**
rhythmic movement	**LILT**
rhythm instrument	**DRUM**
ria	**INLET**
Rialto	**BROADWAY**
Rialto sign	**S.R.O.**

riata	LARIAT, LASSO	rile	ANNOY, IRRITATE, ANGER
rib	BONE, TEASE	rill	STREAM, BROOK, RIVULET
ribbed fabric	REP	rim	BORDER, EDGE, LIP
ribbon	BOW, FILLET	rime	HOAR, HOARFROST, ICE
ribbonlike flag	STREAMER	rimose	CRACKED
ricebird	BOBOLINK	rind	PEEL, PEELING, SKIN
rice field	PADDY	ring	HOOP, CIRCLET, PEAL,
rich	WEALTHY, OPULENT		TOLL
rich cake	TORTE	ring a bell	REMIND
rich in ideas	MEATY	ringed boa	ABOMA
richly ornate	PLUSHY	ringed planet	SATURN
rich milk	CREAM	ringed worm	ANNELID
rich soil	LOAM	ringing device	BELL
rich tapestry	ARRAS	ringing sound	PLINK, TINKLE,
rickety car or truck	JALOPY,		DING, DONG
	RATTLETRAP	ringlet	CURL, TENDRIL, TRESS
ricochet	CAROM, REBOUND	ring of light	HALO, NIMBUS
rid	DISENCUMBER, FREE	ring slowly	TOLL
riddle	ENIGMA	rinky-dink	CHEAP, SHODDY
ride a bike	PEDAL	rinse	WASH
rider	PASSENGER, TRAVELER	rinsing	DREGS
Rider Haggard novel	SHE	Rio's beach	COPACABANA
ride shank's mare	WALK	riot	MELEE, PANDEMONIUM,
ride-sharing plan (2 wds.)			TUMULT
	CAR POOL	rip	TEAR, REND
ride to hounds	HUNT	ripe	MATURE, MELLOW
ridge	CREST	ripen	AGE, MATURE
ridge of rock near water	REEF	riposte	REPARTEE, RETORT
ridge of sand	DUNE	ripped	TORE, TORN
ridicule	DERIDE, MOCK,	ripple	WAVE
	TAUNT, TWIT	rise	ASCEND, CLIMB, STAND,
ridiculous	LUDICROUS,		SOAR, ELEVATE
	ABSURD	rise and fall	HEAVE, TIDE
ridiculous failure	FIASCO	rise up	REBEL
riding costume	HABIT	risible	FUNNY
riding crop	WHIP	risky	CHANCY, PERILOUS
riding exhibition	RODEO	risque	BLUE, NAUGHTY
riding horse	STEED	rissole	MEATBALL
riding shoe	BOOT	rite	CEREMONY, RITUAL
riding stick	CROP	ritual	RITE, LITURGY
riding whip	CROP, QUIRT	ritzy	SWANK
rife	PREVALENT	rivage	BANK, SHORE
rifle	GUN, SHOTGUN	rival	COMPETE, COMPETITOR
rifle noise	SHOT	rive	SPLIT
rift	SPLIT	river	STREAM
rig	OUTFIT	river (Sp.)	RIO
right	FAIR, JUST, CORRECT	river arm	ESTUARY
righteous	VIRTUOUS, PURE	river bank	RIPA
righteously angry	INDIGNANT	river barrier	DAM
rightfully	DULY	river bed	CHANNEL
right-hand page	RECTO	river boat	BARGE, FERRY
right of legal ownership	TITLE	river bottom	BED
right or left part of the		river bottom land	HOLM
body	SIDE	river crossed by Caesar	
right to choose	OPTION		RUBICON
rigid	TENSE, UNYIELDING	river crossing	FORD
rigor	HARDSHIP	river deposit	DELTA
rigorous	SEVERE, STRICT	river dragon	CROCODILE

river duck	**TEAL**
river embankment	**LEVEE**
river fish	**SHAD, TROUT,**
	SALMON
river freighter	**SCOW**
river in Africa	**CONGO, NIGER,**
	NILE, VELÉ
river in Alaska	**YUKON**
river in Arizona	**GILA**
river in Australia	**SWAN**
river in Austria	**ENNS**
river in Bavaria	**ISAR, NAAB**
river in Belgium	**LYS**
river in Bohemia	**ELBE**
river in China	**TARIM, YALU**
river in Egypt	**NILE**
river in England	**AVON, TRENT,**
	THAMES, TEES
river in Ethiopia	**ABBAI**
river in Europe	**DANUBE,**
	SAAR, ODER, YSER,
	RHINE, RHONE, AAR
river in Flanders	**YSER**
river in France	**SEINE, ORNE,**
	EURE, LOIRE
river in Germany	**ELBE, RHINE,**
	RUHR, ODER, WESER
river in Greece	**ARTA**
river in Hades	**STYX**
river in Hungary	**RAAB**
river in India	**INDUS, GANGES**
river in Ireland	**ERNE, BANN**
river in Italy	**ARNO, TIBER, PO**
river in Kansas	**OSAGE**
river inlet	**RIA**
river in Nebraska	**PLATTE**
river in Nigeria	**BENIN**
river in Normandy	**ORNE**
river in Norway	**TANA**
river in Oregon	**KLAMATH**
river in Poland	**WARTA,**
	NAREV(W)
river in Romania	**SIRET**
river in Rome	**TIBER**
river in Russia	**URAL, OKA,**
	NEVA
river in Scotland	**DEE, AYR**
river in South Africa	**VAAL**
river in South America	**APA,**
	AMAZON, PLATA
river in South Carolina	**EDISTO,**
	SANTEE
river in Spain	**EBRO**
river in Sweden	**UME, LULE**
river in Switzerland	**AAR**
river in Texas	**NUECES, RED,**
	PECOS
river in the Congo	**UELE**

river in the Netherlands	**LEX,**
	AMSTEL
river in the Southwest	**PECOS**
river into the Bay of Biscay	
	LOIRE
river in Turkey	**ARAS**
river in Tuscany	**ARNO**
river in Wales and	
England	**WYE**
river in Yorkshire	**LEEDS, AIRE**
river island	**AIT**
river mouth formation	**DELTA**
river nymph	**NAIS**
river passage	**FORD**
river rat	**THIEF**
river sediment	**SILT**
riverside	**BANK**
river siren	**LORELEI**
river through Burgundy	**SAONE**
rivet	**BOLT, PIN**
riviere	**NECKLACE**
rivulet	**BROOK, STREAM**
road	**PIKE, ROUTE, HIGHWAY,**
	AVENUE, STREET,
	BOULEVARD, LANE
road closed at one end	
(2 wds.)	**BLIND ALLEY,**
	DEAD END
roadhouse	**TAVERN, INN**
roadrunner	**CUCKOO**
roadside eatery	**DINER**
roadside hotel	**MOTEL**
roadster	**CAR**
road-surfacing material	
	BLACKTOP
roam	**ROVE, WANDER**
roam about idly	**GAD**
roan	**HORSE**
roar	**BELLOW, HOLLER**
roast	**BAKE**
roasting chamber	**OVEN**
roasting ear	**CORN**
roasting stick	**SPIT**
roast on a spit	**BARBECUE**
roast over a fire	**PARCH**
rob	**PILLAGE, STEAL, THIEVE**
robalo	**SNOOK**
robber	**STEALER, BURGLAR,**
	THIEF, FELON
robe	**HOUSECOAT, DUSTER,**
	WRAPPER, TOGA
robin	**BIRD**
Robin Goodfellow	**PUCK**
Robinson Crusoe's man	
	FRIDAY
roble	**OAK**
robot	**AUTOMATON**
robust	**HALE, LUSTY**

rocambole	**ONION, LEEK**	Roman emperor	**NERO**
rock	**STONE, PEBBLE,**	Roman entrance hall	**ATRIUM**
	BOULDER	Roman fates	**PARCAE**
rocket fuel	**LOX**	Roman galley	**TRIREME**
rock growth	**MOSS**	Roman goddess of plenty	**OPS**
rock hawk	**FALCON**	Roman hearth goddess	**VESTA**
rocking bed	**CRADLE**	Roman highway	**ITER**
rock lobster	**CRAYFISH**	Roman historian	**LIVY**
rock moss	**LICHEN**	Roman household gods	**LARES,**
rock salt	**HALITE**		**PENATES**
rocky crag	**TOR**	Roman judge	**(A)EDILE**
Rocky Mountain park	**ESTES**	Roman matron's wear	**STOLA**
Rocky Mountain range	**TETON**	Roman orator	**CICERO**
Rocky Mountain sheep		Roman patriot	**CATO**
	BIGHORN	Roman philosopher	**SENECA**
rococo	**FLORID, ORNATE**	Roman poet	**OVID, VIRGIL**
rod	**FISHING POLE, FERULE**	Roman prelate	**POPE**
rodent	**RAT, RABBIT, MOUSE,**	Roman river	**TIBER**
	VOLE	Roman road	**ITER**
rodeo	**ROUNDUP**	Roman robe	**TOGA**
roe	**CAVIAR**	Roman shoe	**SANDAL**
Roger Moore role	**SAINT**	Roman statesman	**CATO**
rogue	**RASCAL, SCAMP**	romantic exploit	**GEST**
roil	**ANNOY, DISTURB**	romantic flower	**ROSE**
role	**PART, FUNCTION**	Roman tyrant	**NERO**
roll	**BUN, TURNOVER,**	Roman underworld god	**PLUTO**
	LIST, ROSTER	Romany	**GYPSY**
rollaway	**BED**	Romeo	**LOVER**
roll call answer	**HERE,**	romp	**PLAY, GAMBOL, CAVORT**
	PRESENT	Romulus' brother	**REMUS**
roller	**WAVE, CURLER**	rood	**CROSS**
rollick	**ROMP**	roof	**GABLE**
roll of butter	**PAT**	roof beam	**RAFTER**
roll of cloth	**BOLT**	roof edge	**EAVE**
roll of hair	**RAT, CHIGNON**	roofing liquid	**TAR**
roll of meat	**RISSOLE**	roofing material	**TILE, SLATE,**
roll of parchment	**SCROLL**		**SHINGLE, ASBESTOS**
roll of postage stamps	**COIL**	roof of the mouth	**PALATE**
roll of tobacco	**CIGAR**	roof overhang	**EAVE**
roll tightly	**FURL**	rook	**CASTLE, CROW**
roll up a flag	**FURL**	rookie	**TYRO, NOVICE**
roly-poly	**CHUBBY, PLUMP**	rook's cry	**CAW**
romaine	**COS**	room	**CHAMBER, SPACE**
Roman	**ITALIAN, LATIN**	room entrance	**DOOR**
Roman bishop	**POPE**	roomer	**LODGER**
Roman bronze	**AES**	room in a tower	**BELFRY**
romance	**NOVEL, FICTION**	room of the Last Supper	
Roman comedy writer			**CENACLE**
	TERENCE	room shape	**ELL**
Roman date	**IDES**	room side	**WALL**
Roman deity	**VENUS, MARS,**	room to move	**LEEWAY**
DIANA, MINERVA, JOVE,		roomy	**SPACIOUS**
AURORA, BACCHUS,		roost	**PERCH**
CERES, CUPID, FAUN,		rooster	**COCK**
APOLLO, JUNO, JUPITER,		rooster's mate	**HEN**
MERCURY, JANUS,		rooster's pride	**COMB**
NEPTUNE, VULCAN, DIS,		root	**RADIX, TUBER**
LUNA, AMOR, NONA		rootstock	**TARO**

root vegetable	BEET, RADISH, CARROT, POTATO, TURNIP, PARSNIP	row	LINE, TIER, LAYER, OAR, PADDLE
rope	LASSO, LINE, RIATA, REATA, CORD	rowboat pin	THOLE
rope connection	KNOT	rowdy	HOODLUM
rope fiber	HEMP	rowel	SPUR
rope loop	NOOSE, BIGHT	rowing blade	OAR, PADDLE
rope of flowers	GARLAND, LEI	royal	REGAL, KINGLY, PRINCELY
rope of onions	REEVE	royal headdress	TIARA,
rope to limit animal's range	TETHER		CORONET, CROWN
Rorschach	INKBLOT	royal mace	SCEPTRE
rosary bead	AVE	royal order	EDICT, DECREE
roselike flower	CAMELLIA	royal purple	CRIMSON
rose noble	RYAL	royal residence	PALACE, CASTLE
rose oil	ATTAR	Royal Scottish Academy (abbr.)	R.S.A.
roster	LIST, ROTA, ROLL	rozzer	POLICEMAN, COP
rosy	BLUSHING, RED, CRIMSON	rub	MASSAGE, STROKE
rot	DECAY, SPOIL	rubber	ERASER
rota	COURT, ROSTER	rubber band	ELASTIC
rotary motor	TURBINE	ruber city	AKRON
rotate	SPIN, TWIRL, REVOLVE, TURN, WHIRL	rubber hoop	TIRE
		rubber overshoe	ARCTIC
rotating machine	DYNAMO	rubber rug	MAT
rotating machine part	ROTOR	rubber-soled shoe	SNEAKER
rotating piece	CAM	rubber tree	ULE
rote	REPETITION, ROUTINE	rubber tubing	HOSE
rotisserie skewer	SPIT	rubbish	LITTER, TRASH, GARBAGE
rotund	ROUND, STOUT	rubble	DEBRIS
roue	RAKE	rubdown artist	MASSEUR
rough	UNEVEN	rube	HICK, RUSTIC
rough drawing	SKETCH	rubella	MEASLES
rough hair	SHAG	rubicund	ROSY
rough tire surface	TREAD	rub out	ERASE
round	CIRCULAR	rubric	HEADING, TITLE
roundabout course	DETOUR	rub the wrong way	IRRITATE
rounded lump	NODULE, NODE	rub together	GRATE
rounded roof	DOME, CUPOLA	ruby type	AGATE
round of applause	HAND	ruche	LACE
round platter	DISC	ruckus	TO-DO
Round Table knight	GALAHAD, LANCELOT	ruddy	RED, REDDISH
		rude	DISCOURTEOUS, IMPOLITE, CURT
roundup	RODEO	rude cabin	HOVEL, HUT, SHACK
roundworm	NEMATODE		
rouse from sleep	AWAKE, WAKE, AWAKEN, WAKEN	rude person	BOOR
		rudimental	ELEMENTARY, INITIAL
rouse to action	BESTIR	rue	REGRET
rout	SCATTER, CONQUER	rueful	DISMAL, SAD
route	HIGHWAY, ROAD, WAY	ruffed grouse	PARTRIDGE, PHEASANT
route used by planes (2 wds.)	AIR LANE	ruffian	THUG, RASCAL
routine	ROTE	ruffle	FRILL
routine job	CHORE	rug	MAT, CARPET
rove	ROAM, WANDER	Rugby's river	AVON
rover's friend	FIDO, MAN		

rug fuzz	**LINT**
rugged	**ROBUST, ROUGH**
rugged guy (comp. wd.)	
	HE-MAN
rugged rock	**TOR**
rug surface	**NAP**
ruin	**DESTROY, SPOIL**
ruinous	**FATAL**
rule	**GOVERN, REIGN, LAW,**
	REGULATION
rule out	**EXCLUDE**
ruler	**SOVEREIGN, GOVERNOR,**
	KING
Rumanian city	**BUCHAREST**
rumble	**THUNDER**
rumen	**CUD**
ruminant mammal	**DEER, COW**
ruminate	**REFLECT, PONDER**
rumor	**REPORT**
rumple	**WRINKLE, CRINKLE**
run	**LOPE, GALLOP, TROT,**
	FLOW, HIE, HASTEN,
	HURRY, SCURRY
run after	**CHASE, PURSUE**
run aground	**FOUNDER**
run along	**LEAVE, DEPART**
run away	**FLEE, DECAMP,**
	ESCAPE
run away to marry	**ELOPE**
run before the wind	**SCUD**
run-down	**SUMMARY**
rune	**MYSTERY, SECRET**
run-in	**QUARREL, FIGHT**
run in haste	**SCUTTLE**
run into	**MEET**
run machinery	**OPERATE**
runner	**RACER**
runnered vehicle	**SLED**
runner-up	**LOSER**
run off the track	**DERAIL**
run out	**ELAPSE, EXHAUST**
run out on	**ABANDON, DESERT**
run swiftly, as water	**FLOW**
runt	**DWARF**
runway	**RAMP**
rupture	**BURST, BREAK**
rural	**PASTORAL**
rural backcountry (sl.)	
	BOONDOCKS
rural restaurant	**INN**
ruse	**STRATAGEM, TRICK**
rush	**SURGE**
rush hour	**PEAK**
rush hour at the diner	**NOON**
rusk of wheat grains	**BRAN**
russet	**APPLE**
Russian beer	**KVASS**

Russian beet dish	**BORSCH,**
	BORSCHT
Russian citadel	**KREMLIN**
Russian city	**OREL, MOSCOW**
Russian community	**MIR**
Russian co-op	**ARTEL**
Russian desert	**TUNDRA**
Russian edict	**UKASE**
Russian emperor	**TSAR, CZAR,**
	TZAR
Russian fighter plane	**MIG**
Russian hemp	**RINE**
Russian inland sea	**ARAL**
Russian lake	**ARAL, ONEGA**
Russian log hut	**ISBA**
Russian monetary unit	**RUBLE**
Russian monk	**RASPUTIN**
Russian mountains	**URALS**
Russian news agency	**TASS**
Russian novelist Turgenev	
	IVAN
Russian peninsula	**CRIMEA**
Russian plain	**STEPPES**
Russian river	**NEVA, URAL**
Russian ruler	**TSAR, TZAR,**
	CZAR
Russian satellite	**SPUTNIK**
Russian sea	**ARAL**
Russian secret police	**N.K.V.D.,**
	O.G.P.U.
Russian tea urn	**SAMOVAR**
Russian trade union	**ARTEL**
Russian turnip	**RUTABAGA**
Russian veto word	**NIET, NYET**
Russian village	**MIR**
Russian wolfhound	**BORZOI**
rustable metal	**IRON**
rustic	**PEASANT, RURAL**
rustic retreat	**BOWER**
rustic step	**STILE**
rustic vehicle	**CART**
rustle	**SWISH**
rut	**FURROW, GROOVE**
rutabaga	**TURNIP**
ruthenium (chem. symbol)	**RU**
ruthless	**BRUTAL, CRUEL**
Ruth's husband	**BOAZ**
ruttish	**LUSTFUL**
rye fungus	**ERGOT**

S

sabbath	**SATURDAY, SUNDAY**
sabbatical	**REST, LEAVE**
saber	**SWORD**
sable	**FUR**
sabot	**SHOE**

sabotage	DESTROY
sabra	ISRAELI, CACTUS
sac	BURSA, POUCH
saccharine	SWEET
sachet	POUCH
sack	BAG, POKE, PILLAGE, LOOT
sack material	GUNNY
sacrament	RITE
sacred	HOLY, HALLOW
sacred bird of the Nile	IBIS
sacred book	BIBLE, KORAN, TALMUD, TORAH
sacred Egyptian beetle	SCARAB
sacred Egyptian bull	APIS
sacred flower of India	LOTUS
sacred fruit	LOTUS
sacred hymn	CHORALE
sacred image	ICON
sacred memento	RELIC
sacred song	MOTET, HYMN, CANTATA
sacrifice	OFFERING
sacrilegious	IMPIOUS, PROFANE
sacristy	VESTRY
sad	DOWNCAST, SORROWFUL, UNHAPPY, BLUE
saddleback	HILL, RIDGE
saddlebag	PANNIER
saddle for an elephant	HOWDAH
sad-faced hound	BASSET
safari	HUNT, TREK, JOURNEY
safe	SECURE, VAULT
safecracker	YEGG
safe from harm	SECURE
safe harbor	HAVEN
safekeeping	STORAGE
safety	SECURITY, REFUGE
saffron	YELLOW, ORANGE
saffron plant	CROCUS
sag	DROOP, WILT
saga	TALE, EPIC, EDDA, STORY
sagacious	WISE
sage	HERB, WISE
Sagebrush State	NEVADA
sage hen	GROUSE
sago	STARCH
saguaro	CACTUS
Sahara	DESERT
said further	ADDED
said positively	DECLARED
sail	NAVIGATE, JIB, MAIN
sail against the wind	TACK
sailcloth	CANVAS
sail fast	SCUD
sailing	ASEA
sailing vessel	BARK, BOAT, SHIP, SLOOP, SCHOONER, YACHT, YAWL
sailor	TAR, GOB, SEA DOG, SEAMAN, SALT
sailor's command	AVAST
sailor's holiday (2 wds.)	SHORE LEAVE
sailor's jacket	REEFER, PEA
sailor's mop	SWAB
sailor's patron saint	ELMO
sailor's song	CHANTY
sailplane	GLIDER
sail rope	SHEET
sails, to sailors	SHEETS
sail upward	SOAR
sainte (abbr.)	STE.
saint's tomb	SHRINE
Saint Vitus' dance	CHOREA
salacious	LEWD
salad fish	TUNA, SALMON, SHRIMP, HERRING, LOBSTER
salad green	CRESS, LETTUCE, ENDIVE, ESCAROLE, CHICORY WATERCRESS
salad ingredient	RADISH, TOMATO, LETTUCE, CUCUMBER, AVOCADO, ONION, SCALLION, WATERCRESS, CABBAGE
salamander	EFT, NEWT
salary	PAY, WAGE
salary increase	RAISE
sale	AUCTION
sales figure, before deductions	GROSS
sales representative	AGENT
salient	PROMINENT
salient point	FEATURE
saline	SALTY
saline drop	TEAR
saline solution	BRINE
sally of troops	SORTIE
saloon	BAR, TAVERN, PUB
salt	SEASONING, SAILOR
salt away	SAVE
saltine	CRACKER
salt lake	SALINE
salt marsh	SALINE
saltpeter	NITER
salt water	BRINE
salty	SALINE
salud	TOAST
salutary	HEALTHFUL

salutation	AVE, GREETING, HELLO	sardonic	DERISIVE, BITTER
salvage	SAVE	sash	BELT, OBI, WAISTBAND, CUMMERBUND
salve	ANOINT, BALM	sassy	IMPUDENT
salver	TRAY	Satan	DEVIL
salvo	BURST	satanic	EVIL, VILE
Samantha or Endora	WITCH	Satan's domain	HELL, INFERNO
same	IDENTICAL, LIKE	satchel	VALISE
same (Fr.)	MEME	sate	GLUT, FILL
same thing	ILK	satellite	MOON
Samoan bird	IAO	satellite of Uranus	ARIEL
Samoan city	APIA	satiate	CLOY, FILL, SATE
Samoan seaport	APIA	satire	RIDICULE, BURLESQUE
samovar	URN	satisfaction	CONTENTMENT
Samoyed	SIBERIAN, HUSKY	satisfactory	OK
samp	PORRIDGE, MUSH	satisfy	SATE, SATIATE, GLUT
samphire	GLASSWORT	Saturn	PLANET
sample	TASTE, TRY	Saturn's wife	OPS
Samuel's teacher	ELI	satyr	FAUN
sanctify	BLESS	sauce	ALEC, GRAVY
sanction	ABET, ENDORSE	saucepan	POT
sanctuary	HAVEN, REFUGE	saucer of a kind	COASTER
sanctum	RETREAT	saucer-shaped bell	GONG
sand	GRIT	saucer's mate	CUP
sandal	SHOE	saucy	PERT
Sandalwood island	SUMBA	saucy girl	MINX
sandarac tree	ARAR	sauerkraut	CABBAGE
sand hill	DUNE, DENE	Saul of Tarsus	PAUL
sand lizard	ADDA	sauna	BATH
sandpiper	REE, RUFF, TEREK	saunter	AMBLE
sand trap	HAZARD	saurian	LIZARD
Sandwich Islands	HAWAII	saute	FRY, BROWN
sandwich meat	HAM, PORK, BOLOGNA, BEEF, SPAM, SALAMI, CHICKEN	savage	FERAL
		savage island	NIUE
sandy region	DESERT, SHORE, BEACH	savannah	PLAIN
		savant	SCHOLAR
sane	RATIONAL, SENSIBLE, SOUND	save	RESCUE, ECONOMIZE, SALVAGE, SALT AWAY
sanguine	CONFIDENT	savine	JUNIPER
sanitary	HYGENIC	savior	REDEEMER
sanity	REASON	savoir-faire	TACT, POISE
Sanskrit dialect	PALI	savor	TASTE
Santa's sound	HO	savory	PIQUANT
sap	DRAIN, EXHAUST	savory dish	RELISH
sapajou	CAPUCHIN	savvy	SKILL
sapid	PALATABLE	saw	ADAGE, MAXIM
sapient	WISE	sawbones	DOCTOR, SURGEON
sapling	TREE	sawbuck	TEN
sapor	TASTE	sawfish's snout	SERRA
Saracen	ARAB, MOSLEM	sawing frame	HORSE
Sarah's original name	SARAI	saw lengthwise	RIP
Saratoga	SPA	saw-toothed	SERRATE
Sarazen	GENE	saxhorn	TUBA
sarcasm	IRONY	Saxon serf	ESNE
sarcastic	IRONIC, FACETIOUS	say	SPEAK, DECLARE
sarcastic grin	SNEER	say again	REPEAT, REITERATE
sarcastic remark	TAUNT	say casually	REMARK

say further	ADD	scenic	PICTURESQUE
saying	BYWORD, QUOTE	scenic river	RHINE
scab	STRIKEBREAKER	scenic view	SCAPE
scabbard	HOLSTER, SHEATH	scent	AROMA, ODOR, SMELL,
scalawag	RASCAL, SCAMP		PERFUME, BOUQUET,
scale	CLIMB		SPOOR
scale note	DO, RE, MI, FA,	scented bag	SACHET
	SO, LA, TI, SOL	scepter	STAFF, BATON
scallion	SHALLOT, LEEK	schedule	SCROLL, TIME,
scallop	BIVALVE, MOLLUSK		LIST, AGENDA
scalpel	KNIFE	scheme	PLAN, PLOT
scaly anteater	PANGOLIN	schism	SPLIT
scamp	RASCAL, SCALAWAG,	schnitzel	CUTLET
	ROGUE, IMP	scholar	SAVANT, STUDENT
scampi	PRAWNS, SHRIMP	scholarly	ACADEMIC, ERUDITE
scan	READ, SCRUTINIZE	school	EDUCATE, TEACH,
scandal	DISGRACE, SLANDER		COLLEGE
scandalize	SHOCK	school assignment	LESSON,
Scandinavian	LAPP, NORSE,		HOMEWORK
	FINN, SWEDE, DANE	school book	PRIMER, READER,
Scandinavian capital	OSLO,		SPELLER, TEXT
	COPENHAGEN, HELSINKI,	school cafeteria (2 wds.)	
	STOCKHOLM		LUNCH ROOM
Scandinavian god	ODIN, THOR,	school composition	ESSAY,
	WODEN, BALDER, FRIGGA,		THEME
	LOKI, BRAGI, HEL, FREYA	school (Fr.)	ECOLE, LYCEE
Scandinavian literature	SAGAS	school group	CLASS
scanty	MEAGER	school intermission	RECESS
scapegoat (2 wds.)	FALL GUY	school mark	GRADE
scar	CICATRIX	schoolmaster	DOMINIE
scarab	BEETLE	school of modern art	DADA
scarce	RARE	school of seals	POD
scarcely	HARDLY	school organization (abbr.)	
scare	FRIGHTEN, ALARM		P.T.A.
scared	AFRAID, FRIGHTENED	schoolroom item	CHALK,
scarf	NECKERCHIEF		ERASER, SLATE
scarfskin	EPIDERMIS, CUTICLE	school semester	TERM
scarlet	RED	school sport	TRACK,
scarlet songbird	TANAGER		FOOTBALL, SWIMMING
Scarlett O'Hara's home	TARA	school task	LESSON
scarp	CLIFF	school term	SEMESTER
scary	EERIE	schooner	SHIP, GLASS
scary word	BOO	science	ART
scat	BEGONE, SHOO	science-fiction	
scathing	CAUSTIC,	creature	ROBOT,
	SCORCHING		MUTANT, MONSTER,
scatter	STREW		ANDROID
scatter hay	TED	science-fiction topic	TIME,
scatter seeds	SOW		FUTURE
scatter trash	LITTER	science of government	
scatter water	SPLASH		POLITICS
scaup	DUCK	science of law	
scene	VISTA, VIEW		JURISPRUDENCE
scene of action	ARENA	science of life	BIOLOGY
scene of great disorder		science of reasoning	LOGIC
	SHAMBLES	scientific study of	
scene of the crime	VENUE	lawbreaking	CRIMINOLOGY
scenery	VIEW	scintillate	SPARKLE

scion	SON, HEIR, DESCENDANT	scow	BARGE
scissors	SHEARS	scowl	GLOWER
scoff	SNEER, JEER, DERIDE, GIBE	scrabble piece	TILE
		scramble	JUMBLE, RUSH
		scrambled eggs	OMELET
scold	JAW, NAG, CHIDE, UPBRAID, BERATE, FLAY, RANT, RAIL	scrap	FRAGMENT, ORT, SHRED
		scrape	PREDICAMENT, SCRATCH
scolding woman	SHREW	scraper	STRIGIL
sconce	BRACKET	scratch	MAR, SCORE, SCRAPE, ABRADE
scone	CAKE		
scoop	LADLE, SHOVEL	scratch out	ERASE
scoop of ice cream	DIP	scratch with nails	CLAW
scoop out water	BAIL	scrawl	SCRIBBLE
scope	RANGE	scrawny	LANKY, SKINNY
scorch	CHAR, SEAR, SINGE	scream	SHRIEK, YELL
score	TALLY, TWENTY	screech	SHRIEK
score a victory	WIN	screen	MASK
scoring play in football	TOUCHDOWN	screen from light	SHADE
		screen off	SECLUDE
scoring point	ACE, GOAL	scribble	SCRAWL
scorn	DESPISE	scribble aimlessly	DOODLE
Scot	GAEL	scribe	PENMAN
Scotch accent	BIRR, BURR	scrimp	ECONOMIZE, SAVE
Scotch beret	TAM	scrimshaw	CARVE
Scotch cake	SCONE	scriptural canticle	ODE
Scotch child	BAIRN	scroll	LIST, ROLL
scotch cocktail (2 wds.)	ROB ROY	Scrooge	MISER
		scrounge	PILFER
Scotch cup	TASS	scrub	SCOUR
Scotch Gaelic	ERSE	scruff	NAPE
Scotch hill	BRAE	scruff hair	MANE
Scotch lake	LOCH	scrumptious	DELICIOUS
Scotch musical instrument	BAGPIPE	scruple	QUALM
		scrutinize	SCAN, EYE
Scotch plaid	TARTAN	scuba man	DIVER
Scotch poet	BURNS	scud	SKIM
Scotch river	DEE	scuffle	TUSSLE, MELEE
Scotch uncle	EME	scull	OAR
Scot's tiny	WEE	sculpting plaster	GESSO
Scottish biscuit	SCONE	sculptured piece	BUST
Scottish cap	TAM	scurry	FLURRY, SCAMPER
Scottish fabric	TWEED	sea	OCEAN, CASPIAN, MEDITERRANEAN, RED, BLACK, DEAD
Scottish family	CLAN		
Scottish Gaelic	ERSE		
Scottish girl	LASS		
Scottish heath	MOOR	sea (Fr.)	MER
Scottish highlander	GAEL	sea (Ger.)	MEER
Scottish hillside	BRAE	sea anemone	POLYP
Scottish island	ARRAN	sea bird	ERN, ERNE, TERN, GULL, OSPREY
Scottish landowner	LAIRD		
Scottish skirt	KILT	sea biscuit	HARDTACK
scoundrel	RASCAL, ROGUE	sea bottom	BED
scour	SCRUB	sea calf	SEAL
scourge	BANE	seacoast	SHORE
scouring rush	HORSETAIL	sea cow	DUGONG, MANATEE
scout	SPY	sea dog	SALT, TAR, GOB, SAILOR
scouting group	PATROL		

sea duck	**EIDER**
sea eagle	**ERN, ERNE**
sea eel	**CONGER**
seafaring man	**MARINER,**
	SAILOR
sea food	**SHRIMP, LOBSTER,**
	CLAM, CRAB, CRAYFISH,
	CRAWDAD, OYSTER
sea god	**NEPTUNE**
seagoing vessel	**LINER, SHIP**
sea gull	**COB, MEW**
sea in Central Asia	**ARAL**
seal	**CLOSE, STAMP, SYMBOL**
sealant	**WAX**
sea lettuce	**ALGA, ULVA**
seal's limb	**FLIPPER**
seam	**SUTURE, LINE**
sea mammal	**MANATEE,**
	WHALE, DOLPHIN, SEAL,
	PORPOISE, GRAMPUS,
	ORC
seaman	**MARINE, TAR, GOB,**
	SAILOR
seaman's chapel	**BETHEL**
sea mile	**NAUT**
sea monster	**SERPENT**
seamstress	**DRESSMAKER**
seamy	**SQUALID, SORDID**
seance sound	**RAP**
sea nymph	**NEREID**
sea onion	**SQUILL**
seaport in Alaska	**NOME**
seaport in Algeria	**ORAN**
seaport in Arabia	**ADEN**
seaport in Australia	**BRISBANE**
seaport in Bombay	**SURAT**
seaport in Brazil	**RECIFE**
seaport in Chile	**ARICA**
seaport in Italy	**GENOA,**
	NAPLES
seaport in Oregon	**ASTORIA**
seaport in Samoa	**APIA**
seaport in West Africa	**DAKAR**
seaport of the Philippines	
	ILOILO
sear	**SCORCH, SINGE, CHAR**
search	**HUNT, SEEK, PROBE**
searchlight	**BEAM**
search out	**FERRET**
sea robber	**PIRATE,**
	BUCCANEER
sea's ebb and flow	**TIDE**
sea shell	**CONCH**
seashore	**COAST, BEACH**
seashore attraction	**BEACH,**
	SURF
seashore bird	**GULL**
seashore feature	**SAND**

seaside	**SHORE, COAST**
sea soldier	**MARINE**
season	**SALT**
seasonable	**TIMELY**
seasonal song	**NOEL, CAROL**
seasoned egg dish	
(2 wds.)	**SPANISH OMELET**
seasoning	**CONDIMENT, SALT,**
	PEPPER, SPICE, HERB,
	MACE, SAGE, OREGANO,
	THYME, ROSEMARY,
	CHERVIL, TARRAGON,
	MUSTARD, NUTMEG, DILL,
	GARLIC, CAYENNE,
	PAPRIKA, CLOVE, BASIL,
	BAY LEAF
season of fasting	**LENT**
season of the year	**WINTER,**
	SUMMER, SPRING,
	AUTUMN, FALL
sea spray	**SPINDRIFT**
sea squirt	**ASCIDIAN**
sea swallow	**TERN**
sea swell	**SURF**
seat	**BENCH, CHAIR**
sea term	**AHOY, BELAY**
seat of justice	**BANC**
sea unicorn	**NARWHAL**
sea vessel	**STEAMER, TANKER**
sea wall	**LEVEE**
sea wave	**BREAKER**
seaweed	**ALGA, ALGAE, KELP**
seaweed product	**IODINE**
seaweed substance	**AGAR**
sea wolf	**PIRATE**
seaworthy	**STURDY**
seckel	**PEAR**
seclude	**SCREEN**
secluded	**ALOOF, APART**
secluded valley	**GLEN, VALE,**
	DALE
seclusion	**PRIVACY**
second	**INSTANT, MOMENT,**
	MIN
secondary school	**PREP, HIGH**
secondhand	**USED**
second lieutenant (sl.)	
	SHAVETAIL
second-mentioned	**LATTER**
second of a series	**BETA**
second of two	**OTHER**
second order of angels	
	CHERUB
second person	**YOU**
second-placer (comp. wd.)	
	RUNNER-UP
second selling	**RESALE**
secrecy	**PRIVACY**

secret	MYSTERY	seek	HUNT, SEARCH
secret agent	SPY	seek ambitiously	ASPIRE
secretaire	DESK	seeker of Moby Dick	AHAB
secretary	AMANUENSIS, STENO	seek for by entreaty	SOLICIT
		seel	CLOSE, BLIND
secretary's note	MEMO	seem	APPEAR
secret Chinese society	TONG	seeming	APPARENT
secrete	HIDE	seemingly	QUASI
secreting organ	GLAND	seemly	PROPER, FAIR
secretive	SILENT	seep	OOZE
secret language	CODE	seer	PROPHET
secret scheme	PLOT, CABAL	seeress	SIBYL
secret store	CACHE	seesaw	TEETER
sect	DENOMINATION	seethe	BOIL
sectarian	PAROCHIAL	segment	PART
section	AREA, PART	segment of a curve	ARC
sector	DISTRICT, SEGMENT	sego	LILY, BULB
secular	LAIC	segregate	ISOLATE, SEPARATE
secure	SAFE	seine	NET
secure in place	ANCHOR	seize	GRAB, NAB, GRIP, TAKE, GRASP
securing device	CLEVIS, VISE		
securing pin	TOGGLE	seize forcibly	USURP
security	GAGE, BOND	seizure	ATTACK
sedan	CAR, AUTO	seldom	RARELY
sedate	DIGNIFIED, SOBER, STAID	select	PICK OUT, CHOOSE, ELECT, OPT
sedative	SECONAL, SOOTHING	select group	ELITE
sedentary	FIXED, SEATED	selection	CHOICE
seder	FEAST, ORDER	selective service	DRAFT
sediment	LEES, SILT	self	EGO
sedition	TREASON	self-acting	AUTOMATIC
seditious	INSURGENT, DISLOYAL	self-centered	EGOCENTRIC
seduce	ENTICE, ABDUCT	self-confidence	POISE, APLOMB
seducer	SIREN	self-esteem	PRIDE, EGO
sedulous	BUSY	self-evident	CLEAR
see	BISHOPRIC, ENVISION, OBSERVE, DISCERN, VISUALIZE, WITNESS, PERCEIVE, UNDERSTAND, ESPY	selfish individual	EGOIST
		selfless	ALTRUISTIC
		self-possession	POISE
		self-reproach	REMORSE
		self-righteous person	PRIG
seecatch	SEAL	selfsame	IDENTICAL
seed	GERM, GRAIN, OVULE, SOW	self-satisfied	SMUG
		self-sufficient	INDEPENDENT
seed appendage	ARIL	sell	VEND, RETAIL
seed container	POD	sell direct to consumer	RETAIL
seed covering	ARIL, HULL, POD	selling place	MARKET
		sell out	BETRAY
seedless raisin	SULTANA	semblance	LIKENESS
seedlet	SPORE	semester	TERM
seedling	PLANT	semi-diameter	RADIUS
seed of a mighty tree	ACORN	Seminole chief	OSCEOLA
seed oysters	SPAT	semiprecious gem	OPAL, AGATE, GARNET
seed planter	SOWER		
seedpod	CARPEL, PISTIL	Semite	ARAB, JEW
seed shrimp	OSTRACOD	Semitic deity	BAAL
seedsman	SOWER	Semitic language	ARAMAIC, HEBREW, ARABIC
seedy	SHABBY		

semolina	**MEAL, FLOUR**	series of names	**LIST, ROLL,**
semper	**ALWAYS**		**ROSTER, ROTA**
senate	**ASSEMBLY, COUNCIL**	series of propositions in	
senate attendant	**PAGE**	logic	**SORTIES**
send	**TRANSMIT, DISPATCH,**	series of rooms	**SUITE**
	MAIL	series of steps	**STAIRS**
send a letter	**MAIL**	series of tones	**SCALE**
send away	**DISPATCH**	serin	**BIRD**
send back	**REMAND**	serious	**SOBER, SOLEMN**
send flying	**ROUT**	seriousness	**GRAVITY**
send forth	**EMIT**	sermon	**PREACH, DISCOURSE**
send into exile	**DEPORT**	sermon giver	**PREACHER**
send off	**MAIL, DISMISS**	sermon topic	**TEXT**
send payment	**REMIT**	serpent	**SNAKE, ASP**
senile	**OLD, INFIRM**	serpentine	**SNAKY**
senility	**DOTAGE**	serpent's tooth	**FANG**
senior	**ELDER, OLDER**	serrate	**NOTCHED**
senorita's aunt	**TIA**	serve as a lesson	**TEACH**
sensation	**SENSE, FEELING**	serve food	**CATER**
sensational	**LURID**	server	**TRAY**
sense	**FEEL**	serve tea	**POUR**
senseless	**INANE**	service charge	**FEE**
sense of sight	**VISION**	service station	**GARAGE**
sense of taste	**PALATE**	servile	**MENIAL**
sensible	**SANE**	serving bowl	**TUREEN**
sensitive	**TENDER**	serving dish	**PLATTER**
sentence	**DECREE, JUDGMENT**	serving spoon	**LADLE**
sententious	**CONCISE, TERSE**	serving vessel	**TEAPOT, TRAY**
sentimental person		sesame plant	**TIL**
(colloq.)	**SOFTY**	set	**CLIQUE, GEL, JELL,**
sentinel	**GUARD**		**HARDEN, KIT**
separate	**PART, RIFT, APART,**	seta	**BRISTLE**
	DIVIDE, DETACH	set afloat	**LAUNCH**
separate article	**ITEM**	set aside	**TABLE**
separate from	**ALOOF**	set at liberty	**FREE**
separate from others	**ISOLATE**	set back	**HINDER**
separate metal from		set fire to	**IGNITE, KINDLE**
ore	**SMELT**	set free	**RELEASE, BAIL OUT**
sepia	**DUN, PIGMENT**	Seth's father	**ADAM**
sept	**CLAN**	Seth's son	**ENOS(H)**
sequence of rulers	**DYNASTY**	set into motion	**ACTUATE**
sequestered	**SOLITARY**	set of actors	**CAST**
sequoia	**TREE, REDWOOD**	set of garments	**SUIT**
seraglio	**HAREM**	set of inquiries	
Serb	**EUROPEAN, SLAV**		**QUESTIONNAIRE**
sere	**WITHERED**	set of matched furniture	**SUIT,**
serene	**CALM, PLACID,**		**SUITE**
	TRANQUIL	set of organ pipes	**STOP**
serenity	**COMPOSURE**	set of principles	**CODE**
serf	**ESNE, PEON**	set of three	**TRIO**
serf of Sparta	**HELOT**	set of tools	**KIT**
series	**SEQUENCE**	set of two	**DUAD, PAIR, DUO,**
series of boat races	**REGATTA**		**COUPLE, DUET, BRACE**
series of contests	**TOURNEY,**	set on fire	**IGNITE**
	TOURNAMENT	set out	**START**
series of happenings		setting	**LOCALE**
(3 wds.)	**CHAIN OF EVENTS**	settle	**DECIDE, DETERMINE**
series of heroic events	**EPOS**	settle a bill	**PAY**

settle a question	**DECIDE**	Shakespearean king	**LEAR,**
settle by intercession	**MEDIATE**		**HENRY, RICHARD, JOHN**
settled	**SEDATE**	Shakespearean poem	**ODE,**
settlement	**COLONY**		**SONNET**
settlement in Greenland	**ETAH,**	Shakespearean sprite	**ARIEL**
	THULE	Shakespearean villain	**IAGO**
settler	**PIONEER**	Shakespeare's river	**AVON**
settlings	**DREGS, SEDIMENT**	Shakespeare's wife	**ANNE**
set-to	**FIGHT**	shake the tail	**WAG**
set up	**ESTABLISH**	shake up	**JAR, SHOCK**
setup	**ARRANGEMENT**	shaky	**WOBBLY**
set upon	**ATTACK**	shale	**ROCK**
seven days	**WEEK**	shallow	**SUPERFICIAL**
seventh day	**SABBATH**	shallow area	**SHOAL**
sever	**CUT, SPLIT, DISUNITE**	shallow dish	**PLATE**
several	**VARIOUS, DIVERSE**	shallow river crossing	**FORD**
severe	**STERN, HARSH**	shalom	**GREETING, PEACE**
severe experience	**ORDEAL**	sham	**PRETEND, TRICK, FAKE,**
severely	**SHARPLY**		**COUNTERFEIT, BOGUS**
severe snowstorm	**BLIZZARD**	shamas	**SEXTON**
sew	**BASTE, STITCH**	shame	**FIE, DISHONOR,**
sewage	**WASTE**		**DISGRACE**
sewing implement	**NEEDLE,**	shameless	**BRAZEN**
	DARNER	shamrock	**CLOVER**
sewing machine inventor	**HOWE**	Shandy's creator	**STERNE**
sew lightly	**BASTE**	Shangri-La	**UTOPIA**
sex	**GENDER**	shanty	**HUT**
sgt.	**NCO**	shape	**FIGURE, FORM**
shabby	**SEEDY**	shaped like an egg	**OVATE,**
shabby clothing	**RAGS**		**OVAL**
shack	**CABIN, HUT, HOVEL**	shaped with an ax	**HEWN**
shackle	**FETTER, CHAIN**	shapeless	**AMORPHIC**
shade	**COLOR, HUE, TINT,**	shaping form	**MOLD**
	SHADOW, GHOST,	shard	**FRAGMENT**
	GOBLIN, SPOOK	share	**PARTICIPATE,**
shaded walk	**ARBOR, MALL**		**PORTION, PART**
shade of difference	**NUANCE**	shark	**GATA**
shade of green	**KELLY, OLIVE,**	sharp	**KEEN, ACUTE**
	LEAF, PEA	sharp bark	**YIP, YAP, YELP**
shade of red	**CORAL, CERISE,**	sharp bite	**NIP**
	CRIMSON, SCARLET	sharp blow	**SLAP**
shade of tan	**ECRU, BEIGE,**	sharp disc on a plow	**COLTER**
	KHAKI	sharpen	**HONE, WHET**
shade tree	**ASH, ELM, OAK,**	sharp end	**POINT**
	ELDER	sharpener	**EDGER, STROP**
shadow	**SHADE**	sharp flavor	**TANG**
shadowbox	**SPAR**	sharp mountain ridge	**ARETE**
shady	**DISHONEST, DEVIOUS**	sharpness	**EDGE**
shaft	**POLE**	sharp of mind	**KEEN**
shag	**NAP, PILE**	sharp pain	**STING**
shaganappi	**RAWHIDE**	sharp pointed	**ACUTE**
shaggy	**FURRY, UNKEMPT**	sharp projection	**BARB, JAG,**
shah country	**IRAN**		**SNAG**
shake	**QUIVER, TREMBLE,**	sharp rebuke	**SLAP**
	SHIVER, QUAKE	sharpshooter	**MARKSMAN**
shakedown	**EXTORTION**	sharp-sighted	**ASTUTE**
Shakespearean hero	**ROMEO,**	sharp sound	**PING**
	OTHELLO	sharp spear	**LANCE**

sharp tap	**RAP**	sheltered side	**LEE**
sharp taste	**TANG, NIP**	shelter for bees	**HIVE**
shasta	**DAISY**	shepherd	**PASTOR**
shatter	**DASH, SMASH**	shepherd's pipe	**REED**
shave	**PARE**	sherbet	**ICE**
shavetail	**LIEUTENANT**	sheriff's badge	**STAR**
shaving tool	**RAZOR**	sheriff's band	**POSSE**
shawl	**WRAP, STOLE, SCARF**	sherry	**WINE**
Shawnee Indian chief		shield	**PROTECT, COVER**
	TECUMSEH	shield boss	**UMBO**
shay	**CARRIAGE**	shield from harm	**PROTECT**
she (Fr.)	**ELLE**	shift responsibility (3 wds.)	
sheaf	**BUNDLE, CLUSTER**		**PASS THE BUCK**
shear	**CLIP**	shimmer	**GLEAM, GLINT**
sheath	**SCABBARD, GLOVE**	shin	**SHANK**
sheave	**PULLEY**	shinbone	**TIBIA**
she-bear (Lat.)	**URSA**	shine	**GLEAM, GLOW, GLOSS,**
shed	**HUT, LEAN-TO**		**RADIATE, GLISTEN**
shed feathers	**MOLT, MOULT**	Shinto temple	**SHA**
shed light	**SHINE**	shiny fabric	**SATIN**
shed tears	**SOB, WEEP, CRY**	ship	**BOAT**
sheen	**LUSTER**	ship biscuit	**HARDTACK**
sheep	**EWE, RAM, LAMB**	ship boarding platform	
sheep enclosure	**FOLD**		**GANGPLANK**
sheeplike	**OVINE**	ship bow	**PROW**
sheep's bleat	**BAA, MAA**	shipbuilding wood	**TEAK**
sheep's child	**LAMB**	ship canvas	**SAIL**
sheep's coat	**FLEECE**	ship deck	**POOP, ORLOP**
sheep's hair	**WOOL**	ship deserter	**RAT**
sheep shelter	**COTE**	shipmates	**HEARTIES**
sheepskin	**PELT, DIPLOMA**	ship-model housing	**BOTTLE**
sheepskin shoe	**PAC**	ship mop	**SWAB**
sheer	**STEEP**	ship of Noah	**ARK**
sheer curtain	**SCRIM**	ship of the Argonauts	**ARGO**
sheer fabric	**TOILE, TULLE,**	ship of the desert	**CAMEL**
	VOILE	ship part	**KEEL, RUDDER**
sheerlegs	**SHEARS**	shipping box	**CRATE**
sheet	**ROPE, SHROUD**	shipping unit	**TON**
sheeting fabric	**PERCALE,**	ship prison	**BRIG**
	LINEN, MUSLIN	ship record	**LOG**
sheet of glass	**PANE**	ship's backbone	**KEEL**
sheets and tablecloths	**LINEN**	ship's bed	**BUNK**
sheik's ladies	**HAREM**	ship's boat	**DINGHY**
sheik's land	**ARABIA**	ship's body	**HULL**
sheldrake	**MERGANSER**	ship's cargo space	**HOLD**
shelf	**LEDGE**	ship's clerk	**PURSER**
shell	**ECTOSKELETON**	ship's commanding officer	
shellac	**LAC**		**CAPTAIN**
Shelley	**POET**	ship's complement	**CREW**
Shelley work	**ODE**	ship's contour (naut.)	**HANCE**
shellfish	**ABALONE, CLAM,**	ship's diary	**LOG**
	CRAB, SHRIMP	ship section	**BILGE, HOLD,**
shell out	**PAY**		**GALLEY**
shelter	**HAVEN, LEE**	ship's floor	**DECK**
shelter (Fr.)	**ABRI**	ship-shaped clock	**NEF**
sheltered from wind	**ALEE**	ship's kitchen	**GALLEY**
sheltered glen	**DELL, DALE**	ship's longboat	**GIG**
sheltered nook	**COVE**	ship's lowest deck	**ORLOP**

ship's master	**CAPTAIN**	short	**BRIEF, SMALL**
ship's officer	**MATE, PURSER**	shortage	**DEFICIT**
ship's parking place	**MOORING,**	short and pointed	**TERSE**
	BERTH	short and pudgy	
ship's petty officer	**BOSUN**	(comp. wd.)	**ROLY-POLY**
ship's pole	**MAST, SPAR**	short article	**ITEM**
ship's rope	**HALYARD,**	short blunt end	**STUB**
	HAWSER	short boot	**SHOE**
ship's station	**BERTH**	short business trip	**ERRAND**
ship's tiller	**HELM**	shortcoming	**FAULT**
ship's track	**WAKE**	short dagger	**DIRK**
ships under unified control		short dash	**HYPHEN**
	FLEET	shorten	**ABRIDGE**
shirk	**EVADE**	shortening	**LARD**
shirtwaist	**BLOUSE**	short explosive sound	**POP**
shiver	**SHAKE, TREMBLE**	short firearm	**PISTOL**
shoal	**BANK, REEF**	short for gentleman	**GENT**
shoat	**PIGLET**	short for hurrah	**RAH**
shock	**STARTLE, IMPACT**	short gaiter	**SPAT**
shoe	**FOOTGEAR, SLIPPER,**	short haircut	**BOB, PIXIE,**
	BROGAN, FOOTWEAR,		**BUTCH, CREW**
	OXFORD, PUMP, GILLIE,	shorthand	**STENO**
	SANDAL, LOAFER,	short intermission	**RECESS**
	SNEAKER, SPECTATOR,	short jacket	**ETON, BOLERO**
	CLOG, MULE	short lance	**DART, DAGGER**
shoe bottom	**SOLE**	short-legged hound	**BASSET**
shoe fastener	**LACING, LACES,**	short letter	**NOTE, MEMO**
	BUTTONS, BUCKLES	short-lived style	**FAD**
shoe form	**LAST, TREE**	shortly	**ANON, SOON**
shoe grip	**CLEAT**	short note	**LINE**
shoemaker	**COBBLER**	short pencil	**STUB**
shoe material	**LEATHER**	short period of calm	**LULL**
shoe part	**HEEL, TOE, SOLE,**	short pin	**PEG**
	UPPER, TONGUE	short playlet	**SKIT**
shoestring	**LACE, POTATO**	short poem	**SONNET**
shoe tie	**LACING**	short race	**DASH, SPRINT**
shoji	**PANEL, SCREEN**	shortsighted	**MYOPIC**
shoo	**SCAT**	short skirt	**MINI**
shoofly	**PIE**	short sleep	**NAP, SNOOZE,**
shoot	**TWIG**		**CAT NAP, FORTY WINKS,**
shoot from ambush	**SNIPE**		**DOZE**
shoot game	**POT**	short sock	**ANKLET**
shooting capacity	**FIREPOWER**	short song	**DITTY**
shooting iron	**GUN, PISTOL**	short-spoken	**LACONIC**
shooting marble	**TAW**	short story	**CONTE**
shooting match (Fr.)	**TIR**	short swim	**DIP**
shooting star	**METEOR**	short sword	**ESTOC**
shoot out	**DART**	short-tailed rodent	**HAMSTER**
shop	**STORE, MART, MARKET**	short telegraphic click	**DOT**
shopper's convenience		short-tempered	**EDGY, TESTY**
(2 wds.)	**CHARGE ACCOUNT**	short thick piece	**CHUNK**
shopping center	**MALL**	short tree shoot	**SPUR**
shopping reminder	**LIST**	short visit	**CALL**
shore	**COAST, SEASIDE,**	shortwave	**RADIO**
	BEACH, STRAND	Shoshonean Indian	**UTE**
shore bird	**AVOCET, HERON,**	shotgun	**RIFLE**
	RAIL, TERN	shoulder band	**STRAP**
shore recess	**COVE, INLET**	shoulder blade	**SCAPULA**

shoulder of a road	BERM	shroud	SHEET, VEIL
shoulder ornament	EPAULET	Shrove Tuesday	MARDI GRAS
shoulder scarf	SHAWL, STOLE	shrub	BUSH, PLANT
shout	SCREAM, YELL, HOLLER	shrub of the southwest	
shout of applause	CHEER,		MESQUITE
	BRAVO	shrug off	DISMISS
shout of contempt	HOOT	shuck	SHELL, HUSK
shout of good will (Ital.)	VIVA	shudder	SHAKE, TREMBLE
shout to	HAIL	shuffle along	MOSEY
shout with joy	SING	shun	AVOID
shove	PUSH	shush	HUSH, QUIET
shovel	SPADE	shut	CLOSE
show	DEMONSTRATE, EXHIBIT	shutdown	LAYOFF
show a decline	DROP	shut noisily	SLAM
show appreciation	APPLAUD,	shut out	DEBAR
	CLAP	shutter	BLIND, JALOUSIE
showcase	EXHIBIT	shuttlecock	BIRD
show disapproval	HISS,	shut up	SILENCE
	SNEER, SNORT	shy	COY, TIMID, MODEST,
show displeasure	POUT		BASHFUL
shower	RAIN	shylock	USURER
shower down	CASCADE	Siam	THAILAND
showery	RAINY	Siamese	TAI
showery month	APRIL	Siamese capital	BANGKOK
show favorable reaction		Siamese coin	ATT
	RESPOND	Siamese language	THAI, TAI
showing courage	SPIRITED	Siamese river	ME NAM
showing good judgment	SANE,	sib	RELATIVE
	SENSIBLE, LOGICAL	Siberian city	IRKUTSK
Show-Me State	MISSOURI	Siberian gulf	OB
show of affection	KISS	Siberian mongoloid	TARTAR
show of hands	VOTE	Siberian treeless tract	STEPPE
show ostentatiously	FLAUNT	sibilant sound	HISS
show plainly	EVINCE	sibling	BROTHER, SISTER
show to a seat	USHER	sibyl	SEERESS
show up	SURPASS	sic	THUS
showy	SPORTY	Sicilian harbor	PALERMO
showy clothes	FINERY	Sicilian resort	ENNA
showy covering	VENEER	Sicilian volcano	ETNA
showy feather	PLUME	sick	ILL
showy flower	PEONY, ROSE,	sick bay	INFIRMARY,
	MUM		DISPENSARY
showy red flower	POINSETTIA	sicken	AIL
shred	FRAGMENT, STRIP,	sickly	FEEBLE, INFIRM
	RAG, TATTER, TEAR	Siddhartha	BUDDHA
shrew	VIXEN	side	FLANK
shrewd	ASTUTE, WILY,	side bone	RIB
	CLEVER, WISE, SLY	side by side	TOGETHER
shriek	SCREAM, SCREECH	side dish of greens	SALAD
shrill	SHARP, KEEN	sidekick	COMPANION,
shrill and piping tone	REEDY		PARTNER
shrill cry	SCREECH	side of a room	WALL
shrimp	PRAWN	side post of a doorway	JAMB
shrine	TOMB, ALTAR	sidereal hour angle	
shriner's hat	FEZ	(abbr.)	SHA
shrink	SHRIVEL	sidestep	AVOID, ELUDE,
shrink in fear	COWER		EVADE, SLIDE, GLIDE
shrivel	PARCH, SHRINK	sidetrack	DIVERT, DIGRESS

sideways	ASKANCE
sidewinder	SNAKE, RATTLER
sidewise	LATERAL
sidle along	EDGE
siesta	NAP
sieve	SIFT, STRAINER
sift	DREDGE, SIEVE
sigh	EXHALE, SOB
sight	VISION, SCENE
sight for travelers	RUINS
sight organ	EYE
sight-seeing trip	TOUR
sigil	SEAL, SIGNET
sign	BILLBOARD, BILL, NEON
signal	CUE
signal fire	FLARE
sign at a sellout	S.R.O.
signature	MARK
signet	SEAL, STAMP
significant	IMPORTANT
signify	MEAN, DENOTE, CONNOTE
sign of approaching cold	SNEEZE, SNIFFLE
sign of assent	NOD
sign of disapproval	BOO
sign of fire	SMOKE
sign of full house	S.R.O.
sign of life	PULSE
sign of sorrow	SOB
sign of the future	OMEN
sign of the times	TREND
sign of the zodiac	ARIES, LEO, PISCES, AQUARIUS, GEMINI, CANCER, SCORPIO, TAURUS, LIBRA, VIRGO, SAGITTARIUS, CAPRICORN
sign up	ENROLL, ENLIST
silence	HUSH, STILLNESS
silent	MUM, QUIET, MUTE, TACIT
silhouette	SHADOW
silicate	MICA
silk cotton	KAPOK
silken	SMOOTH
silk fabric	CREPE, GROS
silk net	TULLE
silk voile	NINON
silkworm	ERI, ERIA
sill	LEDGE
silly	APISH, FOOLISH, INANE, GOOFY
silly action	FOLLY
silly bird	GOOSE
silly talk	DRIVEL, PRATTLE
silt	SEDIMENT

silt remover	DREDGE
silver (chem. abbr.)	AG.
Silver State	NEVADA
silvery fish	SMELT
s'il vous plait	PLEASE
simian	APE
similar	AKIN, ALIKE
similar in kind	SUCH, LIKE, AKIN
similarity	ANALOGY, LIKENESS
similarly defined word	SYNONYM
similar to	LIKE
simile	LIKE, AS
simmer	STEW
simpatico	CONGENIAL
simper	SMIRK
simple	STUPID, EASY, MERE, PLAIN
simple song	LAY
simple story	PARABLE
simple substance	ELEMENT
simple sugar	KETOSE
simpleton	NEDDY, OAF, DOLT, DUNCE
simulate	FAKE
sin	ERR, TRANSGRESSION
Sindbad's bird	ROC
since	AS, BECAUSE
sincere	HONEST
sinew	TENDON, THEW
sinewy	ROPY, WIRY
sinful	EVIL, IMMORAL
sing	CROON, VOCALIZE, WARBLE, CHANT
singer Ames	ED
singer Bennett	TONY
singer Boone	PAT
singer Collins	JUDY
singer Como	PERRY
singer Crosby	BING
singer Fitzgerald	ELLA
singer Garland	JUDY
singer Horne	LENA
singer Ives	BURL
singer Jolson	AL
singer Martin	DEAN, TONY
singer Peerce	JAN
singer Presley	ELVIS
singer Sinatra	FRANK
singer's list	REPERTOIRE
singer Stevens	RISE
singer Streisand	BARBRA
singer Torme	MEL
singer Williams	ANDY
singing bird	LARK
singing syllable	TRA, LA

singing voice	**ALTO, BASS,**	situation	**POSITION,**
	SOPRANO, TENOR,		**PREDICAMENT**
	BARITONE, CONTRALTO	Siva's consort	**DEVI**
single	**ONE, SOLE**	six-sided figure	**CUBE**
single-handed	**UNAIDED**	sixth sense (abbr.)	**ESP**
single-hearted	**SINCERE**	sixty-five usually (2 wds.)	
single-masted vessel	**SLOOP**		**RETIREMENT AGE**
singleness	**UNITY**	sixty minutes	**HOUR**
single step	**STAIR**	size	**DIMENSION**
singlestick	**FENCING**	size of paper	**DEMY**
single thing	**ONE, UNIT, ITEM**	size of type	**ELITE, PICA**
single time	**ONCE**	sizzle	**STEAM**
singleton	**LONER, ONE**	skate	**STINGRAY, RAY**
sing like Bing	**CROON**	skate blade	**RUNNER**
singly (4 wds.)		skating arena	**RINK**
	ONE AT A TIME	skean	**DAGGER, DIRK**
sing Swiss style	**YODEL**	skein of yarn	**HANK**
singular	**UNIQUE**	skeleton part	**BONE, SKULL,**
sing under the breath	**HUM**		**RIB, AITCHBONE,**
sinister	**EVIL**		**TIBIA, ULNA**
sinister look	**LEER**	skeptic	**AGNOSTIC**
sinitic	**CHINESE**	sketch	**PLAN, DRAW, INK**
sink	**BASIN, SUBMERGE**	sketcher of comic pictures	
sink down	**SAG, DROOP**		**CARTOONIST**
sink plug	**STOPPER**	sketch through thin paper	
sinuous	**SNAKY**		**TRACE**
sinus cavity	**ANTRUM,**	sketchy	**ROUGH**
Siouan Indian	**OTOE**	skewer	**PIN, ROD**
Siouan language	**TETON,**	skid	**SLIDE**
	DAKOTA	skiff	**BOAT**
Sioux Indian	**CROW, OTOE,**	skilful	**ADEPT, ADROIT**
	TETON	skill	**ART, CRAFT, TALENT**
Sioux State	**NORTH DAKOTA**	skilled	**ABLE, ADEPT, DEFT**
sip	**TASTE**	skillet	**PAN, FRYPAN**
siphon	**TUBE, SUCTION**	skim	**GLANCE, GLIDE**
sire	**FATHER, PROGENITOR**	skimpy	**SCANTY**
siren	**CHARMER, ALARM**	skin	**PELT, HIDE, RIND,**
sire's mate	**DAM**		**PEEL, DERMIS**
sir (Sp.)	**SENOR**	skin ailment	**ACNE**
sir, in India	**SAHIB**	skin decoration	**TATTOO**
sir, in Malaya	**TUAN**	skin diver's attire	
sirloin	**STEAK**	(2 wds.)	**WET SUIT**
sisal	**HEMP**	skinflint	**MISER**
sismo	**SEXTO**	skink	**LIZARD**
sisterhood	**SORORITY**	skin layer	**DERMA**
sister of Orestes	**ELECTRA**	skinned (dial.)	**SKUN**
sister's daughter	**NIECE**	skinny	**THIN, LEAN**
sit	**REST, ROOST**	skin opening	**PORE**
sit back	**RELAX**	skin problem	**ACNE**
sit-down	**STRIKE**	skin tone	**TAN**
site	**LOCATION**	skip	**LEAP, OMIT**
site of 1898 Alsakan		skip on water	**DAP**
gold rush	**NOME**	skip over	**ELIDE**
site of witch trials	**SALEM**	skipper	**CAPTAIN**
sit for a portrait	**POSE**	skipper butterfly	**HESPERID**
sitsang	**TIBET**	skipper of the Pequod	**AHAB**
sitting room	**PARLOR**	ski race	**SLALOM**
situate	**LOCATE**	skirl	**PIPE**

skirmish	**MELEE**	sleep	**NAP, DOZE, REST,**
skirt	**MIDI, MINI, KILT,**		**SLUMBER**
	DIRNDL, BROOMSTICK,	sleeper	**PULLMAN**
	GORE	sleep image	**DREAM**
skirt edge	**HEM**	sleep inducer	**SEDATIVE**
skirt feature	**SLIT, PLEAT,**	sleeping	**DORMANT**
	WAISTBAND	sleeping place	**BED, BEDROOM**
skit	**SKETCH**	sleepless	**ALERT, AWAKE**
skittish	**JITTERY, JUMPY**	sleep lightly	**DOZE**
skittish horse	**SHIER**	sleep noisily	**SNORE**
skoal	**TOAST**	sleepwalker	**SOMNAMBULIST**
skulk	**LURK**	sleepwear	**PAJAMAS,**
skull	**CRANIUM**		**NIGHTGOWN, NIGHTIE,**
skunk	**POLECAT**		**NIGHTSHIRT**
skunk-like animal	**CIVET**	sleepy	**DROWSY**
sky	**HEAVEN**	sleeve	**ARM**
sky-blue	**AZURE**	sleeveless garment	**CAPE,**
skye	**TERRIER**		**CLOAK, VEST**
sky twinkler	**STAR**	sleeve part	**CUFF**
skyward	**UP, ALOFT**	sleigh	**SLED, PUNG**
slack	**LOOSE**	sleight of hand	**MAGIC,**
slacken	**ABATE, RELENT,**		**HOCUS-POCUS**
	RETARD, EASE, LET UP,	slender	**SKINNY, SVELTE,**
	LOOSEN		**LEAN, SLIM,**
slackening bar on a loom			**TENUOUS, THIN**
	EASER	slender candle	**TAPER**
slacks	**PANTS**	slenderize	**REDUCE**
slag	**DROSS, SCORIA**	slender pinnacle	**EPI**
slake	**ALLAY, QUENCH**	slender pipe	**TUBE**
slam	**BANG**	sleuth	**DETECTIVE**
slander	**ASPERSE, DEFAME**	slice	**CARVE, CUT**
slanderous gossip	**DIRT**	slice a roast	**CARVE**
slang	**CANT, ARGOT**	slice of meat	**CUTLET, STEAK,**
slangy affirmative	**YEP, YEAH,**		**CHOP**
	OKAY	slice of toasted bread	**RUSK**
slangy denial	**NOPE**	slick	**SLIPPERY, SMOOTH**
slant	**BIAS, INCLINE, TILT,**	slicker	**RAINCOAT**
	SLOPE, ATTITUDE	slide	**SLIP, SKID, GLIDE,**
slanting	**SLOPING, OBLIQUE**		**SLITHER**
slap	**CUFF, REBUFF, SMACK**	slight	**SMALL, SLIM**
slap-happy	**GIDDY**	slight coloring	**TINT**
slash	**CUT, LASH**	slight depression	**DENT**
slate	**BLACKBOARD, TILE**	slightest	**LEAST**
slattern	**CARELESS**	slighting remark	**SLUR**
slaughter	**CARNAGE, BUTCHER**	slight intentionally	**SNUB**
slaughterhouse	**ABATTOIR**	slightly open	**AJAR**
Slav	**CROAT, SERB**	slightly tapering	**TERETE**
slave	**SERF, ESNE, PEON,**	slightly wet	**DAMP, MOIST**
	BONDSMAN, DRUDGE	slight quarrel	**TIFF, SPAT**
slave owner	**MASTER**	slight sound	**PEEP**
slaver	**SLOBBER, DROOL**	slight taste	**SIP**
slavery	**BONDAGE**	slim	**SLENDER, THIN,**
Slavic language	**CROAT**		**LEAN, SVELTE**
slay	**KILL**	slime	**MUD, OOZE**
slayer of Goliath	**DAVID**	sling	**CAST, FLING**
sled	**COASTER, TOBOGGAN**	slink	**LURK**
sleek	**LUSTROUS**	slinky	**STEALTHY, FURTIVE**
sleek black animal	**PANTHER**	slip	**SLIDE**

slip backwards	**RELAPSE,**	sly fellow	**FOX**
	REGRESS	sly glance	**LEER**
slip by	**ELAPSE**	slyly spiteful	**CATTY**
slipknot	**NOOSE**	sly trick	**WILE**
slip-on garment	**TUNIC**	smack	**SLAP**
slipper	**MULE, SHOE, SCUFF**	small	**LITTLE, PETITE,**
slippery	**EELY, ICY**		**TINY, TEENY, WEE**
slipshod	**SLOVENLY**	small African antelope	**ORIBI**
slip sideways	**SKID**	small amount	**BIT, DAB, DRAM,**
slipsole	**INSOLE**		**IOTA, MITE, MORSEL**
slip the memory	**FORGET**	small anchor	**KEDGE**
slip-up	**ERROR, MISHAP**	small and trim	**PETITE**
slit	**CRACK, SPLIT**	small and unimportant	**DINKY,**
slither	**SLIDE**		**TRIVIAL**
sliver of wood	**SPLINTER**	small antelope	**GAZELLE**
slivovitz	**BRANDY**	small anvil	**TEEST**
slobber	**DROOL**	small aperture	**VENT**
sloe	**PLUM**	small arms	**PISTOLS**
slog	**PLOD, TOIL**	small arrow	**DART**
slogan	**CRY, CATCHWORD,**	small articles case	**ETUI**
	MOTTO	small automobile	**RUNABOUT**
slop	**SPLASH**	small bag	**SATCHEL**
sloping roadway	**RAMP**	small barn	**SHED**
slop over	**SPILL**	small barrel	**KEG**
sloppy person	**SLOB**	small bay	**COVE**
slosh	**SPLASH, SLUSH**	small bed	**COT**
sloth	**AI, UNAU**	small beetle	**WEEVIL**
slothful	**INDOLENT, LAZY**	small bill	**DOLLAR**
slot machine success	**JACKPOT**	small bird	**WREN, TIT**
slouch	**DROOP, SAG**	small bit	**NIP**
slovenly	**UNTIDY, MESSY**	small bit of food	**MORSEL**
slow	**SLUGGISH**	small body of water	**POND**
slow but flowing (mus.)		small bottle	**VIAL**
	ANDANTE	small boy	**TAD**
slow down (2 wds.)	**LET UP**	small branch	**TWIG**
slow-moving mollusk	**SNAIL**	small brook	**RILL**
slow (mus.)	**LENTO, ADAGIO,**	small brown bird	**WREN**
	LARGO	small bunch	**WISP**
slowpoke	**LAGGARD, SNAIL**	small cabin	**HUT**
slow train	**LOCAL**	small candle	**TAPER**
slow-witted	**DULL, STUPID**	small carrying bag	**SATCHEL,**
sludge	**MUD, MIRE**		**GRIP, ETUI**
slug	**SNAIL**	small cask	**KEG**
slugger's special	**HOMER,**	small change	**SILVER**
	KAYO	small chicken	**BANTAM**
sluggish	**LOGY, SLOW**	small child	**TAD, TOT,**
sluggishness	**TORPOR**		**TODDLER**
sluice	**GATE, CHANNEL**	small chunk	**WAD**
sluice gate	**CLOW**	small city	**TOWN**
slumber	**SLEEP**	small coin	**CENT, PENNY,**
slum dwelling	**TENEMENT**		**DIME, NICKEL**
slumgullion	**STEW, HASH**	small compact heap	**WAD**
slump	~~**DROP, FALL**~~	small cord	**STRING**
slur	**INSULT**	small cube	**DIE**
slur over	**ELIDE**	small cuckoo bird	**ANI**
slurp	**SUCK, GULP**	small cushion	**PAD**
slush	**MIRE**	small deer	**ROE**
sly	**CUNNING, WILY, FOXY**	small depression	**DENT**

small distance	**INCH**
small dog	**TERRIER, PUPPY,**
	CHIHUAHUA
small donkey	**BURRO**
small drum	**TABOR**
small duck	**SMEW, TEAL**
small engine	**MOTOR**
smallest	**LEAST**
smallest bit	**IOTA, WHIT**
smallest of the litter	**RUNT**
smallest part	**WHIT, MINIM**
small European fish	**DACE**
small explosion	**POP**
small falcon	**KESTREL**
small field	**CROFT**
small finch	**SERIN, SISKIN**
small fish	**SARDINE, SMELT,**
	MINNOW, GUPPY
small flap	**TAB**
small fly	**GNAT**
small forest ox	**ANOA**
small fragment	**CHIP, SHRED**
small fresh-water duck	**TEAL**
small fried cake	**FRITTER**
small garden spade	**TROWEL**
small glass of brandy	**PONY**
small green finch	**SERIN**
small group of secret	
plotters	**CABAL**
small gull	**TERN**
small harpsichord	**SPINET**
small heavenly body	
PLANETOID, ASTEROID,	
SATELLITE	
small herring	**SPRAT**
small hooter	**OWLET**
small horse	**PONY, COLT**
small hotel	**INN**
small hound	**BEAGLE**
small house	**CABIN, COTTAGE,**
	HUT
small in amount	**SLIGHT**
small in figure	**PETITE**
small inlet	**COVE, CREEK, RIA**
small insect	**GNAT**
small island	**AIT, CAY, ISLE,**
	KEY, ISLET
small jazz group	**COMBO**
small job	**CHORE**
small juicy fruit	**BERRY**
small lace mat	**DOILY**
small lake	**MERE, POND**
small leafy branch	**SPRIG**
small liquid measure	**GILL,**
	PINT
small lizard	**EFT, NEWT**
small mallet	**GAVEL**
small mass	**WAD**

small measure	**OUNCE**
small-minded	**NARROW, PETTY**
small monkey	**TITI**
small mound	**HILL**
small mountain lake	**TARN**
smallmouth	**BASS**
small nail	**BRAD, TACK**
small narrow valley	**RAVINE**
small nocturnal mammal	
	LEMUR
small opening	**FORAMEN,**
	PORE
small orange fruit	**KUMQUAT**
small part	**BIT**
small particle	**ATOM, MOTE**
small photo	**SNAPSHOT**
small piano	**SPINET**
small pie	**TART**
small piece	**BIT, FRAGMENT,**
	MORSEL, SNIP
small piece of food	**MORSEL**
small piece of ground	**PLAT**
small pigeon	**DOVE**
small pillow	**PAD**
small pincers	**PLIER**
small plateau	**MESA**
small pond	**POOL**
small porch	**STOOP**
small potatoes	**UNIMPORTANT**
small pouch	**SAC**
small quantity	**BIT, DAB,**
	DROP, IOTA
small quarrel	**SPAT, TIFF**
small restaurant	**CAFE, DINER**
small river	**STREAM, CREEK,**
	BROOK
small river duck	**TEAL**
small rock	**PEBBLE**
small rodent	**LEROT, MOUSE,**
	VOLE
small roll	**BUN**
small room	**CLOSET**
small rug	**MAT**
small sailing vessel	**LUGGER**
small salamander	**NEWT**
small sample of cloth	**SNIP**
small satellite	**MOONLET**
small-scale	**LIMITED**
small seed	**PIP**
small shelter	**SHED, LEAN-TO**
small ship	**BOAT, TUG**
small shoot	**TWIG**
small shrub	**ELDER**
small sofa	**LOVE SEAT, DIVAN**
small songbird	**WREN,**
	CANARY
small souvenir	**KNICKKNACK**
small spar	**SPRIT**

small spear	**DART**	smoked meat	**HAM**
small spot	**SPECK, DOT**	smoked pork	**BACON**
small steep waterfall	**CASCADE**	smoke flue	**STACK, CHIMNEY**
small stone	**PEBBLE**	smoker	**STAG**
small store	**SHOP**	smoker's item	**CIGARET, PIPE,**
small stream	**CREEK, RILL,**		**CIGARETTE, CIGAR**
	BROOK	smokestack	**CHIMNEY**
small sturgeon	**STERLET**	Smokey	**BEAR**
small Sumatra deer	**NAPU**	smoking tube	**PIPE**
smallsword	**EPEE**	smoky	**HAZY**
small table	**STAND, TABORET**	smoky quartz	**CAIRNGORM**
small talk	**CHAT**	smolder	**SMOTHER, SMUDGE**
small task	**CHORE**	smooch	**KISS, BUSS, NECK**
small taste	**SIP, BITE**	smooth	**EVEN, LEVEL, FLAT,**
small-time	**MINOR, PETTY**		**GLIB, EASY**
small tower	**TURRET**	smoothbore	**GUN**
small-town	**PROVINCIAL**	smooth cotton cloth	**PERCALE**
small tree branch	**TWIG**	smooth-faced	**SHAVEN**
small tropical cuckoo bird	**ANI**	smooth feathers	**PREEN**
small twig	**SPRIG**	smoothing tool	**FILE, PLANE**
small typewriter type	**ELITE**	smoothly courteous	**URBANE**
small valley	**DALE, DELL,**	smooth-spoken	**GLIB**
	GLEN, VALE	smorgasbord	**BUFFET**
small vegetable	**PEA, BEAN**	smother	**STIFLE**
small wagon	**CART**	smudge	**SMEAR, SPOT,**
small weight	**GRAM, OUNCE**		**STAIN, BLUR,**
small wheeled vehicle	**CART**		**DIRTY, SOIL**
small whirlpool	**EDDY**	smug	**COMPLACENT**
small wild ox	**ANOA**	smuggler	**RUNNER**
smalt	**GLASS, BLUE**	smug person	**PRIG**
smart	**INTELLIGENT,BRIGHT,**	smut	**SOOT, DIRT**
	STING, BURN	Smyrna	**IZMIR**
smart in appearance	**CHIC,**	Smyrna figs	**ELEMI**
	NATTY	snack	**BITE**
smart-looking	**TRIG**	snaffle	**BIT**
smash	**SHATTER, BREAK**	snag	**OBSTACLE**
smashup	**WRECK, COLLISION**	snail	**SLUG**
smear	**SMUDGE, DEFAME,**	snail genus	**MITRA, TRITON**
	DAUB	snail-paced	**SLOW**
smell	**ODOR, REEK, SCENT**	snake	**SERPENT, VIPER,**
smelly vegetable	**ONION**		**ADDER, ASP**
smelting by-product	**SLAG**	snake eyes	**TWO, DEUCE**
smelting chamber	**OVEN**	snake-killing mammal	
smelt ore	**REFINE**		**MONGOOSE**
smew	**MERGANSER**	snakeless land	**EIRE**
smile	**GRIN, BEAM**	snakelike fish	**EEL**
smile in a silly manner	**SIMPER**	snakemouth	**POGONIA**
smile scornfully	**SNEER**	snake's sound	**HISS, RATTLE**
smiling	**RIANT**	snakeweed	**BISTORT**
smirch	**TAINT, STAIN, SULLY**	snaky	**SINUOUS**
smirk	**LEER, SIMPER**	snaky letter	**ESS**
smite	**STRIKE**	snap	**CLICK**
smithy	**FORGE**	snap back	**RECOVER**
smock	**CHEMISE, SHIFT**	snappish bark	**YAP**
smog	**MIST**	snappy	**SPICY, LIVELY**
smoke	**REEK, FUME**	snappy comeback	**RETORT**
smoke a cigarette	**PUFF**	snapshot	**PHOTO**
smoke and fog	**SMOG**	snapshot, for short	**PIC**

snare	**NET, TRAP**	soap	**LATHER**
snarl	**TANGLE**	soapbark	**SAPONIN**
snarling dog	**CUR**	soap flake	**CHIP**
snarly	**CROSS**	soap foam	**SUDS**
snatch	**GRAB, NAB**	soap-frame bar	**SESS**
snazzy	**FLASHY**	soap ingredient	**LYE**
sneak	**LURK, STEAL**	soap opera	**SERIAL**
sneaker	**SHOE**	soap plant	**AMOLE**
sneaky	**STEALTHY**	soapstone	**TALC**
snee	**DIRK**	soapweed	**YUCCA**
sneer	**GIBE, SCOFF**	soar	**FLY, RISE**
sneeze	**ACHOO**	sob	**CRY, WEEP**
snicker	**TITTER**	so be it	**AMEN**
snide	**MEAN, LOW**	sober	**SERIOUS, SOLEMN**
sniff	**SMELL, NOSE**	sobriquet	**EPITHET,**
sniffles	**COLD**		**NICKNAME**
snifter	**GOBLET**	sociable	**COMPANIONABLE**
snip	**CLIP**	social	**POLITE**
snitch	**PILFER, INFORM**	social appointment	**DATE**
snivel	**WHINE**	social bud	**DEB**
snobbish	**SNOOTY**	social class	**CASTE**
snood	**NET**	social division	**TRIBE**
snoop	**PRY**	social event	**PARTY, BALL,**
Snoopy's adversary			**RECEPTION, TEA**
(2 wds.)	**RED BARON**	social gathering	**BEE**
snooty person	**SNOB**	social gathering for men	**STAG,**
snooze	**DOZE, NAP**		**SMOKER**
snoozing	**ASLEEP**	social grace	**POISE**
snout	**NOSE**	social group	**CLAN, TRIBE**
snout beetle	**WEEVIL**	social insect	**ANT, BEE**
snowbell	**STYRAX**	social outcast	**PARIAH**
snow coaster	**SLED,**	social rank	**CASTE, CLASS**
	TOBOGGAN	social set	**COTERIE, CLIQUE**
snow field	**NEVE**	social studies	**CIVICS**
snowflake	**CRYSTAL**	society	**UNION, PARTNERSHIP**
snow particle	**FLAKE**	society bud	**DEBUTANTE**
snow removal implement		society game	**POLO, CROQUET**
	SHOVEL, PLOW	society in Chinatown	**TONG**
snow runner	**SKI**	Society of Friends	**QUAKERS**
snow shoe	**PAC**	sock	**ANKLET, PUNCH**
snowslide	**AVALANCHE**	socked in	**FOGGY**
snow slider	**SLED**	sockeye	**SALMON**
snow vehicle	**SLED, SLEIGH,**	sod	**GREENSWARD, TURF**
	TOBOGGAN	soda	**POP**
snowy	**WHITE**	soda sipper	**STRAW**
snub	**IGNORE**	soda water	**SELTZER**
snuffle	**SNIFF, PANT**	sodden	**WET**
snug and warm	**COZY**	sodium chloride	**SAL, SALT**
snuggle	**NESTLE**	sofa	**DAVENPORT, DIVAN,**
snug retreat	**NEST**		**COUCH, SETTEE**
so	**THUS**	sofa bed	**CONVERTIBLE**
soak	**DRENCH, SATURATE,**	so far	**YET**
	SOP	soft	**GENTLE, PLIANT**
soaked	**WET**	soft alkali metallic element	
soak flax	**RET**		**SODIUM**
soak thoroughly	**SATURATE**	soft and pliable	**WAXEN**
soak through	**OOZE**	soft breeze	**ZEPHYR**
soak up	**ABSORB**	soft cap	**BERET**

soft chancre	CHANCROID	soldier's water flask	CANTEEN
soft cheese	BRIE	sole	LONE, ONLY, SOLITARY
soft coal	BITUMINOUS	solecism	BARBARISM
soft drink	COLA, POP, SODA,	solemn	SOBER
	ADE, PUNCH	solemnity	GRAVITY
soft-drink nut	COLA	solemnize	CELEBRATE
soften	ALLAY, ASSUAGE	solemn pledge	VOW, OATH,
softening device	MUTE		PROMISE
soften in temper	RELENT	solemn wonder	AWE
soft feathers	DOWN	solenocyte	FLAGELLUM
soft felt hat	FEDORA	solicit	ASK, REQUEST
soft food	PAP	solicit individually	CANVASS
softgoods	TEXTILES	solicitor	LAWYER
soft hair	FUR	solicitude	CARE
soft hat	CAP	solid	FIRM, HARD
soft in texture	SUPPLE	solid figure	CUBE, CONE
soft leather	CORDOVAN,	solidify	SET, GEL
	SUEDE	soliloquy	MONOLOGUE
softly	LOW, PIANO	solitaire	DIAMOND
soft mass	PULP	solitary	ALONE, LONE, SOLE
soft metal	MERCURY, LEAD,	solitary person	LONER
	TIN	solitude	SECLUSION,
soft metal alloy	SOLDER		LONELINESS
soft mineral	TALC	solo	ALONE
soft mud	SLIME, OOZE	Solomon	SAGE
soft palate	VELUM	so long	TA-TA
soft part of fruit	PULP	solo performance (2 wds.)	
soft pedal	DAMPER		ONE-MAN SHOW
soft plug	WAD	solution	KEY, ANSWER
soft round cap	BERET	solvent	ABOVE WATER
soft-shell	CRAB	soma	BODY
soft-shoe	TAPDANCE	somber	MELANCHOLY
soft-soaper	FLATTERER	sombrero	HAT
soft-spoken	QUIET, SUAVE	some	ANY
software	PROGRAM, DATA	somersault	TUMBLE, FLIP
soggy	WET, MOIST, DAMP	something dependable	
soigne	NEAT, TIDY	(comp. wd.)	STAND-BY
soil	DIRT, EARTH	something easy to	
soil deposit	SILT	accomplish (sl.)	PUSHOVER
soil mixture	LOAM	something extra	ACCESSORY
soil with dirt	BEGRIME	something inferior	PUNK
soirée	PARTY	something landlubbers	
sojourn	ABIDE	lack (2 wds.)	SEA LEGS
sol	SUN	something learned	LESSON
solace	CONSOLE, SOOTHE	something oppressive	BURDEN
solan	GANNET	something remarkable	LULU,
solar disc	ATEN		ONER
solar system model	ORRERY	something similar	ANALOGUE
soldering flux	ROSIN	something small	ATOM, IOTA
soldering piece	LUG	something that entertains	
soldier	PRIVATE, GI		AMUSEMENT, DIVERSION
soldier on guard	SENTRY	something to smoke	CIGAR,
soldier's address (abbr.)	APO		CIGARET, CIGARETTE,
soldiers' meal	MESS		PIPE, TOBACCO
soldier's overcoat	CAPOTE	something unexplained	
soldier's quarters	BARRACKS		MYSTERY
soldier's vacation	LEAVE,	something unique	ONER
	FURLOUGH	something worthless	TRIPE

sometime	**ONCE**
sometime salt ingredient	
	IODINE
sometimes wild card	**DEUCE**
somewhat	**TO A DEGREE,**
	RATHER
somewhat alike	**SIMILAR**
somewhat colorless	**PALISH**
somewhat youthful	**YOUNGISH**
sommelier	**STEWARD**
somnambulist	**SLEEPWALKER**
somniferous	**SOPORIFIC**
somniloquy	**SLEEP-TALK**
somnolent	**SLEEPY**
son	**BOY, HEIR, SCION**
sonance	**TONE**
song	**BALLAD, LAY, TUNE,**
	ARIA, MELODY
songbird	**LARK, SKYLARK,**
	CANARY, TANAGER,
	WREN
song for a diva	**ARIA**
song for a sailor	**CHANTEY**
song for one	**SOLO**
song for two	**DUET**
songlike	**ARIOSO, LYRIC**
song of joy	**PAEN**
songstress Adams	**EDIE**
songstress Bailey	**PEARL**
songstress Brewer	**TERESA**
songstress Cantrell	**LANA**
songstress Della	**REESE**
songstress Diahann	**CARROLL**
songstress Fitzgerald	**ELLA**
songstress Horne	**LENA**
songstress Judy	**GARLAND**
songstress Lanie	**KAZAN**
songstress Lee	**BRENDA,**
	PEGGY
songstress Logan	**ELLA**
songstress Martin	**MARY**
songstress Minnelli	**LIZA**
songstress Page	**PATTI**
songstress Piaf	**EDITH**
songstress Reese	**DELLA**
songstress Shirley	**BASSEY**
songstress Smith	**KATE**
songstress Starr	**KAY**
songstress Stevens	**CONNIE**
songstress Streisand	**BARBRA**
song thrush	**MAVIS**
songwriter	**COMPOSER**
sonnet	**POEM, VERSE**
son of Adam	**SETH, ABEL,**
	CAIN
son of Agamemnon	**ORESTES**
son of Aphrodite	**EROS**
son of Hagar	**ISHMAEL**
son of Isaac	**JACOB, ESAU**
son of Jacob	**LEVI, DAN,**
	JOSEPH, GIDEON,
	ASHER, GAD, JUDAH
son of Judah	**ER**
son of Lancelot	**GALAHAD**
son of Noah	**SHEM, HAM**
son of Obed	**JESSE**
son of Odin	**THOR**
son of Ruth	**OBED**
son of Saul	**JONATHAN**
son of Seth	**ENOS**
sonorous	**RESONANT**
soon	**ANON, PRESENTLY**
Sooner State	**OKALAHOMA**
sooner than	**ERE**
soot	**LAMPBLACK, SMUT, GRIT**
sooth	**TRUTH, FACT**
soothe	**EASE, COMFORT**
soothing ointment	**BALM,**
	SALVE
soothing substance	**BALSAM**
soothing word	**THERE**
soothsayer	**AUGUR**
sop	**DRENCH, SOAK**
sophism	**FALLACY**
sophisticated	**WORLDLY**
	BLASE
soporific	**SEDATIVE, NARCOTIC**
soprano Lehmann	**LOTTE**
sora	**RAIL**
sorcerer	**WIZARD**
sorceress of myth	**CIRCE**
sordid	**FOUL, FILTHY**
sore	**PAINFUL**
sorely	**URGENTLY**
sorghum	**SYRUP**
sorrel	**OCA, OXALIS**
sorrow	**GRIEF, WOE, DOLOR**
sorrowful	**SAD**
sorry	**RUEFUL**
sorry horse	**NAG**
sort	**TYPE, ILK, CLASS,**
	CLASSIFY, KIND
sortie	**FORAY, RAID**
sot	**TOPER, TOSSPOT, DRUNK**
sotto voce	**WHISPER**
souchong	**TEA**
souk	**MARKET**
soul	**SPIRIT, PSYCHE**
soul (Fr.)	**AME**
soul seller	**FAUST**
sound	**NOISE, TONE, VALID**
sound a horn	**TOOT**
sound, as a bell	**RING, PEAL,**
	TOLL
sound detector	**SONAR**
sound equipment of TV	**AUDIO**

sounder	**PLUMB**	source of power	**ATOM, STEAM**
sound from a kennel	**YELP,**	source of revenue	**TAX**
YIP, YAP, WOOF, ROWF,		source of the mighty oak	
BARK, BOWWOW			**ACORN**
sound harshly	**GRATE**	source of wood	**TREE**
sound in harmony	**CHIME**	sourdine	**MUTE**
sound loudly	**BLARE**	sourdough	**BREAD**
sound made by sheep	**BAA,**	sour fruit	**LEMON**
MAA		sour-leaved plant	**SORREL**
soundness of mind	**SANITY**	sour mash	**WHISKEY**
sound of a bell	**DONG, DING**	sousaphone	**TUBA**
sound of a blow	**WHAM**	souse	**PICKLE, BRINE**
sound of a cat	**MEW, MEOW,**	soused	**DRUNK**
MIAW		soutane	**CASSOCK**
sound of a clock	**TICK, TOCK,**	South	**DIXIE**
ALARM, TICKING		south (Fr.)	**SUD**
sound of a cow	**MOO**	South African	**BOER**
sound of a dove	**COO**	South African antelope	**ELAND,**
sound of a rifle shot	**CRACK**		**GNU**
sound of a snake	**HISS,**	South African city	**DURBAN**
RATTLE		South African grassland	**VELDT**
sound of contempt	**BOO, BAH**	South African native	**BANTU**
sound of disapproval	**BOO,**	South African plant	**ALOE**
HISS, CATCALL,		South African republic	
RASPBERRY			**TRANSVAAL**
sound of dismissal	**SCAT,**	South African tribe	**BANTU,**
SHOO			**ZULU**
sound of hesitation	**ER, UM,**	South African village	**KRAAL**
AH, AHEM		South American aborigine	
sound of relief	**SIGH**		**ARAWAK**
sound of rustling skirts	**SWISH**	South American animal	**LLAMA,**
sound of surf	**ROAR**		**TAPIR**
sound of today's music	**ROCK**	South American beast of	
sound quality	**TONE**	burden	**LLAMA**
sound reasoning	**LOGIC**	South American country	**PERU,**
sounds having melody	**MUSIC**		**BRAZIL, CHILE,**
sound system	**STEREO**	**URUGUAY, PARAGUAY,**	
sound the alarm	**ALERT**	**ARGENTINA, VENEZUELA,**	
sound track	**AUDIO**		**COLUMBIA**
soup	**BROTH, BISQUE,**	South American drink	**ASSAI**
CHOWDER		South American Indian	**CARIB,**
soupcon	**SUSPICION, HINT**		**INCA**
soup dish	**BOWL, TUREEN**	South American Indian	
soupfin shark	**TOPE**	group	**INCA**
soup green	**OKRA**	South American knife	
soup ingredient	**ONION, LEEK,**		**MACHETE**
SPLIT PEA, CHICKEN,		South American liberator	
RICE, BARLEY, NOODLE			**BOLIVAR, MARTIN**
sour	**ACID, TART**	South American monkey	**SAI**
source	**ORIGIN, BEGINNING,**	South American mountains	
ROOT, SPRING			**ANDES**
source of honor	**CREDIT**	South American ostrich	**RHEA**
source of income	**REVENUE**	South American parrot	**MACAW**
source of iodine	**KELP**	South American plains	
source of light	**SUN**		**LLANOS, PAMPAS**
source of metal	**ORE**	South American river	**PLATA,**
source of ore	**MINE**		**AMAZON**
source of poi	**TARO**	South American rodent	**PACA**

South American rubber tree **PARA**
South American tree **CACAO**
South American vulture **CONDOR**
South American weapon **BOLAS**
South Dakota city **PIERRE**
southdown **SHEEP**
southeast wind **EURUS**
southern beauty **BELLE**
southern bread **PONE**
southern constellation **ARA, ARGO, LIBRA, CENTAURUS**
southern crop **COTTON, SOYBEANS, PEANUTS, TOBACCO**
southern drink **JULEP, COMFORT**
Southern France **MIDI**
southern general **LEE**
South Pacific island group **SAMOA, HAWAII, FIJI, MICRONESIA**
southpaw **LEFTY**
South Pole bird **PENGUIN**
South Pole region **ANTARCTICA**
South Seas canoe **PROA, PRAU**
South Seas paradise **TAHITI**
South Seas plant **TARO**
Southwestern river **GILA, RED**
Southwestern saloon **CANTINA**
souvenir **RELIC, MEMENTO**
sovereign **RULER**
sovereign authority **DOMINION**
sovereign of Iran **SHAH**
sovereign power **THRONE**
sovereign's domain **EMPIRE**
sovereign's residence **PALACE**
soviet **COUNCIL**
Soviet city **OREL, MOSCOW, LENINGRAD**
Soviet commune **MIR**
Soviet news agency **TASS**
Soviet plane **MIG**
Soviet police **OGPU**
Soviet refusal **NYET, NIET**
Soviet river **URAL, VOLGA, LENA**
sow **SEED, PLANT**
sowbelly **SALT PORK**
space **ROOM**
space beside one **SIDE**
space between two points **DISTANCE**
space for laying up goods **STORAGE, ETAPE**
spaceman **ASTRONAUT**

space of time **INTERVAL**
space vehicle **APOLLO**
space-vehicle booster **SATURN**
spacious **ROOMY, AMPLE**
spade **SHOVEL**
spaghetti **PASTA**
Spain and Portugal **IBERIA**
span **BRIDGE**
spangle **SPARKLE, GLITTER**
Spanish-American laborer **PEON**
Spanish-American priest **PADRE**
Spanish-American shawl **SERAPE**
Spanish article **EL, LA, UNO, LOS**
Spanish aunt **TIA**
Spanish bayonet **YUCCA**
Spanish chaperone **DUENNA**
Spanish cheer **OLE**
Spanish city **CADIZ, TOLEDO, MADRID**
Spanish conqueror **CORTEZ, PIZARRO**
Spanish dance **TANGO, FLAMENCO, BOLERO**
Spanish fleet **ARMADA**
Spanish gambling game **MONTE**
Spanish gentleman **SENOR, CABALLERO**
Spanish gold **ORO**
Spanish hero **CID, EL CID**
Spanish holiday **FIESTA**
Spanish house **CASA**
Spanish jar **OLLA**
Spanish legislature **CORTES**
Spanish mackerel **PINTADO**
Spanish matron **DONA, SENORA**
Spanish nobleman **GRANDEE**
Spanish painter **DALI, GOYA, EL GRECO**
Spanish peninsula **IBERIA**
Spanish river **EBRO, RIO**
Spanish room **SALA**
Spanish sherry **JEREZ**
Spanish title **DON, SENOR**
spanker **SAIL**
spanking **LICKING**
spar **MAST, SHADOWBOX**
spare **EXTRA**
sparing **FRUGAL, CHARY**
spark **FLASH**
sparkle **SHINE, TWINKLE, GLISTEN**
sparrowgrass **ASPARAGUS**

sparse	**SCANT**	speechless	**MUTE, SILENT**
spartan	**SEVERE**	speech to the audience	**ASIDE**
Spartan king	**MENELAUS**	speed	**RUN, SWIFTNESS,**
Spartan slave	**HELOT**		**HASTEN, RACE, HIE**
spasm	**TIC**	speed contest	**RACE**
spasmodic	**FITFUL**	speedily	**APACE, QUICKLY**
spat	**QUARREL**	speed rate	**TEMPO**
spate	**FRESHET**	speed up	**ACCELERATE**
spatter	**SPLASH, SPRINKLE**	speed upward, like a	
spatula	**SCRAPER**	plane	**ZOOM**
spawn	**ROE**	speedy	**FAST, QUICK, RAPID,**
speak	**MOUTH, SAY,**		**HASTY, SWIFT**
	TALK, UTTER	speedy horse	**ARAB**
speak conceitedly	**BOAST,**	spell	**CHARM**
	BRAG	spellbound	**RAPT**
speak eloquently	**ORATE**	spelling contest	**BEE**
speaker	**ORATOR**	spell of cold weather	**SNAP**
speaker's platform	**ROSTRUM**	spelt	**EMMER**
speak from memory	**RECITE**	spelunker's specialty	**CAVE**
speak imperfectly	**LISP**	spencer	**TRYSAIL**
speak in undertone	**MURMUR**	spend	**EXHAUST, DISBURSE**
speak slightingly of	**DEBASE**	spend foolishly	**SQUANDER**
speak slowly	**DRAWL**	spend money	**BUY**
speak tearfully	**SNIVEL**	spend the summer	**VACATION,**
speak wildly	**RAVE**		**(A)ESTIVATE**
spear	**LANCE**	spendthrift	**PRODIGAL**
special	**NOTEWORTHY**	spent	**EXHAUSTED,**
special ability	**TALENT**		**PUT OUT MONEY,**
special approach	**ANGLE**		**EXPENDED**
special edition	**EXTRA**	sphere	**ORB, GLOBE**
special event	**OCCASION**	sphere of action	**ARENA**
specialist	**EXPERT**	sphere of operation	**THEATER**
specialist in crime		spherical	**ROUND**
	SAFECRACKER,	spherical body	**BALL, GLOBE**
	PICKPOCKET	sphinx land	**EGYPT**
species	**KIND, SORT**	spice	**SEASON, PEPPER**
species of deer	**ROE**	spicy	**RACY**
species of moth	**EGGER**	spicy bud	**CLOVE**
species of pheasant	**RINGNECK**	spicy perfume	**INCENSE**
species of water lily	**LOTUS**	spicy quality	**TANG, ZEST**
specific	**EXACT, PRECISE**	spider	**ARACHNID,**
specimen	**SAMPLE**		**TARANTULA**
specious	**PLAUSIBLE, LIKELY**	spider monkey genus	**ATELES**
speck	**DOT, MOTE**	spider's handiwork	**WEB**
speck of dust	**MOTE**	spider trap	**WEB**
speck of moisture from		spieler	**BARKER**
the eyes	**TEARDROP**	spigot	**TAP, FAUCET**
spectacle	**PAGEANT**	spike	**EAR, NAIL**
spectacles	**GLASSES**	spike of corn	**EAR**
spectator	**WITNESS**	spile	**TAP, SPIGOT**
spectator's roofed area		spillikin	**JACKSTRAW**
	GRANDSTAND	spill over	**SLOP**
spectre	**SHADE, GHOST,**	spin	**TWIRL, WHIRL, REEL,**
	HAUNT		**REVOLVE, ROTATE, TURN**
spectrum	**RANGE**	spindle	**AXLE, AXIS**
speculate	**WONDER**	spindrift	**SPRAY**
speech	**ADDRESS, TALK**	spine	**BACKBONE, SETA**
speech impediment	**LISP**	spine bone	**SACRUM**

spinet	**PIANO**	spoor	**TRACK**
spinnaker	**SAIL**	sporadic	**INFREQUENT**
spinner of webs	**SPIDER**	sport	**GAME, PASTIME,**
spinning toy	**TOP**		**BASEBALL, FOOTBALL,**
spinster (2 wds.)	**OLD MAID**		**SQUASH, HOCKEY**
spiny anteater	**ECHIDNA**	sporting a Van Dyke	**BEARDED**
spiny dogfish	**SHARK**	sportive	**PLAYFUL**
spiny-finned fish	**COD**	sport of kings	**RACING**
spire	**STEEPLE, TOWER**	sport of shooting clay	
spire finial	**EPI**	pigeons	**SKEET**
spire ornament	**FINIAL, EPI**	sports enthusiast	**FAN**
spirit	**ELAN, SOUL**	sports field	**ARENA**
sprited	**SPUNKY, BRISK**	sports group	**TEAM**
spirited horse	**STEED**	sports palace	**COLISEUM**
spirit lamp	**ETNA**	sportswear	**SLACKS, JERSEY,**
spiritless	**VAPID**		**SWEATER, SHORTS**
spiritual being	**ANGEL**	sporty	**FLASHY**
spiritualist	**MEDIUM**	spot	**BLOT, STAIN,**
spiritus frumenti	**WHISKEY**		**FLECK, DOT**
spirochete	**BACTERIA**	spot card	**PIP**
spit	**SKEWER, ROD**	spotless	**CLEAN**
spite	**MEANNESS**	spot of color	**BLOB**
spiteful	**VINDICTIVE, MALIGN**	spotted	**DAPPLED**
spiteful woman	**CAT**	spotted dog	**BRINDLE**
Spithead	**SOLENT**	spotted feline	**LEOPARD**
spittoon	**CUSPIDOR**	spotted horse	**PINTO**
splash	**SPLATTER, SPATTER**	spotted wildcat	**OCELOT**
splash through mud	**SLOSH**	spotty	**UNEVEN**
splendid	**SUPERB**	spouse	**MATE, WIFE,**
splendor	**POMP**		**HUSBAND**
splicing machine	**EDITOR**	spout	**GUSH, SPURT**
splinter	**SLIVER**	spout for drawing sap	**SPILE**
split	**CUT, CLEAVE, REND,**	spray	**ATOMIZE**
	RIVE, DIVIDE	spread	**WIDEN, DISPERSE**
split into thin layers	**LAMINATE**	spread abroad	**STREW**
split second	**MOMENT, WINK**	spread between supports	**SPAN**
splotch	**STAIN, SPOT**	spread by rumor	**NOISE**
Spode	**CHINA**	spread defamation	**LIBEL**
spoil	**MAR, ROT**	spread for bread	**BUTTER,**
spoiled child	**BRAT**		**JAM, JELLY**
spoiler of plans	**MARPLOT**	spread for drying	**TED**
spoiler on a plane	**FLAP**	spread on thick	**SLATHER**
spoils	**BOOTY, LOOT,**	spread out	**OPEN**
	PLUNDER	spread out battle line	**DEPLOY**
spoke	**RUNG, BRACE**	spread outward	**FLARE**
spoken	**ORAL, VERBAL**	spread over	**COVER**
spoken exam	**ORAL**	spree	**BINGE, BENDER, TOOT**
sponge	**CADGE**	sprig	**SHOOT, TWIG**
sponger	**MOOCHER, CADGER**	sprightly	**PERT**
sponsor	**BACKER**	sprightly tune	**LILT, AIR**
spontaneous	**IMPULSIVE**	spring	**SOURCE, FONT, LEAP,**
spoof	**PARODY, SATIRE**		**HOP, JUMP, COIL**
spook	**GHOST, HAUNT,**	spring back	**REBOUND**
	GOBLIN, SHADE	spring bloomer	**IRIS, TULIP,**
spooky	**EERIE**		**CROCUS, VIOLET, LILAC,**
spool	**REEL, BOBBIN**		**HYACINTH, LILY**
spoon	**NECK, SMOOCH, LADLE**	spring festival	**EASTER,**
spoonbill	**SHOVELER**		**PASSOVER**

spring-like	**VERNAL**	stage hint	**CUE**
spring month	**MARCH, APRIL,**	stage in development	**PHASE**
	MAY, JUNE	stage of a journey	**LEG, LAP**
spring on one foot	**HOP**	stage of civilization	**CULTURE**
spring suddenly	**BOUNCE**	stage of history	**ERA, EPOCH**
spring up	**ARISE**	stage of insect growth	**LARVA**
springy	**ELASTIC**	stage of travel (obs.)	**GEST**
sprinkle	**SPATTER**	stage parentheses	**ASIDE**
sprinkle a lawn	**WATER**	stage presentation	**REVUE,**
sprinkle with flour	**DREDGE**		**PLAY, DRAMA, REVIEW**
sprinkle with powder	**DUST**	stage setting	**SCENE**
sprint	**RACE, RUN**	stage whisper	**ASIDE**
sprite	**ELF, FAIRY, GOBLIN**	stagger	**REEL**
sprite in *The Tempest*	**ARIEL**	stagnant	**FOUL, INERT**
sprout	**SHOOT, SPRIG**	stagnate	**ROT**
sprout artificially	**MALT**	stag's mate	**DOE**
spruce	**NATTY, TRIM, NEAT,**	staid	**SEDATE, SOBER**
	TIDY, NEATEN	stain	**BLOT, BLEMISH,**
spry	**AGILE, NIMBLE**		**FLAW, SPOT, DYE**
spud	**POTATO**	stair	**STEP**
spun	**WOVE, WOVEN**	stair part	**RISER, TREAD**
spur	**GOAD, ROWEL,**	stair post	**NEWEL**
	IMPEL, STIMULUS	stairwell	**SHAFT**
spurious	**FALSE**	stake	**PEG, WAGER, ANTE**
spurious imitation	**SHAM**	stalactite	**ICICLE**
spurn	**DISDAIN, SCORN**	stale	**OLD, TRITE**
spy	**AGENT**	stalemate	**DRAW**
spy employed by police	**NARK**	stalk	**HUNT, STEM**
spy group (abbr.)	**CIA**	stalk game	**HUNT**
squabble	**QUARREL, BICKER**	stalk of grain	**STRAW**
squalid	**SORDID**	stalk vegetable	**CELERY**
squander	**SPEND, WASTE**	stall	**BOOTH**
square	**CORNY**	stallion	**STUD, HORSE**
square of butter	**PAT**	stalwart	**STRONG, STURDY**
square of three	**NINE**	stamina	**ENDURANCE**
squaring tool	**EDGER**	stammer	**STUTTER**
squash	**GOURD**	stamp	**POSTAGE, SEAL,**
squat	**STUBBY**		**TRAMP, STOMP**
squatter	**NESTER**	stampede	**DEBACLE**
squeal	**TATTLE**	stamping device	**DIE**
squeamish	**DELICATE**	stamp out	**CRUSH**
squeeze	**WRING, PINCH**	stance	**POSE**
squint	**PEER**	stanch	**STOP, STEM**
s-shaped molding	**OGEE**	stand	**RISE, REAR**
stab	**PIERCE**	stand against	**RESIST**
stable	**FIXED, STEADY**	standard	**NORM**
stable compartment	**STALL**	standard of perfection	**IDEAL**
stack role	**NESS**	standard quantity	**UNIT**
stadium cheer	**RAH**	stand by	**AID**
staff	**PERSONNEL, POLE**	standby	**ALTERNATE**
staff officer	**AIDE**	stand for	**REPRESENT**
staff of life	**BREAD**	stand for office	**RUN**
staff of office	**MACE, SCEPTER**	stand in	**SUBSTITUTE**
stag	**DEER, HART**	standing	**STATUS**
stage	**PLATFORM**	stand off	**EVADE**
stage comedy	**FARCE**	stand on edge	**UPEND**
stage direction	**ENTER,**	stannum	**TIN**
	EXEUNT	stanza	**VERSE**

stanza of eight lines **TRIOLET**
staple grain **RICE, WHEAT**
star **TWINKLER, SUN,**
ASTERISK
starch **SAGO**
starchy edible root **TARO**
star cluster **NEBULA**
stare **GAPE, OGLE, GAZE,**
GAWK
stare open-mouthed **GAPE**
stare sullenly **GLOWER**
stark **BARE**
star (prefix) **ASTRO**
star-shaped **ASTRAL,**
STELLATE
start **LEAD, BEGIN, ONSET,**
BEGINNING, INITIATE
start again **REOPEN, RESUME**
start a Model T **CRANK**
start aside **DODGE**
startle **SURPRISE**
start of college cheer **HIP**
start off **LEAD**
start of the fiscal year
(2 wds.) **JANUARY FIRST**
start of the weekend
SATURDAY
start on a cruise **EMBARK**
start out **EMBARK**
start up again **RENEW**
starve **FAMISH**
stash **HIDE**
state **DECLARE, AVER, SAY,**
CONDITION, STATUS
state (Fr.) **ETAT**
state as a fact **POSIT**
state further **ADD**
state in India **ASSAM, SIKKIM**
stately **REGAL, TALL**
stately residence **MANOR**
state meaning of **DEFINE**
statement **ASSERTION**
statement of belief **CREDO**
state of anxiety **SUSPENSE**
state of disorder **MESS**
state-of-emergency crime
LOOTING
state of extreme happiness
(2 wds.) **SEVENTH HEAVEN**
state of feeling **MOOD**
state of health **CONDITION**
state of mind **MOOD, TEMPER**
state of perfection
(comp. wd.)
FARE-THEE-WELL
state of unconsciousness **COMA**
state policeman **TROOPER**
state positively **ASSERT, AVER**

state's leader **GOVERNOR**
state without proof **ALLEGE**
station **TERMINAL, DEPOT**
stationary **FIXED, SET**
stationer's item **INK, PAPER**
station in life **RANK**
station wagon **CAR**
statistics **DATA**
statue **BUST**
statue base **PLINTH**
statue support **PEDESTAL**
statue trunk **TORSO**
stature **HEIGHT**
status **RANK, GRADE**
statute **LAW**
staunch **LOYAL, FAITHFUL**
stave **CUDGEL**
stay **ABIDE, REMAIN**
stay for **WAIT**
stead **LIEU**
steadfast **STAUNCH, FIRM**
steadiness **STABILITY**
steady **STABLE, SOLID**
steady pain **ACHE**
steak **MEAT**
steal **SNEAK, ROB, THIEVE**
steal cattle **RUSTLE**
steal furtively **SLINK**
stealthy **SNEAKY**
steam **VAPOR**
steam bath **SAUNA**
steamer **CLAM**
steamship **LINER**
steamship company **LINE**
steatite **TALC**
steed **HORSE, MOUNT**
steel **HARDEN, INURE**
steel beam **GIRDER**
steelhead **TROUT**
steep **PRECIPITOUS**
steeple **SPIRE**
steeplechase **RACE**
steep slope **SCARP, BLUFF,**
CLIFF
steer **GUIDE, PILOT, DRIVE**
steer clear of **AVOID**
steer enclosure **CORRAL,**
KRAAL
steering apparatus **RUDDER**
steer meat **BEEF**
steersman **PILOT, HELMSMAN**
steeve **LADE, STORE**
stein **MUG**
steinbok **ANTELOPE**
stem **STALK**
stem-like part **STIPE**
stench **ODOR, STINK**

step	PACE, STAIR, TREAD, WALK	stock	STORE
step and hop	SKIP	stockade (Fr.)	ETAPE
step of a ladder	RUNG	stock exchange	BOURSE
steppe	PLAIN	stock farm	RANCH
steps over a fence	STILE	stockholder's unit	SHARE
stereo attachment (2 wds.)	TAPE RECORDER, TAPE DECK	stocking disaster	RUN
		stocking line	SEAM
		stocking mishap	SNAG
stereotype	PATTERN	stocking run (Brit.)	LADDER
sterile	BARREN	stockings	HOSE, HOSIERY, NYLONS
stern	GRIM, SEVERE, REAR, AFT	stockings (Fr.)	BAS
stern-faced	GRIM	stock of goods	LINE
sternward	ABAFT, AFT	stock of wealth	CAPITAL
stevedore union (abbr.)	ILO	stock-quoting machine	TICKER
stew	RAGOUT, SIMMER, OLLA	stogie	CIGAR
stewed fruit	COMPOTE	stoic	UNEMOTIONAL, STAID, STERN
stick	ADHERE, CANE	stoicism	PATIENCE
sticker	LABEL	stoke	FEED
stick out	JUT	stoker	FIREMAN
stick together	COHERE	stole	ROBBED, SHAWL, VESTMENT, WRAP
sticky stuff	GOO, PASTE, GLUE, OOZE, SAP	stolen property	PELF, LOOT, BOOTY
stiff	TENSE, RIGID	stone	ROCK, PEBBLE, GEM, JEWEL
stiff-legged bird	STORK	stonecrop	SEDUM
stiff-necked	STUBBORN	stonecutter	MASON
stifle	CHOKE, SMOTHER	stone monument	STELA(E)
stigma	BLOT, STAIN	stoneware (Fr.)	GRES
still	MOTIONLESS, QUIET, YET, SILENT	stone worker	MASON
		stony	HARD, ROCKY, COLD
still picture	SLIDE, SNAP, PHOTOGRAPH, SNAPSHOT	stooge	FOOL
		stool	SEAT
		stool pigeon	INFORMANT
stimulant	TONIC	stoop	BEND, PORCH
stimulate	STIR, ROUSE	stop	CEASE, HALT, DESIST, QUIT, PAUSE
stimulus to creative thought	INSPIRATION	stop (naut.)	AVAST
		stopgap	RESOURCE
sting	BITE, NIP	stop gradually (2 wds.)	TAPER OFF
stinging insect	BEE, WASP, HORNET	stopper	CORK, PLUG
stinging plant	NETTLE, SMARTWEED	stop talking (2 wds.)	PIPE DOWN, SHUT UP
stingray	SKATE, MANTA	stop up	CLOG, PLUG
stingy	MISERLY, MEAN	stopwatch	TIMER
stink	STENCH, SMELL	storage battery plate	GRID
stint	DUTY	storage bin	GRANARY, MOW
stipend	ALLOWANCE	storage box	BIN
stipulation	PROVISO	storage building	SHED, ETAPE
stir	BUDGE, AROUSE, AGITATE, ROUSE, MIX, MOVE, BUSTLE	storage place	ATTIC
		storage place for weapons	ARMORY
stir the fire	STOKE	storax	BALSAM, RESIN
stitch	SEW	store	ACCUMULATE, SHOP, MARKET, MART
stitched line	SEAM		
St. Louis ball club	CARDINALS		
stoa	PORTICO		
stoat	ERMINE, WEASEL		

store correspondence	**FILE**	strawberry-colored horse	**ROAN**
stored fodder	**ENSILAGE**	straw hat	**PANAMA**
store employee	**CLERK**	straw man	**SCARECROW**
store event	**SALE**	straw rug	**MAT**
store fodder	**ENSILE**	straw vote	**POLL**
store for future use	**STASH,**	stray	**ROAM, ROVE, ERR,**
	SAVE		**RAMBLE, WANDER**
storehouse (Fr.)	**ETAPE**	stray dog	**CUR**
storekeeper	**RETAILER,**	stray from course	**STRAGGLE**
	MERCHANT	streak	**STRIPE**
store label (2 wds.)	**PRICE TAG**	streak in marble	**VEIN**
store up	**AMASS**	stream	**BROOK, RILL, RIVER,**
storm	**GALE, RAGE, RAVE,**		**RIVULET, CREEK**
	FURY, TEMPEST,	stream along	**FLOW**
	CYCLONE, TORNADO,	streamer	**RIBBON**
	HURRICANE	streamlet	**RILL, RUNLET**
storm center	**EYE**	streamline	**ORGANIZE**
stormy	**WINDY**	street	**BOULEVARD, ROAD,**
story	**TALE, YARN, FLOOR**		**AVENUE**
story fabricator	**LIAR**	street (Fr.)	**RUE**
storyteller	**RACONTEUR**	street Arab	**GAMIN, URCHIN**
stout	**ALE, FAT, OBESE**	streetcar	**TRAM**
stouthearted	**BRAVE**	street drain	**SEWER**
stout stick	**BAT**	street peddler	**VENDOR**
stout string	**CORD, TWINE**	street sign	**SLOW, STOP, YIELD**
stove	**COOKER, RANGE, OVEN**	street urchin	**GAMIN**
stove compartment	**OVEN**	strength	**FORCE, POWER,**
stove fuel	**GAS**		**SINEW, THEW**
stow	**PACK, STORE**	strengthen	**BRACE, TOUGHEN**
stow cargo	**STEEVE**	strengthen a levee	**REVET**
straggle	**STRAY, WANDER**	strengthening medicine	**TONIC**
straight	**DIRECT, UNBENT**	strenuous	**SEVERE, ARDUOUS**
straight course	**BEELINE**	stress	**EMPHASIZE, STRAIN,**
straight edge	**RULER**		**ACCENT**
straighten	**ALINE, ALIGN**	stretch	**DISTEND, EXPAND**
straightforward	**CANDID,**	stretched tight	**TAUT**
	FRANK	stretcher	**LITTER**
strain	**STRESS**	stretch injuriously	**SPRAIN**
strained	**TENSE, TAUT**	stretch of land	**TRACT, FIELD**
strainer	**SIEVE**	stretch out	**EKE**
strait	**NECK, NARROW**	stretch the neck	**CRANE**
strand	**ABANDON, MAROON,**	stretchy	**ELASTIC**
	DESERT	strew	**SCATTER**
strange	**FOREIGN, ALIEN,**	stria	**GROOVE, CHANNEL**
	ODD, QUEER, UNUSUAL	striate	**STRIPE, FURROW**
strange (prefix)	**XENO**	strict	**STERN, SEVERE**
strangle	**CHOKE, STIFLE**	strictness	**RIGOR**
strap	**BELT, STROP**	stricture	**CENSURE,**
strap on a falcon's leg	**JESS**		**RESISTANCE**
strapping	**TALL, ROBUST**	stride	**STEP**
strass	**PASTE**	strident	**SHRILL**
stratagem	**RUSE, WILE**	strife	**WAR, TROUBLE**
Stratford's river	**AVON**	strigil	**SCRAPER**
strath	**VALLEY**	strike	**POKE, PUNCH, HIT,**
stratum	**LAYER**		**SMITE, SWAT**
stratum of ore	**VEIN, SEAM**	strikebreaker	**SCAB**
straw	**HAY, SIPPER**	strike lightly	**PAT, TAP, RAP**
strawberry bass	**CRAPPIE**	strike out	**DELE, DELETE**

strike repeatedly	**BEAT**
strike with the hand	**SLAP,**
	SMACK
strike with the head	**BUTT**
strike with violence	**SLAM**
striking	**REMARKABLE**
striking effect	**ECLAT**
string	**CORD, LACE**
stringed instrument	**FIDDLE,**
	HARP, VIOL, VIOLA,
	VIOLIN, LUTE, LYRE,
	UKULELE, BANJO,
	GUITAR, CELLO,
	MANDOLIN, PIANO
stringent	**RIGID, SEVERE**
stringy	**ROPY**
strip	**SHRED, DENUDE**
stripe	**BAR, STREAK**
striped horse	**ZEBRA**
strip of cloth	**TAPE**
strip off skin	**FLAY**
strip of leather	**STRAP, THONG**
strip of wood	**SLAT**
stripling	**LAD**
strive	**AIM, CONTEND**
strive for (2 wds.)	**SHOOT AT**
strive mightily	**STRAIN**
strive with	**VIE**
strobe	**FLASH, LIGHT**
stroke	**PAT, CARESS, PET**
stroke of luck (sl.)	**FLUKE**
stroll	**AMBLE, SAUNTER**
strong	**STURDY, POWERFUL,**
	POTENT
strong affection	**LOVE**
strong and healthy	**ROBUST**
strong and resolute	**STALWART**
strong and tough	**RUGGED**
strongbox	**CHEST**
strong breeze	**WIND**
strong cart	**DRAY**
strong cloth	**SCRIM**
strong cord	**ROPE**
strong cotton	**PIMA**
strong herb	**GARLIC**
stronghold	**FORT**
strong man of myth	**ATLAS,**
	HERCULES, TITAN
strong-minded	**DETERMINED**
strong point	**FORTE**
strong request	**DEMAND**
strong taste	**TANG**
strong upward movement	
	SURGE
strong wind	**GALE**
strong yearning	**ITCHING,**
	ACHE
strop	**STRAP**

strop a razor	**HONE, SHARPEN**
strophe	**STANZA**
structure	**BUILDING, FRAME**
structure on a roof	**CUPOLA**
struggle	**VIE, CONTEND**
strum	**THRUM**
strut	**SWAGGER, PRANCE**
stub	**STUMP**
stubble	**BEARD**
stubborn	**BALKY, DOGGED**
stubborn animal	**MULE,**
	DONKEY, BURRO
stubby	**SHORT**
stuck-up person	**SNOB**
stud	**BUTTON, SCREW**
student	**PUPIL**
student monitor	**PREFECT**
student of an English	
school	**ETONIAN**
student pilot	**CADET**
student's p.m. assignment	
	HOMEWORK
stud for shoe sole	**HOBNAIL**
studio	**ATELIER**
stud with ornaments	**BESET,**
	BEJEWEL
study	**CON, READ, PERUSE,**
	PORE
study closely	**EXAMINE**
study course	**SEMINAR**
stuff	**CRAM**
stuffed shirt	**PRIG**
stuffing	**FILLING**
stuffy	**PRIM, STODGY**
stumble	**TRIP, FALL**
stumbling block	**OBSTACLE**
stun	**AMAZE, DAZE**
stunt	**FEAT, TRICK**
stunted animal	**RUNT**
stupe	**COMPRESS**
stupefy	**DAZE**
stupid	**SIMPLE, IDIOTIC,**
	ASININE
stupid fellow	**SIMPLETON,**
	ASS, OAF, DUNCE
stupidity	**DULLNESS**
stupor	**LETHARGY, TORPOR**
sturdy	**STRONG, STOUT**
sturdy fabric	**DENIM**
sturdy tree	**OAK, MAPLE**
sturgeon roe	**CAVIAR**
stutter	**STAMMER**
sty	**PEN, PIGPEN**
Stygian	**INFERNAL**
style	**FASHION, MODE**
style of singing (2 wds.)	
	BEL CANTO

style of type	ELITE, ROMAN, ITALIC	suburban shopping area	MALL, CENTER
stylet	STILETTO	subvert	SUPPRESS, DEMOLISH
stylish	CHIC, CLASSY	succeed	ENSUE, ARRIVE, MAKE GOOD, WIN
stylish Britisher	TOFF		
stylus	NEEDLE	succeeding	NEXT
styptic	ALUM	success	PROSPERITY, HIT
suave	SOFT, SMOOTH	succession	SERIES
subcontinent of Asia	INDIA, ASIA MINOR	successful move	COUP
		succinct	TERSE, CONCISE
subdivision	SECTION	succotash ingredient	CORN
subdue	TAME, CALM	succulent	TASTY
subject	TEXT, THEME	succulent plant	ALOE
subject of discussion	TOPIC	succumb	SUBMIT, YIELD
subject of verb	NOUN	such and no more	MERE
subject to argument	MOOT	suck	DRAW, INHALE
sublime	GRAND	sucker	DUPE, LOLLIPOP
submarine missile	POLARIS	suckerfish	REMORA
submarine sandwich	HERO	suckle	NURSE
submerge	SINK	suction	INTAKE
submissive	MEEK, TAME, DOCILE	sudden	ABRUPT
		sudden attack	RAID, SORTIE, SWOOP
submit	DEFER, BEND		
submit evidence	PROVE	sudden blast of wind	GUST
subordinate	INFERIOR	sudden blaze	FLARE
subordinate ruler	SATRAP	sudden bump	JOLT
subpoena	SUMMONS	sudden burst of energy	SPURT
		sudden death	OVERTIME
subscription department's delight	RENEWAL	sudden decline	LAPSE, SLUMP
subsequently	AFTER, LATER, THEN, LATER ON		
		sudden downpour	CLOUDBURST, STORM, SHOWER
subside	EBB, SETTLE, ABATE		
subsidiary	AUXILIARY	sudden fear	ALARM, PANIC
subsidy	GRANT, SUPPORT	sudden gush	SPURT
subsist	LIVE	sudden inspiration	BRAINSTORM
substance	GIST		
substance for violin strings	ROSIN	sudden loud noise	BANG
		suddenly, like magic	PRESTO
substantial	MEATY	sudden muscular contraction	TIC, SPASM
substantiate	CONFIRM		
substantive	NOUN, PRONOUN	sudden pain	PANG, TWINGE
substitute	PROXY, SURROGATE	sudden shock	JOLT
substitute in office	DEPUTY	sudden start	JERK
substitute squad (2 wds.)	SCRUB TEAM, SECOND STRING	sudden stroke	COUP
		sudden thrust	STAB
		suds	FROTH
substructure	FOUNDATION	suds maker	SOAP, DETERGENT, SHAMPOO
subterfuge	ARTIFICE, EXCUSE		
subtle	SLY	sue	PLEAD
subtle air	AURA	suet	FAT
subtle sarcasm	IRONY	suffer	ENDURE, BEAR
subtract	DEDUCT	sufferer	VICTIM
suburban builder	DEVELOPER	suffer from heat	SWELTER
suburban residence	VILLA, SPLIT-LEVEL, BUNGALOW, RANCH	suffer remorse	RUE
		suffering	PAIN
		suffice	SERVE
suburban restaurant	INN	sufficient	AMPLE

suffocate	CHOKE, SMOTHER	summon	CALL, CITE
suffrage	FRANCHISE,	summon by name	PAGE
	VOTE	summon forth	EVOKE
sugar	SUCROSE, GLUCOSE	summon together	MUSTER
sugar ladle	SCOOP	summon up	RALLY
sugar portion	CUBE,	sump	PIT
	TEASPOON	sumptuous	LAVISH
Sugar State	LOUISIANA	sumptuous meal	REPAST,
sugar tree	MAPLE		FEAST
sugary	SWEET	sun	STAR, SOL
suggest indirectly	HINT,	sunbeam	RAY
	ALLUDE	sunburn	TAN
suggestion	ADVICE, OPINION	sunburn preventative (2 wds.)	
sui generis	UNIQUE		TANNING LOTION
suit	BEFIT, BECOME	sundae topping	NUTS, SYRUP,
suitable	APT, FIT		CHOCOLATE, CHERRY
suitable for farming	ARABLE	sunday cut of meat	ROAST
suitable place	NICHE	sunday lecture	SERMON
suit at cards	SPADES,	sunday speech (abbr.)	SER
	DIAMONDS,	sunder	TEAR, RIP, SHRED
	HEARTS, CLUBS	sundial arm	GNOMON
suit at law	CASE	sundog	PARHELION
suitcase	GRIP, VALISE,	sundown	EVE, DUSK
	ETUI	sundry	VARIOUS, DIVERS
suitmaker	TAILOR	sunfish	BREAM
suit material	SERGE	Sunflower State	KANSAS
suit of mail	ARMOR	sunken fence	HAHA
suite of rooms	FLAT	sunless spot	SHADE
suitor	SWAIN, BEAU	sunny	BRIGHT, CHEERFUL
sulk	MOPE, POUT, BROOD	sun parlor	SOLARIUM
sulky	SULLEN	sun ring	CORONA
sullen	DOUR, GLUM,	sunrise	SUNUP, DAWN
	MOROSE	sunrise direction	EAST
sully	SMEAR, DEFILE	sun satellite	PLANET
sulphur	BRIMSTONE	sunshade	PARASOL
sultan's wives	HAREM	Sunshine State	FLORIDA,
sultry	HOT, TORRID		NEW MEXICO,
sulu	SARONG		SOUTH DAKOTA
sum	TOTAL, ADD	sunup	DAWN, SUNRISE
sum of money	FUND	Suomi	FINLAND
sum total	ENTIRETY	sup	DINE, EAT
sum up	TOT	super	GREATER, BETTER
summarize	TOT UP,	superannuate	RETIRE
	RECAP	superannuated	OBSOLETE
summary	PRECIS, BRIEF	superb	SPLENDID
summer (Fr.)	ETE	supercilious	SNOBBISH
summer drink	ICED COFFEE,	superego	CONSCIENCE
	ICED TEA, ADE	superficial	CURSORY,
summer flounder	FLUKE		SHALLOW
summer hat	PANAMA,	superfluous	EXCESSIVE,
	BOATER		PROFUSE
summer house	COTTAGE	superior	ABOVE
summer resort area	SHORE,	superlative	MOST
	BEACH, MOUNTAINS	superlative suffix	EST
summer skin tone	TAN	Superman's girl	LOIS
summer tendency	LETHARGY	supermarket	STORE
summit	ACME, APEX,	supernatural	MIRACULOUS
	CREST, PEAK, TOP	supersede	REPLACE

supervise	OVERSEE	surgical probe	STYLET
supervisor	BOSS,	surgical saw	TREPAN
	OVERSEER, DIRECTOR,	surgical stylet	TROCAR
	CONDUCTOR	surgical thread	SETON
supine	INDOLENT,	surly	MOROSE, SULLEN
	LISTLESS	surmise	GUESS
supper	MEAL, DINNER	surmount	CONQUER,
supplant	REPLACE, UPROOT		SUBDUE
supple	PLIANT, ELASTIC,	surmounting	ATOP
	FLEXIBLE	surname	COGNOMEN
supplement	EKE	surpass	EXCEL, OUTDO,
supplementary	ADDITIONAL		BEST
supplicate	PRAY, PLEAD	surplus	EXCESS
supplication	PLEA	surprise	STARTLE
supply	PROVIDE	surprise attack	RAID
supply food	CATER,	surrender	CEDE, YIELD
	NOURISH	surrender rights	WAIVE
supply of money	FUNDS	surround	BESET
supply provisions	PURVEY	surrounded by	AMID
supply station	DEPOT	surrounding (prefix)	PERI
supply with fuel	STOKE	surroundings	DECOR,
supply with funds	ENDOW		ENVIRONMENT
supply with weapons	ARM	surveyor	LINEMAN
support	BEAR, LEG, PROP,	suspend	HANG
	BRACE, MAINTAIN,	suspense	ANXIETY,
	BOOST		UNCERTAINTY
support a motion	SECOND	suspension	DELAY
support for a glass	COASTER		FAILURE
suppose	GUESS, OPINE,	suspicion	DISTRUST
	DEEM, THINK	suspicious	LEERY
supposing (2 wds.)	AS IF	sustain	SUPPORT, ENDURE
supposition	HYPOTHESIS,	sustenance	FOOD
	THEORY	Sutherland specialty	ARIA
suppress	ELIDE, STIFLE,	suture	SEAM
	SIT ON, STOP,	swab	MOP
	ESTOP	swagger	STRUT
supremacy	MASTERY	swaggering pretense of	
supreme	UTMOST	courage	BRAVADO
Supreme Court group	NINE	swain	SUITOR, ADMIRER
supreme Egyptian deity	AMON	swallow	BIRD, GULP
surcease	RESPITE	swallow up	EAT, ENGULF,
sure	IN THE BAG,		DEVOUR
	CERTAIN	swami	PUNDIT
sure-footed	NIMBLE	swamp	BOG, FEN, MARSH,
surf	BREAKERS		MORASS
surface	AREA, TOP	swamp grass	REED
surface a street	PAVE	swampish	MIRY
surface coating	SCUM	swampland tract	
surface depression	DENT		EVERGLADES
surface drain	SEWER	swan	CYGNUS, COB
surface of a gem	FACET	swanky dwelling place	
surfeit	SATE, GLUT	(2 wds.)	
surf roar	ROTE		DUPLEX APARTMENT
surge	TIDE	swansdown	FLANNEL
surge of emotion	THRILL	swap	BARTER, TRADE
surgeon's instrument	SCALPEL	sward	SOD, TURF
surgical compress	STUPE	swarm	TEEM, HIVE
surgical knife	SCALPEL	swarming	ALIVE

swarthy	DARK, DUSKY	swing around	SLUE
swat	STRIKE, SMACK	swinging bed	HAMMOCK
sway	SWING		
sway in the breeze	WAVE	swing music	JIVE
swearword	OATH, CURSE	swipe	STEAL, SWEEP
Swedish beer	OL	swirl	TWIST, EDDY
Swedish canton	LAN	Swiss cabin	CHALET
Swedish city	STOCKHOLM,	Swiss canton	URI, ZUG
	UPSALA	Swiss capital	BERN
Swedish clover	ALSIKE	Swiss city	BASEL,
Swedish Nightingale			ZURICH, GENEVA
	JENNY LIND	Swiss cottage	CHALET
sweet	SUGARY	Swiss district	CANTON
sweet confection	CANDY	Swiss lake	ZUG
sweeten	CANDY, SUGAR	Swiss mountain	ALP
sweetened drink	JULEP	Swiss mountaineer's song	
sweetheart	DREAMBOAT,		YODEL
	LOVER, PARAMOUR,	Swiss river	AAR
	DARLING	switch	CHANGE, DIVERT
sweet liqueur	CREME	sword	RAPIER, SABER
sweetmeat	BONBON	swordfish's snout	SERRA
sweet potato	YAM	sword handle	HILT
sweet roll	BUN	sycophant	PARASITE,
sweet-scented plant	JASMINE		TOADY
sweet-smelling	REDOLENT	sylvan demigod	SATYR
sweet song	BALLAD	symbol	EMBLEM
sweet substance	HONEY,	symbol for tellurium	TE
	SUGAR, SYRUP	symbol for tin	SN
sweet wine	PORT	symbol of bondage	YOKE
swell	EXPAND, DISTEND	symbol of peace	DOVE
swelling	EDEMA	symbol of ruthenium	RU
swell out	BULGE	symbol of victory	PALM,
swerve	SKEW, VEER,		VEE
	CAREEN, DIVERGE	symmetry	BALANCE,
swift	FAST, RAPID, QUICK		HARMONY
swiftly	APACE, FAST,	sympathize	CARE, PITY
	QUICKLY	sympathy	COMPASSION
swiftness	HASTE, SPEED	syncopated rhythm	RAGTIME
swig	DRAFT	synonomous	SAME, SIMILAR
swill	SLOP, GARBAGE	synthetic fabric	ORLON,
swim	FLOAT, FLOOD		RAYON, NYLON,
swim fin	FLIPPER		ARNEL, DACRON
swimming	NATANT	synthetic material	PLASTIC,
swimming mammal	OTTER,		FIBERGLAS, FORMICA
	SEAL, WHALE,	syrup tree	MAPLE
	BEAVER, PORPOISE,	system	METHOD
	DOLPHIN, WALRUS	systematic	REGULAR,
swimming place	POOL		PRECISE
swimming pool	TANK,	system of belief	CREED,
	NATATORIUM		DOGMA
swindle	DUPE, GYP,	system of moral principles	
	BILK, CON		ETHICS
swindling scheme	BUNCO	system of signals	CODE
swine	HOG, PIG, BOAR	system of weights	
swine-like	PORCINE		AVOIRDUPOIS
swing	SWAY	syzygy	PAIR

T

taa	**PAGODA**
tab	**LABEL, TAG, BILL**
tabanid	**HORSEFLY**
tabby	**CAT**
table	**BOARD**
tableau	**SCENE, SKIT**
tablecloth linen	**DAMASK**
table dish	**TUREEN**
table extension	**LEAF**
tableland	**MESA**
table linen	**DAMASK, NAPKIN**
tablemount	**GUYOT**
table of contents	**INDEX**
table protector	**TRIVET**
table scrap	**ORT**
table support	**LEG**
tablet	**PAD, SLATE**
table tennis	**PING PONG**
tabloid	**NEWSPAPER**
taboo	**FORBID, BAN**
tacit	**SILENT, UNSPOKEN**
taciturn	**SILENT**
tack	**NAIL**
tackle	**HARNESS, GEAR**
tact	**DIPLOMACY**
tad	**BOY**
tadpole	**POLLIWOG**
tag	**LABEL, TAB**
tag of lace	**AGLET**
Tahiti capital	**PAPEETE**
tailboard	**ENDGATE**
tailed amphibians	**SALAMANDER, NEWT**
tailless amphibian	**TOAD, FROG**
tailor	**SEW**
taint	**CONTAMINATE, ADULTERATE**
Taiwan	**FORMOSA**
Taj Mahal site	**AGRA**
take	**GRASP, SEIZE**
take a bite	**TASTE**
take a break	**REST**
take a chair	**SIT**
take a chance	**RISK, DARE**
take a dip	**SWIM**
take a direction	**STEER**
take advantage of	**USE**
take advice	**HEED**
take after	**FOLLOW, PURSUE**
take along	**BRING, CARRY**
take a meal	**EAT**
take another spouse	**REWED**

take an upright position	**STAND**
take a shower	**BATHE**
take as one's own	**ADOPT**
take a stroll	**WALK**
take a trip	**TRAVEL, TREK**
take away	**REMOVE**
take away by force	**WREST**
take back	**RECANT, RETRACT**
take by surprise (2 wds.)	**BOWL OVER**
take care	**BEWARE**
take care of	**TREAT, LOOK AFTER, SEE TO, TEND**
take cognizance of	**NOTICE**
take cover	**HIDE**
take evening meal	**DINE, SUP**
take first prize	**WIN**
take five	**REST, BREAK**
take food	**EAT**
take for granted	**ASSUME, PRESUME**
take from	**DEPRIVE, SUBTRACT**
take in oxygen	**BREATHE, INHALE**
take in sail	**REEF**
take into custody	**ARREST**
take it easy	**RELAX, REST**
take long steps	**STRIDE**
take meals for pay	**BOARD**
take notice	**HEED, ESPY, WATCH**
take off	**DOFF**
take offense at	**RESENT**
take on cargo	**LADE**
take out	**DELE**
take-out order (2 wds.)	**TO GO**
take part (2 wds.)	**SIT IN**
take pleasure in	**ENJOY**
take prisoner	**ARREST, CAPTURE**
take the bus	**RIDE**
take the car	**DRIVE**
take the sun	**TAN**
take to court	**SUE**
take to jail	**ARREST**
take to the air	**FLY AWAY, SOAR, FLY**
take turns	**ROTATE, ALTERNATE, SPELL**
take umbrage at	**RESENT**
take up again	**RESUME**
take up weapons	**ARM**
take up with	**BEFRIEND**
taking everything into account	**OVERALL**

tal	CYMBALS	tank	VAT, CISTERN
talc	STEATITE	tankard	STEIN
tale bearer	TATTLER,	tank farming	HYDROPONICS
	GOSSIP	tanned hide	LEATHER
talent	SKILL, GIFT	tansy	WEED
tale of adventure	GEST	tantalize	TEASE
tale of daring	SAGA	Tantalus' daughter	NIOBE
talipes	CLUBFOOT	tantamount	EQUAL
talisman	OMEN, CHARM,	tantara	FANFARE
	AMULET	tantrum	TEMPER
talk	JAW, GAB, CHAT,	tap	FAUCET, SPIGOT
	SPEAK, DISCUSS,	tap down	TAMP
	CONVERSE,	tape	RECORD, BIND
	CHATTER, PRATE	taper	CANDLE
talkative	GARRULOUS,	tapering object	WEDGE
	CHATTY	tapering solid	CONE
talk back	SASS	tapestry	ARRAS
talk foolishly	PRATE	tapioca	CASSAVA
talk idly	GAB, PRATE	tapioca-like food	SALEP
talk imperfectly	LISP,	taproom	BAR, SALOON,
	STUTTER, STAMMER		PUB
talk indistinctly	SPUTTER,	tar	PITCH, SAILOR
	MUMBLE	tarantula	SPIDER
talking bird	MINA,	tarboosh	FEZ
	MYNA, PARROT	tardy	LATE, SLOW
talk slowly	DRAWL	tare	VETCH, WEED
talk up	PROMOTE	target	MARK, OBJECT
talk wildly	RANT, RAVE	target center	EYE,
tall	LOFTY, HIGH		BULLSEYE
tall and thin	LANKY	Tar Heel State	
tall grass stalk	REED		NORTH CAROLINA
tallow	SUET	tariff	DUTY
tall spar	MAST	Tarkington hero	PENROD
tall structure	TOWER,	tarnish	SMUDGE,
	SKYSCRAPER		DISCOLOR
tall tale	YARN, FIB	taro paste	POI
tall wading bird	CRANE	taro root	EDDO
tally	SCORE	tarry	BIDE, LINGER, STAY
Talmud commentary	GEMARA	tarsier	LEMUR
Talmud text	MISHNA	tarsus	ANKLE
talon	CLAW	tart	ACID, SOUR
talus	ANKLE	tartan fabric	PLAID
tamarisk salt tree	ATLE	tartar	CALCULUS
tambour	DRUM	task	CHORE, JOB,
tame	DOMESTICATE,		ERRAND, DUTY
	GENTLE, SUBDUE,	tassel	FRINGE
	DOCILE, HARMLESS	taste	FLAVOR, SAVOR,
tame animal	PET		SAMPLE, SIP
Tamil	DRAVIDIAN	taste a lollipop	LICK
tamp	PACK	taste center	PALATE
tamper	MEDDLE	tasteful luxury	ELEGANCE
tan	BROWN, SUNBURN,	tasteless	INSIPID, VAPID
	ECRU, KHAKI	taste with pleasure	SAVOR
tandem	TEAM, BICYCLE	tasty	SAVORY
tangle	KNOT, SNARL,	ta-ta	GOODBYE
	RAVEL, MAT	Tatar lancer	UHLAN
tangled mass	MOP	tatter	RAG, SHRED
tangy herb	MINT	tatting	LACE

tattle	SQUEAL, RAT ON, TELL, SNITCH	technicality	DETAIL
		technique	METHOD
taunt	TEASE, TWIT, GIBE	tedious	LONG, BORING
taupe	MOLESKIN	tedium	ENNUI
taut	TENSE	tee-hee	TITTER, SNICKER
tavern	PUB, BAR, INN, SALOON	teel	SESAME
		teem	ABOUND
tavern beverage	ALE, BEER	teeming	FULL, REPLETE
tavern employee	BARMAID, BOUNCER	teeny	WEE
		teeter-totter	SEESAW
taw	MARBLE	teetotum	TOP
tawdry	CHEAP, GAUDY	tegula	TILE
tawny	TANNED, DUSKY	Teheran native	IRANI
tax	TOLL, LEVY, TARIFF	tela	TISSUE
taxi	CAB, HACK	telegram	WIRE, MESSAGE
taxi chauffeur	CAB DRIVER, CABBIE	telegraphy inventor	MARCONI
		telephone	CALL
taxi rider	PASSENGER, FARE	telephone book	DIRECTORY
		telephone rod	POLE
taxi ticker	METER	telephone wire	LINE
tax official	ASSESSOR	telescope	GLASS
taxus	YEW	television award	EMMY
T-bone	STEAK	television cabinet	CONSOLE
tea	CHA, OOLONG, PEKOE	television porpoise	FLIPPER
		television sound	AUDIO
teaberry	WINTERGREEN	tell	NARRATE, RELATE
tea cake	SCONE	teller of tall stories	LIAR, FIBBER
teach	EDUCATE, TRAIN, TUTOR		
		telling	VALID
teacher	PROFESSOR	tell secrets	TATTLE
teacher's concern	CLASS, STUDENT, PUPIL, LESSON	tell tales	BLAB, LIE, FIB
		temblor	EARTHQUAKE
		temerity	BOLDNESS, AUDACITY
teaching staff	FACULTY		
tea container	CANISTER	temper	DANDER, MOOD
teak	WOOD	tempera	PAINT
teal	DUCK	temperament	DISPOSITION, MOOD
team race	RELAY		
teamster	CARTER	temperance	MODERATION
team's turn at bat	INNING	temperate	MILD
tear	RIP, REND, RIVE, SPLIT	temper display	RAGE, TANTRUM
tear down	RAZE, DEMOLISH		
tearful	SAD	tempered iron	STEEL
tear into	ATTACK	tempest	STORM, GALE
tear into shreds	TATTER	tempestuous	INCLEMENT
tear out	UPROOT	tempo	PACE, TIME
tear producer	ONION	temporal	SECULAR, EARTHLY
tear roughly	LACERATE		
tear salad greens	SHRED	temporary	TRANSIENT
teary	CRYING	temporary breather	LULL
tease	IRRITATE, TANTALIZE, TAUNT, WORRY, RAZZ, TORMENT, ANNOY, PESTER, BADGER	temporary fashion	FAD, CRAZE
		tempt	ENTICE, LURE
tease wool	TUM	temptress	SIREN
teatime	FOUR	ten	DECAD, DECADE
tea urn	SAMOVAR	tenacious	PERSISTENT

tenant	ROOMER, LODGER, BOARDER, LESSEE, RENTER	term	PERIOD, COURSE
		termagant	SHREW
ten cents	DIME	terminal	STATION, DEPOT
tend	LEAN, LEAD	terminal pole	ANODE, ELECTRODE
tendency	DRIFT, TREND	terminate	END, FINISH
tender	SORE	term in logic	SORITES
tenderfoot	DUDE	term in office	TENURE
tending to arouse feelings	EMOTIVE	terminology	NOMENCLATURE
		termite	ANT
tending to be silent	UNCOMMUNICATIVE, TACITURN	term of address	SIR
		term of imprisonment	SENTENCE
tending to check	REPRESSIVE	term of royal address	SIRE, MAJESTY, HIGHNESS
tending to drive away	REPELLENT	terms	CONDITIONS
tending to wear away	EROSIVE	tern genus	STERNA
ten dollars (sl.)	SAWBUCK	terra alba	MAGNESIA
tendon	MUSCLE, THEW, SINEW	terrace	PATIO, VERANDA
		terra cotta	POTTERY
tendril	SPRIG	terra firma dweller	EARTHMAN
tend to	MIND, NURSE	terrain	LAND
tenebrous	DARK, GLOOMY	terrapin	TURTLE
tenement	FLAT, APARTMENT, SLUM	terrene	EARTHLY, WORLDLY
		terret	RING
tenement pest	RAT, ROACH	terrible	AWFUL, DREADFUL
tenet	DOGMA, DOCTRINE	terrible tsar	IVAN
tennis barrier	NET	terrier	SKYE, FOX
tennis instructor	PRO	terrific	EXCITING
tennis point	ACE	terrify	ALARM, FRIGHTEN, SCARE
tennis pro	ACE		
tennis score	LOVE	territory	AREA
tennis shoe	SNEAKER	terror	PANIC
tennis stroke	LOB	terse	CONCISE, PITHY
tennis term	LOVE, SERVE, FAULT	test	EXAM, EXAMINE, EXAMINATION, TRIAL, TRY
tennis trophy	CUP		
Tennyson hero	ENOCH	test for fit (2 wds.)	TRY ON
tenpenny	NAIL	testify	DEPONE, DEPOSE
tenpins	BOWLING	testimony	ATTESTATION
tense	EDGY TAUT, TIME	testimony weighers in court (2 wds.)	PETIT JURY
tension	STRESS, STRAIN		
tensor	MUSCLE	test ore	ASSAY
tent	TEPEE, WIGWAM	testy	CRANKY
tentacle	FEELER, PALP	Teuton	GERMAN
tentative	PROVISIONAL, TEMPORARY	Texas bronco	MUSTANG
		Texas city	WACO, EL PASO, DALLAS, HOUSTON
tent city	CAMP		
tent-dwelling nomad	ARAB	Texas evergreen shrub	BARETTA
tent show	CIRCUS		
tenth of a decade	YEAR	Texas longhorn	STEER
tenure	TERM	Texas shrine	ALAMO
tenuous	DELICATE, THIN	textiles	MERCERY
ten years	DECADE	text of an opera	LIBRETTO
tepee	TENT, WIGWAM	text of a play	SCRIPT
tepid	LUKEWARM	texture	WALE, GRAIN
teredo	SHIPWORM		
tergal	DORSAL		

Thackeray's Miss
  Sharp **BECKY**
Thailand **SIAM**
Thailand's neighbor **LAOS**
thalium (chemical symbol) **TL**
thankful **GRATEFUL**
thankless person **INGRATE**
thanks (Fr.) **MERCI**
that boy **HE, HIM**
that certain air **AURA**
thatch palm **NIPA**
that girl **HER, SHE**
that is (Lat., 2 wds.) **ID EST**
that is to say **NAMELY**
that place **THERE**
that thing **IT**
that which follows **SEQUEL**
that which gives relief **BALM**
that which must be done **DUTY**
that which one does
  best **FORTE**
that which unlocks **KEY**
thaumaturgy **MAGIC**
thaw **MELT**
the (Fr.) **LE, LA, LES**
the (Ger.) **DAS, DER**
the (Sp.) **LA, EL,**
LOS, LAS
theater **ARENA, STAGE**
theater attendant **USHER**
theater award **TONY**
theater box **LOGE**
theater lobby **FOYER**
theater passageway **AISLE**
theater platform **STAGE**
theater play **DRAMA**
theater sign **SRO, EXIT**
theatrical **DRAMATIC**
theatrical company **TROUPE**
theatrical couple **LUNTS**
theatrical performer **ACTOR**
theatrics **DRAMATICS**
Theban prince **OEDIPUS**
the best within record
  (comp. wd.) **ALL-TIME**
the bounding main **OCEAN**
the briny deep **SEA**
the bull (2 wds., Span.)
EL TORO
the devil **SATAN**
the e in est **EASTERN**
the end **OMEGA, FINIS**
the 400 **ELITE**
theft **ROBBERY, BURGLARY**
the good book **BIBLE**
the inevitable **DESTINY, FATE**
the intellect **MIND**
the last **OMEGA**

the last frontier **ALASKA,**
SPACE
theme **ESSAY, TOPIC,**
SUBJECT
the merchant of Venice
ANTONIO
the m in USMC **MARINE**
the night club set (2 wds.) **CAFE SOCIETY**
theological school **SEMINARY**
the one here **THIS**
the ones here **THESE**
the one there **THESE**
the ones there **THOSE**
theorbo **LUTE**
the Orient **EAST**
theorize **SPECULATE**
theory **CONJECTURE,**
HYPOTHESIS
the p in mph **PER**
the planet earth **TERRA**
the populace **PEOPLE**
the present **NOW**
the present age **TODAY**
therapeutic **CURATIVE**
therapeutic draught **DOSAGE**
there **YONDER**
therefore **ERGO, HENCE, SO**
the r in HRH **ROYAL**
the r in IRS **REVENUE**
therm **CALORIE**
Therma **SALONIKA**
thermal **WARM**
thermos **BOTTLE, JUG**
the same (Lat.) **IDEM**
thesaurus creator **ROGET**
these (Fr.) **CES, CETTES**
thesis **ESSAY**
the smallest bit **IOTA**
thespian **ACTOR**
thespian's signal **CUE**
Thessaly mountain **IDA,**
OSSA
the sun **SOL**
the sun (prefix) **HELIO**
"the terrible" **IVAN**
the thing **IT**
"The Thinker" sculptor **RODIN**
the three wise men **MAGI**
the tube **TELEVISION**
the two of us **WE**
the two together **BOTH**
thew **SINEW, MUSCLE**
the way out **EXIT**
the whole amount **ALL**
thick **DENSE**
thick and short **SQUAT**
thick black liquid **TAR**

thick board	**PLANK**	thinly scattered	**SPARSE**
thick cluster	**CLUMP**	thin metal disk	**PATEN**
thick cord	**ROPE**	thin nail	**BRAD**
thicken	**CLOT**	thinner	**TURPENTINE**
thicket	**COPSE, GROVE**	thin out	**PETER**
thicket fence	**HEDGE**	thin pasteboard	**CARD**
thick mist	**FOG**	thin plate of metal	**LEAF**
thickness	**DIAMETER, PLY**	thin screen	**VEIL**
thick piece	**CHUNK**	thin shelled nut	**PECAN**
thick porridge	**MUSH**	thin silk fabric	**PONGEE**
thick set	**STOCKY**	thin-skinned	**SENSITIVE**
thick skinned	**CALLOUS**	third in number	**TERTIARY**
thick skulled	**STUPID,**	third largest planet	**URANUS**
	OBTUSE	third person	**HE, SHE, THEY**
thick slice	**SLAB**	third power	**CUBE**
thick soup	**PUREE**	third-rate	**INFERIOR**
thick string	**CORD, TWINE,**	thirst quencher	**WATER,**
	ROPE		**DRINK**
thick sweet liquid	**SYRUP**	thirsty	**DRY**
thick wire ropes	**CABLE**	thirteen (2 wds.)	
thighbone	**FEMUR**		**BAKER'S DOZEN**
thimblerig	**CHEAT,**	thirty (Fr.)	**TRENTE**
	SWINDLE	this (Lat.)	**HOC**
thin	**LEAN, SLIM,**	this (Sp.)	**ESTA, ESTE**
	SLENDER, SKINNY	this way	**HERE**
thin and haggard	**GAUNT**	thole	**PIN, OARPIN**
thin and limp	**LANK**	thong	**STRAP**
thin and vibrant	**REEDY**	Thonga	**BANTU**
thin and withered	**WIZENED**	thorn	**BRIAR, SPINE**
thin as air	**RARE**	thorny, as a plant	**SPINY**
thin board	**SLAT**	thorny shrub	**ROSE**
thin cookie	**WAFER**	thorough	**COMPLETE**
thin cord	**STRING**	thoroughfare	**AVENUE,**
thin fog	**MIST**		**STREET, ROAD,**
thing	**OBJECT, ARTICLE**		**BOULEVARD, HIGHWAY**
thing (Lat.)	**RES**	those in office	**INS**
thing abandoned by		those summoned for	
its owner	**DERELICT**	jury duty	**TALESMEN**
thingamajig	**GADGET**	thought	**IDEA, NOTION,**
thing done	**DEED, FEAT,**		**COGITATION**
	FACT	thoughtful	**PENSIVE,**
thing in law	**RES**		**KIND, GENEROUS**
thing of small value	**TRIFLE**	thoughtless	**CARELESS,**
thing of value	**ASSET**		**STUPID**
thing owed	**DEBT**	thousandth	**MIL**
things for sale	**MERCHANDISE**	thrash soundly	**DRUB, TAN,**
things given	**DATA**		**BEAT**
things to be done	**AGENDA**	thread	**FIBER, FILAMENT**
think	**REASON, DEEM,**	threaded nail	**SCREW, BOLT**
	OPINE, SUPPOSE	threaded steel pin	**BOLT**
think ahead	**PLAN**	thread of smoke	**WISP**
think hard	**CONCENTRATE**	thread-winding machine	
think logically	**REASON**		**REELER**
think over	**PONDER**	threaten	**MENACE**
think the world of	**IDOLIZE**	threatening	**OMINOUS**
think twice	**RECONSIDER**	three (Ger.)	**DREI**
thin layer	**FILM**	three (prefix)	**TRI, TRE,**
thinly metallic	**TINNY**		**TER**

three-banded armadillo	**APAR**
three-base hit	**TRIPLE**
three-dimensional	**CUBIC**
three feet	**YARD**
three-fifths of the earth's surface	**OCEAN**
threefold	**TRINE**
three-legged stand	**TRIPOD**
three lines of verse	**TRIPLET**
three-masted vessel	**SCHOONER**
three musicians	**TRIO**
threescore	**SIXTY**
three-sided figure	**TRIANGLE**
threesome	**TRIO**
three-spot card	**TREY**
three-toed sloth	**AI**
three-wheeler	**TRICYCLE**
threnody	**DIRGE, ELEGY**
thresh	**BEAT**
threshing tool	**FLAIL**
threshold	**SILL**
thrice (mus.)	**TER**
thrift	**FRUGALITY**
thriftless	**LAVISH**
thrifty	**ECONOMICAL**
thrill	**SHIVER**
thrill-seeking parachutist (2 wds.)	**SKY DIVER**
thrive	**PROSPER**
throat-clearing word	**AHEM**
throat sound	**RALE**
throaty	**HUSKY, HOARSE**
throb	**PULSE, PULSATE, DRUM, BEAT**
throbbing sound	**PITAPAT**
throes	**PANGS**
throng	**HORDE, HOST, CROWD**
throttle	**CHOKE**
through	**PER**
throw	**CAST, PITCH, LOB, HEAVE, TOSS, SLING, HURL**
throw away	**DISCARD**
throw cold water on	**DISCOURAGE**
throwing rope	**LASSO, REATA**
throw lightly	**TOSS**
throw light upon	**ILLUMINE**
throw off	**EMIT**
throw off the track	**DERAIL**
throw out	**EJECT, EVICT**
throw slowly	**LOB**
thrum	**FRINGE**
thrush	**MAVIS, ORIOLE**
thrust	**PROD, STAB**
thrusting weapon	**SPEAR**
thud	**BLOW**

thug	**HOODLUM**
thumb	**POLLEX**
thumbnail	**BRIEF, CONCISE**
thump	**POUND, KNOCK**
thunder	**RUMBLE**
thunder peal	**CLAP**
thurible	**CENSER**
thus	**SO**
thus (Lat.)	**SIC**
thus far	**YET**
thwart	**FOIL, SPITE**
thyme	**HERB**
thymus	**GLAND**
tiara	**CORONET**
Tibetan capital	**LHASA**
Tibetan chief	**POMBO**
Tibetan gazelle	**GOA**
Tibetan grand lama	**DALAI**
Tibetan guide	**SHERPA**
Tibetan monk	**LAMA**
Tibetan ox	**ANOA, YAK**
Tibet's neighbor	**BURMA**
tibia	**SHIN**
Tibur	**TIVOLI**
tic	**SPASM**
tical	**MONEY**
tick	**OPERATE, WORK**
ticker	**WATCH, HEART**
ticket	**CARD**
ticket (sl.)	**DUCAT**
ticket half	**STUB**
tickle	**TITILLATE**
tidal wave	**EAGRE**
tidbit	**GOODY**
tide	**CURRENT**
tidings	**NEWS**
tidy	**NEAT, TRIM**
tie	**ASCOT, CRAVAT, BIND, FASTEN, TETHER**
tie clasp	**TACK**
tie off	**BELAY**
tier	**LAYER, ROW**
tie the knot	**WED, MARRY**
tie up	**BIND, TRUSS**
tie-up	**JAM**
tiff	**SPAT**
tiffin	**LUNCH**
tiger	**CAT**
tiger cat	**OCELOT, MARGAY**
tight	**TENSE, TAUT**
tightfisted	**STINGY**
tight-lipped	**TACITURN**
tightrope	**WIRE**
tights	**LEOTARD**
til	**SESAME**
tile	**SLATE**
tillable	**ARABLE**

tiller	**HELM**	tint	**DYE, HUE, COLOR,**
till the soil	**FARM,**		**SHADE, TINGE**
	CULTIVATE	tiny	**LILLIPUTIAN,**
tilt	**LEAN, CANT, TIP,**		**SMALL, WEE**
	INCLINE	tiny branch	**SPRIG**
tilt, as a ship	**LIST**	tiny distance	**HAIR, NOSE**
tilted	**ALIST**	tiny morsel	**CRUMB**
tilting match	**JOUST**	tiny parasite	**MITE**
tilting over	**ALOP**	tiny particle	**ATOM, MOTE,**
timber	**LOG, WOOD**		**IOTA**
timber hitch	**KNOT**	tiny speck	**DOT, MOTE**
timber tree	**ASH, OAK, ELM**	tip	**END, GRATUITY,**
timber wolf	**LOBO**		**TILT, LEAN, ADVICE**
timbre	**TONE**	tippet	**SCARF**
time	**DURATION, HOUR**	tipping	**ATILT**
time being	**NONCE**	tipple	**BIB**
time division	**YEAR, DAY,**	tiptoe	**CREEP**
	HOUR, MINUTE,	tirade	**PHILIPPIC,**
	MONTH, WEEK,		**HARANGUE**
	SECOND	tire	**FATIGUE, WEARY**
time gone by	**PAST**	tired	**WEARY, SLEEPY**
time limit	**DEADLINE**	tiresome	**WEARY, TEDIOUS**
timely	**OPPORTUNE**	tire support	**RIM**
time of life	**AGE**	tissue	**TELA**
time of year	**FALL,**	Tisza tributary	**SOMES**
	WINTER, SPRING,	titan	**GIANT**
	SUMMER, SEASON	tithe	**TENTH**
timeout	**REST**	titian	**AUBURN**
timepiece	**CLOCK, WATCH**	titillate	**TICKLE**
timer	**STOPWATCH**	title	**NAME, SIR, MADAM**
timetable	**SCHEDULE**	title role	**LEAD**
time-tested literary work		titter	**GIGGLE, TEEHEE**
	CLASSIC	tittle	**IOTA, JOT**
time waster	**IDLER**	tizzy	**FRENZY**
timeworn	**TRITE**	to	**TOWARD**
timid	**SHY**	toad	**FROG**
timid creature	**MOUSE**	toadstool	**MUSHROOM**
timid person	**FAINTHEART**	toady	**PARASITE,**
timing	**PACING**		**SYCOPHANT**
timing device	**METER**	to a great extent	**LARGELY**
timor	**DREAD, FEAR**	toast	**BROWN, SKOAL**
timorous	**FEARFUL**	toasty	**WARM**
timothy	**HAY**	tobacco chew	**QUID**
timpany	**DRUMS**	tobacco container	**HUMIDOR**
tin	**CAN, METAL**	tobacco disease	**WALLOON**
tin alloy	**PEWTER**	tobacco kiln	**OAST**
tincal	**BORAX**	tobacco pipe	**CORNCOB**
tincture	**MYRRH**	tobacco roll	**CIGAR**
tine	**PRONG**	to be (Fr.)	**ETRE**
tinge	**TINT, HUE**	to be (Lat.)	**ESSE**
tinge deeply	**IMBUE**	to be of use	**AVAIL**
tingle	**PRICKLE**	to be sure	**INDEED**
tingling reaction	**THRILL**	toboggan	**SLED**
tiniest bit	**IOTA**	toby	**JUG**
tinkle	**CLINK**	tocsin	**ALARM**
tinkling sound	**PLINK**	today	**NOW, PRESENT**
tinsel	**GLITTER**	toddler	**TOT**

to-do	**COMMOTION, FUSS**	toot	**BLAST, WHISTLE**
toe ailment	**GOUT**	tooth	**MOLAR, CANINE, INCISOR, FANG**
toe hold	**FOOTING**	tooth covering	**ENAMEL**
toenail beauty treatment	**PEDICURE**	tooth decay	**CARIES**
		tooth doctor	**DENTIST**
toe the line	**OBEY**	toothed wheel	**GEAR, RATCHET**
toff	**DANDY**		
toffee	**CANDY**	tooth of a gear wheel	**DENT**
toga	**ROBE**	toothpaste container	**TUBE**
togetherness	**UNITY**	toothsome	**TASTY**
toggle	**PIN, BOLT**	top	**SUMMIT, APEX, ACME, PEAK**
togs	**CLOTHES**		
toil	**LABOR, WORK**	topaz	**YELLOW**
toilet case	**ETUI**	top banana	**HEADLINER**
tokay	**WINE**	topee	**HELMET, HAT**
token	**SYMBOL**	toper	**SOT**
token move	**GESTURE**	topic	**THEME, SUBJECT**
token of affection	**CARESS KISS**	top military officers	**BRASS**
		top-notch	**BEST**
token of regard	**TESTIMONIAL**	top of altar	**MENSA**
token of right	**TICKET**	top of an apron	**BIB**
token of victory	**PALM**	top of a wave	**CREST**
Tokyo's former name	**EDO**	top of the head	**PATE**
tolerant	**LENIENT, ENDURING**	topper	**HAT**
		topple	**TUMBLE, COLLAPSE**
tolerate	**ENDURE, BEAR, STAND**	topside	**DECK**
		topsy-turvy (2 wds.)	
toll	**RING, TAX**		**UPSIDE DOWN**
tollhouse	**COOKIE**	toque	**HAT, CAP**
toll road	**PIKE**	Torah	**PENTATEUCH**
tomahawk	**HATCHET**	torch	**FLARE**
to make fun of	**DERIDE**	torero	**MATADOR**
to make love	**WOO**	torment	**PESTER, TEASE, TAUNT**
tomato (2 wds.)	**LOVE APPLE**		
tomato relish	**CATSUP, KETCHUP**	tornado	**TWISTER, CYCLONE**
tomb	**CRYPT, VAULT**	torpid	**INERT, NUMB**
tomboy	**HOYDEN**	torpor	**APATHY, LETHARGY**
tomcat	**GIB**	torrent	**DOWNPOUR**
tome	**VOLUME**	torrid	**HOT**
tommyrot	**RUBBISH**	torso	**BODY**
tomorrow (Sp.)	**MANANA**	torte	**CAKE**
tom-tom	**DRUM**	torture	**PAIN, ANGUISH**
tone	**SOUND**	to set in type	**PRINT**
tone color	**TIMBRE**	to some extent (2 wds.)	**IN PART**
tongue	**LANGUAGE**	toss	**THROW, HEAVE, CAST, HURL, FLING**
tonic	**BRACER**		
to no purpose (2 wds.)	**IN VAIN**	toss carelessly	**FLIP**
too	**ALSO, AND**	tossed greens	**SALAD**
tool	**AUGER, PLANE, AWL, HAMMER, SAW, IMPLEMENT**	tot	**TODDLER**
		total	**ADD, ALL, SUM, ENTIRE**
tool for writing	**PENCIL, PEN**	totally	**QUITE**
too much (Fr.)	**TROP**	tote	**CARRY**
toon	**MAHOGANY**	to that time	**UNTIL**
to one side	**APART**	to the larboard	**APORT**

to the left	**HAW**
to the point	**TERSE**
to the rear	**ASTERN**
to the sheltered side	**ALEE**
to this place	**HERE, HITHER**
toucan	**ARACARI**
touch	**FEEL, ABUT**
touch down	**LAND**
touchdown	**GOAL**
touch gently	**DAB, PAT**
touching	**MOVING**
touch up	**FINISH**
touch with color	**PAINT**
touchy	**TESTY**
tough, as meat	**STRINGY**
toughen	**HARDEN, TEMPER**
toughen by exercise	**INURE, ENURE**
tough question	**POSER**
toupee	**WIG**
tourist attraction	**RUINS**
tourist lodging	**MOTEL, HOTEL, RESORT**
tournament	**CONTEST**
tournament bridge award (2 wds.)	**MASTER POINT**
tow	**PULL**
toward	**TO**
toward shelter	**ALEE**
toward the center	**INTO**
toward the front	**ANTERIOR**
toward the interior	**INLAND**
toward the left side (naut.)	**APORT**
toward the stern	**AFT**
towel	**DRY, RUB**
towel fabric	**TERRY**
towel word	**HERS, HIS**
tower	**FORTRESS, SPIRE, STEEPLE, BELFRY**
towering	**TALL**
tower of ice	**SERAC**
towhead	**BLOND**
town (colloq.)	**BURG**
town in New Guinea	**LAE**
town map	**PLAT**
townsman	**CIT**
town's position	**SITE**
town's principal street (2 wds.)	**MAIN STEM**
tow rope	**HAWSER**
toxic	**POISON**
toy	**PLAYTHING**
toy baby	**DOLL**
trace	**VESTIGE**
trace of an ancient animal	**FOSSIL**

trace of color	**TINGE**
tracer	**INQUIRY, BULLET**
trachea	**WINDPIPE**
tracing	**COPY**
track	**TRAIL, SPOOR**
track circuit	**LAP**
track down	**TRACE**
track event	**SELLING RACE, RELAY RACE**
track race	**RELAY**
track runner	**MILER**
tract	**AREA**
tract	**DISSERTATION**
tractable	**DOCILE, PLIANT**
tractate	**TREATISE**
traction	**PULL, FRICTION**
tract of wasteland	**MOOR**
trade	**SWAP, BARTER, EXCHANGE, COMMERCE**
trade center	**MART, MARKET**
trade combination	**MERGER**
trade for money	**SELL**
trademark	**BRAND, LABEL**
trade name	**BRAND**
trade on	**EXPLOIT**
tradesman	**MERCHANT**
trading station	**POST**
tradition	**LEGEND, CUSTOM**
traditional knowledge	**LORE**
traditional restriction	**TABOO**
traditional tale	**SAGA**
traduce	**DEFAME, MALIGN**
traffic	**COMMERCE, TRADE**
traffic light color	**AMBER, RED, GREEN**
traffic route	**LANE**
traffic violation	**SPEEDING**
traffic violation charge	**FINE**
tragedy	**DISASTER, DRAMA**
tragic	**DIRE**
trail	**TRACE, TRACK, SPOOR**
trail blazer	**PIONEER**
trailing plant	**VINE**
train	**TEACH, EDUCATE**
train (Sp.)	**TREN**
train berth (2 wds.)	**BUNK BED**
trainer of wild animals	**TAMER**
train terminal	**DEPOT, STATION**
train track	**RAIL**
train whistle	**TOOT**
traipse	**TRAMP, WANDER**
trait	**MARK**
traitor (sl.)	**RAT**
traitorous	**PERFIDIOUS**

tram	**TROLLEY**
trammel	**ENTANGLE**
tramp	**BUM, HOBO,**
	VAGABOND
tramp vessel	**STEAMER**
trample	**TREAD**
tranquil	**CALM, PEACEFUL,**
	SERENE
tranquility	**PEACE,**
	SERENITY, QUIET
transaction	**SALE**
transcend	**SURPASS**
transcendental	**OBSCURE**
transcribe	**COPY**
transcribe shorthand	**TYPE**
transect	**DIVIDE**
transfer	**SHIFT, MOVE**
transfer sticker	**DECAL**
transfix	**PIERCE**
transform	**CONVERT,**
	CHANGE
transgress	**SIN**
transient	**BRIEF,**
	TEMPORARY
transistor set	**RADIO**
transit	**PASSAGE**
transit coach	**BUS**
transition	**CHANGE,**
	CONVERSION
transitory	**TEMPORAL,**
	FLEETING
translate	**INTERPRET**
translation	**TROT, PONY**
translucent	**LIMPID,**
	CLEAR
transmit	**SEND**
transmit in succession	
	HAND DOWN
transom	**WINDOW**
transparent	**CLEAR, SHEER**
transparent liquid	**WATER**
transpire	**HAPPEN, OCCUR**
transplant	**GRAFT**
transport	**CARRY**
transportation charge	**FARE**
transportation to the	
top floor	**ELEVATOR**
transpose	**REVERSE**
transverse	**BEAM, AXIS**
trap	**SNARE, CAPTURE**
trap door	**DROP**
trapeze artist	**ACROBAT**
trappings	**GEAR**
trash	**WASTE, RUBBISH**
trauma	**SHOCK**
travail	**LABOR, WORK**
travel	**TOUR, RIDE,**
	JOURNEY, VISIT

travel across snow	**MUSH**
traveler	**FARER**
traveler's choice	**TOUR,**
	TRAIN, BUS, PLANE,
	SHIP, CAR, JET
traveler's concern (2 wds.)	
	DEPARTURE DATE
traveler's home	**HOTEL,**
	MOTEL
travel fast (2 wds.)	**MAKE TIME**
traveling bag	**VALISE,**
	SUITCASE
traveling salesman	**DRUMMER**
travel on foot	**WALK,**
	HIKE, MARCH
travel on horseback	**RIDE**
traverse	**CROSS**
travesty	**PARODY, SATIRE**
tray	**SALVER, SERVER**
treacherous	**FALSE**
tread	**STEP, TRAMPLE**
treasure box	**CHEST**
Treasure State	**MONTANA**
treat	**AMUSE, ENTERTAIN**
treaty	**PACT**
treble	**SOPRANO, TRIPLE**
treble clef	**GEE**
tree	**ASH, CEDAR,**
	CHESTNUT, FIR, LARCH,
	OAK, POPLAR,
	SAPLING, ELM,
	PINE, MAPLE,
	LINDEN, WALNUT
tree (Ger.)	**BAUM**
tree branch	**LIMB**
tree covering	**BARK**
tree dwelling	**NEST**
tree exudation	**LAC, RESIN**
tree fluid	**SAP**
tree groups	**GROVE**
treeless	**UNWOODED,**
	BARE
treeless Arctic plain	**TUNDRA**
tree-snake	**LORA**
tree stump	**STUB**
treetop chatter (2 wds.)	
	BIRD TALK
treetop home	**NEST**
tree trunk	**BOLE**
trek	**TRAVEL, TOUR**
trellis	**ARBOR, LATTICE**
tremble	**QUAKE, SHAKE,**
	SHIVER, QUIVER,
	VIBRATE
trembling tree	**ASPEN**
tremendous	**HUGE**
tremor	**VIBRATION**

trench	**DITCH**	Trojan king	**PRIAM**
trenchant	**KEEN, CUTTING**	Trojan mountain	**IDA**
trencherman	**EATER**	trolley	**TRAM**
trend	**DIRECTION, TURN**	trophy	**AWARD, PRIZE**
trepidation	**FEAR**	tropical	**HOT, TORRID**
trespass	**INTRUDE**	tropical arum plant	**TARO**
tresses	**HAIR, CURLS**	tropical basket fiber	**ISTLE**
trestle	**BRIDGE**	tropical cuckoo	**ANI**
triad	**THREE**	tropical fruit	**BANANA,**
trial	**TEST**		**DATE, FIG, MANGO,**
trial package	**SAMPLE**		**PAPAW, PINEAPPLE**
triangle side	**LEG**	tropical grouper	**MERO**
triangular piece in skirts	**GORE**	tropical lizard	**AGAMA**
tribal emblem	**TOTEM**	tropical nut	**KOLA**
tribe	**CLAN, FAMILY,**	tropical plant	**ALOE**
	BAND	tropical tree	**EBOE, PALM**
tribulation	**WOE**	tropical vine	**LIANA**
tribunal	**COURT**	tropical water lily	**LOTUS**
tributary	**ARM**	trot	**CANTER, JOG, LOPE**
tribute	**PRAISE**	troth	**LOYALTY, PROMISE**
trice	**INSTANT**	trottoir	**SIDEWALK**
trick	**RUSE, HOAX, SHAM,**	troubador	**MINSTREL**
	WILE, DUPE	trouble	**AIL, WOE, ANNOY,**
trickle	**SEEP**		**ADO, ILL**
trifle	**FIG, JOT**	trouble (Scot.)	**FASH**
trifle fault	**PECCADILLO**	troublesome plant	**RAGWEED,**
trifling	**PETTY, TRIVIAL**		**WEED**
trig	**SPRUCE, TRIM**	troublesome weed	**TARE**
trigonometric function	**SINE,**	trough	**CONDUIT, CHUTE**
	COSINE	trough to hold hay	**MANGER**
trill	**QUAVER, WARBLE**	trounce	**DEFEAT**
trim	**DECORATE, NEAT**	trousers	**PANTS**
trimming	**RUCHE, FRINGE**	trousers' fabric	**TWILL**
trim off branches	**LOP,**	trousers' pocket	**FOB**
	PRUNE	trove	**TREASURE**
trim the hair	**CLIP**	Troy	**ILIUM**
trim trees	**PRUNE**	truce	**ARMISTICE**
Trinacria	**SICILY**	trucker	**HAULER,**
trine	**THREEFOLD**		**TEAMSTER**
trinity	**TRIAD**	truculent	**SAVAGE, FIERCE**
trinket	**BEAD**	trudge	**PLOD**
trip	**JOURNEY, STUMBLE,**	true	**LOYAL, REAL,**
	TREK, FALL,		**GENUINE, CORRECT**
	VOYAGE, TOUR	true to fact	**LITERAL**
triple	**THREE**	truffle	**TUBER**
tripod	**EASEL, TRIVET**	truism	**AXIOM**
trireme	**GALLEY**	truly	**YEA, VERILY**
Tristan's beloved	**ISOLDE**	Truman's opponent	**DEWEY**
trite	**BANAL, HACKNEYED,**	trump	**RUFF**
	CORNY	trumpet	**HORN**
triton	**EFT, NEWT**	trumpet fanfare	**TANTARA**
triumph	**WIN, VICTORY**	trumpet sound	**BLARE**
triumphant exclamation	**AHA,**	trunk of a body	**TORSO**
	EUREKA	trust	**BELIEVE, CREDIT**
trivial	**PETTY**	trustworthy	**RELIANT**
troche	**LOZENGE**	truth	**FACT, HONESTY**
Trojan hero	**PARIS,**	truthful	**HONEST**
	AENEAS		

try	**TEST, ATTEMPT**
trying age	**TEENS**
try to secure (2 wds.)	**GO FOR**
tub activity	**BATH**
tube	**CYLINDER, PIPE**
tuberous vegetable	**POTATO**
tug	**HAUL, DRAG**
tumble	**FALL**
tumbledown dwelling	**SHACK, SHANTY**
tumbler	**GLASS**
tumid	**POMPOUS**
tumult	**RIOT, STIR**
tumultuous	**TURBULENT, VIOLENT**
tune	**AIR, MELODY, SONG**
tune in secretly	**WIRETAP**
Tunisian ruler	**BEY, DEY**
turbid	**MUDDY**
turbine power	**STEAM**
turbulent	**DISTURBED, RESTLESS**
turf	**PEAT, SOD, SWARD**
turgid	**SWOLLEN, BLOATED**
Turk	**OTTOMAN**
turkey gobbler	**TOM**
Turkish caliph	**ALI**
Turkish cap	**FEZ**
Turkish capital	**ANKARA**
Turkish cavalryman	**SPAHI**
Turkish decree	**IRADE**
Turkish governor	**PASHA**
Turkish gulf	**COS**
Turkish hat	**FEZ**
Turkish inn	**IMARET**
Turkish judge	**CADI**
Turkish money	**LIRA, PARA**
Turkish mountain	**ARARAT**
Turkish name	**ALI**
Turkish standard	**ALEM**
Turkish title	**AGA, AMIR, EMIR**
Turkish tobacco	**LATAKIA**
Turkish vessel	**SAIC**
turmoil	**ADO, MELEE**
turn	**REVOLVE, ROTATE, SPIN, WHIRL**
turn about	**SLUE**
turn aside	**AVERT, DETER**
turn away	**REPEL**
turn back	**REVERSE**
turn down	**VETO**
turn for help	**RESORT**
turning part of a dynamo	**ROTOR**
turn in trading stamps	**REDEEM**
turn of duty	**SPELL**

turn on axis	**ROTATE**
turn on pivot	**SWIVEL**
turn outward	**EVERT**
turn over	**OVERSET, REVERSE, FLOP**
turn over a new leaf	**REFORM**
turnpike	**ROAD, HIGHWAY**
turnpike charge	**TOLL**
turnpike exit	**RAMP**
turn sharply	**VEER**
turpentine distillate	**RESIN**
turret	**TOWER**
turtle shell	**CARAPACE**
tusk	**FANG, TOOTH**
tusk material	**IVORY**
tussle	**STRUGGLE, WRESTLE**
tuxedo (2 wds.)	**DINNER COAT**
TV emcee Linkletter	**ART**
TV emcee Mack	**TED**
TV emcee Parks	**BERT**
TV in England	**TELLY**
TV outlet	**CHANNEL**
TV part	**TUBE**
TV program	**NEWS, SERIES, SOAP OPERA, WESTERN, SPECIAL**
TV repeat show	**RERUN**
TV sponsor's concern	**RATINGS**
TV statuette	**EMMY**
TV's Uncle Miltie	**BERLE**
twang	**NASALITY**
tweak	**PINCH**
tweedle	**CAJOLE, WHINE**
tweet	**CHIRP**
tweezers	**PINCERS**
twelfth of a year	**MONTH**
twelve inches	**FOOT**
twelvemonth	**YEAR**
twenty four hours	**DAY**
twice	**BIS**
twig	**SHOOT, SPRIG**
twilight	**EVENING**
twilled woolen fabric	**SERGE**
twin	**DOUBLE**
twine	**CORD**
twine about	**ENLACE**
twinge	**PANG, QUALM**
twining shoot	**BINE**
twining stem	**VINE**
twinkle	**WINK**
twirl	**SPIN**
twirlers wand	**BATON**
twist	**WIND**
twist about	**SLEW, SLUE**
twisted	**WRY**
twister	**TORNADO, CYCLONE**

twist out of shape	WARP
twist to one side	SLUE
twist together	ENTWINE
twit	TEASE, TAUNT
twitch	JERK
twitter	CHATTER, GIGGLE
two	DUET, DUO, PAIR,
two below par, in golf	EAGLE
two bit gambler (sl.)	PIKER
two cups	PINT
two door auto	COUPE
two family quarrel	FEUD
twofold	DOUBLE,
	DUAL, TWIN, TWICE
two-footed animal	BIPED
two-masted vessel	YAWL,
	KETCH
two pints	QUART
two (poetic)	TWAIN
two (quartets)	OCTET
two singers	DUO, DUET
twosome	DUO, PAIR
two spot	DEUCE
two times	TWICE, BIS,
	DOUBLE
two-toed sloth	UNAU
two-wheeled vehicle	CART,
	SCOOTER, BIKE
tycoon	SHOGUN
tyke	SHAVER
type	SORT, KIND, CLASS,
	ILK, GENRE
type collection	FONT
type measure	EM, EN
type of agent	UNDERCOVER
type of beer	LAGER,
	PILSNER
type of cabbage	KALE
type of canoe	PIROGUE,
	PROA, DUGOUT
type of car	SEDAN, COUPE
type of cross	TAU
type of drapery	VALANCE
type of employment	
(comp. wd.)	PART-TIME,
	FULL-TIME
type of fabric	LENO
type of fastener	HASP
type of fuel	COAL, GAS,
	OIL, PEAT
type of glazed paper	GLASSINE
type of jacket	ETON,
	EISENHOWER, IKE
type of joke	PUN

type of magazine	
	PERIODICAL, GLOSSY,
	MONTHLY, WEEKLY,
	ANNUAL
type of ode	PINDARIC
type of painting	OIL COLOR,
	PORTRAIT,
	WATER COLOR,
	LANDSCAPE, STILL LIFE
type of pay	DAY RATE,
	PIECE WORK
type of perfection	PARAGON
type of piano	GRAND,
	UPRIGHT,
	BABY GRAND
type of poem	ODE, SONNET
type of puzzle	JIGSAW
type of race	RELAY
type of race track	SPEEDWAY
type of record player	STEREO
type of rock	SANDSTONE,
	SHALE
type of rubber	LATEX
type of ruby	SPINEL
type of skylight	LUNETTE
type of waistcoat	JERKIN
type of word game	FILL-IN,
	CROSSWORD, LOTTO
type of wrench	SPANNER
type row	LINE
type size	ELITE, PICA
typewriter bar	SPACER,
	PLATEN
typhoon	CYCLONE
typical	REGULAR, NORMAL
typographer	PRINTER
tyrant	DESPOT, DICTATOR
Tyre king	HIRAM
Tyrian	PURPLE
tyro	NOVICE
tzigane	GYPSY

U

u-boat	SUBMARINE,
	SUB
ugly	HOMELY, HIDEOUS
ugly old woman	HAG, CRONE
uh-huh	YES
uh-uh	NO
ukase	EDICT, DECREE
ulna	BONE
ulster	COAT
ultimate	EVENTUAL
ultimate end	GOAL
ultimately (2 wds.)	IN FINE
ultra	EXTREME

ululate	HOWL, WAIL
umber	PIGMENT
umbrage	HATRED, CONTEMPT, OFFENSE
umpire	REFEREE, ARBITER
unable	CANNOT
unabridged	COMPLETE, UNCUT
unaccompanied	ALONE
unadorned	BARE, PLAIN
unadulterated	PURE
unaffected	SINCERE
unanimity	ACCORD, UNITY
unanimously	SOLIDLY
unapt	DULL, SLOW
unaroused	ASLEEP, DORMANT
unaspirated	LENE
unassisted	ALONE
unassumed	NATURAL
unattached	SINGLE
unbalanced	ALIST, ALOP
unbelievable	INCREDIBLE
unbeliever	INFIDEL, HERETIC
unbend	RELAX
unbroken	INTACT
unburden	EASE, RELIEVE
unburnt and dried brick	ADOBE
unbusy	IDLE
uncanny	EERIE
unceremonious	ABRUPT, INFORMAL
uncertain	DOUBTFUL
unchecked	FREE, RAMPANT
uncivil	RUDE, IMPOLITE, CRUSTY
unclaimed ground (comp. wd.)	NO-MAN'S-LAND
uncle (Scot.)	EME
uncle (Sp.)	TIO
unclean	DIRTY
unclose (poetic)	OPE
unclosed	OPEN
unclothed	NUDE, NAKED, BARE
uncommon	ODD, RARE
uncomplaining	STOICAL
uncomplicated	EASY
uncompromising	RIGID
unconcealed	BARE, OPEN
unconcerned	DETACHED
unconcerned, ethically	AMORAL
unconditional	ABSOLUTE
unconfined	LOOSE

unconfirmed gossip	RUMOR
unconfused	CALM, CLEAR
unconventional (Fr.)	OUTRE
uncooked	RAW
uncopied	ORIGINAL
uncouth	CRASS, RUDE
uncovered	BARE, OPEN
unctuous	OILY, GUSHY
uncultivated	FALLOW, WILD
uncultivated plant	WEED
uncultured	CRUDE
undaunted	BOLD, BRAVE
undecided (4 wds.)	UP IN THE AIR
undecorated	BARE
undeniable	TRUE
under	BENEATH
under an assumed name	INCOGNITO
undercover	SECRET
undercover man	SPY, AGENT
underground hollow	CAVE
underground plant part	ROOT
underground worker	MINER
underhand	SECRETLY
underling	MENIAL, INFERIOR
underlying reason	RATIONALE
undermine	SAP
undershirt	VEST
undersized	TINY, SMALL, WEE
undersized animal	RUNT
understand	SEE, REALIZE, KNOW
understanding	KEN
understood	TACIT
understood by a select few	ESOTERIC
undertake	ASSUME, ENGAGE
undertaker	MORTICIAN
undertaking	TASK
under tension (sl.)	UPTIGHT
under the weather	ILL
undertone	ASIDE
underwater	AWASH
underworld	HADES, SHEOL
underworld god	DIS
underworld of myth	HADES
undetermined	VAGUE
undeveloped stem	BUD
undiluted, as liquor	NEAT
undisguised	NAKED
undistinguished multitude	RUCK

undivided	ENTIRE, ONE, UNITED	uniform	MEASURED
undo knitting	RAVEL	uniform ornament	EPAULET
undoing	RUIN, DOWNFALL	unilateral	ONE-WAY
undomesticated	WILD, FERAL	unimaginative	DULL, PROSAIC
undue hurry	HASTE	unimportant	ONE-HORSE, PETTY
undulate	SWAY, RIPPLE	uninformed	IGNORANT
unearned cash (2 wds.)	EASY MONEY	union weapon	STRIKE
		unique	RARE, CHOICE
unearth	UNCOVER, EXHUME	unique person	ONER
unearthly	EERIE	unison	HARMONY, CONCORD
uneasy	RESTIVE, RESTLESS	unit	ONE
unemotional	STOIC	unite	WELD, WED, JOIN, ALLY, MARRY, SPLICE, MERGE
unemployed	OUT OF WORK, IDLE		
unencumbered	FREE	united	ONE, WED
unequal	UNEVEN, DIFFERENT	unit of cavalry	TROOP
		unit of energy	ERG, DYNE
unequal things	ODDS	unit of heat	THERM, CALORY, CALORIE
unequivocal	PLAIN, SINCERE		
		unit of heredity	GENE
unerring	SURE, TRUE	unit of illumination	LUX, PHOT
unescorted male	STAG		
uneven	ROUGH, EROSE	unit of length	METER, FOOT, YARD, INCH, MILE
unexpected difficulty	SNAG		
unexpected stroke of luck	WINDFALL	unit of light	LUX, PYR
		unit of weight (India)	SER
unexpected win	UPSET	unit of work	ERG
unexplored region	FRONTIER	unity	ONE
unfamiliar	STRANGE	universal	GENERAL, TOTAL
unfasten	UNDO		
unfavorable	ADVERSE, BAD	universal language	IDO
unfeeling	STONY, COLD	universal remedy	PANACEA
unfettered	LOOSE	universe	COSMOS
unfit	INEPT, INCOMPETENT	university post	
unfold	OPEN		PROFESSORSHIP
unfortunate	ILL	unkempt	SHAGGY, TOUSLED
unfounded report	RUMOR	unkind	CRUEL, MEAN
unfreeze	THAW, MELT	unkind remark	SLUR
unfrequented	COOL, HOSTILE	unlawful	ILLEGAL
unfriendly	COOL, HOSTILE	unlawful act	CRIME
unfruitful	BARREN	unleavened corn cake	
unfulfilled desire	WISH		TORTILLA
unfurl	SPREAD, UNROLL		
ungainly	CLUMSY, AWKWARD	unlighted	DARK, DIM
		unlock	OPEN
ungentlemanly man	CAD, LOUT, BOOR	unlucky	UNTOWARD
		unmarried	SINGLE
unhappy	SAD	unmarried woman	MAIDEN
unhappy expression	FROWN	unmetered writing	PROSE
unharmed	INTACT	unmixed	PURE
unhealthy color	SALLOW	unmounted	AFOOT
unhealthily pallid	PASTY	unmoved	FIRM
unheard of	STRANGE	unnamed person	SOMEONE
unheeding	DEAF	unnecessary	NEEDLESS
unheralded	UNSUNG	unnerve	UPSET

unobtrusive	**MODEST, RETIRING**	untidy person	**SLOVEN**
unoccupied	**EMPTY, IDLE**	untidy pile	**HEAP**
unpaved road edges		untidy woman	**SLATTERN**
	SHOULDER, BERM	untie	**LOOSEN**
unpleasant	**NASTY**	until now (2 wds.)	**SO FAR**
unpretentious	**MODEST**	untoward	**UNLUCKY**
unreasoning fear	**PANIC**	untrammeled	**FREE**
unrefined	**CRUDE**	untried	**NEW, GREEN**
unrefined metal	**ORE**	untrue	**FALSE**
unresisting	**PASSIVE**	untutored	**ILLITERATE**
unrestrained pleasure	**FLING, SPREE**	untwist	**RAVEL**
		unused	**NEW**
unrestricted	**OPEN**	unusual	**NOVEL, RARE,**
unrhymed poetry (2 wds.)			**UNCOMMON, ODD,**
	BLANK VERSE		**OUTLANDISH, STRANGE**
unripe	**GREEN**	unusually good	**EXCELLENT**
unroll	**OPEN**	unusually sensitive	**ALLERGIC**
unruffled	**CALM**	unusual person (sl.)	**ONER**
unruly	**RESTIVE**	unveil	**REVEAL**
unruly child	**BRAT**	unverified report	**RUMOR**
unruly crowd	**MOB, HORDE**	unwanted plant	**WEED**
unsatisfactory, as		unwarranted	**UNDUE**
an excuse	**LAME**	unwavering	**RESOLUTE**
unsavory	**TASTELESS**	unwearied	**TIRELESS**
unseal	**OPEN**	unwelcome person	**INTRUDER**
unseam	**RIP**	unwieldy	**BULKY**
unseat a monarch	**DEPOSE**	unwieldy object	**HULK**
unseemly	**INAPT, IMPROPER**	unwilling	**AVERSE**
		unwooded	**TREELESS**
unseen	**HIDDEN**	unwrap	**OPEN**
unselfish	**ALTRUISTIC**	unyielding	**FIRM, RIGID**
unsightly	**UGLY**	up	**ALOFT, ABOVE, OVER**
unskilled worker (2 wds.)		up and around	**ACTIVE**
	DAY LABORER	upbraid	**SCOLD**
unskillful	**INEPT**	upheave	**LIFT, REAR**
unsoiled	**CLEAN**	uphold	**BACK, ABET**
unsophisticated	**NAIVE, CORNY**	uplift	**RAISE**
		uplift spirits	**ELATE**
unsound	**INSECURE**	upon	**ATOP, ON, ONTO**
unsparing	**PROFUSE**	upper	**HIGHER, BERTH**
unspecified amount	**SOME, ANY**	upper air	**ETHER**
		upper Canada	**ONTARIO**
unspecified person	**ONES**	upper-case letter	**CAPITAL**
unspecified time	**WHENEVER**	upperclassman	**JUNIOR, SENIOR**
unspoiled	**FRESH**		
unspoken	**TACIT**	uppercut	**PUNCH, BLOW**
unstable	**ERRATIC**	upper end	**TOP**
unsteady glaring light	**FLARE**	upper house of the	
unsuitable	**INEPT, UNFIT**	legislature	**SENATE**
unsung	**UNHERALDED**	upper limb	**ARM**
unswerving in allegiance	**LOYAL**	uppermost	**TOP**
untamed	**FERAL, WILD**	upper Nile native	**NILOT**
untanned hide	**PELT**	upper part	**TOP**
unthankful person	**INGRATE**	upper story	**ATTIC**
untidy	**MESSY**	uppish person	**SNOB**
untidy heap	**MESS**	uppity	**SNOOTY**
		upright	**ERECT**

uprightly	**RECTLY**
uprising	**RIOT, REVOLT, MUTINY**
uproar	**CLAMOR, DIN, HURLY-BURLY, RIOT**
uproarious	**RIOTOUS**
uproot	**ERADICATE**
upset	**OVERTURN**
upshot	**RESULT, OUTCOME**
upside down	**INVERTED**
upstanding	**UPRIGHT, HONORABLE**
upstart	**PARVENU**
up to	**UNTIL**
up-to-date	**MODERN**
up to now (2 wds.)	**SO FAR**
up to the time of	**UNTIL**
up to this point	**AS YET, SO FAR**
urban area	**CITY**
urbane	**SUAVE, POLISHED**
urban eyesore	**SKID ROW, SLUM**
urban need (2 wds.)	**RAPID TRANSIT**
urchin	**TAD, GAMIN**
urd	**BEAN**
urge	**COAX, IMPEL, PROD, SPUR, EGG ON, PERSUADE**
urgent	**PRESSING**
urgent wireless signal	**SOS**
urn	**VASE**
ursa	**BEAR**
urticate	**STING**
Uruguay river	**PLATA**
us	**WE**
usable	**FIT**
usage	**HABIT, CUSTOM**
use	**EMPLOY, UTILIZE**
use a broom	**SWEEP**
use a chair	**SIT**
use a crayon	**DRAW**
use a gun	**SHOOT**
use a hammer	**NAIL**
use a knife	**SLICE, CARVE, STAB**
use a lever	**PRY**
use a loom	**WEAVE**
use a needle	**SEW**
use an oven	**BAKE, ROAST**
use a pencil	**WRITE**
use a phone	**CALL, DIAL**
use a razor	**SHAVE**
use a shovel	**DIG**
use a sieve	**SIFT**
use a spade	**DIG**

use bad posture	**SLOUCH**
use boat oars	**ROW**
used	**SECONDHAND**
used up (2 wds.)	**PLAYED OUT**
use dynamite	**BLAST**
use experimentally	**TRY**
useful	**HELPFUL, UTILE**
useful quality	**ASSET**
useless plant	**WEED**
use hindsight (comp. wd.)	**SECOND-GUESS**
use logic	**REASON**
use money	**SPEND, BUY**
use needlessly	**WASTE**
use oars	**ROW**
use pressure	**EXERT**
use scissors	**SNIP, CUT**
use sparingly	**STINT, RATION**
use subterfuge	**CHICANE**
use the brain	**THINK**
use up	**CONSUME, EAT**
U.S. flag	**OLD GLORY, STARS AND STRIPES**
U.S. frigate Constitution (2 wds.)	**OLD IRONSIDES**
usher	**SEATER, ESCORT**
using speech	**ORAL**
U.S. president's home (2 wds.)	**WHITE HOUSE**
U.S. service branch	**NAVY, ARMY, AIR FORCE, MARINES**
U.S. symbol	**EAGLE**
usual	**NORMAL, FAMILIAR**
usually	**GENERALLY**
usurp	**SEIZE, CLAIM**
Utah's flower	**SEGO**
Ute	**INDIAN**
utensil	**TOOL, IMPLEMENT**
utilitarian	**ECONOMIC, PRACTICAL**
utility	**USE**
utmost	**SUPREME**
utopian	**IDEAL**
utopian region	**EDEN**
utter	**SAY, SPEAK, SHEER**
utter affectedly	**MINCE**
utter a shrill cry	**YELP**
utter brokenly	**GASP**
utter confusion	**CHAOS**
utter in a low tone	**MUTTER**
utterly	**TOTALLY, FULLY**
utterly perplexed and confounded (4 wds.)	**AT ONE'S WITS' END**

utter musical tones	**SING**	vaporizing easily	**VOLATILE**
uxorial	**WIFELIKE**	vaquero	**COWBOY**
		vaquero's rope	**RIATA**
		vaquero's weapon	**BOLA**
V		variable	**PROTEAN**
		variable star in Cetus	**MIRA**
v-shaped cut	**NOTCH**	variation	**DEVIATION**
vacancy	**GAP, BLANK,**	variegated	**PIED**
	OPENING	variety	**DIVERSITY, MEDLEY**
vacant	**EMPTY, UNRENTED**	variety of agate	**ONYX**
vacate	**EVACUATE, LEAVE**	variety of apple	**WINESAP,**
vacation	**HOLIDAY, RECESS**		**DELICIOUS, McINTOSH**
vacation specialist (2 wds.)		variety of beet	**CHARD**
	TRAVEL AGENT	variety of cabbage	
vacation spot	**RESORT, SPA**		**CAULIFLOWER, KALE**
vacillate	**WAVER**	variety of cheese	**EDAM,**
vagabond	**TRAMP, HOBO,**		**BRIE, GOUDA,**
	GYPSY		**CHEDDAR**
vagrant	**HOBO, TRAMP,**	variety of grape	**MALAGA**
	BUM, ROVER	variety of moth	**LUNA**
vague	**OBSCURE, DIM**	variety of wheat	**SPELT**
vain	**IDLE, TRIVIAL**	various	**SEVERAL, SUNDRY,**
vain bird's mate	**PEAHEN**		**ASSORTED**
valentine's day archer	**CUPID**	varlet	**SCOUNDREL, KNAVE**
valentine symbol	**HEART**	varmint	**PEST**
valet	**MANSERVANT**	varna	**CASTE**
valiant	**BRAVE, DARING**	varnish	**ELEMI, LAC,**
valid	**COGENT, SOUND**		**RESIN**
valise	**GRIP, SUITCASE**	vary	**DIFFER, ALTER**
valley	**DALE, VALE, DELL**	varying weight of India	**SER,**
valley of Argolis	**NEMEA**		**SEER**
valley on the moon	**RILLE**	vase	**JAR, URN**
valor	**PROWESS, COURAGE**	vase-shaped jug	**EWER**
valorous person	**HERO**	vase with a pedestal	**URN**
valuable	**DEAR, PRECIOUS**	vassal	**SLAVE**
valuable card	**TRUMP, ACE**	vast	**HUGE, ENORMOUS**
valuable fur	**ERMINE, MINK**	vast desert	**SAHARA**
	SABLE	vast expanse	**OCEAN, SEA**
valuable moth larva	**SILKWORM**	vast number	**MYRIAD**
valuable possession	**ASSET**	vast period of time	**EON,**
valuable violin	**AMATI, STRAD**		**AEON**
value	**WORTH**	vat	**CALDRON, TUB**
value highly	**TREASURE**	vault	**LEAP, SAFE**
vamoose	**SCRAM**	vaulter's shaft	**POLE**
vampire	**LAMIA**	vaunt	**BOAST, BRAG**
van	**TRUCK, FRONT**	veal	**MEAT**
vandal	**HUN**	veal steak	**CHOP**
Van Druten character	**MAMA**	veer	**SWERVE**
vane	**COCK**	vega	**STAR**
Van Gogh	**ARTIST**	vegetable	**BEET, KALE,**
vanish	**DISAPPEAR**		**LEEK, PEA, BEAN,**
vanity	**CONCEIT, PRIDE**		**POTATO, CARROT,**
vanity box	**ETUI**		**RADISH, CORN,**
van man	**MOVER**		**LETTUCE, CABBAGE,**
vanquish	**CONQUER**		**TOMATO, OKRA,**
vapid	**INSIPID, BLAND**		**SQUASH, LEGUME**
vapor	**GAS, STEAM,**	vegetable box	**BIN**
	FUME, SMOKE		

vegetable ferment **YEAST**
vegetable oyster **SALSIFY**
vegetable punk **AMADOU**
vegetable silk **KAPOK**
vehemence **FURY, RAGE**
vehicle **AUTO, BUS, TRAIN, TRUCK**
vehicle dispatch man **STARTER**
vehicle for hauling **TRUCK**
vehicle on runners **SLED, SLEIGH**
veil **SCREEN, VELUM**
veiling material **TULLE**
veil of gauze **VOLET**
vein **LODE, STREAK, VESSEL**
vein of a leaf **RIB**
vellum **PARCHMENT**
velocity **SPEED**
velvet-like fabric **PANNE, VELURE**
venal **MERCENARY**
vend **SELL, RETAIL**
vendetta **FEUD**
vendue **AUCTION**
veneer **SURFACE**
venerable **OLD, WISE, AUGUST**
venerate **REVERE**
veneration **AWE, RESPECT**
Venetian blind part **SLAT**
Venetian boat **GONDOLA**
Venetian painter **TITIAN**
Venetian red **SIENA**
Venetian resort **LIDO**
Venetian ruler **DOGE**
Venetian water taxi **GONDOLA**
vengeful Greek goddess **ERIS**
venom **POISON**
venomous ill-will **SPITE**
venomous snake **ADDER, ASP, COBRA**
venomous spider **TARANTULA**
vent **OPENING, OUTLET**
ventilate **AIR**
ventilator **AIR SHAFT**
venture **DARE, RISK**
venturesome **BOLD**
Venus' son **CUPID**
Venus' sweetheart **ADONIS**
veracity **TRUTH, REALITY**
veranda **PORCH, STOOP, TERRACE, PATIO**
verb form **TENSE**
verbatim **WORD FOR WORD**
verbose **WORDY**

verboten **FORBIDDEN**
verdant **LUSH, GREEN**
verdict **FINDING, DECISION**
Verdi opera **AIDA**
verge **BRINK**
verglas **GLAZE**
verify **AVER, CONFIRM**
verily **AMEN, TRULY**
veritable **ACTUAL, REAL**
vermilion **RED**
Vermont tree **MAPLE**
vernacular **NATIVE**
vernal **SPRING**
Verne hero **NEMO**
versatile **ADAPTABLE**
verse **POEM, ODE, SONNET**
verse maker **POET, BARD**
version **RENDITION**
versus **AGAINST**
vertical **ERECT**
vertigo **DIZZINESS**
verve **ELAN**
very **EXTREMELY, EXCEEDINGLY**
very (Fr.) **TRES**
very cold **ICY**
very dry **ARID**
very eager **AVID**
very fat **OBESE**
very good **FINE**
very heavy **LEADEN**
very hot **TROPICAL**
very important persons (abbr.) **VIPS**
very impressive **AWESOME**
very large **HUGE**
very large nail **SPIKE**
very nervous (4 wds.) **ON PINS AND NEEDLES**
very pale **ASHY**
very powerful **POTENT**
Very signal **FLARE**
very skillful **EXPERT**
very small **TEENY, TINY, WEE**
very small (prefix) **MICRO**
very small paintings **MINIATURE**
very small quantity **IOTA**
very thin **SHEER, SKINNY, LEAN, GAUNT**
very unpleasant **NASTY**
very warm **HOT**
very wealthy person **MILLIONAIRE**
very wet **SOPPY**
vesicate **BLISTER**
vesicle **SAC, CAVITY**

vespers (2 wds.) **EVENING PRAYER**
vespid **WASP, HORNET**
vessel **CRAFT, BOAT, VEIN, BOWL**
vessel for preserves **JAR**
vessel in Genesis **ARK**
vessel's bow **PROW**
vessel's frame **HULL**
vest **WAISTCOAT**
vestal **CHASTE, PURE**
vestibule **ENTRY, HALLWAY, FOYER**
vestige **TRACE**
vestment **STOLE, ALB, COPE**
vestry **SACRISTY**
vetch **ERS, TARE**
veteran sailor **TAR**
veto **DENY, NYET, PROHIBIT**
vex **IRK, RILE, PESTER, ANNOY, NETTLE**
vexed **SORE, ANNOYED**
via **WAY, ROUTE**
viable **LIKELY, WORKABLE**
viaduct **TRESTLE, BRIDGE**
vial **BOTTLE, PHIAL**
vibrant **ALIVE, VITAL**
vibrate **SWING, QUIVER**
vibration **TREMOR**
vicar **PARSON**
vice **CRIME, EVIL**
vicinity **AREA**
vicious **MEAN**
victim **PREY, SLAVE**
victor **WINNER**
victory **WIN, TRIUMPH, CONQUEST**
victory symbol **LAUREL, VEE**
victrola **PHONOGRAPH**
victuals **FOOD**
video's predecessor **RADIO**
vie **CONTEND**
view **LOOK, VISTA, SCENE**
vigil **WAKE, WATCH**
vigilant **ALERT, AWAKE**
vignette **PICTURE**
vigor **ENERGY, PEP, VIM**
vigorous **ENERGETIC, HARDY**
vigorous colloquial language **SLANG**
vigorous scuffle **TUSSLE**
viking **NORSEMAN**
vile **BASE, FOUL**
vilify **ABUSE, DEFAME**
village **HAMLET**
village in Ireland **TARA**

village in South Africa **STAD**
village square in ancient Greece **AGORA**
villain in "Othello" **IAGO**
villainous **VICIOUS**
villain's exclamation **AHA**
villain's nemesis **HERO**
vim **ENERGY**
vindicate **AVENGE**
vindictive **MALICIOUS, VENGEFUL**
vine **IVY, LIANE, LIANA**
vine fruit **BERRY**
vinegar **ACETUM**
vinous **WINY**
vintage **YEAR**
vinyl square **TILE**
viola **ALTO**
violate **DESECRATE**
violation of law **CRIME**
violence **FEROCITY, RAGE, FORCE**
violent **FURIOUS, RAGING**
violent anger **RAGE**
violent downpour **TORRENT**
violent outbreak **ERUPTION**
violent pain **PANG, THROE**
violent storm **TEMPEST**
violent wind **SIMOON(M), TYPHOON, HURRICANE, TORNADO, TWISTER, CYCLONE, MONSOON**
violet **MAUVE**
violin **FIDDLE**
violin bar **FRET**
violin maker **AMATI**
viper **ADDER, ASP, SNAKE**
Virgil's poem **AENEID**
Virginia willow **ITEA**
virile **MANLY**
virtue **EXCELLENCE, PURITY**
virtuous **PURE, CHASTE, MORAL**
virulent **DEADLY**
visage **FACE**
viscid **STICKY, WAXY**
viscid liquid **TAR**
viscous **THICK, VISCID**
visible **SEEN**
visible outline **SILHOUETTE**
visible vapor **STEAM**
Visigoth king **ALARIC**
vision **DREAM**
visit **CALL, SEE**
visit a pawnbroker **HOCK**
visit frequently **HAUNT**
visitor **CALLER**

vison	**MINK**
vista	**SCENE, VIEW**
visual	**SEEN**
visualize	**SEE**
vital	**ALIVE**
vital organ	**HEART, LIVER,**
	KIDNEY
vitality	**VIGOR**
vitamin B₁	**THIAMIN**
vitamin B₂	**RIBOFLAVIN**
vitriolic	**CAUSTIC, SCATHING**
vivid	**LIVELY, BRIGHT,**
	INTENSE, BRILLIANT,
	ACTIVE, STRONG,
	DARING, CLEAR
vixen	**SCOLD, SHREW**
vocal	**ORAL**
vocalize	**SING**
vocation	**PROFESSION, CAREER**
vociferous	**BLATANT, LOUD**
vogue	**STYLE, MODE**
voice	**SPEECH**
voice box	**LARYNX**
voice inflection	**TONE**
voice of the people	
(Lat., 2 wds.)	**VOX POPULI**
void	**EMPTY**
void court proceeding	
	MISTRIAL
volatile	**LIGHT, AIRY,**
	UNSTABLE
volcanic ash	**LAVA**
volcanic cavity	**CRATER**
volcanic rock column	**BASALT**
volcanic scoria	**SLAG**
volcano in Italy	**ETNA**
volcano mouth	**CRATER**
volcano of Martinique	**PELEE**
vole	**RODENT**
Volga tributary	**KAMA, OKA,**
	SAMARA
volition	**WILL**
volley	**BARRAGE**
voluble	**GLIB, CHATTY**
volume	**TOME, BOOK**
volume of maps	**ATLAS**
voluntary	**INTENTIONAL**
volunteer	**ENLIST**
Volunteer State	**TENNESSEE**
voluptuous	**SENSUAL**
voracious	**GREEDY, HUNGRY**
voracious eel	**MORAY**
vortex	**EDDY**
vote against	**CON**
vote down	**DEFEAT**
vote into office	**ELECT**
voting place	**POLLS**

vouch	**ATTEST**
vouchsafe	**GRANT, GIVE**
vow	**OATH, SWEAR, PROMISE**
vowel combination	**DIPHTHONG**
Vulcan's creation	**TALOS**
vulgar	**COMMON, RUDE**
vulgarity	**OBSCENITY**
vulnerable	**WEAK**
vying	**COMPETING,**
	STRUGGLING

W

wad	**LUMP, BALL, MASS,**
	PLUG, STUFF
wading bird	**CRANE, CURLEW,**
	HERON, IBIS, RAIL,
	STILT, STORK
wafer	**BISCUIT, CAKE**
waff	**PUFF, GUST**
waft	**BLOW, BREEZE, BECKON**
wag	**HUMORIST**
wage	**SALARY**
wager	**BET**
wages	**SALARY, PAY**
wagon	**CART**
wagon journey	**TREK**
wagon track	**RUT**
wagtail	**LARK**
wahoo	**PETO**
waif	**STRAY, ORPHAN**
wail	**HOWL, BAWL**
wainscot	**PANELING**
waist	**BLOUSE**
waist band	**BELT, SASH**
waistcoat	**VEST**
wait	**LINGER, TARRY, BIDE**
wait close by	**HOVER**
waiter	**SERVANT, GARCON**
waiter at a drive-in	**CARHOP**
waiter's item	**TRAY**
waiter's reward	**TIP**
waiting	**EXPECTANT**
wait on tables	**SERVE**
waive	**RELINQUISH**
wake	**ROUSE**
wale	**WELT, WEAL, RIDGE**
walk	**PACE, TRED, STEP,**
	STRIDE
walk back and forth	**PACE**
walk clumsily	**LUMBER**
walk drunkenly	**STAGGER**
walk fast	**RUN**
walk for pleasure	**HIKE,**
	STROLL, AMBLE
walk heavily	**TRAMP, TREAD,**
	LUMBER

walking shorts	**BERMUDAS**
walking stick	**CANE**
walk in water	**WADE**
walk lamely	**LIMP**
walk leisurely	**AMBLE, STROLL**
walk like a duck	**WADDLE**
walk off with	**STEAL**
walk on	**TREAD**
walkout	**STRIKE**
walk out on	**ABANDON**
walk over	**TRAMPLE**
walk pompously	**STRUT**
walk softly	**TIPTOE**
walk the floor	**PACE**
walk uncertainly	**TOTTER**
walk wearily	**TRUDGE**
walk with an easy gait	**LOPE**
wall	**BASTION, RAMPART**
wallaba tree	**APA**
wall border	**DADO**
wall bracket	**SCONCE**
wall covering	**PLASTER, VINYL,**
	MURAL
wall end	**GABLE**
wallet	**PURSE, BILLFOLD**
walleye	**FISH, HORSE**
wall hanging	**TAPESTRY**
wall lining	**WAINSCOT**
wall ornament	**PLAQUE**
wallow	**FLOUNDER**
wall painting	**MURAL**
wall recess	**NICHE**
Walt Disney elephant	**DUMBO**
waltz	**DANCE**
wampum	**BEADS**
wan	**PALE, ASHEN**
wand	**BATON, ROD**
wander	**ERR, ROAM, ROVE,**
	GAD, MEANDER, STRAY
wander aimlessly	**MEANDER**
wanderer	**NOMAD, ROVER,**
	VAGRANT, VAGABOND
wanderer from duty	**TRUANT**
wander from subject	**DIGRESS**
wandering	**ERRANT, ERRATIC**
wandering laborer	**MIGRANT**
wane	**DECREASE, DECLINE**
wangle	**MANIPULATE**
want	**DESIRE, LACK, NEED,**
	CRAVE, WISH
want and expect	**HOPE**
wanting	**ABSENT, LACKING**
wanting in color	**PALE**
wanton	**LOOSE, OBSCENE**
wanton look	**LEER**
wapiti	**DEER, ELK**
war	**BATTLE, HOSTILITY**
warble	**SING, TRILL**
war club	**MACE**
ward	**DISTRICT, DIVISION**
ward off	**AVERT**
wardrobe	**CLOSET**
warehouse	**DEPOT, STORAGE,**
	ETAPE
wares	**MERCHANDISE,**
	GOODS, PRODUCTS
war fleet	**ARMADA**
war hero	**ACE, AVIATOR**
war horse	**STEED**
warlike	**HOSTILE**
warlock	**SORCERER, WIZARD**
warm	**TEPID, HOT, HEAT**
war machine	**TANK**
warmhearted	**TENDER**
warm season	**SUMMER**
warmth	**HEAT**
warmth of color	**GLOW**
warm up a motor	**REV**
warm up an oven	**PREHEAT**
warm wind	**SOUTHERLY**
warn	**ALARM, ALERT**
warning	**CAUTION**
warning device	**HORN, SIREN,**
	ALARM
warning sound at sea	**FOGHORN**
warp	**DISTORT, PERVERT,**
	CORRUPT
warrant	**PERMIT, WRIT,**
	GUARANTEE
warrior	**SOLDIER**
Warsaw citizen	**POLE**
wary	**LEERY, CAUTIOUS**
wash	**LAVE, LAUNDER,**
	CLEANSE
wash away	**ERODE, RINSE**
wash basin	**LAVABO, SINK**
washbowl	**SINK, BASIN**
wash by draining	**LEACH**
washday	**MONDAY**
wash for gold	**PAN**
washing bar	**SOAP**
Washington ballplayer	
	SENATOR
Washington city	**SEATTLE**
Washington sound	**PUGET**
wash lightly	**RINSE**
wash the hair	**SHAMPOO**
wash vigorously	**SCRUB,**
	SCOUR
washy	**PALE, DILUTED**
wasp	**HORNET**
waspish	**TESTY**
waste	**LOSS, SQUANDER**
waste allowance	**TRET**

waste away	**MOLDER, DECAY, CRUMBLE**
waste cloth	**RAG**
wasteful	**EXTRAVAGANT**
wasteland	**DESERT**
waste matter	**DROSS, SLAG**
wastepaper receptacle	**BASKET**
waste time	**DALLY, LOAF, IDLE**
watch	**OBSERVE, REGARD, VIGIL**
watch chain	**FOB**
watch closely	**EYE**
watch face cover	**CRYSTAL**
watch for	**AWAIT**
watchful	**ALERT, AWAKE, VIGILANT**
watchman	**GUARD**
watch over	**TEND**
watch pocket	**FOB**
watch secretly	**SPY**
watch sound	**TICK, TOCK**
watchtower	**BEACON**
watchword	**CRY**
water	**WET, IRRIGATE, SPRINKLE**
water (Fr.)	**EAU**
water after liquor (colloq.)	**CHASER**
water barrier	**DAM**
water bird	**PELICAN, ERNE, TERN, GULL, DUCK, SWAN**
water bottle	**CARAFE**
water channel	**FLUME**
water cow	**MANATEE**
water craft	**SHIP, BOAT**
water down	**WEAKEN**
water drain	**SEWER, SUMP**
water eagle	**OSPREY**
watered silk	**MOIRE**
water enthusiast (2 wds.)	**SKIN DIVER**
waterfall	**CATARACT**
waterfall (Scot.)	**LINN**
water flask	**CANTEEN**
waterfront	**HARBOR, DOCK**
water grass	**REED**
water hole	**WELL**
watering place	**SPA**
watering tube	**HOSE**
water jug	**OLLA**
water lily	**LOTOS, LOTUS**
waterless	**ARID, BONE-DRY**
waterlogged	**SOAKED**
water main	**PIPE**
water moccasin	**COTTONMOUTH**

water monster's home (2 wds.)	**LOCH NESS**
water nymph	**NAIAD**
water passage	**CANAL**
water (pharm.)	**AQUA**
water pipe	**MAIN, SPOUT**
water pitcher	**EWER**
water plant	**LOTUS**
water rat	**MUSKRAT**
water sound	**SPLASH**
water sprite	**NIX, NIXIE**
water vapor	**MIST, STEAM**
waterway	**CANAL**
waterway under a road	**CULVERT**
water willow	**OSIER**
water witch	**DOWSER**
watery	**AQUEOUS**
watusi or frug	**DANCE**
wave	**FLUTTER, FLICKER, BREAKER**
wave (Fr.)	**ONDE**
waver	**TEETER, VACILLATE, REEL, FALTER**
wave (Sp.)	**OLA**
wave to and fro	**FLAP**
wavy	**CURLY**
wax	**CERE**
wax (Lat.)	**CERA**
waxy ointment	**CERATE**
waxy substance in cork	**CERIN**
way	**METHOD, ROUTE, SYSTEM**
way of behaving	**MANNER**
waylay	**AMBUSH**
way out	**EXIT**
wayside hotel	**INN, TAVERN, MOTEL**
way train	**LOCAL**
wayward	**ERRATIC**
weak	**NERVELESS, VULNERABLE**
weaken	**ENERVATE, SAP**
weakness	**DEBILITY**
weak point	**FOIBLE**
weal	**WALE, WELT**
wealth	**RICHES, ABUNDANCE**
wealthy	**OPULENT, RICH, AFFLUENT, ABUNDANT**
weapon	**GUN, RIFLE, ARROW, DART, ARM, SWORD**
weapons	**ARMS**
wear and tear	**DAMAGE**
wear at edge	**FRAY**
wear away	**ERODE**
wear down	**EXHAUST**
weariness	**FATIGUE**

wearing apparel **SUITS, CLOTHES, DRESSES, ATTIRE, CLOTHING**
wearing boots **SHOD**
wearing clothes **CLAD**
wearisome **TEDIOUS, FATIGUING**
wear out **TIRE**
weary **TIRED, BORED**
weasel **STOAT, ERMINE**
weathercock **VANE**
weather condition **CLIMATE**
weather forecast **FAIR, SUNNY, RAIN, CLOUDY, HOT, COLD, MILD, SLEET, SNOW, WARM, HUMID, CLEAR**
weave **INTERLACE**
weaving device **LOOM**
webbing **MEMBRANE**
web-footed bird **GOOSE, DUCK**
web spinner **SPIDER**
wed **MARRY**
wedding **MARRIAGE, NUPTIALS, UNION**
wedding attendant **USHER, BRIDESMAID**
wedding band **RING**
wedding grain **RICE**
wedding party member **BEST MAN, BRIDESMAID, MAID OF HONOR**
wedding proclamation **BANNS, BANS**
wedding ring **BAND**
wedge in **JAM**
wedlock **MATRIMONY**
wed secretly **ELOPE**
wee **SMALL, TINY**
weed **TARE**
weeding implement **HOE**
wee drink **NIP**
weep **CRY**
weep aloud **SOB**
weeping daughter of Tantalus **NIOBE**
weevil **BOLL, RICE, PEA, SEED**
weft **WOOF, FILLING, WEB**
weigh **SCALE**
weigh down **BURDEN**
weighing device **SCALE**
weigh in mind **PONDER**
weight **OUNCE, POUND, TON**
weight allowance **TARE**
weight for gems **CARAT**
weight of India **SER**
weight system **METRIC**

weighty **MASSIVE, BULKY**
weir **DAM, FENCE**
weird **EERIE, EERY, MACABRE, STRANGE**
weird sisters **FATES**
welcome **GREET**
weld **UNITE**
welfare **PROSPERITY**
well **HEALTHY**
well-being **WELFARE, PROSPERITY**
well-bred **GENTEEL**
well done! **BRAVO**
well-heeled **RICH**
well-informed **LEARNED**
well-known **FAMOUS**
well-liked **POPULAR**
well-skilled **ADEPT, ABLE**
well-to-do **RICH**
well-ventilated **AIRY**
well-worn course **PATH, TRAIL**
Welsh dog **CORGI**
welt **SLASH, STRIP**
wench **MAIDEN**
went back over **RETRACED**
went before **LED**
went beyond the mark **OVERSHOT**
went by car **RODE**
went by ship **SAILED**
went past one's bedtime (2 wds.) **SAT UP**
went quickly **SPED**
went to bed (2 wds., colloq.) **TURNED IN**
went to the bottom **SANK**
weskit **VEST**
west **OCCIDENT**
western **OMELET, MOVIE, FILM**
Western farm **RANCH**
Western halter **HACKAMORE**
Western lily **SEGO**
Western marsh plant **TULE**
Western mountains **SIERRAS**
Western resort **TAHOE, ASPEN**
Western rope **LASSO, REATA, RIATA, LARIAT**
Western show **RODEO**
Western shrub **SAGE**
Western song (4 wds.) **HOME ON THE RANGE**
Western weed **LOCO**
West German capital **BONN**
West Indian magic **OBE(AH)**
West Indian product **RUM**
West Indian volcano **PELEE**
West Indies rodent **AGOUTI**

West Point freshman	**PLEBE**	whir	**BUZZ, VIBRATE**
West Point student	**CADET**	whirl	**ROTATE, SPIN, SWIRL,**
wet	**MOIST, DAMP, WATER**		**TURN, EDDY, REEL,**
wet behind the ears	**YOUNG**		**GYRATE, REVOLVE**
wet earth	**MUD**	whirligig	**PINWHEEL**
wet falling sound	**PLOP**	whirlwind	**CYCLONE, TORNADO**
wet ground	**BOG, MIRE,**	whirlybird	**HELICOPTER,**
	SWAMP		**COPTER, CHOPPER**
wet sludge	**MIRE**	whisk	**TUFT, WISP**
wet smack	**SPLAT**	whiskers	**BEARD**
wet thoroughly	**DRENCH**	whisper	**MURMUR**
whack	**SLAP**	whistle sound	**TOOT**
whale	**CETE, SPERM**	whit	**BIT, IOTA**
whale school	**GAM, POD**	white	**PALE, WAN**
whale secretion	**AMBERGRIS**	white admiral	**BUTTERFLY**
whale's passenger	**JONAH**	white and shining	**PEARLY**
whammy	**JINX**	white ant	**TERMITE**
wharf	**DOCK, PIER**	whitebait	**SMELT**
whatever the meal is	**POTLUCK**	white bear	**POLAR**
what for	**WHY**	white beet	**CHARD**
what person	**WHO**	whitecap	**WAVE**
wheat	**GRAIN**	white coal	**WATER**
wheat chaff	**BRAN**	whitefish	**BELUGA**
wheedle	**COAX, CAJOLE**	white flower	**GARDENIA**
wheel animalcule	**ROTIFER**	white frost	**RIME, HOAR**
wheel covering	**TIRE**	white jade	**ALABASTER**
wheel edge	**RIM**	white lie	**FIB**
wheel hoop	**TIRE**	white merganser	**SMEW**
wheel hub	**NAVE**	whiten	**BLEACH, PALE**
wheelman	**HELMSMAN**	white-plumed heron	**EGRET**
wheel projection	**CAM**	white poplar	**ABELE**
wheel rut	**TRACK**	white sheep	**MERINO**
wheel shaft	**AXLE**	white vestment	**ALB**
wheel stopper	**TRIG**	whitewall	**TIRE**
wheel track	**RUT**	white walnut	**BUTTERNUT**
wheeze	**GASP**	white water	**RAPIDS**
whelk	**SNAIL**	white whale	**BELUGA**
when	**AS, UNTIL**	white with age	**HOARY**
wherewithal	**MEANS**	whiting	**CHALK**
whet	**HONE, SHARPEN**	whitlow	**FELON**
which	**THAT**	whittle	**CUT**
which thing	**WHAT**	whizz	**EXPERT**
whiff	**GUST, PUFF, SNIFF**	whoa	**STOP**
Whig's opponent	**TORY**	whole	**ALL, ENTIRE, TOTAL,**
while	**AS**		**INTACT**
whilom	**FORMER**	wholehearted	**SINCERE,**
whim	**CAPRICE**		**EARNEST**
whimper	**PULE, WHINE**	whole number	**INTEGER**
whimsical	**FANCIFUL**	wholesome	**HEALTHY,**
whin	**FURZE, GORSE**		**VIGOROUS**
whine	**SNIVEL, WHIMPER**	wholly engrossed	**RAPT**
whining complainer		whoop	**HOOT, CHEER**
(arch.)	**PULER**	whoop-de-do	**HOOPLA,**
whinny	**NEIGH**		**BALLYHOO**
whip	**CANE, BEAT**	whooping cough	**PERTUSSIS**
whip handle	**CROP**	whopper	**LIE**
whipping boy	**SCAPEGOAT**	whorl	**SPIRE**

wick	FUSE	wild iris	FLAG
wicked	BAD, EVIL	wild mustard	CHARLOCK
wickedness	EVIL	wild ox	YAK, ANOA
wicker basket	HAMPER,	wild party	ORGY
	PANNIER	wild pig	BOAR
wicker container	BASKET	wild plum	SLOE
wicker cradle	BASSINET	wild rabbit	HARE
wicket	WINDOW, GATE	wild rose	SWEETBRIER
wide	BROAD	wild sheep	ARGAL
wide-awake	ALERT	wild talk	RAVING
wide-brimmed hat	SOMBRERO	wild turnip	RUTABAGA
wide extent	EXPANSE	wild west show	RODEO
wide inlet	BAY	wile	STRATEGEM, TRICK
widely accepted	PREVALENT	will	VOLITION, MIND
widemouthed jug	EWER	willful	INTENTIONAL
widen	DILATE, ENLARGE,	willing	AGREEABLE
	BROADEN	willow	OSIER
wide smile	GRIN	Wilson's thrush	VEERY
widespread	GENERAL	wilt	DROOP, SAG
wide stream	RIVER	wily	ARTFUL, SHREWD,
wide street	AVENUE,		CRAFTY, SLY
	BOULEVARD	win	TRIUMPH, PREVAIL
widgeon	SMEE, DUCK	wince	CRINGE, FLINCH
widget	GADGET	winch	HOIST, HAUL
width	GIRTH, DIAMETER	wind	BREEZE, AIR
width of a circle	DIAMETER	wind (prefix)	ANEM(O)
wield	BRANDISH, PLY	wind about	COIL
wiener	HOT DOG, FRANK	windbreaker	JACKET
wife	SPOUSE, MATE	windflower	ANEMONE
wife of Abraham	SARAH	wind gauge	VANE
wife of Chuchulain	EMER	windhover	KESTREL
wife of Hiawatha	MINNEHAHA	wind indicator	VANE
wife of Jason	MEDEA	winding sheet	SHROUD
wife of Zeus	HERA	wind instrument	BUGLE, OBOE,
wig	PERUKE, TOUPEE		TUBA, FLUTE, HORN,
Wight	ISLE		SAX, CLARINET
wigwam	TEPEE, TENT	windlass	WINCH
wild	FERAL, SAVAGE,	windmill sail	AWN
	UNTAMED	window compartment	PANE
wild allspice	SPICEBUSH	window covering	BLIND,
wild animal	BEAST		SHADE, DRAPE,
wild arum	CUCKOOPINT		SHUTTER, AWNING
wild banana	PAWPAW	window curtain material	SCRIM,
wild beast's covert	LAIR, DEN		LACE
wild buffalo of India	ARNA	window part	SASH, SILL, PANE
wild disorder	RIOT	windpipe	TRACHEA
wild dog of Australia	DINGO	windshield gadget	WIPER
wild donkey	ONAGER	wind spirally	COIL
wildebeest	GNU	windstorm	GALE
wilderness	DESERT	windy	STORMY
wild fancy	VAGARY	Windy City	CHICAGO
wild goat	IBEX	windy month	MARCH
wild grape vine	LIANA	wine barrel	CASK, TUN
wild headlong flight	STAMPEDE	wine bottle	DECANTER
wild hog	BOAR	wine cask deposit	TARTAR
wild horse	MUSTANG	wine colored	PURPLE
wild indigo	BAPTISIA	wine cup	CHALICE

winesap	APPLE	wise bird	OWL
wing	ALA	wise counselor	NESTOR
winged	ALAR, ALATE	wisecrack	GIBE, RETORT
winged god	EROS	wise king of Pylos	NESTOR
winged horse	PEGASUS	wise lawgiver	SOLON,
winged insect	BEE, FLY,		SOLOMON
	BUTTERFLY, WASP	wisely cautious	PRUDENT
winged monster	HARPY	wise man	SAGE, SEER
winglet	ALULA	wisent	BISON
winglike	ALAR	wise saying	ADAGE
winglike part	ALA	wisest Greek in the	
wing movement	FLUTTER	Trojan War	NESTOR
wing-shaped	ALARY, ALATE,	wise to	AWARE
	ALAR	wish	DESIRE, HOPE, WANT
wing tip	SHOE	wish undone	RUE
wink	BLINK	wish well	BLESS
winner	CHAMPION, VICTOR	wishy-washy (comp. wd.)	
winnow	SEPARATE, SIFT		NAMBY-PAMBY
winsome	CHARMING,	wisp	STRAND
	ATTRACTIVE	wist	KNOW, GAME
winter apple	WINESAP	wistful	LONGING
winter bird food	SUET	wit	CLEVERNESS, HUMOR,
wintergreen	SHINLEAF		HUMORIST
winter hand warmer	MUFF,	witchcraft	SORCERY
	MITTEN, GLOVE	witch trial city	SALEM
winter jacket	PARKA	with (Fr.)	AVEC
winter melon	CASABA	withdraw	RETRACT, RETREAT,
winter moisture	SNOW		SECEDE
winter sport	SLEDDING,	withdraw a statement	RECANT
	SKATING, SKIING	withdraw from	
winter vehicle	SLED, SLEIGH,	association	SECEDE
	SNOWMOBILE, TOBOGGAN	withdraw from business	RETIRE
winter weapon	SNOWBALL	with force	AMAIN
winter white stuff	SNOW, ICE	withhold	DENY
win the regatta	OUTSAIL	wither	SEAR, WILT
wintry	HIEMAL	with ice cream, as pie	
wintry glaze	ICE	(3 wds.)	A LA MODE
wipe	DRY, RUB, CLEAN	within	IN
wipe out	ERASE	within the time of	DURING
wipe the dishes	DRY	with less hair	BALDER
wire	CABLE, TELEGRAM	with one	ALONG
wire fastener	NAIL	without (Fr.)	SANS
wirehair	TERRIER	without (Lat.)	SINE
wireless communication	RADIO	without charge	FREE, GRATIS
wire measure	MIL	without company	ALONE
wire nail	BRAD	without emotion	DULLY
wire rope	CABLE	without end	ETERNAL
wire-stitching machine		without energy	LANGUID
	STAPLER	without equal	PEERLESS
wiretap device	DETECTAPHONE	without face value	
wireless signal	SOS	(comp. wd.)	NO-PAR
wiry	RANGY, SINEWY	without fat	LEAN
Wisconsin city	OSHKOSH,	without knowledge	IGNORANT
	MADISON	without much meat	BONY
wisdom	SAGACITY	without purpose	AIMLESS, IDLY
wise	SAGACIOUS, SAPIENT,	without reason	NEEDLESS
	SENSIBLE, SHREWD	without vigor	SPIRITLESS

without warning **SUDDENLY**
without work **IDLE**
withstand **RESIST, OPPOSE, HOLD OFF**
with the mouth wide open **AGAPE**
with unlimited power **PLENIPOTENTIARY**
witless **FOOLISH, STUPID**
witness **SEE**
witticism **MOT**
witty **CLEVER**
witty answer **REPARTEE**
witty person **WAG**
wizard **SORCERER, MAGICIAN**
wizen **DRY UP, WITHER, SHRIVEL**
wobble **SHAKE**
woe **GRIEF, SORROW**
woeful **SAD, WRETCHED**
woe is me **ALAS**
wolf **LOBO**
wolfhound **BORZOI**
wolfish **LUPINE**
wolfram **TUNGSTEN**
wolfsbane **ACONITE**
Wolverine State **MICHIGAN**
woman **LADY, FEMALE**
woman entertainer **HOSTESS**
woman hater **MYSOGYNIST**
woman in the U.S. Army **WAC**
womanish **FEMALE**
womanless party **STAG, SMOKER**
womanly **FEMININE**
woman of breeding **LADY**
woman of rank **DAME**
woman's crowning glory **HAIR**
woman's dress **GOWN**
woman's dressing gown **NEGLIGEE**
woman's dressing jacket **CAMISOLE**
woman's fur garment **STOLE, WRAP**
woman's garment **SLIP, BRA, SKIRT, BLOUSE, DRESS, COAT**
woman singer (Fr.) **CHANTEUSE**
woman's secret **AGE**
women's patriotic society (abbr.) **D.A.R.**
womera (2 wds.) **SPEAR THROWER**
wonder **MARVEL**
wonderful **AMAZING, MARVELOUS**

wonderful thing **MIRACLE**
wonderland girl **ALICE**
wondrous **MARVELOUS**
wont **HABIT, CUSTOM**
woo **COURT**
wood **LUMBER, OAK, TEAK, EBONY, WALNUT, CHERRY, BIRCH**
wood alcohol **METHANOL**
wood bundle **FAGOT**
wood carver **HEWER**
woodchopper **LOGGER, AXEMAN**
wood chopping tool **AXE, AX**
wood clearing **GLADE**
woodchuck **MARMOT**
wood coal **CHARCOAL, LIGNITE**
wood deities **FAUNS, SATYRS**
wood-eating ant **TERMITE**
wooded valley **GLEN**
wooden box **CRATE**
wooden container **BARREL, CASE**
wooden joint part **TENON**
wooden match **FUSEE, FUZEE**
wooden nail **PEG**
wooden shoe **SABOT, CLOG**
wooden tub **SOE**
wood knot **GNARL, KNUR**
woodland **FOREST**
woodland animal **DEER**
woodland deity **FAUN, SATYR**
wood plant **TREE**
wood sorrel **OCA**
wood strip **LATH, SLAT**
woodwind instrument **FLUTE, OBOE, REED, CLARINET, BASSOON**
woodwork **MOLDING**
woodworking tool **ADZE**
woody plant **TREE**
wooer **SUITOR**
woof **FILLING, WEFT**
wool **FLEECE**
wool blemish **MOTE**
woolen cap **TAM**
woolen dress fabric **DELAINE**
wool fat **LANOLIN**
wool fiber **NEP**
woolly **LANATE**
woozy **DIZZY, FAINT**
wordbook **DICTIONARY, LEXICON**
word for opening doors **SESAME**
word for word **LITERAL, VERBATIM**

word game **LOTTO, SCRABBLE**
wordiness **VERBIAGE**
wording **DICTION**
word in Japanese ship names **MARU**
word inventor **COINER**
wordless actor **MIME**
word of action **VERB**
word of approval **BRAVO**
word of assent **YES**
word of disgust **BAH**
word of division **INTO**
word of farewell **ADIEU, ADIOS**
word of gratitude **THANKS**
word of greeting **HELLO, HI**
word of honor **PAROLE, OATH**
word of negation **NOT**
word of regret **ALAS**
word of reproof **TUT**
word on a towel **HIS, HERS**
word on the wall **MENE, TEKEL**
word puzzle **REBUS, CROSSWORD, ACROSTIC**
words of understanding (2 wds.) **I SEE**
word to call attention **HEY**
word with silver or glass **WARE**
wordy **PROLIX, VERBOSE**
work **LABOR, TOIL**
workaday **COMMON, ORDINARY**
work at **PLY**
work cattle **OXEN**
work crew **GANG**
work diligently **DRILL, PEG**
work dough **KNEAD**
worker with rattan **CANER**
worker's concern (2 wds.) **LIVING WAGE**
worker's cooperative **ARTEL**
worker's meal (2 wds.) **BOX LUNCH**
work for **SERVE**
work for a candidate **ELECTIONEER, CAMPAIGN**
working class **PROLETARIAT**
working space (2 wds.) **ELBOW ROOM**
work into a mass **KNEAD**
workman **ARTISAN, LABORER**
work of art **ETCHING, OPUS**
work of charity (3 wds.) **ACT OF LOVE**
work of fiction **NOVEL**
work of sculpture **FOUNTAIN, STATUE, BUST**
workout **EXERCISE**

work out **SOLVE**
workplace for students (2 wds.) **DAY SCHOOL**
work soil **TILL**
work too hard **OVERDO**
work unit **ERG**
work with **COOPERATE**
work with a needle **SEW, KNIT**
work with oils **PAINT**
world **UNIVERSE, EARTH**
world goal **PEACE**
worldly **MUNDANE, EARTHLY**
world of canines **DOGDOM**
world of illusions **DREAMLAND**
world's highest mountain **EVEREST**
world-wide **UNIVERSAL**
world-wide complex of statutes **INTERNATIONAL LAW**
worm **ERIA**
worn and gaunt **HAGGARD**
worn away **EROSE**
worn out **EFFETE, TIRED, JADED**
worn trail **PATH**
worrisome offspring (2 wds.) **PROBLEM CHILDREN, ENFANT TERRIBLE**
worry **FRET, FUSS, TEASE**
worry at persistently **NAG**
worsen **DETERIORATE**
worship **ADORE, LOVE, REVERE, IDOLIZE, VENERATE**
worsted suit fabric **SERGE**
worth **MERIT**
worthless **TRIVIAL, PALTRY**
worthless bit **ORT**
worthless plant **WEED**
worthy **RELIABLE, VIRTUOUS**
worthy of belief **CREDIBLE**
would-be socialite (comp. wd.) **NAME-DROPPER**
would-be-smoker's tobacco (2 wds.) **CORN SILK**
wound **INJURY, HARM**
wound covering **BANDAGE, SCAB**
wound mark **SCAR, SCAB**
woven container **BASKET**
wrack **TORTURE, CONVULSE**
wraith **GHOST, SPECTRE**
wrangle **SPAR**
wrangler **COWBOY**
wrap **CAPE, SWADDLE, COAT**

wraparound **SKIRT**
wrap in bandage **SWATHE**
wrapper **ENVELOPE**
wrap up **FOLD, PACKAGE, END**
wrath **IRE, ANGER**
wreak **INFLICT, CAUSE**
wreath **GARLAND, LEI**
wreathe **ENTWINE, COIL**
wreath of honor **LAUREL**
wreck **SMASHUP**
wrecker (2 wds.) **TOW CAR**
wren **BIRD**
wrench **TWIST, TEAR**
wrest **EXTORT**
wrestle **GRAPPLE**
wrestling pad **MAT**
wretched hut **HOVEL**
wretched (sl.) **RATTY**
wriggle **SQUIRM, WRITHE**
wriggly fish **EEL**
wrinkle **CREASE**
wrist **CARPUS**
wristwatch feature
(2 wds.) **RADIUM DIAL**
write **INSCRIBE, PEN**
write by machine **TYPE**
write carelessly **SCRAWL,**
SCRIBBLE
write down **PEN**
write hastily **SCRAWL, JOT,**
SCRIBBLE
write music **COMPOSE**
write off **CANCEL, AMORTIZE**
writer of drama **PLAYWRIGHT**
writer of fiction **NOVELIST,**
AUTHOR
writer of plays **DRAMATIST**
writer of travesty **PARODIST**
writer of verse **POET**
writing **DOCUMENT,**
MANUSCRIPT
writing desk **SECRETARY**
writing fluid **INK**
writing implement **PEN, NIB,**
PENCIL, BALL-POINT
writing master **STYLIST,**
CALLIGRAPHER, PENMAN,
ENGROSSER
writing material **PAPER,**
PARCHMENT
writings **LITERATURE**
writing sheet **PAPER**
writing table **DESK**
written acknowledgment
of a debt **IOU**
written agreement **CARTEL**
written characters **SCRIPT**

written communication **NOTE,**
EPISTLE, LETTER, MEMO
written in verse **POETIC**
wrong **AMISS, INCORRECT**
wrong (prefix) **MIS**
wongdoing **EVIL**
wrong name **MISNOMER**
wry **TWISTED, ASKEW**
wurst **SAUSAGE**
WW II area **ETO**
Wyandotte abode **NEST**
Wyoming city **LARAMIE,**
CASPER
Wyoming mountain range
TETON

X

xanthic **YELLOWISH**
Xanthippe **SHREW**
xebec **BOAT**
xeres **SHERRY**
xylograph **WOODCUT**
xyloid **WOODY**

Y

yabber **TALK, JABBER**
yacht basin **MARINA**
yachting affair **REGATTA**
Yale man **ELI**
yam (2 wds.) **SWEET POTATO**
yank **JERK, PULL**
Yannigan **ROOKIE, RECRUIT**
yard (2 wds.) **THREE FEET**
yard entrance **GATE**
yardstick **RULER**
yarn **TALE, STORY**
yarn fluff **LINT**
yawn **GAPE**
yawning fissure **CHASM**
yea **TRULY**
year **TWELVEMONTH**
yearbook **ALMANAC, ANNUAL**
yearling **COLT**
yearn **PINE, LONG, ACHE**
years of life **AGE**
years thirteen to nineteen
TEENS
yeast **FERMENT, LEAVEN**
yell **CRY, SHOUT, HOLLER**
yellow **GOLDEN, SAFFRON**
yellow-belly **COWARD**
yellow bugle **IVA**

yellow condiment	**MUSTARD**
yellow fever mosquito	**AEDES**
yellow gem	**TOPAZ**
Yellowhammer State	**ALABAMA**
yellowish-green pear	**BOSC**
yellowjacket	**WASP, HORNET**
yellow metal	**BRASS, GOLD**
yellow of an egg	**YOLK**
yellow pigment	**OCHER, OCHRE**
yellow poplar	**TULIPWOOD**
yellow root	**CARROT**
yellow shade	**AMBER**
Yellowstone attraction	**GEYSER**
yelp	**ULULATE, YIP**
Yemenite	**ARAB**
yen	**DESIRE, URGE,**
	HANKERING
yeoman	**EXON**
yes	**AYE**
yes (Sp.)	**SI**
yesterday (Fr.)	**HIER**
yet	**HOWEVER, STILL**
yield	**CEDE**
yield a result (2 wds.)	
	PAN OUT
yield control (2 wds.)	
	HAND OVER
yielding	**SUBMISSIVE**
yield under pressure	**SAG**
yock	**YAK, LAUGH**
yoke	**HARNESS, BIND**
yokel	**RUSTIC**
yonder	**THERE**
yore	**PAST**
Yorkshire river	**AIRE, URE**
you and I	**WE, US**
you don't say (2 wds.)	**DO TELL**
young	**JUVENILE, FRESH**
young animal	**PUP, CUB**
yound bear	**CUB**
young bird	**NESTLING**
young blood	**YOUTH, VIGOR**
young boy	**LAD**
young chicken	**FRYER**
young child	**TOT, TODDLER**
young conger	**ELVER**
young cow	**CALF**
young deer	**FAWN**
young dog	**PUP, PUPPY**
young fellow	**CHAP**
young flower	**BUD**
young girl	**LASS**
young goat	**KID**
young hog	**SHOAT, SHOTE**
young horse	**COLT, FOAL**
young lady	**GIRL, LASS,**
	DAMSEL, MAID

young man	**BOY, LAD**
young pig	**SHOAT, PIGLET,**
	SHOTE
young salmon	**GRILSE, PARR,**
	SMOLT
young seal	**PUP**
young sheep	**LAMB**
young socialite, for short	**DEB**
youngster	**CHILD, TOT**
young tough	**PUNK**
young tree	**SEEDLING**
young woman	**GIRL, LASS,**
	MAID, MAIDEN
yours and mine	**OURS**
youth	**BOY, LAD**
youthful years	**TEENS**
yowl	**HOWL, CRY**
Yugoslav city	**BELGRADE,**
	ZAGREB
Yugoslav commune	**STIP**
Yugoslav leader	**TITO**
Yugoslav money	**DINAR**
Yugoslav region	**BOSNIA,**
	SLAVONIA
Yugoslav river	**DANUBE, SAVA,**
	MORAVA, DRAVA
yukata	**KIMONO**
Yule	**CHRISTMAS, NOEL**
yummy	**TASTY, DELICIOUS**

Z

zany	**CLOWN, BUFFOON,**
	SIMPLETON, COMICAL,
	FOOLISH, CRAZY
zeal	**ARDOR**
zealot	**FANATIC**
zealous	**EARNEST**
zenith	**APEX**
zephyr	**BREEZE**
Zeppelin	**DIRIGIBLE**
zero	**NAUGHT, NIL,**
	NOTHING, CIPHER
zest	**PEP**
zesty flavor	**TANG**
zibeline	**SABLE**
zigzag	**OBLIQUE, AWRY**
zilch	**NOTHING, ZERO**
zing	**SPIRIT, VIM**
zip	**PEP, FLY**
zodiac sign	**ARIES, LEO, LIBRA,**
	PISCES, VIRGO, CANCER,
	AQUARIUS, TAURUS,
	SAGITTARIUS, GEMINI,
	CAPRICORN, SCORPIO
Zohar	**CABALA**

Zola heroine	**NANA**	zoo resident	**ANIMAL**
zombie	**CORPSE**	Zoroastrian	**PARSEE, PARSI**
zone	**REGION, SECTOR**	zounds	**EGAD**
zoo	**MENAGERIE**	zowie	**WOW**
zoo animal	**LION, TIGER, APE,**	Zsa Zsa's sister	**EVA**
	PANDA, BEAR, SEAL	zucchini	**SQUASH**
zoo enclosure	**CAGE**	zwieback	**RUSK, BISCUIT**
zoology	**FAUNA**		

HISTORY, ECOLOGY, & HUMAN DRAMA

A PRIVATE BATTLE   04564 $2.95
by Cornelius Ryan & Kathryn Morgan Ryan
   An intimate and dramatic account of the famous author's struggle against cancer.

MIDNIGHT EXPRESS   04302 $2.25
by Billy Hayes with William Hoffer
   True story of life in a Turkish prison. The basis for the motion picture.

PEOPLE WHO LIVE IN SOLAR HOUSES   04441 $2.25
by Chester and Martha Davis
   The owners and occupants of 32 solar houses give you a clear look at what may be your home of the future.

THE BATTLE FOR JERUSALEM   04326 $2.50
by General Mordechai Gur
   Military history by the Israeli chief of staff and field commander of the battle.

THE THIRTEENTH TRIBE   04242 $2.25
by Arthur Koestler
   An account of the Khazar people and their conversion to Judaism in the eighth century A.D.